The Encyclopedia of
WORLD MILITARY WEAPONS

The Encyclopedia of
WORLD MILITARY WEAPONS

Editors: Chris Bishop and Ian Drury

CRESCENT BOOKS
New York

Copyright © Aerospace Publishing Limited 1988

Produced by Aerospace Publishing Ltd
179 Dalling Road, Hammersmith, London W6 0ES

First published 1988 by Temple Press
an imprint of The Hamlyn Publishing Group Limited
a division of Octopus Publishing Group
Michelin House, 81 Fulham Road,
London SW3 6RB.

First published in book form 1988

Reprinted 1989

This edition published by
Crescent Books and distributed by
Crown Publishers, Inc.

Produced by Mandarin Offset
Printed and Bound in Hong Kong

ISBN 0-517-65341-9

CONTENTS

Surface to Surface Missiles

Ever since the dropping of the atom bombs on Japan in 1945 the defence of the big powers has been based on the mutual fear of nuclear warfare, and missile forces have been the main agents of those in command. Deterrence seemed absolute, but the emergence of smaller mobile battlefield nuclear weapons has destabilized the once-simple equation. Do these weapons maintain our security or produce a dangerous and potentially deadly insecurity?

Land-based missile systems are usually classed as strategic, theatre, or tactical. Strategic normally refers to those missiles which have intercontinental ranges (more than 3,350 miles/5400 km), and as such are termed Inter-Continental Ballistic Missiles (ICBMs). Only three countries possess this class of missile. The USA deploys over 1000 and the USSR nearly 1500 ICBMs of various types, classified as light, medium or heavy depending upon size, range, and payload (or 'throw weight'). China had deployed less than 20 missiles by 1986, and is currently involved in a active research and development programme to increase this force level in order to provide a credible deterrent against the USSR.

Theatre area missiles are those missiles that have ranges restricted to specific geographical areas, such as West and East Europe. They can be called either Medium-Range Ballistic Missiles (MRBMs) with ranges between 700 and 1,725 miles (1125 and 2775 km) or Intermediate-Range Ballistic Missiles (IRBMs) with ranges between 1,725 and 3,350 miles (2775 and 5400 km). The USA did at one time deploy IRBMs, but withdrew them as her ICBM programmes matured. The largest operator of theatre systems is the USSR, which created a peak force of some 700 missiles in the 1960s for use against possible targets in Europe, the Middle East and China. The USSR has also pioneered the use of the mobile IRBM system. The second major operator is China with some 100 MRBMs and IRBMs currently deployed against Soviet targets. France maintains a small 18-round IRBM force as its land-based deterrent force

Lance is the only battlefield guided missile of NATO armies, and it is a relatively small weapon. At launch the dense smoke from its on-board gas generator is expelled through tangential ports to spin the missile, adding stability. One of Lance's good features is that it can be fitted with a variety of different warheads, including nuclear.

contribution.

Missiles which have ranges of less than 1125 km (700 miles) are called Battlefield Support Systems and are intended to be used in direct support of the ground forces. Most users of such weapons outside the USA, USSR and China are NATO or Warsaw Pact members, but numbers have been supplied to Soviet or American allied states such as Libya, North Korea, Syria, Israel and Taiwan. Both sides in the Gulf War have used such missiles operationally with conventional warheads.

Countries reported to be developing their own surface to surface weapons of this type include Argentina, Brazil, Israel and Taiwan. Israel is also reputed to have developed atomic and thermo-nuclear warheads to arm the missiles.

Looking down into a Minuteman ICBM silo. The silo is extremely strongly built to withstand nuclear attack, but large enough for the giant flame from the first-stage motor to escape past the missile without damaging it. Minuteman is over 20 years old and a very small missile compared with the much more numerous Soviet ICBMs.

The Militarization of Space

One of the most basic principles of military philosophy is to 'take the high ground', giving your troops an advantage over the enemy. To the modern military mind, it has been obvious from the start that space is the new high ground, and to that end military involvement in space research has been considerable.

Below: Following the disaster which overtook the US Space Shuttle programme in the January 1986 Challenger explosion, the subsequent suspension of Shuttle launches has forced the USAF to fall back on the Titan launchers kept in reserve, and to propose modifying surplus Titan ICBMs.

Much has been said recently about the militarization of space by the American 'Star Wars' programme and all it entails. The sad fact remains that despite all this rhetoric such a process actually started the day that the Soviets launched their Sputnik I satellite back in 1957. The respective superpower photo-reconnaissance and Elint satellite networks which evolved from that day now monitor the forces and validate the claims of its rival with almost unnerving accuracy to produce what has in effect become an overall stabilizing influence on world events and on the strategic issues which condition such events.

First priority

In a global war, however, the priority for each side would become the need to destroy these prying eyes as quickly as possible so that military intentions would not be assessed before they could take effect. Thus in the 1960s both the Soviets and the Americans embarked on the development first of suitable ground-based tracking systems to watch the skies for satellite orbits, and then of the means to destroy them. The US armed forces leaned towards the use of what is known as a direct-ascent anti-satellite (ASAT) weapon which is fired under radar guidance straight at a target and then uses a command-detonated nuclear warhead with its prompt radiation and resultant EMP to destroy or disable the satellite.

Two systems were developed to deployment status. The first was based on the US Army's DM-15B series Nike Zeus ABM and codenamed Programme 505. Deployed at the Kwajalein Atoll test site in the Pacific, it employed a new DM-15S series Nike Zeus missile, which carried a high kiloton yield thermonuclear warhead to intercept satellites out to a maximum orbit of around 555 km (345 miles). By late 1963 an installation with one DM-15S always on operational alert had been completed.

However, from mid-1966 Programme 505 was slowly phased out because of the availability of the USAF's direct-ascent ASAT Program 437 at Johnson Island, 1150 km (715 miles) south of Honolulu. This used two LV-2D Thor IRBM conversions on launch pads, each armed with a 1.4-megaton yield W49 thermonuclear warhead with a satellite-killing distance of 8 km (5 miles). Capable of attacking targets out to 1300 km (808 miles) orbital distance and with a horizontal range of some 2780 km (1,725 miles), the Thors remained the sole American ASAT asset until mid-1970, when the programme was reduced to a 30-day stand-by status. The project was finally terminated in 1972 after a hurricane hit the island and devastated the installations.

Soviet ASAT

Two years before the Americans first set up an operational ASAT system in 1966, the Soviets created a special ASAT branch of the PVO-Strany air defence force known as the PKO (Protivo Kosmicheskaya Oborona, or Against Cosmic Attack). By 1966 the Soviets were assessed as having a direct-ascent weapon possibly based on a development ver-

Above: The US Air Force has established Space Launch Complex 6 at Vandenburg AFB in California as the west coast (and main military) launch site for the Space Transportation System (Shuttle). Here the shuttle Enterprise *is moved to the launch pad.*

sion of the ABM-1A 'Galosh' ABM. The Soviets also paralleled this by developing an orbital ASAT system which was carried by the F-1-r booster version of the SS-9 'Scarp' ICBM and first flown on 27 October 1967. The ASAT tests lasted until 1971 and utilized an initial parking orbit for the powered interceptor and then either a co-orbit or fast fly-by terminal attack profile to destroy the target satellite. The tests then came to a halt and did not resume until February 1976 following a significant advance in China's space programme.

These new trials introduced the third terminal attack profile into the Soviet ASAT programme, which required less than one orbit from launch to target interception. This gave the Soviets a genuine fast-reaction capability to destroy American satellites whilst out of ground-based tracking range and, more importantly, to hit manoeuvring satellites trying to take evasive action. In 1977 the US DoD confirmed that the Soviets had a fully operational ASAT weapon armed with a conventional HE-fragmentation type warhead. At the same time it was recognized that the ASAT weaponry was also directed against the Chinese with their newly acquired photo-reconnaissance capability. As a counter to the Soviet system the Americans went back to their design boards and came up with the Project 1005 Vought Miniature Vehicle ASAT that could be carried and launched by a McDonnell Douglas F-15 Eagle fighter. Tested in the early 1980s after

several delays (and given Congressional willingness to deploy it) the Vought ASAT weapon should be available to two squadrons of Eagles based in the USA by the end of the decade and under the command and control of the US Space Command.

By 1980 the Soviets had resumed their own ASAT testing again following a three-year hiatus, flying the first prototype of a new interceptor using an IR guidance system instead of the more normal radar. This weapon demonstrated the capacity for inspecting a target before actually attacking. American intelligence also indicated that the Soviets had brought into service a new direct-ascent ASAT weapon armed with a nuclear warhead and the ability to destroy previously safe high-orbit geosynchronous communication, early warning and Elint satellites.

Manned programmes

Concurrently with the ASAT testing of both sides, the superpowers also began to exploit their manned space programmes for military use. The Soviets developed a specialized military version of their Salyut space station which was flown on several occasions during the flight series, whilst the unmanned Salyut-6/Cosmos 1287 space link up in June 1982 was interpreted by American intelligence agencies as the first testing of a space station defence system armed with small IR-guided interceptor missiles to prevent possible American interference with Soviet satellites or space stations in a war scenario. On the American side the Space Transportation System (STS, more commonly known as the Space Shuttle) was built during the 1970s as a NASA project heavily subsidized by the American military.

Below: SLC-6 at Vandenburg, with the Enterprise *on the pad. In spite of the* Challenger *disaster, too many DoD and NASA eggs are in the shuttle basket to consider cancellation of the programme, although launches have been set back many months.*

Surface to Surface Missiles

With one-third of its flights scheduled for military purposes before the January 1986 *Challenger* disaster, and with the special Vandenburg AFB military space port for it just about to be completed, President Reagan also chose the STS for use as the space test bed for much of the technology to be derived from his Strategic Defense Initiative (SDI) plans. Not to be outdone by the Shuttle (and despite the vehement propaganda aimed at its use for military purposes) the Soviets are known to be developing a similar spacecraft plus a smaller manned spaceplane. This is far more important as the latter is known to have several military roles including those of a mobile space station defence fighter and a manned ASAT system. This finally validates the Soviet 1964 definition of the role of the PKO, which stated that it will be equipped with special spacecraft and vehicles controlled either from the ground or by special crews to attack enemy space systems. Coupled with this is the Soviets' own prodigious research and development into the technology envisaged for the American SDI programme.

Advanced technology

The Soviets are known to have an operational particle beam R&D facility at Semipalatinsk using power generated by a small nuclear explosion. They also have a conventional HE-powered iodine pulse laser installation at the ABM test site at Sary-Shagan near the Soviet-Sino border. This latter has now been joined by several air-defence test lasers and an ASAT-capable laser weapon. Yet another laser of the electron beam pumped carbon dioxide gas-dynamic type has been identified at an installation near Moscow for ASAT use, whilst programmes involving research on radio-frequen-

Above: The USSR has had an operational anti-satellite interceptor system based at Tyuratam since 1971. Capable of reaching targets in orbits out to 5000 km (3,100 miles), it destroys other satellites by means of a giant 'shotgun blast' of pellets.

Below: The launch and manning of the new Soviet 'Mir' space station speaks eloquently of the effort made by the USSR in Earth orbit. When the Soviet shuttle equivalent becomes operational, one of its roles will be to service increasingly sophisticated manned space complexes.

cy signals to interfere with or to destroy electronic components of ICBMs or satellites, and on kinetic-energy weapons using the high-speed collision of small mass with a target have also been identified. By the 1960s the Soviets had already developed an experimental gun assembly that could shoot streams of high-density metals such as tungsten or molybdenum at 25 km (15.5 miles) per second in air and over 60 km (37.3 miles) per second in a vacuum. By the 1990s American intelligence expects that many of the research programmes will have resulted in operational systems both on the ground and on space-based satellites, space stations and spaceplane fighters, whilst the SDI is not expected to result in any deployable systems (if at all) before the turn of the century.

Above: The Sary Shagan proving ground by Lake Balkhash in Kazakhstan is one of the sites where directed energy weapons such as high-powered lasers and particle beams are being developed.

Left: The shuttle deploys a long duration satellite on the end of its remote manipulator arm. Such systems are designed to remain in operation until retrieval by another shuttle mission up to a year later. The shuttle is the only means of doing this and returning it undamaged to earth for analysis.

Below and bottom; Before and after shots of a Titan I booster during the first laser lethality test conducted for the Strategic Defense Initiative. The laser (the most powerful continuous wave system outside the USSR) was the Mid-Infra Red Advanced Chemical Laser (MIRACL), which was in operation for several seconds.

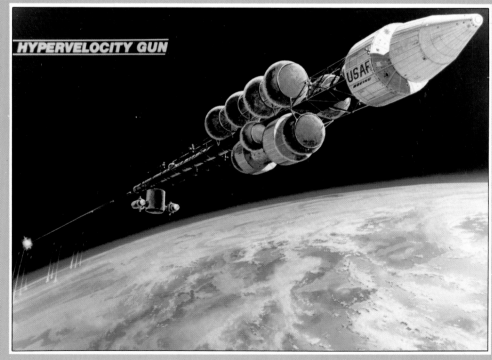

HYPERVELOCITY GUN

Left: The space-based Hypervelocity Launcher, or Railgun, launches projectiles by means of an electro-magnetic accelerator at velocities of up to 29000 km/h (18,000 mph). Using 'Smart' warheads, targets could be destroyed by kinetic energy alone.

Lance Short Range Battlefield Tactical Support Missile System

The **MGM-52** Lance battlefield support missile was first conceived in 1962 when the Vought Corporation was chosen as the prime contractor for the programme. In 1963 the research and development contract was placed and in March 1965 the first test firing of a trials missile was conducted. After problems with the propulsion system and rocket engine had been overcome, the first production models were delivered to the US Army in 1971 for service trials. The missile was type-classified as 'standard' in 1972, with the first training battalion being activated in April of that year. The missile provides nuclear fire support at the corps level. The US Army has eight battalions in service at present. The Lance has also replaced most of the Honest John short-range missiles in service with various NATO armies. Current operators of the Lance are: USA (65 M572 launchers), UK (18 M572 launchers), West Germany (24 M572 launchers), Netherlands (nine M572 launchers), Italy (nine M572 launchers), Belgium (nine M572 launchers) and Israel (18 M572 launchers).

The Lance has a two-part Rocketdyne concentric pre-packed storable liquid-propellant motor, the outer section of which provides the thrust during the initial boost phase of the flight when the missile is under the control of the onboard simplified inertial guidance system; once this system detects that the cruise velocity has been attained, the inner propellant section is ignited to take over the propulsion until the guidance unit commands it to shut down so as to leave the missile in free flight for the terminal phase of its trajectory. The missile is spin-stabilized in flight by the expulsion of propellant gases through canted vents in the missile body. The Lance system is normally carried on two tracked derivatives of the M113 APC family: the M752 self-propelled erector-launcher vehicle carries one ready-to-fire missile, and the M688 loader-transporter vehicle carries two reload missiles (minus their fins) and a loading hoist. A

single-rail lightweight launcher has also been developed for delivery by helicopter or parachute into the battle area.

The warhead options for the Lance include the NATO standard 212-kg (467-lb) M234 10- to 100-kiloton optional yield weapon. The US Army is replacing some of these with a version based on the W70-4 weapon that has built-in features allowing it to operate as a ½-kiloton low-yield enhanced-radiation (neutron) device that minimizes blast damage and residual radiation but maximizes the output of fast radiation at the time of detonation to increase personnel casualties. This effect is of considerable use when large concentrations of tanks and APCs are engaged by nuclear weapons. All the NATO nuclear warheads for Lance are held by the Americans under a dual-key arrangement. Israel does not have any nuclear warheads for Lance but uses the M251 cluster munition warhead instead. The M251 is also used by the US Army and the Netherlands. This air-burst warhead is filled with 836 0.43-kg (0.95-lb) sphere-shaped anti-personnel/anti-matèriel fragmentation bomblets that can saturate a 820-m (900-yard) diameter circle with lethal fragments. This is of particular use to Israel as a possible air-defence suppression system that does not risk any personnel casualties in its use.

Vought is currently developing an **Improved Lance** to meet the US Army's Corps Support System programme requirement. The new missile will be compatible with the current Lance systems and will be effective into the 1990s. Improved Lance will have three times the range, six times the accuracy and a 30 per cent increase in payload when compared to the present missile.

Specification
MGM-52C Lance
Length: 6.17 m (20 ft 3 in)
Diameter: 0.56 m (1 ft 10 in)
Weight: 1530 kg (3,373 lb) with nuclear

warhead, and 1778 kg (3,920 lb) with conventional warhead
Warhead weight: 212 kg (467 lb) nuclear, and 454 kg (1,000 lb) conventional
Warhead types: 10/100-kiloton M234 nuclear, M251 conventional cluster and training
Minimum range: 4.8 km (3 miles)
Maximum range: 121 km (75 miles) with nuclear warhead, and 70 km (43 miles) with conventional warhead
CEP: 455 m (500 yards)
Launch vehicle: tracked M572
Propellant type/guidance: liquid/simplified inertial

Lance is a mobile battlefield missile with a range of up to 120 km (75 miles) with a nuclear warhead. This Lance of the US Army is mounted on a lightweight heli-portable launcher which can also be dropped by parachute.

A US Army Lance is carefully lowered onto an M752 launch vehicle. The missile is widely employed by NATO, with a variety of warheads including tactical nuclear types.

Pershing Short Range Battlefield Support Missile System

The two-stage solid-propellant **MGM-31 Pershing I** missile was first deployed in 1962, and the entire system was carried on four XM474 tracked vehicles. The first deployment to Europe occurred in 1964 when the missile served in the Quick Reaction Alert role for the Central European theatre of operations and as a general nuclear delivery system for field armies. The Pershing was grouped into battalions comprising a headquarters battery, a service battery and four firing batteries. The West German air force also adopted the Pershing I, receiving a total of 72 launchers. Because of the poor mobility characteristics of the tracked vehicles, in 1966 a development contract was placed with Martin-Marietta to improve the system and the missile's capabilities.

In November 1967 production started of the improved **Pershing Ia** to replace the Pershing I in both the US Army and West German air force. The first operational Pershing Ia was deployed in 1969. The most obvious improvement was the replacement of the XM474 tracked vehicles by wheeled vehicles derived from the M656 5-ton truck chassis. This greatly enhanced the system's mobility over paved roads and across country. It also allowed the warhead to be carried with the missile rather than on its own vehicle as had been the case with the Pershing I. The system's firing unit now consisted of an articulated truck and trailer combination that served as the erector-launcher, a transporter for the programme tester and generator units, a firing battery control centre vehicle and a radio terminal set vehicle with an inflatable aerial. A series of subsequent system improvements has allowed the reaction time to be reduced still further, and the introduction of an automatic reference system and sequential launch adapter in 1976-7 allows the Pershing unit commander to fire up to three missiles from a single control station at previously unsurveyed launch sites. The current US Army inventory of Pershing systems is 164 launchers, of which 108 are in Western Europe. The West Germans replaced their Pershing I systems on a one-for-one basis by the Pershing Ia.

In 1978 the advanced development programme of the **MGM-31B Pershing II** system was successfully completed.

First and second stages fall away after boosting payload into required trajectory

Re-entry vehicle manoeuvred over target area by onboard inertial guidance unit

Terrain scanning radar activated Image compared with reference area held in on board computer memory

Pershing II launched with updated launch position in inertial guidance memory

Target

Reference area
Area of radar scan

First stage   Second stage   Guidance and re-entry vehicle control

Low yield ground penetrating nuclear warhead

Narrow beam terrain mapping radar

Specification
MGM-31B Pershing II
Dimensions: length 10.50 m (34.45 ft); diameter 1.00 m (3.28 ft)
Weight: 7439 kg (16,400 lb)
Warhead: 5/50-kiloton selectable yield W85 nuclear
Range: 1300 km (808 miles)
CEP: see text
Launch: wheeled M656 truck and trailer combination
Guidance: inertial with RADAG terminal homing

This missile is a modular modernization of the solid-propellant Pershing Ia with considerably enhanced accuracy and range. Achieving initial operational capability in late 1984, a total of 108 launchers have been deployed by the US Army in West Germany as part of the NATO theatre nuclear forces modernization programme. The launchers are centred in a brigade of three battalions, each of which has four firing batteries that are further subdivided into three firing platoons with three mobile launchers apiece. In peacetime one platoon of each battalion is on 'quick reaction alert' at all time, whilst in wartime all the batteries would disperse into the heavily wooded areas where a launcher requires only a 1.83-m (6-ft) diameter clear space above the missile for a successful launch. After a launch the unit would quickly relocate to another area and set up again for the despatch of the next missile. A further training battalion with eight firing platoons is located in the USA.

The Pershing II's RADAG terminal-guidance system depends on an all-weather radar correlation unit in its ceramic nose cone to compare returns from an area (initially of 906 km²/350 sq miles) surrounding the target with a pre-stored onboard radar profile map of the same region. Several such correlations are made during the descent phase to update the RV's inertial guidance system and so generate course corrections to ensure the best CEP value attainable. Values of between 20 and 45 m (66 and 148 ft) have been achieved during the trials phase.

Left: A Pershing II launcher is assembled from its travelling configuration. The Pershing force in Germany is centred around the brigade of three battalions; with three launchers per firing platoon, and three platoons in each of the batteries of the battalion, the brigade has a firing strength of 108 launchers.

Above: An early Pershing II is launched from Cape Canaveral. Now fully deployed in West Germany, the highly accurate system poses a considerable threat to Soviet command and control centres far behind the Central Front, being capable of reaching targets deep within the USSR itself.

MGM-118 Peacekeeper Heavy ICBM Missile System

USA

Serious development of the **MGM-118A Peacekeeper** missile began in 1974 under President Ford's Administration and has progressed well in spite of a number of non-technical problems. The first test rounds were fired in 1983 and the first production rounds were deployed in 1986. The four-stage solid-propellent missile has been designed to have considerably improved accuracy, range and payload features when compared with ICBMs. The missile is encased at the time of its assembly in a protective launch canister compatible with a variety of basing options. When the missile is fired a solid-propellant unit in the base of the canister is ignited to eject the missile in a cold launch clear of the protective casing. The first-stage propulsion motor system is then fired automatically once the missile is some 24-30 m (80-100 ft) clear. A protective shroud over the nose assembly and a 6 mm (¼ in) thick rubber-like skin over the missile's surface protects it from dust and debris.

The first stage is powered by Thiokol rockets and burns out at an altitude about 24385 m (80,000 ft). The second-stage Aerojet propulsion unit then takes over. This stage burns out at about 85345 m (280,000 ft), whereupon the final solid-propellant Hercules Aerospace motor ignites. The nose shroud is then jettisoned at around 97-km (60-mile) altitude to uncover the MIRV payload. Final third-stage burn out occurs around 116-km (72-mile) altitude when the fuel load has been totally exhausted. During all three powered flight stages the guidance system has constantly modified the flight path so that all the solid fuel aboard is consumed, this meaning that no propulsion cut-off system is required on the third stage.

The fourth-stage Rockwell International RS-34 assembly is then released. This carries a post-boost liquid-propellant propulsion motor with multiple-burn capability, the Northrop advanced inertial reference sphere guidance system, attitude-reference systems, and the Avco re-entry package of 10 MIRVs with penetration aids. The rocket motor is used to target the MIRVs. Once the course of the dispensing bus is set a warhead is released and the RS-34 backs away. The newly released MIRV is then spin-stabilized by the two small rockets it carries. As soon as the warhead is well clear of the RS-34 the motor re-ignites and the assembly changes course to engage the next target. The process is repeated until all 10 MIRVs have been launched.

The payload to be carried is now known to be 10 Mk 21 (formerly ABRV) MIRVs, each of which has a 300-kiloton yield W87 warhead which can, if required, be upgraded to 475-kiloton yield. The warheads can be individually fused for one of five actuation modes depending upon the target type to be engaged: these modes are a high-altitude airburst, a medium-altitude airburst, a low-altitude airburst, a proximity surface burst and a contact surface burst. The dispensing MIRV bus has room for 12 warheads without stacking, but the spare capacity is used for penetration aids of various types. An automatic retargeting capability allows for the reprogramming of target information to compensate for missiles which are destroyed in their silos by an enemy attack or which malfunction in flight.

Although an engineering and technological success, the Peacekeeper programme has been dogged by Congressional hostility which has hampered attempts to establish a viable basing mode. 1986 saw the first 12 of 50 missiles deployed in modified Minuteman III silos at Warren AFB, Wyoming. The upgraded silos have new shock isolation, command, control and com-

The Peacekeeper is smaller than comparable Soviet missiles but is extremely accurate. The nose cone can take a dozen warheads easily, but the usual load will be ten with the remaining space used for penetration aids and decoys.

munications, but have not received any additional hardening. It is planned that a second batch of 50 missiles are to be based on railcars, two to a train. The Reagan administration hopes to have the first mobile missiles ready by 1991 with deployment complete in 1993.

Peacekeeper has replaced the obsolete, liquid-fuelled Titan II heavy ICBM, the last of which was withdrawn in 1986. The Peacekeeper is accurate enough to threaten all types of hardened Soviet targets, from fourth generation ICBM silos and their associated super-hardened launch control centres through to the very heavily protected bunkers which would shelter the civil and military leadership of the USSR in time of war.

Specification
MGM-118A Peacekeeper
Dimensions: length 21.60 m (70.87 ft); diameter 2.34 m (7.67 ft)
Weight: 87545 kg (193,000 lb)
Warhead: 10 300-kiloton MIRVs
Range: 14001 km (8,700 miles)
CEP: 60 to 90 m (65 to 100 yards)
Launch: silo with cold-launch system
Guidance: inertial

Above: Peacekeeper is cold launched, the missile being popped out of its silo under gas pressure before the first stage ignites. To ensure a tight fit in the silo, the missile is surrounded by a gas seal, which drops away once out of the tube.

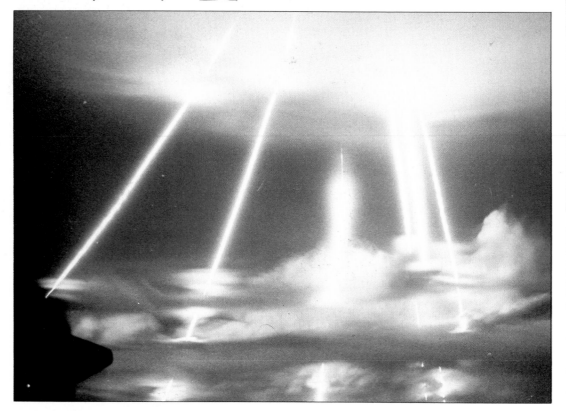

Left: MGM-118A Peacekeeper re-entry vehicles pass through a cloud layer over their target at the Kwajalein missile range, more than 4,000 nautical miles from the missile's launch at Vandenburg AFB, California.

14

Minuteman Lightweight ICBM Missile System

The **Minuteman** family of ICBMs comprised four variants, of which only the **Minuteman II** and **Minuteman III** remain in service. The original **LGM-30A Minuteman I** equipped one Strategic Air Command missile wing in 1963. An improved **LGM-30B Minuteman I** with increased range and of longer length was then brought into service with the next four wings formed, whilst the sixth was equipped in 1966 with the **LGM-30F Minuteman II**. Both the Minuteman II and the **LGM-30G Minuteman III**, introduced in 1970, then replaced the two Minuteman I variants. The 450 Minuteman IIs and 550 Minuteman IIIs are deployed in six strategic missile wings in Montana, North and South Dakota, Missouri and Wyoming.

The wings are dispersed over wide geographical areas and are organized in squadrons of five flights each with 10 hardened missile silos and an underground launch control centre. If the control centre is incapacitated for any reason, launch control is passed either to one of two control centres within the squadron that can also serve as a squadron control centre or, in the case of some 200 or so missiles, to a specially configured Strategic Air Command airborne command post aircraft that carries an airborne launch control and retargeting system.

The three-stage solid propellant LGM-30F Minuteman II is essentially an upgraded Minuteman I with increased range and a more sophisticated guidance system. The latter has an eight-target selection capability giving increased accuracy and a single Mk 11G thermonuclear RV with Tracor Mk 1A chaff-dispenser penetration aids. Several of the Minuteman IIs are specially configured to carry communications equipment instead of a warhead to act as Emergency Rocket Communications Systems for the back-up role of crisis communication to surviving nuclear strike forces in a post-nuclear exchange environment.

The improvements of the LGM-30G Minuteman III over its predecessor are confined mainly to the third stage and the warhead re-entry system. The main feature is the introduction of three MIRVs as the payload. The post-boost bus has been fitted with a small Bell Aerosystem liquid-propellant rocket motor, four smaller roll rockets and six slightly larger pitch stabilizer jets. All of these are under the command of the onboard Rockwell International inertial guidance system. Currently 250 of the Minuteman III force have the Mk 12 re-entry vehicle containing three W62 165-kiloton yield warheads with chaff and decoy penetration aids.

The remaining 300 missiles have been further modernized by the installation of the improved Mk 12A re-entry vehicle. This is about 16 kg (35 lb) heavier than the Mk 12 but as a result of the miniaturization of certain components remains identical in size. It is able to carry three W78 335-kiloton yield warheads with slightly better CEP capability. The associated penetration aids also remain. Considerable effort is being devoted to sustain the Minuteman force's operational capabilities and survivability prospects during any nuclear-exchange scenario.

All Minutemen IIIs will receive guidance software improvements, and improved protection from electro-magnetic pulse is being developed. The whole Minuteman force is involved in the US ICBM Modernization Program, which entails increased site security, improved and hardened communication systems at all Minuteman Wings, improved emergency power systems, and upgrading of launch complex control centre facilities. In addition, the replacement of third stage motors on the Minuteman II force is well under way, which will allow the missile to remain effective to the year 2000. Minuteman IIIs are to receive chaff and decoy launchers, more sophisticated penetration aids and a manoeuvrable re-entry vehicle (MARV) which is currently under development. These improvements will enable the Minuteman force to overcome potential threats from Soviet ABM defences and remain a credible deterrent into the next century.

Specification
LGM-30F Minuteman II and LGM-30G Minuteman III
Length: 18.20 m (59 ft 8½ in)
Diameter: LGM-30F 1.83 m (6 ft 0 in); LGM-30G 1.85 m (6 ft 0⅘ in)
Weight: LGM-30F 31750 kg (70,000 lb); LGM-30G 34500 kg (76,058 lb)
Warhead type: LGM-30F single 1.2-megaton thermonuclear RV; LGM-30G three 165- or 335-kiloton nuclear MIRVs

Minuteman III was the ultimate development of the neat Minuteman developed in 1958-60 as the first solid-propellant ICBM. Among its new features were multiple independently targeted warheads (up to three 335-kiloton units) and a Command Buffer System for rapid retargeting. A total of 550 of this version was put into silos.

Range: LGM-30F 12510 km (7,775 miles); LGM-30G 14000 km (8,700 miles)
CEP: LGM-30F 370 m (405 yards); LGM-30G 280 m (305 yards) with Mk 12 or 220 m (240 yards) with Mk 12 RVs
Launch facility: hardened silo
Launch: hot type
Propellant type/guidance: solid/inertial

Right: The ignition of a Minuteman's motors in the silo forces smoke and gas hundreds of feet into the air. The resulting titanic smoke-ring is passed by the rapidly accelerating missile within seconds.

Below: A Minuteman is launched from a test silo on the Vandenberg Air Force Base in California. Suitably modernized, the Minuteman force will present a credible deterrent well into the 21st Century.

American Ground-Launched Cruise Missile System

For many years the only cruise missiles in service have been Russian, but because of the combined efforts of Western protesters and the Western media the term 'cruise' today means a quite small and slow missile which the USAF deployed in Europe. Actually called the **BGM-109G**, and a member of the versatile **General Dynamics Tomahawk** family, it has been developed to give the NATO alliance its previously missing theatre nuclear strike capability against important fixed targets such as major airfields, naval bases and hardened missile silos. It makes sense to use a super-accurate missile against such targets, because it frees manned aircraft for use in the conventional role against moving targets which at present only they can attack.

Unlike today's aircraft, the BGM-109G is not itself based on a fixed location, and thus does not invite easy retaliation. In any time of crisis between the East and West one of the first things to happen would be that the cruise missiles would be driven out of their normal storage bases to new positions in remote areas. These positions have already been selected and surveyed. Each offers the maximum concealment, and special measures have obviously been taken to guard against their location becoming known in advance by spying, because this would render them vulnerable to mining or other forms of sabotage at the crucial time. Obviously, roads would be sealed for a time behind the dispersing fire units to prevent enemy agents from following them. The problems in the West are greater than in the Warsaw

Pact powers, where the population as a whole are not mobile and the area available for concealing mobile long-range missiles far greater.

The other big question mark hanging over such slow-flying missiles is their ability to penetrate hostile airspace. Hitler's V-1 was an ancestor to modern cruise missiles, yet the piston engined fighters of the RAF and USAF rapidly gained the upper hand in 1944. Modern radar systems, computers, jet interceptors and precision missiles combine to form a defence network that a 805-km/h (500-mph) missile would certainly find very difficult to pierce.

The BGM-109G, otherwise known as the **GLCM** or ground-launched cruise missile, was developed as part of the NATO theatre nuclear force modernization programme, and along with the Pershing II ballistic missile is designed to counter Soviet deployment of their SS-20 mobile IRBM system. It can be used against fixed strategic targets (such as lines of communication, logistics dumps, airfields, and command and control centres) or against stationary tactical targets such as troop staging or assembly areas. The GLCM reached IOC (initial operational capability) with the US Air Force in December 1983, and began to equip bases in Great Britain, Belgium, Holland, Italy and West Germany thereafter. The original plans called for a total of 464 missiles to be based in Europe by 1988, but any US/Soviet agreement on the reduction of theatre weapons will naturally affect that figure.

The GLCM is deployed in firing un-

its of 16 missiles carried on four TELs with two mobile LCCs in attendance. The unit is in peace located in a hardened concrete shelter at its home base, but will deploy to pre-surveyed firing positions offering good natural concealment at distances of about 160 km (100 miles) from the base if hostilities seem imminent. Escorts from the host nation's armed forces will accompany the unit to provide security during the dispersal operation and to provide ground defence at the launch site. Both the TEL and the LCC have good cross-country capabilities. To fire a missile the launcher-container is first elevated and then a solid-propellant booster on the missile is ignited to boost it to its cruise speed. Once this has been attained the booster is jettisoned, the missile wings and fins unfold, the engine inlet is deployed and the turbofan engine ignited in order to sustain flight. Guidance throughout the mission is by an inertial navigation guidance system updated by a terrain contour matching (Tercom) unit at periodic intervals.

The GLCM carries a 123-kg (270-lb) W84 nuclear warhead with a yield of 200 kilotons to a maximum range of 2800 km (1,740 miles). The CEP value over that range is estimated to be a phenomenal 18.3 m (60 ft), and is solely due to the inertial/Tercom guidance system. The major advantage of the GLCM is its ability to fly most of the mission at low altitude to avoid radar detection and air defence systems. Its major disadvantage is its slow speed (Mach 0.7), which makes for long mission times to extreme-range targets. Thus if the Russians field enough high-

performance low-level detection an air defence-missile systems, and an craft with look-down radars, then th credibility of the cruise missile in i present form becomes questionab! The next generation of cruise missile is already under development. Th ACM, or advanced cruise missile, w initially replace current air-launche weapons and will be constructed fro low observability, or stealth materia

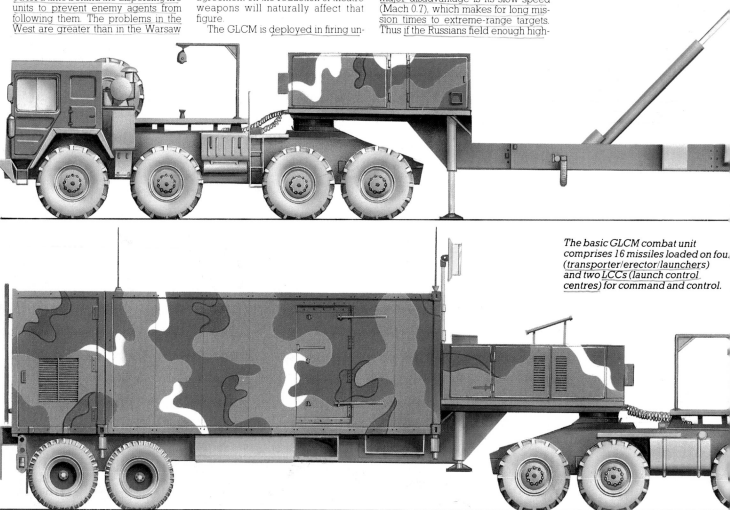

The basic GLCM combat unit comprises 16 missiles loaded on fou. (transporter/erector/launchers) and two LCCs (launch control centres) for command and control.

…dramatic launch picture of a GLCM …ring a test firing (probably at …hite Sands Missile Range, New …exico). The missile is popped from … tube by a short-burn rocket, …ving it enough energy to keep …asting upwards as it unfolds its …ngs, tail and engine inlet, and fires … the small turbojet on which it …uises.

…ecification
…GM-109G Tomahawk
…ngth: 6.4 m (21 ft 0 in)
…ameter: 0.53 m (1 ft 8⁹⁄₁₀ in)
…eight: 1200 kg (2,645 lb)
…arhead weight: 123 kg (270 lb)
…arhead type: 200-kiloton nuclear, …d training
…inimum range: not available
…aximum range: 2780 km (1,725 miles)
…EP: 18.3 m (60 ft)
…unch vehicle: wheeled transporter-…ector-launcher
…opellant type/guidance: solid boos-…r plus turbofan main engine/inertial …th Tercom updating

…ere the TEL is shown parked in the …ring mode with the quad missile …ox elevated. The LCC seen below …ntains all systems needed for a …o-man crew to target and fire.

Small Lightweight ICBM programme

The inability of Strategic Air Command to find an acceptable long-term basing mode for the MGM-118 Peacekeeper ICBM resulted in the engineering study of a possible alternative in the form of a small highly dispersable lightweight land-based ICBM with a single 300/500-kiloton yield warhead that would have a projected CEP of between one and two times that of its larger brother. At least three different possibilities have been studied to date. The first, known as the **Midgetman**, was around 15.24 m (50 ft) long, had a launch weight of 9072 to 13608 kg (20,000 to 30,000 lb) and a range of 11265 km (7,000 miles). Between 3,000 and 4,000 missiles were projected as being deployed in small blast-resistant silos spaced about 1.6 km (1 miles) apart over an area of some 11660 km² (4,500 sq miles). The major problems discovered for such a system were, however, the high cost and potential difficulties with the guidance system.

The second weapon was Boeing Aerospace's three-stage **Small ICBM** (**SICBM**), which was to be about 11.58 m (38.0 ft) long and 1.07 m (3.5 ft) in diameter, weigh some 11340 to 15876 kg (25,000 to 35,000 lb) and have a 453.6-kg (1,000-lb) throw-weight. This version was to be deployed in some 3,350 super-hardened silos about 457 to 610 m (1,500 to 2,000 ft) apart on existing military bases throughout the western USA or at Minuteman missile fields.

The third system studied was a major modification of the Martin Marietta Pershing II, to be known as the **Pershing III**, using additional third and fourth stages to give intercontinental range. With the same throw-weight as the SICBM, the 13.11-m (43-ft) long, 1.02-m (3.33-ft) diameter missile would have a maximum range of 12875 km (8,000 miles).

The SICBM and Pershing III are also projected as having alternate road-mobile Tractor-Erector-Launcher (TEL) basing. Both Boeing and General Dynamics are investigating the possibilities, the later firm developing a specially armoured carrier/launcher under the codename 'Armadillo'.

The lightweight ICBM has now evolved into an augmentation system for Peacekeeper rather than a replacement, with an initial operational capability date of 1992. The chosen design for production will be picked in the latter part of the decade and will probably be assigned the popular name Midgetman when it finally comes into service.

The new small ICBM currently under research and development for the US Air Force is shown in this cutaway drawing as it might appear when it enters service in the 1990s. Very likely to be given the popular name Midgetman, the small ICBM will supplement MGM-118 Peacekeeper.

Both Boeing and Vought have developed HML (Hard Mobile Launcher) Test Beds for the Small ICBM programme. Boeing's wheeled example has been selected for further development in preference to Vought's tracked model.

FROG series/SS-21 Tactical Surface-to-Surface Missile Systems

The **FROG** (Free Rocket Over Ground) missiles are described by the Russians as tactical missile systems, and are known in Soviet army service by the name **Luna**. First deployed in 1957, the FROG has undergone an extensive development programme that has resulted in seven versions of the missile, known by the NATO designations FROG-1 to FROG-7. Of these the tracked vehicle-mounted **FROG-1** to **FROG-5** are considered obsolescent, although the **FROG-3** is still used in training units and held in the Soviets reserve war stocks. The **FROG-6** is a non-operational training round, and the **FROG-7** is the current system. Introduced into service in 1965, the FROG-7 is carried on a ZIL-135 wheeled erector-launcher vehicle and is found at divisional level in both the Soviet and Warsaw Pact armies. Each tank division and motorized rifle division has a FROG battalion with a headquarters battery and two firing batteries (each equipped with two FROGs on their launchers and two reload vehicles with a further six missiles). Two variants of the FROG-7 have been identified: the nuclear-armed **FROG-7a** with a 550-kg (1,213-lb) warhead, and the **FROG-7b** with a 390-kg (860-kg) chemical warhead. The latter is believed to contain the thickened persistant nerve gas agent VR-55, and other types of agents may also be carried. The FROG series has been extensively exported and has also been used in combat. The Egyptians used both FROG-3 and FROG-7 missiles with HE warheads in the 1973 war with Israel. Fired initially against fixed targets in the Sinai and then against the Israeli bridgehead over the Suez Canal, the missiles caused relatively little damage. At least one FROG-7 was claimed as shot down by the Israeli battlefield air defence system. The Syrians used FROG-2 and FROG-3 missiles during their Golan Heights assault, but because of their inaccuracy the missiles impacted mainly on civilian areas. The most recent use of the FROG has been by Iraq against Iran in the Gulf War. Iraq has been using the FROG-7 as a long-range bombardment system targeted against Iranian cities immediately behind the battle zone.

FROG-7 is a single-stage spin-stabilized solid-propellant unguided rocket that uses speed brakes as its main inflight control system. The rocket, weighing 2300 kg (5,071 lb), takes about 30 minutes to prepare for firing and is aimed by adjusting the elevation of the launcher arm. Meteorological radars are required for maximum effect. In the nuclear role the Soviets will fire single FROG rounds with airburst nuclear warheads (50-200 kilotons) against battlefield nuclear delivery systems, forward and reserve troop concentrations, forward headquarters and communication facilities, the large-yield warheads used making up for the FROG's lack of accuracy.

The replacement for the FROG-7 (Soviet designation R-75, Luna-M) tactical missile is the NATO-designated **SS-21 'Scarab'** (Soviet name Tockha, or point) which was initially deployed in 1976 in small numbers. By late 1985 the total had grown to some 250 launchers. The missile is carried within the belly of a derivative of the three-axle 6×6 ZIL-167 vehicle that has already been used for the SA-8 'Gecko' SAM system.

The tractor-erector-launcher (TEL) is fully amphibious, and the inertially-guided solid-propellant single-stage missile is moved into the vertical position for launching whilst the vehicle is stabilized by four hydraulic jacks lowered to the ground. The SS-21 can be armed with a nuclear, chemical or cluster-munition warhead. The SS-21 is also in service with the Syrian (one regiment of 12 launchers), Iraqi (one brigade of 18 launchers) and is replacing the FROG-7 in the Czech and East German armies. Current users of FROGs include the other Warsaw Pact members, Cuba, Egypt, Iraq, North Korea, Libya, Syria and Yugoslavia. China is reported to be developing a version of the FROG-7.

Specification
SS-21 'Scarab'
Dimensions: not known
Weight: not known
Warhead: 10- or 100-kiloton nuclear, chemical or cluster munition
Ranges: minimum 14 km (8.7 miles) and maximum 120 km (74.6 miles)
CEP: 50-100 m (55-110 yards)
Launch: wheeled TEL based on the ZIL-167
Guidance: inertial

Specification
FROG-7
Length: 9.1 m (29 ft 10¼ in)
Diameter: 0.55 m (1 ft 9⅔ in)
Weight: 2300 kg (5,071 lb)
Warhead weight: 550-kg (1,213-lb) nuclear, 550-kg (1,213-lb) HE, or 390-kg (860-lb) chemical
Warhead type: 10-, 100- and 200-kiloton nuclear, HE, chemical and training
Minimum range: 11 km (6.8 miles) nuclear and HE, and 14 km (8.7 miles) chemical
Maximum range: 70 km (43 miles)
CEP: 450-700 m (490-765 yards) depending on range
Launch vehicle: wheeled ZIL-135
Propellant type/guidance: solid/none

Since 1956 the Soviet armies have deployed several thousand free-flight artillery rockets called FROG by NATO (from Free Rocket Over Ground). There have been successive improved rockets and launch vehicles, this example being a 'FROG 7' carried on a ZIL-135 cross-country prime mover. Range is up to 70 km (43 miles)

19

SS-1 'Scud' and SS-23 'Spider' Short Range Ballistic Missile Systems

The **SS-1 'Scud'** guided missiles are classed as operational/tactical-level missile systems by the Soviets. The original 4400-kg (9,700-lb) 'Scud-A' was first employed in 1957. Carried on a variant of the IS-III heavy tank chassis, the missile was limited to a 130-km (81-mile) range with a 40-kiloton nuclear warhead as its payload. In 1965 the improved 6370-kg (14,043-lb) **'Scud-B'** was introduced on an eight-wheeled MAZ-543 erector-launch vehicle for greater mobility. By 1970 the 'Scud-B' constituted three-quarters of the 300 'Scud' launchers deployed. Around this time the longer range **'Scud-C'** was first deployed, this being an improvement over the 'Scud-B' in terms of propellant efficiency but at the expense of a worse CEP at long ranges. By 1978 all the 520 or so 'Scud' launchers deployed in the Soviet army were carrying the 'Scud-B' or 'Scud-C' versions.

In Soviet service the 'Scud-B' and 'Scud-C' are deployed at army and army group levels in brigades consisting of a headquarters battery with three firing batteries each of three launcher vehicles and three reload vehicles carrying single missiles. Alternative 1000-kg (2,205-lb) HE or chemical warheads are available to replace the nuclear type. The 'Scud-A' and 'Scud-B' have been exported to all the Warsaw Pact nations, Egypt, Syria, Libya, Iraq and South Yemen. 'Scud-C' has been exported only to Libya, which is the largest operator of the 'Scud' outside the USSR with some 70 'Scud-B' and 'Scud-C' weapons in service by late 1986. Egypt fired Scuds against Israel in the 1973 Yom Kippur War, and both Iraq and Iran (the latter acquiring the missiles via North Korea and possibly Libya) have used Scuds operationally in the Gulf War.

The SS-1B/C 'Scud' (Soviet designations R-17 and R-17E respectively) operational/tactical missile replacement is the inertially-guided single-stage **SS-23 'Spider'**, which uses an eight-wheeled MAZ chassis with an environmental protection chamber as the TEL. The missile can be fitted with a nuclear, chemical or cluster-munition warhead. The first SS-23s entered service with the Soviet army in early 1980 and, as a consequence of its new solid-propellant powerplant, has reduced the reaction and refire times of both Soviet army and front missile brigades by perhaps 66 per cent. By late 1985 over 100 TELS were in service with the Soviet army.

Specification
SS-1 'Scud-B'
Length: 11.4 m (37 ft 4¾ in)
Diameter: 0.84 m (2 ft 9 in)
Weight: 6370 kg (14,043 lb)
Warhead weight: 1000 kg (2,205 lb)
Warhead type: 40-/100-kiloton nuclear, HE, chemical and training
Minimum range: 80 km (50 miles)
Maximum range: 180 km (112 miles) with nuclear warhead, and 280 km (174 miles) with HE or chemical warhead
CEP: 930 m (1,015 yards) at 180 km (112 miles), reducing with further range
Launch vehicle: wheeled MAZ-537
Propellant type/guidance: liquid/inertial

Originally fielded on a massive tracked chassis derived from the Stalin Tank, Scud is now transported and fired from the MAZ 543 8×8 transporter, which has exceptional mobility.

Specification
SS-23 'Spider'
Dimensions: not known
Weight: not known
Warhead: 200-kiloton nuclear, chemical or cluster munition
Ranges: minimum 80 km (50 miles) and maximum 500 km (311 miles)
CEP: 280 m (305 yards)
Launch: wheeled TEL based on the MAZ 8×8 vehicle

SS-12 'Scaleboard'/SS-22 Short Range Ballistic Missile Systems

The **SS-12 'Scaleboard'** was introduced into Soviet army service in 1969 as an operational/strategic-level missile system. Deployed only at army group level in brigades of one headquarters battery and three firing batteries each of three erector-launcher vehicles and three reload vehicles carrying single missiles, the 'Scaleboard' provides the Front (army group) commander with his only organic nuclear system capable of hitting both the enemy corps and army group rear areas. The only other Soviet systems tasked with strikes into the army rear areas are held by the Strategic Rocket Forces and by the Long Range Air Force. The single-stage 8800-kg (19,400-lb) 'Scaleboard' is an inertially guided missile carried enclosed in a ribbed split casing on a MAZ-543 eight-wheeled vehicle similar in appearance to that carrying the 'Scud-B' and 'Scud-C' missiles. The 'Scaleboard' is elevated to the vertical from the horizontal shortly before firing. The propellant used is of the solid type, and the warhead carried has a yield of 800 kilotons. The CEP at the maximum range of 800 km (497 miles) is estimated to be 480 m (525 yards). The peak number of 'Scaleboard' missiles deployed was 120 throughout the mid-1970s.

The last of the trio of replacement missiles is the operational/tactical inertially-guided two-stage **SS-12M 'Scaleboard'** (formerly the SS-22) which entered service in 1979 as a variant of the original SS-12 with reduced reaction time, and improved range and accuracy. By 1984 SS-12M systems had been forward-deployed to Soviet army bases in both East Germany and Czechoslovakia as counters to NATO's INF systems. Each modified MAZ 8×8 SS-12M TEL has a reload round in the front or army's missile brigade supply train. A total of 80 of the original SS-12 launchers had been modified for the new missile by late 1985.

SS-12 is a powerful battlefield mobile weapon with a range of 800 km (500 miles). It is gradually being replaced by the SS-22, which has improved range and accuracy.

Specification
SS-12 'Scaleboard'
Length: 11.25 m (36 ft 11 in)
Diameter: 1.05 m (3 ft 5⅓ in)
Weight: 8800 kg (19,400 lb)
Warhead weight: 1250 kg (2,756 lb)
Warhead type: 800-kiloton nuclear
Minimum range: 220 km (138 miles)
Maximum range: 800 km (497 miles)
CEP: 480 m (525 yards)
Launch vehicle: wheeled MAZ-537
Propellant type/guidance: solid/inertial

USSR
Soviet Cruise Missile

Cruise missiles are not new. The idea of attacking targets with small explosive pilotless aircraft dates back at least to the First World War, though it was not until the Second World War and the arrival of Hitler's V-1 over the skies of Europe that the concept saw extensive operational testing. The German scientists and their programmes were eagerly snapped up by the victorious allies, who were keen to make best use of German wartime research. Cruise missiles became the subject of a series of development programmes on both sides of the Iron Curtain and pilotless aircraft such as the tactical Martin Matador and the huge Northrop Snark (the world's first strategic missile) began to be deployed. Before long, however, ballistic missiles proved more effective for the strategic nuclear mission, and soon the only cruise-type weapons in operation were the pioneering Soviet naval systems, designed mainly for anti-ship use. In spite of their considerable experience with this type of missile, the only Soviet ground launched applications were as coastal defence systems. The most capable of the conversions from ship- or air-launched missiles was the SS-C-1B 'Sepal', a derivative of the SS-N-3 'Shaddock' naval anti-ship system, which has a secondary surface-to-surface role. This 10.5 ton, 11 m (almost 36 ft) long missile has a maximum speed of Mach 1.4 and a maximum

range of about 450 km (280 miles). Some versions may be equipped with a radio altimeter, which would give it a limited terrain following capability. Unofficial sources estimate that there are about 100 SS-C-1s in use as part of the defences of major Soviet ports and naval bases. 'Sepal' is thought to be able to carry a variety of warloads, including 350 or 800 kiloton yield nuclear warheads, chemical warheads containing either the non-persistant blood agent Hydrogen Cyanide or VR-55, which is a thickened form of the nerve agent Somun. A later coastal missile currently in service with Warsaw Pact countries, Yugoslavia, Syria (but *not* with the USSR) is the SSC-3 system using the widely available SS-N-2 'Styx' naval missile.

The American cruise missile programmes in the 1970s appears to have spurred the Soviets into matching schemes, however. The first to be fielded appears very similar to the American Tomahawk family, with the air launched AS-15 achieving IOC in 1984, and the submarine launched SS-N-21 probably being fielded in 1986. The land based version of this 3000 km range missile has been designated SSC-4, and may be deployed as part of the Soviet Theatre Nuclear Forces in support of the SS-20 IRBM. As such, it could be affected by any US/Soviet arms reduction agreements, (although the first units are thought to be oper-

ational in four-round mobile launchers in the Far East and may not be covered by such an understanding.

According to the Pentagon, the Soviets are in the process of developing a much larger system than the Tomahawk equivalent AS-15/SSC-4/SS-N-21 family. This 13m (over 42ft) long missile may be developed in a ground launched version in addition to the submarine launched system designated SS-NX-24, currently under test in

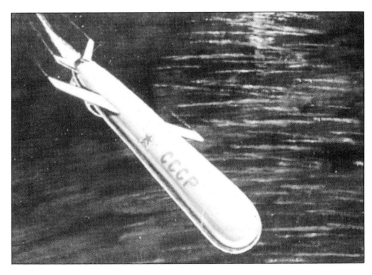

The US Department of Defense has released artist's impressions of recently deployed Soviet cruise missiles, which according to the Americans bear a marked resemblance to the BGM-109 Tomahawk series.

a modified 'Yankee' class SSBN. The ground launched missile could be operational by 1990 and will almost certainly be nuclear armed.

USSR
SS-4 MRBM Missile System

The Soviet SS-4 (NATO reporting name 'Sandal') is a development of the SS-3 'Shyster' missile. Deployed initially in 1959, the SS-4 rapidly became the standard operational/strategic-level MRBM of the Soviet Strategic Rocket Forces (Raketnyye Voyska Strategicheskovo Natnacheniya, or RVSN). In fact all Soviet land-based missiles with ranges exceeding 620 miles (1000 km) are assigned to the Strategic Rocket Forces whilst those missiles with ranges of under 620 miles (1000 km) are assigned to the Rocket Troops and Artillery branch of the Soviet army. Both the MRBM and IRBM forces are designed to deliver nuclear strikes against Western Europe, the

Middle East, Japan and China. The SS-4 and SS-20 systems targets include those in the immediate enemy army group rear areas lying some 310 to 375 miles (500 to 600 km) behind the battle zone, whilst the remaining targets for the SS-4, SS-5 and SS-20 missiles lie at distances in excess of 620 miles (1000 km) and include strategic theatre headquarters and communications facilities, airfields, ports, logistical centres and selected politico-economic targets such as oil refineries.

The SS-4 gained a certain notoriety in 1962 as the main Soviet missile deployed to Cuba during the Cuban Missile Crisis. It was during this deployment that it was noticed that the gui-

dance had been changed from command to an inertial system. The complete SS-4 firing unit consists of around one dozen tractor vehicles and associated trailers. The missile can be fired either from a fixed hardened site or from a soft launch pad. At the latter site a reload capacity is known to exist. The SS-4 force peaked at its maximum during the 1960s, but fell to 500 in the period 1971-7. From the latter year the numbers started to decline as the SS-20 was introduced until in late 1985 only some 112 were in service, based primarily in the Western Soviet states and targeted towards NATO and the Middle East. Replacement by the SS-20 continues.

The SS-4 was also developed into the B1 small utility satellite launch-vehicle by fitting a second stage. First

use of the B1 was in 1962, and the type has been used to launch Kosmos and Interkosmos series satellites from the Kapustin Yar space centre.

Specification
SS-4 'Sandal'
Length: 21.0 m (68 ft 10¾ in)
Diameter: 1.6 m (5 ft 3 in)
Weight: 27000 kg (59,525 lb)
Warhead type: single 1.2-megaton thermonuclear RV, or high explosive
Range: 2200 km (1,367 miles)
CEP: 2300 m (2,515 yards)
Launch facility: hardened silo or fixed soft launch pad
Launch: hot type (reload capability at soft site)
Propellant type/guidance: liquid/inertial

USSR
SS-9 Heavy ICBM Missile System

The SS-9 heavy ICBM (NATO reporting name 'Scarp') entered service in its initial form with the Strategic Rocket Forces in 1965 as the largest ICBM in the world. The missile was a three-stage inertially-guided liquid-propellant type. The Soviets then developed another three variants of which only one, the Model 4, actually entered service in some numbers from 1971 onwards. The SS-9 Model 1 carried a 25-megaton warhead; the briefly-deployed SS-9 Model 2 had a 20-megaton warhead; and the SS-9 Model 4 had three MRVs of 3.5-megaton yield each. The Model 3 or F-1-m satellite launch-vehicle version was employed as the test vehicle for a depressed trajectory role and Fractional Orbital Bombardment System (FOBS). The first flight of a FOBS missile was in 1966, the uppermost stage being a new fourth stage acting as the suborbital

warhead-carrier that attained a temporary orbit close to the Earth's surface before a retro-rocket unit was activated to bring the carrier back into the atmosphere over the target zone. Such a missile can be fired in any direction to hit its target without alerting the defending early warning systems until just before impact. However, the penalty incurred is a reduction in accuracy that is offset somewhat by the high-yield multi-megaton warhead carried. A three-stage FOBS variant is also believed to have been developed, possibly using the uppermost stage of the SS-10 'Scrag' ICBM for the suborbital warhead carrier. The FOBS test flights lasted until 1971.

All the SS-9 ICBM variants can loosely be described as bottle-shaped in appearance with the first stage having six fixed thrust nozzles and four vernier nozzles. The SS-9 Model 3 has

also appeared in the F-1-r satellite launcher form. This is the main Soviet anti-satellite hunter/killer missile and carries a manoeuvring final stage with multiple-burn capacity to attack US near-Earth orbit reconnaissance and communications satellites by detonating an onboard high explosive frag-

SS-9 is 34.5 m (113 ft) long and has a launch weight of 200 tonnes. This version, seen on parade through Red Square in 1967, has a single 25-megaton warhead, by far the largest ever produced for any missile.

mentation charge near them.

The numbers of SS-9s deployed peaked at 308 in the period 1972-4, but declined from then as the first of the even larger SS-18 ICBMs became operational. By 1980-1 the SS-9 had been totally replaced in their silos on a one-for-one basis, although it is known that 18 launch pads remain operational at the Tyuratam space centre to launch the F-l-r. It is also likely that several

F-1-m missiles remain available for use in a strategic nuclear exchange.

Specification
SS-9 'Scarp'
Length: Model 1 34.5 m (113 ft 2¼ in); Model 2 34.5 m (113 ft 2¼ in); Model 4 35.0 m (114 ft 10 in)
Diameter: 3.05 m (10 ft 0 in)
Weight: 200000 kg (440,920 lb)
Warhead type: Model 1 single 25-

megaton thermonuclear; Model 2 single 20-megaton thermonuclear; Model 4 three 3.5-megaton MRVs
Range: Models 1 and 2 11000 km (6,835 miles); Model 4 12000 km (7,455 miles)
CEP: Models 1 and 2 740 m (810 yards); Model 4 1850 m (2,025 yards)
Launch facility: hardened silo
Launch: hot type
Propellant type/guidance: liquid/inertial

First of the really global missiles to be deployed in substantial numbers, the SS-9 carried either a 25-megaton warhead or three 3.5-megaton MRVs. It has now been replaced by the SS-18.

USSR

SS-11 Lightweight ICBM System

The **SS-11** (NATO reporting name 'Sego') was introduced into service in 1966. By 1970 some 970 had been deployed, making this the most numerous of all ICBMs deployed. The two-stage storable liquid-propellant missile was developed in four versions: the basic **Model 1** with a single RV, the **Model 2** first seen in the late 1960s but non-operational although fitted with a single RV and advanced penetration aids, the **Model 3** deployed in 1973 with three MRVs, and the **Model 4** seen in the late 1970s with three or six small MIRVs but not deployed operationally.

By 1975 the number of the deployed SS-11 Model 1 and Model 3 variants dropped slightly to 960 as the first of the SS-17 and SS-19 replacement systems were fielded. By 1977 the number had dropped to 850 and then by 1979 to 650. By mid-1982 the number had stabilized at around 570 with only a small number believed to be of the Model 3 type. By 1986 the Soviets had begun to dismantle SS-11 silos to allow deployment of the first SS-25 mobile ICBM systems. As a result, numbers of 'Segos' deployed fell to 486, mostly Mod 2 and Mod 3. Since the more modern systems have been deployed, the remaining SS-11 warheads have been re-targeted on major cities, airfields and ports throughout Western Europe (incidentally making the argument about the deployment of the SS-20 somewhat academic). It is expected that the final 'Sego' will be withdrawn from service by the middle of the 1990s.

The SS-11 has been periodically shown in the Moscow military parades but only enclosed in a tubular container carried on the rear of a wheeled tractor-trailer combination. The only physical features of the missile to be seen are four thrust nozzles on the first stage and the tip of the nose cone. The container is believed to be raised to the vertical over a silo for loading. The Americans credit the SS-11 force with a limited reload capability as the hot-launched missile is accommodated within a launch container inside the silo. This and the silo design are common to the SS-11, SS-17, SS-18 and SS-19 systems, and limit damage during main-engine ignition and launch. Refurbishment and reloading probably take several days. Provision for the delivery of reserve missiles, warheads and propellants to a number of SS-11 and SS-19 hot-launch ICBM complexes, together with all the cold-launch SS-17 and SS-18 missiles, is known to exist. None of the extra missiles or warheads is reckoned under the SALT agreements, only the launchers being counted.

We in the West still have only a rough idea of what SS-11 looks like, but this is the missile that has since 1966 increasingly been targeted on every city, airfield and port in Western Europe. By 1972 there were 970 known SS-11 silos, with 66 more then being built.

Specification
SS-11 'Sego'
Length: 20.0 m (65 ft 7⅓)
Diameter: 2.5 m (8 ft 2½ in)
Weight: 45000 kg (99,205 lb)
Warhead type: Model 1 single 950-kiloton RV; Model 3 three 250-kiloton MRVs
Range: Model 1 10000 km (6,214 miles); Model 3 10600 km (6,587 miles)
CEP: Model 1 1400 m (1,530 yards); Model 3 1110 m (1,215 yards)
Launch facility: hardened silo
Launch: hot type (limited reload capability)
Propellant type/guidance: liquid/inertial

Pictured from left to right:
SS-4 was operational in 1959 but has been superseded by SS-20.
SS-11, first deployed in 1966, at one time the most numerous ICBM with almost 1000 in place.
SS-9, once the largest ICBM, now replaced by the even larger SS-18.

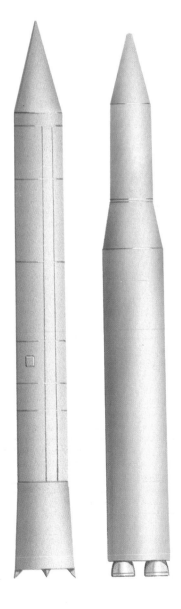

SS-13 and SS-16 Lightweight ICBM Missile Systems

The **SS-13** and **SS-16** are the first solid-propellant ICBMs to have been developed by the Soviets, probably by the VN Nadradze missile design bureau that specializes in such solid-fuel missiles. The SS-13 (NATO reporting name 'Savage') was first deployed in 1969, although it was actually first seen in public in 1965. By 1970 the number deployed operationally had risen to 20, with 40 operational in 1971 and the maximum 60 the following year. The Soviets claim the advanced SS-25 mobile ICBM now entering service is a derivative of the Savage, but the Americans do not agree. Savage is a three-stage inertially-guided missile comparable with the Minuteman missile in terms of performance and capabilities. The upper two stages of the SS-13 were used in the development of the **SS-14** 'Scapegoat' mobile IRBM system.

Between 1972 and 1975 a next generation replacement for the SS-13 was tested, becoming operational in 1978. The **SS-16** 'Sinner' (Soviet designation **RS-14**) was deployed at Plesetsk until 1985. A total of some 60 were built. The three-stage SS-16 has an advanced guidance system believed to be of the stellar-inertial type, and a post-boost bus vehicle usually associated with MIRVs. However, the missile carries only a single RV. The 'Sinner' can be silo-launched or operate from mobile transporter-erector-launch vehicles as a true mobile ICBM, in violation of SALT II agreements. No reload capability for the system is believed to exist. The upper two stages of the SS-16 have been used to form the SS-20 mobile IRBM missile.

Specification
SS-13
Length: 20.0 m (65 ft 7⅓ in)
Diameter: 1.7 m (5 ft 7 in)
Weight: 34000 kg (74,955 lb)
Warhead type: single 600-kiloton RV
Range: 8000 km (4,970 miles)
CEP: 1850 m (2,025 yards)
Launch facility: silo
Launch: hot type
Propellant type/guidance: solid/inertial

Specification
SS-16
Length: 20.5 m (67 ft 3 in)
Diameter: 1.7 m (5 ft 7 in)
Weight: 36000 kg (79,365 lb)
Warhead type: single 650-kiloton RV
Range: 8750 km (5,435 miles)
CEP: 480 m (525 yards)
Launch facility: silo or mobile launcher
Launch: hot type
Propellant type/guidance: solid/stellar-inertial

Only a few (about 60) were put into service of the SS-13, the first of the Soviet Union's solid-propellant strategic missiles. Smaller than SS-11, it is very like a Minuteman III, and has a launch weight of 34 tonnes and range of over 8000 km (5,000 miles), usually carrying a warhead of 600-kT yield

Right: SS-17, an accurate ICBM which replaces some older SS-11 missiles.

SS-17 Lightweight ICBM Missile System

The **SS-17** 'Spanker' lightweight ICBM was first deployed in 1975 as the second two-stage storable liquid-propellant successor to part of the SS-11 'Sego' force, the other part being the SS-19. The SS-17 is slightly longer than the SS-11 and has an increased volume. The most important features, however, are its cold-launch technique and, in its **Model 1** and **Model 3** forms, the four-MIRV warhead it carries. The **Model 2** introduced in 1977 has a single medium-yield thermonuclear warhead, whilst the Model 3 was introduced in the early 1980s because of its increased accuracy over the Model 1 version. The number of the different versions fielded was 20 Model 2 plus 130 Model 1 and Model 3 ICBMs in mid-1986. No further upgrading of the SS-17 force is envisaged for the foreseeable future. Two missile fields contain the SS-17: Yedrovo and Kostroma.

The accuracy of the force makes feasible attacks on some hardened American targets. The use of the MIRVed warhead allows a single Model 1 or Model 3 missile to attack individual targets throughout an area covering several tens of thousands of square miles, whereas the older Soviet SS-11s equipped with MRVs can only attack a single target within a few thousand square kilometres by creating a nuclear explosion 'footprint' around it with its warheads to maximize the blast and radiation damage. The SS-17 has yet to appear at a Moscow parade.

Specification
SS-17
Length: 24.0 m (78 ft 9 in)
Diameter: 2.5 m (8 ft 2½ in)
Weight: 65000 kg (143,300 lb)
Warhead type: Model 1 four 750-kiloton MIRVs; Model 2 single 6-megaton thermonuclear RV; Model 3 four 750-kiloton MIRVs
Range: Model 1 10000 km (6,215 miles), Model 2 11000 km (6,835 miles); Model 3 10000 km (6,215 miles)
CEP: Model 1 440 m (480 yards); Model 2 425 m (465 yards); Model 3 350 m (385 yards)
Launch facility: hardened silo
Launch: cold type (confirmed reload capability)
Propellant type/guidance: liquid/inertial.

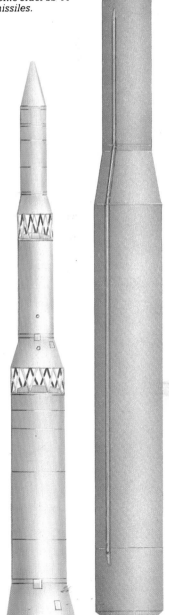

SS-18 Heavy ICBM Missile System

The **SS-18** 'Satan' ICBM (Soviet designation **RS-20**) entered service in its initial form in 1974. Since then three other versions have been deployed, the **Model 2** in 1976, the **Model 3** in 1977 and the **Model 4** in 1979. By 1980-1 the four versions had replaced the 308 SS-9 missiles. In mid-1982 the number breakdown for the four versions was: Models 1 and 3 total 26, Model 2 total 162 and Model 4 total 120. By 1986, all 308 SS-18s operationally deployed were Model 4s, carrying more than 3000 MIRVed 500kT warheads. The Model 1 carries a single 27-megaton warhead, whilst the longer-range and improved-accuracy Model 3 carries a single 20-megaton warhead. The Model 2 has a spin-stabilized computer-controlled warhead bus carrying 8 to 10 900-kiloton yield MIRVs. The later Model 4 is also MIRVed but carries up to 14 warheads (usually 10 500-kiloton MIRVs and four dummies plus other advanced penetration aids). The SS-18 Models 3 and 4, together with the most accurate version of the SS-19, can destroy hard targets. This effectively means the American Minuteman ICBM force in its silos. Hence the Soviets have a credible first-strike capability if they require it. Although all SS-18s are now MIRVed, the USSR has continued testing missiles with single massive warheads.

A fifth model has been reported having ten 750-kiloton MIRVed warheads, and US intelligence have reported two even larger missiles (tentatively called **SS-X-26** and **SS-X-27** under test for the 1990s).

The SS-18 is a cold-launched two-stage liquid-propellant missile. The launch technique is so called because the missile is ejected from its silo by a gas generator system before the main engines are fired. This allows the silo to be reused within a day or so after the missile has been fired. The Russians have been monitored doing this during Strategic Rocket Force exercises. The reload capability is of significant importance to the Russians in their protracted nuclear-exchange warfighting scenario. The SS-18 missile fields are known to be located in the following areas: Kartaly, Dombarovskiy, Imeni Gastello, Aleysk, Zhangiz Tobe and Uzhur.

Specification
SS-18
Length: 35.0 m (114 ft 10 in)

SS-13   *SS-17*

SS-18 Heavy ICBM Missile System (continued)

Diameter: 3.0 m (9 ft 10 in)
Weight: 225000 kg (496,030 lb)
Warhead type: Model single 27-megaton RV; Model 2 8-10 900-kiloton MIRVs; Model 3 single 20-megaton RV; Model 4 10 500-kiloton MIRVs
Range: Model 1 12000 km (7,455 miles); Model 2 11000 km (6,835 miles); Model 3 16000 km (9,940 miles); Model 4 11000 km (6,835 miles)
CEP: Model 1 425 m (465 yards); Model 2 425 m (465 yards); Model 3 350 m (385 yards); Model 4 260 m (285 yards)
Launch facility: hardened silo
Launch: cold type (confirmed reload capability)
Propellant type/guidance: liquid/inertial

SS-19 Lightweight ICBM Missile System
USSR

The **SS-19 'Stiletto'** lightweight ICBM entered service in 1975 as the first of the SS-11 'Sego' replacements, the other being the SS-17. The SS-19 is a two-stage liquid-propellant missile with an onboard computer, a MIRV payload and a combined 'fly-the-wire' inertial guidance system similar to that fitted on the SS-17 and SS-18 missiles. The computer determines the deviations from the preprogrammed course and either corrects it or computes a new course if the circumstances require it. The SS-19 is slightly larger than the SS-17 and has been fielded in three versions: the basic **Model 1** with six MIRVs, the **Model 2** (deployed in 1978) with a single high-yield thermonuclear warhead, and the improved-accuracy **Model 3** (introduced in 1980) with the same MIRV payload as the original version. In 1981 the numbers of each version deployed were 180 Model 1, 40 Model 2 and 80 Model 3 ICBMs. By 1982 the Model 3 total had risen to 90 and in 1986 the SS-19 force level was estimated at 360 Model 3 missiles replacing part of the SS-11 'Sego' force. SS-19 missile fields are located in the Derazhnya, Kozelsk, Pervomayek and Tatischchevo areas.

Because of its accuracy, the Model 3 together with the most accurate versions of the SS-18 are considered to be counterforce weapons capable of destroying practically all the American hardened missile silos by using a two warhead-to-one silo ratio.

The Soviets in their weapon improvement programmes follow an incremental policy: they improve those components of the system that require improving whilst retaining those portions that have demonstrated their reliability to a satisfactory level. For the current ICBM force this policy has meant a considerable improvement in both its reliability and capabilities. The fourth-generation SS-17, SS-18 and SS-19 deployment was primarily into converted third-generation silos. During the process of conversion the silo hardness was greatly enhanced to improve the survivability factor, existing communications systems were upgraded and where necessary new ones added, and silo-based launch-control facilities built.

Specification
SS-19
Length: 27 m (88 ft 6 in)
Diameter: 2.75 m (9 ft 0 in)
Weight: 78000 kg (171,960 lb)
Warhead type: Model 1 six 550-kiloton MIRVs; Model 2 single 10-megaton thermonuclear RV; Model 3 six 550-kiloton MIRVs
Range: Model 1 9600 km (5,965 miles); Model 2 10000 km (6,215 miles); Model 3 10000 km (6,215 miles)
CEP: Model 1 390 m (425 yards); Model 2 260 m (285 yards); Model 3 280 m (305 yards)
Launch facility: hardened silo
Launch: hot type (limited reload capability)
Propellant type/guidance: liquid/inertial

SS-20 Mobile IRBM System
USSR

Design of the missile known in the West as the **SS-20 'Saber'** began in about 1967 when the Soviet Union looked to the long-term replacement for it's intermediate range SS-4 and SS-5. The programme was allocated to the VN Nadradze design bureau, which specializes in solid propellant rockets and had experience with mobile IRBMs. It had designed the **SS-14 'Scapegoat'**, carried in a container nicknamed the 'Iron Maiden' (rather confusingly the whole system of missile and launcher was assigned a separate reporting name by NATO, and was known as 'Scamp'), and the large **SS-15 'Scrooge'** which like the SS-14 used a modified JS-III heavy tank chassis as transporter-erector-launcher. Both missiles were briefly deployed in Soviet Central Asia.

The SS-20, (basically the first two stages of the SS-16 mobile ICBM) first flew in 1974, and by 1977 had entered service with the Strategic Rocket Forces. It is classed as an operational/strategic missile, able to undertake the support of Soviet Military operations in Western Europe or China, and at the same time to threaten traditional strategic targets. SS-20 fields are located in three geographical areas; in the Western USSR, near the Urals and along the Chinese border in central Asia. Most American facilities in the Pacific are within range of the SS-20, and if bases were established in the extreme north-east of Siberia then Hawaii and the West coast of the USA itself would be vulnerable.

SS-20s are grouped in brigades of nine transporter-erector-launcher vehicles (TELs) located at central control and maintenance bases but which would disperse to pre-surveyed and secret launch positions in time of war. Each SS-20 is carried in a tubular container on the back of it's TEL. Three other vehicles complete the SS-20 system, one carrying a reload round and the other two housing the operators, launch control, testing equipment, generators and communications gear.

More than 440 missiles, with over 1,300 nuclear warheads, were in place by 1986 (35% based in the Far East).

Below: SS-19 was deployed first in 1975, along with SS-17. Both are intended as replacements for SS-11, and are among the most accurate of Soviet ICBMs.

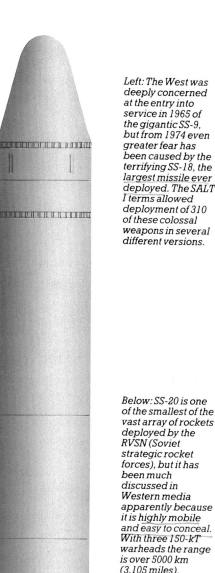

Left: The West was deeply concerned at the entry into service in 1965 of the gigantic SS-9, but from 1974 even greater fear has been caused by the terrifying SS-18, the largest missile ever deployed. The SALT I terms allowed deployment of 310 of these colossal weapons in several different versions.

Below: SS-20 is one of the smallest of the vast array of rockets deployed by the RVSN (Soviet strategic rocket forces), but it has been much discussed in Western media apparently because it is highly mobile and easy to conceal. With three 150-kT warheads the range is over 5000 km (3,105 miles), covering all Europe.

ICBM Nuclear Warhead Development

The original ICBM single re-entry vehicle (SRV) was a large-yield relatively inaccurate warhead designed to be used against large-scale area targets such as cities or industrial areas. Its capacity to devastate such targets lay principally in its blast effect, which is normally measured in pounds per square inch (psi) overpressure (i.e. pressure greater than normal atmospheric). Such warheads would almost certainly be detonated in the air above the target to give what is known as an air-burst explosion. With the advent of better guidance systems terminal accuracy increased and this allowed the large-yield warheads to be retargeted as ground-burst weapons against point targets such as the enemy's military and political strategic command, control and communications (C^3) facilities located in deeply buried and hardened underground bunker complexes. Destruction of some or all of these facilities would cause considerable confusion and delay to the opposing side in any nuclear exchange until new lines of command and control could be activated.

blast damage caused; the resulting pattern of nuclear explosions is known as the nuclear footprint. The USA deployed this type of warhead only on its Polaris submarine-launched ballistic missile force and did not use it on any ICBM.

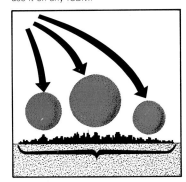

Multiple Re-entry Vehicles (MRVs). Each missile could deliver a number of warheads (usually three) whose combined airburst footprint could obliterate a city.

The USA decided to field the multiple independently-targeted re-entry vehicle (MIRV) warhead system instead. The MIRV is highly accurate and independently targeted, which means that each MIRV-equipped missile can engage a number of widely separated targets equivalent to the number of MIRV warheads it carries. The accuracy of the MIRV is usually sufficient for the carrying missile to be targeted against the enemy's hardened missile silos. Usually two warheads are assigned from different missiles in a cross-targeting tech-

There was a time when threatened nuclear force seemed to consist of a single blunt instrument of undeniable devastation. But defence strategists and scientists have now developed a range of warheads, and methods of delivery which have greatly complicated the discussions of nuclear comparability and security.

nique in order to ensure that the kill probability approaches the certainty value. Both the Soviets and the Americans use MIRV-equipped ICBMs. The current Soviet SS-18 Model 4 and SS-19 Model 3 MIRVed ICBMs are considered to be the world's most lethal missiles in terms of accuracy, and given the numbers deployed the Russians can destroy most of the American Minuteman ICBM force in their silos by expending only a fraction of the warheads they carry for a first-strike situation.

The Americans, however, have developed a follow-on to the MIRV. This is known as the manoeuvring re-entry vehicle (MARV), and is capable both of inflight manoeuvring to avoid anti-missile defences and of terminal in-atmosphere guidance to give very low CEP (circular error probable, a measure of statistical accuracy) values in the order of tens of metres. The technology

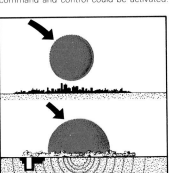

Single Re-entry Vehicles (SRVs). Early generation single warheads airburst over their targets to achieve devastation by blast. Later more accurate warheads were designed to groundburst against hardened targets, such as silos or command bunkers.

Both the USA and USSR currently have ICBMs fitted with thermonuclear warheads of sufficient accuracy to achieve these results.

The attacks against soft city, industrial and military targets were then, in the case of the Soviet ICBM force, assigned to the models equipped with a multiple re-entry vehicle (MRV) package as the payload. This effectively provides for landing several warheads, usually two or three, which have separated in the final stage of the flight in the same area as the target to maximize the

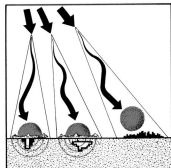

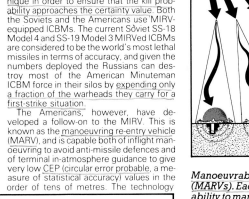

Manoeuvrable Re-entry Vehicles (MARVs). Each warhead has an ability to manoeuvre itself through defences and onto its assigned target.

for the MARV is available for eventual deployment on all American strategic ballistic missile systems if required.

The Americans also have available the technology of the Pershing II earth-penetrator theatre nuclear missile warheads. If the Americans were to combine the low-yield earth-penetrator design with MARV technology then the possibility is opened up of the eventual deployment of an ICBM carrying a large number (20 or more) of super-accurate warheads capable of attacking any type of target. Such a development would have a considerable effect on the strategic forces of both sides as a radical rethinking of fixed-base missiles and command facilities would have to be undertaken.

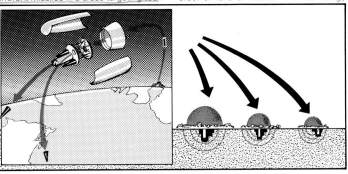

Multiple Independently-targeted Re-entry Vehicles (MIRVs). The independent accurate targeting of a number of warheads enables MIRVs to be groundburst against hardened targets.

SS-20 continued

The total deployed in the future would of course depend upon the success (or lack of success) of any US/Soviet theatre arms reduction talks. Very little unclassified hard fact about the SS-20 is available in the West. For instance, there is some discussion as to the nature of the payload of the missile. The general consensus is that the Model 1 version, entering service in 1977, had a single warhead of between 650 kT and 1 mT yield, but is likely to have been entirely replaced by the Model 2. This entered service at the same time but has three 150 kT MIRVs. A third model, with a single 50 kT warhead, was tested in 1985. The increased range and enhanced accuracy of this development has led some sources to consider it a new missile, with the designation **SS-X-28**. If deployed, it would probably become operational in about 1990.

Specification
SS-20
Length: 16.0 m (52 ft 6 in)
Diameter: 1.7 m (5 ft 7 in)
Weight: 25000 kg (55,115 lb)
Warhead type: Model 1 single 650-kiloton nuclear RV; Model 2 three 150-kiloton nuclear MIRVs; Model 3 single 50-kiloton nuclear RV
Range: Model 1 5000 km (3,105 miles); Model 2 5000 km (3,105 miles); Model 3 7000 km (4,350 miles)
CEP: 425 m (465 yards)
Launch facility: wheeled transporter-erector-launcher
Launch: cold type (reload capability confirmed)
Propellant type/guidance: solid/inertial

SS-20 is being deployed in increasing numbers in Europe and the Far East. The US Department of Defense visualizes highly mobile units operating from easily prepared concealed positions, as shown here.

SS-24 medium ICBM

Initially deploying into 100 former SS-11 'Sego' silo complexes, the three-stage solid-propellant **SS-24** medium ICBM entered operational service in 1985. By 1988 it will also be deployed as a mobile system on 26-m (85.3-ft), 120000-kg (264,550-lb) class 4×4 heavy-duty rail truck missile-launchers, which will be located in a series of hardened railway tunnels that are being constructed in various areas of the USSR where the standard 1.52-m (5-ft) broad-gauge railway system has no overhead power cables. The tunnels will also house the support railway stock comprising 29.5-m (96.78-ft) TSMVO-66 class launch-control vans and smaller KVZ-TsNII two-axle personnel accommodation trucks. The launcher truck is fitted with electrically-powered hydraulic rams to erect the missile capsule into the launch position, a side-folding roof, a missile-ejector unit, and four hydraulically-operated outriggers to stabilize the vehicle during firing.

The SS-24 was first identified under the Western codename **PL-04** (Plesetsk Test Range Missile No. 4), first round being launched in October 1982 but suffering a first-stage failure according to Western intelligence sources. By the tenth flight on 6 September 1983 six further failures had occurred, although the problems had apparently been solved by the time of its deployment. The maximum throw-weight of the missile is assessed at 3600 kg (7,937 lb) for its MIRV payload.

Specification (provisional)
SS-24
Dimensions: length 21.25 m (69.72 ft); diameter 2.0 m (6.56 ft)
Weight: 100000 kg (220,459 lb)
Warhead: 10 350-kiloton MIRVs
Range: 10000 km (6,215 miles)

CEP: 200 m (220 yards)
Launch: silo or mobile railway-based type with a cold-launch system for rapid reload facility
Guidance: stellar inertial

The fifth generation SS-24 ICBM, while replacing SS-11 'Sego' missiles in silos, is expected to be mobile on special trains by the end of the 1980s. Flight tests have been completed at the Plesetsk test facility, and deployment of the system has begun.

SS-25 lightweight ICBM

Formerly known as the **PL-05** because it was the fifth new missile design detected at the Plesetsk launch complex, the **SS-25 'Sickle'** lightweight ICBM began to be deployed by the Strategic Rocket Forces of the Soviet Union in 1986. It has been designed by the V.N. Nadradze bureau who are specialists in solid-fuelled rockets. The Soviets claim that it is a modified SS-13 'Savage' (also designed by Nadradze), and so permitted under the SALT II agreements. The Americans say it exceeds the 5% improvement in throw-weight allowable under SALT, however, and should be considered an entirely new system in violation of the agreements, rather than the modernization of an older type. The Americans also claim that telemetry during flight tests has been encrypted in order to baffle US monitors, which if true is another clear breach of the agreements. In spite of this, the Department of Defense has established that the SS-25 has a greater HTKP (hard-target kill probability) than any preceding system, because of its greater accuracy.

Treaty violation or not, the SS-25 began to replace the SS-13s in their 60 silos at the Yoshtar Osa missile field as the initial deployment. Up to 200 additional silo-launched SS-25s are to be deployed at former SS-11 'Sego' sites with either a single 550-kiloton yield RV or three/four 150-kiloton yield MIRVs as the payload. In the mobile version a total of 20 sites (each for 10 off-road launchers based on the MAZ-548/7910 heavy-duty wheeled truck chassis) are being prepared at SS-20 IRBM fields. Intended to replace additional SS-22 launchers, the sites consist

Approximately the size of the US Minuteman, the SS-25 could be an improved version of the first Soviet solid propellant ICBM, the SS-13. Unlike the US missile, however, the SS-25 seems to have been intended from the outset for mobile deployment, and two mobile bases have been built.

of a number of buildings with sliding roofs, concrete hard stands and enclosed vehicle parking facilities for support vehicles. The launch vehicles can either fire from within their own buildings or, if time permits, deploy to presurveyed sites many miles away. A reload capability is available, and individual missile throw-weight is assessed at up to 1000 kg (2,205 lb). Flight testing of the SS-25 began during 1982, with one test on 30 May 1983 involving the maximum four-MIRV payload.

The SS-25 is being deployed at a very fast rate, the 18 emplaced by the autumn of 1985 growing to more than 70 by the spring of 1986. The SS-25 is now beginning to replace the SS-11 with the Strategic Rocket Forces. The next model is likely to have a MIRVed payload.

Specification (provisional)
SS-25
Dimensions: length 19.0 m (62.34 ft);

diameter 1.7 m (5.58 ft)
Weight: 37000 kg (81,570 lb)
Warhead: three or four 150-kiloton MIRVs or one 550-kiloton RV
Range: 9000 km (5,590 miles)
CEP: 200 m (220 yards)
Launch: hardened silo or wheeled TEL type with cold-launch system for rapid reload facility
Guidance: stellar inertial

Currently the Soviets operate around Moscow the world's only operational ABM system. Deployed initially in 1968, the system began an upgrading and expansion programme in 1980 to bring it up to the maximum limit of 100 launchers set by the 1972 ABM treaty with the USA. The original single-layer defence system relied on 64 reloadable above-ground launchers for the liquid-propellant three-stage exo-atmospheric **ABM-1A/B 'Galosh'** (Soviet designation **UR-96**) missiles in four complexes with six 'Try Add' tracking and guidance radars at each plus two 'Dog House' and 'Cat House' battle-management radars south of the capital to control the engagements and assign targets.

The modified ABM system will be operational by 1989 and comprise modified **ABM-1C 'Galosh'** interceptor missiles emplaced in hardened silos for exo-atmospheric attacks, and a new **SAH-08 'Gazelle'** high-performance endo-atmospheric missile of similar concept to the US high-acceleration Sprint. A reload capability for both systems has been demonstrated, whilst to control the new weapons the Soviets have built a new large phased-array battle-management radar at Pushkino, north east of Moscow, to serve both the original complexes and the new ones under construction.

Initial launch detection of an American, NATO or Chinese ICBM attack is currently handled by a launch detection satellite network and two over-the-horizon radars which can provide a warning of up to 30 minutes and pinpoint the general origin of the attack. Actual confirmation, determination of its size and composition, and provision of target-tracking data to the relevant ABM battle-management radar is then carried out by six peripheral radar sites equipped with a total of 11 'Hen House' ballistic missile early warning radars. This network is being upgraded by the addition of six new phased-array radars that can track more targets with greater accuracy. Five of the sites duplicate or supplement the coverage of the 'Hen House' whilst the sixth, at Krasnoyarsk in Siberia, closes the only gap in missile EW coverage of the USSR.

It is also apparent that the Soviets are developing a mobile ABM system which could be ready for deployment in the early 1990s at any desired location to provide a countrywide ABM defence network rather than one simply for the capital and its surroundings. The Soviets have also tested SAM air defence radars in ABM related exercises and could use their **SA-5 'Gammon'**, **SA-10 'Grumble'** and **SA-12 'Gladiator'** SAMs to intercept some types of strategic missile re-entry vehicles. A massive research programme in using advanced technology such as lasers and particle beam weapons is also under way for possible deployment late in the next decade.

Specification
ABM-1B 'Galosh'
Dimensions: length 19.8 m (64.96 ft); diameter 2.57 m (8.43 ft)
Weight: 32700 kg (72,090 lb)
Warhead: 5-megaton thermonuclear
Range: 740 km (460 miles)
Guidance: radar command

Right: An American impression of the missile at the heart of the world's only operational ABM system, known to NATO as the ABM-1 'Galosh'. It is deployed in 100 launchers around Moscow.

Right: The upgrading of Moscow's ABM defence has seen the emplacement of a new hypersonic missile type, presumably intended for endo-atmospheric interception, in association with upgraded models of the ABM-1. The parallel to the cancelled US Sentinel system is clear.

Below: The phased array radar at Krasnoyarsk is claimed by the USA to violate the 1972 ABM treaty in that it is designed for ballistic missile detection and tracking, and not purely for space tracking.

Chinese MRBM/IRBM/ICBM Missile Systems

The Chinese have had a strategic missile development programme under way since the early 1960s. All development of these systems is the responsibility of a design bureau located at the Shuang-Chengzi missile test centre in the Gobi desert.

The first missile produced was the **Dong Feng 1** (**DF-1**, or **East Wind-1**) SRBM, a locally designed variant of the Soviet SS-2 'Sibling', which was itself an updated German V-2 development. Armed with a conventional HE warhead, the missile was 16-m (52.49-ft) long and 1.65-m (5.41-ft) in diameter, and the single-stage 20500-kg (45,194-lb) missile was pushed to a range of between 560 and 740 km (348 and 460 miles) by a liquid-propellant rocket. The type was deployed in limited numbers during the 1960s and early 1970s, its life being extended into the late 1970s by the retrofitting of the nuclear warhead of the DF-2.

The **DF-2** (Western designation **T-1** or **CSS-1**) MRBM was the first major missile to be produced in China, the type's development starting in 1959-60 on the basis of technology derived from the Soviet SS-3 'Shyster' MRBM. The DF-2 was initially deployed in the north eastern and north western areas of China during 1966. Some 100 rounds were produced between 1966 and 1969, although only 50 or so concrete pad-type launch sites were actually used. It is believed that the DF-2 is now being phased out because of its obsolescence. The DF-2 was the subject of a full-scale test in 1966 using an armed nuclear warhead.

The third missile deployed was the **DF-3** (**T-2** or **CSS-2**) IRBM, which was developed at the beginning of the 1960s using technology derived from the Soviet SS-5 'Skean' but actually following the DF-2 onto the production line from 1970 to late 1974. Operationally deployed in 1972, it is also fired from a fixed site and some 70 are currently believed to be in service. Modified DF-3s were used in April 1970 and March 1971 to launch China's first two satellites.

The first Chinese ICBM, the limited-range **DF-4** (**T-3** or **CSS-3**) entered the development phase in 1967. The first rounds were produced in 1973 but deployment did not start until 1975. Believed to be a two-stage variant of the DF-3, the DF-4 was slow to build, construction of some 25 rounds taking until 1983. The weapon has recently been the subject of a major product improvement programme to upgrade its electronics, to enhance its range and targeting capabilities, and to fit what may be China's first attempt at a MRV or MIRV warhead system. The DF-4 is also the basis of the three-stage **Changzheng-1** (**CZ-1** or **Long March-1**, Western designation **CSL-1**) satellite booster rocket, which was used to put several satellites into orbits up to 265 km (165.7 mile) high during the mid-1970s. Only 10 DF-4s are in service with II Artillery Corps, based in 20.4 bar (300-lb/sq in) hardened concrete silos.

The next ICBM began development in 1973 as the two-stage largely experimental **DF-5** (**T-4** or **CSS-4**) with four liquid-propellant rocket motors powering the first stage and one motor the second. Initially tested in 1980, the DF-5 also formed the basis of the two-stage **CZ-2** (**CSL-2**) and three-stage **CZ-3** (**CSL-3**) boosters that are capable

of launching close-orbit and geosynchronous satellites respectively. The former has been used to launch China's first photo-reconnaissance satellites. Although rivalled in size by only the Soviet SS-18 series, the CSL-3 has a maximum throw-weight of only a meagre 2000 kg (4,409 lb), which is a reflection of China's relatively inefficient propellant industry. The operational version of the DF-5 is thought to be the slightly modified **DF-6** (**T-5** or **CSS-5**) to give a longer range. Deployed in central China in five underground missile silos, the DF-6 represents the current state of the art in Chinese strategic missile production.

Specification
DF-2
Dimensions: length 22.8 m (74.8 ft); diameter 1.6 m (5.25 ft)
Weight: 26000 kg (57,319 lb)
Warhead: 15-kiloton fission or conventional HE
Range: 1200 km (746 miles)
CEP: 2780 m (3,040 yards)
Launch: pad with hot-launch system
Guidance: radio command and inertial

Specification
DF-3
Dimensions: length 20.6 m (67.59ft); diameter 2.46 m (8.07 ft)
Weight: 27000 kg (59,524 lb)
Warhead: 200-kiloton thermonuclear
Range: 13200 km (1,988 miles)
CEP: 1390 m (1,520 yards)
Launch: pad with hot-launch system
Guidance: radio command and inertial

Specification
DF-4
Dimensions: length 26.8 m (87.93ft); diameter 2.46 m (8.07 ft)
Weight: 50000 kg (110,229 lb)
Warhead: (initial version) 3-megaton thermonuclear or (later version) three/four 200-kiloton MRVs or MIRVs
Range: (initial version) 5000 km (3,107 miles) or (later version) 6960 km (4,325 miles) for later version
CEP: 1930 m (1,015 yards)
Launch: silo with hot-launch system
Guidance: (initial version) radio command and inertial or (later version) inertial

Specification
DF-5 and DF-6
Dimensions: length 32.5 m (106.63ft); diameter 3.35 m (10.99 ft)
Weight: 200000 kg (440,917 lb)
Warhead: (DF-5) 4-megaton thermonuclear or (DF-6) 5-megaton thermonuclear
Range: (DF-5) 10000 km (6,214 miles) or (DF-6) 13000 km (8,078 miles)
CEP: 1930 m (1,015 yards)
Launch: silo with hot-launch system
Guidance: inertial

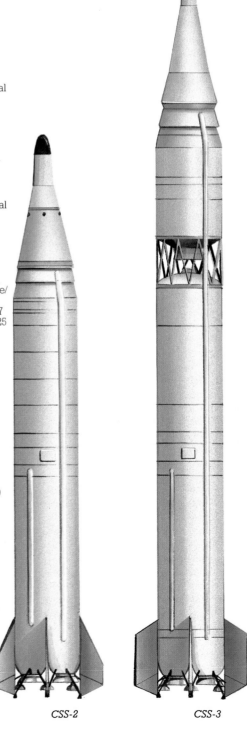

CSS-2   CSS-3   CSS-4

Pluton Short Range Battlefield Tactical Support Missile System

Developed in the late 1960s, the **Pluton** was placed in production during 1972. The first deliveries to the French army began in early 1974. Since then the French have deployed five regiments of the missiles to provide tactical nuclear support to their field armies. Each of the regiments has six launcher vehicles based on the AMX-30 main battle tank chassis, several command vehicles and the appropriate support and resupply sections. A total of 42 launcher vehicles has been produced. The missile and warhead are supplied separately to the operational units. The single-stage dual-thrust solid-propellant Pluton is fitted with a simplified inertial guidance package that is based on a SFENA semi-strapdown system. Two warheads have been developed for the missile: one is the AN-51 for use against rear-area targets and containing the same 25-kiloton MR50 nuclear weapon as the French air force's AN-52 tactical nuclear gravity bomb; the other is a 15-kiloton warhead designed as an air-burst weapon for use in the main battle zone area. As has been the case with most French nuclear weapons the design, testing and production of the systems was carried out totally by the French themselves.

In mid-1977 the French defence ministry disclosed that consideration of a 'Super Pluton' tactical missile was already in hand for deployment in the late 1980s. This missile would have a considerably improved performance in terms of accuracy and range as well as having an improved warhead. By 1983, the project received the go-ahead with Aérospatiale conducting the first flight tests during 1987/88. Now known as **Hades**, the missile will be deployed in an autonomous division of

Carried on a modified AMX-30 MBT chassis, Pluton is a modern and effective weapon; it went into service with the French army in 1974.

the French Army. The missile is about 8.5 m (27.8 ft) long, and has a maximum range of c.350 km. The warhead is likely to be of between 10 and 25 kT yield and possibly of enhanced radiation, or neutron bomb, type. Hades will be launched from wheeled TELs (Transporter-Erector-Launcher) each of which will carry two missiles.

Specification
Pluton
Length: 7.64 m (25 ft 0¾ in)
Diameter: 0.55 m (1 ft 9⅔ in)
Weight: 2350 kg (5,181 lb)
Warhead weight: 350-500 kg (772-1,102 lb)
Warhead type: 15-kiloton nuclear, 25-

kiloton nuclear, or training
Minimum range: 10 km (6.2 miles)
Maximum range: 120 km (75 miles)
CEP: 330 m (360 yards)
Launch vehicle: tracked AMX-30 MBT chassis
Propellant type/guidance: solid/inertial.

French IRBM Missile Systems

From the deployment of the first squadron in 1971, the main land-based component of France's *Force de Frappe* became 18 **SSBS S2** IRBMs. The SSBS S2 was a two-stage inertially-guided solid-propellant missile with a CEP value of 900 m (985 yards) and was deployed in two squadrons each of nine missiles. Located on the Plateau d'Albion east of Avignon in Haute Provence in hardened underground silos, the squadrons were controlled by two heavily protected subterranean fire-control centres that had special communications links direct to the French strategic air force headquarters. The 14.8 m (48 ft 7 in) long and 1.5 m (4 ft 11 in) diameter missile had a launch weight of 31900 kg (70,325 lb) and a maximum range of 2750 km (1,708 miles), and carried a 150-kiloton yield nuclear warhead.

In 1973 a new IRBM development programme was initiated to produce a second-generation missile to replace the S2. The new missile, the **SSBS S3**, was developed by Aérospatiale under five contracts spanning the years 1974-80, and uses the same first stage as the S2. The second stage is, however, of higher performance with a warhead that includes a hardened thermonuclear charge and advanced penetration aids to counter anti-ballistic missile defences. The first test launch was in December 1976, the test firing trials being completed in the summer of 1979. Ini-

tial S3 deployment began in 1980 and by 1982 the missile had completely replaced the S2 in the two IRBM squadrons. During the deployment the ground facilities of the silo complexes were improved to allow modernization of some systems and to increase missile reliability while reducing maintenance costs. Reaction time of the S3 is said to be around 200 seconds from the order to fire.

Specification
SSBS S3
Length: 13.8 m (45 ft 3⅓ in)
Diameter: 1.5 m (4 ft 11 in)
Weight: 25800 kg (56,880 lb)
Warhead: single 1.2-megaton thermonuclear RV
Range: 3.500 km (2.175 miles)
CEP: 830 m (908 yards)
Launch facility: hardened silo
Launch: hot type
Propellant type/guidance: solid/inertial

Launch of an SSBS, probably of the new S-3 type which is now replacing the S-2 in the same silos on the Plateau d'Albion in southern France. S-3 has a range of 3500 km (2,175 miles) with a single large Aérospatiale warhead with a yield of 1.2 megatons. The entire silo and missile are hardened against nuclear attack.

Modern Main Battle Tanks

Although many other weapon systems have been developed for land combat since World War II, the main battle tank is still the dominant factor in that environment. It possesses the armour protection, mobility/agility and firepower which is essential to its survival on today's battlefield, and of all army weapons it is the only one capable of offensive and defensive operations

Tanks have dominated the incessant post-war conflicts in the Arab lands. Despite all the revolutionary advances made in other weapon systems, it is the tank formations that carry out the battles, relegating other weaponry to more or less support roles.

During World War II most of the major powers developed and deployed three classes of tank (light, medium and heavy) and in the immediate post-war period this tendency continued with the USA and the USSR each developing new generations of tanks that included all three types. In the case of the United States it was the M41 Walker Bulldog light tank, the M47 and M48 Patton medium tanks and the M103 heavy tank. The USSR developed the PT-76 light amphibious tank, T-54 medium tank and T-10 heavy tank.

By the 1950s the idea of having three types of tank had lost ground, however, and almost without exception the industrialized countries built just one type of tank which became known as the Main Battle Tank (MBT). France built the AMX-30 (36 tonnes), West Germany the Leopard 1 (40 tonnes), Japan the Type 74 (38 tonnes), the UK the Chieftain (55 tonnes), Sweden the unconventional Stridsvagn 103 or S-tank (39 tonnes), Switzerland the Pz 61 (38 tonnes), the USSR the T-62 (40 tonnes), and the United States the M60 (46 tonnes). As can be seen from these weights, there were significant differences in weight: the British Chieftain is the heaviest of them and would by earlier standards be classed as a heavy tank. The lighter tanks have fairly thin armour and rely on their mobility for protection.

Whereas most first-generation MBTs weighed about 40 tonnes and, in the case of the Leopard 1, had a power-to-weight ratio of 21 hp (15.7 kW) per tonne, second-generation MBTs are much heavier but also have much more powerful engines. The Leopard 2 weighs just over 55 tonnes, but thanks to its 1,500-hp (1119-kW) MTU diesel has a power-to-weight ratio of just over 27 hp (20 kW) per tonne, and therefore much improved cross-country mobility and hence greater survivability, as it is able to move from one fire position to another more quickly and is in direct line of fire with enemy weapons for a shorter period.

For many years most MBTs have been fitted with a NBC (nuclear, biological and chemical) system to enable them to continue to operate in a NBC-contaminated area; but the first generation of infra-red night-vision equipment is now giving way to thermal and passive systems which are a dramatic improvement. All tanks now have a weapon-stabilization system which enables the main armament to be laid and fired whilst the vehicle is moving across country. Fire-control systems now always include a laser rangefinder and a ballistic computer which virtually guarantee a first-round hit on both stationary and moving targets at most battlefield ranges. The widespread introduction of electronic devices into AFVs has, however, increased the cost of the vehicle and increased the demands on the already overworked maintenance personnel.

Apart from the unconventional S-tank designed in Sweden, tank design has not changed dramatically in the last 50 years or so. It may well be that we are now seeing the last MBT as we know it. Already the United States, West Germany and Sweden are experimenting with externally-mounted guns fed by automatic loaders. This enables the crew to be reduced to three men (commander, gunner and driver) seated in the hull under the maximum possible armour protection.

The General Dynamics M1 Abrams MBT is the first tank in the world to enter production fitted with a gas turbine. Although this is much smaller than a diesel, it does have much higher fuel consumption and has to carry additional fuel. Even so, the Abrams is the most mobile of current tanks.

ARGENTINA
TAM Medium Tank

For many years the World War II Sherman tank was the backbone of Argentinian armoured units. By the early 1970s these were becoming increasingly difficult to maintain and a decision was taken to obtain a new tank. Most of the tanks available at that time weighed 40 tonnes or more and were therefore too heavy to pass safely over many of the bridges in the country. A decision was then taken to have a new tank designed specifically to meet the requirements of the Argentinian army, and the development contract for this was subsequently awarded to the West German company of Thyssen Henschel, which was at that time building the Marder MICV (mechanized infantry combat vehicle) for the West German army. The first prototype of the new tank, called **TAM** (Tanque Argentino Mediano) was completed in 1976, a further two vehicles being completed the following year. This tank was accepted for service with the Argentinian army and a factory for production of the vehicle was established near Buenos Aires. Some 200 tanks were to be built, along with 300 related VTCP armoured personnel carriers, but constraints on the hard pressed Argentine economy meant that production ceased when about 350 out of the 500 vehicles had

been completed.

The hull of the TAM is based on that of the Marder MICV, of which well over 2,000 are now in service with the West German army. The driver is seated at the front of the vehicle on the left with the powerpack (engine and transmission) to his right. The glacis plate is well sloped to give the best possible protection within the weight limits of the vehicle. The armour does not compare very well with that fitted to MBTs such as the Leopard 1 and AMX-30, however. The three-man all-welded turret is at the rear of the vehicle, with the commander and gunner on the right and the loader on the left. The main armament comprises a 105-mm gun fitted with an extractor to remove fumes when the gun is fired; this has an elevation of +18° and a depression of −7°. A 7.62-mm (0.3-in) machine-gun is mounted co-axially with the main armament, and a similar weapon can be mounted on the turret roof for anti-aircraft defence. Four Wegmann dischargers can be fitted on each side of the turret, and these fire smoke or fragmentation grenades.

One variant which has been actively promoted is a 155-mm self-propelled howitzer housed in an Italian Palmaria turret and mounted on a widened and lengthened chassis. The project has

been delayed by Argentina's economic difficulties (though all 25 turrets have been delivered).

Specification
Crew: 4
Weight: 30.5 tonnes (loaded)
Engine: MTU 6-cylinder diesel developing 720 hp (537 kW)
Dimensions: length (with gun forward) 8.23 m (27 ft 0 in); length (hull) 6.77 m (22 ft 2½ in); width 3.25 m (10 ft 8 in); height (turret top) 2.42 m (7 ft 11¼ in)

The TAM tank has been designed by the West German company of Thyssen Henschel for the Argentinian army and is based on the chassis of the Marder MICV. Well over 100 of these have now been built in Argentina.

Performance: maximum road speed 75 km/h (46.6 mph); maximum range 550 km (342 miles); fording 1.4 m (4 ft 7 in); gradient 65%; vertical obstacle 1 m (3 ft 3⅓ in); trench 2.5 m (8 ft 2½ in)

CHINA
Type 59 Main Battle Tank

Following the ending of the Chinese civil war in 1949, the Communist Chinese army was based on a more permanent basis, but much of its equipment was obsolete or in urgent need of repair including a number of American and Japanese tanks of World War II vintage. The USSR soon supplied large numbers of armoured vehicles including T-34/85 tanks, SU-100 100-mm tank destroyers, and BTR-40 and BTR-152 armoured personnel carriers. In the early 1950s these were followed by a quantity of T-54 MBTs, and production of the type was subsequently undertaken in China under the designation **Type 59** MBT. The first production models were very austere and were not fitted with a stabilization system for the 100-mm Type 59 gun or with any night-vision equipment. Later vehicles were fitted with a full range of infra-red night-vision equipment for the commander, gunner and driver, as well as a stabilization sytem. The 7.62-mm (0.3-in) bow-mounted and 7.62-mm (0.3-in) co-axial machine-guns are designated Type 59T, while the Russian-designed 12.7-mm (0.5-in) DShKM machine-gun mounted on the loader's cupola is designated Type 54 by China. The British company MEL has provided small quantities of pas-

sive night-vision equipment for the Type 59 MBT, including the driver's periscope and the commander's and gunner's sights. More recently a number of Type 59s have been observed with a laser rangefinder mounted externally above the gun mantlet. This is in a very exposed position, however, and is therefore vulnerable to small arms fire and shell splinters.

The Type 59 has been exported in some numbers and is known to be in service with Albania, the Congo, Kampuchea, North Korea, Pakistan, Sudan, Tanzania and Vietnam. It has seen combat with Pakistan, Vietnam and, of course, China when she invaded Vietnam in 1979.

The Type 59 has been replaced in production by the Type 69, which has a new 100-mm smooth-bore gun. Other improvements include more sophisticated fire-control systems. Both tanks can be fitted with versions of a highly effective British 105-mm gun, a copy of which is now built in China.

Early in 1983 it was reported that China was supplying, via Saudi Arabia, large quantities of Type 69 MBTs to Iraq to make up for some of its losses in the heavy fighting with Iran. American intelligence reports have stated that between 1977 and 1981 Chinese tank

production amounted to about 3,500 vehicles, the vast majority being the Type 69 MBT with the remainder the Type 62 light tank.

Specification
Crew: 4
Weight: 36 tonnes
Engine: V-12 diesel developing 520 hp (388 kW)
Dimensions: length (with gun forward) 9.0 m (29 ft 6 in); length (hull) 6.17 m (20 ft 3 in); width 3.27 m (10 ft 9 in); height 2.59 m (8 ft 6 in)
Performance: maximum road speed 50 km/h (31 mph); maximum range 400 km (249 miles); fording 1.4 m (4 ft

The Chinese-built Type 59 is essentially a Soviet T-54. Later production Type 59s have infra-red night vision equipment and an externally mounted laser rangefinder.

7 in); gradient 60%; vertical obstacle 0.79 m (2 ft 7 in); trench 2.68 m (8 ft 9½ in)

Early T-59s lacked main armament stabilization and night vision equipment, but later models have had these deficiencies made good. Some have been seen with what is probably a laser rangefinder.

Type 80 Main Battle Tank

NORINCO, the China North Industries Corporation, have announced the latest Chinese Main Battle Tank. The **Type 80** could be described as a progressive development of the Type 69, although the introduction of a new chassis, a new gun and a new engine make it a very different vehicle.

At first sight the Type 80 looks like the Type 69 as the turret is almost identical, but closer examination will quickly reveal an extra road wheel on each side. The longer hull houses a more powerful engine, the V-12 turbo-charged diesel having a power output of 730 hp (540 kW) in climates from tropical to Himalayan. Torsion bars are used for suspension, and side skirts are fitted for added protection and to keep road dust from the turret optical devices.

The main gun is a new thermal-sleeved 105-mm (4.14 in) weapon believed to be based on the highly successful British L7 series. Reports have suggested that the original made its way to China via Israel. A stabilized rangefinder and computerized fire-control system can inject an aiming point into the gunner's optical sight within ten seconds of a moving target being engaged. The tank can carry and fire up to 44 rounds of APFSDS, HESH and HEAT ammunition. There is a 12.7 mm (0.50 in) heavy machine-gun mounted on the turret cupola for anti-aircraft use and there is a 7.62 mm (0.30 in) machine-gun co-axial with the main armament.

Other innovations include a full collective NBC system, automatic fire-extinguishing, and infra-red smoke screen dischargers around the turret. The armour seems thicker than that of the Type 69 although no figures are yet available. However, Chinese sources have referred to a composite armour plate that can be applied to the front of the hull. Deep wading in water depths of 5 m (16 ft 5 in) is possible by fitting a schnorkel tube.

Many of the improved features of the Type 80 can be retro-fitted into Type 59 and Type 69 tanks in a package being offered by NORINCO.

Specification
Crew: 4
Weight: 38 tonnes
Engine: V-23 turbo-charged diesel developing 730 hp (540 kW)
Dimensions: length with gun 9.33 m (30 ft 7 in); hull length 6.33 m (20 ft 9 in); width 3.37 m (11 ft 0.75 in); height to turret top 2.3 m (7 ft 6.4 in)
Performance: maximum road speed 60 km/h (37.3 mph); maximum range 430 km (267 miles); fording 1.4 m (4 ft 7 in); gradient 60%; vertical obstacle 0.8 m (2 ft 7½ in); trench 2.7 m (8 ft 10 in)

The Type 80 retains the appearance of preceding Chinese tank designs, but minor external differences hide a much improved fighting machine.

Type 74 Main Battle Tank

The **Type 74** MBT has been designed to meet the requirements of the Japanese Ground Self-Defense Force (JGSDF) by Mitsubishi Heavy Industries. The first prototype, called the **STB**, was completed in 1969, and the first production vehicles followed in 1975. By early 1983 about 300 Type 74 MBTs had been completed, and production was expected to continue until at least the mid-1980s.

The main armament consists of the proven British Royal Ordnance Factories 105-mm L7A1 gun, for which a total of 55 rounds of ammunition are carried; there are also a 7.62-mm (0.3-in) co-axial machine-gun and a 12.7-mm (0.5-in) machine-gun on the roof for anti-aircraft defence. Three smoke dischargers are mounted on each side of the turret, firing forwards. The fire-control system includes a ballistic computer and a laser rangefinder to enable the exact range to the target to be determined, so increasing the possibility of a first-round hit. Some models have an infra-red/white-light searchlight mounted to the left of the main armament, and the driver is also provided with infra-red night-vision equipment.

The most unusual feature of the Type 74 is its hydro-pneumatic suspension, which enables the driver quickly to adjust the height of the vehicle to suit the type of ground being crossed or to meet different tactical situations. The ground clearance can be varied from 0.2 to 0.65 m (7.9 to 25.6 in), and the driver can even tilt the nose or back of the tank, or have one side of the tank higher than the other. The 105-mm gun has an elevation of +9.5° and a depression of −6.5°, but with the suspension raised at the front and lowered at the rear this can be increased to +15°, the reverse producing a depression of −12.5°; this is a very useful feature when the tank is firing from behind a crest or from a reverse slope.

As a result of Japan's prohibition of the export of weapons the Type 74 MBT has not been exported. The only variant of the Type 74 is the **Type 78** armoured recovery vehicle, which has a hydraulic dozer/stabilizing blade at the front of the hull, a winch, and a hydraulic crane on the right side of the hull for changing engines and other components in the field. The chassis of the vehicle will also be used for the projected twin 35-mm **AW-X** self-propelled anti-aircraft gun which is expected to enter service in the second half of the 1980s.

For the future the **Type 88** MBT is being developed under the direction of the Japanese Self-Defense Agency's Technical Research Headquarters. This will have advanced armour, be fitted with a smooth-bore 120-mm gun and weigh about 43 tonnes. At least 600 of these are expected to be built to replace the old Type 61 MBTs, which are rapidly becoming obsolete.

Specification
Crew: 4
Weight: 38 tonnes (loaded)
Engine: Mitsubishi 10-cylinder diesel developing 750 hp (560 kW)
Dimensions: length (with gun forward) 9.41 m (30 ft 10½ in); length (hull) 6.7 m (21 ft 11¾ in); width 3.18 m (10 ft 5¼ in); height (overall) 2.67 m (8 ft 9 in)
Performance: maximum road speed 53 km/h (33 mph); maximum range 300 km (186 miles); fording 1 m (3 ft 3⅓ in); gradient 60%; vertical obstacle 1 m (3 ft 3⅓ in); trench 2.7 m (8 ft 10¼ in)

The Type 74 MBT entered service in 1976. An unusual feature of the vehicle is its hydro-pneumatic suspension, allowing the driver to adjust the height of the suspension to suit the type of terrain being crossed.

AMX-30 Main Battle Tank

When the French army was re-formed after the end of World War II its initial tank fleet comprised Sherman tanks and a few French-designed ARL 44s. All of these were replaced from the mid-1950s by the American M47, which was supplied to France in large numbers by the United States under the Mutual Defense Aid Program (MDAP). In 1956 France, West Germany and Italy drew up a requirement for a new MBT lighter and more powerfully armed than the M47 which was then being used by all three countries. France and West Germany each went ahead and built prototypes of a new MBT to meet this specification, the French contender being the **AMX-30**, and the West German vehicle the Leopard 1. It was expected that one of these two tanks would be adopted by both countries, but in the end each adopted its own tank. The AMX-30 was designed by the Atelier de Construction d'Issy-les-Moulineaux (AMX), which has designed most French AFVs since World War II. The first prototypes were completed in 1960, and the first production tanks were completed by the Atelier de Construction Roanne in 1966. By 1982 some 2,000 had been built, half for the French army and half for export. The AMX-30 is also manufactured under licence in Spain for the Spanish army.

The AMX-30 is the lightest of the first generation of NATO tanks, and has a hull of rolled steel plates welded together; the three-man turret is of cast construction. The main armament consists of a 105-mm gun with a 20-mm cannon co-axial with the main armament and a 7.62-mm (0.3-in) machine-gun on the commander's cupola. The co-axial weapon is unusual in that it can be elevated independently of the main armament to +40°, enabling it to be used against low-flying aircraft and helicopters. A total of 47 rounds of ammunition is carried for the 105-mm gun, of which 19 are in the turret and

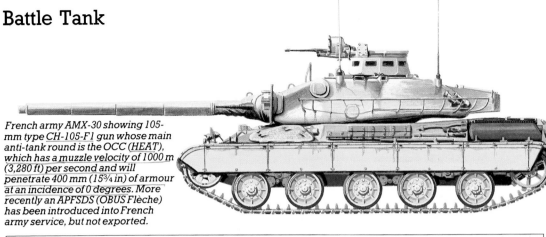

French army AMX-30 showing 105-mm type CH-105-F1 gun whose main anti-tank round is the OCC (HEAT), which has a muzzle velocity of 1000 m (3,280 ft) per second and will penetrate 400 mm (15¾ in) of armour at an incidence of 0 degrees. More recently an APFSDS (OBUS Flèche) has been introduced into French army service, but not exported.

Main armament of the AMX-30 is a 105-mm rifled gun, which can fire standard NATO ammunition as well as French-designed rounds.

the remaining 28 in the hull. Totals of 1,050 rounds of 20-mm and 2,050 rounds of 7.62-mm ammunition are also carried. Types of ammunition fired by the 105-mm gun include HEAT, HE, Smoke and Illuminating, while a new APFSDS round has been introduced recently. The latter is called the Obus Flèche, and with a muzzle velocity of 1525 m (5,005 ft) per second will penetrate 150 mm (5.9 in) of armour at an angle of 60° at a range of 5,000 m (5,470 yards). The current production model of the AMX-30 for the French army is the **AMX-30 B2**, which has a number of improvements including an integrated fire-control system that includes a laser rangefinder and a LLLTV system; its automotive improvements include a new transmission.

The basic AMX-30 chassis has given birth to a very large family of related vehicles. The **AMX-30D** armoured recovery vehicle is designed to recover and repair damaged vehicles in the field, and has a dozer/stabilizer blade mounted at the front of the hull, two winches, and an hydraulic crane on the right side of the hull for changing engines and other components in the field. The **AMX-30 bridgelayer** has a scissors bridge which can be used to span gaps of up to 20 m (65 ft 7½ in). The chassis is also used to carry and launch the Pluton surface-to-surface tactical nuclear missile, which is used only by the French army. The combat engineer tractor, the **AMX-30 EBG**, is still under development and will be used by the French corps of en-

gineers. The chassis is also used for the French version of the Euromissile Roland SAM system and the SA-10 Shahine SAM system which has been developed by Thomson-CSF to meet the requirements of the Saudi Arabian army. A twin 30-mm self-propelled anti-aircraft gun system, the AMX-30-S 401 A, has also been developed for Saudi Arabia, this providing close-in protection for the Shahine batteries. The AMX-30 and its derivatives are in service with France, Spain, Chile, Greece, Iraq, the United Arab Emirates, Saudi Arabia and Venezuela.

The AMX-30 has been the mainstay of French armoured forces since its introduction in 1966, but is now outclassed by later designs.

AMX-30 of the French army showing its cross-country mobility. This is one of the few Western MBTs that is not now fitted with a stabilization system for the main armament, and cannot therefore fire on the move.

Specification
Crew: 4
Weight: 36 tonnes
Engine: Hispano-Suiza 12-cylinder diesel developing 720 hp (537 kW)
Dimensions: length (with gun forward) 9.48 m (31 ft 1 in); length (hull) 6.59 m (21 ft 7 in); width 3.1 m (10 ft 2 in); height (overall) 2.86 m (9 ft 4 in)
Performance: maximum road speed 65 km/h (40 mph); maximum range 500 to 600 km (311 to 373 miles); gradient 60%; vertical obstacle 0.93 m (3 ft 0⅔ in); trench 2.9 m (9 ft 6 in)

AMX-40 Main Battle Tank

Unlike West Germany, the UK and the USA, France has not developed a second-generation MBT such as the Leopard 2, Challenger or M1/M1A1. The standard French army MBT is still the AMX-30, whose design can be traced back to the late 1950s. This is now being modernized until the new French army MBT, the so called Engin Principal de Combat (recently renamed the Futur Char, or future tank) enters production.

GIAT realized that there would be a big gap between the end of AMX-30 production and the beginning of EPC production, so a decision was taken to build a new MBT specifically for the export market.

The first tank built was the so called AMX-32, which was based on the AMX-30 but fitted with a 120-mm (4.72-in) gun, new armour, improved fire-control system and some automotive improvements. Its crucial power-to-weight ratio was below that of the AMX-30, however, and the AMX-32 has not been sold. It is now offered only with the standard 105-mm (4.13-in) gun as installed in the AMX-30.

In 1983 GIAT unveiled the **AMX-40** MBT, which is a brand new design and has significant improvements over the earlier AMX-30 in the three key areas of tank design: armour, mobility and firepower. The AMX-40 has been designed specifically for the export market and by early 1986 four prototypes had been completed and one of these is believed to have been tested in the Middle East. The AMX-40 has also been offered to the Spanish army, which has a requirement for new MBT with a 120-mm gun.

The armour over the frontal part is of the laminate type and provides protection against HEAT (High Explosive Anti-Tank) rounds with a calibre of up to 100 m (3.94 in).

The layout of the AMX-40 is similar to that of other French MBTs, with the driver at the front left, the turret in the centre (with the commander and gunner on the right and the loader on the left) and the engine and transmission at the rear.

The AMX-40 is powered by a Poyaud diesel engine which gives a power-to-weight ratio of around 25 hp (18.6 kW) per tonne, a very significant improvement over current French MBTs. The engine is coupled to a West German ZF automatic transmission for ease of handling and reduced driver fatigue.

The main armament comprises a 120-mm smoothbore gun which fires

Above: The AMX-40 carries laminate armour over the hull front to give improved protection against HEAT ammunition. It carries its ammunition in the turret bustle, which, if penetrated, will explode upwards and away from the crew compartment.

Right: The French army is still stuck with a first-generation tank, the AMX-30, and the promised 'future tank' is still a long way off. GIAT has developed a much-improved MBT for the export market, the AMX-40, which is armed with a 120-mm smooth-bore gun.

ammunition with combustible cartridge case. Ammunition stowed in the turret bustle is separated from the crew compartment by bulkheads and if a round penetrates the turret bustle the force of the exploding ammunition is vented upward rather than into the crew compartment.

Mounted co-axially with the main armament is a 20-mm cannon for dealing with lightly armoured targets, while mounted on the commander's cupola is a 7.62-mm machine-gun which can be aimed and fired from within the safety of the tank.

The integrated fire-control system includes a laser rangefinder and low-light-level TV with screens at both the commander's and gunner's positions. The commander also has a roof-mounted SFIM stabilized sight, which enables him to aim and fire the main armament.

Specification
AMX-40
Crew: 4
Weights: empty 41000 kg (90,388 lb); loaded 43000 kg (94,798 lb)
Powerplant: one Poyaud 12-cylinder diesel developing 1,100 hp (820 kW)
Dimensions: length, gun forward 10.04 m (32 ft 11.3 in) and hull 6.80 m (22 ft 3.7 in); width 3.36 m (11 ft 0.3 in);

height overall 3.08 m (10 ft 1.3 in)
Performance: maximum road speed 70 km/h (44 mph); range 600 km (373 miles); fording 1.30 m (4 ft 3 in); vertical obstacle 0.9 m (2 ft 11½ in); trench 3.20 m (10 ft 6 in); gradient 70 per cent; side slope 30 per cent

Although heavier than the AMX-30, the AMX-40 is still a very agile MBT thanks to its Poyaud diesel engine, which gives a power-to-weight ratio of 18.6 kW per tonne. Its automatic transmission reduces driver fatigue.

Leclerc Main Battle Tank

Following the collapse of a joint Franco German MBT project in 1982 France was faced with the prospect of a tank force consisting of outdated AMX-30s until the end of the century. As a result, a programme was set up to develop the **Engin Principal de Combat** with the aim of producing a modern battle tank by the early 1990s.

Named **Leclerc** after the general who liberated Paris in 1944, the first 'functional prototype' of the new tank was unveiled in January 1987. This is largely a technology demonstrator, and will be followed by six more prototypes around the end of 1988.

The Leclerc will be the first western production tank to incorporate an automatic loader and three man crew. The gun will be an advanced version of the current GIAT 120-mm smoothbore, designed to handle the increased firing chamber pressures future high performance ammunition will produce. A new, high-velocity APFSDS round is currently under development. Ammunition storage is likely to be 40 rounds, 24 of which will be in the auto loader and the remainder in the hull. A 7.62-mm MG on the turret roof will probably be joined by a co-axial MG in the production tank.

The Leclerc is a notably low and compact design. Although smaller

than the Leopard 2 and the M1 Abrams, the 53 tonne Leclerc weighs about the same, indicating heavy armour protection. The armour itself is of the laminated type, having no structural function, and is added on to the load carrying framework. This means that armour plates can be repaired after battle damage or replaced by newer, more effective protection. The 1,500 hp (1100 kW) supercharged V-8 Diesel engine developed for the Leclerc gives the tank an excellent power-to-weight ratio, which should be reflected in superb combat agility, and an ability to handle the inevitable weight increase arising from

future armour improvements. The suspension is likely to be an advanced form of the conventional torsion bar type, though tests have been carried out with a new oleo-pneumatic system.

Although the Leclerc will have advanced armour, armament and propulsion, the French feel that the most innovative aspect of the tank will be in the electronics. All main functions will be computer controlled, from thermal imaging sensors, gun stabilization and the multiple target capable fire-control to engine monitoring, communications and real-time data transmission.

The first Leclercs should be deployed by the French army by 1991.

Stridsvagn 103 (S-tank) Main Battle Tank

In the period immediately after World War II, light tanks formed the bulk of the Swedish army's tank strength. To meet the country's immediate requirements for tanks some 300 Centurions were purchased from the UK. Development of a heavy tank (the KRV) armed with a 150-mm smooth-bore gun was started with Landsverk responsible for the chassis, Volvo for the powerpack and Bofors for the armament. At the same time Sven Berge of the Swedish army was designing a new concept in AFVs in that the gun was fixed to the chassis and not mounted in a turret. Traverse was to be obtained by turning the tank on its vertical axis and elevation/depression by lowering or raising the suspension at front or back. Test rigs proved the basic concept and in 1958 Bofors was awarded a contract for two prototypes of the turretless tank. At the same time development of the KRV was stopped. The first two prototypes were completed in 1961 but so certain was the Swedish army that the concept was sound that it had, in 1960, placed a pre-production order for a further 10 vehicles. Total development costs of the **Stridsvagn 103** tank, which is commonly known as the **S-tank**, was under £9 million. The first production vehicles, which differed only in minor details from the prototypes, were completed in 1966 and production continued until 1971, by which time 300 had been built.

Main armament is a derivative of the British 105-mm L7, fed from a 50-round magazine in the hull rear and capable of firing up to 15 rounds per minute. A 7.62-mm MG is mounted on the cupola and two more fire forwards from the hull. Two Lyran illumination launchers are also fitted.

Originally powered by a Rolls-Royce multi-fuel engine and a Boeing 553 gas turbine, 200 S-tanks are

Bofors S-tank showing external stowage boxes at hull rear and dozer blade in retracted position under nose. Flotation screen is in lowered position.

undergoing a modernization programme where a Detroit Diesel has been fitted along with an improved transmission. The diesel is still used for normal operations, with the turbine engaged for combat or cross-country use.

The driver sits to the left of the powerplant at the front with the radio operator behind him facing to the rear. The commander has a periscope/binocular sight to which has recently been added a laser rangefinder. A Bofors fire-control computer is also part of the modernization programme.

The suspension is of the hydro-pneumatic type and allows the armament/hull to have an elevation of +12° and a depression of −10°. The main drawback of the S-tank is that it cannot fire on the move. This is of no great drawback to Sweden, however, as her armed forces will probably be engaged in defensive rather than offensive operations.

Mounted under the nose of the tank is a dozer blade which is used to prepare defensive positions. Carried around the top of the hull is a flotation screen which can be erected in 20 minutes, and the tank is then propelled in the water by its tracks at a speed of 6 km/h (3.7 mph).

Specification
Crew: 3
Weight: 39 tonnes
Engines: diesel developing 240 hp (179 kW) and a Boeing 553 gas turbine developing 490 shp (366 kW)
Dimensions: length (with gun) 8.99 m (29 ft 6 in); length (hull) 7.04 m (23 ft 1 in); width 3.26 m (10 ft 8⅓ in); height (overall) 2.5 m (8 ft 2½ in)
Performance: maximum road speed 50 km/h (31 mph); maximum range 390 km (242 miles); fording 1.5 m (4 ft 11 in); gradient 60%; vertical obstacle

Bofors Strv 103B (or S-tank), which has a 105-mm gun fixed to the hull with the weapon being aimed in elevation and depression by adjusting the hydro-pneumatic suspension. The gun is fed by an automatic loader, enabling 15 rounds per minute to be fired.

0.9 m (2 ft 11½ in); trench 2.3 m (7 ft 6½ in)

Centurion Main Battle Tank

The **Centurion** was developed during World War II as a cruiser tank under the designation **A41**, the first prototypes being completed early in 1945 and armed with the 17-pounder gun. The A41 was subsequently renamed the Centurion and entered production shortly after the end of the war. By the time production was completed in 1962, some 4,423 examples had been completed at four plants, namely the Royal Ordnance Factories at Leeds and Woolwich (early vehicles only), Leyland Motors at Leyland and Vickers at Elswick. The **Centurion Mk 1** and **Mk 2** were armed with the 17-pounder (76.2-mm gun), and the **Centurion Mk 3** with the 20-pounder (83.4-mm) gun. A total of 13 basic marks of Centurion were fielded, many of these having no less than three submarks. For example, the **Centurion Mk 10** was a **Mk 8** with more armour and a 105-mm L7 gun, the **Centurion Mk 10/2** was Mk 10 with ranging machine-gun. All through its British army life the Centurion had the standard Rolls-Royce Meteor petrol engine which was a development of the Merlin aero engine. The Centurion was replaced as a gun tank in the British army by the Chieftain, though it remained in service with the Royal Artillery until recently as an armoured observation post. From there gun-

armed Centurions were passed to the Royal Engineers, where they are known as AVRE 105s because they retain their 105mm ordnance.

Centurions were sold to many nations, and saw considerable amount of service. Gun tanks are still being operated by Austria in the static defence role, Denmark, Israel, Jordan, Singapore, South Africa, Somalia, Sweden and Switzerland. Israel has extensively modernized its Centurions, the refit of 105-mm guns, diesel engines and automatic transmission ensuring the **Upgraded Centurion** remains effective into the 1990s. South Africa has a similar Centurion programme, the improved tanks being known as **Olifants**, and Swedish tanks have had advanced fire-control fitted.

There have been many specialized versions of the Centurion, including a variety of self-propelled weapons including the 25-pounder, 5.5-in and 180-mm guns, and a 120-mm tank destroyer. Versions that remain in service include the **Centurion Mk 2 ARV** fitted with large spades at the hull rear and a winch with a capacity of 31 tonnes, which with snatch blocks can be increased to 90 tonnes. The **Centurion/AVRE (Assault Vehicle Royal Engineers)** is used only by the British

army and is fitted with a turret-mounted 165-mm demolition gun for the destruction of battlefield fortifications and a dozer blade at the front of the hull. It can also carry a fascine (large bundle of wood) which can be dropped into anti-tank ditches to enable following vehicles to cross, as well as tow a trailer carrying the ROF Giant Viper mine-clearance equipment. The **Centurion BARV (Beach Armoured Recovery Vehicle)** is another specialized version unique to the British, and this is used to recover disabled vehicles on an invasion beach, as well as to push landing craft off the beach. The BARV was successfully used during the British landings at San Carlos Water in the Falklands. Other versions include the **Centurion AVLB (armoured vehicle-launched bridge)** and target tanks, while the Israelis have fitted a number of vehicles with special dozer blades and roller-type mine-clearing equipment.

The reason why the Centurion has been such a successful design is that it has been able to accept more armour and a larger gun (from the 17-pounder to the 20-pounder and finally to the famous 105-mm L7 gun) as the threat and technology have changed. All models have been fitted with a gun

stabilization system which keeps the gun on the target when the tank is moving across country, and many countries today are now installing advanced fire-control systems which include a laser rangefinder. The Centurion has seen combat with the British army in Korea, with the Australian army in Vietnam, with the Indian army against Pakistan, and with the armies of Israel, Egypt and Jordan in the Middle East. To many people, the Centurion has been the most successful tank design in the history of armoured warfare.

Specification
Crew: 4
Weight: 51.82 tonnes
Engine: Rolls-Royce Meteor Mk IVB V-12 petrol developing 650 bhp (485 kW)
Dimensions: length (with gun forward) 9.854 m (32 ft 4 in); length (hull) 7.823 m (25 ft 8 in); width 3.39 m (11 ft 1½ in); height (without AA MG) 3.009 m (9 ft 10½ in)
Performance: maximum road speed 34.6 km/h (21.5 mph); range 190 km (118 miles); gradient 60%; vertical obstacle 0.914 m (3 ft 0 in); trench 3.352 m (11 ft 0 in)

Centurion Main Battle Tank

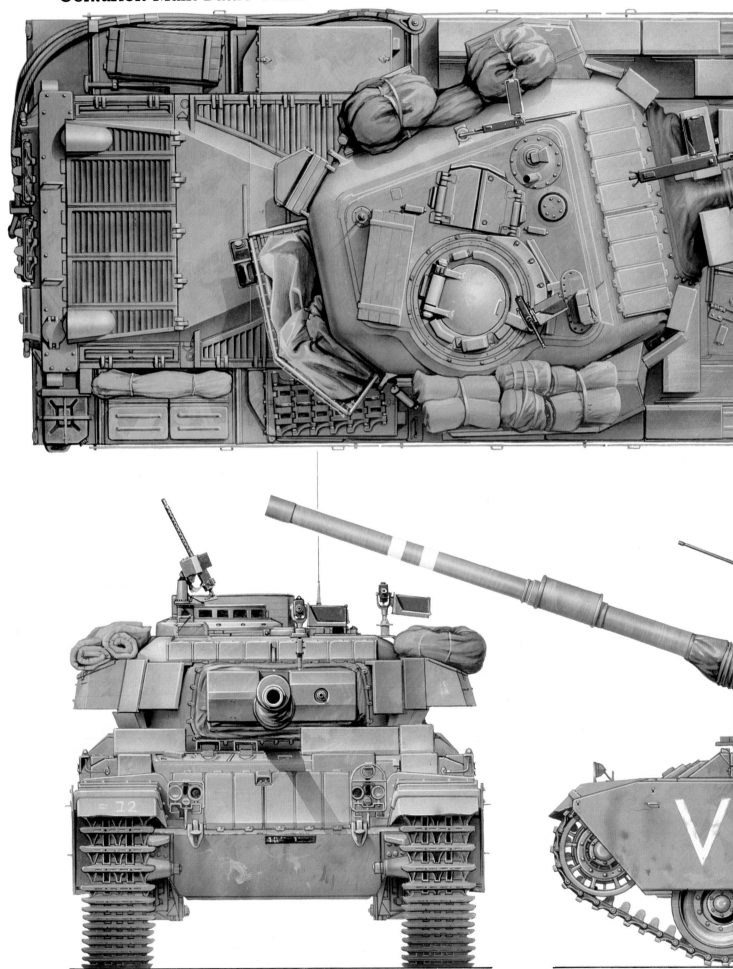

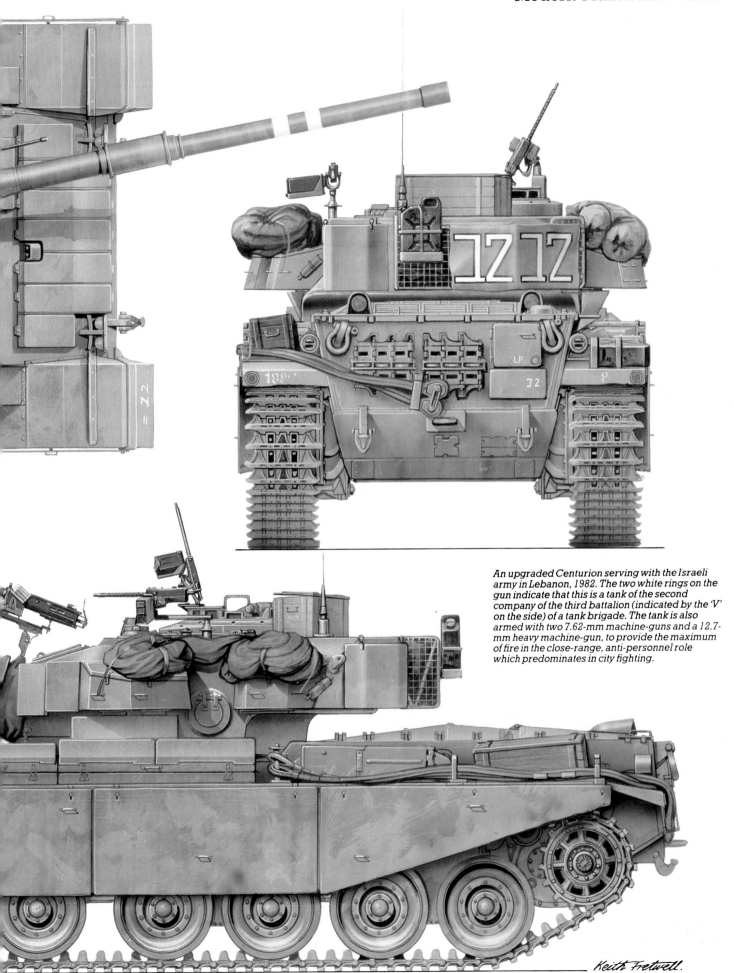

An upgraded Centurion serving with the Israeli army in Lebanon, 1982. The two white rings on the gun indicate that this is a tank of the second company of the third battalion (indicated by the 'V' on the side) of a tank brigade. The tank is also armed with two 7.62-mm machine-guns and a 12.7-mm heavy machine-gun, to provide the maximum of fire in the close-range, anti-personnel role which predominates in city fighting.

Keith Fretwell.

Chieftain Mk 5 Main Battle Tank

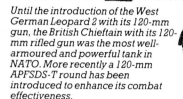

The **Chieftain** MBT was designed by the Fighting Vehicles Research and Development Establishment (now the Military Vehicles and Engineering Establishment) in the late 1950s as a successor to the Centurion tank. The first prototype was completed in late 1959 with a further six prototypes following in 1961-62. The Chieftain was accepted for service with the British army in May 1963 and two production lines were laid down, one at the Royal Ordnance Factory Leeds and the other at Vickers at Elswick (Newcastle-upon-Tyne). Until the introduction of the Leopard 2 into the West German army in 1980, the Chieftain was the best armed and armoured MBT in the world. About 900 Chieftains were built for the British army, Kuwait also ordering 165, and Oman taking delivery of a small quantity in 1981. But the largest export order was placed by Iran, which ordered over 700 MBTs, plus ARVs and bridgelayers as well as 187 Improved Chieftains. In 1974 Iran ordered 125 **Shir 1** and 1,225 **Shir 2** MBTs (the latter a new design) but this order was cancelled by the new regime. The Shir 1 became the Khalid and further development of the Shir 2 resulted in the Challenger which entered service with the British Army in 1983.

The layout of Chieftain is conventional, with the driver at the front, turret in the centre (with the commander and gunner on the right and the loader on the left), and the engine and transmission at the rear. To reduce overall height, the driver sits in a reclined position, lying almost horizontal when driving with the hatch closed. The turret is of all-cast steel construction with the front well sloped to provide the maximum possible protection. The commander has a cupola that can be traversed through 360°, and mounted externally on this is a 7.62-mm (0.3-in) machine-gun which can be aimed and fired from within the turret.

The main armament of the Chieftain is a 120-mm L11A5 series rifled gun designed by the Royal Armament Research and Development Establishment at Fort Halstead. This weapon fires separate-loading ammunition (projectile and charge). The main advantages of this type of ammunition over the conventional fixed round is that the ammunition is easier to handle in the cramped confines of the tank turret, and that as the bagged charges are stowed in special water-filled containers below the turret ring, there is less risk of an explosion. Types of projectile that can be fired include APDS-T (training round is DS-T), HESH (training round is SH/Practice) and Smoke. Soon to be introduced into service is the APFSDS-T projectile which will have a long rod-penetrator and will be capable of penetrating the armour of all known MBTs in service today.

British army Chieftains are now being fitted with the Marconi Space and Defence systems Improved Fire Control System (IFCS) which, when used in conjunction with the laser rangefinder manufactured by Barr and Stroud, enables targets to be hit at ranges of well over 2010 m (2,200

British Chieftain MBT with 120-mm L11A5 rifled tank gun, which has a thermal sleeve to reduce distortion, and is also used by Iran, Kuwait, Oman and probably Iraq.

Until the introduction of the West German Leopard 2 with its 120-mm gun, the British Chieftain with its 120-mm rifled gun was the most well-armoured and powerful tank in NATO. More recently a 120-mm APFSDS-T round has been introduced to enhance its combat effectiveness.

yards).

Mounted co-axially with the 120-mm gun is a 7.62-mm (0.3-in) machine-gun and located on each side of the turret is a bank of six electrically-operated smoke dischargers. A total of 64 rounds of 120-mm ammunition (projectiles and charges) and 6,000 rounds of 7.62-mm (0.3-in) machine-gun ammunition are carried. The NBC pack is mounted on the turret bustle, and a fire detection and extinguishing system is mounted in the engine compartment. Night-vision equipment is of the infra-red type with an infra-red/white light searchlight mounted on the left of the turret with a range of 1000-1500m (1,100-1,640 yds) in the I-R or white light role. A project to update in-service Chieftains with thermal imaging equipment, improved sights and other detail changes began in 1983. Most recently, Chieftains in Germany have had an extra armour belt applied around the turret in a programme codenamed 'Stillbrew'.

Variants of the Chieftain include an export model known as **Chieftain 900** which was introduced in 1984 but which won no orders, an armoured repair and recovery vehicle with hydraulic crane, an armoured recovery vehicle, and a bridgelayer which can span gaps of up to 22.86m (75ft).

Specification
Crew: 4
Weight: 55 tonnes
Engine: Leyland 6-cylinder multi-fuel developing 750 bhp (560 kW)
Dimensions: length (with gun forward) 10.795 m (35 ft 5 in); length (hull) 7.518 m (24 ft 8 in) width 3.657 m (11 ft 8½ in); height (overall) 2.895 m (9 ft 6 in)
Performance: maximum road speed

The Chieftain has been the strength of the British Army's armoured force for two decades, and it's potent combination of heavy armour and powerful gun will serve it well up to the end of the century.

48 km/h (30 mph); maximum road range 400 to 500 km (250 to 310 miles); fording 1.066 m (3 ft 6 in); gradient 60%; vertical obstacle 0.914 m (3 ft 0 in); trench 3.149 m (10 ft 4 in)

Challenger Main Battle Tank

In 1974 Iran ordered 125 Shir 1 and 1,225 **Shir 2** MBTs from Royal Ordnance Factory Leeds. The Shir 1 was essentially a late-production Chieftain, already entering service with Iran in large numbers, with a new powerpack consisting of a 1,200-bhp (895-kW) Rolls-Royce diesel, coupled to a David Brown TN37 automatic transmission and fitted with an Airscrew Holden cooling system. Armament was the 120-mm L11A5 rifled gun connected to a Marconi Space and Defence Systems Improved Fire Control System (IFCS) and a Barr and Stroud laser rangefinder. The Shir 2 was a brand new design and had the same powerpack, armament and fire-control system as the Shir 1, but had a hull and turret of Chobham armour which would provide a high degree of protection against all battlefield weapons, especially missiles with their HEAT warheads. It also had hydrogas suspension which gave an excellent ride across rough country as well as being easy to maintain and repair in the event of battlefield damage.

The British army was to have replaced its Chieftains with a British/West German design, but this fell by the wayside in March 1977 and the UK went ahead on its own with a new project designated MBT-80. With the fall of the Shah of Iran the massive Iranian order was cancelled before deliveries could start, although by that time the Shir 1 was already in production at the Royal Ordnance Factory Leeds. Jordan eventually placed an order for 278 Khalid MBTs essentially similar to the Shir 1; deliveries of these began in 1981, and are still under way.

In 1980 the British Ministry of Defence announced that the MBT-80 project had been cancelled as not only was it getting too expensive but its in-service date was slipping. Instead an

initial order was placed with Leeds for 243 examples of the **Challenger** MBT, this being basically the Shir 2 with modifications to suit it for a European rather than Middle Eastern climate. The first production Challengers were handed over to the British army in March 1983, and four regiments are expected to be equipped with the tank within the British Army of the Rhine. It is anticipated that a further order will be placed to enable at least half of the Chieftains of the Royal Armoured Corps to be replaced.

The first production vehicles are fitted with the standard Royal Ordnance Factory Nottingham 120-mm L11A5 rifled gun but at a later date this will be replaced by the new high-technology gun now under advanced development by the Royal Armament Research and Development Establishment (RARDE) at Fort Halstead. This weapon will be of electro-slag refined steel (ESR) with a new split breech design, and will be able to fire projectiles with a much higher muzzle velocity, providing increased penetration compared with current projectiles. It will also be able to fire, as will the current L11A5, the new Royal Ordnance Factory Birtley APFSDS-T projectile which will defeat all known armours.

The original production order for 243 vehicles has since been increased. All Challengers in service are to be retro-fitted with a new transmission system, a micro-processor based engine control unit and a new, longer lasting track. Challengers in Germany have been equipped with the Barr and Stroud TOGS (Thermal Observation and Gunnery System), which uses thermal imaging for surveillance and gun sighting.

The only Challenger variant so far ordered is the **Armoured Repair and**

Recovery Vehicle (ARRV), which is necessary because the earlier Chieftain ARRV cannot cope with the greater weight of Challenger. The first new ARRV is due for service in 1988. Other Challenger variants which have reached the trials stage include a 155-mm self-propelled howitzer using the Vickers Shipbuilding and Engineering GBT 155 turret, and an anti-aircraft tank mounting the Marconi Command and Control Systems Marksman twin 35-mm anti-aircraft system.

Specification
Crew: 4
Weight: 60 tonnes
Engine: Rolls-Royce 12-cylinder

One of the first Challenger MBTs for the British army, which accepted the tank in March 1983. This retains the 120-mm gun of the earlier Chieftain but has a new powerpack and Chobham armour.

diesel developing 895 kW (1,200 hp)
Dimensions: length (with gun forward) 11.55 m (37 ft 10¾ in); length (with gun to rear) 9.87 m (32 ft 4⅔ in); width 3.51 m (11 ft 6¼ in); height 2.89 m (9 ft 5¾ in)
Performance: maximum road speed 56 km/h (35 mph); maximum range (estimated) 500 km (310 miles); fording 1.07 m (3 ft 6 in); gradient 60%; vertical obstacle 0.91 m (3 ft 0 in); trench 3 m (9 ft 10 in)

The Royal Hussars, seen here on exercise in Germany, were the first British tank regiment to completely re-equip with Challenger. The tank's Chobham armour and 120-mm gun make it one of the most powerful of modern battlefield weapons.

Vickers Mk III Main Battle Tank

Vickers' Elswick facility built many of the 4,423 Centurion MBTs built by 1961, but the company realized that for many countries Centurion's successor, the Chieftain, would be too heavy and too expensive. At about the same time the Indian army issued a requirement for a new MBT, and in 1961 the Vickers proposal was accepted. This was based on the company's private-venture design which had become known as the Vickers Main Battle Tank (VMBT). This used the proven 105-mm L7 series gun as well as some of the components of the Chieftain MBT, which was then about to enter production at both Royal Ordnance Factory Leeds and Vickers' Elswick facility, including the 12.7-mm (0.5-in) ranging machine-gun, Leyland L60 engine, TN12 transmission, auxiliary engine, brakes and steering. The first two prototypes were completed in 1963 and by the following year a production line had been established in India, the first tank being completed in 1965 from components supplied by Vickers. But as time went on India produced more and more of the tank and by 1982 some 1,200 had been built, with production continuing. In 1968 Kuwait ordered 70 Vickers Mk I MBTs which were delivered between 1970 and 1972.

Vickers continued development of the tank with its own funds, the first stage being the replacement of the L60 engine by a Detroit Diesel, followed by a new all-cast turret with a welded bustle which could be fitted with different types of fire-control system. In 1977 Kenya ordered 38 Vickers Mk III MBTs plus three ARVs; these were delivered by 1980, and a second order was placed in 1978 for a further 38 MBTs plus four ARVs, all these being delivered by late 1982.

In 1981 Nigeria ordered 36 MBTs plus six ARVs and five AVLBs. These were built at Vickers Defence Systems' new Armstrong Works, which were opened late in 1982. The famous old Elswick works, which produced armoured fighting vehicles and artillery pieces for some 100 years, has now been closed down and demolished.

The Mk III is also armed with the 105-mm L7 mounted in a turret which can be traversed through 360° and provides the gun with elevation of +20° and depression −10°. A 7.62-mm (0.3-in) machine-gun is mounted co-axially with the main armament, and a similar weapon is mounted on the commander's cupola. The latter can be aimed and fired from within the turret and be elevated to +90°. A bank of six electri-

cally-operated smoke dischargers is mounted on each side of the turret. The Nigerian vehicles are fitted with the Marconi Radar SFCS-600 (Simplified Fire Control System) which gives a high probability of a first-round hit. This system is now being fitted to some of the Indian Mk I MBTs. The commander has a Pilkington PE Condor day/night sight which enables him to lay and fire the main armament. As usual a whole range of optional equipment can be fitted to the Vickers Mark III MBT, including various radio installations, passive night-vision equipment, fire extinguishing system, an 0.5-in (12.7-mm) M2 HB machine-gun to replace the standard 7.62-mm (0.3-in) co-axial machine-gun, deep fording kit, full air filtration and pressurization, heater and so on.

The Vickers Armoured Bridge-laying Vehicle (VABV) is fitted with a bridge 44 ft (13.41 m) long, which is launched hydraulically over the front of the vehicle. The Vickers Armoured Recovery Vehicle (VARV) is provided with a front mounted dozer/stabilizing blade and a winch with a maximum capacity of 25 tonnes which can be increased to 65 tonnes if required. Some vehicles have a hydraulic crane to enable them to change powerpacks (engine and transmission) in the field.

Vickers Mk I MBT with turret traversed to the right firing its 105-mm L7 rifled tank gun during a demonstration at the Royal Armoured Corps gunnery range at Lulworth. The Mk I is in service with Kuwait and India and is also manufactured in the latter country under the name of the Vijayanta; over 1200 have been built there.

Vickers Mk I Main Battle Tank cutaway drawing key

1 QF 105-mm high-velocity gun
2 Smoke dischargers
3 Gunner's periscope sight
4 Gunner's seat
5 Loader's periscope
6 Commander's seat
7 Commander's cupola
8 First-aid box
9 Map board
10 Access to engine and transmission
11 Literature stowage
12 7.62-mm (0.3-in) magazine stowage
13 Hand-grenade stowage
14 Slewing ring
15 7.62-mm (0.3-in) and 12.7-mm (0.5-in) ammunition feed tray
16 105-mm ammunition 6-round bin
17 105-mm ammunition 25-round bin
18 Anti-gas equipment bin
19 Driver's seat
20 Spray unit water bottle
21 Fire extinguisher
22 Sight stowage
23 Storage bin
24 12.7-mm (0.5-in) ranging machine-gun
25 7.62-mm (0.3-in) machine-gun

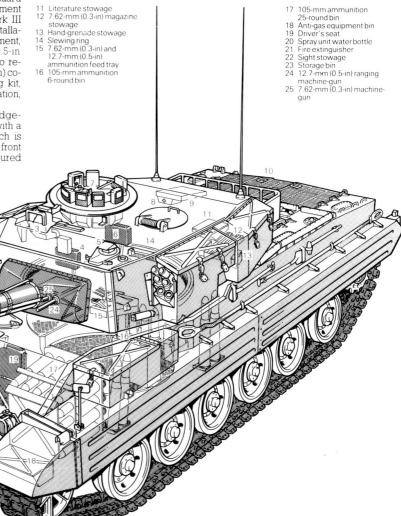

The hull of the Vickers Mk III MBT can also be fitted with the Vickers Shipbuilding and Engineering Limited turret armed with a 155-mm howitzer which can fire an HE round to a maximum range of 26,250 yards (24000 m), or to 32,800 yards (30000 m) with a rocket-assisted projectile (RAP).

Specification
Crew: 4
Weight: 38.7 tonnes
Engine: 12-cylinder diesel developing 720 hp (537 kW)
Dimensions: length (with gun forward) 32 ft 1¾ in (9.788 m); length (hull) 24 ft 9¾ in (7.561 m); width 10 ft 4¾ in (3.168 m); height (overall) 10 ft 2 in (3.099 m)
Performance: maximum road speed 31 mph (50 km/h); range 375 miles (600 km); gradient 60%; vertical obstacle 3 ft 0 in (0.914 m); trench 8 ft 0 in (2.438 m)

Vickers Mk III MBT of the Kenyan army, who took delivery of 76 vehicles plus seven armoured recovery vehicles between 1979 and 1982. It is now in production for Nigeria, who have also ordered the ARV plus the bridgelayer tank. The Mk I is powered by the Detroit Diesel engine.

Vickers Mk 7 Main Battle Tank

In the late 1970s Vickers Defence Systems designed and built as a private venture the Valiant MBT which made its first public appearance during the 1980 British Army Equipment Exhibition. This was armed with a 120-mm (4.72-in) Royal Ordnance tank gun and a Marconi fire-control system, and was designed to have the new Chobham armour. The Valiant was demonstrated in the Middle East but no orders were placed.

Vickers Defence Systems then discovered that a number of customers believed that the turret of the Valiant could be married to a chassis incorporating automotive components of the Leopard 2 MBT currently in service with the West German and Dutch armies, and also ordered by the Swiss army. The first prototype of this tank, called the **Vickers Mk 7**, was completed in mid-1985 and later in that year went to Egypt for trials. This tank has been designed specifically for the export market as the British army is already taking delivery of the heavier Challenger MBT armed with the same gun.

The Vickers Mk 7 is fitted with the standard Royal Ordnance 120-mm L11A5 tank gun, a McDonnell Douglas Helicopters 7.62-mm (0.3-in) Chain Gun being mounted co-axial with the main armament. A total of 38 rounds of 120-mm and 3,000 rounds of machine-gun ammunition are carried.

As an alternative to the L11A5 a West German Rheinmetall 120-mm smoothbore gun can be installed.

The Vickers Mk 7 has a Marconi Command and Control Systems Centaur 1 fire-control system: both the commander and gunner can aim and fire the gun, and the main armament is stabilized in both elevation and traverse. The commander is provided with a roof-mounted French SFIM panoramic sight that allows him to scan through 360° without moving his head. The sight also incorporates a laser rangefinder. The gunner has a Vickers telescopic laser sight and a roof-mounted periscope head.

Also mounted on the turret roof is a Philips UA9090 gyro-stabilized panoramic sight which provides a thermal picture on a TV screen at both tank commander's and gunner's positions. A very useful auto-scanning device is fitted: this scans a pre-set arc, and if there is a change in the thermal picture an alarm sounds, so alerting the crew.

The MTU diesel engine is coupled to Renk HSWL 354/3 automatic transmission with four forward and two reverse gears.

Standard equipment includes an NBC pack and a fire-extinguishing system for engine compartment, while optional equipment includes a roof-mounted anti-aircraft machine-gun, a fully automatic fire detection and suppression system for the crew compartment, and an air-conditioning system which is considered to be essential for operations in the Middle East.

The Vickers Mk 7 is a private venture by the company aimed purely at the export market. It combines the turret of the Valiant MBT, which failed to gain any orders, with automotive components of the German Leopard 2. It carries the powerful Royal Ordnance 120-mm (4.72-in) gun.

Specification
Vickers Mk 7
Crew: 4
Weights: empty 52640 kg (116,050 lb); loaded 54641 kg (120,460 lb)
Powerplant: one MTU MB 873 Ka 501 12-cylinder turbocharged diesel developing 1,500 bhp (1119 kW)
Dimensions: length, gun forward 10.95 m (35 ft 11 in) and hull 7.72 m (25 ft 4 in); width 3.43 m (11 ft 3 in); height overall 3.00 m (9ft 10 in)
Performance: maximum road speed 72 km/h (45 mph); range 500 km (310 miles); fording 1.7 m (5 ft 7 in); vertical obstacle 1.1 m (3 ft 7 in); trench 3.0 m (9 ft 10 in); gradient 60 per cent, side slope 30 per cent

The turret developed for the Vickers Valiant carries the British L11 rifled 120-mm gun as used in the Chieftain and Challenger, but this can be replaced by a Rheinmetall 120-mm smoothbore cannon as fitted to the Leopard 2 and to the M1A2 Abrams of the US Army.

OF-40 Main Battle Tank

The standard tank of the Italian army during the 1950s was the American-supplied M47. The country did take part in the formulation of the requirement which eventually led to the production of the French AMX-30 and West German Leopard 1 MBTs. Italy decided to make the American M60A1 under licence instead, and 200 of these were made by OTO Melara; another 100 were supplied direct from the USA. In 1970 Italy placed an order with West Germany for 200 Leopard 1s, and at the same time OTO Melara obtained a licence to undertake production of the vehicle in Italy. By 1982 some 720 had been completed for the Italian army and a further 160 of three specialized versions (ARV, AVLB and AEV) were due to be completed by the mid-1980s.

Under the terms of the Leopard 1 licence OTO Melara could not export the tank, so the company designed a new tank specifically for the export market under the designation **OF-40**, the O in the designation standing for the prime contractor (OTO Melara) and the F for Fiat which supplies the complete powerpack (engine, transmission and cooling system); 40 stands for the empty weight of the vehicle, 40 tonnes.

The first prototype was completed in 1980, and the first production contract was placed by the United Arab Emirates, which received its first production vehicles in 1981.

The hull and turret of the OF-40 are of all welded steel construction and are divided into three compartments, with the driver's at the front, fighting in the centre, and engine and transmission at the rear.

The main armament comprises an OTO Melara-designed 105-mm rifled gun which is fitted with a falling-wedge breech-block, concentric buffer and spring recuperator. When the gun recoils the breech-block automatically opens and ejects the empty cartridge cases into a bag under the breech of the weapon. Towards the rear of the turret on the left is a circular hatch which can be used to dispose of the empty shell cases or to resupply the vehicle with ammunition. A total of 61 rounds of ammunition is carried, 42 to

the left of the driver and the remainder in the turret for ready use.

A 7.62-mm (0.3-in) machine-gun is mounted co-axially with the main armament, and a similar weapon is mounted on the turret roof for anti-aircraft defence. Four smoke/fragmentation grenade launchers are mounted on each side of the turret, firing forwards. The OF-40 has a Officine Galileo OG14LR fire-control system which includes a computer and a Selenia laser rangefinder. As an option, a fully stabilized fire-control system can be fitted, enabling the OF-40 to engage enemy tanks when moving at speed across country. The commander has a roof-mounted French SFIM stabilized sight, which is used for both

surveillance and target acquisition. Standard equipment on the OF-40 MBT includes night-vision equipment and an NBC pack which is mounted to the left of the driver.

Italy is developing a new generation MBT called the C1, for service in the 1990s. The first prototype was unveiled in the summer of 1987.

Specification
Crew: 4
Weight: 43 tonnes
Engine: 10-cylinder diesel developing 830 hp (619 kW)
Dimensions: length (with gun forward) 9.22 m (30 ft 3 in); length (hull) 6.89 m (22 ft 7¼ in); width 3.51 m (11 ft 6¼ in);

OF-40 MBT of the Dubai army (part of the United Arab Emirates), which has ordered 18 vehicles with an option on a further 28. This MBT uses automotive components of the West German Leopard 1 and is armed with a 105-mm gun and two 7.62-mm (0.3-in) MGs. The fire-control system includes a laser rangefinder and a ballistic computer.

height (turret top) 2.45 m (8 ft 0⅓ in)
Performance: maximum road speed 60 km/h (37.3 mph); maximum range (road) 600 km (373 miles); fording 1.2 m (3 ft 11¼ in); gradient 60%; vertical obstacle 1.15 m (3 ft 9¼ in); trench 3 m (9 ft 10 in)

Leopard 1 Main Battle Tank

When the West German army was reformed it was initially equipped with American M47 and M48 tanks, both of which were armed with a 90-mm gun. A decision was soon taken that the former would be replaced by a more modern tank armed with a 105-mm gun, and two design teams (called A and B) were selected to build prototypes of vehicles for comparative trials. At the same time France built prototypes of the AMX-30 to replace its American-supplied M47s. It had been expected that either the West German MBTs or the French AMX-30 would become the common MBT of both armies, but in the end each country went its own way. In the case of West Germany, further development of the team A design resulted in the standardization of the vehicle as the **Leopard 1**. The first production tanks were completed by Krauss-Maffei of Munich in September 1965 and production continued until 1979. A total of 2,437 MBTs

was built for the West German army in four basic models designated **Leopard 1A1** (with additional armour this became the **Leopard 1A1A1**), the **Leopard 1A2**, the **Leopard 1A3** (with a new welded turret) and the **Leopard 1A4** (with a new welded turret and new fire-control system). The Leopard 1 was also adopted by Australia (90 vehicles), Belgium (334), Canada (114), Denmark (120), Italy (920, of which 720 were built in Italy by OTO Melara), the Netherlands (468) and Norway (78). Production was resumed by Krauss Maffei and Krupp MaK in 1982 to meet further orders from Greece (106) and Turkey (77).

The Leopard 1 is armed with the proven British Royal Ordnance Factories Nottingham L7 series 105mm (4.14in) rifled tank gun, and can fire a variety of ammunition including APDS, APFSDS, HEAT, HESH and Smoke, a total of 60 rounds being carried. A 7.62mm (0.3-in) machine-gun is

mounted co-axially with the main armament, a similar weapon is mounted on the turret roof for use in the anti-aircraft role, and four three-barrelled smoke dischargers are mounted on each side of the turret, firing forwards. A gun stabilization system is fitted, enabling the main armament to be laid and fired whilst the tank is moving across country. Leopard 1s have an NBC system and a full set of night-vision equipment for the commander, gunner and loader. When originally introduced, the latter was of the first-generation infra-red type but this is now being replaced by the second-generation passive type.

A wide range of optional equipment has also been developed for the Leopard 1 including a schnorkel which enables the tank to ford deep rivers and streams to a maximum depth of 4 m (13 ft 1½ in). A hydraulic blade can be mounted at the front of the hull and this is operated by the driver to clear or prepare battlefield obstacles. Most West German and Dutch Leopards are having appliqué armour

fitted to their turrets to give increased armour protection against missiles and HEAT projectiles.

The basic Leopard 1 chassis has been the basis for a complete family of vehicles which have been designed to support the MBT on the battlefield. All of the specialized versions, with the exception of the Gepard, have been designed and built by MaK of Kiel who have also built a few of the Leopard 1 MBTs.

Specification
Crew: 4
Weight: 40 tonnes
Engine: MTU 10-cylinder diesel developing 830 hp (619 kW)
Dimensions: length (with gun forward) 9.543 m (31 ft 4 in); length (hull) 7.09 m (23 ft 3 in); width 3.25 m (10 ft 8 in); height (overall) 2.613 m (8 ft 7 in)
Performance: maximum road speed 65 km/h (40.4 mph); maximum range 600 km (373 miles); fording 60%; vertical obstacle 1.15 m (3 ft 9¼ in); trench 3 m (9 ft 10 in)

Leopard 2 Main Battle Tank

In the late 1960s West Germany and the USA were jointly developing a new MBT designated MBT-70. In 1970 this was cancelled as a result of rising costs, and West Germany went ahead to develop a new MBT eventually known as the **Leopard 2**. This is fact incorporated the engine, transmission and certain other components of the MBT-70. A total of 16 hulls and 17 turrets was built to test various suspension, armaments (105-mm or 120-mm smooth-bore guns) and fire-control combinations. A special version was also built at a later date to meet the requirements of the US Army; this was called the **Leopard 2(AV)** and was armed with the standard 105-mm L7 rifled gun.

After troop trials had been carried out in both West Germany and abroad, the Leopard 2 was accepted for service by the West German army, and in 1977 an order was placed for a total of 1,800 Leopard 2 MBTs, of which Krupp MaK built 810 and Krauss Maffei of Munich the remaining 990. The first production tanks were handed over in 1979, and production has continued through 1986. The Leopard 2 has replaced the ageing Centurions and AMX-13s in Dutch service, 445 tanks having been delivered in a contract worth over DM 2,100 million. Leopard 2 has also won a Swiss order, in competition with the American M1 Abrams, for some 380 vehicles most of

The Leopard 2 follows the German tradition of mobility, but it is also well protected with Chobham type armour and has a very powerful gun.

Leopard 2 MBT of the West German army, which will take delivery of 1,800 vehicles by 1986. The 7.62-mm (0.3-in) MG3 machine-gun can be mounted at the commander's or loader's station and provides short range anti-aircraft protection. On either side of the turret is a bank of eight electrically-operated smoke dischargers.

which will be licence built in Switzerland. The British Vickers Mk 7 MBT uses a Leopard 2 hull and running gear with a British 120-mm turret.

The Leopard 2 is armed with a Rheinmetall-developed 120-mm smooth-bore gun which fires two main types of ammunition, namely HEAT-MP-T (High Explosive Anti-Tank Multi-Purpose Tracer) and APFSDS-T (Armour-Piercing Fin-Stabilized Discarding-Sabot Tracer); in each case there is also a practice round. The former is used against all battlefield targets, including field fortifications and lighter vehicles, while the latter is the main tank-killing round and is said to be able to penetrate the frontal armour of all current tanks including the Soviet T-64 and T-72. The ammunition, also developed by Rheinmetall, is unusual in that it has a combustible cartridge case, so that after the gun is fired all that remains of the cartridge is the base stub which is ejected into a bag under the breech of the gun. A total of 42 rounds of 120-mm ammunition is carried, compared with 60 rounds for the first-generation Leopard 1 with its 105-mm gun. This is

not a great drawback as the 120-mm round has greater penetration and the fire-control system gives a much greater hit probability. A 7.62-mm (0.3-in) machine-gun is mounted co-axially with the main armament, and a similar weapon is mounted on the turret roof for anti-aircraft defence. On each side of the turret are eight smoke dischargers, firing forwards.

The commander of the Leopard 2, who sits on the right of the turret, is provided with a stabilized roof-mounted sight which has a variable magnification of ×2 and ×8; this can be traversed through 360° for observation and can also be used to lay and fire the main armament. The gunner, who is seated forward and below the commander, also has a stabilized sight, but his incorporates a laser rangefinder and a thermal image unit, both of which are linked to the fire-control system. The main armament is fully stabilized and standard equipment includes passive night-vision equipment, an NBC system, a fire extinguishing system and a schnorkel for deep wading.

The hull and turret of the Leopard 2 incorporate advanced armour which

gives it a high degree of battlefield survivability, especially against anti-tank weapons with HEAT warheads. The Leopard 2 is powered by a multi-fuel engine developing 1,500 hp (1119 kW), which gives the Leopard 2 a power-to-weight ratio of 27 hp (20 kW) per tonne compared with just under 20 hp (15 kW) per tonne for the final production models of the Leopard 1. This gives the tank greater acceleration and improved cross-country mobility, which promote survivability on the battlefield.

Specification

Crew: 4
Weight: 55.15 tonnes
Engine: MTU 12-cylinder multi-fuel developing 1,500 hp (1119 kW)
Dimensions: length (with gun forward) 9.668 m (31 ft 8⅔ in); length (hull) 7.772 m (25 ft 6 in); width 3.7 m (12 ft 1⅔ in); height (overall) 2.79 m (9 ft 1¾ in)
Performance: maximum road speed 72 km/h (45 mph); maximum range 550 km (342 miles); gradient 60%; vertical obstacle 1.1 m (3 ft 7¼ in); trench 3 m (9 ft 10 in)

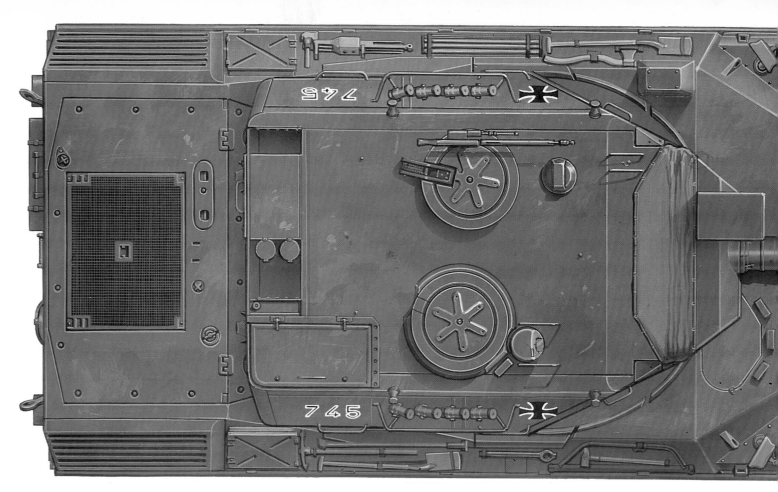

Four-view illustration of the Leopard 1A4, the final production model for the West German army with a new all-welded turret with improved armour protection and a stabilized sight for the commander. The rear view shows the tank fitted with a schnorkel for deep fording operations, with which the Leopard 1 can ford to a depth of 2.25 m (7 ft 4½ in).

Leopard 1A4 Main Battle Tank

Keith Fretwell

M48A3 Main Battle Tank

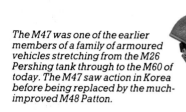

When the Korean War broke out in 1950, the USA had no medium tanks in production. As an interim measure the turret of the T43 medium tank then under development was put onto the chassis of the M46A1 tank and this entered production as the M47, well over 8,000 being built. The M47 has long been phased out of US Army service but remains in service with many countries including Greece, Italy, Spain, Pakistan and Portugal, to name but a few. Design work on a new medium tank, also armed with a 90-mm gun, started in the early 1950s under the designation T48, and this was ordered into production even before the first prototypes had been completed. The first production vehicles were completed at the Delaware Tank Plant, operated by the Chrysler Corporation, in July 1952, when the widow of General George Patton christened

The M47 was one of the earlier members of a family of armoured vehicles stretching from the M26 Pershing tank through to the M60 of today. The M47 saw action in Korea before being replaced by the much-improved M48 Patton.

M48A2 of the US Army with commander's and loader's hatch in the open position. By late 1983 the US Army still had over 2,000 of these vehicles on strength.

the type **Patton**. With such a short development period, which was justified by the international situation at that time, there were many problems with the early M48s, including poor reliability and a very short operating range of only 70 miles (113 km). The M48 was followed by the **M48A1, M48A2** and finally **M48A3**. The last had many modifications as a result of problems with the earlier vehicles, and was powered

by a Teledyne Continental AVDS-1790-2A diesel which increased the operational range of the tank to some 288 miles (463 km).

Production of the M48 series continued until 1959, by which time over 11,700 had been built. The M48 was succeeded in production by the M60 series, which itself is a further development of the M48. The M48 is still used by many countries around the world including Greece, Iran, Israel, Jordan, South Korea, Lebanon, Morocco, Norway, Pakistan, Portugal, Somalia, Spain, Taiwan, Thailand, Tunisia, Turkey, the USA and West Germany. The M48, M48A1, M48A2 and M48A3 are all armed with a 90-mm gun, with a 7.62-mm (0.3-in) machine-gun mounted co-axially with the main armament and a 0.5-in (12.7-mm) machine-gun mounted in the commander's cupola. To extend the type's operational life, the **M48A5** was developed in the mid-1970s. This is essentially any one of the earlier models rebuilt and fitted with a 105-mm M68 gun (as fitted to the M60 series), a 7.62-mm (0.3-in) M60D machine-gun on the turret roof, a new powerpack and many other detailed modifications. From 1975 Anniston Army Depot converted well over 2,000 of the older M48 series MBTs to the M48A5 configuration, and apart from two battalions in Korea these are all deployed in the USA. The United States has also supplied many countries with kits to enable them to convert their existing

stocks of M48s to M48A5 standard. The West German company Wegmann has converted some 650 M48A2 tanks into the **M48A2GA2** version for the West German army. These have the British 105-mm L7A3 gun, new ammunition racks, new commander's cupola, passive night-vision equipment, Wegmann smoke dischargers and modifications to the fire-control system.

The automotive components of the M48 were also used in the **M88** ARV and the **M53** and **M55** self-propelled artillery weapons. Variants of the M48 include the **M67**, **M67A1** and **M67A2** flamethrower tanks (none of which are at present in front-line service) and the **M48 AVLB** which is widely used in the US Army and has a scissors bridge launched over the front of the vehicle.

The M48 series has seen combat with the United States and Vietnamese armies in South Vietnam, with the Pakistani army against India, and with the Israeli army against Jordan, Egypt and Syria. It has now proved to be a reliable tank, and when fitted with the 105-mm L7A3 or M68 gun can counter most tanks likely to be encountered on the battlefield today, especially when firing the new types of APFSDS-T ammunition developed by the United States, Israel and the United Kingdom. Although the last M48s will be withdrawn from the US National Guard by the end of the decade, the type will remain in service worldwide well into its fifth decade. One variant that will *not* be seen is the ill-fated Sergeant York self-propelled AA system, based on the M48 chassis, which was cancelled in 1986 after millions of dollars of development money had been wasted.

Specification
Crew: 4
Weight: 47.17 tonnes
Engine: Continental AVDS-1790-2A 12-cylinder diesel developing 750 bhp (560 kW)
Dimensions: length (with gun forward) 8.686 m (28 ft 6 in); length (hull) 6.882 m (22 ft 7 in); width 3.631 m (11 ft 11 in); height 3.124 m (10 ft 3 in)
Performance: maximum road speed 48.2 km/h (30 mph); maximum range 463 m (288 miles); fording 1.219 m (4 ft 0 in); gradient 60%; vertical obstacle 0.915 m (3 ft 0 in); trench 2.59 m (8 ft 6 in)

An early production M60 tank crosses a pontoon bridge. The M60 was virtually an upgunned M48 with an improved engine; it was quickly replaced by the M60A1, which had a completely redesigned turret.

M60A1 Main Battle Tank

In 1956 a decision was taken to develop an improved version of the M48 tank to incorporate a new engine and a larger-calibre main armament. The former was the Teledyne Continental AVDS-1790-P while the latter was the British 105-mm L7A1 barrel fitted with an American-designed breech. The L7A1 was subsequently made under licence in the United States under the designation M68 and fitted to all production examples of this M60 series (with the exception of the M60A2) and is also fitted to the new M1 MBT which is also produced by General Dynamics.

The M60 entered service with the US Army in 1960 but was soon succeeded in production by the **M60A1** which had a number of modifications including a redesigned turret which offered greater ballistic protection. The **M60A2** was fitted with a new turret armed with a 152-mm weapon system which could fire the Shillelagh missile or a range of conventional ammunition with a combustible cartridge case. A total of 526 M60A2s was built, but the type has now been phased out of service, the chassis being stored for conversion to specialized vehicles.

The current production model is the **M60A3**, which is produced at the Detroit Tank Plant now operated by the Land Systems Division of General Dynamics who took over Chrysler Defense Inc. during 1982. The M60A3 has many improvements over the earlier M60A1, including a Hughes Aircraft Laser Tank Fire Control System, Tank Thermal Sights, main armament stabilized in both elevation and traverse, AVDS-1790-2A RISE (Reliability Improved Selected Equipment) engine, new tracks with replaceable pads, new searchlight over the main armament, thermal sleeve for main arma-

The M60A3 is the most widely used American MBT and is the latest development of the M60, which entered service in 1960. It is armed with a 105-mm M68 gun and has an advanced fire control system that includes a stabilization system, passive night vision equipment, laser rangefinder and a ballistic computer.

ment, new co-axial 7.62-mm (0.3-in) machine-gun and British six-barrelled smoke dischargers mounted on each side of the turret, to name but a few. Many of these improvements have now been retrofitted into the M60A1, which is then redesignated the M60A3.

The M60A3 carries a total of 63 rounds of ammunition for the 105-mm gun, of which 26 are carried in the forward part of the hull, 13 in the turret for ready use, 21 in the turret bustle and three under the gun. A 7.62-mm (0.3-in) machine-gun is mounted co-axially with the main armament, and a 0.5-in (12.7-mm) machine-gun is mounted in the commander's cupola.

By 1986, production of the M60 series had passed 15,000 units for the home and export markets. M60s equip the US Army and Marines, and armies in Austria, Bahrein, Egypt, Iran, Israel, Italy (including 200 built under licence by OTO-Melara), Jordan (who have had a number supplied by Iraq after being taken from Iran in the Gulf War), Morocco, Saudi Arabia, Sudan, Tunisia, and North Yemen.

There are only two main variants of the M60, namely the **M60 AVLB** and

the **M728 CEV**. The M60 AVLB has a scissors bridge on top of the hull, and this is launched over the front of the vehicle to span gaps of up to 60 ft 0 in (18.288 m). The M728 Combat Engineer Vehicle has a hull and turret similar to those of the M60A1, but is armed with a 165-mm demolition gun which fires a HESH (High Explosive Squash Head) round to demolish battlefield fortifications and pillboxes. Mounted at the front of the vehicle is an hydraulic dozer blade to clear battlefield obstacles and prepare fire positions for other AFVs, and pivoted at the front of the hull is an A-frame which lies back over the rear when not required.

Israeli M60s have been modified with a new lower profile commanders cupola, and most can now be fitted with the Israeli Military Industries Blazer reactive armour, first seen publically during Israel's 1982 invasion of the Lebanon. Since then the US Army has also tested M60s with applique armour, although whether this is reactive or passive has not been disclosed. Teledyne Continental developed a so-called 'Super M60' with improved protection and mobility as a private ven-

ture, but the project did not go ahead.

Specification
Crew: 4
Weight: 48.98 tonnes
Engine: Continental AVDS-1790-2A 12-cylinder diesel developing 750 bhp (560 kW)
Dimensions: length (with gun forward) 9.436 m (30 ft 11½ in); length (hull) 6.946 m (22 ft 9½ in); width 3.631 m (11 ft 11 in); height 3.27 m (10 ft 8¼ in)
Performance: maximum road speed 48.28 km/h (30 mph); maximum road range 500 km (310 miles); fording 1.219 m (4 ft 0 in); gradient 60%; vertical obstacle 0.914 m (3 ft 0 in); trench 2.59 m (8 ft 6 in)

M60s of the US Army await loading aboard a cargo ship on the east coast of America before a desert exercise in North Africa. Still the most numerous tank in the US inventory, the M60 will remain in front-line use for many years.

M1 Abrams Main Battle Tank

In the 1960s West Germany and the USA started the joint development of a new MBT known as the MBT-70, but this was cancelled in July 1970 for a variety of reasons. The United States then went on to develop a more austere version called the XM803, but this too was soon cancelled as it was felt that it would be too expensive and too sophisticated. Two years later the Detroit Diesel Allison Division of the General Motors Corporation and the Defense Division of the Chrysler Corporation were each awarded contracts to design a new MBT which would have much improved armour protection and greater mobility than the M60 then in production. After extensive trials the design from Chrysler was accepted and in 1976 the company was awarded a full-scale development contract including the construction of 11 pilot vehicles which were completed in 1978. The **XM1** was eventually standardized as the **M1 Abrams** MBT, the first production tank being completed at the Lima Army Tank Plant, Ohio, in 1980. Production started at the Detroit Tank Plant in 1982 and by early 1983 over 700 M1 MBTs had been built and each plant was turning out 30 tanks a month. The US Army has a requirement for 7,058 M1s by fiscal year 1988.

The hull and turret of the M1 are of advanced Chobham type armour and provide the greatest degree of protection ever incorporated into an American MBT. Main armament comprises the proven 105-mm M68 gun as mounted in the current M60 series, but a much improved fire-control system has been installed, this system including a laser rangefinder and thermal imaging system that allows the tank to engage targets by both day and night. The gun is fully stabilized in both elevation and traverse, and so can be aimed and fired while the vehicle moving across country. A total of 55 rounds of 105-mm ammunition is carried, of which 52 are compartmentalized. Of the latter 44 are in the turret bustle (22 on each side) and separated from the crew by sliding doors. A 7.62-mm (0.3-in) machine-gun is mounted co-axially

The M1 Abrams, with its 105-mm M68 rifled gun, advanced armour and gas turbine, is now operational with the US 7th Army in West Germany. Its fire control system, incorporating thermal sights, laser rangefinder and stabilization system, enables it to engage and destroy enemy tanks in a variety of environmental conditions.

with the main gun, and a similar weapon is mounted at the loader's hatch. The commander has a 0.5-in (12.7-mm) machine-gun that can be traversed through 360° and elevated to +65°. Mounted on each side of the turret is a bank of six smoke dischargers.

The M1 Abrams MBT is the first such vehicle to be powered by a gas turbine engine, and was installed following trials in an M48 tank. The gas turbine takes up much less room than a diesel, and is easier to service or replace in the field if it breaks down, but it uses more fuel than a diesel engine, a factor which tends to negate the space saved in the first place. The West Germans installed the same gas turbine in the Leopard 2 for trials purposes, but stuck to the MTU diesel for all production vehicles.

Some years ago the USA decided to adopt the West German Rheinmetall 120-mm (4.72-in) smoothbore gun already selected for the Leopard 2 MBT for an improved version of the M1, which was given the development designation **M1E1**. After the usual trials and modifications, this vehicle was accepted for service as the **M1A1 Abrams**, the first two production vehicles being completed by August 1985. Other armament is a 12.7-mm (0.5-in) commander's machine-gun and a 7.62-mm (0.3-in) loader's machine-gun.

The 120-mm Rheinmetall gun is built under licence in the USA under the designation M256, with Honeywell responsible for the complete range of ammunition together with its combustible cartridge case. In addition to the making of the West German APFSDS-

T (Armour-Piercing Fin-Stabilized Discarding-Sabot – Tracer) and HEAT-MP-T (High Explosive Anti-Tank – Multi-Purpose – Tracer), Honeywell has also developed new types with much improved armour-penetration characteristics.

In addition to the 120-mm gun, the M1A1 has a number of other improvements including increased armour protection and an integrated NBC system which not only provides the four-man crew with conditioned air for breathing but also supplied cooling or heating as long as the crew are wearing their protective suits and masks.

At one time both the Detroit Arsenal Tank Plant and the Lima Army Tank Plant were producing both the M1 and M1A1, but from early 1986 only the M1A1 was in production. At present there are no plans for the 105-mm armed M1 to be upgunned with the 120-mm gun.

As the M1/M1A1 will remain in service until the 21st century many other

Like the Challenger and the Leopard 2, the Abrams is clad in advanced Chobham type laminated armour. This gives much greater protection against all kinds of anti-tank rounds than armour plate.

improvements are already under development, including a new and safer laser rangefinder, an improved commander's weapon station with panoramic sight, and a rapid refuelling capability.

The M1 Abrams has already been evaluated by Saudi Arabia and Switzerland, but so far no export orders have been placed.

At present there are no variants of the M1/M1A, although under development by BMY is the **Heavy Assault Bridge** which uses an M1 chassis. It is probable that an armoured recovery vehicle will be developed on the M1 chassis as the current M88A1 is not powerful enough to handle the M1A1.

Undergoing trials is the **Tank Test Bed** which is an M1 chassis with an externally-mounted 120-mm gun, the three-man crew being safely seated within the hull.

Specification
Crew: 4
Weight: 54.432 tonnes
Engine: Avco Lycoming AGT-1500 gas turbine developing 1119kW (1,500hp)
Dimensions: length with gun forward 9.766m/32.04ft (M1A1 9.828m/32.25ft); hull length 7.918m (25.98ft); width 3.655m (12ft); overall height 2.885m (9.46ft)
Performance: maximum road speed 72.4km/h or 45mph (M1A1 66.77km/h or 41.45 mph); max road range 450km/280 miles (M1A1 465km/288 miles); fording 1.219m (4ft); gradient 60%; vertical obstacle 1.244m/4.08ft (M1A1 1.066m/3.5ft); trench 2.743m (9ft)

The combination of 120-mm gun-power, Chobham protection and gas-turbine powered mobility allied to advanced electronics and computerized fire-control makes the M1 Abrams one of the most formidable of modern battlefield weapon systems.

Merkava Main Battle Tank

In the 1960s the backbone of the Israeli Armoured Corps was the British-supplied Centurion MBT (which was subsequently rebuilt and fitted with a 105-mm gun to become known as the Upgraded Centurion), Sherman (most of which have now been rebuilt for specialized roles such as command vehicles, ambulances, recovery vehicles, mortar carriers and self-propelled howitzers) and the American M48. After the 1967 Middle East war Israel became concerned that in the future she would not be able to obtain AFVs from her traditional suppliers (the UK, France and the USA). Moreover, many of the tanks from these sources did not meet Israel's unique requirements.

Under the direction of General Tal, Israel started to develop its own MBT, named **Merkava** (or Chariot). This was announced in 1977, and the first production vehicles were completed in 1979. It was estimated that by 1982 at least 250 vehicles had been built. The Merkava was used in action for the first time against Syrian armoured units operating in southern Lebanon in the summer of 1982.

The layout of Merkava is unique in that the whole front of the vehicle is occupied by the engine, transmission, cooling system and fuel tanks. The driver is seated just in front of the turret on the left. The turret, which is of cast and welded construction, is situated well to the rear of the hull with the commander and gunner on the right and the loader on the left. The turret is well sloped to give the greatest possible degree of armour protection and its small cross section makes it a very difficult target. At the rear of the hull is a compartment which can be used to carry additional ammunition or (supposedly) four stretcher patients or 10 fully equipped infantrymen. A hatch is

Israeli army Merkava MBT armed with a 105-mm M68 gun, as fitted to the M48A5 and M60 series of MBT. The Merkava was first used in combat in the 1982 invasion of the Lebanon, when it engaged and defeated Syrian T-72s. It can carry infantrymen, additional ammunition or a number of stretcher patients in the hull rear.

provided in the hull rear to allow for the rapid exit of the tank crew or infantrymen. Standard equipment includes a full range of night-vision equipment, an NBC system and a special fire detection and extinguishing system which is automatically activated when a projectile penetrates the vehicle.

The main armament is the proven 105-mm rifled tank gun, which can fire a wide range of ammunition including the new APFSDS-T round (the M111) developed by Israel Military Industries. During the fighting in the Lebanon this round proved capable of penetrating the Soviet T-62 and T-72 MBTs over their frontal arc. The 105-mm gun has an elevation of +20° and a depression of −8.5°. Turret traverse and gun elevation/depression are electro-hydraulic, with manual controls for emergency use. A stabilization system is fitted, enabling the gun to be aimed accurately and fired while the vehicle is moving across country. The Elbit fire control system includes a computer and laser rangefinder.

Compared with other MBTs developed in recent years, the Merkava has a very low speed and poor power-to-weight ratio, but it has been designed for a different tactical situation

to that found in Central Europe. It should also be remembered that Israel has had more experience of successful armoured warfare since World War II than any other country. In designing the Merkava the Israelis have placed great emphasis on crew survivability. With a national population of only four million, every trained crew man is a very valuable person who must be given the maximum possible protection.

The **Merkava Mark 2** entered production in 1983. This has a number of improvements, most obviously in the extra armour carried on turret front and sides and the chains fitted to the turret bustle designed to ensure the early detonation of incoming HEAT warheads. Less obviously, the Mark 2 has an improved sensor fit (including a thermal gunner's sight) and more efficient transmission allowing greater range. Some sources have reported that engine power has been increased to some 1,200 hp (895 kW) with consequent increase in battlefield mobility. **Merkava Mark 3** is under development, and is expected to be fielded in the late 1980s. It is to have new armour, improved fire-control, improved suspension, an engine developing up to

1,500 hp (1120 kW) and possibly a smoothbore 120-mm gun in a new low-profile three-man turret.

Specification
Crew: 4
Weight: 56 tonnes
Engine: V-12 diesel developing 900 hp (671 kW)
Dimensions: length (with gun forward) 8.36 m (27 ft 5¼ in); length (hull) 7.45 m (24 ft 5¼ in); width 3.72 m (12 ft 2½ in); height (roof) 2.64 m (8 ft 8 in)
Performance: maximum road speed 46 km/h (28.6 mph); maximum range 500 km (311 miles); gradient 60%; vertical obstacle 1 m (3 ft 3⅓ in); trench 3 m (9 ft 10 in)

Israel's unparalleled experience in modern armoured warfare has contributed to the design of the Merkava, a tank in which protection and hitting power are paramount. Later models maintain these strengths while markedly improving battlefield mobility.

T-54 Main Battle Tank

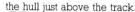

The T-54 tank was developed in the late 1940s and has probably been produced in greater numbers than any other Soviet tank in the post-war period. It has also been produced in China, Poland and Czechoslovakia and has seen combat in countless campaigns since World War II, especially in the Middle East, where it has been used by the Arab states against Israel.

In 1946 the USSR designed a new medium tank called the T-44, and this was produced in small numbers between 1945 and 1949 although it was not considered to be a satisfactory design. In 1946 prototypes of a new design, the T-54, were completed and this type entered production several years later. The T-54 and its variants were built in larger numbers than any other Russian tank to appear after World War II, and by the time production of the improved T-55 was completed in 1980-1 it is estimated that well over 50,000 vehicles had been built. The series was also built in Czechoslovakia and Poland for both the home and export markets, while the Chinese produced an almost identical version designated Type 59. Further development of the T-54 and T-55 resulted in the T-62.

The T-54 has an all-welded hull divided into three compartments (driver's at the front, fighting in the centre, and engine and transmission at rear). The driver is seated at the front of the hull on the left and steers the tank with conventional sticks. An unusual feature of the T-54 is that it has a 7.62-mm (0.3-in) machine-gun fixed in the centre of the glacis plate to fire forwards, this being fired when the driver presses a button on his right steering lever. The commander and gunner are seated on the left of the turret, with the loader on the right. The turret is a casting with the top welded into position. One of the major weaknesses of the T-54 series has been its engine and transmission, which have proved very unreliable in service.

The main armament consists of a 100-mm gun, which was developed from a naval weapon of the same calibre and also used in a modified form in the SU-100 tank destroyer developed in World War II. A well-trained crew can fire about four rounds per minute, and the types of ammunition that can be fired includes AP-T, APC-T, HE, HE-FRAG, HEAT-FS and HVAPDS-T. The last was introduced some time after the T-54 entered production and will penetrate well over 200 mm (7.9 in) of armour at a range of 1000 m (1,095 yards). A total of 34 rounds of 100-mm ammunition is carried, a poor quantity when compared with contemporary Western tanks. One of the major drawbacks of the T-54 family is that the main armament can only be depressed to −4°, which makes firing from a hill or reverse slope almost impossible. A 7.62-mm (0.3 in) SGMT is mounted co-axially with the 100-mm gun, and a similar weapon is mounted in the bow. A 12.7-mm (0.5-in) DShKM anti-aircraft machine-gun is mounted on the loader's hatch. The tank does not have smoke dischargers as it can lay its own smoke screen by injecting diesel fuel into the exhaust pipe on the left side of the hull just above the track.

The basic T-54 was improved as the years went by. The T-54A included stabilization of the 100-mm gun in the vertical plane. The T-54B was the first production model to incorporate infra-red night-vision equipment, subsequently retrofitted to earlier vehicles, and its armament was stabilized in both the horizontal and vertical planes. The T-54C was not fitted with an AA MG, although such a weapon was refitted at a later date. The T-55 succeeded the T-54 in production in the late 1950s and has numerous improvements including more ammunition stowage, new 7.62-mm (0.3-in) machine-guns, and improved NBC protection. There have been countless versions of the T-54 family, including a flamethrower tank, armoured recovery vehicles (including Russian, Polish and Czech versions), bridgelayers (built by East Germany, Czechoslovakia and the USSR), dozer tanks, a combat engineer vehicle fitted with an hydraulic crane and front-mounted dozer blade, and mine-clearing vehicles fitted with rollers, ploughs and rocket-assisted devices, to name but a few. In recent years the T-54/T-55 series has been fitted with improved fire-control systems, including an externally mounted laser rangefinder.

The T-54/T-55 series has seen extensive combat in the Middle East, North Africa, Angola and the Far East. On a one-for-one basis Western tanks of the same period, such as the British Centurion and American M48, have proved more than a match for the T-54/T-55, especially during the fighting between Israel and Egypt and Syria.

Specification
Crew: 4
Weight: 36 tonnes
Engine: V-12 diesel developing 520 hp (388 kW)
Dimensions: length (with gun forward) 9 m (29 ft 6⅓ in); length (hull) 6.45 m (21 ft 2 in); width 3.27 m (10 ft 8¾ in); height (turret roof) 2.4 m (7 ft 10½ in)
Performance: maximum road speed 48 km/h (30 mph); maximum range 400 km (249 miles); fording 1.4 m (4 ft 7 in); gradient 60%; vertical obstacle 0.8 m (2 ft 7½ in); trench 2.7 m (8 ft 10¼ in)

Soviet T-54 series tanks lined up in a street in Prague during the unrest in Czechoslovakia in 1968. The white stripes have been a common marking on Soviet vehicles when invading other countries.

Soviet T-54 with turret traversed to the rear, and the loader manning the 12.7-mm DShKM anti-aircraft machine-gun. The tank can also lay its own smokescreen by injecting diesel fuel into the exhaust outlet.

T-54/55 tanks spearhead a combined arms attack with infantry having emerged from their personnel carriers in support.

T-62 Main Battle Tank

The T-62 is a further development of the T-54/T-55 tank with a slightly longer hull to accommodate the turret with its 115-mm smooth-bore gun. The T-62 was first seen in public during a parade held in Red Square (Moscow) during 1965, although it is now known to have entered production in about 1961. The T-62 remained in production until the early 1970s and a number were also produced under licence in Czechoslovakia, mainly for the export market. The T-62 was more expensive to produce than the earlier T-54/T-55 and for this reason the T-55 remained in production for many years after the more modern T-62 had been phased out of production.

The 115-mm U-5TS smooth-bore gun is fitted with a bore evacuator and is fully stabilized in both elevation and traverse. An unusual feature of the T-62 is that it has an integral shell case ejection system which is activated by the recoil of the gun. This ejects the empty case out through a trapdoor in the turret rear, but this has reduced the rate of fire to about four rounds a minute as the gun has to elevate to +3° 30′ for this to be carried out.

Three main types of ammunition are fired by the 115-mm gun, namely HE-FRAG-FS, or High Explosive Fragmentation Fin-Stabilized, with a muzzle velocity of 750 m (2,460 ft) per second; HEAT-FS, or High Explosive Anti-Tank Fin-Stabilized, with a muzzle velocity of 900 m (2,955 ft) per second and capable of penetrating over 430 mm (16.9 in) of armour at any range; and the deadly APFSDS, or

Armour-Piercing Fin-Stabilized Discarding-Sabot, with a muzzle velocity of 1680 m (5,510 ft) per second and a very flat trajectory, and capable of penetrating 330 mm (13 in) of armour at a range of 1000 m (1,095 yards). A total of 40 rounds of 115-mm ammunition is carried, of which four are ready rounds in the turret, and of the rest 16 are to the right of the driver and 20 in the rear of the fighting compartment. A 7.62-mm (0.3-in) PKT machine-gun is mounted co-axially with the main armament; for this weapon 2,500 rounds of ammunition are carried.

Standard equipment on all T-62s includes infra-red night-vision equipment for the commander, gunner and driver, an unditching beam which is carried at the rear of the hull, a turret ventilation system to remove fumes when the gun is fired, a nuclear collective protection system, and the capability of injecting diesel fuel into the exhaust to provide smoke screen. The vehicle carries 675 litres (148.5 Imp gal) of fuel internally with a further 285 litres (63 Imp gal) externally on the running boards, and this total gives the T-62 a road range of 450 km (280 miles). A further two drum-type fuel tanks can be fitted on the hull rear; these each hold some 200 litres (44 Imp gal) of fuel, increasing road range to some 650 km (404 miles). All T-62s can ford rivers to a depth of 5.5 m (18 ft 0½ in) with the aid of a schnorkel erected over the loader's hatch. A centralized fire-extinguisher system is provided for the engine and fighting compartments, and this can be oper-

ated automatically or manually by the commander or driver.

The T-62A has a revised turret, a new laser rangefinder and a digital fire-control system. There are also armoured recovery and flamethrower variants in service. The T-62 is still very widely used, being operated by Afghanistan, Angola, Algeria, Egypt, Iran, Iraq, Israel, North Korea, Libya, Mongolia, Syria, Vietnam and South Yemen in addition to the large numbers still in the Soviet inventory. The US Army has managed to acquire some examples which are used for training.

Specification
Crew: 4
Weight: 40 tonnes

Soviet T-62 tanks advance through an artillery barrage during training exercises. This tank was first used operationally in the Middle East.

Engine: V-12 water-cooled diesel developing 580 hp (433 kW)
Dimensions: length (with gun forward) 9.335 m (30 ft 7½ in); length (hull) 6.63 m (21 ft 9 in); width 3.3 m (10 ft 10 in); height 2.395 m (7 ft 10¼ in)
Performance: maximum road speed 50 km (31 mph); maximum road range 650 km (404 miles); gradient 60%; vertical obstacle 0.8 m (2 ft 7½ in); trench 2.85 m (9 ft 4¼ in)

A Soviet T-62 with added armour applied to the turret is seen being withdrawn from Afghanistan during a token withdrawal in 1986.

T-64 Main Battle Tank

In the 1960s the Russians built prototypes of a new MBT which became known as the **M-1970** in the West in the absence of any known Soviet designation. This vehicle had a new suspension consisting of six small dual road wheels with the drive sprocket at the rear, idler at the front and four track return rollers supporting the inside of the track only. All previous MBTs designed in the USSR since World War II (the T-54, T-55 and T-62) had been characterized by larger road wheels with no return rollers. The turret of the M-1970 was similar to that of the T-62 and was armed with the same 115-mm smooth-bore gun. Further development of the M-1970 resulted in the **T-64** MBT which was placed in production at one tank plant in the USSR. Production vehicles were armed with a 125-mm gun which was later fitted to the T-62 MBT. So far the T-64 has not been identified as being in service with any other country whereas the later T-72 has been exported on a wide scale, both within the Warsaw Pact and overseas with production now being undertaken both in Czechoslovakia and Poland. Developed in parallel with the T-72, the T-64 incorporated so many advanced features that early models were plagued by technical problems. It was the first major MBT to feature a three-man crew and an automatic loader, and it saw the introduction of an exceptionally powerful smoothbore 125-mm gun.

The layout of the T-64 is similar to that of the T-72, with the driver's compartment at the front, turret in the centre and engine and transmission at the rear. The driver is seated in the centre with a well-shaped glacis plate (probably of laminate armour) to his front. A vee-type splashboard on the glacis plate stops water rushing up when the vehicle is fording a deep stream. When driving in the head-out position, the driver can quickly erect a cover

over his position to protect himself against rain and snow.

The turret is similar to that on the T-72, with gunner to the left of the gun and the commander to the right. One major early problem was an unnerving fault in the auto-loader which saw it grabbing and trying to load convenient parts of the gunner into the breech instead of 125-mm rounds!

Armament is identical to that of the T-72 and consists of a fully stabilized 125-mm smooth-bore gun, a 7.62-mm (0.3-in) machine-gun co-axial with the main armament, and a 12.7-mm (0.5-in) machine-gun on the commander's cupola. The T-64 has an NBC system and a full range of night-vision equipment and, like most other Russian MBTs, it can be fitted with a front-mounted dozer blade and various types of mine-clearing systems such as

roller or plough.

The **T-64B** is the model currently in service with the Group of Soviet Forces in Germany. It has an advanced fire-control system, and one variant can fire the Kobra gun-launched anti-tank missile, known as the AT-8 'Songster' to NATO. The T-64K is a command tank with a large telescopic radio mast. The most recent addition to the T-64 has been appliqué armour. The Soviet version looks very like Israeli Blazer reactive armour. Examples of this may have been acquired via Syria after the 1982 operations in the Lebanon.

Specification
Crew: 3
Weight: 38 tonnes
Engine: 5-cylinder diesel developing 700 to 750 hp (522 to 560 kW)

The T-64 was at first thought to be a failure by Western sources, as none were exported, but the large numbers being used by Category One Soviet divisions in Germany would seem to indicate otherwise. It may be that the T-64 was too advanced to be allowed out of Soviet hands.

Dimensions: length (overall) 9.10 m (29 ft 10¼ in); length (hull) 6.40 m (21 ft 0 in); width (without skirts) 3.38 m (11 ft 1 in); height 2.30 m (7 ft 6½ in)
Performance: maximum road speed 70 km/h (43 mph); maximum range 450 km (280 miles); fording 1.4 m (4 ft 7 in); gradient 60%; vertical obstacle 0.915 m (3 ft 0 in); trench 2.72 m (8 ft 11 in)

T-72 Main Battle Tank

The T-72 MBT was seen in public for the first time during a parade held in Red Square (Moscow) during November 1977, although it is now known to have entered production in 1971. In April 1978 American reports stated that production of the T-64 and T-72 was running at the rate of some 2,400 units a year and rising, with up to 30,000 tanks built by 1987. The T-72 is also built under licence, in Czechoslovakia, Poland, India and Yugoslavia. By 1986 the T-72 was known to be in service with Algeria, Bulgaria, Cuba, Czechoslovakia, Finland, East Germany, Hungary, India, Iraq, Libya, Poland, Romania, Syria, and of course the Soviet Union. The T-72 was first used in combat in the Lebanon and in the Gulf War. Even though the later T-80 is now in production for the Soviet Union, the T-72 is still being built in large numbers in at least four factories, and is likely to remain in production for export for several years to come.

The layout of the T-72 is conventional, with the driver's compartment at the front, the turret in the centre, and the engine and transmission at the rear. The hull may incorporate some type of advanced armour (especially on the glacis plate), although the turret is believed to be of conventional cast steel

Provisional drawing of T-72 MBT with the commander's cupola fitted with 12.7-mm AA MG traversed rear. At hull rear are the long range fuel tanks that can be quickly jettisoned. Side skirts provide defence against ATGWs with their HEAT warheads.

armour construction. The commander is seated on the right and the gunner on the left, the former being provided with a cupola that can be traversed through 360°, and on this is mounted a 12.7-mm (0.5-in) machine-gun for anti-aircraft defence.

The crew has been reduced to three as in the T-64. It has a similar automatic loader, mounted in the lower part of the hull beneath the turret with the rounds fitting upright into a magazine like a carousel with the projectiles in the lower part and the cartridge, which is believed to have a combustible case, in the upper part. Some reports have indicated that the automatic loader has not proved reliable in service and in some instances has tried to place the

gunner in the breech instead of the ammunition! A total of 40 rounds of 125-mm ammunition is carried, a typical load consisting of 12 APFSDS, 22 HE and six HEAT. The APFSDS has a muzzle velocity of 1615 m (5,300 ft) per second and will penetrate 300 mm (11.8 in) of armour at a range of 1000 m (1,095 yards), while the HEAT-FS has a muzzle velocity of 900 m (2,955 ft) per second and will penetrate 475 mm (18.7 in) armour at a similar range. A 7.62-mm (0.3-in) PKT machine-gun is mounted co-axially with the main armament.

The fire-control system includes an optical rangefinder mounted in the forward part of the turret roof, in front of the commander's cupola; more recent production vehicles have a laser

rangefinder.

The suspension is of the torsion-bar type, with six large road wheels, the idler at the front, drive sprocket at the rear and three track-return rollers, the last supporting the inside of the track only. When the tank is in action, four spring-loaded skirts are fitted over the forward part of the track on each side and spring forward to give some protection against HEAT attack, notably from missiles.

As on all Russian tanks, long-range fuel tanks can be mounted at the hull rear; in the case of the T-72 these increase its road operating range from 480 km (298 miles) to 700 km (435 miles). Standard equipment includes an NBC system, infra-red night-vision equipment and a schnorkel for deep fording. Mounted under the nose of the T-72 is a dozer blade for clearing obstacles or preparing fire positions.

Specification
Crew: 3
Weight: 41 tonnes
Engine: V-12 diesel developing 780 hp (582 kW)
Dimensions: length (with gun forward) 9.24 m (30 ft 3¾ in); length (hull) 6.95 m (22 ft 9¾ in); width (without skirts) 3.6 m (11 ft 9¾ in); height (without AA MG) 2.37 m (7 ft 9⅓ in)
Performance: maximum road speed 60 km/h (37.25 mph); maximum range 480 km (298 miles); fording 1.4 m (4 ft 7 in); gradient 60%; vertical obstacle 0.915 m (3 ft 0 in); trench 2.9 m (9 ft 2¼ in)

A T-72 of the Finnish army displays the notably low lines which have characterized Soviet tank designs since the end of the Second World War. The T-72 is no match for current Western designs, but is available in vastly greater numbers.

T-80 Main Battle Tank

The **T-80** has been the source of considerable confusion in the West ever since first rumours of a new Soviet tank design began to emerge from intelligence sources. At various times the T-80 designation has been applied to variants of the T-72 and to an apparently imaginary machine looking like a Soviet version of the M1 Abrams (although the illustration in the US DoD's publication *Soviet Military Power 1981* might just appear as an entirely new design in the 1990s). Today it appears that the T-80 is a revised and improved version of the T-64B. Between them the T-80 and the T-64 make up much of the front line strength of the Soviet armies in Europe, with over 7,500 of the newer model built by 1986.

The T-80 may have entered production as long ago as 1976, and is obviously the product of much experience with the problems of the T-64. Some are thought to mount the same 125-mm smoothbore cannon and autoloader as the preceding tanks, but later versions have a different weapon of the same calibre. This can fire a slim, laser-guided anti-tank missile thought to be called Kobra by the Soviets, which has received the NATO designation AT-8 'Songster'. The AT-8 is propelled from the muzzle at about 150 metres/sec by a small charge, and is accelerated after leaving the barrel by a rocket sustainer. Maximum speed is 1800 km/h (over 1,100 mph) and maximum range has been quoted as 5000 m, which the missile could cover in 10 seconds or less. The tank has a laser designator on the turret roof, and there have been suggestions that the missile is a beam-rider, following the designator beam to the target. The missile firing tanks are distributed through each Tank Division, possibly to provide some protection against NATO anti-armour helicopters armed with long range anti-tank missiles.

The fire-control system is probably

similar to that of the T-64B, with added night fighting capability. There is no external evidence of the passive night vision or thermal imaging systems common to current Western types, although low-light TV systems have made an appearance on Soviet battlefield helicopters. The hull armour is probably an advanced laminate although this would be impossible to fit onto the cast turret. No pictures have been released of T-80s with anchoring points for Blazer type reactive armour, but reports from East Germany suggest that some T-80s have been so fitted along with large numbers of T-64s. The rubber-tyred road wheels are larger than those of the T-64, and the troublesome suspension of the earlier tank has probably been changed. The engine of the T-80 may be a multi-fuel gas turbine delivering about 985 hp (735 kW) making this fastest and most agile of Soviet tanks. As with all Soviet designs, the T-80 carries a Schnorkel tube for river crossings and has mounting plates on the hull front for mine rollers.

The T-80 appears to be a result of lessons learnt with the T-64 series, and already provides a significant proportion of the strength of the Category I divisions of the Group of Soviet Forces in Germany. A recent photo released by the US Department of Defense shows a T-80 with reactive armour very similar to the Israeli Blazer system.

T-72 M1980/1

This improved model of the T-72 was first observed at a parade in Berlin in 1981, and it subsequently appeared at the November Parade in Moscow. Early T-72s had a pronounced hood in front of the right-hand (commander's) cupola; the absence of this on the latest model indicates that optical equipment has been replaced by a laser rangefinder. The full details of the construction of the T-72 will not be revealed until several examples of the tank have been brought to the West intact, for example after Syrian T-72s have been overrun by the Israelis. However, the controversy might not end there, as the Soviets often remove some of the more sensitive equipment from tanks or aircraft which are intended for export; these are referred to as 'monkey models' in Soviet jargon. Soviet T-72s are known to be very well protected from nuclear contamination, carrying a skin layer of a lead-based foam; this lining is not fitted to exported T-72s. It is also to be expected that the fire control systems and possibly the automatic loaders are different in Soviet and export T-72s.

Brazilian Main Battle Tanks

Since the early 1970s the ENGESA company has built over 4,000 of its 4×4 scout cars, EE-9 Cascavel 6×6 armoured cars and EE-11 Urutu 6×6 armoured personnel carriers, sales having been made to virtually every continent. Several years ago the company decided to design and build a new MBT which would meet the needs of both the home and export markets. The first prototype, armed with the combat-proven British Royal Ordnance 105-mm (4.13-in) rifled tank gun, was completed in 1985. This was demonstrated in Saudi Arabia late in 1985 and the second prototype, armed with a French GIAT 120-mm (4.72-in) smoothbore gun, was completed early in 1986. Vickers Defence Systems of the UK designed both the 105-mm and 120-mm turrets specifically to meet the requirements of ENGESA.

The **EE-T1 Osorio** has an all-welded hull and turret. The conventional layout locates the driver at front left, the turret in the centre, and the engine and transmission at the rear. The 12-cylinder turbocharged diesel is coupled to a fully automatic transmission with four forward and two reverse gears.

The suspension is of the hydro-pneumatic type and has been designed by Dunlop of the UK. It has six road wheels with the drive sprocket at the rear and idler at the front; there are three track-return rollers.

Turret traverse is electric, and controls are provided for both tank commander and gunner. At present two fire-control systems are available for the EE-T1 Osorio. The first option is an integrated fire-control system in which the gunner has a day/night sight with a laser rangefinder and the commander a day/night sight. The second fire-control option includes a stabilization system for the main armament allowing the gun to be fired against moving targets while the tank itself is moving across country. The tank commander has a roof-mounted SFIM stabilized periscopic sight with a laser rangefinder, while the gunner also has an SFIM stabilized sight with laser rangefinder. To enable targets to be

Osorio is offered with a choice of armament, either the proven British 105-mm gun used all over the world or the French GIAT 120-mm smoothbore. The turrets for both weapons were designed by Vickers Defence Systems to ENGESA's requirements.

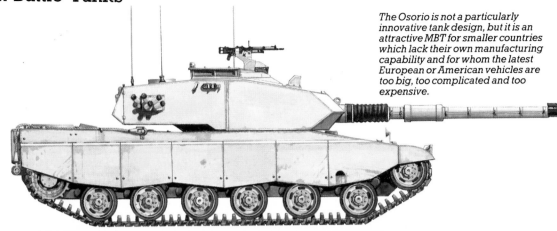

The Osorio is not a particularly innovative tank design, but it is an attractive MBT for smaller countries which lack their own manufacturing capability and for whom the latest European or American vehicles are too big, too complicated and too expensive.

detected and engaged at night, mounted on the turret roof is a Philips stabilized thermal camera which provides a TV picture on screens at the commander's and gunner's positions.

Mounted on each side of the turret is a bank of electrically-operated smoke-dischargers, and optional equipment (apart from the choice of main armament and fire-control systems) includes an NBC system, a fire detection and suppression system, a land navigation system, a laser detector and indirect fire control equipment.

Using components of the EE-T1 Osorio, ENGESA is now developing other variants including an armoured recovery vehicle, a bridgelayer, and an anti-aircraft gun vehicle.

The Brazilian Army's requirement

for 500 tanks has seen the Osorio in competition with the Bernardini **MB-3 Tamoio**. The Bernardini company upgraded 300 M41 tanks for the Army, and the experience led them to develop a medium tank of their own design.

The Tamoio has an all-welded hull of conventional layout, with an all-welded three-man turret mounting a 90-mm gun with 68 rounds. A 12.7-mm M2HB coaxial machine gun and a 7.62-mm AA machine gun on the turret roof complete the armament. A Brazilian built Saab-Scania diesel powers the vehicle, although production models may be equipped with a 736 hp (549 kW) Detroit Diesel and the hydro-mechanical transmission fitted to the M2 Bradley.

Three MB-3 Tamoio prototypes are seen at night. Smaller and lighter than the latest MBTs, the Tamoio is more suited to less sophisticated armies in the Third World.

Specification
EE-T1 Osorio
Crew: 4
Weights: empty 37000 kg (81,570 lb); loaded 39000 kg (85,979 lb)
Powerplant: one 12-cylinder diesel developing 1,000 hp (745 kW)
Dimensions: length, gun forward 9.995 m (32 ft 9.5 in) and hull 7.08 m (23 ft 2.75 in); width 3.26 m (10 ft 8.3 in); height 2.371 m (7 ft 9.3 in)
Performance: maximum road speed 70 km/h (43.5 mph); maximum range 550 km (342 miles); fording 1.20 m (3 ft 11 in); vertical obstacle 1.15 m (3 ft 9 in); trench 3.0 m (9 ft 10 in); gradient 60 per cent; side slope 30 per cent

Specification
MB-3 Tamoio
Crew: 4
Weights: empty 28000 kg (61,728 lb); combat 30000 kg (66,137 lb)
Powerplant: one eight-cylinder diesel developing 500 hp (373 kW)
Dimensions: length, gun forwards 8.77 m (28.77 ft); hull length 6.5 m (21.3 ft); width 3.22 m (10.56 ft); overall height 2.5 m (8.2 ft)
Performance: maximum road speed 67 km/h (41.6 mph); road range 550 km (341.7 miles); fording 1.3 m (4.26 ft); vertical obstacle 0.71 m (2.33 ft); trench 2.4 m (7.87 ft); gradient 60%

Modern Light Tanks and Reconnaissance Vehicles

Modern reconnaissance vehicles no longer have a clear-cut role to themselves as many of their traditional cavalry tasks, especially the gathering of information, are being carried out by newer means. As a result, differing theories on the employment of light armour in combat today have led to a bewildering variety of vehicle types and armament.

The original role of armoured cars in World War I was the gathering of information on the strength, position and movement of enemy forces, and in such a role armoured cars would normally act ahead and on the flanks of the main forces. This was satisfactory in a fluid battle situation, but once the lines of the opposing forces had become established there was often little the armoured car could do as it lacked the firepower, armour protection and mobility of the tank. In the years following World War II some NATO countries (for example the UK and France) have continued the development of armoured cars or developed light tracked vehicles that have much improved off-the-road performance when compared with their wheeled counterparts (a good example is the British Alvis Scorpion), while other countries see little need for armoured cars to carry out the reconnaissance role, and so employ tanks for this purpose.

Today there are many other means of carrying out the reconnaissance role, such as aircraft, helicopters and more recently RPVs. Some of these can send back real-time information about the whole battlefield, whereas the armoured car or other surface reconnaissance vehicle is limited to a mere portion of the battlefield.

It is also apparent that countries often place a different emphasis on their concept of reconnaissance vehicles. The West German 8×8 Spähpanzer Luchs has excellent cross-country mobility, is fully amphibious, has a high road speed and is possessed of exceptional operational range, but is armed with only a 20-mm cannon. The French 6×6 AMX-10RC on the other hand is fully amphibious, has a good road speed and is armed with a 105-mm (4.13-in) gun. There is a school of thought that believes that to give a reconnaissance vehicle too heavy an armament may tempt the crew to engage the enemy rather than report the same enemy's position back to the next link in the chain of command.

In many African, South American and Far Eastern countries the armoured car is often the main offensive force of the army and is also heavily engaged in internal security operations. For this reason there has been a trend in recent years to put the heaviest possible gun onto the chassis of the armoured car.

Scorpion reconnaissance vehicle on patrol in the Middle East. Over 3000 of these vehicles and variants have been sold to some 16 countries. It has exceptional cross-country mobility and is armed with a potent Royal Ordnance 76-mm (3-in) gun.

SK-105 Light Tank/Tank Destroyer

The **Jagdpanzer SK-105** was designed by Steyr in the mid-1960s to meet an Austrian army requirement for a highly mobile and hard-hitting tank destroyer suitable for operation in Austria's unique terrain. The first prototype was completed in 1967, and production began in the early 1970s. By early 1983 about 400 vehicles had been built, 150 for the Austrian army and the remainder for the export market, in which sales have been made to Argentina, Bolivia, Morocco, Nigeria and Tunisia. The engine, transmission, tracks, suspension and many other automotive components are identical to those of the Steyr-Daimler-Puch family of tracked vehicles, which have also been exported in large numbers.

The hull of the SK-105 is of all-welded steel armour, with the driver's compartment at the front, the turret in the centre, and the engine and transmission at the rear. Over its frontal arc the vehicle has complete protection from attack by all weapons up to 20-mm calibre, protection against small arms fire being provided over the remainder of the vehicle.

The turret is a modified version of the French Fives-Cail-Babcock FL-12 as installed on the AMX-13 light tank, and is of the oscillating type, with the gun fixed to the upper part, which pivots on the lower part. The commander is seated on the left and the gunner on the right, both with a hatch cover and observation devices. The main armament comprises a 105-mm (4.13-in) gun fitted with a thermal sleeve and a muzzle-brake; elevation is +13° and depression −8°, and turret traverse is 360°. Ammunition stowage is provided for totals of 44 105-mm (4.13-in) main armament rounds and 2,000 rounds of 7.62-mm ammunition for the co-axial machine-gun. The 105-mm (4.13-in) gun is fed by two revolver-type magazines in the turret bustle, this enabling the gun to fire until the ammunition is exhausted. One of the crew then has to leave the vehicle in order to reload the magazines. The empty brass cartridge cases are ejected from the turret through a small trap in the bustle. The

fire-control system includes telescopes for both the commander and gunner, with an infra-red/white-light searchlight above this. The latter enables targets to be engaged at night. Mounted on each side of the turret is a bank of three electrically-operated smoke-dischargers.

The engine and transmission are at the rear, the latter being a ZF manual box with six forward and one reverse gears. Suspension is of the torsion-bar type, and consists of five dual rubber-tyred road wheels with the drive sprocket at the rear, idler at the front and three track-return rollers. Standard equipment includes an NBC system and a heater.

Variants of the SK-105 include the **Greif** armoured recovery vehicle, a pioneer vehicle and a driver training vehicle. The improved A2 model of the **Kürassier**, as the SK-105 is nicknamed, is equipped with a digital fire-control computer, stabilized turret, and full night fighting capability.

Specification
Crew: 3
Weight: 17.5 tonnes
Dimensions: length (including gun) 7.763 m (25 ft 5⅔ in); length (hull) 5.58 m (18 ft 3⅔ in); width 2.50 m (8 ft 2½ in); height 2.529 m (8 ft 3½ in)
Powerplant: one Steyr 6-cylinder

The SK-105 light tank/tank destroyer climbs an incline, showing the French laser rangefinder on the turret roof at the rear with an infra-red/white-light searchlight mounted above. The 105-mm (4.13-in) gun is fed by two revolver-type magazines, each of which hold six rounds of fixed ammunition for ready use.

diesel developing 320 hp (239 kW)
Performance: maximum road speed 65 km/h (40 mph); maximum range 520 km (325 miles); fording 1.00 m (3 ft 3 in); gradient 75%; vertical obstacle 0.80 m (2 ft 7½ in); trench 2.41 m (7 ft 11 in)

ENGESA EE-9 Cascavel Armoured Car

For many years the standard armoured car of the Brazilian army was the US 6×6 M8 Greyhound that was developed in the early 1940s and armed with a 37-mm gun. By the late 1960s spares for the vehicle were becoming difficult to obtain, and its armament was obviously inadequate. The São Paulo company ENGESA had already converted many trucks, for example from 6×4 to 6×6 configuration, so giving them an excellent cross-country mobility. ENGESA then went on to develop two armoured vehicles to meet the requirements of the Brazilian army: these were the 6×6 **EE-9 Cascavel** armoured car and the 6×6

The latest production ENGESA EE-9 Cascavel armoured car, showing the laser rangefinder mounted externally over the 90-mm (3.54-in) gun and 7.62-mm machine-gun mounted externally at the commander's station. This vehicle has been widely used by the Iraqi army during the conflict with Iran.

EE-11 Urutu armoured personnel carrier, which shared many common automotive components although their layouts are quite different. The first prototype of the EE-9 Cascavel, named after a Brazilian snake, was completed in 1970 and was followed by a batch of pre-production vehicles before the first production vehicles were completed at the company's new facility at São José dos Campos in 1974. Since then large numbers have been built not only for the Brazilian army but also for many other countries around the world including Bolivia, Chile, Colombia, Cyprus, Gabon, Iraq, Libya, Tunisia and Uruguay, to name a few. The Cascavel has been used operationally by the Iraqi army in the war with Iran and by Libya in Chad.

Although some five different marks of the Cascavel have now been produced, the layout of all EE-9s is essentially the same. The armour is of an unusual design developed by the company in conjunction with the University of São Paulo, and consists of an outer layer of hard steel with an inner layer of softer steel roll-bonded and heat-treated to give the maximum possible protection within the weight limit of the vehicle; increased protection is provided over the frontal arc.

The driver is seated at the front of the vehicle on the left, with the two-man turret in the centre, and the engine and transmission at the rear. The engine is either a Detroit Diesel or a Mercedes-Benz diesel, coupled to an automatic or manual transmission. Spare parts for both the engine and transmission are available from commercial sources all over the world. All six wheels are powered, power-assisted steering is provided on the front two wheels. The rear suspension is of the ENGESA-designed Boomerang type that gives excellent cross-country mobility.

The initial **Cascavel Mk I** had the same gun as the M8, but all of these vehicles have now been rebuilt with the ENGESA turret armed with a 90-mm (3.54-in) gun. The **Cascavel Mk II** was for export only, and has a French Hispano-Suiza H-90 turret armed with a 90-mm (3.54-in) DEFA gun. The other models, the **Cascavel Mks III, IV and V**, have a two-man ENGESA-designed turret armed with a 90-mm (3.54-in) Cockerill Mk III gun (produced in Brazil by ENGESA), a 7.62-mm machine-gun mounted co-axially with the main armament, and a 12.7-mm or 7.62-mm machine-gun mounted on the roof for anti-aircraft defence.

As with most armoured cars today, a wide range of optional equipment can be fitted to the Cascavel, including a fire-control system, a laser rangefinder mounted externally over the main armament, a laser rangefinder operating through the gunner's sight, day/night sights for commander and gunner, an NBC system, and a ventilation system. All current models have a central tyre-pressure regulation system to enable the driver to adjust the ground pressure to suit the terrain.

Specification
Crew: 3
Weight: 12 tonnes
Dimensions: length (gun forward) 6.22 mm (20 ft 5 in); length (hull) 5.19 m (17 ft 0⅓ in); width 2.59 m (8 ft 6 in); height 2.29 m (7 ft 6 in)
Powerplant: one Detroit Diesel 6V-53 6-cylinder diesel developing 212 hp (158 kW)
Performance: maximum road speed 100 km/h (62 mph); maximum range 1000 km (620 miles); fording 1.00 m (3 ft 3 in); gradient 60%; vertical obstacle 0.60 m (1 ft 11⅔ in); trench not applicable

---

Type 63 Light Tank

After the end of World War II the USSR supplied China with a significant amount of military equipment including T-54 MBTs and PT-76 light amphibious tanks. Further development of the latter by China resulted in the **Type 63** light tank, which has been in service with the Chinese army for many years and has seen combat in the hands not only of the Chinese army but also of the Pakistani army (against India) and of the North Vietnamese army (against South Vietnam).

In many respects the Type 63 has a number of significant improvements over the original Soviet PT-76, including a four-man crew, increased firepower and (as it has a more powerful engine) a greater power-to-weight ratio which gives much improved road and water speeds.

The hull of the Type 63 is, like that of the PT-76, very large to allow the vehicle to float without any preparation apart from erecting the trim vane at the front of the hull and switching on the bilge pumps. The Type 63 is propelled in the water at a maximum speed of 12 km/h (7.5 mph) by two water jets mounted at the rear of the vehicle.

Main armament comprises an 85-mm (3.34-in) gun which fires a variety of ammunition including armour-piercing HE, HE, HEAT and smoke; 47 rounds of ammunition are carried. A 7.62-mm (0.3-in) machine-gun (for which 1,000 rounds are carried) is mounted co-axial with the main armament, and a 12.7-mm (0.5-in) machine-gun (for which 500 rounds are carried) is mounted on the turret roof for anti-aircraft defence.

The turret and hull are of welded steel construction with a maximum thickness of 14 mm (0.55 in), which is sufficient to provide protection against small arms fire and shell splinters only. If the armour was any thicker then the vehicle would require a flotation screen to be amphibious.

Suspension is of the torsion bar type, and consists of six large rubber-tyred road wheels with the idler at the front and drive sprocket at rear; there are no track-return rollers.

In the Chinese army four Type 63 light tanks can be found in the reconnaissance platoon of each armoured regiment, while there are 10 in the reconnaissance company of each armoured division. The vehicle is also in service with Pakistan, Sudan, Tanzania and Vietnam, and is now being offered for sale to other countries.

Specification
Type 63
Crew: 4
Weights: empty 16700 kg (36,816 lb); loaded 18700 kg (41,226 lb)
Powerplant: one Type 12150-L 12-cylinder diesel developing 400 hp (299 kW)
Dimensions: length, gun forward 8.437 m (27 ft 8.2 in) and hull 7.125 m (23 ft 4.5 in); width 3.20 m (10 ft 6 in); height without machine-gun 2.522 m (8 ft 3.3 in)
Performance: maximum road speed 64 km/h (40 mph); range 370 km (230 miles); fording amphibious; vertical obstacle 0.87 m (2 ft 10 in); trench 2.9 m (9 ft 6 in); gradient 60 per cent; side slope 30 per cent

Above: The Type 63 amphibious light tank was one of the first AFVs to be produced by China. Sharing many components with the Type 77 armoured personnel carrier, it is a development of the Soviet PT-76 and has seen action in Vietnam and Pakistan.

Below: The Type 63 needs only to erect its trim vane and switch on the bilge pumps before entering the water. It has a more powerful engine than the PT-76, which gives it correspondingly faster speeds both on land and in the water.

Close Combat Vehicle – Light

The Ordnance Division of the FMC Corporation of San Jose, California, is the largest manufacturer of tracked vehicles in the West, having produced over 70,000 units in the M113 series of armoured personnel carriers and over 2,000 Bradley Infantry Fighting Vehicles, plus large numbers of armoured amphibious tracked vehicles, reconnaissance vehicles, M59s and Armoured Infantry Fighting vehicles.

Several years ago the company realized that the US Army would require a highly mobile armoured vehicle armed with a 105-mm (4.13-in) standard tank gun for use with its light divisions. A decision was then taken to design and build a prototype of the **Close Combat Vehicle – Light (CCV – L)** with company money.

The prototype cost $26 million to build, of which around $14 million came from FMC and the remainder from the many subcontractors involved in the project.

A version of this vehicle, with a less sophisticated three-man turret has been developed and is being marketed by Vickers in the UK as the **Vickers Mark 5**. It retains the low-recoil 105-mm gun of the CCV L but can accept other guns.

To reduce development time and cost, proven automotive components have been used in the design of the CCV – L: for example, the engine uses many parts of the 8V-92TA engine installed in the Heavy Expanded Mobility Tactical Truck which has been in service with the US Army for some

The three-man CCV-L has been built by FMC's ordnance division as a private venture intended for the US Army's light divisions. It carries a modified version of the 105-mm gun carried by M48s, M60s and M1s but has a West German low recoil system and an automatic loader.

years, the transmission is from the FMC-built Bradley IFV, and parts of the suspension are from the M113A2.

The main armament comprises a 105-mm M68A1 gun of the type installed in the M48A5, M60/M60A1/M60A3 and M1 MBTs already in service with the US Army, but in this application fitted with a West German Rheinmetall low recoil system. The automatic loader for the main armament has been designed by FMC Northern Ordnance Division, which has some 40 years of experience in designing and building automatic loaders mainly for naval applications. The automatic loader makes possible a rate of fire of 12 rounds per minute. Nineteen rounds are carried in the automatic loader, with a further 24 rounds carried elsewhere in the hull.

The turret traverse and weapon elevation systems are based on those installed in the M1. The gunner has a stabilized day/night sight with laser rangefinder, while the commander has periscopes for all-round observation and an independent thermal viewer which can be traversed through 360° and has a day/night capability.

The US Army has a requirement for a vehicle it calls the Armoured Gun System (AGS) and hoped to get some funding for this in the FY87 budget, but this has been disapproved. So far three US companies have built vehicles which could meet the AGS requirement: these are the FMC Close Combat Vehicle – Light, the Cadillac Gage Stingray and the Teledyne Continental Motors General Products Division TCM-20.

Specification
CCV – L
Crew: 3
Weights: empty 17509 kg (38,600 lb); loaded 19414 kg (42,800 lb)
Powerplant: one Detroit Diesel Model 6V-92 TA 6-cylinder diesel developing 552 hp (412 kW)
Dimensions: length, gun forward 9.37 m (30 ft 9 in) and hull 6.20 m (20 ft 4 in); width 2.69 m (8 ft 10 in); height 2.36 m (7 ft 9 in)
Performance: maximum road speed 70 km/h (43.5 mph); range 483 km (300 miles); fording 1.32 m (4 ft 4 in); vertical obstacle 0.76 m (2 ft 6 in); trench 2.13 m (7 ft 0 in); gradient 60 per cent; side slope 40 per cent

---

Stingray Light Tank

Since the early 1960s the Cadillac Gage Company has built over 3,500 of its Commando range of 4×4 multi-mission vehicles, most of which have been exported. More recently the company has developed and placed in production the V-300 6×6 and Commando Scout 4×4 vehicles, while the Commando Ranger 4×4 light armoured personnel carrier has been built in large numbers for the the US Air Force base protection role.

Some years ago Cadillac Gage realized that there was a need for a light tank with good cross-country mobility, the combat-proved 105-mm (4.13-in) tank gun, and simplicity of operation and maintenance. With this requirement in mind the company designed and built the **Stingray** light tank, whose prototype was unveiled for the first time late in 1984.

To reduce development and procurement costs, proved and in-production automotive components have been used wherever possible: for example, the suspension is the same as that on the M109 self-propelled howitzer used by more than 20 countries.

The turret and hull are of all-welded steel armour construction providing complete protection from small arms fire and shell splinters. If required, additional armour can be added, for example of the reactive type which provides protection against HEAT projectiles.

Main armament is a low recoil version of the combat proven Royal Ordnance L7 105-mm, which fires the same ammunition as the proven L7/M68 gun used in many MBTs (including the Leopard 1, M48A5, M60, M1,

The Stingray light tank weighs little over 17 tons, but has the firepower of a main battle tank. Costs have been minimized by the use of automotive parts already in production; for example, the suspension is the same as that of the M109 SP gun.

Merkava and some models of the Centurion) and including the recent APFSDS-T (Armour-Piercing Fin-Stabilized Discarding-Sabot – Tracer).

Mounted co-axial with the main armament is a 7.62-mm (0.3-in) machine-gun for the engagement of soft targets such as trucks or infantry, while a 7.62-mm or 12.7-mm (0.5-in) machine-gun is mounted on the roof for anti-aircraft defence. Mounted on each side of the turret is a bank of electrically-operated smoke-dischargers.

The turret has power controls, and the prototype Stingray has a Marconi Command and Control System computerized digital Fire-Control System, which gives a high first-round hit probability. As an option a stabilization system can be installed, allowing the main armament to be laid and fired while the Stingray is moving across country.

As with most armoured vehicles today, a wide range of optional equipment is available to suit different user's requirements: for example, a land

Right: Given the vulnerability of many MBTs to HEAT warheads, the light armour of Stingray is not necessarily a great disadvantage. A stabilization system can be fitted, enabling the main armament to be aimed and fired while the vehicle is moving.

navigation system, a laser rangefinder, an NBC system, and a fire detection and suppression system.

So far the Stingray is still at the prototype stage, but a number of countries are showing more than a passing interest in this vehicle, which has the mobility and firepower of a MBT but is much cheaper.

Specification
Stingray
Crew: 4
Weights: empty 17237 kg (38,000 lb);

loaded 19051 kg (42,000 lb)
Powerplant: one Detroit Diesel Model 8V-92 TA diesel developing 535 hp (399 kW)
Dimensions: length, gun forward 9.35 m (30 ft 8 in) and hull 6.30 m (20 ft 8 in); width 2.71 m (8 ft 11 in); height overall 2.54 (8 ft 4 in)
Performance: maximum road speed 69 km/h (43 mph); range 483 km (300 miles); fording 1.22 m (4 ft 0 in); vertical obstacle 0.76 m (2 ft 6 in); trench 1.69 m (5 ft 7 in); gradient 60 per cent; side slope 30 per cent

Lynx Command and Reconnaissance Vehicle

When the M113 armoured personnel carrier entered production at FMC's facility at San Jose in 1960, it was realized that in addition to being used for a wide range of roles its automotive component could also be used in other armoured vehicles. At that time the US Army had already selected the M114 vehicle to carry out the role of command and reconnaissance, but the M114 did not prove a successful design and it has long been phased out of service, and it was never sold overseas. FMC then designed and built a command and reconnaissance vehicle using automotive components of the diesel-powered M113A1, and this was subsequently selected by Canada, which ordered 174 vehicles under the name Lynx, and by the Netherlands, which ordered 250 vehicles. all of these were delivered by 1968. The vehicle is often called the M113 and a half!

In comparison with the M113 the Lynx has a lower-profile hull, the powerpack repositioned to the rear, and one road wheel less on each side. The hull is of all-welded aluminium construction that provides the crew with complete protection from small arms fire and shell splinters. The driver is seated at the front of the vehicle, with the commander to his rear and right. The radio operator/observer is seated to the left rear of the commander. The engine compartment is at the rear of the hull on the right side, with access hatches in the roof and hull rear.

Suspension is of the torsion-bar type, and consists of four dual rubber-tyred road wheels on each side with the drive sprocket at the front and the idler at the rear; there are no track-return rollers. The Lynx is fully amphibious, being propelled in the water by its tracks at a speed of 5.6 km/h (3.5 mph). Before the vehicle enters the water a trim vane is erected at the front of the hull, electric bilge pumps are switched on, and rectangular covers erected around the air inlet and exhaust louvres on the hull top to stop water entering the engine compartment, the vehicle having very limited freeboard. Vehicles such as the M113 and the Lynx can cross only calm rivers and lakes, open-sea landings almost inevitably resulting in swamping.

The commander of the Lynx has an M26 hand-operated turret, with vision blocks for all-round observation and an externally-mounted standard 12.7-mm M2HB machine-gun for which

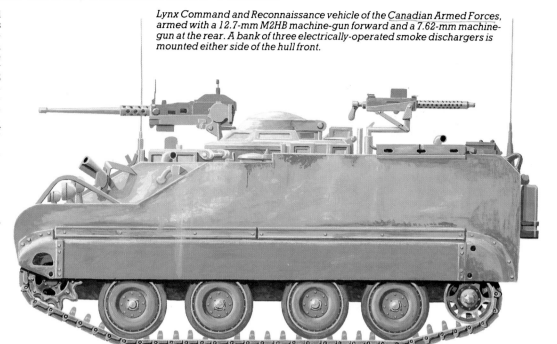

Lynx Command and Reconnaissance vehicle of the Canadian Armed Forces, armed with a 12.7-mm M2HB machine-gun forward and a 7.62-mm machine-gun at the rear. A bank of three electrically-operated smoke dischargers is mounted either side of the hull front.

1,155 rounds of ammunition are carried. The radio operator/observer has a pintle-mounted 7.62-mm machine-gun with 2,000 rounds. In addition a bank of three electrically-operated smoke-dischargers is mounted at the front of each side of the hull firing forwards.

The Dutch vehicles have a slightly different internal layout, and as originally supplied were slightly lighter. More recently all of these vehicles have been fitted with a Swiss Oerlikon-Buhrle GBD-AOA one-man turret armed with a 25-mm KBA-B cannon. This has three rates of fire: single-shot, 175 rounds per minute and 570 rounds per minute. Two hundred rounds of ready-use ammunition are carried for the cannon, of which 120 are high explosive and the other 80 armour-piercing. An added advantage for the Dutch is that this Oerlikon cannon (in a different one-man power-operated turret) is also installed in the FMC-designed armoured infantry fighting vehicles of the Dutch army, so assisting in ammunition commonality.

Specification
Crew: 3
Weight: 8.775 tonnes

Dimensions: length 4.597 m (15 ft 1 in); width 2.413 m (7 ft 11 in); height (including armament) 2.171 m (7 ft 1½ in)
Powerplant: one Detroit Diesel Type 6V53 6-cylinder diesel developing 215 hp (160 kW)
Performance: maximum road speed 70.8 km/h (44 mph); maximum range 523 km (325 miles); fording amphibious; gradient 60%; vertical

All Dutch vehicles have now been fitted with a Swiss Oerlikon-Buhrle one-man turret armed with a 25-mm KBA-B cannon. This is also fitted to the Dutch army's Armoured Infantry Fighting Vehicles, thus ensuring ammunition supply on the battlefield.

obstacle 0.609 m (2 ft 0 in); trench 1.524 m (5 ft 0 in)

Daimler Ferret Scout Car

Following the success of the Daimler Dingo scout car in World War II, the British War Office issued a requirement for a new scout car in 1946 and in the following year Daimler Ltd of Coventry was awarded the development contract. The first prototype was completed in 1949, and after user trials the vehicle was accepted for service as the Ferret scout car, although it was at one time to be called the Field Mouse. Production continued at Daimler for the home and export markets until 1971, by which time just over 4,400 vehicles had been built. In 1983 the Ferret was still being used in some numbers by the British army and by some 30 other countries in almost every part of the world with the exception of the Americas.

All versions of the Ferret have the same basic layout, with the driver at the front, the commander/gunner in the centre, and the engine and transmission at the rear. The all-welded steel hull has a maximum thickness of 12 mm (0.47 in) and provides the crew

A Daimler Ferret Mk 1 scout car (left) armed with a Bren light machine-gun, and a Ferret Mk 2/3 on the right armed with a 7.62-mm machine-gun. A total of 4409 vehicles were built for home and export markets by the time production was completed in 1971.

Daimler Ferret Scout Car (continued)

with complete protection from small arms fire and shell splinters. Steering is on the front four wheels but is not power assisted.

The **Ferret Mk 1** has an open top and is armed simply with a pintle-mounted 7.62-mm Bren or a Browning machine-gun. The **Ferret Mk 1/2** has a three-man crew and a low-profile turret with an externally-mounted machine-gun. The **Ferret Mk 2/3** has a one-man turret armed with a 7.62-mm machine-gun with an elevation between −15° and +45°, turret traverse being 360°. This turret is almost the same as that fitted to the Alvis Saracen armoured personnel carrier. The **Ferret Mk 2/2** was an interesting model developed locally in the Far East, and was a Ferret Mk 2 with an extension collar between the hull top and turret base to give the commander much improved all-round observation. As far as it is known none of this particular model remain in service. The **Ferret Mk 2/6** was the Ferret Mk 2/3 with a British Aircraft Corporation (now British Aerospace) Vigilant ATGW mounted on each side of the turret, a further two missiles being carried in reserve on the left side of the hull. The Vigilant was a first-generation wire-guided missile and had a maximum range of 1375 m (1,500 yards), and could be launched from within the vehicle or away from the vehicle with the aid of a separation sight and cable. The **Ferret Mk 3** and **Ferret Mk 4** were essentially earlier versions rebuilt to incorporate stronger suspension units, larger tyres and a flotation screen carried collapsed around the top of the hull; this could be quickly erected by the crew to make the vehicle fully amphibious, being propelled in the water by its wheels.

The **Ferret Mk 5** was the final version, and all of these were rebuilds of earlier vehicles. It had the stronger suspension, larger tyres, flotation screen and a turret in each side of which were two launcher bins for the British Aerospace Dynamics Swingfire ATGW with a range of 4000 m (4,375 yards). These could knock out the heaviest tank, and could be launched from within the vehicle or away from

the vehicle with the aid of a separation cable and sight. The Ferret Mk 5 was also armed with a 7.62-mm machine-gun and, like all Ferrets, smoke-dischargers. This model is no longer in service with the British army and was not exported.

The Ferret Mk 2/3 has a one-man turret armed with a 7.62-mm machine-gun. In addition to being used as a scout car, it is widely used in the internal security role.

Specification
Daimler Ferret Mk 2/3
Crew: 2
Weight: 4.395 tonnes
Dimensions: length 3.835 m (12 ft 7 in); width 1.905 m (6 ft 3 in); height 1.879 m (6 ft 2 in)
Powerplant: one Rolls-Royce 6-cylinder petrol engine developing 129 hp (96 kW)
Performance: maximum road speed 93 km/h (58 mph); maximum range 306 km (190 miles); fording 0.914 m (3 ft 0 in); gradient 46%; vertical obstacle 0.406 m (1 ft 4 in); trench 1.22 m (4 ft 0 in) with one channel

Ferrets head a column of the FV 432 armoured personnel carriers of an British army infantry battalion in Germany in the 1970s. The Ferret has been largely phased out of British service today but remains in use around the world.

Fox Light Armoured Car

The **FV721 Fox** light armoured car arose out of a British army requirement for reconnaissance vehicles. Developed by the Daimler company from 1965, the Fox design is based upon the rebuilt Ferret Mark 4 and Mark 5, but unlike the Ferret has a welded aluminium hull and turret providing protection against heavy machine-gun fire and shell splinters.

The two-man turret mounts a 30-mm cannon with co-axial 7.62-mm machine gun. The RARDEN cannon is normally used in rapid single shots but six round bursts can also be fired. It can handle a variety of ammunition including APDS, HE Incendiary, AP Smoke, and standard Oerlikon HE and AP rounds. The RARDEN is an accurate weapon, 1-metre groups being recorded on targets at 1000 m range.

The Fox is powered by a militarised Jaguar XK series engine, and with the erection of the flotation screen can be propelled and steered across rivers by its wheels. Three Foxes can be car-

ried in a C-130 Hercules, or two if dropped by parachute.

The Fox is used by the British army, Malawi and Nigeria.

Specification
Crew: 3
Weight: 6120 kg (13,492 lb)
Dimensions: length 5.08 m (16 ft 8 in) including gun; width 2.134 m (7 ft); height overall 2.2 m (7 ft 2½ in)
Powerplant: one Jaguar 4.2 litre 6-cylinder petrol engine developing 190 bhp (141 kW)
Performance: maximum road speed 104 km/h (64.6 mph); maximum road range 434 km (270 miles); fording 1 m (amphibious with preparation); gradient 58%; vertical obstacle 0.5 m (1 ft 8 in); trench with channels 1.22 m (4 ft)

The Fox is a Jaguar-powered development of the late production Ferret family.

Alvis Scorpion Reconnaissance Vehicle

In the late 1960s the British army decided to build two new reconnaissance vehicles, one tracked and the other wheeled, and these became known as the **Combat Vehicle Reconnaissance (Tracked)** or **Scorpion** and the **Combat Vehicle Reconnaissance (Wheeled)**, or **Fox**. In 1967 Alvis was awarded a contract to build 17 prototypes of the Scorpion, the first of which was completed in 1969. Trials were so successful that it was accepted for service the following year. Late in 1970 the Scorpion was also ordered by Belgium and an assembly line for the vehicle was set up at Malines in Belgium. First production Scorpions were delivered to the British army in 1972, and by 1983 total orders had passed the 3,000 mark and production was continuing. In addition to being used by the United Kingdom (army and Royal Air Force Regiment) and Belgium, the Scorpion is also used by Brunei, Eire, Honduras, Iran, Kuwait, Malaysia, New Zealand,

Nigeria, Oman, Tanzania, Philippines and the United Arab Emirates.

The Scorpion has a hull and turret of all-welded aluminium construction. The driver is seated at the front on the left, the engine is to his right, and the two-man turret is at the rear. Suspension is of the torsion-bar type, and consists of five road wheels with drive sprocket at the front, idler at the rear; there are no track-return rollers. A flotation screen is carried collapsed around the top of the hull, and once this has been erected the vehicle is propelled in water by its tracks at a speed of about 6 km/h (3.7 mph).

The basic Scorpion has a 76-mm (3-in) gun (a lightened version of that carried in the Saladin armoured car) with an elevation of −10° to +35°; turret traverse is 360°. A total of 40 rounds of ammunition is carried, and this can be a mixture of canister, HESH, HE, smoke (base ejection) and illuminating. A 7.62-mm machine-gun is mounted co-axial with the main arma-

ment, and the machine-gun can be used as a ranging as well as a secondary weapon; a total of 3,000 rounds of ammunition are carried for this weapon. The vehicle is also available with a diesel engine in place of the standard petrol engine, and this model has a much increased operating range.

On the same basic chassis a complete family of light tracked vehicles has been developed. **Striker** is the anti-tank model and has five British Aerospace Swingfire ATGWs in the ready-to-launch position. **Spartan** is the troop carrier and can carry four fully equipped troops in addition to its three-man crew. The ambulance model, which is unarmed, is called the **Samaritan**, while the command model, which like Samaritan has a much higher roof, is called the **Sultan**. The recovery model, which uses the same hull as the Spartan, is called the **Samson** and has winches, spades and other specialized equipment. The **Scimitar** has

the same hull as the Scorpion but has a two-man turret armed with the same 30-mm Rarden cannon as fitted to the Fox CVR(W). More recently the **Stormer** armoured personnel carrier and the **Streaker** high-mobility load-carrier have been developed, both based on the chassis of the Spartan and developed with company rather than government money.

The Stormer has an extra road wheel each side to provide increased chassis length and thereby increase the internal capacity (it can hold up to eight troops). It can be armed with various roof-mounted gun turrets. 151 Stormers have been ordered by the British army to carry multiple launchers for the Short Starstreak air defence missile. The British army has also ordered a roof turret carrying Milan anti-tank missile launchers to be fitted to some of their in-service Spartan armoured personnel carriers.

Specification
Crew: 3
Weight: 8.073 tonnes
Dimensions: length 4.794 m (15 ft 8¾ in); width 2.235 m (7 ft 4 in); height 2.102 m (6 ft 10¾ in)
Powerplant: one Jaguar 4.2-litre petrol engine developing 190 hp (142 kW)
Performance: maximum road speed 80 km/h (50 mph); maximum range 644 km (400 miles); fording 1.067 m (3 ft 6 in); gradient 60%; vertical obstacle 0.50 m (1 ft 8 in); trench 2.057 m (6 ft 9 in)

Left: Scorpion has been tested in action from the deserts of the Middle East to the cold wastes of the Falklands and has proved highly successful.

Below: Seen supporting the Royal Marines in northern Norway, these Scimitars are armed with the high-velocity 30-mm RARDEN cannon

The Alvis Scorpion

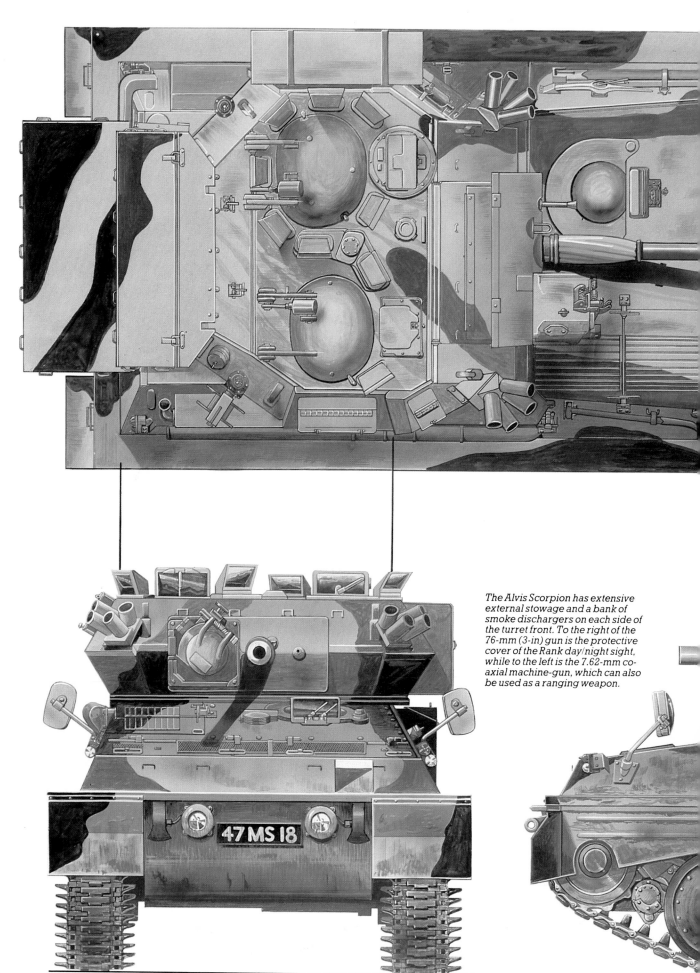

The Alvis Scorpion has extensive external stowage and a bank of smoke dischargers on each side of the turret front. To the right of the 76-mm (3-in) gun is the protective cover of the Rank day/night sight, while to the left is the 7.62-mm co-axial machine-gun, which can also be used as a ranging weapon.

47 MS 18

47MS18

Rex Nicholls
Swanston Graphics

Alvis Saladin Armoured Car

UK

Following the success of the AEC Mk III and Daimler Mk II armoured cars during World War II the British army issued a requirement for a new armoured car with a 2-pdr gun. But it was soon decided that this weapon would be ineffective against the newer vehicles expected in the 1950s, and the Armament Research and Development Establishment then designed a new 76-mm (3-in) gun called the L5.

The chassis of the **Saladin**, or **FV601**, is very similar to that of the FV603 Saracen armoured personnel carrier, which was also under development by Alvis at that time. Because of needs of the guerrilla war in Malaya, development of the Saracen was given precedence over that of the Saladin, and because of the high work load at Alvis the first six preproduction Saladins were built by Crossley Motors at Stockport in Cheshire.

The Saladin was accepted for service with the British army in 1956, and production started two years later at Alvis in Coventry. Production continued for the home and export markets until 1972, by which time 1,177 vehicles had been completed. In British army service the Saladin has now been replaced by the Alvis Scorpion tracked vehicle, which is armed with a new version of the 76-mm (3-in) gun called the L23. A small number of Saladins remain in service in Cyprus with the British army, and the type is also used by Bahrain, Ghana, Honduras, Indonesia, Kenya, Kuwait, Lebanon, Libya, Nigeria, Portugal, Sierra Leone, Sri Lanka, Sudan, Tunisia, United Arab Emirates and both North and South Yemen, although in some cases spares must be a major problem as the UK is no longer handling spares for some countries as a result of political considerations.

The hull of the Saladin is of all-welded steel armoured construction that varies in thickness from 8 mm (0.31 in) up to 16 mm (0.63 in); the turret has a maximum thickness of 32 mm (1.25 in) at the front and 16 mm (0.63 in) at the sides and rear. The driver sits at the front of the vehicle with excellent vision to his front and sides. The other two crew members are seated in the turret with the commander, who acts as the loader, on the right and the gunner on the left. The engine and trans-

mission are at the rear of the hull. All six wheels of the Saladin are powered, with steering on the front four wheels. The vehicle can still be driven with one wheel blown off.

The 76-mm (3-in) gun is mounted in a turret that can be traversed manually through 360°; the gun itself can be elevated from −10° to +20°. A total of 42 rounds of fixed ammunition can be carried, the type being identical to those used in the L23 gun of the Scorpion and including canister, HESH, SH/P, HE, HE/PRAC, smoke (both base ejection and phosphorus) and illuminating. A 7.62-mm machine-gun is mounted coaxial with the main armament, and a similar weapon is mounted on the turret roof for anti-aircraft defence. A total of 2,750 rounds of 7.62-mm ammunition is carried. Mounted on each side of the turret is a bank of six electrically-operated smoke-dischargers.

There were very few variants of the Saladin, one of the more interesting ones being the amphibious model. This was fitted with a flotation screen around the top of the hull, and when this had been erected the vehicle could propel itself on water with its wheels.

The Alvis Saladin armoured car shares many common automotive components with the Saracen 6×6 APC. A few Saladins remain in service with the British army in Cyprus.

Specification
Crew: 3
Weight: 11.59 tonnes
Dimensions: length (including gun) 5.284 m (17 ft 4 in); length (hull) 4.93 m (16 ft 2 in); width 2.54 m (8 ft 4 in); height 2.93 m (9 ft 7⅓ in)
Powerplant: one Rolls-Royce B80 8-cylinder petrol engine developing 170 bhp (127 kW)
Performance: maximum road speed 72 km/h (45 mph); maximum range

The Saladin is armed with a 76-mm (3-in) gun; a lightened version is fitted in the more recent Scorpion, and fires the same range of fixed ammunition. Between 1958 and 1972 Alvis of Coventry built 1177 Saladins for the home and the lucrative overseas markets.

400 km (250 miles); fording 1.07 m (3 ft 6 in); gradient 46%; vertical obstacle 0.46 m (1 ft 6 in); trench 1.52 m (5 ft 0 in)

AMX-13 Light Tank

FRANCE

The **AMX-13** light tank was one of the three armoured vehicles designed in France immediately after the end of World War II, the other being the Panhard EBR heavy armoured car and the AMX-50 MBT which did not enter service as large numbers of M47s soon became available from the United States. The AMX-13 was designed by the Atelier de Construction d'Issy-les-Moulineaux, the numeral 13 in the designation being the originally specified design weight in tonnes. The first prototype was completed in 1948 and production was under way at the Atelier de Construction Roanne (ARE) by 1952. The AMX-13 continued in production at the ARE until the 1960s, when space was needed for the AMX-30 MBT and AMX-10P IFV family. Production of the whole AMX-13 family, including the light tank, was transferred to Creusot-Loire at Chalon-sur-

Saône, where production continues to this day. By early 1983 over 3,000 vehicles had been built and the type remains in service with Algeria, Argentina, China, Djibouti, Dominican Republic, Ecuador, France, El Salvador, Indonesia, Ivory Coast, Lebanon, Morocco, Nepal, Peru, Singapore, Tunisia and Venezuela. The AMX-13 was also used by a number of other countries such as India, Israel, the Netherlands and Switzerland, but most of these have now been sold. The chassis of the

The AMX-13 light tank is fitted with an oscillating turret in which the gun is fixed in the upper part, which in turn pivots on the lower part. The gun can fire until its 12 rounds of ready-use ammunition are exhausted, and then two six-round magazines have to be reloaded manually from outside the vehicle by a crewman.

Modern Light Tanks and Reconnaissance Vehicles

AMX-13 (extensively modified in many cases) has been used as the basis for one of the most complete family of vehicles ever developed; this includes the 105-mm (4.13-in) Mk 61 self-prop-

AMX-13 light tank fitted with an FL-10 two-man turret armed with a 75-mm (2.95-in) gun. Other versions were armed with 90-mm (3.54-in) or 105-mm (4.13-in) guns.

elled howitzer, 155-mm (6.1-in) Mk F3 self-propelled gun, AMX-13 DCA twin 30-mm self-propelled anti-aircraft gun system, AMX VCI infantry fighting vehicle and its countless variants, AMX VCG engineer vehicle, AMX-13 armoured recovery vehicle and the AMX-13 armoured bridge-layer.

The original model of the AMX-13 was fitted with the FL-10 turret armed with a 75-mm (2.95-in) gun and a 7.62-mm co-axial machine-gun. This turret is of the oscillating type and the 75-mm (2.95-in) gun is fed by two revolver-type magazines, each of which holds six rounds of ammunition. The basic types of ammunition were fixed HE and HEAT, the latter capable of penetrating 170 mm (6.7 in) of armour. This model was used in some numbers by Israel during the 1967 Middle East war, but its gun was found to be ineffective against the frontal armour of the Soviet T-54/T-55 MBTs supplied to Syria and Egypt, so it was soon phased out of service, most ending up in Singapore or Nepal.

At a later date all 75-mm (2.95-in) models of the French army were fitted

with a 90-mm (3.54-in) gun which would fire canister, HE, HEAT and smoke projectiles, although more recently an APFSDS projectile has been developed that can penetrate a triple NATO tank target at an incidence of 60° at a range of 2000 m (2,190 yards). The 105-mm (4.13-in) gun model was designed specifically for the export market and had the heavier FL-12 turret, which is also fitted to the Austrian SK-105 light tank/tank destroyer.

The basic AMX-13 is powered by a

petrol engine but upgrades in France, Singapore, Argentina, Peru and Venezuela have had diesel engines of similar power fitted giving greater range and enhanced fire safety.

Specification
AMX-13 (90-mm gun)
Crew: 3
Weight: 15 tonnes

Dimensions: length (including gun) 6.36 m (20 ft 10⅓ in); length (hull) 4.88 m (16 ft 0 in); width 2.50 m (8 ft 2½ in); height 2.30 m (7 ft 6½ in)
Powerplant: one SOFAM 8Gxb 8-cylinder petrol engine developing 250 hp (186 kW)
Performance: maximum road speed 60 km/h (37 mph); maximum range 350-400 km (220-250 miles); fording 0.60 m (1 ft 11⅔ in); gradient 60%; vertical obstacle 0.65 m (2 ft 1⅔ in); trench 1.60 m (5 ft 3 in)

FRANCE
AMX-10RC Reconnaissance Vehicle

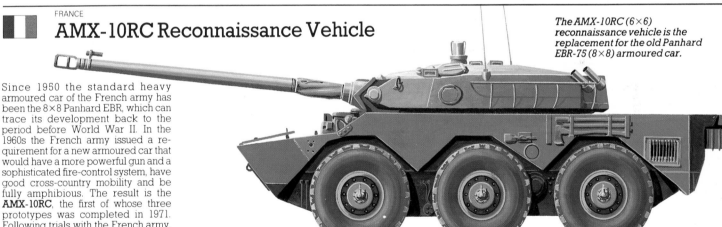

The AMX-10RC (6×6) reconnaissance vehicle is the replacement for the old Panhard EBR-75 (8×8) armoured car.

Since 1950 the standard heavy armoured car of the French army has been the 8×8 Panhard EBR, which can trace its development back to the period before World War II. In the 1960s the French army issued a requirement for a new armoured car that would have a more powerful gun and a sophisticated fire-control system, have good cross-country mobility and be fully amphibious. The result is the **AMX-10RC**, the first of whose three prototypes was completed in 1971. Following trials with the French army, the type was accepted for service and production got under way at the Atelier de Construction Roanne, where the AMX-10P MICV and the AMX-30 MBT family are produced. The first French army units were issued with the vehicle in 1979.

The AMX-10RC has two major drawbacks: firstly, it is more expensive than some MBTs and, secondly, it is very sophisticated. For this reason the French army has trimmed back its original requirements and is now looking at cheaper alternatives.

The hull and turret of the AMX-10RC are of all-welded aluminium construction, with the driver seated at the front left, the turret in centre and engine, and transmission at the rear. The 6×6 suspension is unusual in that the driver can adjust its ground clearance to suit the type of ground being crossed and even tilt it from side to side. For example, when travelling on roads the ground clearance is 330 mm (13 in), while for cross-country travel it is

470 mm (18½ in).

The vehicle is fully amphibious, being propelled in the water by two waterjets at the rear of the hull. Designed in the UK but manufactured in France under licence, this propulsion produces a maximum water speed of 7.2 km/h (4.5 mph). Before the vehicle enters the water a trim vane is erected at the front of the hull and the bilge pumps are switched on.

The commander and gunner are seated on the right on the turret, with the loader on the left. The main armament comprises a 105-mm (4.13-in) gun with an elevation of +20° and a depression of −8°; turret traverse is 360°. A 7.62-mm machine-gun is mounted co-axial with the main armament. Totals of 40 105-mm (4.13-in) and 4,000 7.62-mm rounds are carried. Two electrically-operated smoke dischar-

gers are mounted on each side of the turret rear and fire forwards.

The fire-control system is the most sophisticated of its type installed in any vehicle of this class, and includes a laser rangefinder, a computer and a low-light TV system with a screen for both the commander and driver. This fire-control system enables stationary and moving targets to be engaged by day and night.

At present, two types of main-armament ammunition can be fired, namely HEAT and HE. The former has a muzzle velocity of 1120 m (3,675 ft) per second and will penetrate 350 mm (13.78 in) of armour at an incidence of 0° or 150 mm (5.91 in) of armour at an incidence of 60°. The HEAT round is ineffective against the new generations of armour, however, and for this reason an APFSDS projectile is now

being developed.

The last AMX-10RCs were delivered in 1987 with a new, more powerful and fuel efficient Baudouin diesel, which will be retrofitted to all French army examples.

Specification
Crew: 4
Weight: 15.8 tonnes
Dimensions: length (gun forward) 9.15 m (30 ft 0¼ in); length (hull) 6.35 m (20 ft 10 in); width 2.95 m (9 ft 8 in); height 2.68 m (8 ft 9½ in)
Powerplant: one 8-cylinder diesel developing 260 hp (194 kW)
Performance: maximum road speed 85 km/h (53 mph); maximum range 800 km (500 miles); fording amphibious; gradient 60%; vertical obstacle 0.70 m (2 ft 3¼ in); trench 1.15 m (3 ft 9 in)

Panhard ERC Sagaie Armoured Car

For many years the backbone of the Panhard armoured vehicle production has been the 4×4 AML light armoured

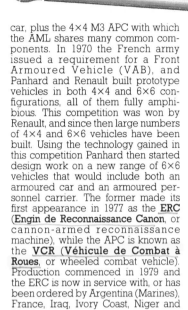

car, plus the 4×4 M3 APC with which the AML shares many common components. In 1970 the French army issued a requirement for a Front Armoured Vehicle (VAB), and Panhard and Renault built prototype vehicles in both 4×4 and 6×6 configurations, all of them fully amphibious. This competition was won by Renault, and since then large numbers of 4×4 and 6×6 vehicles have been built. Using the technology gained in this competition Panhard then started design work on a new range of 6×6 vehicles that would include both an armoured car and an armoured personnel carrier. The former made its first appearance in 1977 as the **ERC** (**Engin de Reconnaissance Canon**, or cannon-armed reconnaissance machine), while the APC is known as the **VCR** (**Véhicule de Combat à Roues**, or wheeled combat vehicle). Production commenced in 1979 and the ERC is now in service with, or has been ordered by Argentina (Marines), France, Iraq, Ivory Coast, Niger and Mexico.

The vehicle can be fitted with a wide range of turrets on the same basic chassis. The driver is seated at the front, the turret is in the centre, and the engine and transmisson are at the rear. All six road wheels are powered; power-assisted steering is provided on the front two wheels. An unusual feature of the ERC is that the centre pair of wheels can be raised off the ground for road travel and lowered again for cross-country travel. The basic vehicle is fully amphibious, being propelled in the water at a speed of 4.5 km/h (2.8 mph) by its wheels, or by two optional waterjets at a speed of 9.5 km/h (5.9 mph). Before the vehicle enters the water a trim vane is erected at the front of the hull

and two schnorkels are erected at the rear.

The basic vehicle can be fitted with a wide range of turrets including the GIAT TS-90, Hispano-Suiza Lynx 90, Hispano Suiza 60-20 Serval and EMC 81-mm mortar turrets, and a two-man turret with twin 20-mm or 25-mm cannon for use in the anti-aircraft role is also available.

The model selected by the French army (for use by its rapid intervention force) is fitted with the GIAT TS-90 turret and called the **ERC-90 F4 Sagaie**. This is armed with the long-barrelled 90-mm (3.54-in) gun with an elevation of +15° and a depression of −8°. The gun can fire the following types of fixed ammunition: canister, HE, HEAT, smoke and APFSDS. The last has a muzzle velocity of 1350 m (4,430 ft) per second and will penetrate 120 mm (4.72 in) of armour at an incidence of 60°. A 7.62-mm machine-gun is mounted co-axial with the main armament, and two electrically-operated smoke-dischargers are mounted on each side of the turret. Twenty rounds of 90-mm (3.54-in) and 2,000 rounds of 7.62-mm machine-gun ammunition are carried.

Panhard's private venture range of 6×6 armoured cars has attracted a number of export orders as well as interest from the French army. The ERC 90 has seen action in Chad's interminable civil war, and now equips part of the French rapid deployment force.

In 1985 Panhard announced that it had developed the Sagaie 2 armoured car and that one overseas country had already placed an order for the vehicle. The Sagaie 2 has a slightly longer and wider hull, and instead of the 90-mm GIAT TS-90 turret it is fitted with the SAMM TTB-1900 turret, which has the same gun as the TS-90 turret. The SAMM turret has much improved armour protection, however, and is available with a wide range of turret controls, fire-control systems and optical devices. Two types of ammunition stowage are available, one having 35 rounds of 90-mm ammunition of which 13 are ready for immediate use, and the other 32 rounds of which 10 are for ready use.

The original Panhard Sagaie 1 was powered by a single Peugeot V-6 petrol engine developing 155 hp (116 kW), but the Sagaie 2 is powered by two Peugeot XD 3T 4-cylinder turbocharged diesels which develop a total of 196 hp (146 kW); these engines are also used in the Panhard VBL 4×4 light armoured vehicle. As an alternative the Sagaie 2 can be powered by two V-6 petrol engines developing a total of 290 hp (216 kW) which gives an exceptionally high power-to-weight ratio.

Optional equipment includes an air-conditioning system, additional ammunition stowage, laser rangefin-

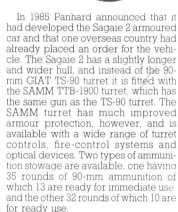

The Panhard ERC Sagaie armoured car is fitted with a GIAT TS-90 turret, armed with a 90-mm (3.54-in) gun.

der, passive night-vision equipment, NBC system, anti-aircraft machine-gun, additional elevation of the 90-mm (3.54-in) gun to +35°, various types of fire-control system and a land navigation system, the last being essential when the vehicle is operating in the desert.

Specification
Crew: 3
Weight: 7.65 tonnes (Sagaie) or 10 tonnes (Sagaie 2)
Dimensions: length gun forward 7.693 m/25 ft 3 in (Sagaie) or 7.97 m/26 ft 2 in (Sagaie 2); hull length 5.083 m/16 ft 8 in (Sagaie) or 5.87 m/19 ft 3 in (Sagaie 2); width 2.495 m/8 ft 2 in (Sagaie) or 2.7 m/8 ft 10 in (Sagaie 2); height 2.07 m/6 ft 9 in (Sagaie) or 2.3 m/7 ft 7 in (Sagaie 2)
Powerplant: one Peugeot V-6 petrol engine developing 155 hp (116 kW) in Sagaie; two Peugeot XD 3T 4-cylinder diesels delivering 196 hp (146 kW) or two Peugeot V-6 petrol engines developing 290 hp (216 kW)
Performance: Maximum road speed 90 kmh/56 mph (Sagaie) or 100 kmh/62 mph (Sagaie 2); maximum road range 800 km/500 miles (Sagaie) or 600 km/373 miles (Sagaie 2); fording amphibious (Sagaie) or 1.2 m/3 ft 11 in (Sagaie 2); vertical obstacle 0.8 m/2 ft 8 in; trench 1.1 m/3 ft 8 in (Sagaie) or 0.8 m/2 ft 8 in (Sagaie 2); gradient 60% (Sagaie) or 50% (Sagaie 2)

Panhard AML-90 Armoured Car

The French army used large numbers of British-built 4×4 Daimler Ferret scout cars in North Africa in the 1950s, and decided to procure a similar vehicle but with a wider range of armament installations. After evaluation of prototype vehicles, the design from Panhard was selected. Production commenced in 1960 under the designation **AML (Automitrailleuse Légère**, or light armoured car), and since then well over 4,000 vehicles have been built in several variants, with production continuing to this day for export. The type is also built in South Africa by Sandock Austral for the South African army, which calls the type the **Eland**. The AML, which is in service with well over 30 countries, shares 95 per cent of its automotive components with the Panhard M3 armoured personnel carrier, and many countries operate fleets of M3s and AMLs with the obvious financial, logistical and training advantages.

The layout of all variants is similar, with the driver at the front, the two-man turret in the centre (with an entry door in each side of the hull), and the engine and transmission at the rear.

One of the most common models is the **AML-90**, the latest version of this being called the **Lynx 90**. This has a two-man turret designed and built by Hispano-Suiza and armed with a GIAT 90-mm (3.54-in) DEFA gun, a 7.62-mm co-axial machine-gun and a 7.62-mm anti-aircraft machine-gun. The 90-mm (3.54-mm) gun can fire a wide range of fixed ammunition, including HEAT,

HE, smoke and canister. The HEAT round will penetrate 320 mm (12.6 in) of armour at an incidence of 0° or 120 mm (4.72in) of armour at an incidence of 65°. Totals of 21 rounds of 90-mm (3.54-in) and 2,000 rounds of 7.62-mm ammunition are carried. Optional equipment for this turret includes passive night-vision equipment, powered controls and a laser rangefinder.

The **HE 60-7** turret has a 60-mm breech-loaded mortar and two 7.62-mm machine-guns, the **HE 60-12** turret a similar mortar and a 12.7-mm machine-gun, and the **HE 60-20** turret has the 60-mm mortar and a 20-mm cannon. The breech-loaded mortar is used both in the indirect and direct fire modes, and is very useful in guerrilla-type operations as it can be fired over hills and buildings.

One of the more recent models is the **HE 60-20 Serval** turret with a 60-mm long-barrel mortar mounted in the turret front with a 20-mm cannon and 7.62-mm machine-gun mounted externally at the turret rear. For the export market an anti-aircraft model of the AML was developed fitted with a two-man **SAMM S530** turret armed with twin 20-mm cannon, each with 300 rounds of ready-use ammunition. Turret traverse and weapon elevation is powered so enabling aircraft and helicopters to be engaged successfully.

More recently, scout car versions of the AML have been developed that are fitted with various combinations of 7.62-mm and 12.7-mm machine-guns on pintle mounts or in turrets. These

have a lower profile than the 90-mm (3.54-in) gun models, are lighter, much cheaper and well suited for the light reconnaissance role.

As usual a wide range of optional equipment can be fitted, including passive night-vision equipment, an air-conditioning system and a complete NBC system. An amphibious kit was developed, but as far as is known this was not produced in quantity.

The AML has been used operationally by a number of armies and in a variety of terrain. It has seen action in the Falklands (with Argentina), Chad (with the French and the armies of Chad), with Iraq in the Gulf War, with Morocco and Polisario in the former Spanish Sahara, in Namibia and Angola with the South Africans, and in a number of internal security operations and counter-terrorist actions in Latin America and Africa. It has also seen combat with nations which no longer operate the type, such as Cambodia, Ethiopia, Israel and the Lebanon.

The AML-90 has been one of the most successful wheeled AFVs in the post-war era, with over 4000 being built in France and South Africa. This model has a 90-mm (3.54-in) gun.

Specification
Crew: 3
Weight: 5.5 tonnes
Dimensions: length (including gun) 5.11 m (16 ft 9¼ in); length (hull) 3.79 m (12 ft 5¼ in); width 1.97 m (6 ft 5½ in); height 2.07 m (6 ft 9½ in)
Powerplant: one Panhard 4-cylinder petrol engine developing 90 hp (67 kW)
Performance: maximum road speed 90 km/h (56 mph); maximum range 600 km (375 miles); fording amphibious; gradient 60%; vertical obstacle 0.30 m (1 ft 0 in); trench 0.80 m (2 ft 7½ in) with one channel

South Africa builds it's own modified version of the AML-90. Known as the Eland, it has been used extensively in Namibia and Angola.

Panhard VBL Scout Car

Some years ago the French army issued a requirement for a small, light and fast armoured vehicle which would be able to carry out two basic roles on the battlefield: anti-tank armed with the Euromissile Milan anti-tank guided weapon, and reconnaissance/scout armed with machine-guns. Five manufacturers submitted designs for this competition, and Panhard and Renault were each awarded a contract to deliver three prototypes for trials with the French army.

Following these trials the **Panhard VBL** (Véhicule Blindé Leger) was accepted for service although no immediate production order was placed because of a shortage of funding. The total French army requirement is for a total of 3,000 vehicles (1,000 in the anti-tank role and the remaining 2,000 in the scout/reconnaissance role).

Panhard was convinced that its design would win the French army competition, so it built additional prototypes with its own funds and embarked on an intensive overseas marketing drive which involved the despatch of vehicles to many parts of the world. This marketing effort was successful to the extent that Mexico placed an order for 40 VBLs in 1984, an these had all been delivered by late 1985. Of these 40 vehicles, 32 were armed with machine-guns and the remaining eight with Milan anti-tank guided weapons.

The hull of the Panhard VBL is of all-welded steel armour and provides the crew with protection from small arms fire and shell splinters. The small size and rapid acceleration of the vehicle also increases its survivability on the battlefield.

To reduce both initial procurement costs and life cycle costs, proven commercial automotive parts have been used in the design of the VBL: for example, the diesel engine is from the Peugeot 505 and 605 civilian cars and the Peugeot P4 4×4 light vehicle already entering service with the French army in significant numbers as the replacement for the Hotchkiss M201 jeep, while the West German ZF fully automatic transmission is used in many civilian cars.

The layout of the vehicle is conventional, with the engine and transmission at the front, the driver and commander in the centre, and space for a third man, weapons or other specialized equipment in the rear. Bulletproof windows (providing the same degree of protection as the hull) are provided for all crew members, and standard equipment on French army vehicles will include an NBC system, heater and communications equipment. The combat tyres allow the VBL to travel a distance of 50 km (31 mph) at a speed of 30 km/h (19 mph) after they have been damaged by enemy fire.

The vehicle is fully amphibious with very little preparation, and is moved in the water by a propeller at the rear of the hull.

The Panhard light armoured vehicle is designed as a reconnaissance scout car and anti-tank guided weapons platform carrying Milan missiles. It is fully amphibious and is fitted with an NBC system and combat tyres.

The anti-tank model has a three-man crew and is armed with a Milan anti-tank guided missile launcher with six missiles and a 7.62-mm (0.3-in) machine-gun with 3,000 rounds of ammunition. The scout model normally has additional communications equipment, a two-man crew and armament comprising a 7.62 mm or 12.7-mm (0.5-in) machine-gun.

Panhard is already proposing a wide range of variants of the VBL including a police/internal security version, a battlefield model carrying various surveillance or air-defence radars, and an AA vehicle armed with surface-to-air missiles.

The Panhard VBL has a propeller at the rear of the hull and needs little preparation to enter the water. Many proven commercial automotive parts are used in the VBL, including the engine from the Peugeot 505 car.

Specification
VBL
Crew: 2 or 3
Weights: empty 2850 kg (6,283 lb); loaded 3550 kg (7,826 lb)
Powerplant: one Peugeot XD 3T 4-cylinder turbocharged diesel developing 105 hp (78 kW)
Dimensions: length 3.82 m (12 ft 6.4 in); width 2.02 m (6 ft 7.5 in); height without weapons 1.70 m (5 ft 6.9 in)
Performance: maximum road speed 100 km/h (62 mph); range 1000 km (621 miles); fording amphibious; gradient 50 per cent; side slope 30 per cent

The first examples of the VBL for French observation and security forces in the Lebanon. Variants of the VBL have been offered to the US Army for the new light divisions of the 1990s.

BRDM-1 Amphibious Scout Car

In the period immediately after World War II the BA-64 light armoured car (developed in 1942) remained the standard reconnaissance vehicle of its type in the Soviet army. From the late 1950s this was rapidly replaced by the 4×4 **BRDM-1** amphibious scout car, which was also used by the Warsaw Pact countries and exported to a number of countries in Africa and the Middle East. It was not used by Hungary, however, as that country decided to build a similar vehicle called the **FUG** (or **OT-65**), which is very similar in appearance but has the engine at the rear instead of the front. The FUG is also used by Czechoslovakia and Poland. In most Soviet units the BRDM-1 has now been replaced by the much improved BRDM-2 vehicle.

The layout of the BRDM-1 is similar to that of a car with the engine and transmission at the front, driver and commander in the centre and a small crew compartment at the rear. The only means of entry are by hatches in the roof and rear of the crew compartment. Between the front and rear wheels on each side of the hull are two belly wheels, which are powered and lowered to the ground by the driver when the vehicle is crossing ditches or rough terrain. This feature was also adopted by the later BRDM-2. A central tyre pressure regulation system is standard, and this allows the driver to inflate or deflate the tyres according to the conditions: for example, the tyres are deflated for sand crossings, while on roads they are fully inflated. The BRDM-1 is fully amphibious, being propelled in the water at a speed of 9 km/h (5.6 mph) by a single waterjet at the rear of the hull. Before the vehicle enters the water, a trim vane is erected at the front of the hull and the bilge pumps are switched on.

The BRDM-1 is normally armed with a single 7.62-mm SGMB machine-gun mounted on the forward part of the roof with a total traverse of 90° (45° left and right) elevation being from −6° to +23.5°. A total of 1,070 rounds of

ammunition is carried. Some vehicles have been observed with a similar weapon at the rear and a 12.7-mm DShKM machine-gun at the front.

The **BRDM-U** command vehicle has additional communications equipment, while the **BRDM-rkh** radiological/chemical reconnaissance vehicle is used to mark lines through contaminated areas. Mounted at the rear of the hull are two racks that contain the marking poles and pennants; when required, these racks swing through 90° over the rear of the vehicle so allowing the poles with their attached pennants to be put into the ground.

There are also three versions of the BRDM-1 fitted with ATGWs. The first model has three AT-1 'Snapper' ATGWs with a range of 2500m (2,725 yards). The missiles on their launcher arms are carried under armour protection and raised above the roof of the vehicle for launching. The second model is similar but has four 'Swatter' missiles with a range of 3000 m (3,280 yards); for some reason this mounting was not exported outside the Warsaw Pact. The last model to enter service has six 'Sagger' ATGWs with a maximum range of 3000 m (3,280 yards); additional missiles are carried in the hull. This wire-guided missile, which proved to be highly effective in the 1973 Middle East war, can be launched from within the vehicle or up to 80 m (87.5 yards) away from it with the aid of a separation sight.

Specification
Crew: 5
Weight: 5.6 tonnes
Dimensions: length 5.70 m (18 ft 8½ in); width 2.25 m (7 ft 4⅔ in); height 1.90 m (6 ft 2¾ in)
Powerplant: one 6-cylinder petrol engine developing 90 hp (67 kW)
Performance: maximum road speed 80 km/h (50 mph); maximum range 500 km (310 miles); fording amphibious; gradient 60%; vertical obstacle 0.40 m (1 ft 3¾ in); trench 1.22 m (4 ft 0 in)

Above: Soviet BRDM-1 (4×4) amphibious scout cars, with roof hatches open, ford a stream. The vehicle is propelled in the water by a single waterjet at the rear of the hull, which gives it a maximum speed of 9 km/h (5.6 mph). When travelling across rough country belly wheels are lowered between the front and rear axles.

Below: A Soviet BRDM-1 with four AT-2 'Swatter' ATGWs in the foreground, and a BRDM-1 with three AT-1 'Snappers' in the background. The 'Snapper' has a maximum range of 2500 m (2,735 yds), while the 'Swatter' has a range of 3000 m (3,280 yds). Both missiles have a HEAT (High Explosive Anti-Tank) warhead.

BRDM-2 Amphibious Scout Car

The 4×4 **BRDM-2** amphibious scout car was developed as the successor to the earlier **BRDM-1**, and was first seen in public in 1966, although it entered service some years before that date. The most significant improvements of the BRDM-2 over the earlier vehicle can be summarized as better vision for the commander and driver, more powerful armament mounted in a fully enclosed turret, a more powerful engine that gives higher road and water speeds, an NBC system, and longer operational range.

The BRDM-2 has now replaced the BRDM-1 in most Soviet units, and is also in service with over 40 countries all over the world, seeing action in such places as Angola, Egypt, Iraq, Syria and Vietnam.

The all-welded steel hull of the BRDM-2 is only 7 mm (0.275 in) thick, apart from the nose plate which is 14 mm (0.55 in) thick, and the underside of the belly which is only 2 or 3 mm (0.08 or 0.12 in) thick and makes the vehicle very vulnerable to mine explosions. The driver and commander are seated at the front of the vehicle. Each has to his front a windscreen

that is covered in combat by an armoured hatch. Over each of their positions is a single-piece hatch cover that opens vertically; these are the only means of entry into the vehicle for the four-man crew. The turret, which has no roof hatch, is the same as that fitted to the Soviet 8×8 BTR-60PB and Czech 8×8 OT-64 Model 2A armoured personnel carriers, and is armed with a 14.5-mm KPV heavy machine-gun and a co-axial 7.62-mm PKT machine-gun. The weapons have an elevation of +30° and a depression of −5°, and turret traverse is 360°. Totals of 500 rounds of 14.5-mm and 2,000 rounds of 7.62-mm ammunition are carried. The KPV is a highly effective weapon and can fire an API projectile that will penetrate 32 mm (1.26 in) of armour at a range of 500 m (545 yards).

A BRDM-2 ATGW carrier, with a launcher for six AT-3 'Sagger' ATGWs in the raised position, ready for firing. This model was used successfully by the Egyptian army in the 1973 Middle East campaign. The missiles can be launched from or away from the vehicle.

The engine and transmission are at the rear of the vehicle. Like the earlier BRDM-1 the BRDM-2 has two belly wheels that can be lowered to the ground on each side of the hull to enable ditches and rough country to be crossed with ease. The vehicle also has a central tyre pressure regulation system, infra-red night-vision equipment, an NBC system, radios, a navigation system and a winch mounted internally at the front of the hull.

The basic BRDM-2 chassis has formed the basis for a whole family of more specialized vehicles including the **BDRM-2-rkh** radiological/chemical reconnaissance vehicle and the **BRDM-2U** command vehicle, which does not have a turret.

The first ATGW model was armed with six 'Sagger' ATGWs with a range of 3000 m (3,280 yards), and this **BTR-40PB 'Sagger'** model was widely used by Egypt during the 1973 Middle East war. A version with 'Swatter' ATGWs is also in service, but the latest model is armed with five 'Spandrel' ATGWs in the ready-to-launch position on the hull top. These missiles, which operate in a similar manner to the Euromissile HOT, have a range of at least 4000 m (4,375 yards). The SA-9 'Gaskin' sur-

Most BRDM-2 ATGW versions were armed with 'Sagger', but some carried the earlier 'Swatter' missile.

face-to-air missile also uses the BRDM-2 chassis and has four missiles in the ready-to-launch position; each Soviet armoured and motorized rifle division has 16 of these systems. The SA-9 has also been used in combat in the Middle East, most recently with the Syrian forces during the Israeli invasion of the

Lebanon in the summer of 1982.

Specification
Crew: 4
Weight: 7 tonnes
Dimensions: length 5.75 m (18 ft 10⅓ in); width 2.35 m (7 ft 8½ in); height 2.31 m (7 ft 7 in)

Powerplant: one V-8 petrol engine developing 140 hp (104 kW)
Performance: maximum road speed 100 km/h (62 mph); maximum range 750 km (465 miles); fording amphibious; gradient 60%; vertical obstacle 0.40 m (1 ft 3¾ in); trench 1.25 m (4 ft 1 in)

USSR

PT-76 Amphibious Tank

The PT-76 light tank is now being replaced in many Soviet units by special models of the BMP-1 (reconnaissance) vehicle.

The Soviet Union developed light tanks with an amphibious capability in the 1920s and these were used with varying degrees of success during World War II. The **PT-76** light amphibious tank was designed in the immediate post-war period by the design team responsible for the IS series of heavy tanks. For many years the PT-76 was the standard reconnaissance vehicle of the Soviet army, and was used alongside the 4×4 BRDM-1 and BRDM-2 amphibious scout cars. In many Soviet units the type has now been replaced by MBTs such as the T-62, T-64 and T-72. Although production of the PT-76 was completed many years ago, the tank is still used by at least 25 countries. It has seen action with the Indian army during the conflict with Pakistan, with the Egyptian army during the 1967 Middle East war, with the North Vietnamese army during the Vietnamese War and more recently with the Angolan army during operations against South African incursions from Namibia. Most recently it has been used by Iraq in the Gulf War, especially in the marshes of the south where an amphibious tank can be most usefully employed.

The hull of the PT-76 is of all-welded steel construction and provides the crew with protection from small arms fire only: any additional armour would have increased the type's weight to the point that it would not have been amphibious. The driver is seated at the front in the centre, the two-man turret is in the centre of the vehicle, and the engine and transmission are at the rear. The torsion-bar suspension consists of six single road wheels, with the drive sprocket at the rear and the idler at the front; there are no track-return rollers.

The main armament consists of a 76-

mm (3-in) D-56T gun with an elevation of +30° and a depression of −4°, turret traverse being 360°. A 7.62-mm SGMT machine-gun is mounted co-axial with the main armament, and more recently some vehicles have been observed fitted with a 12.7-mm DShKM anti-aircraft machine-gun on the turret roof. Totals of 40 rounds of 76-mm (3-in) and 1,000 rounds of 7.62-mm ammunition are carried. Several types of fixed ammunition can be fired, namely AP-T, API-T, HE-FRAG, HEAT and HVAP-T. The HEAT projectile can penetrate 120 mm (4.72 in) of armour at 0°, while the HVAP-T projectile can punch through 58 mm (2.28 in) of armour at 1000 m (1,095 yards) or 92 mm (3.62 in) at 500 m (545 yards). The lack of armour penetration against more recent tanks must have been one of the reasons why the PT-76 has been phased out of service with many Soviet units.

The most useful feature of the PT-76 is its amphibious capability, which is the reason why the type has also been used by the Polish and Soviet marines. In the water the tank is powered by two waterjets at a maximum speed of 10 km/h (6.2 mph). The only preparation required before entering the water is the raising of the trim vane at the front of the hull, the activation of the bilge pumps and the engagement of

the waterjets. Maximum waterborne range is about 65 km (40 miles). To enable the driver to see forwards when afloat his centre periscope can be raised above the hatch cover. Standard equipment includes infra-red lights, but no NBC system is installed.

Specification
Crew: 3
Weight: 14 tonnes
Dimensions: length (with armament) 7.625 m (25 ft 0¼ in); length (hull) 6.91 m (22 ft 8 in); width 3.14 m (10 ft 3⅔ in); height 2.255 m (7 ft 4¾ in)
Powerplant: one V-6 6-cylinder diesel

developing 240 hp (179 kW)
Performance: maximum road speed 44 km/h (27 mph); maximum range 260 km (160 miles); fording amphibious; gradient 60%; vertical obstacle 1.10 m (3 ft 7⅓ in); trench 2.80 m (9 ft 2 in)

PT-76 Model 2 light amphibious tanks come ashore from landing craft of the Red Banner Northern Fleet. Note the turret hatch cover open and the trim vane at the front in the raised position. Main armament comprises a 76-mm (3-in) gun and 7.62-mm co-axial machine gun.

Wiesel Air-portable Armoured Vehicle

Today the West German army has one three-brigade airborne division, and this uses the Faun Kraka 4×2 light cross-country vehicle for a wide range of roles including the carriage of TOW and Milan anti-tank guided weapons.

Many years ago the West German army issued a requirement for a new light armoured tracked vehicle for use by the airborne brigades, and Porsche was subsequently awarded a development contract. After prototypes had been built and tested, the whole project was shelved as the West German ministry of defence found that it could not fund all of its projects.

More recently this **Wiesel** has been tested by the US Army, while in 1984 the West German army announced that it was to fund final development of the Wiesel air-portable armoured vehicle and to purchase 312 production variants with first deliveries due in 1989.

Two basic models of the Wiesel are to be produced, one armed with a Hughes TOW anti-tank guided missile and the other with a 20-mm cannon.

The first of these has a three-man crew and is armed with a Hughes TOW anti-tank guided missile launcher on an elevating pedestal which can be traversed 45° to each side of the centreline, and elevated and depressed 10°. Seven TOW missiles are carried, of which two are for ready use. In action, as soon as it has launched two missiles, the vehicle changes its firing position (to avoid being detected by the enemy) and loads another pair of TOWs.

The second model is armed with a Rheinmetall 20-mm dual-feed cannon in a turret which can be traversed 110° left and right while the cannon has an elevation of +45° and a depression of −10°. Some 400 rounds of 20-mm ammunition are carried, of which 160 rounds are for ready use and the remainder in reserve. This version has a two-man crew.

As the Wiesel has been designed for air transport it is very compact and difficult to detect on the battlefield. A Sikorsky CH-53 helicopter, as used by West Germany, can carry two Wiesel vehicles, while a Lockheed C-130 Hercules transport aircraft can carry three internally and the Transall C.160 four.

The Wiesel will provide West German paratroops with the sort of mobile fire support the ASU light tanks provide for the Soviet airborne forces. Two models are planned: one with a 20-mm cannon, seen here, and another mounting TOW anti-tank guided missiles.

The manufacturer has suggested that the Wiesel could be adopted for a wide range of other missions, all using the same basic chassis or a slightly longer chassis with an additional road wheel on each side. These variants include an anti-tank model with a turret for HOT missiles in the ready-to-launch position, an anti-aircraft model with Stinger surface-to-air missiles, a recovery vehicle, an ambulance, a reconnaissance vehicle, a command and control vehicle, a battlefield surveillance model and an armoured personnel carrier, to name but a few.

Specification
Wiesel (with TOW launcher)
Crew: 3
Weights: empty 2030 kg (4,475 lb); loaded 2750 kg (6,063 lb)
Powerplant: one 5-cylinder turbocharged diesel developing 86 hp (64 kW)

Dimensions: length 3.265 m (10 ft 8.5 in); width 1.82 m (5 ft 11.7 in); height 1.875 m (6 ft 1.8 in)
Performance: maximum road speed 80 km/h (50 mph); range 200 km (124 miles); vertical obstacle 0.4 m (1 ft 4 in); trench 1.2 m (3 ft 11 in); gradient 60 per cent; side slope 30 per cent

Spähpanzer 2 Luchs Reconnaissance Vehicle

The Spähpanzer Luchs continues the German tradition of 8×8 reconnaissance vehicles with an exceptional operational range. It has a four-man crew and is fully amphibious.

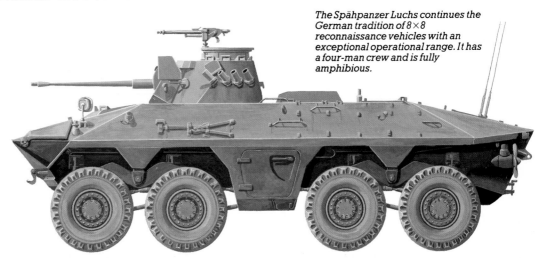

When the West German army was reformed in the 1950s it had insufficient time to have equipment designed to meet its own requirements, and it therefore had to take what was on offer from the American or European manufacturers. To meet its requirement for a reconnaissance vehicle it selected the French Hotchkiss carrier fitted with a turret armed with a Hispano-Suiza 20-mm cannon, this variant being designated the **SPz 11-2**. This suffered from a number of drawbacks as it was not amphibious and its petrol engine gave an operating range of only about 400 km (250 miles).

In the mid-1960s a complete family of 4×4, 6×6 and 8×8 trucks, 4×4 and 6×6 (later to become the Transportpanzer, or Fuchs) armoured amphibious load-carriers, and an 8×8 amphibious armoured reconnaissance vehicle were developed, all sharing many common automotive compo-

Modern Light Tanks and Reconnaissance Vehicles

The Lüchs Armoured Amphibious Reconnaissance Vehicle has excellent cross-country mobility, which allied to the low noise levels emitted makes for a very effective reconnaissance car. Fully amphibious, the only preparation required before entering the water is the erection of a trim vane (done hydraulically) and the switching on of three bilge pumps.

nents that were in most cases already in production for a civilian application. Prototypes of the 8×8 amphibious armoured reconnaissance vehicle were designed and built by Daimler-Benz and a consortium of companies known as the Joint Project Office (JPO) in 1968, and in 1971 the Daimler-Benz model was selected for production. For a variety of reasons production was undertaken by Thyssen Henschel, which built a total of 408 vehicles called the **Spähpanzer 2 Luchs** for the West German army between 1975 and 1978. The Spz 2 was offered on the export market, but for most countries it proved too expensive.

The hull of the Luchs is of all-welded steel construction, with the front part of the turret and the hull providing protection against attacks from 20-mm projectiles and the remainder proof against small arms fire and shell splinters. The driver is at the front left, the two-man turret in the centre, the engine at the rear on the right side, and the co-driver, who also operates the radio, on the rear on the left side, seated facing the rear. In an emergency the rear driver can quickly take control and drive the vehicle out of trouble. The Luchs has a maximum speed of 90 km/h (56 mph) in both directions. It also has an exceptionally large operating range of 800 km (500 miles).

The Rheinmetall TS-7 turret is armed with a dual-feed Rheinmetall MK 20 Rh 202 cannon, for which 375 rounds of ammunition are carried in the turret. Turret traverse and weapon elevation (from −15° to +69°) is powered, turret traverse being 360°. A 7.62-mm MG3 machine-gun is mounted on the turret roof for anti-aircraft defence and 1,000 rounds of ready-use ammunition are provided for this weapon. On each side of the turret is a bank of four electrically-operated smoke-dischargers, all firing forward.

The driver has powered steering to reduce fatigue when driving over long distances or across rough country, and he can select either steering on the front four wheels or on all eight wheels; the latter turning radius is only 11.5 m (37 ft 8¾ in).

The Luchs is fully amphibious, being propelled in the water at a speed of 9 km/h (5.6 mph) by two steerable propellers mounted under the hull at the rear, one on each side. Before the vehicle enters the water the trim vane is erected at the front of the hull and the three bilge pumps are switched on.

The Luchs also has an NBC system, and the original range of infra-red night-vision equipment is now being replaced by the passive type. Standard equipment includes a pre-heater for the batteries, engine and transmission oil and cooling liquid, all essential for winter operations in Germany.

Specification
Crew: 4
Weight: 19.5 tonnes
Dimensions: length 7.743 m (25 ft 4¾ in); width 2.98 m (9 ft 9⅓ in); height (including AA MG) 2.905 m (9 ft 6⅓ in)
Powerplant: one 10-cylinder diesel developing 390 hp (291 kW)
Performance: maximum road speed 90 km/h (56 mph); maximum range 800 km (500 miles); fording amphibious; gradient 60%; vertical obstacle 0.60 m (1 ft 11⅔ in); trench 1.90 m (6 ft 3 in)

ITALY

FIAT Type 6616 Armoured Car

During World War II the Italian army used scout cars and armoured cars on quite a large scale, but in the post-war period no vehicles of this type were developed as the Italian army did not have an operational requirement for a vehicle of this type. Then in the early 1970s FIAT and OTO-Melara developed the **Type 6616** armoured car and the **Type 6614** armoured personnel carrier. In both cases FIAT was responsible for the powerpack and automotive components, plus final assembly, while OTO-Melara supplied the armoured hull and turret. The first prototype of the Type 6616 was completed in 1972, and 50 vehicles were subsequently ordered by the Italian government for the Carabinieri. Since then sales have also been made to Peru, Somalia and several other undisclosed countries.

The hull of the Type 6616 is of all-welded steel construction with a uniform thickness of 8 mm (0.315 in), somewhat thin when compared with other vehicles in this class. The driver is seated at the front of the vehicle on the left, with vision blocks giving good vision to the front and sides. The two-man turret is in the centre of the vehicle, with the engine and transmission at the rear.

The Type 6616 is fully amphibious, being propelled in the water by its wheels at a speed of 5 km/h (3.1 mph); all the preparation that is required before entering the water is to switch on the bilge pumps and pressurize the submerged mechanical components. Unlike most other comparable vehicles, the Type 6616 requires no trim vane at the front of the hull.

The commander is seated on the left and the gunner on the right of the turret, each man being provided with an adjustable seat, observation equipment and a single-piece hatch cover. The communications equipment is mounted in the turret bustle. The main armament comprises a West German Rheinmetall 20-mm Mk 20 Rh 202 cannon with an elevation of +35° and a depression of −5°; turret traverse is 360°. Turret control is electric, with traverse at a maximum of 40° per second and weapon elevation at a maximum of 25° per second. A total of 400 rounds of 20-mm ammunition is carried, of which 250 are for ready use and 150 in reserve. A useful feature of the weapon, which is also installed in the West German 8×8 Luchs amphibious reconnaissance vehicle and the Marder MICV is that the empty cartridge cases are ejected outside the turret automatically, and therefore do not clutter up the crew compartment. A 7.62-mm machine-gun is mounted co-axial with the main armament, and 1,000 rounds are carried for this. Mounted on each side of the turret is a bank of three forward-firing electrically-operated smoke-dischargers.

Standard equipment includes a front-mounted winch with a capacity of 4500 kg (9,921 lb), while optional equipment includes an NBC system, a full range of passive night-vision equipment for commander, gunner and driver, and a fire-extinguishing system.

One of the main drawbacks of this vehicle on the export market is its small-calibre gun. More recently FIAT has fitted the basic Type 6616 chassis with a new two-man OTO-Melara turret armed with a 90-mm (3.54-in) Cockerill Mk III gun and a co-axial 7.62-mm machine-gun, so giving the vehicle the capability to engage much heavier vehicles than in the past.

Specification
Crew: 3
Weight: 8 tonnes

The FIAT Type 6616 armoured car is a joint development between FIAT and OTO Melara, and shares many common components with the Type 6614 APC. It is, however, under-armed, and for this reason a model with a 90-mm (3.54-in) two-man turret has been built. This has the Belgian Cockerill gun used in many AFVs.

Dimensions: length 5.37 m (17 ft 7½ in); width 2.50 m (8 ft 2½ in); height 2.035 m (6 ft 8 in)
Powerplant: one FIAT diesel developing 160 hp (119 kW)
Performance: maximum road speed 100 km/h (62 mph); maximum range 700 km (435 miles); fording amphibious; gradient 60%; vertical obstacle 0.45 m (1 ft 5¾ in); trench not applicable

Modern Tracked Infantry Vehicles

Arising out of a need for infantry to accompany tanks in action, the armoured personnel carrier has for a long time been little more than an 'armoured bus', delivering infantry to the battlefield where they fought on foot. In recent years, however, a dramatic change has taken place, with the evolution of the infantry fighting vehicle.

Modern infantry play a key part in the combined arms concept of mechanized warfare that also includes tanks and reconnaissance vehicles, artillery, anti-tank systems, engineers, logistic support and army aviation. In order to keep up and operate with tanks the infantry has to be carried in tracked or wheeled armoured vehicles. Some countries, for example France and the Soviet Union, have a mix of wheeled armoured personnel carriers and tracked armoured personnel carriers/mechanized infantry combat vehicles. The former are cheaper to build and operate, and have greater strategic mobility as they can travel at high speeds on roads. The full-tracked vehicles, on the other hand, normally have much improved armour protection, greater cross-country mobility and heavier armament than their wheeled counterparts.

In the 1960s armoured personnel carriers such as the M113 used in SE Asia were only armed with a 7.62-mm (0.3-in) or 12.7-mm (0.5-in) machine-gun in an unprotected mount to provide suppressive fire while the infantry dismounted and fought on foot. The more modern mechanized infantry fighting vehicle (or infantry fighting vehicle as it is also called) not only has improved armour protection but is usually fitted with a turret-mounted weapon that can range from 20 mm (for example the West German Marder and French AMX-10P) right up to 73 mm (the Soviet BMP). It also has a co-axial machine-gun to engage softer targets, and some even have anti-tank guided weapons on their turrets so that they can also engage enemy tanks. In addition the embarked infantrymen are provided with firing ports and vision devices to enable them to engage unprotected infantry as the vehicle crosses the battlefield, although the actual value of this feature is open to debate. The modern personnel carrier of whatever type also has a full range of night-vision

The years since independence have seen Israel's army become possibly the most highly mechanized in the world. In order for infantry to support the tank forces, Israel operates the M113 in numbers second only to the United States.

equipment for the commander, gunner and driver and an NBC system to enable it to operate on a contaminated battlefield; and in many cases it is fully amphibious.

Very often the armoured personnel carrier is the basic member of a whole family of vehicles that share many components, with obvious cost and logistical advantages to the user.

In a number of recent conflicts in the Middle East, tanks have tried to fight alone without the use of mechanized infantry. In almost every case they have failed: without the infantry, tanks cannot always take their objective, and moreover (perhaps even more important) if they do take it they cannot subsequently hold it against an all-arms counterattack.

The M113 has become the most widely used personnel carrier in the world, with more than 50 nations operating the vehicle. Since 1960 more than 75,000 have been produced, with new models still being developed. It has seen action many times, most notably in the Middle East and with the US Army in South East Asia.

AMX-10P mechanized infantry combat vehicle

The **AMX-10P** is the replacement for the AMX-VCI, and was designed by the Atelier de Construction d'Issy-les-Moulineaux in the mid-1960s, production being undertaken from 1972 at the Atelier de Construction Roanne (ARE), where production of the AMX-30 MBT is undertaken together with that of the AMX-10RC (6×6) reconnaissance vehicle which is automotively related to the AMX-10P even though it is a wheeled vehicle. First production vehicles were completed in 1973, and since then more than 2,000 vehicles have been completed for the French army and for export to countries such as Greece, Indonesia, Qatar, Saudi Arabia and the United Arab Emirates.

The AMX-10P has a hull of all-welded aluminium, with the driver at the front left, engine to his right, two-man turret in the centre and troop compartment at the rear. The eight troops enter and leave the vehicle via a power-operated ramp in the hull rear; there is a two-part roof hatch above the troop compartment. Apart from the roof hatches and two firing ports in the ramp, there is no provision for the troops to use their rifles from within the vehicle. The power-operated turret is armed with a 20-mm dual-feed (HE and AP ammunition) cannon with a co-axial 7.62-mm (0.3-in) machine-gun; mounted on each side of the turret are two smoke-dischargers. The weapons have an elevation of +50° and a depression of −8°, turret traverse being 360°. Totals of 800 rounds of 20-mm and 2,000 rounds of 7.62-mm (0.3-in) ammunition are carried.

The AMX-10P is fully amphibious, being propelled in the water by water-jets at the rear of the hull, and is also fitted with an NBC system and a full range of night-vision equipment for the commander, gunner and driver.

Variants of the AMX-10P include an ambulance, a driver training vehicle, a repair vehicle with crane for lifting engines, an anti-tank vehicle with four HOT ATGW in the ready-to-launch position, an **AMX-10PC** command vehicle, a RATAC radar vehicle, artillery observation and fire control vehicles, an **AMX-10TM** mortar tractor towing 120-mm (4.72-in) Brandt mortar and carrying 60 mortar bombs, 81-mm

Above: The AMX-10P has a two-man power-operated turret armed with a 7.62-mm (0.3-in) machine-gun and a dual-feed 20-mm cannon. In the future it is probable that the latter will be replaced by a 25-mm weapon, which will have improved penetration characteristics against more recent vehicles.

Right: French infantry dismount from the rear of their AMX-10P MICV, which forms the basis for a complete family of vehicles including command post, HOT anti-tank, mortar tractor, fire control, artillery observation, repair vehicle, ambulance, radar and fire support.

(3.19-in) fire-support vehicle and the **AMX-10 PAC 90** fire-support vehicle. The last has already been adopted by the Indonesian marines and has a GIAT TS-90 two-man turret armed with a 90-mm (3.54-in) gun, for which 20 rounds of ammunition are carried, and a 7.62-mm (0.3-in) co-axial machine-gun. As with most turrets today, a wide range of options is offered including an anti-aircraft machine-gun and various types of fire-control equipment. In addition to its three-man crew of commander, gunner and driver, the AMX-10 PAC 90 carries four infantrymen in the rear. The vehicles delivered to In-

donesia have improved amphibious characteristics and they are meant to leave landing craft offshore rather than just cross rivers and streams, as is the basic vehicle. Indonesia also took delivery of a number of AMX-10Ps with the original two-man turret replaced by a new one-man turret at the rear armed with a 12.7-mm (0.5-in) M2 HB machine-gun.

Specification
AMX-10P
Crew: 3+8

Weight: 14200 kg (31,305 lb)
Powerplant: one HS-115 V-8 water-cooled diesel developing 280 hp (209 kW)
Dimensions: length 5.778 m (18 ft 11 in); width 2.78 m (9 ft 1 in); height (hull top) 1.92 m (6 ft 4 in) and (overall) 2.57 m (8 ft 5 in)
Performance: maximum road speed 65 km/h (40 mph); maximum range 600 km (373 miles); fording amphibious; gradient 60 per cent; vertical obstacle 0.70 m (2 ft 4 in); trench 1.60 m (5 ft 3 in)

AMX VCI infantry combat vehicle

To meet a French army requirement for an infantry combat vehicle Hotchkiss, which is no longer involved in the design, development or production of vehicles, built a number of prototypes in the early 1950s, but these were all rejected. It was then decided to build an IFV based on the chassis of the AMX-13 light tank, which was then already in large scale production for both the French and other armies. Following trials with prototype vehicles, the **AMX VCI** was adopted by the French army, first production vehicles being completed at the Atelier de Construction Roanne in 1967. Since then some 3,000 vehicles have been built for the home and export markets. Once the Atelier de Construction Roanne (ARE) started to turn out the AMX-30 MBT, production of the AMX-13 light tank family, including the VCI, was transferred to Creusot-Loire at

Chalon-sur-Saone, where the VCI remains in production today at a low level. The French army currently calls the vehicle the Vehicule de Combat d'Infanterie (infantry fighting vehicle), although it had a number of earlier names. In many respects the VCI was an advance on other Western vehicles of its period as not only was it fitted with a machine-gun turret for suppressive fire, but the infantry could also use their rifles from within the vehicle. The major drawback of the VCI was its lack of amphibious capability, and when originally deployed it was not fitted with an NBC system or night-vision equipment. The VCI remains in service with the French army, although it is being replaced by the AMX-10P, and is also used by Argentina, Belgium, Ecuador, Indonesia, Italy, Kuwait, Lebanon, Morocco, Venezuela and the United Arab Emirates.

AMX VCI infantry fighting vehicle of the French army fitted with a cupola mounted machine-gun. The troop compartment at the rear of the hull is provided with firing ports. In the French army this is now slowly being replaced by the amphibious AMX-10P MICV.

The AMX VCI is of all-welded steel construction, with the driver at the front left, engine to his right, commander and gunner in the centre and the troop compartment at the rear. The last are provided with doors in the rear, and hatches in the side are provided with four firing ports each. Torsion-bar suspension consists of five single rubber-tyred road wheels, with the drive sprocket at the front and idler at the rear; there are four track-return rollers.

In addition to the basic VCI, which carries 10 fully equipped troops as well as its three-man crew, there were also ambulance, command, cargo, combat engineer, anti-tank (with EN-TAC wire-guided missiles), RATAC radar, artillery fire-control, mortar-carrier (both 81-mm/3.19-in and 120-mm/4.72-in weapons) and support vehicles, the last carrying the remainder of the gun crew and additional ammunition for the 155-mm (6.1-in) Mk F3 self-propelled gun.

More recently the manufacturer has offered a diesel conversion package for the VCI and all other members of the AMX-13 light tank family. In this the original petrol engine is replaced by the well-known Detroit Diesel 6V-53T engine developing 280 hp (208 kW) for improved operational range, slightly higher speed and reduced fire risk.

Specification
AMX VCI
Crew: 3+10
Weight: 15000 kg (33,069 lb)
Powerplant: one SOFAM 8-cylinder petrol engine developing 250 hp (186 kW)
Dimensions: length 5.70 m (18 ft 8 in); width 2.67 m (8 ft 9 in); height (hull top) 2.1 m (6 ft 11 in) and (overall) 2.41 m (7 ft 11 in)
Performance: maximum road speed 60 km/h (37 mph); maximum range 350 km (218 miles); fording 1.00 m (3 ft 3 in); gradient 60 per cent; vertical obstacle 0.65 m (2 ft 2 in); trench 1.60 m (5 ft 3 in)

UK
FV432 armoured personnel carrier

After the end of World War II various prototypes of full-tracked armoured personnel carriers were built in the UK, but it was not until 1962 that one of these, the **FV432**, was accepted by the British army. The FV432 is member of the **FV430** series of vehicles which also includes the **FV433** Abbot 105-mm (4.13-in) self-propelled gun built by Vickers at its Elswick facility in Newcastle between 1964 and 1967. Production of the FV432 and its many variants was undertaken by GKN Sankey between 1963 and 1971, about 3,000 being built in all. Although offered overseas it was never purchased by any country as by that time the very similar American M113 APC was already in volume production for the US Army, and this was much cheaper than the FV432. For a short period the FV432 was commonly known as the **Trojan**.

The basic role of the FV432 is to transport British infantry across the battlefield; when close to its objective the infantry dismount and continue the assault on foot. The main difference between the M113 and the FV432 is that the latter has a hull of welded steel construction while the former has a hull of welded aluminium. The driver is seated at the front on the right, with the commander to his rear and the power-pack to his left. The troop compartment is at the rear of the hull, with entry to this compartment via a large single door in the hull rear. Hatches are provided over the top of the troop compartment, but there is no provision for the infantry to use their weapons from within the vehicle. The 10 infantrymen carried are seated five on each side of the hull facing each other on seats that can be quickly folded up to enable cargo to be carried. The vehicle is fitted with night-vision equipment and was also one of the first vehicles of its type to be fitted with an NBC system, which supplies clean air to the troops and crew. When introduced into service the FV432 was fitted with a flotation screen attached to the top of the hull; when this was erected the vehicle could propel itself across lakes and rivers with its tracks. These screens have now been removed as they were easily damaged and prone to damage in time of war from small arms fire and shell splinters. The basic vehicle is fitted with a 7.62-mm (0.3-in) machine-gun in an unprotected mount, but many vehicles have now been fitted with a turret-mounted 7.62-mm (0.3-in) machine-gun over the troop compartment.

In addition to being used as a troop carrier, the FV432 is also used for a wide range of other roles including ambulance, command with extensive

An FV432 fitted with a Peak Engineering one-man turret armed with a 7.62-mm (0.3-in) machine-gun and four electrically-operated smoke dischargers on either side. When fitted with this turret the roof hatches over the troop compartment cannot be used. The FV432 is in service only with the British army.

communications equipment installed, 81-mm (3.19-in) mortar carrier, minelayer towing the Bar minelaying system and fitted with the Ranger anti-personnel mine scatter on the roof, radar carrier (such as the ZB 298 surveillance radar or the Cymbeline mortar/artillery-locating system), artillery fire-control vehicle with the Field Artillery Computer Equipment (FACE), and specialized vehicles for the Royal Signals. The maintenance carrier is called the **FV434** and can change Chieftain engines in the field.

From 1987 the FV432 has been succeeded in front line service, but not entirely replaced, by the Warrior mechanized combat vehicle.

Specification
FV432
Crew: 2+10
Weight: 15280 kg (33,686 lb)
Powerplant: one Rolls-Royce K60 6-cylinder multi-fuel engine developing 240 bhp (190 kW)
Dimensions: length 5.251 m (17 ft 3 in); width 2.80 m (9 ft 2 in); height (with machine-gun) 2.286 m (7 ft 6 in)
Performance: maximum road speed 52.2 km/h (32 mph); maximum range 483 km (300 miles); fording 1.066 m (3 ft 6 in); gradient 60 per cent; vertical obstacle 0.609 m (2 ft 0 in); trench 2.05 m (6 ft 9 in)

An FV432 APC at speed. In many respects this vehicle is similar to the American M113, but it has steel rather than aluminium armour and, as built, was fitted with a multi-fuel engine and a complete NBC system.

Warrior mechanized combat vehicle

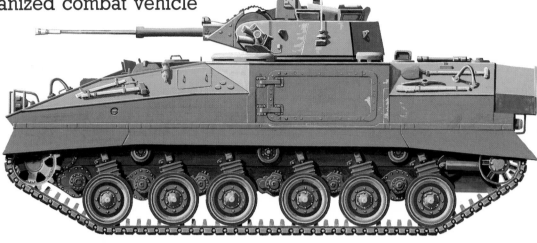

The **Warrior** infantry combat vehicle has been developed to meet the requirements of the British army by GKN Sankey, which built all of the FV432 series of vehicles which are currently used to transport infantry in the British Army of the Rhine. After exhaustive trials with prototype vehicles, early in 1984 the British Ministry of Defence ordered the MCV-80, as it was then called, into full-scale production. Compared with the FV432 the Warrior has greater armour protection, mobility and firepower.

The hull of the vehicle is all-welded aluminium, with the driver at the front on the left and the powerpack to his right. The two-man power-operated turret is in the centre of the hull, with the commander on the left and the gunner on the right. Main armament comprises a 30-mm Rarden cannon which is already in service with the British army in the CVR(W) Fox light armoured car and the Scimitar, which is a member of the CVR(T) Scorpion family of vehicles. Mounted co-axially with the main armament will be a Hughes Helicopters 7.62-mm (0.3-in) Chain Gun which is manufactured under licence in the United Kingdom by the Royal Ordnance Factory at Enfield in North London. Unlike the American Bradley and Soviet BMP series, the Warrior will not be fitted with an ATGW as the British believe that anti-tank warfare is best left to a dedicated vehicle. The troop compartment is at the rear of the hull, and the eight infantrymen leave via two large doors in the hull rear. Over the top of the troop compartment are roof hatches, but there is no provision for the infantry to aim and fire their weapons from within the vehicle as is the case with the American M2 Bradley, West German Marder and Soviet BMP. There is ample room in the vehicle to carry sufficient supplies of food and ammunition for a 48-hour period. Suspension is of the torsion-bar type with six road wheels, and the drive sprocket is at the front with the idler at the rear; there are three track-return rollers. The Warrior is not amphibious as this was not a requirement of the

Above: The GKN Warrior is in production for the British army in order to supplement the FV432 APC. It is fitted with a two-man power-operated turret armed with a 30-mm Rarden cannon and a 7.62-mm (0.3-in) co-axial machine-gun.

British army; it is fitted with an NBC system and a full range of night-vision equipment.

In addition to the basic IFV armed with a 30-mm cannon, it is expected that a number of more specialized versions will enter service with the British army, including a platoon vehicle with a turret mounted 7.62-mm (0.3-in) machine-gun, a recovery vehicle, an 81-mm (3.19-in) mortar vehicle, an engineer vehicle, a forward repair vehicle and an artillery command post vehicle.

GKN Sankey believes that the basic chassis is suitable for a wide range of other applications, especially for the export market, and is now proposing a complete family of vehicles including a light tank with a turret-mounted 105-mm (4.13-in) L7 series gun, an anti-aircraft vehicle with twin 30-mm cannon, a tank destroyer armed with missiles such as TOW or HOT, an anti-aircraft vehicle with missiles, a reconnaissance vehicle with 76-mm (3-in) or 90-mm (3.54-in) gun, a cargo carrier

and a multiple rocket-launcher.

Specification
Warrior
Crew: 2+8
Weight: 24500 kg (54,012 lb)
Powerplant: one Rolls-Royce CV-8 diesel developing 550 hp (410 kW)
Dimensions: length 6.34 m (20 ft 10 in); width 3.034 m (9 ft 11 in); height (overall) 2.735 m (9 ft 0 in)
Performance: maximum road speed 75 km/h (47 mph); maximum range

Unlike the American M2 Bradley and West German Marder, the British MCV-80 does not have any firing ports in the rear troop compartment as there was no British army requirement for this feature. It is fitted with an NBC system and a full range of night vision equipment.

500 km (310 miles); fording 1.32 m (4 ft 3 in); gradient 60 per cent; vertical obstacle 0.75 m (2 ft 6 in); trench 2.49 m (8 ft 2 in)

VCC infantry armoured fighting vehicle

OTO Melara of La Spezia, well known as a manufacturer of naval weapons, have been engaged in the design and production of armoured vehicles since the 1960s and have built several thousand M113 armoured personnel carriers for the Italian army under licence from FMC of the United States. While the M113 is an excellent vehicle, it suffers from the major drawback of having an unprotected 12.7-mm (0.5-in) machine-gun mounting and no provision for the infantry to fire their weapons from within the vehicle with any degree of safety. The Automotive Technical Service of the Italian army subsequently modified the M113, and after trials this was adopted by the Italian army under the designation of the **VCC-1**, or more commonly the **Camillino** and well over one thousand of these have now been delivered to the Italian army, with final deliveries taking place in 1983. From 1983 there were delivered to Saudi Arabia 200 vehicles fitted with the Emerson Improved

TOW launcher as fitted to the M901 Improved TOW Vehicle (ITV).

The forward part of the VCC-1, which was deployed to the Lebanon in 1983, is identical to the M113, with the driver at the front left and the engine to his right. The rest of the vehicle is new, the commander being seated to the rear of the driver and provided with a cupola and periscopes. The 12.7-mm (0.5-in) machine-gun is to the right of the driver in a cupola that can be traversed through 360°, lateral and rear armour protection being provided. The troop compartment is at the rear and in each side of the hull top, which is chamfered inwards on its upper part, are two firing ports each surmounted by a vision block. There is a

An Italian OTO Melara Infantry Armoured Fighting Vehicle with a roof-mounted 20-mm cannon. This is a further development of the M113, which has been built under licence by the company.

further firing port in the power-operated ramp in the hull rear. In the centre of the hull at the rear is a machine-gunner, who has an externally mounted 7.62-mm (0.3-in) machine-gun. To make more room in the troop compartment the fuel tank has been removed and the diesel fuel is now carried in two panniers externally at the hull rear, one on each side of the ramp. When the infantry fire their weapons from within the troop compartment there is a considerable build-up of fumes, which can be dangerous, so two roof-mounted fans are fitted to remove these fumes.

The first prototypes of a new infantry combat vehicle, the VCC-80, were completed in 1985 after development by OTO-Melara and Fiat. Weighing just under 20 tonnes, the VCC-80 is a low-profile vehicle with a high power-to-weight ratio and has a 25-mm cannon in a two man turret. It has better cross-country ability than current Italian MBTs, and is expected to match any tank introduced before the end of the century. For export, OTO-Melara has recently developed the OTO C13 infantry fighting vehicle which can carry nine troops and a crew of three. By 1986, five prototypes had been completed with a variety of weapon fits ranging from a basic machine-gun armed APC to a 90-mm armed version.

Specification
VCC
Crew: 2+7
Weight: 11600 kg (25,573 lb)
Powerplant: one GMC Model 6V-53 6-cylinder water-cooled diesel developing 215 bhp (160 kW)
Dimensions: length 5.041 m (16 ft 6 in); width 2.686 m (8 ft 10 in); height (12.7 mm MG) 2.552 m (8 ft 4 in) and (hull top) 1.828 m (6 ft 0 in)
Performance: maximum road speed 64.4 km/h (40 mph); maximum range 550 km (342 miles); fording amphibious; gradient 60 per cent; vertical obstacle 0.61 m (2 ft 0 in); trench 1.68 m (5 ft 6 in)

Marder mechanized infantry combat vehicle

When the West German army was re-formed in the 1950s its first mechanized infantry combat vehicle was the SPz 12-3 based on a Swiss chassis and subsequently manufactured both in England and West Germany. A decision was taken at an early stage that a complete family of vehicles would be developed that would use the same basic chassis. The first members of this family to enter service were the Jagd-panzer Kanone with a 90-mm (3.54-in) gun and the Jagdpanzer Rakete armed with SS.12 ATGWs (recently replaced by HOT). After many different prototypes had been built and subjected to extensive tests one of these was finally adopted by the West German army as the Marder Schützenpanzer Neu M-1966, and Rheinstahl (now Thyssen Henschel) was selected as prime contractor with MaK of Kiel as the second source. First production vehicles were delivered late in 1970 and production continued until 1975, by which time 3,000 vehicles had been built. The Marder was not exported overseas although recently Saudi Arabia has shown some interest in the vehicle.

At the time of its introduction the Marder was the most advanced MICV in the West, and even today it is matched only by more recent designs such as the M2 Bradley. The Marder has excellent armour protection and a high cross-country speed to enable it to operate with the Leopard 1 and Leopard 2 MBTs as part of the combined-arms team.

The driver is seated at the front left with one infantryman to his rear and the engine to his right. The two-man power-operated turret (commander and gunner) is in the centre of the vehicle with the troop compartment at the rear. The infantry enter and leave via a power-operated ramp in the hull rear, and on each side of the troop compartment are two spherical firing ports, each with a roof-mounted periscope above it to enable infantrymen to aim and fire their rifles from within the vehicle.

The turret is armed with a dual-feed 20-mm Rh 202 cannon and a co-axial 7.62-mm (0.3-in) machine-gun. These can be elevated from −17° to +65°,

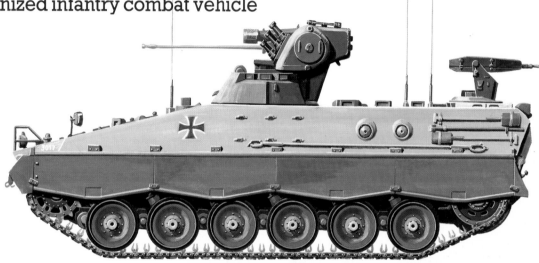

turret traverse being 360°. In the future the 20-mm cannon will be replaced by a Mauser 25-mm weapon firing ammunition with better armour-piercing characteristics to enable it to combat recent Soviet vehicles such as the BMP. Some Marders have been fitted with a Euromissile MILAN ATGW launcher on the turret to enable them to engage MBTs out to a maximum range of 2000 m (2,190 yards). Mounted above the rear troop compartment is a remote-controlled 7.62-mm (0.3-in) machine-gun.

Variants of the Marder in service with the West German army include the Roland SAM system with two missiles in the ready-to-launch position and a further eight in reserve, and another model with a surveillance radar on a hydraulically-operated arm that can be raised above the top of the vehicle for increased radar coverage.

The chassis of the Marder is also used as the basis for the Argentine

Above: Recently many Marders have been fitted with new passive night vision equipment and a Euromissile MILAN ATGW system. In the future the 20-mm cannon will be replaced by a 25-mm weapon to enable the vehicle to defeat the latest Soviet light combat vehicles, such as the BMP-2.

TAM medium tank and its variants, including the VCTP infantry combat vehicle and the VCTM 120-mm (4.72-in) mortar carrier; none of these vehicles were used during the Falklands campaign of 1982.

Specification
Marder
Crew: 4+6
Weight: 28200 kg (62,169 lb)
Powerplant: one MTU MB 833 6-cylinder diesel developing 600 hp (447 kW)
Dimensions: length 6.79 m (22 ft 3 in);

The Marder was the first MICV to enter service in the West, and is fitted with a two-man power-operated turret armed with a 20-mm cannon and a 7.62-mm (0.3-in) machine-gun. It has not so far been exported.

width 3.24 m (10 ft 8 in); height (overall) 2.95 m (9 ft 8 in)
Performance: maximum road speed 75 km/h (46.6 mph); maximum range 520 km (323 miles); fording 1.50 m (4 ft 11 in); gradient 60 per cent; vertical obstacle 1.00 m (3 ft 3 in); trench 2.50 m (8 ft 2 in)

Pbv armoured personnel carrier

Although the Swedish army deployed tanks well before World War II, it was not until the post-war period that the first full-tracked armoured personnel carriers were fielded. These were called the Pbv 301 and were essentially the older Strv m/41 light tank stripped down to the basic chassis and rebuilt as an armoured personnel carrier. This was armed with a 20-mm cannon and could carry eight fully-equipped infantrymen as well as the two-man crew. The conversion work for the Pbv 301 was carried out by Hägglund & Söner between 1962 and 1963. Even before this work had started the Swedish army realized that this would only be an interim solution as the basic chassis was so old. Design work on the new Pbv 302 armoured personnel carrier started in 1961 and progress was so quick that the first prototypes were completed in the following year. After the usual trials the company was awarded a full-scale production contract and production was undertaken from 1966 to 1971. The Pbv 302 was not sold abroad, although it was offered to several countries. The main reason for this lies with the fact that the export of defence equipment is subject to such strict controls that Sweden can deal with only a very few countries.

In some respects the Pbv 302 is very similar in layout to the American M113, although the Swedish vehicle has some noticeable features that, when the vehicle was introduced, put it some way ahead of its competitors. The hull is of all-welded steel armour with the driver in the centre at the front, the gunner to the left rear and the commander to the right rear. Main armament comprises 20-mm Hispano cannon mounted in a turret with a traverse of 360°, weapon elevation being from −10° to +60°. The cannon can fire either high explosive (in belts of 135 rounds) or armour-piercing (in 10-round magazines) ammunition. The same turret has also been fitted to a number of other vehicles including M113s of the Swiss army and EE-11 (6×6) vehicles of Gabon. The troop compartment is at the rear of the hull, with the 10 infantrymen seated five along each side facing inwards. No firing ports are provided, although hatches over the troop compartment allow the troops to fire their weapons from within the vehicle. The infantry enter and leave the vehicle via two doors in the hull rear. The Pbv 302 is fully amphibious, being propelled in the water by its tracks.

The basic vehicle can also be used as an ambulance or a cargo carrier, while more specialized versions include an artillery command vehicle, an armoured observation vehicle and a fire direction-post vehicle. The prototype of the **Pbv 302 Mk 2**

Above: The Pbv 302 APC is only used by the Swedish army, and is fitted with a turret-mounted 20-mm cannon. Before entering water the bilge pumps are switched on and the trim vane erected at the front.

armoured personnel carrier has been built by Hägglund & Söner as a private venture. This has a separate cupola at the rear for the squad commander, a Lyran flare system and other minor modifications. The company has also proposed that the vehicle be converted into a mechanized infantry fighting vehicle with 25-mm cannon and sloping hull sides (like those of the Italian IFV) provided with firing ports and vision blocks.

Specification
Pbv 302
Crew: 2 + 10
Weight: 13500 kg (29,762 lb)
Powerplant: one Volvo-Penta Model THD 100B 6-cylinder inline diesel developing 280 hp (209 kW)

Dimensions: length 5.35 m (17 ft 7 in); width 2.86 m (9 ft 5 in); height (turret top) 2.50 m (8 ft 2 in) and (hull top) 1.90 m (6 ft 3 in)

Performance: maximum road speed 66 km/h (41 mph); maximum road range 300 km (186 miles); fording amphibious; gradient 60 per cent;

Swedish infantrymen dismount from the rear of their Pbv 302 armoured personnel carrier. The Pbv 302 was one of the first vehicles of its type to enter production with a fully enclosed weapon station.

vertical obstacle 0.61 m (2 ft 0 in); trench 1.80 m (5 ft 11 in)

FV90 (Fighting Vehicle 90)

The 1000 or more Pbv 302 armoured personnel carriers operated by the Swedish Army were built by Hägglund and Söner between 1966 and 1971. Although a good design for its time, being more advanced in some ways than the contemporary M113 or the British FV 432, the changing face of battle means that a new design must take its place.

Prototypes of product improved Pbv 302s were tested, as were examples of other vehicles on the market such as the British Scorpion, but it was decided to develop a whole new family of Swedish vehicles under the general designation **Stridsfordon 90**, or **Fighting Vehicle 90 (FV90)**.

Prime Contractor for the FV90 is HB Utveckling AB of Stockholm. AB Bofors and Hägglund & Söner are the principal sub-contractors.

When compared with the Pbv 302, the FV90 will be a dramatic advance in the three vital areas of protection, firepower and mobility, ensuring much greater battlefield survivability.

At the moment, the Swedish army plans on fielding seven members of the FV 90 family. The **Pbv L** is the basic APC, with a three-man crew and able to carry eight troops. The two-man turret will be fitted with a 25-mm rapid fire cannon, while a Bofors BILL top-attack wire-guided anti-tank missile

will be fitted over the roof of the rear troop compartment. However, unlike the Soviet BMP or the US M2 Bradley designs there will be no provision for infantry to use their weapons from within the troop compartment. The **Pbv G** will be like the basic model, but the two-man turret will be fitted with a larger automatic cannon as well as a 7.62mm machine-gun. A version of Bofors well known 40mm L70 anti-aircraft gun is under consideration for the main weapon, as is the Israeli IMI 60mm hyper-velocity gun. The **Lvkv A2** will be a key component in the low-level air defence of Swedish ground forces. It will have the same hull, turret and gun as the Pbv G, but it

will be optimized for air defence with the addition of an Ericsson 3D radar to the turret rear. This was developed for the ARMAD system, which uses the RBS-70 missile, and is able to detect hovering helicopters. The **Stripv** armoured command post will be fitted with extensive communications equipment, and the **Epbv** armoured observation post will be the eyes and ears of Swedish artillery units. The **Bgbv** armoured recovery vehicle has a front-mounted hydraulically operated bulldozer blade, a powerful winch and an hydraulic crane for engine changing. The final variant currently envisaged will be the **Grkbv** mortar carrier, armed with a 120mm mortar firing the

FFV Strix guided mortar projectile which is under development.

All vehicles will have a common chassis and running gear (engine, tracks, transmission and torsion bar suspension). For ease of supply and maintenance, standard commercial components will be used wherever possible. The engine will be a diesel of about 370 kW (500 hp) built by Volvo or Saab-Scania, and it will be fitted with fully automatic transmission.

The first five prototypes were ordered in the summer of 1985, with the first completed in 1988. If the trials are successful, the first production vehicles will be with the Swedish Army by 1992.

NVH1 mechanized infantry combat vehicle

For many years the Chinese produced copies of Soviet armoured personnel carriers but during the latter stages of the Vietnam war numbers of a new type of all-Chinese tracked armoured personnel carrier began to appear. This was the Type **YW 531** which has numerous variants such as the enlarged YW 534, the YW 750 ambulance, the WZ 701 command vehicle and many others, including the Type 54-1 which carries a 122mm (4.8-in) howitzer. All these vehicles are simple armoured boxes on tracks capable of carrying a crew of up to four plus 10 troops and armed with a 12.7mm (0.50-in) machine-gun in a small roof turret.

In order to convert the YW 531 series of armoured personnel carriers into mechanized infantry combat vehicles, NORINCO (China North Industries Corporation, the Chinese manufacturers) teamed with the British Vickers concern and developed a modified and enlarged YW 531 chassis to carry a new Vickers-designed two-man turret mounting either a 30mm (1.18-in) RARDEN cannon or an Oerlikon 25mm (0.98-in) KBB cannon together with a co-axial 7.62mm (0.30-in) machine-gun. Smoke grenade dischargers are fitted to either side of the turret.

The resultant vehicle, known as the **NVH1**, carries a crew of three (commander, driver and gunner) and eight troops who are provided with seven firing ports in the hull for them to fire their weapons from under cover. A large door in the rear is used for access and egress and there are vision devices in the roof and sides. The usual Chinese-produced ex-Soviet engine has been replaced by a licence-produced turbocharged Deutz power pack. A simple manual gearbox is fitted. Torsion bars with linear dampers are used for the suspension.

The NVH1 is amphibious (with preparation) and there is an enlarged version known as the NVH4 which is amphibious without preparation – it can carry an extra two troops. Various optional equipment such as air conditioning or a full NBC suite can be fitted to the NVH1. Passive night vision equipment is another option and it is possible to instal image intensification equipment for the gunner and driver.

Specification NVH1
Crew: 3+8
Weight: (combat) 17000 kg (37,478 lb)
Powerplant: Deutz air-cooled turbocharged diesel developing 320 hp (239 kW)
Dimensions: length 6.125 m (20 ft 1.1 in); width 3.06 m (10 ft 0.5 in); height (top of turret) 2.77 m (9 ft 1 in)
Performance: maximum road speed 65 km/h (40.4 mph); road range

The NVH1 uses the latest western electronics and weaponry to produce a highly capable infantry combat vehicle. Armament can include the British 30 mm Rarden cannon shown.

500 km+ (over 310 miles); fording, amphibious with preparation; gradient 31 degrees; vertical obstacle 0.6 m (1 ft 11.6 in); trench 2.2 m (7 ft 2 in)

MOWAG Tornado mechanized infantry combat vehicle

The MOWAG company has been engaged in the design and development of tracked and wheeled vehicles since just after World War II, and in the early 1960s it was awarded a contract from the West German government for the construction of prototypes of a mechanized infantry combat vehicle that eventually became known as the Marder. In the 1970s the company developed as a private venture the very similar **Tornado** MICV, whose latest version, called the **Improved Tornado**, was announced in 1980. At this time the Swiss army's standard APC is the American M113, though many of these have been fitted with a Swedish turret armed with a 20-mm cannon. With the recent decision to order 420 Leopard 2 MBTs there is an obvious requirement for a MICV to work with this vehicle as part of the combined-arms team.

The hull of the Improved Tornado is of all-welded steel construction and probably has better protection against armour-piercing projectiles than most vehicles on the market today as its sides and front are so well sloped for the maximum possible protection. The driver is at the front of the vehicle on the left, with the commander to his rear and the engine and transmission to his right. In the centre of the hull can be mounted a wide range of armament installations depending on the mission

requirement. One of the most powerful installations is the Swiss Oerlikon-Bührle two-man power-operated Type GDD-AOE turret, which has an externally mounted 35-mm KDE cannon fed from two ready-use magazines each holding 50 rounds. One could hold armour-piercing rounds to engage other vehicles while the other could hold high explosive rounds for use against softer target such as trucks. Mounted co-axially with the 35-mm cannon is a 7.62-mm (0.3-in) machine-gun with 500 rounds of ready-use ammunition for the engagement of soft targets. The infantrymen are seated in the troop compartment at the hull rear, and enter and leave via a power-operated ramp. On each side of the troop compartment are spherical firing ports that allow some of the troops to fire their weapons from within the vehicle. If required, two remote-controlled 7.62-mm (0.3-in) machine-guns can be fitted (one on each side) at the rear on the troop compartment roof. These are almost identical to those fitted to the Marder, also built by MOWAG. Each mount can be traversed through 230° and the machine-guns can be elevated from −15° to +60°.

As with most vehicles of its type, the Improved Tornado is fitted with an NBC system and night-vision equip-

ment. The design of the chassis is such that it can be adopted for a wide range of other roles such as command vehicle, missile carrier, recovery vehicle, mortar carrier and so on, but as far as it is known none of these have reached even the prototype stage.

Specification
MOWAG Tornado
Crew: 3+7
Weight: 22300 kg (49,162 lb)
Powerplant: one Detroit Diesel Model 8V-71T diesel developing 390 hp (290 kW)
Dimensions: length 6.70 m (22 ft 0 in);

The Tornado MICV has been developed by MOWAG of Switzerland as a private venture. This particular Tornado has a turret-mounted 25-mm cannon and two machine-guns at the rear.

width 3.15 m (10 ft 4 in); height (hull top) 1.75 m (5 ft 9 in) and (turret top) 2.86 m (9 ft 5 in)
Performance: maximum road speed 66 km/h (41 mph); maximum road range 400 km (249 miles); fording 1.30 m (4 ft 3 in); gradient 60 per cent; vertical obstacle 0.85 m (2 ft 9 in); trench 2.20 m (7 ft 3 in)

Standard APC of the US Army for over 20 years, the M113 has recently been the subject of a product improvement programme. The M113A2 has a considerably improved engine and suspension performance, and the 5,300 M113s and 12,700 M113A1s to be converted will be joined by a 2,660 new-built M113A2s, to give a total of more than 20,000 in service by 1989. While the M2 Bradley is to replace the M113 in many roles, they will not be exchanged on a one-to-one basis, and the M113 will continue to serve for years to come.

M113 armoured personnel carrier

The **M113** series of armoured personnel carriers can lay claim to being the most widely-used vehicle of its type for at the end of 1984 some 72,787 of all variants had been produced and many more have been produced since.

The prototype of the M113 was the **T113** which used an aluminium hull. This became the **M113** in 1960, followed by the **M113A1** in 1963 and the **M113A2** in 1978. The latest model is the **M113A3**, production of which commences in 1987.

The basic M113 is an amphibious tracked armoured box carrying a crew of two and up to 11 men; passengers enter via a powered ramp at the rear and are seated along each side wall. It is a simple vehicle that has proved reliable and sturdy and it is also adaptable. The basic M113 is not armed but can have various types of machine-gun mounted by the commander's cupola on the roof and more weapons can be mounted by the roof hatch. The engine is at the right-hand front.

The M113 has been used as the basis for just about every armoured vehicle function imaginable. Production has been carried out in Italy as well as in the United States where the main contractor is the Food Machinery Corporation (FMC) of San Jose.

M113 variants include reconnaissance vehicles (it was widely used as such in Vietnam), anti-tank missile carrier (the main variant being the TOW-armed **M901** with its elevating launcher arm), mortar carrier, Vulcan air defence gun carrier (the **M163**), command post (**M577** series), fire support vehicle, combat engineer vehicle, recovery vehicle, fitters vehicle, ambulance, flamethrower (**M132**) and so on. Many of the user nations have added their own modifications such as extra armour (especially in Israel where the M113 is known as the Zelda) or gun turrets. The result has been a wide array of M113 variants that are too numerous to list. The **M548** tracked cargo carrier is just one M113 variant and even the British Tracked Rapier

vehicle has M113 origins.

The **M113A1** is basically a product-improved basic version that became the **M113A2**. The M113A3 features increased stand-off armour and many other detail changes. Development trials are being carried out with stretched M113A2s having an extra road wheel each side so the development life of the M113 is still very far from over.

Specification
M113A2
Crew: 2 + 11
Weight: 11261 kg (24,826b)
Powerplant: GMC Detroit Diesel 6V-53 diesel developing 215 bhp (160 kW)
Dimensions: length 4.863 m (15 ft 11.4 in); width 2.686 m (8 ft 10 in); height (overall) 2.52 m (8 ft 3.2 in)
Performance: maximum road speed 67.6 km/h (42 mph); maximum road range 595 km (369.7 miles); fording, amphibious; gradient 60 per cent; vertical obstacle 0.61 m (2 ft); trench 1.68 m (5 ft 6 in)

M2 Bradley Infantry Vehicle

The US Army requirement for a mechanized infantry vehicle emerged in the 1960s, as did a requirement for a reconnaissance scout vehicle. Prototypes of tracked and wheeled vehicles were built before a single vehicle for both roles was decided upon. The **XM723** which FMC developed from 1972 became the basis for the **M2 Infantry Fighting Vehicle** and the **M3 Cavalry Fighting Vehicle**. Collectively called the Fighting Vehicle System,

The M2 Bradley is almost identical to the M3 except that the latter has no Omar N. Bradley. The first production vehicles were completed in 1981, equipping a battalion at Fort Hood in March 1983 and reaching Europe later that year. By 1987 nearly 3000 Bradleys had been delivered, out of a planned procurement of 6,882 vehicles. The M2 Bradley is almost identical to the M3 except that the latter has no firing port, carries a total of five men (compared with 10 in the M2) and is provided with much more ammunition.

The M2 Bradley is almost identical to the M3 except that the latter has no firing port, carries a total of five men (compared with 10 in the M2) and is provided with much more ammunition.

The hull of the M2 is of welded aluminium armour with an additional layer of spaced laminate armour fitted to the hull front, sides and rear to give much increased protection against most battlefield weapons. The driver is at the front of the hull on the left, with the powerpack to his right. The two-man power-operated turret is in the centre of the hull with the commander on the right and gunner on the left. The main armament is a Hughes Helicopter 25-mm dual-feed Chain Gun which can defeat Soviet light armoured vehicles when firing APDS ammunition; there is also a 7.62-mm (0.3-in) co-axial machine-gun and a twin launcher on the left side of turret for the Hughes TOW ATGWs. A stabilization system is fitted which allows the gunner to aim and fire the 25-mm cannon while moving at speed across country. The troop compartment is at the rear and provided with six firing ports and periscopes to allow the embarked men to fire their 5.56-mm (0.22-in) weapons from within the vehicle. A full range of night-vision equipment is fitted for the commander, gunner and driver, and there is an NBC system. The Bradley is a highly effective vehicle and plays a key role in the US Army's combined-

Above: An M2 Bradley Infantry Fighting Vehicle with the twin TOW launcher retracted. This vehicle is entering service in increasing numbers with the US Army.

arms team concept. It has many critics, though, who say that it is too large, expensive and difficult to maintain, and will be unable to operate with the M60 and M1 tanks as it has much inferior armour protection to these MBTs.

The upgraded **M2A1** and **M3A1** entered production in 1985, first deliveries being in 1986. These Block 1 improved vehicles have enhanced NBC protection, and can fire the larger diameter TOW 2 missile. Improvements have also been made to the fuel system and the fire suppression system. Further significant changes are expected in the Block 2 improved vehicles due in the 1990s. Other variants in the Fighting Vehicle System include the base vehicle for a number of entries in the US Army's Forward Area Air Defence programme, the M993 MLRS carrier, and the M987 Carrier (itself forming the basis for a whole series of armoured support vehicles).

Specification
M2 Bradley
Crew: 3+7
Weight: 22666 kg (49,970 lb)
Powerplant: one Cummins VTA-903T 8-cylinder diesel developing 500 hp (373 kW)
Dimensions: length 6.453 m (21 ft 2 in); width 3.20 m (10 ft 6 in); height (overall) 2.972 m (9 ft 9 in)
Performance: maximum road speed 66 km/h (41 mph); maximum range 483 km (300 miles); fording amphibious; gradient 60 per cent; vertical obstacle 0.914 m (3 ft 0 in); trench 2.54 m (8 ft 4 in)

The M2 Bradley IFV has been designed to operate alongside the M1 Abrams Main Battle Tank on the modern battlefield. The twin TOW missile launcher gives the Bradley a significant anti-tank capability.

Armoured Infantry Fighting Vehicle

The shortcomings of the M113 armoured personnel carrier were realized by the US Army in the late 1960s, and in 1967 FMC was awarded a contract to build two prototypes of a new vehicle called the **XM765**. This was essentially an M113 with a fully-enclosed weapon station and with the troop compartment at the rear modified for firing ports and observation devices in the upper part of an inward-sloping hull top. The US Army did not adopt this vehicle, however, going on to develop a much heavier and more complex vehicle eventually standardized as the M2 Bradley Infantry Fighting Vehicle, which is also built by FMC Corporation.

FMC realized, though, that the new US Army infantry fighting vehicle would be too complex, heavy and expensive for many countries around the world, so with company funds started a development of the XM765 which finally resulted in the **Product Improved M113A1**. This was not placed in production but did result in another vehicle with rearranged interior layout called the **Armoured Infantry Fighting Vehicle**. Following a number of demonstrations in Europe and elsewhere, the Netherlands became (in 1975) the first country to adopt the

The Dutch army uses a version of the AIFV fitted with the Emerson twin TOW launcher, as fitted to the M901 Improved TOW Vehicles of the US army, which has two missiles in the ready-to-launch position.

vehicle with an initial order for 850 vehicles. This was followed by the Philippines with an order for about 30 vehicles and in 1981 Belgium ordered 514 AIFVs and 525 M113A2s which are now being built under licence in Belgium.

Like the M113 series, the hull of the AIFV is of welded aluminium armour construction, but in addition has a layer of appliqué steel armour added to the front, sides and rear for increased protection. The driver is at the front left, with the engine to his right and the commander to his rear. The commander has a cupola with observation devices. The power-operated turret is to the right of the commander and is armed with a 25-mm Oerlikon dual-feed cannon; a 7.62-mm (0.3-in) machine-gun is mounted co-axially to the left of the 25-mm cannon. The turret is provided with both day and night observation devices. The seven infantrymen are seated in the rear of the vehicle and enter via a power-operated ramp as in the standard M113. A hatch is provided above the troop compartment, and there are five firing ports with observation devices. A wide range of optional equipment can be fitted including an NBC system, heater and different armament options.

The basic vehicle is fully amphibious, being propelled in the water by its tracks. Compared with the earlier

M113 the AIFV has improved armour protection, improved fire power (25-mm cannon in turret instead of a 12.7-mm/0.5-in machine-gun in an unprotected mount) and improved mobility (improved suspension and more powerful engine).

The Dutch army is using the AIFV as the basic member of a whole family of vehicles including an anti-tank vehicle with the Emerson Improved TOW system, a command vehicle, a tractor for the 120-mm (4.72-in) Brandt mortar, a

radar vehicle, a cargo carrier and an ambulance.

Specification
AIFV
Crew: 3+7
Weight: 13687 kg (30,175 lb)
Powerplant: one Detroit Diesel 6V-53T V-6 diesel developing 264 hp (197 kW)
Dimensions: length 5.258 m (17 ft 3 in); width 2.819 m (9 ft 3 in); height (overall) 2.794 m (9 ft 2 in)
Performance: maximum road speed

The Armoured Infantry Fighting Vehicle has been developed by the FMC Corporation specifically for the export market, and fills the gap between the basic M113 APC and the more expensive M2 Bradley IFV.

61.2 km/h (38 mph); maximum range 490 km (305 miles); fording amphibious; gradient 60 per cent; vertical obstacle 0.635 m (2 ft 1 in); trench 1.625 m (5 ft 4 in)

JAPAN

Type 73 armoured personnel carrier

When the Japanese Ground Self-Defense Force was formed in the 1950s its first armoured personnel carriers were half-tracks supplied by the United States. The first Japanese-designed vehicle to enter service was the **Type SU 60** APC which was produced by Mitsubishi Heavy Industries and the Komatsu Manufacturing Corporation, final deliveries being made in the early 1970s. The Type SU 60 is not amphibious, has a four-man crew and can carry six fully equipped troops. Over 400 of these are in service and variants include an NBC detection vehicle, 81-mm and 107-mm (3.19-in and 4.2-in) mortar-carriers and a dozer. The **Type 73** is now supplementing the Type SU 60 but production is at a very low rate, sometimes as low as six per year, and by 1987 some 200 were in service.

The Type 73 has a hull of all-welded aluminium armour with the commander, driver and bow machine-gunner at the front. The 7.62-mm (0.3-in) machine-gun in the bow is unique and can be traversed 30° left, right, up and down, and a similar weapon is installed in the earlier Type SU 60 APC. The engine is towards the front on the left, with troop compartment at the rear. Entry is via two doors rather than a power-operated ramp as in the M113 APC and M2 Bradley IFV. One of the nine infantrymen normally mans the roof-mounted 12.7-mm (0.5-in) machine-gun, which is on the right side of the vehicle and can be aimed and fired from within the vehicle. The cupola can be traversed through 360° and the weapon elevated from −10° to +60°. The infantry are seated on benches down each side of the troop compartment facing each other; the ben-

ches can be folded up to allow stores and other equipment to be carried. On each side of the troop compartment are two T-type firing ports, although these have a limited value compared with the firing ports/vision blocks fitted to vehicles such as the West German Marder. Another unusual feature of the Type 73 is that mounted on the very rear of the hull roof on each side is a bank of three electrically-operated smoke-dischargers, which fire forwards. In action these would be fired when the vehicle was under attack so that it could withdraw to the rear.

The Type 73 has night-vision equipment and an NBC system, but is only amphibious after lengthy preparation. This preparation includes flotation aids along side of the hull and attached to the road wheels, a trim vane mounted at the front of the hull, and boxes fitted

around the air inlet, air outlet and exhaust pipes on the roof of the vehicle. If the last were not fitted any surge of water over the roof would soon get into the engine.

Unlike many current APCs there is only one known variant of the Type 73, namely the **Type 75** self-propelled ground-wind measuring unit that is used with the 130-mm (5.12-in) multiple rocket-launcher and uses some automotive components of the Type 73.

The replacement for the Type 73 began development in 1981, with the first of four prototypes of the **Type 88 MICV** running in 1984. The Type 88 will have a two-man turret with an Oerlikon 35mm cannon and two new Japanese Chyu-MAT medium range laser guided anti-tank missiles. It may enter service before 1990.

The Japanese Type 73 APC and the earlier Type SU 60 APC are the only vehicles of their type with a bow-mounted 7.62-mm (0.3-in) machine-gun.

Specification
Type 73
Crew: 3+9
Weight: 13300 kg (29,321 lb)
Powerplant: one Mitsubishi air-cooled diesel developing 300 hp (224 kW)
Dimensions: length 5.80 m (19 ft 1 in); width 2.80 m (9 ft 2 in); height (with MG) 2.20 m (7 ft 3 in) and (hull) 1.70 m (5 ft 7 in)
Performance: maximum road speed 70 km/h (45 mph); maximum range 300 km (186 miles); fording amphibious; gradient 60 per cent; vertical obstacle 0.70 m (2 ft 4 in); trench 2.00 m (6 ft 7 in)

Steyr 4K 7FA armoured personnel carrier

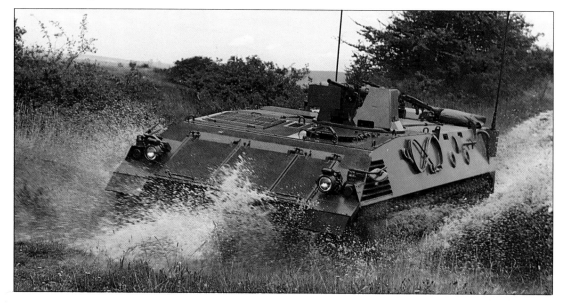

Between 1961 and 1969 Oesterreichische, which was taken over by Steyr-Daimler-Puch in 1970, built 450 full-tracked armoured personnel carriers for the Austrian army, the final production model being **Schützenpanzer 4K 4FA** with a more powerful engine. In addition to the usual specialized versions, the Austrian army uses two basic models of the 4K 4FA, the **SPz G2** fitted with an Oerlikon-Bührle one-man turret armed with a 20-mm cannon and the **SPz G1** fitted with a 12.7-mm (0.5-in) M2 HB machine-gun.

In 1976 Steyr-Daimler-Puch completed the prototype of the **SPz 4K 7FA** APC which had improved armour protection as well as the more powerful engine and upgraded transmision of the SK-105 tank destroyer with 105-mm (4.13-in) gun that by then was already in production for the Austrian army and was subsequently adopted by many other countries. The first production 4K 7FA APCs were completed in 1977, and since then sales have been made to Austria, Greece (where the vehicle is manufactured under licence as the **Leonidas**), Nigeria and Bolivia.

The all-welded steel hull of the SPz 4K 7FA provides the crew with protection from 20-mm projectiles over the frontal arc, and accommodates the driver at the front left with the engine to his right and the troop compartment at the rear. The gunner is seated to the rear of the driver, and his cupola is provided with a two-part hatch cover that when in the vertical position provides protection to his sides, the 12.7-mm (0.5-in) machine-gun being provided with a shield to provide frontal protection. On the rear of the gunner's cupola are four smoke-dischargers firing to the rear. The eight troops enter and leave the vehicle through twin doors in the hull rear, and sit in two

rows of four down the middle of the vehicle facing outwards. Over the top of the troop compartment is a two-piece hatch cover that opens to each side, and around the roof can be mounted up to four 7.62-mm (0.3-in) machine-guns; to fire these weapons the troops have to expose their heads and shoulders above the roof. Standard equipment includes heating and ventilating systems, and passive night-vision equipment can be installed if required.

As usual the chassis has been used as the basis for a complete family of vehicles. The infantry fighting vehicle has ball mounts for two rifles in each side of the hull with periscopes above for aiming the weapons. The fire-support model, which has yet to enter

production, has a GIAT TS-90 turret armed with a long-barrelled 90-mm (3.54-in) gun that fires APFSDS-T ammunition. There are also command, ambulance (unarmed), mortar-carrier (81-mm/3.19-in and 120-mm/4.72-in) and two anti-aircraft vehicles. Neither of the latter has yet entered production. One is fitted with the French ESD turret and armed with twin 20-mm cannon, while the other has a complete surveillance and tracking system and is armed with twin 30-mm cannon in a turret designed by Thomson-CSF.

Specification
SPz 4K 7FA
Crew: 2+8
Weight: 14800 kg (32,628 lb)
Powerplant: one Steyr 6-cylinder

The Steyr-Daimler-Puch 4K 7FA-K SPz infantry fighting vehicle is a further development of the basic 4K 7FA which is used by Austria, Greece (manufactured under licence), Morocco, Nigeria and Tunisia. It shares many common components with the SK 105 tank destroyer.

liquid-cooled diesel developing 320 hp (238 kW)
Dimensions: length 5.87 m (19 ft 3 in); width 2.50 m (8 ft 2 in); height (without MG) 1.69 m (5 ft 7 in)
Performance: maximum road speed 63.6 km/h (41 mph); maximum range 520 km (323 miles); fording 1.00 m (3 ft 3 in); gradient 75 per cent; vertical obstacle 0.80 m (2 ft 7 in); trench 2.10 m (6 ft 11 in)

M-980 mechanized infantry combat vehicle

The first Yugoslav-designed and -built armoured personnel carrier to enter service was the **M-60P**. In appearance and role this was similar to other vehicles developed in this period, such as the American M113, and was designed to transport men across the battlefield where they would dismount and fight on foot. Realizing the obvious shortcomings of this vehicle, Yugoslavia then started design work on a mechanized infantry combat vehicle which finally appeared in 1975 under the designation **M-980**. The short development period was made possible by the decision to incorporate a number of proven components from other sources, often from outside the country. For example, the engine came from Renault (formerly Saviem) of France and is also installed in the GIAT AMX-10P vehicle, while the road wheels are similar to those of the Soviet PT-76 light amphibious tank family and the 'Sagger' ATGW is fitted to a wide number of Soviet vehicles including MICVs, APCs and tank destroyers.

In many respects the design of the M-980 is very similar to that of the Soviet BMP-1, which is also used by Yugoslavia in small numbers. The driver is seated at the front of the vehicle on the left, with the vehicle commander to his rear and the engine to his right. The one-man turret is in the cen-

tre of the vehicle and armed with a 20-mm cannon with an elevation of +75° and a depression of −5°; mounted co-axially to the right of this is a 7.62-mm (0.3-in) machine-gun. The high elevation of these weapons enables them to be used against low-flying aircraft and helicopters. Mounted externally on the right rear of the turret are two Soviet AT-3 'Sagger' wire guided anti-tank missiles. The troop compartment is at the rear, and entry to this is via two doors in the hull rear. Over the top of the troop compartment are roof hatches and firing ports (with periscopes above) to enable the troops to fire their weapons from within the vehicle.

The M-980 is fully amphibious, being propelled in the water by its tracks; before the vehicle enters the water a trim vane is erected at the front of the hull and the bilge pumps are switched on. It is also fitted with a fire-extinguishing system, an NBC pack and a smokelaying system.

As far as it is known there are no variants of the M-980, although command vehicles and other specialized versions probably exist. In some respects this vehicle is an improvement over the Soviet BMP-1 as it has two rather than one 'Sagger' missile in the ready-to-launch position, and its 20-mm cannon is probably more suited to

the role of the vehicle than the 73-mm (2.87-in) gun of the BMP-1. It is of note that the latest Soviet BMP has had the 73-mm (2.87-in) weapon replaced by a smaller 30-mm calibre gun, and most Western vehicles of this type are armed with weapons in the 20- to 30-mm range rather than heavy weapons such as the 73-mm (2.87-in) gun of the BMP-1.

Specification
M-980
Crew: 2+8
Weight: 13000 kg (28,660 lb)
Powerplant: one HS 115-2 V-8 diesel

A Yugoslav M-980 mechanized infantry combat vehicle, showing the twin launcher for AT-3 'Sagger' ATGWs above the turret roof. The engine is as used in the French AMX-10P.

developing 260 hp (194 kW)
Dimensions: length 6.40 m (21 ft 0 in); width 2.59 m (8 ft 6 in); height (overall) 2.50 m (8 ft 2 in)
Performance: maximum road speed 60 km/h (37 mph); maximum range 500 km (310 miles); fording amphibious; vertical obstacle 0.80 m (2 ft 8 in); trench 2.20 m 7 ft 3 in)

BMD airborne combat vehicle

USSR

The Soviet Union has for some time placed great emphasis on its airborne forces, and for many years has had at least seven airborne divisions maintained at full strength. In the past the only armoured vehicles these divisions have used have been the 57-mm ASU-57 or the 85-mm (3.35-in) ASU-85 or the 85-mm (3.35-in) ASU-85 self-propelled anti-tank guns. To give these units increased firepower and mobility once they have been landed behind enemy lines the **BMD** airborne combat vehicle was designed, and this entered service in 1970. Today each Soviet airborne rifle division has 330 of these vehicles in various configurations, although it is uncertain whether or not all seven of these divisions have their full complement of vehicles. The BMD was used to spearhead the invasion of Afghanistan in 1979, and there is also evidence that it has been used by Cubans in the Ogaden.

The layout of the vehicle is unusual, the driver being seated at the front of the hull in the centre with the commander to his left and the bow machine-gunner to his right. The latter operates the two single 7.62-mm (0.3-in) machine-guns mounted internally at the front of the hull, one on each side. The turret, which is identical to that fitted to the BMP-1, is in the centre of the hull and is armed with a 73-mm (2.87-in) gun, a 7.62-mm (0.3-in) co-axial machine-gun and a launcher rail for the AT-3 'Sagger' ATGW mounted above the main gun. To the rear of the turret is a small compartment with seats for the senior gunner, the grenade-launcher and his assistant; the only means of entry to this compartment is via the concertina type roof hatch. The independent suspension of the BMD consists of five road wheels,

with drive sprocket at the rear and idler at the front; there are four track-return rollers. An unusual feature of this suspension is that a hydraulic system is incorporated that allows the ground clearance of the vehicle to be altered from 100 mm to 450 mm (4 in to 18 in), a factor of some importance for airborne operations.

The BMD is fitted with an NBC system and a full range of night-vision equipment. It is also fully amphibious, the only preparation required being the erection of the trim vane at the front of the hull and the engagement of the bilge pump.

The command version of the BMD is called the **BMD-U** (command), and this has a longer chassis with six road wheels on each side and no turret. There is also an 82-mm (3.23-in) mortar

version that has seen action in Afghanistan. More recently some BMDs have been observed with the launcher rail for the 'Sagger' ATGW replaced by that for a shorter-range AT-4 'Spigot' on the turret roof; if required the launcher can be dismounted for use in the ground role. The missile has the Soviet designation 9K111. There is a BMD with the same 30mm gun as the BMP-2. The **BMD-2** is an extended version, with the six roadwheels of the BMD-U, and a version of that, known as the **SO-120**, has been seen with a 120mm breech loading mortar in a new turret.

Specification
BMD
Crew: 7
Weight: 6700 kg (14,771 lb)

The BMD airborne combat vehicle is used only by the Soviet Air Assault Divisions and has been operated extensively in Afghanistan. Its turret is similar to that fitted to the BMP-1 MICV, although some BMDs have a roof-mounted Spigot ATGW in place of the AT-3 'Sagger' ATGW.

Powerplant: one V-6 liquid-cooled diesel developing 240-hp (179 kW)
Dimensions: length 5.40 m (17 ft 9 in); width 2.63 m (8 ft 8 in); height 1.62 m to 1.97 m (5 ft 4 in to 6 ft 6 in)
Performance: maximum road speed 70 km/h (43 mph); maximum range 320 km (200 miles); fording amphibious; gradient 60 per cent; vertical obstacle 0.80 m (2 ft 8 in); trench 1.60 m (5 ft 3 in)

BMP-1 mechanized infantry fighting vehicle

USSR

The **BMP-1** was developed as the replacement for the BTR-50 armoured personnel carrier and caused a major stir throughout Western armies when it rolled through Red Square for the first time in 1967. Previous armoured personnel carriers simply transported the infantry to a point near the scene of action, where it dismounted to attack the objective on foot. The BMP-1 not only has firing ports that allow all of the embarked troops to fire their weapons from within the vehicle in relative safety, but also a 73-mm (2.87-in) cannon and a wire-guided anti-tank missile. Since the introduction of the BMP-1 several countries have also developed mechanized infantry combat vehicles: the West German Marder (20 mm cannon), the French AMX-10P (20-mm cannon) and most recently the US M2 Bradley (25-mm cannon) are all good examples. The Marder has recently been fitted with an externally mounted MILAN ATGW, but although this is more accurate than the 'Sagger' fitted to the BMP-1 it has a shorter range. The M2 has a twin launcher for the TOW ATGW which has a longer range than the 'Sagger' and is much more accurate.

The layout of the BMP-1 is unusual, with the driver at front left, the commander to his rear and the engine on the right. The turret is in the centre of the hull and the infantry compartment at the rear. The eight infantrymen are

seated four down each side, back to back, and enter the vehicle via twin doors in the hull rear. Over the top of the troop compartment are roof hatches. The main drawback of this arrangement is that the troop commander is out of immediate contact with the men he must command in battle. The 73-mm (2.87-in) gun is fed from a magazine that holds 40 rounds of HEAT (high explosive anti-tank) or HE-FRAG (high explosive fragmentation) ammunition, and there is a 7.62-mm (0.3-in) co-axial machine-gun. Turret traverse is electric, with manual controls for emergency use. The main drawbacks of the 73-mm (2.87-in) low-pressure gun are its low muzzle velocity and its lack of accuracy in high winds. To fire with any chance of a first-round hit the BMP-1 must first halt. The 'Sagger' ATGW is mounted on a launcher rail over the 73-mm (2.87-in) gun and controlled (via a joystick) by the gunner. The missile has a maximum range of 3000 m (3,280 yards), but takes 27 seconds to reach this range.

The BMP-1 is fitted with a full range of first-generation infra-red night-vision equipment for the commander, gunner and driver, as well as an NBC system. It is fully amphibious, with hardly any preparation, being propelled in the water by its tracks.

In addition to the basic BMP-1 there are also command versions of the vehicle, a radar carrier fitted with two-man cle, a radar carrier fitted with two-man

turret armed with a 7.62-mm (0.3-in) machine-gun and carrying a 'Small Fred' mortar/artillery-location radar on turret rear, and a reconnaissance vehicle that has a new two-man turret fitted with the same 73-mm (2.87-mm) gun. The BMP is widely used, over 30,000 having been built and supplied to over 20 countries, and has seen extensive combat with the Soviet forces in Afghanistan. It is used by both sides in the Gulf War, and has been in action in the Lebanon, Ethiopia and with the Libyan backed forces in Chad.

Soviet BMP-1 mechanized infantry combat vehicles in support of their dismounted infantry. In this photograph none of the vehicles have the AT-3 'Sagger' wire-guided anti-tank missile mounted above the 73-mm gun.

Specification
BMP-1
Crew: 3+8
Weight: 13500 kg (29,762 lb)

Powerplant: one 6-cylinder diesel developing 300 hp (224 kW)
Dimensions: length 6.74 m (22 ft 1 in); width 2.94 m (9 ft 8 in); height (overall) 2.15 m (7 ft 1 in)
Performance: maximum road speed 80 km/h (50 mph); maximum range 500 km (248 miles); fording amphibious; gradient 60 per cent; vertical obstacle 0.80 m (2 ft 8 in); trench 2.20 m (7 ft 3 in)

BMP-2 mechanized infantry combat vehicle

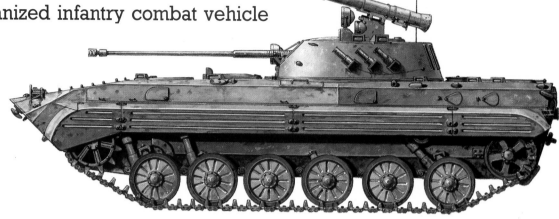

The **BMP-2** mechanized infantry fighting vehicle is a further development of the BMP-1 and was first observed in public during a parade held in Red Square, Moscow, late in 1982, although it entered service with the Soviet army several years before that. Since then it has also been observed in service with the Czech army.

The basic chassis of the BMP-2 is very similar to that of the original BMP-1 which entered service with the Soviet army in the early 1960s, but has a new turret and different crew positions. On the BMP-1 the commander was seated behind the driver and therefore had poor observation to the right side of the vehicle. In the BMP-2 the commander now sits in the much enlarged turret alongside the gunner, and has excellent all-round battlefield observation.

The BMP-1 is armed with a 73-mm (2.87-in) weapon that fires a fin-stabilized HEAT (High Explosive Anti-Tank) or HE-FRAG (High Explosive Fragmentation) round, with a 7.62-mm (0.3-in) co-axial machine-gun, and with a 'Sagger' wire-guided anti-tank weapon mounted above the main armament. The 73-mm gun suffered from a number of drawbacks and is ineffective in high winds, while the first-generation 'Sagger' missile needed a well-trained gunner to ensure a first-round hit.

These major disadvantages have been overcome in the BMP-2, as the armament now comprises a 30-mm rapid-fire automatic cannon which can be elevated to +74°, so enabling it to be used against low-flying aircraft and helicopters. The gunner can select either single shots or one of two rates of automatic fire (200/300 or 500 rounds per minute) and 500 rounds of HE-T (High Explosive – Tracer) and AP-T (Armour-Piercing – Tracer) are carried. A 7.62-mm PKT machine-gun is mounted co-axial with the main armament.

Mounted on the turret roof is an AT-4 'Spigot' anti-tank guided weapon which has a maximum range of 2000 m (2,187 yards) and is fitted with a HEAT

warhead. All the operator has to do to ensure a hit is to keep the crosswires of his sight on the target. (On the earlier AT-3 'Sagger' he had to operate a small joystick.)

In addition to being able to inject diesel fuel into the exhaust to lay its own smoke screen, the BMP-2 has a bank of three electrically-operated smoke-dischargers mounted on each side of the turret towards the rear. More recent BMP-2s have appliqué armour on their turret sides.

Seven fully-equipped infantrymen are carried, compared with eight in the earlier vehicle: one man is seated to the rear of the commander, and the other six in the troop compartment at the rear facing outwards, each being provided with a firing port with an observation periscope above.

Like the BMP-1, the BMP-2 is fully amphibious, being propelled in the water by its tracks. Before entering the water a trim vane is erected at the front of the vehicle and the bilge pumps are switched on.

Specification
BMP-2
Crew: 3+7
Weight: loaded 14600 kg (32,187 lb)
Powerplant: believed to be one Type 5D20 turbocharged 6-cylinder water-cooled diesel developing 350 hp (261 kW)
Dimensions: length 6.71 m (22 ft 0.2 in);

width 3.09 m (10 ft 1.7 in); height 2.06 m (6 ft 9 in)
Performance: maximum road speed 60 km/h (37.3 mph); range 500 km (311 miles); fording amphibious; vertical obstacle 0.7 m (2 ft 3 in); trench 2.0 m (6 ft 7 in); gradient 60 per cent; side slope 30 per cent

Above: The BMP-2 is a new version of the BMP Mechanized Infantry Combat Vehicle, and substitutes a 30-mm cannon for the 73-mm smooth-bore gun of the first model. It also carries AT-4 'Spigot' ATGMs in place of outdated AT-3 'Sagger' missiles.

Below: A close up of a BMP-2 on parade in Prague shows details of the rapid-firing 30-mm cannon which has replaced the troublesome 73-mm gun of the BMP-1. It has the added advantage of being usable and effective in the anti-aircraft role.

Below: Like most Soviet AFVs, the BMP-2 is able to lay a smokescreen by injecting diesel fuel directly into the exhaust, but it also carries a bank of electrically operated smoke dischargers on the turret sides. Some BMP-2s have been sporting appliqué armour on their sides.

BTR-50PK armoured personnel carrier

The **BTR-50P** was the first full-tracked armoured personnel carrier to enter service with the Soviet army in the mid-1950s, and is essentially the chassis of the PT-76 amphibious light tank with its turret removed and a superstructure added to the forward part. The commander and driver are seated under armour protection at the front of the vehicle, while the 10 infantrymen are seated in the troop compartment on bench seats that run across the width of the vehicle. The main drawback of this model is the complete lack of any overhead armour protection for the infantry carried and additionally there is no NBC system. The main armament consists of a 7.62-mm (0.3-in) machine-gun on a pintle mount at the front of the crew compartment. On the rear engine decking ramps are provided so that a 57-mm (2.24-in) or 85-mm (3.35-in) anti-tank gun could be carried and, if required, even fired from the vehicle. The next major model to enter service was the **BTR-50PK**, which has a fully enclosed troop compartment and is fitted with an NBC system. Armament consists of a roof-mounted 7.62-mm (0.3-in) machine-gun that provides no protection for the gunner. The Czechs have also built an improved version of the BTR-50PK called the **OT-62**, this being distinguishable from the Soviet vehicle by its lack

of chamfer between the side and top of the hull. There are two command versions of the vehicle called the **BTR-50PU** (command) **Model 1** and **BTR-50PU Model 2**. Both of these have a fully enclosed crew compartment, the former having one projecting bay and the latter two. These command vehicles have additional communications equipment and can be recognized by their radio aerials, external stowage and a generator; the last removes the need for the main engine to be run when the vehicle is being used in the static mode.

The basic vehicle has been out of production for some time, and in many Soviet units the type has been replaced by the BMP-1 MICV. Two new versions have recently been noticed by Western intelligence, however, these being the **MTK** mine-clearing vehicle and the **MTP** technical support vehicle. The former is fitted with a launcher on the rear deck that fires explosive tubes across the minefield: these fall to the ground and are then detonated, hopefully detonating the mines in the process. In concept this is similar to the British Giant Viper system. The MTP has much higher roof with chamfered sides and supports the BMP in the forward battlefield area, it having better cross-country capability than the trucks normally used in this

role.

Even in 1984, the BTR-50P and its variants are still used by some 30 countries in Europe, the Middle East and elsewhere. The type was used in Vietnam by the North Vietnamese army and in the Middle East campaigns by Syria and Egypt. The last used the BTR-50P with some success in crossing the Suez Canal during 1973. Whereas most western APCs (such as the American M113 and British FV432) are propelled in the water by their tracks, the BTR-50P is propelled in the water by waterjets at a speed of 11 km/h (6.8 mph).

Specification
BTR-50PK
Crew: 2+10
Weight: 14200 kg (31,305 lb)
Powerplant: one Model V-6 6-cylinder inline water-cooled diesel developing 240 hp (179 kW)
Dimensions: length 7.08 m (23 ft 3 in); width 3.14 m (10 ft 4 in); height (without armament) 1.97 m (6 ft 6 in)
Performance: maximum road speed 44 km/h (27 mph); maximum range 400 km (250 miles); fording amphibious; gradient 70 per cent; vertical obstacle 1.10 m (3 ft 7 in); trench 2.80 m (9 ft 2 in)

Soviet BTR-50PK armoured personnel carriers. This model has overhead armour protection for the troop compartment. The original BTR-50P has an open-topped troop compartment, which makes the 10 seated infantrymen very vulnerable to shells and mortar bombs bursting overhead.

MT-LB multi-purpose tracked vehicle

In the period immediately after World War II the Soviets introduced the AT-P armoured tracked artillery tractor, which could tow anti-tank guns and howitzers up to 122 mm (4.8 in) in calibre. This has now been replaced by the **MT-LB** multi-purpose armoured vehicle, which is used for a wide range of roles in addition to its role of towing anti-tank guns such as the 100-mm (3.9-in) T-12.

The crew compartment is at the front, with the engine to the rear of this on the left and the troop compartment at the rear. The 11 infantrymen are seated on canvas seats down each side of the troop compartment that can be folded up to allow cargo to be carried. The infantry can quickly leave the vehicle through two large doors in the hull rear, and two hatches are provided over the top of their compartment. Mounted at the front of the hull on the right side is a manually-operated turret armed with a 7.62-mm (0.3-in) machine-gun. The road wheels are similar to those on the PT-76 amphibious light tank and the BTR-50 series armoured personnel carrier. The torsion-bar suspension consists of six road wheels, with the drive sprocket at the front and idler at the rear. The MT-LB is normally fitted with 350-mm (13.8-in) wide tracks, but when operating on snow-covered ground these can be replaced by the much wider 565-mm (22.25-in) wide tracks, which give a lower ground pressure and therefore better mobility.

The MT-LB is fully amphibious, being propelled in the water by its tracks at a speed of between 5 and 6 km/h (3 to 4 mph), and has infra-red night vision equipment and an NBC system.

In some areas of the Soviet Union where terrain is swampy or normally covered by snow, the MT-LB is used in

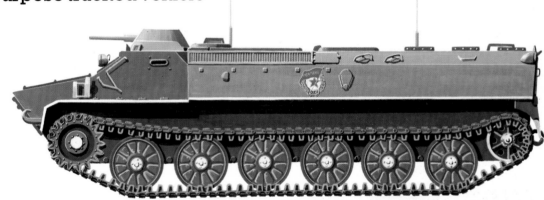

Above: The MT-LB multi-purpose armoured vehicle is a member of a family of vehicles that all share the same automotive components.

place of the BMP mechanized infantry combat vehicle.

As usual the MT-LB chassis has been used for a number of specialized applications including the **MT-LBU** (command), **MT-SON** with 'Pork Trough' radar mounted on roof, MT-LB with 'Big Fred' artillery/mortar locating radar on roof at rear, MT-LB armoured engineer vehicle with dozer blade and **MTL-LB** repair vehicle. The last is used (front) with an A-frame, plus a winch in the forward area and fitted (at the front) with an A frame, plus a winch and a full range of tools and other specialized equipment. The chassis is also used as the basis for the SA-13 surface-to-air missile system that has four missiles in the ready-to-launch position. Automotive components of the MT-LB, including the engine and transmission, are also used in the 122-mm (4.8-in) 2S1 self-propelled howitzer which entered service in the 1970s and is now widely used by the Soviet Union as well as

being exported to many countries.

Specification
MT-LB
Crew: 2+11
Weight: 11900 kg (26,235 lb)
Powerplant: one V-8 diesel developing 240 hp (179 kW)
Dimensions: length 6.454 m (21 ft 2 in); width 2.85 m (9 ft 4 in); height (turret) 1.865 m (6 ft 2 in)

The MT-LB amphibious vehicle is used for a wide range of roles such as artillery prime mover, command post, cargo carriers and an armoured personnel carrier.

Performance: maximum road speed 61.5 km/h (38 mph); maximum range 500 km (310 miles); fording amphibious; gradient 60 per cent; vertical obstacle 0.70 m (2 ft 3 in); trench 2.70 m (8 ft 10 in)

Modern Wheeled Armoured Personnel Carriers

In spite of the rise in importance of the tracked vehicle in the armies of the world, the wheeled APC remains a vital item in the military inventory. It is particularly useful in second-echelon tasks and for the increasingly important internal security role.

Many armoured personnel carriers are today fitted with long range anti-tank guided weapons, so turning them into highly effective tank destroyers. This Panhard VCR (6×6) has a Euromissile UTM-800 turret with four Euromissile HOT missiles ready to launch.

For many years wheeled armoured personnel carriers possessed only limited cross-country mobility compared with their tracked counterparts, and therefore were often limited to roads, being used to transport troops from the rear area to points near the front line where the men dismounted to fight on foot. Some countries, including the United States, had no requirement for wheeled armoured personnel carriers at all, and it was not until the Vietnam conflict that the US Army purchased large numbers of the private venture Cadillac Gage V-100 4×4 Commando range of multi-purpose vehicles . It should be noted, however, that these were used mainly for escorting convoys of supplies from one camp to another or patrolling high risk areas such as airports, fuel dumps and ammunition compounds, rather than for transporting troops into action.

The Soviet Union, on the other hand, has continued to develop both tracked and wheeled armoured personnel carriers on an almost continual basis, and the two types are complementary. The tracked vehicles have excellent cross-country mobility and are therefore capable of keeping up with tanks and other armoured fighting vehicles moving across country, while the wheeled armoured personnel carriers have a greater road speed and therefore better strategic mobility, so that troops can be quickly brought up from the rear areas to exactly where they are needed, or switched from one area to another at short notice.

The United Kingdom started development programmes for full-tracked armoured personnel carriers soon after the end of World War II, but it was the Alvis Saracen 6×6 vehicle which entered service first, this

sharing many components with the Alvis Saladin 6×6 armoured car developed at the same time. The Saracen was rushed into production as it was urgently needed in Malaya during the early 1950s. Many of the modern wheeled armoured personnel carriers described here use the same automotive components as an armoured car developed by the same company (the M3 has 95 per cent common automotive components with the AML armoured car, for example) with obvious logistical training and financial savings for the operators.

For the internal security role special versions of wheeled armoured personnel carriers have been developed, these normally equipped with barricade-clearing equipment, CS gas dispensers or water cannon, and special protection against petrol bombs which can easily cause a vehicle to catch fire, so forcing the occupants to leave their vehicle. Instead of using heavily armoured wheeled armoured personnel carriers, many countries use modified light vehicles such as the Land Rover, these being normally provided with protection from small arms fire and nail bombs. They do not provide the same degree of protection as vehicles like the VAB or Transportpanzer, but their small size makes them useful in most riot-control situations, where the employment of larger vehicles, often clearly identified as military, can make the situation even worse.

A convoy of South African Ratel APCs departs at dawn from the Operational Area in Namibia for a raid deep into Angola. These raids are often large operations supported by artillery, aircraft and helicopters, and the Ratel has been designed for use in this testing environment.

Transportpanzer 1 armoured personnel carrier

In the mid-1960s the West German army decided to develop a complete new range of vehicles sharing many common components; the range included 4×4, 6×6 and 8×8 trucks, an 8×8 armoured reconnaissance vehicle and 4×4 and 6×6 armoured personnel carriers. The 8×8 armoured reconnaissance vehicle finally emerged as the Luchs, of which 408 were built between 1975 and 1978. In the end only the 6×6 armoured personnel carrier entered production as the **Transportpanzer 1**. In 1977 Thyssen Henschel was awarded a production contract for 996 vehicles, the first of which was completed in 1979. The 4×4 was then developed into the APE amphibious engineer reconnaissance vehicle by EWK, but this was never placed in production. In 1983 Venezuela ordered about 10 Transportpanzer vehicles fitted with a 12.7-mm (0.5-in) and a 7.62-mm (0.3-in) machine-gun, and these were delivered by late 1983.

When used as an armoured personnel carrier the Transportpanzer can carry 10 fully equipped troops in addition to the commander and driver. In the West German army, however, the Transportpanzer is normally used for more specialized roles. The NBC reconnaissance vehicle, of which 140 are being built, is fitted with NBC detection equipment, and devices for taking soil samples and for marking the ground. The engineers have 220 vehicles which they use for carrying mines and demolition equipment about the battlefield. The electronic warfare version is the **TPz-1 Eloka** and has a large number of antennae on the roof and a generator to provide sufficient power to run the equipment. The supply units have 220 vehicles to supply forward units with ammunition and other essential supplies, and this model can also be used as a forward ambulance carrying up to four stretcher patients. The radar carrier has a RASIT battlefield surveillance radar mounted on a hydraulic arm which is raised above the roof of the vehicle, and this can be operated up to 30 m (98 ft) from the vehicle by remote control. There is also a command and control model with extensive communications equipment and a generator at the rear. The West German army vehicles are normally armed with a 7.62-mm (0.3-in) machine-gun above the commander's position but other weapons can be fitted on the roof of the troop compartment, including a 20-mm cannon. Mounted on the left side of the hull is a bank of six smoke dischargers firing forwards.

The commander and driver are seated at the front of the Transportpanzer

Above: Thyssen-Henschel of Kassel had by 1986 completed 996 Transportpanzer 1 (6×6) Fuchs amphibious vehicles for the West German army, which are used in a wide range of roles including that of NBC reconnaissance vehicle, load carrier and engineer vehicle.

Right: The Transportpanzer 1 is fully amphibious, being driven through water at up to 10.5 km/h (6.5 mph) by twin propellers. The twin vane seen extended at the front is built into the vehicle.

with the engine immediately behind them on the left and the troop compartment at the rear; a small aisle connects the front and rear compartments. The latter has seats down each side, and these seats can be quickly folded to allow cargo to be carried. The compartment has two doors in the rear, roof hatches and three vision blocks. The Transportpanzer is fully amphibious, being propelled in the water by two propellers at the rear of the hull for a maximum water speed of 10.5 km/h (6.5 mph). All West German vehicles have an NBC system and passive night-vision equipment. Steering is power assisted on the front two axles.

Though the last Transportpanzer was built in 1986, the manufacturers could resume production if any further orders were placed. As is usual with modern APCs, a wide variety of weapon systems can be fitted for export versions.

Specification
Transportpanzer 1
Crew: 2+10

Combat weight: 17000 kg (37,479 lb)
Powerplant: one Mercedes-Benz OM 402A V-8 diesel developing 320 hp (239 kW)
Dimensions: length 6.76 m (22 ft 2.1 in); width 2.98 m (9 ft 9.3 in); height without armament 2.30 m (7 ft 6.5 in)
Performance: maximum road speed 105 km/h (65 mph); maximum range 800 km (497 miles); fording amphibious; gradient 70 per cent; trench 1.6 m (5 ft 3 in)

Condor armoured personnel carrier

Following the success of the UR-416 armoured personnel carrier, Thyssen Henschel decided to develop a new vehicle with improved armour protection, greater speed and range, increased load-carrying capability, fully amphibious performance and able to mount heavier armament installations. The first prototype of this vehicle, called the **Condor**, was completed in 1978 and an initial sale was soon made to Uruguay. In 1981 Malaysia placed its largest ever order for armoured vehicles when 459 Condors were ordered

from Thyssen Henschel and 186 SIB-MAS 6×6 vehicles from Belgium.

The Condor has an all-welded steel hull which provides the crew with protection from small arms fire and shell splinters. Wherever possible standard automotive components (such as the engine and transmission) are taken from commercial sources to keep costs to a minimum. The Condor has a three-man crew consisting of the commander, who would normally dismount with the troops, the gunner and the driver, and carries nine fully equipped

infantrymen. The driver is seated at the front left with the commander to his rear, each having a single-piece hatch cover that opens to the rear. The driver has excellent vision to his front and sides through large bullet-proof windows. In the combat area these would normally be covered by quickly erectable armoured shutters, forward observation then being maintained via a roof-mounted periscope. The engine compartment is to the right of the driver, and the troop compartment at the rear. Entry to the latter is effected via

three doors, one in each side and one in the rear. The infantry sit on individual seats and can use their weapons from within the vehicle via firing ports and/or vision blocks. The main armament installation is normally in the centre of the hull, and can range from a turret with one or twin 7.62-mm (0.3 in) machine-guns right up to a power-operated turret with a 20-mm cannon. For the anti-tank role the vehicle has already been fitted, for trials purposes, with the Euromissile HOT turret with four ATGWs in the ready-to-launch

Left: A Thyssen Henschel Condor (4×4) armoured personnel carrier with a Rheinmetall TUR-1 one-man turret armed with twin 7.62-mm (0.3-in) machine-guns. In 1981 Malaysia ordered a total of 459 Condors, and all of these have now been delivered. The vehicle is fully amphibious.

Right: A Thyssen Henschel Condor (4×4) armoured personnel carrier fitted with a one-man turret armed with a 20-mm cannon and co-axial 7.62-mm (0.3-in) machine-gun. In addition to its three-man crew of commander, gunner and driver it can also carry 9 fully-equipped troops and their supplies.

position, additional missiles being carried in the hull. When fitted with a one-man turret accommodating a 20-mm cannon and a 7.62-mm (0.3-in) machine-gun, totals of 220 rounds of 20-mm and 50 rounds of 7.62-mm (0.3-in) ready-use ammunition are carried. The turret can also be fitted with smoke-dischargers or grenade-launchers on each side.

The Condor is fully amphibious, being propelled in the water by a single rear-hull propeller at a speed of 8 km/h (5 mph); before the vehicle enters the water a trim vane is erected at the front of the hull and the bilge pumps are switched on. The Condor can be equipped with a wide range of optional equipment such as passive night-vision devices, an NBC and/or air-conditioning system, various intercoms and radios, and a winch. The last is suggested as standard equipment for many parts of the world, for

although the Condor has excellent amphibious capability, like most other vehicles it sometimes needs assistance in order to leave a river when the banks are very steep.

Specification
Condor
Crew: 3+9
Combat weight: 12000 kg (26,455 lb)
Powerplant: one Daimler-Benz OM

352A 6-cylinder diesel developing 168 hp (125 kW)
Dimensions: length 6.05 m (19 ft 10.2 in); width 2.47 m (8 ft 1.2 in); height without armament 2.10 m (6 ft 10.7 in)
Performance: maximum road speed 100 km/h (62 mph); maximum range 900 km (559 miles); fording amphibious; gradient 60 per cent; vertical obstacle 0.55 m (1 ft 9.7in); trench not applicable

WEST GERMANY
UR-416 armoured personnel carrier

The Daimler-Benz Unimog 4×4 was developed originally as a civilian vehicle in the period after World War II and soon established an excellent reputation for its cross-country capabilities. Development has continued, and the Unimog range of trucks, with typical payloads of one to four tonnes, is today used by many armed forces around the world, including those of Argentina, West Germany, New Zealand and Australia to name but a few.

In the early 1960s Rheinstahl Maschinenbau (now part of the Thyssen group) saw that there was a considerable overseas market for an armoured personnel carrier based on the chassis of the Unimog 4×4 truck, and the first **UR-416** prototype was completed in 1965. Production got under way four years later. By 1984 almost 1,000 vehicles had been completed, with sales made to countries in Black Africa, North Africa, South and Central America and the Far East, as well as to some European countries. European operators employ the type mainly for airport patrol and riot control, while other countries use them for reconnaissance as well as their designed roles of carrying troops. The UR-416 is a relatively inexpensive vehicle and is simple to maintain and operate. Spare parts are not a problem as the chassis is identical to that of the Mercedes-Benz Unimog light truck.

The all-welded hull is 9 mm (0.35 in) thick and provides the crew with protection from small arms fire and shell splinters. The commander and driver are seated at the front with the eight fully equipped troops to their rear, three down each side facing outwards and two at the rear facing the rear. Firing ports are provided in the hull sides and rear to allow the troops to fire their rifles from inside the vehicle, and if required these standard ports can be replaced by spherical firing ports and an observation block which allows each man to fire his rifle or submachine gun from within the vehicle in

complete safety. The UR-416 has two roof hatches, the forward one normally being fitted with a 7.62-mm (0.3-in) machine-gun that can also be provided with a shield.

As with most vehicles of this type, the UR-416 can be fitted with a wide range of optional equipment such as a rear-mounted winch with a capacity of 5000 kg (11,023 lb), passive or active night-vision equipment, an obstacle-clearing blade at the front of the hull, a public address system, flashing lights, a heater, a fire extinguisher, an air-conditioning system and run-flat tyres. In addition to the normal pintle-mounted 7.62-mm (0.3-in) machine-gun, other armament installations that can be fitted include a turret with one or two 7.62-mm (0.3-in) machine-guns, a turret with a 20-mm cannon, or a special cupola for use in internal security roles with vision devices and the ability to mount a rifle to engage snipers. More specialized versions include a repair vehicle complete with jib crane

and a complete set of tools, an ambulance, and a command vehicle with extensive communications equipment. It was also proposed that the UR-416 could be fitted with a recoilless rifle or anti-tank guided missiles for use in the anti-tank roles, but as far as is known neither of these were placed in production.

Specification
UR-416
Crew: 2+8
Combat weight: 7600 kg (16,755 lb)
Powerplant: one Daimler-Benz OM 352 6-cylinder diesel developing 120 hp (89 kW)
Dimensions: length 5.21 m (17 ft 1 in); width 2.30 m (7 ft 6.5 in); height without armament 2.225 m (7 ft 3.6 in)
Performance: maximum road speed 85 km/h (53 mph); maximum range 600 to 700 km (373 to 435 miles); fording 1.4 m (4 ft 7 in); gradient 75 per cent; vertical obstacle 0.55 m (1 ft 9.7 in); trench not applicable

Above: Thyssen Maschinenbau UR-416 armoured personnel carrier.

The Thyssen Maschinenbau UR-416 armoured personnel carrier is based on the chassis of the Mercedes-Benz Unimog (4×4) vehicle, which has exceptional cross-country mobility and is easy to maintain and operate.

TM 170 armoured personnel carrier

Using company money, Thyssen Maschinenbau of Witten-Annen has developed three light armoured personnel carriers of the wheeled variety, all of them using proven and common commercial components to keep procurement and operating costs to an absolute minimum. The vehicles are the **TM 170**, **TM 125** and the **TM 90**. The largest member of the family is the TM 170, which has a two-man crew and can carry 10 fully equipped infantrymen, although more often than not it is used in the internal security role for the rapid and safe transport of riot squads to spots at which they are needed.

In the early 1960s Bussing and Henschel in West Germany built some 600 of the Swiss-designed MOWAG MR 8 series of 4×4 armoured personnel carriers for the Federal German border police, although at a later date some of these were transferred to the state police. By the early 1980s it had been decided to start replacing this old vehicle with a more modern type, and after looking at the various vehicles on offer, the border police and state police selected the TM 170 under the designation **SW1** being the SW1 being the basic MR 8, the SW2 being the same vehicle with a turret-mounted 20-mm cannon and the SW3 an armoured version of the Mercedes-Benz light jeep type vehicle. At least 250 examples of the SW4 are required, although funding problems have meant that the initial order was for only 87 vehicles, the first of these being delivered in 1983.

The TM 170 has a hull of all-welded steel construction with the engine at the very front of the hull and coupled to a manual gearbox with four forward and one reverse gear. For road use the driver would normally select 4×2 (rear wheels only) drive, while for cross country the front axles would also be engaged for 4×4 (all wheel) drive. The commander and driver have bullet-proof windows to their front, and in combat these are covered by armoured shutters, observation then being obtained through roof-mounted periscopes. An entry door is provided in each side of the hull and rear, and firing ports and/or vision blocks enable the troops or police to aim their weapons safely from inside the vehicle. The basic vehicle is fully amphibious, being propelled in the water by its wheels; before the vehicle enters the water a trim vane is erected at the front of the hull. For increased water speed the TM 170 can be fitted with waterjets, which give a maximum speed of 9 km/h (5.6 mph). A variety of armament stations can be fitted on the roof including turret- or pintle-mounted 7.62-mm (0.3-in) machine-guns or even 20-mm cannon. Specialized equipment for the riot-control role includes a hydraulically-operated dozer blade at the front of the hull (for clearing street barricades and pushing cars and other obstacles out of the way) and a special observation cupola.

The latest production model is the

Armoured Special Vehicle TM 170 **Hardliner** which has a number of detail improvements on earlier models, although it is no longer amphibious. The TM 125 and TM 90 are no longer offered.

Specification
TM 170
Crew: 2+12
Combat weight: 9500 kg (20,944 lb)
Powerplant: one Daimler-Benz OM 352 supercharged diesel developing 168 hp (125 kW)
Dimensions: length 6.10 m (20 ft 0 in); width 2.45 m (8 ft 0.5 in); height 2.22 m

A Thyssen Maschinenbau TM 170 (4×4) armoured personnel carrier with the hatches over the windscreen in the lowered position. The TM 170 has been selected by the West German Border Guard and State Police to replace the old SW1 and SW2 vehicles.

(7 ft 3.4 in)
Performance: maximum road speed 100 km/h (62 mph); maximum range 670 km (416 miles); fording amphibious; gradient 80 per cent; vertical obstacle 0.5 m (1 ft 7.7 in); trench not applicable

---

PSZH-IV armoured personnel carrier

In the 1960s Hungary developed the FUG 4×4 amphibious scout car, which it uses in place of the Soviet BRDM vehicle. Further development resulted in a vehicle which was seen in the mid-1960s and called the **FUG-66** or **FUG-70**. It was originally thought that this was the replacement for the original FUG and that it would be used in place of the Soviet BRDM-2 4×4 amphibious scout car. After some time it was discovered that the new vehicle was in reality called the **PSZH-IV** and that its role was that of a personnel carrier.

The hull of the PSZH-IV is of all-welded steel construction with a maximum thickness of 14 mm (0.55 in). The commander and driver are seated at the front of the vehicle, each being provided to his front with a windscreen that can be quickly covered by an armoured shutter with an integral periscope. Above their position is a single-piece roof hatch and to each side is a vision block. Mounted in the centre of the roof is a one-man turret armed with a 14.5-mm (0.57-in) KPVT machine-gun with a 7.62-mm (0.3-in) PKT machine-gun mounted co-axially to the left. Both weapons have an elevation of +30° and a depression of −5°, turret traverse being 360°. Totals of 500 rounds of 14.5-mm (0.57-in) and 2,000 rounds of 7.62-mm (0.3-in) ammunition are carried. The turret is of Hungarian design and is not the same as that fitted to the Soviet BRDM-2 amphibious scout car.

The troops enter and leave the PSZH-IV through a door in each side of the hull; each door is in two parts, upper and lower, and opens towards the front of the vehicle. The engine, which

is the same as that installed in the earlier FUG amphibious scout car, is mounted at the rear of the hull. The PSZH-IV is fully amphibious, being propelled in the water at a speed of 9 km/h (5.6 mph) by two waterjets at the rear of the hull. Before the vehicle enters the water the bilge pumps are switched on and a trim vane is erected at the front of the hull (when not required the latter is stowed on the glacis plate). Like most Warsaw Pact vehicles developed in recent years, the PSZH-IV is fitted with a central tyre-pressure regulation system (allowing the driver to adjust the tyre pressure to suit the type of ground being crossed), an NBC system and infra-red night-vision equipment for the gunner and commander.

There are a number of variants of the PSZH-IV including two command vehicles (one with and the other without the turret), an ambulance model (although loading of stretchers cannot be considered to be an easy occupation) and an NBC reconnaissance vehicle. The last is probably provided with equipment to detect NBC agents and then drop pennants into the ground to mark a path through the contaminated area. The PSZH-IV is operated by Bulgaria, Czechoslovakia, East Germany, Hungary and Iraq.

Specification
PSZH-IV
Crew: 3+6
Combat weight: 7500 kg (16,535 lb)
Powerplant: Caspel 4-cylinder diesel

When the PSZH-IV was first seen in the early 1960s its role was believed to be that of a reconnaissance vehicle, but it was later discovered that it was in fact an armoured personnel carrier and carried six troops in addition to its three-man crew consisting of a commander, gunner and driver.

developing 100 hp (74.57 kW)
Dimensions: length 5.70 m (18 ft 8.4 in); width 2.50 m (8 ft 2.4 in); height 2.30 m (7 ft 7 in)
Performance: maximum road speed 80 km/h (50 mph); maximum range 500 km (311 miles); fording amphibious; gradient 60 per cent; vertical obstacle 0.4 m (1 ft 3.7 in); trench 0.6 m (1 ft 11.6 in)

Renault VAB armoured personnel carrier

Some years ago the French army decided to issue its infantry battalions with both tracked and wheeled armoured personnel carriers, the former being the AMX-10P built by the ARE. To meet the requirement for the wheeled vehicle, designated **VAB** (*Véhicule de l'Avant Blindé*, or front armoured vehicle), prototypes were built by Panhard and Saviem/Renault in both 4×4 and 6×6 configurations. In May 1974 the Renault design was selected, and first production vehicles were delivered to the French army in 1976. The total French army requirement is for at least 4,000 vehicles, and production is already running at between 30 and 50 vehicles per month. Over a thousand had been exported by 1987 to countries including the Ivory Coast, Cyprus, Lebanon, Mauritius, Morocco, Oman, Qatar and the United Arab Emirates. Of these Morocco is the largest operator, having purchased over 400 vehicles; some of these have already been lost in the fighting in the Sahara against the Polisario guerrillas.

The VAB is currently produced in 4×4 and 6×6 configurations, the latter costing about 10 per cent more but having greater cross-country capability. At present the French army uses only the 4×4 model.

The VAB has a hull of all-welded steel armour construction with the driver and commander at the front (the latter also operating the roof-mounted 7.62-mm/0.3-in machine-gun), the engine compartment to their immediate rear, and the troop compartment at the rear of the hull; an aisle connects the front of the vehicle with the troop compartment. The infantry enter and leave via two doors in the hull rear, and the troops are seated five down each side facing the centre. The VAB is fully amphibious, being propelled in the water by its wheels or, as an option, by two waterjets at the rear of the hull. Standard equipment on French army vehicles includes an NBC system and passive night-vision equipment.

French army VABs are fitted with a cupola-mounted 7.62-mm (0.3-in) machine-gun, but a wide range of other armament options is available, including turret-mounted 12.7-mm (0.5-in) machine-guns and 20-mm cannon. The basic vehicle has also been adopted for a wide range of other roles including a forward ambulance, internal security vehicle, command vehicle, repair vehicle, 81-mm mortar carrier, 120-mm (4.72-in) mortar tower, anti-aircraft vehicle (with twin 20-mm rapid-fire cannon or short range SAMs) and anti-tank vehicle. There

are two versions of the latter, the **UTM 800** and the **Mephisto**. The former has a turret with four HOT ATGWs in the ready-to-launch position, while the latter has a similar number of HOT ATGWs on a launcher retracted flush along the top of the hull until it is required for action.

To reduce operation and procurement costs, well tried commercial components have been used in the design of the VAB range of armoured vehicles. Using the same automotive components, Renault has designed the **VBC 90** 6×6 armoured car which is now in service with Oman, the UAE and the French Gendarmerie.

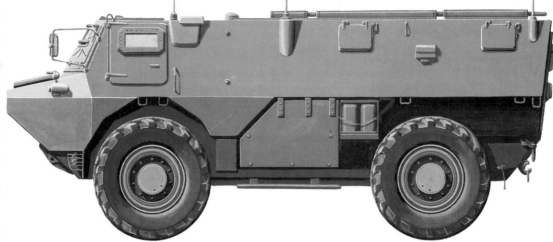

Above: At present the French army uses only the 4×4 VAB, which is slightly cheaper than the 6×6. This particular VAB is not fitted with water jets under the hull at the rear, or with a roof-mounted weapon station, which normally carries a 7.62-mm (0.3-in) MG.

Above: A Renault VAB (6×6) for the export market, fitted with the new Creusot-Loire one-man turret armed with a 20-mm cannon. The VAB can be fitted with a wide range of armament systems to enable it to undertake different roles on the battlefield.

Below: A Renault VAB (4×4) vehicle used by the French army and fitted with the RATAC (Radar de Tir pour Artillerie de Campagne) radar on the roof. This can detect, identify, locate and automatically track a variety of ground targets, including armoured vehicles.

Specification
VAB (4×4 model)
Crew: 2+10
Combat weight: 13000 kg (28,660 lb)
Powerplant: one MAN 6-cylinder inline diesel developing 235 hp (175 kW)
Dimensions: length 5.98 m (19 ft 7.4 in); width 2.49 m (8 ft 2 in); height without armament 2.06 m (6 ft 9 in)
Performance: maximum road speed 92 km/h (57 mph); maximum road range 1000 km (621 miles); fording amphibious; gradient 60 per cent; vertical obstacle 0.6 m (2 ft 0 in); trench not applicable

---

Berliet VXB-170 armoured personnel carrier

After World War II Berliet was a major supplier of trucks to the French army, and in the late 1960s designed and built the prototype of a wheeled APC called the **BL-12** which used a number of standard heavy duty commercial components. Further development of this resulted in the **VXB-170** which was subsequently adopted by the French Gendarmerie as well as Gabon and Senegal. In 1975 Berliet was taken over by the Renault group, who had by then already built prototypes of 4×4 and 6×6 vehicles to meet the French army VAB requirement. With the accept-

ance of the Renault/Saviem vehicle to meet this requirement, production and marketing of the VXB-170 ceased as there was no point in two parts of the same group producing vehicles of a

A Berliet VXB (4×4) armoured personnel carrier at speed with armoured shutters over the driver's windscreens in the open position. When in a combat zone these cover the windscreens, and the driver then sees the terrain ahead through three roof-mounted periscopes.

similar nature.

The hull of the VXB-170 is of all-welded steel construction with a maximum thickness of 7 mm (0.27 in). The driver is seated at the front of the hull in the centre with a large windscreen to his front and a smaller one on each side. In an internal security situation these windscreens are covered by armoured flaps and the driver then observes the terrain ahead through three roof-mounted periscopes. The troops enter the vehicle through three doors, one in each side and the third in the hull rear on the right side. Hatches are provided in the roof, and as usual a wide range of armament installations could be fitted. The vehicles used by the French Gendarmerie have a small SAMM one-man turret armed with a 7.62-mm (0.3-in) machine-gun and a 40-mm grenade-launcher which can be elevated from −15° to +60°; the grenade-launcher is normally used to launch tear gas grenades to disperse crowds.

The engine compartment is at the rear of the vehicle on the right side, and the diesel engine is coupled to a pre-selective gearbox with six forward and one reverse gear and a two-speed transfer case. Steering is power-assisted to reduce driver fatigue, and the suspension consists of helical springs and hydraulic shock absorbers. The VXB-170 is fully amphibious, being propelled in the water by its wheels at a speed of 4 km/h (2.5 mph); waterjets were offered as an option,

but as far as it is known these were never fitted to any production APCs. Vehicles used by the French Gendarmerie have a hydraulically-operated obstacle-clearing blade at the front of the hull, and optional equipment includes bullet-proof tyres, night-vision equipment, a winch and a heater.

Berliet offered three families of the VXB-170: one was for internal security use and the two others were the light reconnaissance vehicle and the light combat vehicle. These were offered with a wide range of weapon options including the Hispano-Suiza turret armed with twin 7.62-mm (0.3-in) machine-guns and a 60-mm breech/muzzle-loaded mortar, and the H-90 turret armed with a 90-mm (3.54-in) gun and a 7.62-mm (0.3-in) co-axial machine gun; both turrets were at that time standard for the Panhard AML-90 light armoured car.

Specification
VXB-170
Crew: 1+11
Combat weight: 12700 kg (27,997 lb)
Powerplant: one Berliet V 800 M V-8 diesel developing 170 hp (127 kW)
Dimensions: length 5.99 m (19 ft 8 in); width 2.50 m (8 ft 2.4 in); height without armament 2.05 m (6 ft 8.7 in)
Performance: maximum road speed 85 km/h (53 mph); maximum road range 750 km (466 miles); fording amphibious; gradient 60 per cent; vertical obstacle 0.3 m (1 ft 0 in); trench not applicable

Infantry armed with 9-mm MAT 49 sub-machine guns remount their Berliet VXB 170 (4×4) armoured personnel carrier while the 7.62-mm *(0.3-in) machine-gunner prepares to give covering fire if required. The largest user of the VXB is the French Gendarmerie.*

A Berliet VXB-170 (4×4) armoured personnel carrier with all roof hatches open. When the Berliet company was taken over by Renault *the VXB family was phased out of production as the Renault VAB (4×4 and 6×6) series had more scope for further development.*

FRANCE

Panhard VCR armoured personnel carrier

Following the success of its AML and M3 range of 4×4 armoured vehicles, Panhard went on to develop the ERC 6×6 armoured car and **VCR** 6×6 armoured personnel carrier, which share over 90 per cent common automotive components such as engine, transmission, suspension, steering and wheels. The first prototype of the VCR (*Véhicule de Combat à Roues*, or wheeled combat vehicle) was shown in 1977, the first production vehicles being completed just two years later. The VCR has been designed specifically for the export market, and known sales have been made to Argentina, Iraq and the United Arab Emirates.

The VCR has an all-welded hull which varies in thickness from 8 to 12 mm (0.315 to 0.47 in), the very front of the vehicle being almost identical with that of the Panhard M3 4×4 armoured personnel carrier. The driver is seated at the front with the engine to his right rear and the commander to his left rear. Both have a single-piece

hatch cover and periscopes for observation. The troop compartment is at the rear and has twin doors in the hull rear, with roof hatches and firing/observation ports in the upper part. The main armament is normally mounted over the forward part of the troop compartment and can consist of a pintle-mounted 7.62-mm (0.3-in) or 12.7-mm (0.5-in) machine-gun, or a turret with similar weapons or a 20-mm cannon. An unusual feature of the VCR is its wheel arrangement as all six wheels are powered, with power-assisted steering on the front wheels only. When the VCR is travelling on roads, the centre road wheel on each side is normally raised off the ground. The VCR is fully amphibious, being propelled in the water by its wheels at a speed of 4 km/h (2.48 mph). Optional equipment includes an air-conditioning system, passive night-vision equipment, an NBC system and a front-mounted winch for self-recovery or assisting other vehicles.

The first model to enter production

was the **VCR/TH** anti-tank vehicle, of which 106 have been supplied to Iraq. This is fitted with the Euromissile UTM 800 turret with four HOT ATGWs in the ready-to-fire position and a further 10 missiles in the hull. Mounted over the rear part of the troop compartment is a remote-controlled 7.62-mm (0.3-in) machine-gun. This model has a crew of four and has been used in the fighting between Iraq and Iran. The ambulance version is the **VCR/IS**, and has a higher roof so the medical staff can stand up. This can carry six seated and two stretcher patients or four stretcher patients plus the three-man crew consisting of commander, driver and medical orderly. The ambulance version is known to have been supplied to the United Arab Emirates. The command post version is the **VCR/PC**, which has communications equipment and mapboards. The repair vehicle is the **VCR/AT**, fitted with a block and tackle for lifting out engines and other components; it carries a full range of spares and tools, but no winch.

The **VCR TT 2** is a private venture from Panhard, using many of the components of the Sagaie 2 armoured car. It is larger and more powerful than it's predecessor, and can be fitted with the usual wide variety of armament. There is also a 4×4 version of the VCR, which has only been sold to Argentina.

Specification
VCR
Crew: 3+9
Combat weight: 7000 kg (15,432 lb)
Powerplant: one Peugeot PRV V-6 petrol engine developing 155 hp (115.6 kW)
Dimensions: length 4.565 m (14 ft 11.7 in); width 2.495 m (8 ft 2.2 in); height without armament 2.03 m (6 ft 8 in)
Performance: maximum road speed 100 km/h (62 mph); maximum range 800 km (497 miles); fording amphibious; gradient 60 per cent; vertical obstacle 0.8 m (2 ft 7.5 in); trench 1.1 m (3 ft 7.3 in)

A standard Panhard VCR/TT armoured personnel carrier with a 20-mm cannon over the forward part of the troop compartment and a 7.62-mm (0.3-in) machine-gun at rear.

The Panhard VCR/TH anti-tank vehicle is fitted with a Euromissile UTM-800 one-man turret armed with four Euromissile HOT long-range anti-tank weapons.

The Panhard ENC 81-mm mortar gun carrier is a member of the ERC range of armoured cars which shares common components with the VCR range of APCs.

This Panhard VCR/TT armoured personnel carrier is fitted with a one-man turret armed with a 20-mm cannon. All VCRs are fully amphibious without preparation.

Panhard M3 armoured personnel carrier

FRANCE

The **M3** armoured personnel carrier was designed as a private venture by Panhard, and the first production vehicles were completed in 1971. The vehicle uses 95 per cent common automotive components with the Panhard AML armoured car, of which some 4,000 have now been built by Panhard or manufactured under licence in South Africa by Sandock-Austral. This enables a country to purchase a fleet of armoured cars and personnel carriers which share the same components, permitting significant savings in training and spare parts holdings. Over 25 countries have now purchased the vehicle, some for army use and some for police use.

The hull of the M3 is of all-welded steel armour construction which varies in thickness from 8 to 11 mm (0.315 to 0.43 in). The driver is seated at the front of the hull, with the engine to his immediate rear. The engine is coupled to a manual gearbox with six forward and one reverse gear, and power is transmitted to the four road wheels by drive shafts that run inside the hull. The troop compartment is at the rear of the hull, a single door being provided in each side of the hull and twin doors in the hull rear. In the upper part of the hull side, which slopes inwards, are three hatches hinged at the top, these enabling troops to use their small arms from within the vehicle. The main armament is normally mounted in the roof to the rear of the engine compartment, this armament ranging from a turret with single or twin 7.62-mm (0.3-in) machine-guns to a power-operated turret with a 20-mm cannon.

The M3 is fully amphibious, being propelled in the water by its wheels at a speed of 4 km/h (2.48 mph), but it can only operate in lakes and rivers with a slow current. Many vehicles are fitted with channels which can be quickly removed and placed in front of the vehicle to allow it to cross ditches and other battlefield obstacles. If required, the M3 can be fitted with passive night-vision equipment for the driver, an air-conditioning system (essential in the Middle East) and smoke dischargers. The basic M3 has also been adopted for a number of more specialized roles. The anti-aircraft model is called the **M3 VDA** and is fitted with a power-operated turret armed with twin 20-mm cannon. The **M3 VAT** repair vehicle has a full range of tools and is fitted with a jib for lifting engines in the field. The **M3 VPC** command vehicle has extensive communications equipment. The ambulance model of the family is

This Panhard M3 armoured personnel carrier has the driver's hatch open and is fitted with a Creusot-Loire STB shield with a 7.62-mm (0.3-in) machine-gun. Designed as a private venture, the M3 has been purchased by more than 25 countries, with more than 4000 vehicles in service.

A standard Panhard M3 armoured personnel carrier showing rear troop doors and a roof-mounted 7.62-mm (0.3-in) machine-gun. All M3s are fully amphibious.

The anti-aircraft member of the family is called the M3 VDA and is fitted with a one-man turret armed with twin 20-mm cannon.

This Panhard M3 is used in the fire support role and is fitted with a Brandt Type HB 60-mm breech/muzzle loaded mortar in a special mount.

called the **M3 VTS** and is unarmed. The engineer vehicle version is the **M3 VLA**, and is fitted with a hydraulically-operated dozer blade at the front of the hull for clearing obstacles.

The M3 is no longer in production, having been replaced by a much improved model known as the **Buffalo**. This has greatly increased external stowage and a choice of petrol or diesel engines. First ordered by Be-

nin, it will probably be built in as many versions as the M3.

Specification
M3
Crew: 2+10
Combat weight: 6100 kg (13,448 lb)
Powerplant: one Panhard Model 4 HD 4-cylinder petrol engine developing

90 hp (67 kW)
Dimensions: length 4.45 m (14 ft 7.2 in); width 2.40 m (7 ft 10.5 in); height without armament 2.00 m (6 ft 6.7 in)
Performance: maximum road speed 90 km/h (56 mph); maximum range 600 km (373 miles); fording amphibious; gradient 60 per cent; vertical obstacle 0.3 m (11¾ in); trench with one channel 0.8 m (2 ft 7.5 in) or with three channels 3.1 m (10 ft 2 in)

ACMAT armoured personnel carrier

FRANCE

For well over 25 years the Ateliers de Construction Mécanique de l'Atlantique (ACMAT) have been building a wide range of 4×4 and 6×6 cross-country trucks which have exceptional range and durability. These have been sold to more than 30 countries in Africa, the Middle East and the Far East. The company also realized that there was a market for an armoured personnel carrier on the same chassis and has produced the 4×4 **TPK 4.20 VSC**, which is in service with a number of the countries using the VLRA light truck and reconnaissance vehicle.

The layout of the TPK 4.20 VSC is similar to that of a truck, with the en-

gine at the front, commander and driver in the centre and the troop compartment at the rear. The commander and driver each have a windscreen to their front which can be quickly covered by an armoured shutter, a side door with a bullet-proof window in its upper part, and a single-piece hatch cover above their position.

An ACMAT VSC armoured personnel carrier with an open-topped troop compartment, in which can be mounted an 81-mm mortar or other types of weapons. The ACMAT armoured vehicles have exceptional range and durability.

The troops are seated on bench seats down each side of the vehicle, and can exit quickly through the two doors in the hull rear. If required, firing ports and/or vision blocks can be provided in the sides and rear of the troop compartment, and a 7.62-mm (0.3-in) or 12.7-mm (0.5-in) machine-gun turret can be mounted on the roof of the vehicle to give covering fire while the infantry dismount from the vehicle. Another model of the vehicle has an open-topped rear troop compartment with sides that can quickly folded down on the outside.

The well proven Perkins six-cylinder diesel engine is coupled to a manual gearbox with four forward and one reverse gear and a two-speed transfer case. Steering is of the worm and nut type, and the exceptional operating range of 1600 km (994 miles) results from the large-capacity fuel tank, which holds 370 litres (81.4 Imp gal). A spare wheel and tyre is normally carried on the wall to the immediate rear of the commander's and driver's position. Optional equipment includes an air-conditioning system, essential in many parts of the world if the infantry

are to arrive at their objective in any condition to fight, and different radio systems. Other armament options include a Euromissile MILAN ATGW system with additional missiles carried internally in the troop compartment, and an 81-mm Brandt mortar firing to the rear. In most infantry battalions six or eight mortars are normally issued to provide immediate and close-range support for the infantry. Artillery support is normally not organic to an infantry battalion, although for some missions (for example a long-range patrol in North Africa by a battalion of infantry in ACMAT trucks), it would often have a battery of four 105-mm (4.13-in) howitzers towed by similar vehicles.

Specification
TPK 4.20 VSC
Crew: 2+8
Combat weight: 7300 kg (16,094 lb)
Powerplant: one Perkins Model 6.354.4 6-cylinder diesel developing 125 hp (93 kW)
Dimensions: length 5.98 m (19 ft 7.4 in); width 2.07 m (6 ft 9.5 in); height 2.21 m (7 ft 3 in)
Performance: maximum road speed

95 km/h (59 mph); maximum range 1600 km (994 miles); fording 0.8 m (2 ft 7.5 in); gradient 60 per cent; trench not applicable

An ACMAT VBL light armoured car with all hatches closed and fitted with a one-man Creusot-Loire turret armed with one machine-gun.

BMR-600 infantry fighting vehicle

In the early 1970s the Spanish army issued a requirement for a 6×6 infantry fighting vehicle which was subsequently developed by ENASA and the Spanish army under the designation **Pegaso 3.500**, later **BMR-600** (*Blindado Medio de Ruedas*, or wheeled medium armoured vehicle). This was tested alongside the Swiss MOWAG Piranha 6×6 and French Renault VAB 6×6 vehicles, and accepted for service against a total requirement for at least 500. The company have now developed a complete family of vehicles using the same basic chassis, namely the **Pegaso 3560/1** armoured personnel carrier, the **Pegaso 3560/3** 81-mm mortar carrier, the **Pegaso 3560/4** 120-mm mortar towing vehicle, the **Pegaso 3560/5** battalion command vehicle and the **Pegaso 3564** fire-support vehicle which can be fitted with a variety of turrets such as the French TS-90 (two-man turret armed with a 90-mm (3.54-in) gun. The **Pegaso 3562 VEC** cavalry scout vehicle has a brand new hull but uses the same automotive components as the basic infantry fighting vehicle, and is fitted with a two-man power-operated turret armed with a 20-mm or 25-mm cannon; this model is already in service with the Spanish army.

The hull of the BMR-600 armoured personnel carrier is of all-welded aluminium construction which provides complete protection against 7.62-mm (0.3-in) armour-piercing rounds over the frontal arc and 7.62-mm (0.3-in) ball over the remainder of the vehicle. The driver is seated at the front of the vehicle on the left with the machine-gunner/radio operator to his rear and the engine compartment to their right. The troop compartment is at the rear of the hull, and has accommodation for 11 fully equipped troops who enter and leave the vehicle through a power-operated ramp in the hull rear. Depending on the model, firing ports and/or vision blocks are provided in the troop compartment to allow the troops to fire their weapons from within the vehicle. The main armament normally

comprises a 7.62-mm (0.3-in) externally-mounted machine-gun, although other weapon stations can be fitted.

The vehicle is fully amphibious, and if required can be delivered with waterjets which give it a maximum water speed of 10 km/h (6.2 mph). Steering is powered to reduce driver fatigue, and is unusual in that it is on both the front and rear axles. The engine is coupled to an automatic transmission with six forward and one reverse gear, torque converter and hydraulic retarder.

Vehicles used by the Spanish army have a machine-gun with an elevation of +60° and a depression of −15° in a turret capable of 360° traverse. Some 2,500 rounds of ammunition are carried for this weapon. For trials purposes a BMR-600 has been fitted with the Euromissile HCT turret with four HOT wire-guided anti-tank missiles in the ready-to-launch position, additional missiles being carried in reserve. An anti-aircraft version with a 20-mm Meroka cannon or missiles is also being proposed.

Specification
BMR-600
Crew: 2+11
Combat weight: 13750 kg (30,313 lb)
Powerplant: one Pegaso 9157/8 6-cylinder diesel developing 306 hp (228 kW)
Dimensions: length 6.15 m (20 ft 2.1 in); width 2.50 m (8 ft 2.4 in); height to hull top 2.00 m (6 ft 6.7 in)
Performance: maximum road speed 100 km/h (62 mph); maximum range 700 km (435 miles); fording amphibious; gradient 68 per cent; vertical obstacle 0.8 m (2 ft 7.5 in); trench 1.2 m (3 ft 11.2 in)

A BMR-600 used in the fire support and anti-tank role, and fitted with the French GIAT TS-90 turret armed with the long-barrelled 90-mm gun which can fire a wide range of fixed ammunition, including APFSDS.

A BMR-600 infantry fighting vehicle as used by the Spanish army and fitted with a one-man turret armed with a remote-controlled 12.7-mm (0.5-in) M2 HB machine-gun. An unusual feature of this vehicle is that both the front and rear axles can be steered and the suspension adjusted to suit the type of terrain being crossed.

Ratel 20 infantry fighting vehicles

For many years the British-supplied Alvis Saracen 6×6 armoured personnel carrier was the standard vehicle of its type in the South African army. When it became apparent that future supplies of armoured vehicles and their all-essential spare parts were in some doubt, the South Africans decided to build a new vehicle to meet their own requirements. Then as now, Sandock-Austral was building a modified version of the Panhard AML 4×4 light armoured car for the South African army under the name Eland, and the task of designing and building the new vehicle was given to this company. The first prototype was completed in 1976, the first production vehicles being completed just two years later, a remarkable achievement by any standards. Since then some 1,000 examples of the **Ratel** have been built for the home market and for export to Morocco. The South African army used the type operationally for the first time in Operation 'Reindeer' in May 1978, and since then Ratels have been used on many of the deep strikes into Angola, where the type's large operating range has proved to be very useful. The Moroccans have used them against the Polisario guerrillas in the Sahara desert.

The basic vehicle is called the **Ratel 20** and carries a total of 11 men in the form of the commander and gunner in the turret, the driver at the front, the anti-aircraft machine-gunner at the rear and seven fully equipped infantry. The two-man turret is armed with a French-designed 20-mm dual-feed cannon and co-axial 7.62-mm (0.3-in) machine-gun, a similar weapon being located on the turret roof for anti-aircraft defence. Mounted on each side of the turret are two smoke-dischargers, and there is a 7.62-mm (0.3-in) anti-aircraft machine-gun at the right rear of the hull roof. The **Ratel 60** has a similar crew, but has a two-man turret armed with a 60-mm breech-loaded mortar, a 7.62-mm (0.3-in) co-axial and a 7.62-mm (0.3-in) anti-aircraft machine-gun. The **Ratel 90** is

the fire-support vehicle and has a two-man turret armed with the same 90-mm (3.54-in) gun as fitted to the Eland light armoured car, together with a 7.62-mm (0.3-in) co-axial and 7.62-mm (0.3-in) anti-aircraft machine-gun. Some 69 rounds of 90-mm (3.54-in) ammunition are carried, 29 in the turret and 40 in the hull, these being of the HEAT (high explosive anti-tank) or HE (high explosive) types. The command member of the family has a nine-man crew consisting of the commander, driver, main gunner and six command staff, and is armed with a turret-mounted 12.7-mm (0.5-in) M2 HB machine-gun and two 7.62-mm (0.3-in) anti-aircraft machine-guns.

Production of the Ratel has now ceased as it is being replaced by two new series of armoured vehicle. The last Ratel in production is a turretless mortar carrier, with an 81mm mortar mounted on a turntable and stowage for up to 180 mortar bombs. All Ratels can be converted to recovery vehicles by the addition of a small crane jib on the hull rear. One example of an 8×8 logistics support vehicle based on the Ratel was produced. It was designed to carry fuel, water, ammunition and supplies on long operations, but the job will now be done by a version of the new AC.200.

Specification
Ratel 20
Crew: 11
Combat weight: 19000 kg (41,888 lb)
Powerplant: one Model D 3256 BTXF 6-cylinder diesel developing 282 hp (210 kW)
Dimensions: length 7.212 m (23 ft 8 in); width 2.516 m (8 ft 3 in); height overall 2.915 m (9 ft 6.8 in)
Performance: maximum road speed 105 km/h (65 mph); maximum range 1000 km (621 miles); fording 1.2 m (3 ft 11.2 in); gradient 60 per cent; vertical obstacle 0.35 m (1 ft 1.7 in); trench 1.15 m (3 ft 9.3 in)

Above and below: The Ratel command vehicle is fitted with a two-man manually-operated turret armed with a 12.7-mm (0.5-in) M2 HB Browning and a 7.62-mm (0.3-in) machine-gun. The commander and gunner each have a raised cupola which give good all-round observation. This model has a nine-man crew consisting of a driver, commander, gunner and six command-post staff. Internally it has extensive communications equipment, intercom, lighting and map boards.

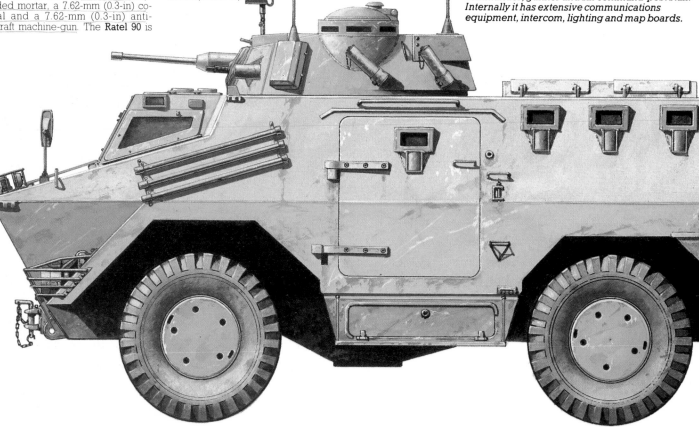

Above: South African infantrymen mount their Ratel (6×6) infantry fighting vehicle. This was designed by Sandock-Austral to meet very demanding requirements, including an operational range of 1000 km (621 miles) and excellent cross-country mobility.

BLR-600 armoured personnel carrier

The **BLR-600** (*Blindado Ligero de Ruedas*, or wheeled light armoured vehicle) is one of two armoured vehicles of the wheeled type currently being produced by Empresa Nacional de Autocamiones, the other being the BMR-600 6×6 infantry fighting vehicle. The BLR 4×4 vehicle is designed mainly for internal security operations, however, and is used in this role by the Spanish army and Spanish civil guard. Many of the automotive components are taken from standard commercial vehicles already in production.

The layout of the BLR is unusual, the commander and driver being seated at the front of the vehicle with excellent observation to the front and sides, an essential requirement for an internal security vehicle. The 12 fully equipped men are seated to the rear of the commander and driver and along the sides of the hull at the rear. The engine, coupled to an automatic transmission with torque converter and transfer case, is in the centre of the hull at the rear. No less than four doors are provided, one in each side and two in the rear, so that in the event of an ambush the troops quickly leave the vehicle through at least one of the doors. There are four hatches in the roof in addition to a cupola located on the forward part of the roof and armed with a 7.62-mm (0.3-in) machine-gun, with a shield to protect the gunner from enemy small arms fire. Depending on the actual model, firing ports and/or vision blocks are provided in the sides and rear of the troop compartment to allow the men to fire their weapons from within the vehicle.

The basic BLR is fitted with a six-cylinder water-cooled diesel developing 220 hp (164 kW), but the type is also available powered by a diesel engine developing only 170 hp (127 kW).

In many riot situations, petrol bombs are thrown at the internal security vehicles, and in addition to being fitted with the normal fire-suppression system in its engine compartment, the BLR has in each of the four road wheels hub outlets for fire suppressant in case the tyres catch fire. The tyres are fitted with puncture-proof Hutchinson O-rings. The commander's and driver's windows can be quickly covered by shutters, and each is provided with a standard water washer and another one filled with solvent to deal with paint or other liquids on the windscreens.

In addition to the less powerful engine already mentioned, the BLR can also be fitted with a wide range of optional equipment including a manual transmission in place of the automatic transmission, CS gas dischargers, loudspeakers (also essential in IS operations to warn crowds to disperse), power-take-off and so on.

Specification
BLR-600
Crew: 3 + 12
Combat weight: 11600 kg (25,574 lb)
Powerplant: one Pegaso 9220 6-cylinder diesel developing 220 hp (164 kW)
Dimensions: length 5.65 m (18 ft 6.4 in); width 2.5 m (8 ft 2.4 in); height without armament 1.99 m (6 ft 6.3 in)
Performance: maximum road speed 86 km/h (53.4 mph); maximum range 800 km (497 miles); fording 1.1 m (3 ft 7.3 in); gradient 75 per cent; vertical obstacle 0.6 m (1 ft 11.6 in); trench not applicable

A BLR (4×4) armoured personnel carrier from the rear with all of its doors in the open position. The large number of doors and hatches allows the 12 troops carried to quickly leave the vehicle in the event of an ambush. Firing ports and vision blocks are fitted.

The BLR (Blindado Ligero de Ruedas) was designed by Empresa Nacional de Autocamiones (who also build the BMR-600 IFV) mainly for use in the internal security role. It is now used by the Spanish army and Civil Guard. Armament normally comprises a 7.62-mm (0.3-in) or 12.7-mm (0.5-in) machine-gun.

AC 200 Armoured Support Vehicle

Sandock-Austral have combined the design knowledge acquired in building the Ratel series of infantry fighting vehicles with the South African Defence Force's operational experience in the **AC 200 Armoured Support Vehicle** prototype. It will replace the Ratel in production and almost certainly with the SADF.

The basic AC 200 is a mine protected 6×6 APC with a crew of three and able to carry ten troops in a troop compartment to the rear. This will have small bullet proof windows and firing ports to enable the troops to use their weapons from within the vehicle. There are doors in the hull rear and on the right side, and five hatches on the roof. The hull is V-shaped to deflect mine blasts away from the occupants. The driver sits in the front right position with the gunner to his left.

In the prototype the main weapon is a 7.62 mm machine-gun mounted in a small turret on the roof of the cab, but provision has been made for the fitting of a 20 mm cannon or a 60 mm breech-loading mortar (both currently in use on variants of the Ratel). Behind and above the gunner, the commander's position has vision blocks for all round observation and a one piece hatch.

The AC 200 is driven by a turbocharged V-8 diesel coupled with automatic transmission, and has a very long operational range.

The 6×6 APC is intended to be the progenitor of a family of vehicles which will share a large number of common components. A 4×4 APC will also be suitable for internal security applications. At least two 8×8 models are proposed, one being an armoured recovery vehicle and the other an armoured logistics vehicle. The ARV will have an armoured cab and a hydraulic crane on a flatbed rear. The logistics vehicle is designed to support a troop of four AC 200s on extended operations. It will carry a number of modular containers for fuel, water, ammunition and food and will have space for spare parts such as wheels and a number of useful extras

(such as a field shower unit). Other possible variants include ambulance, command, and logistic versions of the 6×6 and troop transporter and technical support variants of the 8×8.

The **AC 100 Amphibious Infantry Combat Vehicle** is another Sandock-Austral design, being developed in parallel with the AC 200. The AC 100 has been designed to take any of the weapons currently fitted to the Ratel, as well as a new two-man turret with a shortened version of the OTO-Melara 76 mm naval gun (which equips South Africa's 'President' class Fast Missile Craft). It too is intended to be the basis for a series of variants, although when the design was announced in 1986 the only other variant disclosed was a 4×4 APC.

All the new vehicles are tailored to suit the rugged conditions prevailing in the deserts and bush which go to make up so much of South Africa's very long borders. This means that they have good ground clearance, high speed and considerable operating range and are designed for ease of maintenance in the field.

Specification
AC 200 6×6
Crew: 3 + 10
Weight: 18000 kg (39,683 lb)
Engine: V-8 turbocharged diesel coupled with fully automatic transmission delivering 370 hp (276 kW)
Dimensions: Not yet available
Armament: See text
Performance: Maximum road speed 108 km/h (67 mph); road range 1,000 km (621 miles) at steady 80 km/h; fording 1.2 m (3.93 ft); gradient 60 per cent; vertical obstacle 0.6 m (1.96 ft); trench 1.2 m (3.93 ft)

BTR-152 armoured personnel carrier

The Soviet Union did not employ a tracked or wheeled armoured personnel carrier during World War II, and her infantry normally went in on foot or were carried on tanks. The **BTR-152** was first seen in public during 1951, but probably entered service several years before this. The vehicle consists basically of a ZIL-151 truck chassis fitted with a fully armoured body, later production vehicles from the BTR-152V1 onwards being based on the improved ZIL-157 truck chassis. From the early 1960s it was replaced in front-line Soviet motorized rifle divisions by the BTR-60 series of 8×8 armoured personnel carriers, which have better cross country capabilities. The BTR-152 and its variants have been widely exported by the Soviet Union, and even in 1986 the type remained in service with some 30 countries all over the world, and the BTR-152 has seen action in the Middle East (with Syria, Iraq and Egypt), Africa and the Far East.

The first model to enter service was the BTR-152, and has an open-topped troop compartment, in which the 17 troops sit on bench type seats running across the hull. The second model to enter service was the **BTR-152V1**, which retained the open-topped troop compartment but was fitted with a front-mounted winch and a central tyre-pressure regulation system with external air lines. The latter system enables the driver to adjust the tyre pressure to suit the type of ground being crossed. The **BTR-152V2** was not fitted with a winch, but did have a tyre-pressure regulation system. The **BTR-152V3** had winch, infra-red night-vision equipment and a central tyre-pressure regulation system with internal air lines more robust than those of the external system. The main drawback of these versions was the open-topped troop compartment, which left the infantry vulnerable to overhead shell bursts. This was rectified with the introduction of the **BTR-152K** which had full overhead protection. In all ver-

Above: A BTR-152 (6×6) armoured personnel carrier fitted with a central tyre pressure regulation system that allows the driver to adjust the pressure to suit the type of ground being crossed.

Right: Soviet BTR-152 (6×6) armoured personnel carriers being supported by T-54 tanks. Until the introduction of the BTR-60 (8×8) armoured personnel carrier in the 1960s the BTR-152 was the standard vehicle of the Soviet motorized rifle divisions.

sions of the BTR-152 firing ports are provided in the sides and rear of the troop compartment. The infantry enter and leave the vehicle via two doors in the rear of the hull.

The command version is called the **BTR-152U** and has a much higher roof so the command staff can work while standing; it also has an armoured roof. The anti-aircraft model is the **BTR-152A**, which has at its rear a mount with twin 14.5-mm (0.57-in) KPV heavy machine-guns that can be elevated from −5° to +80° with turret traverse through 360°. During the fighting in the Lebanon in 1982, the Israeli army captured a number of BTR-152s from the

PLO: these vehicles had the towed ZU-23 twin 23-mm mounted in the rear, these being much more effective than the 14.5-mm (0.57-in) KPVs.

The first armoured personnel carrier to be deployed by the Soviet Union after World War II was in fact the **BTR-40** 4×4 vehicle, which was based on a modified GAZ-63 truck chassis. This could carry eight troops in addition to its two-man crew and was also used as a reconnaissance vehicle until the introduction of the BRDM-1 in the 1950s. Both the BTR-40 and BTR-152 were normally armed with a pintle-mounted 7.62-mm (0.3-in) machine-gun.

Specification
BTR-152V1
Crew: 2+17
Combat weight: 8950 kg (19,731 lb)
Powerplant: one ZIL-123 6-cylinder petrol engine developing 110 hp (82 kW)
Dimensions: length 6.83 m (22 ft 4.9 in); width 2.32 m (7 ft 7.3 in); height 2.05 m (6 ft 8.7 in)
Performance: maximum road speed 75 km/h (47 mph); maximum road range 780 km (485 miles); fording 0.8 m (2 ft 7.5 in); vertical obstacle 0.6 m (1 ft 11.6 in); trench 0.69 m (2 ft 3.2 in)

BTR-60P series armoured personnel carrier

The BTR-152 6×6 armoured personnel carrier introduced into the Soviet army during the 1950s had a number of major shortcomings, including poor cross-country mobility (as it was based on a truck chassis) and lack of an amphibious capability. In the late 1960s the **BTR-60P** was introduced, and this and later variants have now replaced almost all BTR-152s used by the Soviet army, in which the BTR-60 series is normally used by the motorized rifle divisions while the tank divisions have the BMP-1 tracked MICVs. The BTR-60 series has been exported to some 30 countries, and Romania has produced a modified version under the designation **TAB-72**. The BTR-60 has seen action in many parts of the world.

The members of the BTR-60 series are all fully amphibious, being propelled in the water by a single waterjet under the rear of the hull at a speed of 10 km/h (6.2 mph), and have a similar layout with the commander and driver at the front, troop compartment in the centre and the two petrol engines at the rear. Each engine drives one side of the vehicle. Power-assisted steering is provided on the front two axles.

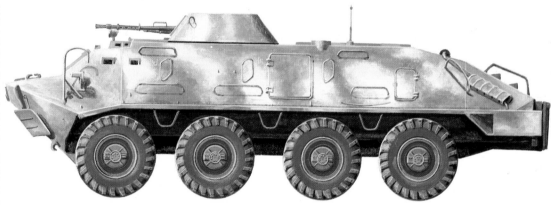

The first model to enter service was designated BTR-60P, and has an open-topped troop compartment. This carried a total of 16 infantrymen who were seated on bench seats across the hull. Armament normally consisted of one 12.7-mm (0.5-in) and two 7.62-mm (0.3-in) machine-guns. This was soon replaced in production by the **BTR-60PA**, which has a fully enclosed troop compartment and carries a maximum of 16 troops, although its normal comple-

ment is 12. This model is generally armed with a pintle-mounted 7.62-mm (0.3-in) machine-gun. The **BTR-60PB** is similar to the BTR-60PA but is fitted with the same one-man manual turret as installed on the BRDM-2 4×4 scout car and the Czech OT-64C(1) armoured personnel carrier, used by Czechoslovakia and Poland (as the SKOT-2A) in place of the Soviet vehicle. The infantry carried by the BTR-60PA and BTR-60PB can aim and

A BTR-60PB (8×8), which has the same turret as fitted to the BRDM-2 (4×4) scout car and the Czech OT-64C (8×8) vehicle.

fire their weapons from within the vehicle, although they normally have to dismount by climbing through the roof hatches. The command version of the vehicle is called the **BTR-60PU** and has additional communications equipment; there is also a forward air control

BTR-60P series APC (continued)

vehicle, basically the BTR-60PB with the armament removed and an observation window in the forward part of the turret.

The BTR-60PB is now being replaced in the Soviet Union by the **BTR-70**, which is very similar in appearance and has the same turret, but introduces a slightly more powerful engine and has improved seating and exit arrangements for the infantry, the roof hatches being supplemented by a small door in the lower part of the hull between the second and third road wheels. The BTR-70 has seen action in Afghanistan, where a number have been fitted with a 30-mm grenade-launcher on the roof.

The single diesel engine of the latest **BTR-80** is more powerful and safer than older models, and a new hatch arrangement allows troops to de-bus more efficiently.

Specification
BTR-60PB
Crew: 2+14
Combat weight: 10300 kg (22,708 lb)

A BTR-60PB (8×8) armoured personnel carrier, powered by two petrol engines each of which drives four wheels on one side of the vehicle. When afloat the vehicle is propelled in the water by a single water jet mounted in the hull rear.

Powerplant: two GAZ-49B 6-cylinder petrol engines each developing 90 hp (67 kW)
Dimensions: length 7.56 m (24 ft 9.6 in); width 2.825 m (9 ft 3.2 in); height to top of turret 2.31 m (7 ft 6.9 in)
Performance: maximum road speed 80 km/h (50 mph); maximum road range 500 km (311 miles); fording amphibious; gradient 60 per cent; vertical obstacle 0.4 m (1 ft 3.7 in); trench 2.0 m (6 ft 7 in)

A BTR-60PB (8×8) armoured personnel carrier swims ashore from a landing ship of the Soviet navy during exercises in the Red Banner Caucasian Military District.

CZECHOSLOVAKIA
OT-64 armoured personnel carrier

Rather than employ the Soviet BTR-60P series of 8×8 armoured personnel carriers, Czechoslovakia and Poland decided to develop their own vehicle. This entered service in 1964 and in addition to being used by Czechoslovakia and Poland has also been exported to Hungary, India, Libya, Morocco, Sudan, Syria and Uganda. The main advantages of the **OT-64** over the Soviet vehicle are that the former is powered by a diesel instead of two petrol engines (giving a longer operational range and reduced risk of fire) and that the troop compartment is fully enclosed. The OT-64 is heavier than the Soviet vehicle, however, and has a lower power-to-weight ratio. Many of the automotive components of the OT-64 are also used in the TATRA 813 range of 8×8 cross-country vehicles, which are widely used for civil and military applications.

The hull of the OT-64 is of all-welded steel construction that provides protection from small arms fire and shell splinters, maximum hull armour thickness being 10 mm (0.39 in). The commander and driver are seated at the front of the vehicle with the engine to their immediate rear. The troop compartment is at the rear of the hull, and access to this is gained via two doors in the hull rear. Roof hatches are provided over the top of the troop compartment, and firing ports are located in the side and rear. The OT-64 is fully amphibious, being driven in the water by two propellers mounted under the hull rear at a speed of 9 km/h (5.6 mph); before the vehicle enters the water a trim vane is erected at the front of the hull and the bilge pumps are switched on. All vehicles have night-vision equipment, front-mounted winch and an NBC system.

The original member of the family, the **OT-64A** (or **SKOT** in Poland) was sometimes fitted with a roof-mounted 7.62-mm (0.3-in) machine-gun. The **OT-64B (SKOT-2)** has on the roof to the rear of the engine compartment a plinth on which is mounted a 7.62-mm (0.3-in) or 12.7-mm (0.5-in) machine-gun fitted with a shield. The **OT-64C(1)**

or **SKOT-2A** has a one-man turret identical with that fitted to the BTR-60PB 8×8 APC and the BRDM-2 4×4 scout car; this turret is armed with a 14.5-mm (0.57-in) and a 7.62-mm (0.3-in) machine-gun. Some vehicles have been fitted with a wire-guided 'Sagger' ATGW on each side of the turret to give the vehicle an anti-tank capability. The **OT-64C(2)** or **SKOT-2AP** is used by Poland and has a new turret with a distinctive curved top which has the same armament as the turret of the OT-64C(1) but with an elevation of +89.5° to enable them to engage aircraft and helicopters. Other more specialized versions include a recovery vehicle and at least two command vehicles designated **R-2** and **R-3**.

Czechoslovakia also still uses a number of **OT-810** half-track vehicles. During World War II the Germans made the SdKfz 251 half-track at the Skoda plant in Pilsen, where production continued after the end of the war. In the 1950s many of these vehicles, by then designated the OT-810, were rebuilt and fitted with a diesel engine and overhead armour protection for the troop compartment. Most of the OT-810s have now been fitted with the 82-mm (3.23-in) M59A recoilless gun for use in the anti-tank role.

Above: The OT-64C(1) armoured personnel carrier and its earlier models are used by Czechoslovakia and Poland in place of the Soviet BTR-60 series.

Below: The OT-64C(1) armoured personnel carrier has the same one-man turret as fitted to the Soviet BRDM-2 (4×4) and BTR-60PB (8×8) vehicles.

Specification
OT-64C(1)
Crew: 2+15
Combat weight: 14500 kg (31,967 lb)
Powerplant: one Tatra V-8 diesel engine developing 180 hp (134 kW)
Dimensions: length 7.44 m (24 ft 5 in); width 2.55 m (8 ft 4.4 in); height overall 2.06 m (6 ft 9 in)
Performance: maximum road speed 94.4 km/h (59 mph); maximum road range 710 km (441 miles); fording amphibious; gradient 60 per cent; vertical obstacle 0.5 m (1 ft 7.7 in); trench 2.0 m (6 ft 7 in)

DAF YP-408 armoured personnel carrier

Since well before World War II DAF has been a major supplier of wheeled vehicles to the Royal Netherlands army, and in 1958 it built prototypes of an eight-wheeled armoured personnel carrier. With a number of modifications and the replacement of the Hercules JXLD petrol engine by a more powerful DAF diesel engine, this was accepted for service as the **DAF YP-408**, the first production vehicles being delivered in 1964 and final deliveries taking place in 1968. A total of 750 vehicles were built for the Dutch army and five are used by Surinam, these latter being passed on when the Dutch withdrew in the 1970s. In the Dutch army the YP-408 is now rapidly being replaced by the YPR-765, which is the Dutch version of the FMC Armoured Infantry Fighting Vehicle, and it is expected that all YP-408s will have been phased out of service by 1988.

The hull of the YP-408 is of all-welded steel construction which varies in thickness from 8 mm (0.315 in) to 15 mm (0.59 in). The engine is at the front, the commander and driver are to the rear of the engine compartment, and the troop compartment is at the rear. The diesel engine is coupled to a manual gearbox with five forward and one reverse gear and a two-speed transfer box. The YP-408 has a total of eight road wheels (four on each side), but only six of these are powered, making the YP-408 an 8×6 vehicle; it is the second pair of road wheels which is unpowered. Steering is power-assisted on the front four wheels, and the tyres have reinforced side walls that enable the vehicle to be driven for a distance of 50 km (31 miles) at a reduced speed after they have been punctured. The driver is seated on the left with the commander/machine-gunner to his right. The 12.7-mm (0.5-in) M2 machine-gun can be traversed through 360° and elevated from −8° to +70°.

The 10 fully equipped troops enter and leave the YP-408 through two doors in the hull rear, and are seated five down each side facing each other. Hatches are provided over the top of the troop compartment. Standard equipment includes a heater, but the YP-408 lacks an NBC system and amphibious capability. If required, infra-red equipment can be fitted for the driver and the machine-gunner.

The basic armoured personnel carrier is called the **PWI-S(GR)**, this standing for the **Pantser Wagen Infanterie-Standaard(Groep)**; the platoon commander's vehicle is the **PWI-S(PC)**, and has a crew of nine and additional communications equipment; and the battalion or company commander's vehicle is the **PWCO**, this having a crew of six, additional communications equipment and mapboards. The ambulance model, which is unarmed, is the **PW-GWT** which can carry two stretcher patients and four seated patients plus its three-man crew (driver and two medical orderlies). The **PW-V** freight carrier can transport 1500 kg (3,307 lb) of freight. The **PW-MT** has a seven-man mortar team and tows a French 120-mm (4.72-in) Brandt mortar and 50 mortar bombs. More recent versions are the **PWRDR** radar carrier, which is fitted with the British Marconi Avionics ZB 298 ground surveillance radar, and the **PWAT** anti-tank vehicle which has the Hughes TOW ATGW system.

Specification
YP-408
Crew: 2+10
Combat weight: 12000 kg (26,455 lb)
Powerplant: one DAF Model DS 575 6-cylinder diesel developing 165 hp (123 kW)
Dimensions: length 6.23 m (20 ft 5.3 in); width 2.40 m (7 ft 10.5 in); height (including MG) 2.37 m (7 ft 9.3 in)
Performance: maximum road speed 80 km/h (50 mph); maximum road range 500 km (311 miles); fording 1.2 m (3 ft 11 in); gradient 60 per cent; vertical obstacle 0.7 m (2 ft 4 in); trench 1.2 m (3 ft 11 in)

First produced in 1968, the 8×6 DAF YP-408 is soon to be replaced by the tracked FMC infantry fighting vehicle. With a crew of two, the YP-408 can transport up to 10 fully-equipped infantrymen, but has no NBC protection or amphibious capability.

The YP-408MT tows a French-built Brandt 120-mm mortar, and transports the seven-man mortar team as well as up to 50 mortar bombs. The machine-gun is a Browning M2 HB 12.7-mm and is operated by the vehicle commander.

MOWAG Roland armoured personnel carrier

The **MOWAG Roland** 4×4 is the smallest vehicle currently produced by the MOWAG company of Kreuzlingen, Switzerland, and is used mainly in the internal security role. The first prototype was completed in 1963, the first production vehicles being completed the following year. Known operators of the Roland include Argentina, Bolivia, Chile, Greece, Iraq, Mexico and Peru. The hull of Roland is of all-welded steel armour construction that provides the crew with complete protection from 7.62-mm (0.3-in) small arms fire. The driver is at the front, the crew compartment is in the centre and the engine at the rear on the left side; there is also an aisle in the right side of the hull that leads to a door in the hull rear. The driver has a roof hatch, and there is a single door in each side of the hull. In each of the three doors is a firing port (with a vision block above) which allows three of the embarked infantrymen to fire their rifles or sub-machine guns from within the vehicle in safety.

The basic Roland was designed from the outset for relatively easy conversion to a number of roles, including those of personnel, cargo or ammunition carrier, reconnaissance, command and communications post or, as illustrated, for the ambulance role.

MOWAG Roland APC (continued)

In the centre of the roof is installed the main armament; this is normally a simple cupola with an externally mounted 12.7-mm (0.5-in) or 7.62-mm (0.3-in) machine-gun. One of the alternative weapon stations is a turret on top of which is a remotely-controlled 7.62-mm (0.3-in) machine-gun fired from within the turret.

The petrol engine is coupled to a manual gearbox with four forward and one reverse gear and a two-speed transfer case. More recent production Rolands are offered with an automatic gearbox to reduce driver fatigue.

When used in the internal security role, the Roland is normally fitted with an obstacle-clearing blade at the front of the hull, a public address system, wire mesh protection for the head-lamps and sometimes the vision blocks as well, a siren and flashing lights. Another option is MOWAG bulletproof cross-country wheels. These consist of metal discs on each side of the tyre, the outside ones having ribs which assist the vehicle when crossing through mud.

In the late 1960s the company designed and built another 4×4 armoured personnel carrier called the **MOWAG Grenadier**, which can carry a total of nine men including the commander and driver. This model was sold to a number of countries but is no longer offered, having been replaced by the Piranha range of 4×4, 6×6 and 8×8 armoured vehicles. Typical armament installations for the Grenadier included a one-man turret armed with a 20-mm Hispano-Suiza cannon and a turret with twin 80-mm (3.15-in) rocket-launchers. The vehicle is fully amphibious, being propelled in the water by a propeller under the rear of the hull. Waterborne steering is accomplished by turning the steering wheel in the normal manner to move two parallel rudders mounted to the immediate rear of the propeller.

Specification
Roland
Crew: 3+3
Combat weight: 4700 kg (10,362 lb)
Powerplant: one V-8 petrol engine

developing 202 hp (151 kW)
Dimensions: length 4.44 m (14 ft 6.8 in); width 2.01 m (6 ft 7 in); height (with turret) 2.03 m (6 ft 8 in)
Performance: maximum road speed 110 km/h (68 mph); maximum range 550 km (341 miles); fording 1.0 m (3 ft 3.4 in); gradient 60 per cent; vertical obstacle 0.4 m (1 ft 4 in); trench not applicable

The anti-tank Roland is armed with three Messerschmitt-Bölkow-Blohm Mamba wire-guided anti-tank missiles. The equipment is mounted directly onto the remote-controlled 7.62-mm machine-gun turret.

SWITZERLAND

✚ MOWAG MR 8 series armoured personnel carriers

Since the end of World War II the MOWAG company has manufactured a wide range of tracked and wheeled armoured fighting vehicles aimed mainly at the export market, and has also built prototypes of armoured vehicles for foreign governments. For example, MOWAG built some of the prototypes of the West German Marder mechanized infantry combat vehicle. In the 1950s a 4×4 series of armoured vehicles were designed and built under the company designation **MOWAG MR 8**, and this was subsequently adopted by the West German border police in two configurations, the **SW1** and the **SW2**. The first batch of 20 or so vehicles was supplied direct by MOWAG, but main production was undertaken in West Germany by Henschel and Büssing. Total production in West Germany amounted to about 600 vehicles.

The SW1 (**geschützter Sonderwagen Kfz 91**) is the armoured personnel carrier model and accommodates five men plus the commander and driver, while the SW2 has a slightly different hull top and is fitted with a one-man turret armed with a 20-mm Hispano-Suiza cannon plus four smoke-dischargers mounted on each side of the turret to fire forwards.

The same basic hull is used for both the SW1 and SW2, with slight differences to the roof. In the SW1 the commander and driver are seated at the front of the hull with a windscreen in front of each man; these windscreens can be quickly covered by armoured shutters with integral vision blocks. The driver also has a roof hatch above his position for driving in the head-out position. The troop compartment is at the rear of the hull with the engine compartment to its left. In each side of the hull is a two-part door that opens left and right; each door has a vision block and a firing port. Over the top of the troop compartment are two roof hatches and an unusual cupola. The latter is fixed but split down the middle so that it can be opened vertically if required; in each half are three fixed vision blocks. When the cupola is in

the normal position complete visibility is possible through 360°.

Unlike more recent MOWAG wheeled armoured vehicles, the MR 8 series vehicles have no amphibious capability and are not fitted with an NBC system or any type of night vision equipment, although both of the latter could have been fitted if so required by the user.

MOWAG continued to develop the MR 8 series for other export markets, and these variants included the **MR 8-09** sporting a one-man turret armed with a 20-mm cannon, the **MR 8-23** that had a two-man turret armed with a 90-mm (3.54-in) gun and a 7.62-mm (0.3-in) co-axial machine-gun, and the **MR 9-32** fitted with a 120-mm (4.72-in) mortar at the rear of the hull. The last version had an open-top hull, and before the mortar could be fired it had to be lowered to the ground. Two multiple rocket-launchers were also designed and built, one with a launcher fitted with 20 145-mm (5.7-in) barrels and the other with two 80-mm (3.15-in) rocket projectors fed by an automatic loader which enabled a cyclic rate of 500 rounds per minute to be achieved. None of these models entered production.

Specification
MR 8
Crew: 2+5
Combat weight: 8200 kg (18,078 lb)
Powerplant: one Chrysler Type R 361 6-cylinder petrol engine developing 161 hp (120 kW)
Dimensions: length 5.31 m (17 ft 5 in); width 2.2 m (7 ft 3 in); height (hull) 1.88 m (6 ft 2 in)
Performance: maximum road speed 80 km/h (50 mph); maximum range 400 km (248 miles); fording 1.1 m (3 ft 7 in); gradient 60 per cent; vertical obstacle 0.4 m (1 ft 4 in); trench not applicable

West German Bundesgrenzschutz (BSG, or Federal Border Police) parade with their armoured but unarmed MR 8 (model SW1) personnel carriers. The first Swiss-built models were delivered in 1959/60, and were subsequently built in the Federal Republic.

The SW2 model of the MR 8, also used by the BSG, differs in being armed with an Hispano 20-mm cannon and having a crew of four instead of seven. Smoke dischargers are mounted on each side of the 20-mm turret.

✚ MOWAG Piranha armoured personnel carrier

The **MOWAG Piranha** range of 4×4, 6×6 and 8×8 armoured personnel carriers was designed by MOWAG in the late 1960s, and the first prototype was completed in Switzerland in 1972, with first production vehicles following four years later. As with all recent MOWAG vehicles, the Piranha family was a private venture and developed without government support. In 1977 Canada decided to adopt the 6×6 version and production was undertaken in Canada by the Diesel Division of General Motors Canada, 491 being built for the Canadian Armed Forces between 1979 and 1982. Canada uses three versions of the 6×6 Piranha: the 76-mm (2.99-in) **Cougar Gun Wheeled Fire Support Vehicle**, which has the same two-man turret as the British Combat Vehicle Reconnaissance (Tracked) Scorpion; the **Grizzly Wheeled Armoured Personnel Carrier**, which has a one-man turret armed with a 12.7-mm (0.5-in) and a 7.62-mm (0.3-in) machine-gun and has a three-man crew consisting of commander, gunner and driver plus six fully equipped troops; and the **Husky Wheeled Maintenance and Recovery Vehicle**, which supports the other vehicles in the field. In addition to being used by Canada, the Piranha range of vehicles is used also by Chile (licence production), Ghana, Liberia, Nigeria and Sierra Leone, and in 1983 the 6×6 model was evaluated by the Swiss army as an anti-tank vehicle fitted with the Hughes TOW anti-tank system. After evaluating a number of different vehicles both tracked and wheeled, the USA selected the 8×8 version of the Piranha to meet its requirement for a Light Armored Vehicle (LAV) and the first of these was completed for the US Marine Corps in late 1983. These have a two-man power-operated turret armed with a Hughes Helicopters 25-mm cannon (as fitted to the Bradley) and a co-axial 7.62-mm (0.3-in) machine-gun. Variants required by the US Marines include a logistics support vehicle, a command vehicle, a repair vehicle, a mortar carrier and an anti-tank model. The US Army withdrew from the programme early in 1984.

The hull of the Piranha is of all-welded steel construction, which provides protection from small arms fire. On the six-wheeled version the driver is at the front on the left with the commander to his rear and the engine to the right. The troop compartment is at the rear of the hull, and entry to this is gained via two doors in the hull rear. Armament depends on the role, but can range from a single-man turret up to a two-man power-operated turret armed with a 90-mm (3.54-in) Cockerill gun. If a heavy weapon such as this is fitted, however, the commander is normally in the turret and a reduced number of troops is carried.

All members of the Piranha family are fully amphibious, being propelled in the water by two propellers at the rear of the hull. Optional equipment includes such things as night vision equipment, an NBC system, an air-conditioning system (essential in the Middle East) and so on.

Specification
Piranha (6×6 version without armament)
Crew: 2+12
Combat weight: 10500 kg (23,148 lb)
Powerplant: one Detroit Diesel 6V-53T developing 300 hp (224 kW)
Dimensions: length 5.97 m (19 ft 7 in); width 2.50 m (8 ft 2.4 in); height 1.85 m (6 ft 1 in)
Performance: maximum road speed 100 km/h (62 mph); maximum range 600 km (373 miles); fording amphibious; gradient 70 per cent; vertical obstacle 0.5 m (1 ft 8 in); trench not applicable

The 4×4 version of the Piranha has a maximum load of 10 infantrymen and, as here, can be armed with a remote-controlled 7.62-mm machine-gun mount. All of the Piranha family are fully amphibious, being driven by twin propellers in water.

Armed with the Belgian Cockerill 90-mm gun, the 6×6 Piranha is capable of fulfilling the infantry support role so often required of the modern infantry fighting vehicle. Such a large weapon is mounted at the expense of the number of troops carried.

🇺🇸 Dragoon armoured personnel carrier

In the late 1970s the US Army Military Police issued a requirement for a vehicle which would be airportable in a Lockheed C-130 Hercules transport aircraft and be suitable for both air base protection and convoy escort. The requirement lapsed, but the Verne Corporation went ahead and with its own money built two prototypes of a vehicle which was eventually called the **Dragoon**. In appearance the Dragoon is very similar to the Cadillac Gage V-100 and V-150 range of 4×4 multi-mission vehicles, but shares many common components with the M113A2 full-tracked armoured personnel carrier and the M809 6×6 5-ton truck, which are used all over the world. From the M113A2 the Dragoon uses the engine, starter, periscopes, bilge pumps, switches, electrical and hydraulic components (to name but a few), with the obvious logistical advantages.

The hull of the Dragoon is of all-welded steel construction which provides the crew with complete protection from 5.56-mm (0.22-in) and 7.62-mm (0.3-in) small arms fire and shell splinters. The driver is seated at the front on the left with another crew member to his right, the main crew

Although apparently very similar to the well established Cadillac Gage Commando range, the Dragoon is designed for maximum commonality with the existing US Army inventory. As is usual today, a variety of weapons can be fitted, including the Arrowpointe 90-mm turret with the Mk III Cockerill 90-mm gun.

Dragoon armoured personnel carrier (continued)

compartment is in the centre, and the engine is at the rear of the hull on the right side (on the Cadillac Gage vehicles it is on the left side), and an aisle connects the main crew compartment with the door in the hull rear. The troops normally enter and leave the vehicle via a door in each side of the hull, the lower part of each door folding down to form a step while the upper part hinges to one side. Firing ports with a vision block above are provided in the sides and rear of the crew compartment. The diesel engine is coupled to an automatic transmission with five forward and one reverse gear and a single-speed transfer case, and steering is hydraulic on the front axle. The Dragoon is fully amphibious, being propelled in the water by its wheels at a speed of 4.8 km/h (3 mph), with three bilge pumps extracting any water that seeps in through the door and hatch openings.

When being used as a basic armoured personnel carrier the Dragoon is normally fitted with an M113 type cupola with a pintle-mounted 12.7-mm (0.5-in) or 7.62-mm (0.3-in) machine-gun to allow the maximum number of troops to be carried. Other armament installations are available, however, including two-man power-operated turrets armed with a 25-mm cannon or a 90-mm (3.54-in) gun, 7.62-mm (0.3-in) co-axial and 7.62-mm (0.3-in) anti-aircraft machine-guns. More specialized versions include command, engineer, anti-tank (with TOW

ATGWs), recovery and internal security vehicles.

In 1982 six Dragoons were supplied to the US Army and a smaller number to the US Navy. The former are used by the 9th Infantry Division High Technology Test Bed in two roles, electronic warfare and video optical surveillance vehicle. The first of these has extensive communications equipment and a hydraulically-operated mast which can be quickly extended for improved communications. The US Navy uses its vehicles for patrolling nuclear weapons storage areas in Alaska and the continental United States. More recently it is reported that Venezuela placed an order for a number of Dragoons.

Specification
Dragoon
Crew: typically 3+6
Combat weight: typically 12700 kg (27,998 lb)
Powerplant: one Detroit Diesel Model 6V-53T diesel developing 300 hp (224 kW)
Dimensions: length 5.588 m (18 ft 4 in); width 2.438 m (8 ft 0 in); height (hull top) 2.133 m (7 ft 0 in) but varies with weapon fit
Performance: maximum road speed 116 km/h (72 mph); maximum road range 1045 km (650 miles); fording amphibious; gradient 60 per cent; vertical obstacle 0.99 m (3 ft 3 in); trench not applicable

The electronic warfare Dragoon is undergoing trials with the US Ninth Infantry division. Roles include the jamming of high speed communications, and advanced battlefield direction finding.

Seen on deployment to Egypt, the long-range video optical surveillance vehicle offers commanders a highly mobile, armoured observation capacity, giving real-time communication.

Cadillac Gage V-150 Commando armoured personnel carrier

In the early 1960s the Cadillac Gage Company of Detroit, Michigan, started to design a multi-purpose armoured vehicle which was finally unveiled in 1963 as the **Cadillac Gage V-100 Commando**. Trials were so successful that the type entered production the following year for the export market. The conflict in South Vietnam soon showed that there was an urgent need for a wheeled vehicle for patrolling air bases, fuel dumps and other high risk areas as well as escorting convoys from one base to another, and soon significant numbers of vehicles were shipped to South Vietnam for use by the South Vietnamese army and the United States forces (including the military police and US Air Force).

The first model was powered by a Chrysler petrol engine, and was followed by the much larger **V-200 Commando** with a more powerful engine, greater weight and increased load-carrying capability. The V-200 was sold only to Singapore and is no longer offered by the company. In the early 1970s the V-100 and V-200 were replaced in production by the **V-150 Commando**. The V-150 introduced a number of improvements, the most significant of which is the installation of a diesel engine which gives the vehicle a much increased range of action as well as reducing the risk of fire. So far over 4,000 V-100, V-150 and V-200 armoured vehicles have been built, and known purchasers have included Bolivia, Botswana, Cameroun, Dominican Republic, Ethiopia, Haiti, Gabon, Guatemala, Indonesia, Jamaica, Kuwait, Malaysia, Oman, Panama, Philippines, Saudi Arabia, Singapore, Somalia, Sudan, Taiwan,

Thailand, Tunisia, Turkey, United States and South Vietnam. The stretched model of the V-150, the **V-150 S**, was entered in the Light Armored Vehicle (LAV) competition together with the new 6×6 Cadillac Gage V-300 Commando, but this competition was won by the Canadian 8×8 vehicle based on the Swiss Piranha. The V-150 S is the current production model.

The V-150 Commando is called a multi-mission vehicle as it can be used for a wide range of roles. In the basic armoured personnel carrier model it has a three-man crew (commander, gunner and driver) and can carry nine fully equipped troops, who enter and leave the vehicle via doors in the hull

sides and rear. A very wide range of armament installations can be fitted, including a one-man turret with various combinations of 7.62-mm (0.3-in) and 12.7-mm (0.5-in) machine-guns; a two-man power-operated turret with 90-mm (3.54-in) or 76-mm (2.99-in) gun and 7.62-mm co-axial and 7.62-mm (0.3-in) anti-aircraft machine-guns; and a turret with 20-mm cannon and 7.62-mm co-axial and 7.62-mm anti-aircraft machine-guns. There is also an anti-aircraft vehicle with a 20-mm Vulcan six-barrelled anti-aircraft weapon, a mortar carrier with an 81-mm mortar, an anti-tank vehicle with the Hughes TOW anti-tank guided weapon, a command vehicle with raised roof to allow

the command staff to work in the upright position, a riot control vehicle, and a recovery vehicle.

Specification
V-150 Commando
Crew: 3+9
Combat weight: 9888 kg (21,800 lb)
Powerplant: one V-8 diesel developing 202 bhp (151 kW)
Dimensions: length 5.689 m (18 ft 8 in); width 2.26 m (7 ft 5 in); height (hull top) 1.981 m (6 ft 6 in);
Performance: maximum road speed 88.5 km/h (55 mph); maximum range 643 km (400 miles); fording amphibious; gradient 60 per cent; vertical obstacle 0.609 m (2 ft 0 in)

Developed from the V-100 of 1962, the V-150 entered production in 1971. A wide range of armament can be fitted, including the two-man 25-mm gun turret.

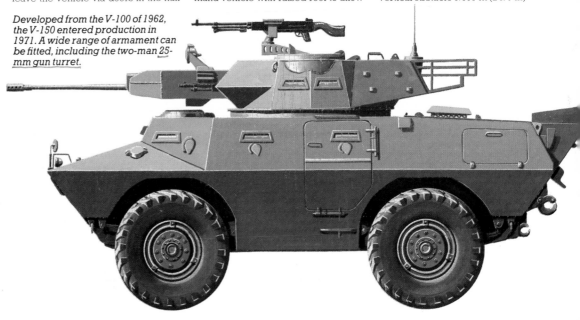

Cadillac Gage V-300 Commando armoured personnel carrier

In the last 20 years the Cadillac Gage Company of Detroit, Michigan has built some 4,000 of its Commando range of 4×4 multi-mission vehicles in three models: the V-100, V-150 (current production model) and V-200. In recent years, however, there has been a trend to 6×6 vehicles with their increased load-carrying capabilities, and for this reason in 1979 the company as a private venture built two prototypes of the **Cadillac Gage Commando V-300** 6×6 vehicle which can be used for a wide range of roles, including use as an armoured personnel carrier. In 1982 Panama placed an order for 12 V-300 vehicles, which were all delivered the following year. Four different models were selected by Panama: a fire-support vehicle with 90-mm (3.54-in) Cockerill gun, a recovery vehicle, and two types fitted with different machine-gun installations. Cadillac Gage also supplied three V-300s for the US Army and US Marine Corps Light Armored Vehicle (LAV) competition; of these one was fitted with a two-man turret armed with a 90-mm (3.54-in) Cockerill Mk III gun, while the other two were fitted with a two-man turret armed with the Hughes Helicopters 25-mm Chain Gun as installed in the FMC M2 and M3 tracked vehicles. In the end, however, the LAV programme was won by General Motors of Canada with an 8×8 version of the MOWAG Piranha. In 1984 Kuwait ordered 62 V-300 Commandos.

The layout of the V-300 is quite different from that of the V-150. The driver is seated at the front left with the engine to his right. The engine is coupled to a fully automatic Allison MT-643 transmission with four forward and one reverse gear and a two-speed transfer case. In addition to his roof hatch the driver also has a small hatch in the left side of the hull. The troop compartment is at the rear, and the troops enter and leave via the two doors in the hull rear; in addition there are hatches in the roof and firing ports with a vision block in the sides and rear.

The V-300 can be fitted with a wide range of armament installations, all in a turret designed and built by Cadillac

Gage. Among the two-man installations is a turret armed with a 90-mm (3.54-in) Cockerill Mk III gun, or British ROF 76-mm (2.99-in) gun or 25-mm Hughes Helicopters Chain Gun, or 20-mm cannon; there is also a one-man turret with a 20-mm cannon, and in all of these a 7.62-mm (0.3-in) machine-gun is mounted co-axial with the main armament and a similar weapon can usually be mounted on the roof for anti-aircraft defence. The one-man turret can have single or twin 7.62-mm (0.3-in) machine-guns or a combination of 7.62-mm (0.3-in) and 12.7-mm (0.5-in) machine-guns. A simple alternative to the turrets is a ring mounting with a 7.62-mm (0.3-in) or 12.7-mm (0.5-in) machine-gun.

Variants of the V-300 include an ambulance with a higher roof, an armoured recovery vehicle, an anti-tank vehicle fitted with the same TOW launcher as fitted to the M901 Improved TOW Vehicle (ITV), and a 81-mm mortar carrier.

The vehicle is fitted with a front-mounted winch and is fully amphibious, being propelled in the water by its wheels at a speed of 5 km/h (3 mph).

Specification
V-300 Commando
Crew: 3+9 (commander, gunner, driver and 9 infantry)
Combat weight: typically 13137 kg (28,962 lb)
Powerplant: one VT-504 V-8 turbocharged diesel developing 235 hp (175 kW)

The Hughes Helicopter 25-mm Chain Gun has been fitted to the V-300 Commando. The two-man turret has a co-axial 7.62-mm machine-gun,

Dimensions: length 6.40 m (21 ft 0 in); width 2.54 m (8 ft 4 in); height (hull top) 1.981 m (6 ft 6 in) but varies with weapon fit
Performance: maximum road speed

and smoke dischargers have been mounted on the side. An extra machine-gun can be fitted on top of the turret.

93 km/h (58 mph); maximum road range 700 km (435 miles); fording amphibious; gradient 60 per cent; vertical obstacle 0.609 m (2 ft 0 in); trench not applicable

The V-300 has been developed as a private venture by Cadillac Gage. Heaviest of the wide range of weapons operable is the Cockerill Mk III 90-mm gun, mounted in a Cadillac Gage two-man turret.

Cadillac Gage Commando Ranger armoured personnel carrier

The US Air Force has hundreds of vast bases spread all over the world, and in recent years these have become possible targets for terrorists and other fringe groups as these bases not only contain highly expensive aircraft and/or missiles but also radars and other surveillance devices, fuels and all types of ordnance ranging from ammunition and conventional aircraft bombs up to nuclear warheads. To protect these assets the US Air Force issued a requirement for a vehicle which it called a Security Police Armored Response/Convoy Truck which, in addition to carrying out patrols on air bases, would also escort convoys carrying ordnance to and Continued on page 110

Developed to meet USAF base security requirements, the Ranger is also tasked with escorting ordnance convoys.

Cadillac Gage Commando

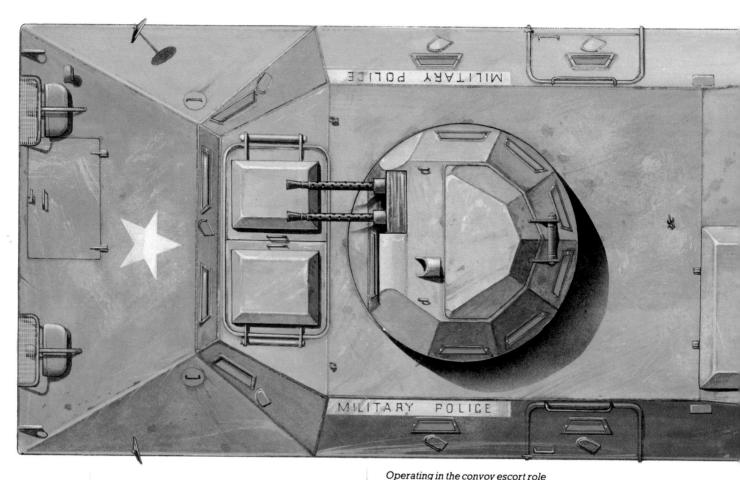

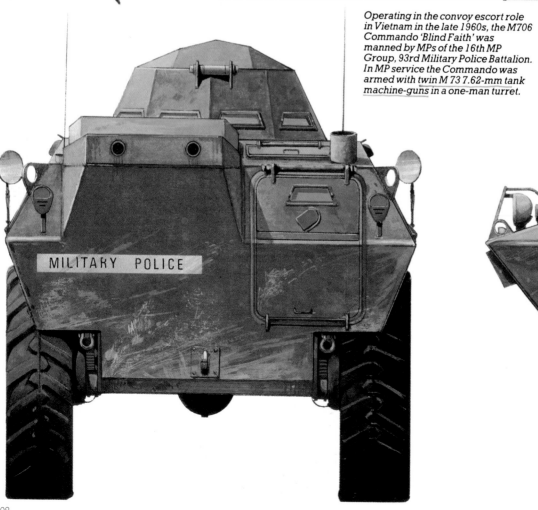

Operating in the convoy escort role in Vietnam in the late 1960s, the M706 Commando 'Blind Faith' was manned by MPs of the 16th MP Group, 93rd Military Police Battalion. In MP service the Commando was armed with twin M 73 7.62-mm tank machine-guns in a one-man turret.

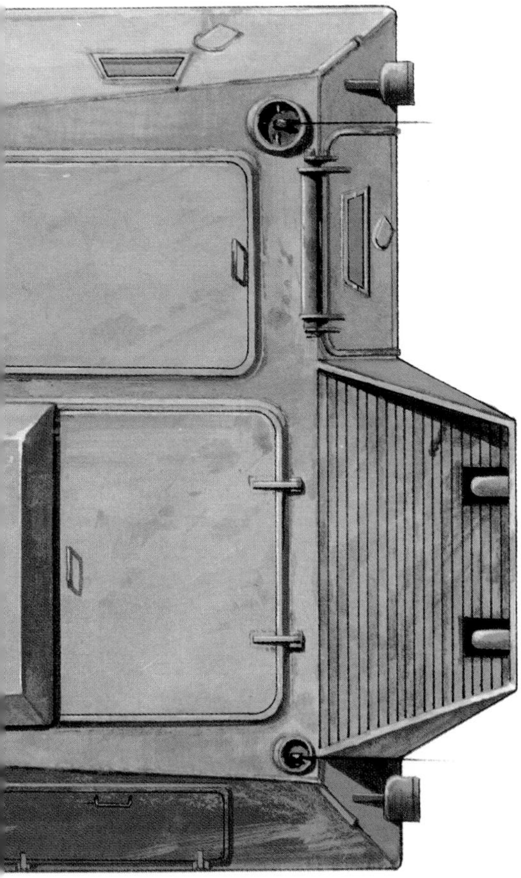

16 MP6P
93P

560P
X-61

MILITARY POLICE

BLINDFOLDED

PETER SARSON/TONY BRYAN

MILITARY POLICE

from bases, or even from the storage dump on the airfield to the aircraft itself.

After studying a number of proposals, in early 1979 the US Air Force selected the **Cadillac Gage Commando Ranger** armoured personnel carrier to meet its requirements. The first of these was handed over in the following year, and by 1984 some 700 had been delivered. The US Air Force calls the vehicle the **Peacekeeper**, and sales have also been made by the company to Luxembourg (these are the only armoured vehicles operated by this country) and more recently some have been sold to Indonesia together with a number of Cadillac Gage Commando Scout 4×4 reconnaissance vehicles.

The Commander Ranger is based on a standard Chrysler truck chassis suitably modified and with a shorter wheelbase. (The wheelbase of a vehicle is the distance between the first and last axles.) The full armoured body provides the crew with protection from small arms fire and shell splinters. The engine is at the front of the vehicle and coupled to an automatic transmission with three forward and one reverse gear and a two-speed transfer case. Steering is integral with pump

assistance, and suspension front and rear consists of leaf springs and double-acting hydraulic shock absorbers.

The commander and driver are seated to the rear of the engine, each being provided with a bulletproof window to his front and a rearward-opening side door that has a bulletproof vision block and a firing port underneath; in addition there is a firing port between the driver's and commander's windscreens.

The six men sit three down each side in the rear, and enter via two doors in the hull rear. Each of these doors has a firing port, and the left one also has a vision block. In each side of the troop compartment is a vision block and a firing port. In the roof is a hatch on which a variety of light armament installations can be fitted, including a simple shield with a 7.62-mm (0.3-in) machine-gun or a turret with twin 7.62-mm (0.3-in) machine-guns.

Standard equipment includes internal lighting, an air-conditioning system, a heater, two-speed wipers and a windscreen defogger. Optional equipment includes 24-volt electrics in place of the normal 12-volt system, and a winch. Specialized versions include a command vehicle and an ambulance.

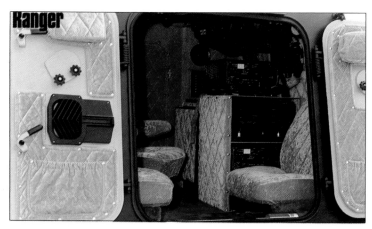

Specification
Commando Ranger
Crew: 2+6
Combat weight: 4536 kg (10,000 lb)
Powerplant: one Dodge 360 CID V-8 petrol engine developing 180 hp (134 kW)
Dimensions: length 4.699 m (15 ft 5 in); width 2.019 m (6 ft 7.5 in); height 1.981 m (6 ft 6 in)
Performance: maximum road speed 112.5 km/h (70 mph); maximum range

The Ranger interior is insulated and air-conditioned, lessening crew fatigue considerably. The interior can be fitted for command and communication equipment or for two crew and six passengers.

556 km (345 miles); fording 0.457 m (1 ft 6 in); gradient 60 per cent; vertical obstacle 0.254 m (10 in); trench not applicable

Humber 'Pig' armoured personnel carrier

UK

When World War II was over, the British army drew up its requirements for a complete new generation of wheeled military vehicles including a 1-ton truck which was eventually produced by Humber/Rootes. In the early 1950s the Alvis Saracen 6×6 armoured personnel carrier started to enter service, but as there would clearly be insufficient of these to go around it was decided to build an armoured personnel carrier on the **Humber FV1600** series truck chassis. This armoured personnel carrier was not designed to operate with tanks, but rather to transport the infantry from one part of the battlefield to another, where they would dismount and fight on foot. About 1,700 vehicles were eventually built, the bodies being provided by GKN Sankey and the Royal Ordnance Factory at Woolwich. By the 1960s the FV432, also designed and built by GKN Sankey, was entering service in increasing numbers so the **Humber 'Pigs'** were phased out of service and placed in reserve or scrapped. The flare-up in Northern Ireland in the late 1960s meant that many of these vehicles were returned to service, and in 1987 these remain in use with the British army in Northern Ireland.

Many of the 'Pigs' in Northern Ireland have now been specially modified for use in the internal security role, being fitted with additional armour protection to stop 7.62-mm (0.3-in) armour-piercing rounds and barricade-removal equipment at the front of the hull. Variants include the 'Holy Pig' which has a hole in the roof surrounded by perspex screens, the 'Winged Pig' which has side mounted screens to protect foot personnel from missile-throwing mobs, and the 'Kremlin Pig' which is covered in wire mesh for protection against rocket grenades. Some 'Pigs' in the border 'Bandit Country' have acquired machine gun turrets.

The basic armoured personnel car-

Above: The FV1609 model of the Humber one-ton armoured personnel carrier entered service in the early 1950s. With an open top, capacity was two crew and up to eight troops.

rier model is the **FV1611**, and normally carries six or eight men in the rear with the commander and driver sitting at the front to the rear of the engine. Both the commander and driver are provided with a door in the side, and there are twin doors in the rear. A total of six firing ports/observation blocks are provided in the rear troop compartment, (two in each side and one in each of the rear doors).

Specification
FV1611 'Pig'
Crew: 2+6 (or 2+8)
Combat weight: 5790 kg (12,765 lb)
Powerplant: one Rolls-Royce B60 Mk 5A 6-cylinder petrol engine developing 120 bhp (89 kW)

Dimensions: length 4.926 m (16 ft 2 in); width 2.044 m (6 ft 8.5 in); height 2.12 m (6 ft 11.5 in)
Performance: maximum road speed 64 km/h (40 mph); maximum range 402 km (250 miles); trench not applicable

The 'Pig', as it has come to be known, had been withdrawn from service but heightening civil disorder in Northern Ireland required its return. Some 500 are still in use in the internal security role in Ulster.

Alvis Saracen armoured personnel carriers

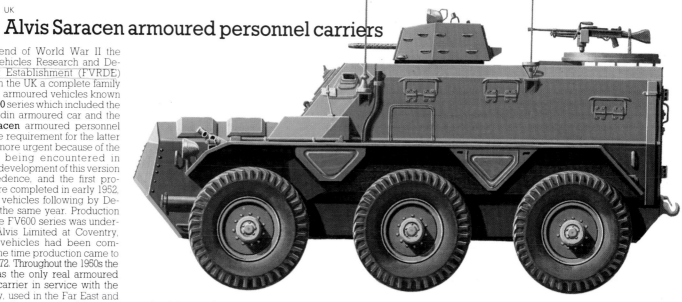

After the end of World War II the Fighting Vehicles Research and Development Establishment (FVRDE) designed in the UK a complete family of wheeled armoured vehicles known as the FV600 series which included the FV601 Saladin armoured car and the **FV603 Saracen** armoured personnel carrier. The requirement for the latter was much more urgent because of the guerrillas being encountered in Malaya, so development of this version took precedence, and the first prototypes were completed in early 1952, production vehicles following by December of the same year. Production of the whole FV600 series was undertaken by Alvis Limited at Coventry, and 1,838 vehicles had been completed by the time production came to an end in 1972. Throughout the 1950s the Saracen was the only real armoured personnel carrier in service with the British army, used in the Far East and Middle East (for example Aden and Libya) as well as in the United Kingdom and with the British Army of the Rhine. From the early 1960s replacement of the Saracen in the BAOR started by the FV432 full-tracked armoured personnel carrier, which has better cross-country performance, improved armour protection and longer operational range.

Although the FV603 Saracen had the same automotive components as the FV601 Saladin 6×6 armoured car, its layout was quite different with the engine at the front and troop compartment at the rear. The driver is seated in the centre, with the section commander to his left rear and radio operator to his right rear. To their rear are the eight infantrymen, who are seated on individual seats (four down each side of the hull facing inwards). The troops enter and leave via twin doors in the hull rear, and firing ports are provided in the sides and rear. On the forward part of the roof is a manually-operated turret with a 7.62-mm (0.3-in) machine-gun (this turret is identical with that fitted to some Ferret scout cars), and over the rear part of the troop compartment is a 7.62-mm (0.3-in) Bren light-machine gun for air defence.

Steering is hydraulically assisted on the front four wheels, and the vehicle

can be driven with one wheel missing from each side. Some vehicles supplied to the Middle East were not fitted with a roof.

There were not many variants of the Saracen as the **FV602** ambulance was cancelled fairly early on in the development programme. The **FV604** is a command vehicle, while the **FV610** is also a command vehicle with a much higher roof to allow the command staff to work standing up. The **FV611** is an ambulance model and also has a higher roof.

The Saracen was sold to a number of countries, and remains in service with Indonesia, Jordan, Kuwait, Lebanon, Nigeria, South Africa, Thailand and Uganda. They are no longer used by the British in Northern Ireland, but a small number of Territorial Army command posts, Royal Engineer remote control bomb-disposal vehicles and RAF mobile air traffic control units are still operational.

Specification
Saracen
Crew: 2 + 10
Combat weight: 8640 kg (19,048 lb)
Powerplant: one Rolls-Royce B80 Mk 6A 8-cylinder petrol engine

developing 160 hp (119 kW)
Dimensions: length 5.233 m (17 ft 2 in); width 2.539 m (8 ft 4 in); height (overall) 2.463 m (8 ft 1 in)
Performance: maximum road speed 72 km/h (44.7 mph); maximum road range 400 km (248 miles); fording 1.07 m (3 ft 6 in); gradient 42 per cent; vertical obstacle 0.46 m (1 ft 6 in); trench 1.52 m (5 ft 0 in)

First produced in 1952, the FV 603 Saracen APC was a member of a family of 6×6 vehicles. The turret mounts a 0.30-calibre machine-gun.

Versions of the Saracen include the FV 604 command vehicle, seen landing from a Mexefloat while on exercise with the 13/18 Hussars in Cyprus. Notice the extensive external stowage, the auxiliary generator on the front wing and the lack of the machine-gun turret.

GKN Saxon armoured personnel carrier

Saxon was produced to a British Army requirement and can carry up to ten troops.

In the early 1970s GKN built the **AT100** 4×2 and **AT104** 4×4 vehicles as a private venture, these being aimed mainly at the internal security role. The former never entered production, but about 30 AT104s were built for the Dutch state police and Royal Brunei Malay Regiment. These were followed by the **GKN AT105** which was subsequently called the **Saxon**. This is a completely new design and uses many common automotive components from the Bedford MK 4×4 4-tonne truck, which is the standard vehicle in its class in the British army and many other armed forces around the world. Production of the AT105 started by 1976, and by 1984 about 200 had been sold to Bahrain, Kuwait, Malaysia and Oman. The British army purchased three for evaluation purposes in the 1970s, and in 1983 placed an order for 50 further vehicles. The first of these were delivered early

GKN Saxon (continued)

in 1984 and are issued to infantry battalions in the United Kingdom who, in time of war, will be sent to West Germany to reinforce the British Army of the Rhine (BAOR). At present these battalions use standard Bedford MK 4×4 trucks for this purpose. The British army requirement is for up to 1,000 AT105s.

The AT105 Saxon has a hull of all-welded steel construction that provides complete protection against small arms fire and shell splinters, including 7.62-mm (0.3-in) armour-piercing rounds; indeed the vehicle is one of the best armoured vehicles of its type available in the world today. Both left-hand and right-hand drive models are available, the driver being seated right at the front of the vehicle with the engine to his left or right. The troop compartment is at the rear of the hull, and twin doors are provided in the hull rear and a single door in each side to allow for the rapid exit of troops. British army vehicles do not have the left door installed as external bins are fitted for the stowage of personnel kit and supplies. The commander's cupola in the roof of the Saxon is fixed and fitted with an observation block in each of the four sides for all-round observation; a 7.62-mm (0.3-in) machine-gun is mounted on a DISA mount for ground and anti-aircraft fire. A wide range of other armament in-

stallations can be fitted, including turret-mounted 7.62-mm (0.3-in) and 12.7-mm (0.5-in) machine-guns or anti-riot weapons. If required firing ports and/or vision blocks can be installed in the troop compartment. An unusual feature of the Saxon is that its mudguards are of light sheet steel construction which will blow off in the event of the vehicle hitting a mine so that the blast is not contained under the hull.

Variants of the Saxon proposed by the manufacturer include a command vehicle, a mortar carrier, an armoured ambulance and various anti-riot versions, including one with an obstacle-clearing blade at the front of the hull. GKN has also designed the **Simba**

range of armoured vehicles which can be used as armoured personnel carriers or as weapon carriers with a wide range of armament installations up to 90 mm (3.54 in) in calibre.

Specification
Saxon
Crew: 2×8
Combat weight: 10670 kg (23,523 lb)
Powerplant: one Bedford 500 6-cylinder diesel developing 164 bhp (122 kW)
Dimensions: length 5.169 m (16 ft 11.5 in); width 2.489 m (8 ft 2 in); height 2.86 m (9 ft 4.6 in)

The AT105P, seen outside the UK Ministry of Defence, has a commander's cupola with pintle-mounted 7.62-mm GPMG. The cupola can be removed and replaced by one of a number of alternative armament installations.

Performance: maximum road speed 96 km/h (60 mph); maximum range 510 km (317 miles); fording 1.12 m (3 ft 8 in); gradient 60 per cent; vertical obstacle 0.41 m (1 ft 4 in); trench not applicable

---

BRAZIL

ENGESA EE-11 Urutu armoured personnel carrier

In 1970 the Brazilian company ENGESA, which had for some years been successfully converting 6×4 and 4×2 trucks into 6×6 and 4×4 models for increased cross-country mobility, turned its attention to the development of a range of 6×6 wheeled vehicles to meet the requirements of the Brazilian armed forces. In 1970 prototypes of the ENGESA EE-9 Cascavel armoured car and **ENGESA EE-11 Urutu** armoured personnel carrier made their first appearance. Production of these started in 1974 at a new plant at São José dos Campos, and by early 1984 some 3,000 EE-9s and EE-11s had been built, most of them for export, especially to the Middle East.

The layout of both vehicles is quite different although they both share many common automotive components such as engine, transmission and suspension. In the EE-11 the driver is seated at the front on the left side with the engine to his right and the troop compartment to his rear. The troops can enter the vehicle via a door in the side of the hull or through two doors in the hull rear. Over the top of the troop compartment are four roof hatches, two on each side, which open outwards, while forward of this is the main armament installation. This can range from a pintle- or ring-mounted 12.7-mm (0.5-in) M2 HB machine-gun, via a turret armed with a 20-mm cannon and a co-axial 7.62-mm (0.3-in) machine-gun, right up to a two-man turret armed with a 90-mm (3.54-in) gun, 7.62-mm (0.3-in) co-axial and 7.62-mm (0.3-in) anti-aircraft machine-gun. This turret is similar to that fitted to the EE-9 armoured car, but has no bustle and the 90-mm (3.54-in) gun has a reduced recoil length. Firing ports and/or vision blocks can be installed in the troop compartment to enable the troops to

fire their weapons from within the vehicle if required. The infantry sit on seats down each side of the hull facing each other, and these seats can be folded up to allow cargo to be carried. The EE-11 is fully amphibious, being propelled in the water at a speed of 8 km/h (5 mph) by two propellers at the hull rear. Before the vehicle enters the water a trim vane is erected at the front of the hull by the driver, who does so without leaving his seat, and the electric bilge pumps are switched on. The **EE-11 Mk 2** is available with a Detroit Diesel or a Mercedez-Benz diesel engine coupled to an automatic transmission, although the original **EE-11 Mk 1** had a manual transmission. All models now have a central tyre pressure regulation system that enables the driver to adjust the tyre pressure to suit the type of ground being crossed, and optional equipment includes a winch, night vision equipment. an NBC system and various radio installations.

A whole range of versions of the basic vehicle has now been designed by the company, including ambulance, cargo, command, recovery, anti-tank and anti-aircraft vehicles. The anti-tank model has MILAN or HOT ATGWs, while the anti-aircraft has a French ESD turret with twin 20-mm cannon and a surveillance radar. When fitted with the two-man 90-mm (3.54-in) turret the EE-11 is known as the **Urutu Armoured Fire Support Vehicle** (AFSV), and this is known to be used by Tunisia. The recovery vehicle has a hydraulically-operated crane for changing components in the field, and a winch for recovering other vehicles.

Specification
EE-11
Crew: 2+12 (commander, driver and 12 infantry)

Combat weight: 13000 kg (28,660 lb)
Powerplant: one Detroit Diesel 6V-53N 6-cylinder diesel developing 212 hp (158 kW)
Dimensions: length 6.15 m (20 ft 2 in); width 2.59 m (8 ft 6 in); height (without armament) 2.09 m (6 ft 10.3 in)
Performance: maximum road speed 90 km/h (56 mph); maximum road range 850 km (528 miles); fording amphibious; gradient 60 per cent; vertical obstacle 0.6 m (1 ft 11.6 in); trench not applicable

The ENGESA EE-11 Urutu armoured personnel carrier has a crew of two and can carry up to 12 fully armed infantrymen. Basic armament is a 12.7-mm (0.50-in) M2 HB heavy machine-gun.

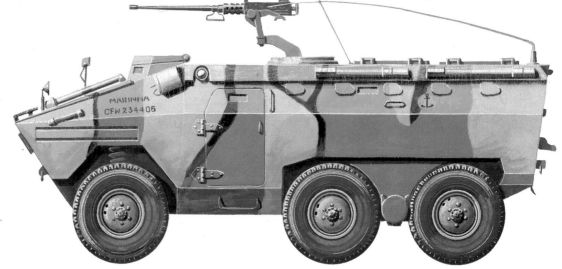

Left: The EE-11, in production since 1974 has been successful in the export market. This version is equipped with a Swedish-designed Hagglunds turret armed with a 20-mm cannon from Hispano. A 7.62-mm machine-gun can also be fitted.

Above: The 3,000 or more Urutus manufactured have carried a wide variety of weapon systems. This model is equipped with a Euromissile MILAN ATGW system and a 7.62-mm M1919 machine-gun.

 BELGIUM
SIBMAS armoured personnel carrier

In the mid-1970s the Belgian company B N Constructions Ferroviaires et Métalliques started development, as a private venture, of a 6×6 armoured personnel carrier which would have a number of common and proven commercial components. The first **SIBMAS** prototype was completed in 1976, the second following in 1979. One of these was tested by the Royal Malaysian army in competition with a number of vehicles submitted from other European, North American and South American companies. In the end Malaysia selected two vehicles to meet its requirements, namely the Condor 4×4 from Thyssen Henschel of West Germany and the Belgian SIBMAS 6×6. The order for the latter, valued at about £50 million, was placed in 1981, and the first vehicles were delivered in 1983. Two versions have been ordered by Malaysia: 24 examples of the **SIBMAS Armoured Recovery Vehicle (ARV)** and 162 examples of the **SIBMAS Armoured Fire Support Vehicle 90 (AFSV-90)**. The latter has a two-man turret designed and built by Cockerill and armed with a 90-mm (3.54-mm) Cockerill Mk III gun, 7.62-mm (0.3-in) co-axial and 7.62-mm (0.3-in) anti-aircraft machine-gun, and fitted with an OIP fire-control system.

The hull of the SIBMAS is of all-welded steel construction which provides the crew with complete protection from small arms fire and shell splinters. The driver is seated at the front of the vehicle, with the crew compartment in the centre and the engine at the rear of the vehicle on the left side, an aisle connecting the troop compartment with a door in the hull rear being fitted on the right side. Doors are provided in each side of the hull, and there are hatches over the troop compartment. Depending on the model, firing ports and/or vision blocks can be fitted in the sides and rear of the troop compartment. The engine is coupled to a fully automatic ZF transmission with six forward and one reverse gear and a hydrodynamic torque converter. Steering is power-assisted on the front wheels, and if required the vehicle can be fitted with a hydraulically-operated winch to assist in self-recovery or in the recovery of other vehicles.

The basic model is fully amphibious without preparation, being propelled in the water by its wheels at a speed of 4 km/h (2.4 mph). The SIBMAS can also be fitted with two propellers at the hull rear to provide a maximum water speed of 11 km/h (6.8 mph). Other optional equipment includes night vision equipment, an air-conditioning system, a heater and an NBC system.

Following a 1985 reorganization of the Belgian armaments industry, SIBMAS was transferred from BN to Belgian Mechanical Fabrication SA, who are building tracked IFVs for the Belgian Army. BMF no longer have the SIBMAS in production, but retain the prototypes for customer demonstrations. Further developments are aimed at reducing production and operating costs, and production could begin again if an order was received.

Specification
SIBMAS
Crew: 3+11
Combat weight: 14500 kg to 16500 kg (31,967 to 36,376 lb) depending on role and armament

Powerplant: one MAN 6-cylinder turbocharged diesel developing 320 hp (239 kW)
Dimensions: length 7.32 m (24 ft 0 in); width 2.50 m (8 ft 2.4 in); height (hull) 2.24 m (7 ft 4.2 in)
Performance: maximum road speed 100 km/h (62 mph); maximum road range 1000 km (621 miles); fording amphibious; gradient 70 per cent; vertical obstacle 0.6 m (1 ft 11.6 in); trench 1.5 m (4 ft 11 in)

The SIBMAS 6×6 APC was designed as a private venture. It can be armed with the French SAMM TTB 120 20-mm two-man turret.

The major export success to date for the SIBMAS has been the 186 vehicle sold to Malaysia. Most of the vehicles have been the Cockerill Mk III armed AFSV-90 version, for use as Armoured Fire Support Vehicles.

UK/BELGIUM
BDX/Valkyr armoured personnel carrier

In the early 1970s Technology Investments of Ireland designed and built the prototype of a 4×4 armoured personnel carried called the **Timoney**, and after trials with several prototype vehicles the Irish army finally ordered 10 vehicles in two batches of five. In 1976 Beherman Demoen of Belgium obtained a licence from Technology Investments to manufacture the Timoney armoured personnel carrier in Belgium. The Belgian government placed an order for a total of 123 vehicles under the designation **BDX**, and these were all built between 1978 and 1981. Of the 123, 43 were delivered to the Belgian air force for the defence of air bases, while the remainder were supplied to the Gendarmerie. All of the air force vehicles have a 7.62-mm (0.3-in) machine-gun, while the Gendarmerie vehicles comprise 13 fitted with an 81-mm mortar, 41 in the armoured personnel carrier role and the remaining 26 fitted with a front-mounted dozer blade.

The BDX was also tested in a number of other countries including Malaysia, but the only order obtained was placed by Argentina, which ordered five vehicles for use in the internal security role.

More recently Vickers Defence Systems of the United Kingdom have undertaken further development of the BDX which has resulted in the **Valkyr**, whose first two prototypes were completed in 1982 and the third in 1984. The Valkyr has many significant improvements over the original vehicle and is considered by many to be a new vehicle. It is powered by a proven

General Motors Model 4-53T diesel coupled to a fully automatic AT-545 transmission with four forward and one reverse gear. Two basic models of the Valkyr are being offered, an armoured personnel carrier and a weapons platform which has a slightly lower profile and has already been experimentally fitted with a variety of weapons stations including a French turret armed with a 90-mm (3.54-in) gun and the Belgian CM-90 Cockerill turret armed with the 90-mm (3.54-in) Cockerill Mk III gun, 7.62-mm (0.3-in) co-axial and 7.62-mm (0.3-in) anti-aircraft machine-guns.

When used as an armoured personnel carrier the vehicle normally has a two-man crew consisting of the commander/machine-gunner and driver, and can carry 10 fully equipped troops, who can rapidly leave the vehicle via twin doors in the hull rear. If required the Valkyr can be fitted with firing ports and/or vision blocks and a wide range of options including air-conditioning, riot-control equipment and night vision devices. It is fully amphibious, being propelled in the water by its wheels, although as an option waterjets can be fitted to provide a much higher water speed.

In addition to armoured personnel carrier and fire-support vehicle models, a wide range of other variants are possible such as forward ambulance, command post vehicle, mortar carrier, and anti-tank vehicle fitted with turret mounted ATGWs.

Specification
BDX
Crew: 2+10

Combat weight: 10700 kg (23,590 lb)
Powerplant: one Chrysler V-8 water-cooled petrol engine developing 180 hp (134 kW)
Dimensions: length 5.05 m (16 ft 7 in); width 2.50 m (8 ft 2.4 in); height (hull top) 2.06 m (6 ft 9 in)
Performance: maximum road speed 100 km/h (62 mph); maximum range (road) 500 to 900 km (310 to 560 miles);

The Vickers Valkyr, while based upon the Timoney/BDX design, is of significantly improved capability. As has become the norm with modern APCs, the Valkyr can be fitted with a wide range of weapon systems.

fording amphibious; gradient 60 per cent; vertical obstacle 0.4 m (1 ft 4 in); trench not applicable

---

ITALY
Tipo 6614 armoured personnel carrier

Some years ago Fiat and OTO-Melara designed and built prototypes of a 4×4 armoured car (the Tipo 6616) and a 4×4 armoured personnel carrier (**Tipo 6614**), both of which had identical automotive components although their layouts were quite different. Many of the automotive components of these vehicles are taken from standard commercial vehicles to keep costs to a minimum as well as making spare parts easier to obtain on a worldwide basis. The Tipo 6616 is used in small numbers by the Italian police, and known export customers include Libya, Peru, Somalia and Tunisia. It is estimated that about 400 vehicles at least had been built by 1984, and licence production is also undertaken in the Republic of Korea by Asia Motors Incorported, who call the vehicle the **KM900**.

The hull of the Tipo 6614 armoured personnel carrier is of all-welded steel construction that varies in thickness from 6 mm (0.24 in) to 8 mm (0.315 in), and this provides protection against 7.62-mm (0.3-in) small arms fire and light artillery splinters. The driver is seated at the very front of the vehicle on the left side with the engine to his right. The troop compartment is toward the rear, and the 10 fully equipped troops, including the commander, sit on individual bucket type seats that can be quickly folded up. The troops enter and leave via a door in each side of the hull, or over a power-operated ramp in the hull rear. A total of 10 firing ports is provided, with a vision block above each; four of these ports are in

each side of the hull (including one in the door) and one on each side of the rear ramp. Over the top of the troop compartment is a two-part roof hatch that opens to each side, while to the front of this is the main armament installation. This is normally an M113-type cupola with a single-piece hatch cover that opens to the rear, periscopes for all-round observations and a 12.7-mm (0.5-in) M2 HB machine-gun. A turret armed with twin 7.62-mm (0.3-in) machine-guns can also be installed. One of the more unusual versions offered has a multiple rocket launcher, this consisting of an Italian 48-round 51-mm system which can be fired by remote control at a rate of 10 rounds per second. Other variants include a mortar carrier which is known to be used by Peru, an ambulance and a command vehicle.

The Fiat engine is coupled to a manual gearbox with five forward and one reverse gear and a two-speed transfer case. The Tipo 6614 is fully amphibious, being propelled in the water by its wheels at a speed of 4.5 km/h (2.8 mph), and before the vehicle enters the water the four electrically-operated bilge pumps are switched on to pump out any water that enters the vehicle through the door or ramp seals. As usual a range of optional equipment is available apart from the different weapon stations, these including various types of passive night vision equipment, a spare wheel and holder (often mounted on the roof of the troop compartment), smoke dischargers, an air-conditioning system, a

fire extinguishing system, and a front-mounted winch with a capacity of 4500 kg (9,221 lb) and 40 m (131 ft) of cable. This last would be used to recover other vehicles or to assist in self-recovery.

Specification
Tipo 6614
Crew: 1+10
Combat weight: 8500 kg (18,739 lb)
Powerplant: one Model 8062.24 supercharged liquid-cooled diesel developing 160 hp (119 kW)
Dimensions: length 5.86 m (19 ft 2.7 in);

width 2.50 m (8 ft 2.4 in); height (hull top) 1.78 m (5 ft 10 in)
Performance: maximum road speed 100 km/h (62 mph); maximum range 700 km (435 miles); fording amphibious; gradient 60 per cent; vertical obstacle 0.4 m (1 ft 4 in); trench not applicable

Seen fording a stream, the Type 6614 APC (left) shares many components with the Type 6616 armoured car. The APC can transport 10 men in addition to the driver, with usual armament being a 12.7-mm MG.

Armoured Vehicle General Purpose/Light Armored Vehicle

A Canadian Armed Forces requirement for an **Armoured Vehicle General Purpose** was issued in 1974. 14 proposals were examined, and three vehicles were subject to engineering tests and trials in the field. Eventually the 6×6 version of the Swiss MOWAG Piranha, built under licence by the Diesel Division of General Motors of Canada, was selected by the CAF for use in continental Canada. 350 vehicles were ordered in 1977, the first being delivered in 1979. The order was increased several times, until the last of 491 units were delivered in September 1982.

Used by both regulars and the militia, the AVGP has been built in three models. The **Cougar 76mm Wheeled Fire Support Vehicle** is a 6×6 Piranha fitted with the 76mm gun and turret of the British Scorpion reconnaissance vehicle. 10 rounds of 76mm ammunition are carried in the turret and a further 30 rounds in the hull. 195 of this model were built, along with 269 of the **Grizzly Wheeled Armoured Personnel Carrier**. This version is equipped with a Cadillac Gage 1-metre one-man turret with a 12.7mm and a 7.62mm machine-gun, and can carry six or eight troops in addition to its crew of three. The troop compartment has had vision blocks and firing ports fitted in the sides and rear. The third variant is the **Husky Wheeled Maintenance and Recovery vehicle**, 27 of which were delivered. All vehicles are heated and have cold-start aids to cope with the Canadian winter. All have passive night vision devices for the driver.

In 1981, GM Canada entered an 8×8 version of the Piranha for the US **Light Armored Vehicle (LAV)** competition. An airportable vehicle of this type was needed in the evolving doctrine of rapid US intervention worldwide, and the winner of the competition could anticipate orders for close to a thousand vehicles for the US Army and the US Marine Corps. In the event, the Canadian bid was successful and the first orders were placed late in 1982 with the first 60 vehicles delivered to the Marines in 1983. Even though the Army withdrew from the project in 1984, production for the Marines over five years is expected to reach nearly 800.

The Marines have received six main variants. The **LAV-25** is the base vehicle, equipped with a Delco two man turret armed with a stabilized 25mm Chain Gun, a co-axial 7.62mm machine-gun and a pintle mount for an M60 7.62mm machine-gun. It can carry six fully equipped Marines in addition to the crew of three, and is provided with vision blocks in the troop compartment. The **Logistics Vehicle** has a higher roof on which is mounted a cargo crane, and two roof hatches for quick loading and unloading. The **Mortar Carrier** has a five-man crew operating an 81mm mortar firing through a three-part roof hatch. The **Light Armored Recovery Vehicle** also has a crew of five to operate its fuel transfer system, 1800kg capacity crane and 13608kg capacity winch. The **Command and Control Vehicle** has the same large hull as the logistic vehicle, to house the extensive communications gear carried. The **Anti-tank Vehicle** has an Emerson twin TOW launcher with 14 reload missiles in the hull. Other projected models include an anti-aircraft variant and an EW support

variant. Two out of four LAV prototypes were completed as assault guns, and though this was not built a requirement for such a fire-support vehicle still exists. It is likely that some LAV-25s will be converted by the addition of a high-velocity gun of between 60mm and 90mm calibre mounted in a new turret.

Specification
Grizzly WAPC
Crew: 3+6/8
Combat weight: 10,500kg (23,148lb)
Powerplant: one GM Detroit Diesel 6-cylinder diesel developing 215hp (160kW)
Dimensions: length 5.968m (19.6ft); width 2.53m (8.3ft); height to hull roof 1.85m (6.06ft)
Performance: maximum road speed 101.5km/h (63mph); maximum water speed 7km/h (4.3mph); maximum road range 603km (375 miles); fording-amphibious; gradient 60 per cent; vertical obstacle 0.5m (1.66ft); trench 0.4m (1.31ft)

Specification
LAV-25
Crew: 3+6
Combat weight: 12882kg (28,399lb)
Powerplant: one GM Detroit Diesel 6-cylinder diesel developing 275hp (205kW)
Dimensions: length 6.393m (20.97ft); width 2.499m (8.2ft); height overall 2.692m (8.83ft)
Performance: maximum road speed 100km/h (62.2mph); maximum water speed 10.46m/h (6.5mph); maximum range 668km (415 miles); fording-amphibious; gradient 70 per cent; vertical obstacle 0.5m (1.64ft); trench 2.057m (6.75ft)

Above: A Marine Corps LAV-25 undergoes trials at the Marine Corps Air-Ground Combat Center, Twenty Nine Palms, California. The arid wastes of the Mojave Desert provide much the same kind of environment as any force rapidly deployed to the Middle East would encounter, and are a true test of men and equipment.

Below: Marines must be ready to make assaults onto beaches from the arctic to the tropics, so the LAV has to be fully amphibious. The Marine Corps has three current LAV battalions, at Camp LeJeune North Carolina, Camp Pendleton California and at Twenty Nine Palms. A further company is stationed in Okinawa.

Modern Self-Propelled Guns and Howitzers

Used in Vietnam to provide long range fire support, the M107 has since been phased out of American service to be converted to 203-mm (8-in) M110A2 howitzer systems. Many other armies who use the equipment are likely to follow suit.

Since the end of World War II the self-propelled gun and howitzer has become an essential part of the modern battlefield scene. As one of the vital components of the combined arms concept, self-propelled artillery has a vast array of fire control aids and types of ammunition available in order to produce exactly the amount of fire to suit any situation.

Self-propelled guns and howitzers are by no means a new invention as in World War I the British developed a version of the tank that could transport a towed artillery piece across the battlefield. Between the world wars much work was done on self-propelled artillery weapons but hardly any of these were in service by the time that World War II broke out. During this conflict Germany and the United States devoted considerable resources to the development and production of self-propelled guns and howitzers and some of these, such as the M7 'Priest', remain in service today.

After the war Western armies became increasingly mechanized and, as towed guns could not be expected to keep up with these units, self-propelled guns and howitzers were developed and deployed on a large scale. These were mostly of the 203-mm (8-in) 155-mm (6.1-in) and 105-mm (4.13-in) calibres, although by the 1960s the last was being phased out in most countries due to preference for the more effective 155-mm (6.1-in) weapon which could also fire a nuclear projectile.

It is only in recent years that the Soviet Union has started to deploy self-propelled guns and howitzers on a large scale, although specialized tank destroyers and assault guns have been in service for many years.

The recent conflicts in the Middle East have again proved that there is no substitute for self-propelled artillery, which is now an essential part of the combined arms concept with armour, infantry, engineers and helicopters. For a variety of reasons towed rather than self-propelled artillery was used in the Falklands campaign of 1982 but there is little doubt that this was one of the deciding factors in the rapid collapse of Argentinian morale.

Sweden was the first country to deploy a self-propelled gun with an automatic loading system: the Bandkanon 1A, but this was never exported. France has recently deployed the 155-mm (6.1-in) GCT self-propelled gun that can fire at the rate of eight rounds per minute until its ammunition is exhausted; this weapon has already been exported to Iraq and Saudi Arabia. Italy, West Germany and the United Kingdom were to have replaced their M109s from the late 1980s with the tri-national SP-70, but this automatic loading 155-mm system ran into so many development problems it was cancelled in 1986. The introduction of artillery- and mortar-locating systems such as the American AN/TPQ-36 and AN/TPQ-37 has meant that artillery weapons can now easily be located and identified and counter-battery fire quickly brought to bear. This means that in future conflicts artillery will fire only for a short period before moving off to a new fire position, for static location will surely entail neutralization.

Self-propelled artillery weapons are of little use without the full range of fire-control aids that now include surveillance and locating radars, sound-ranging equipment, battalion and battery computers, position and azimuth determining systems, RPVs and surveillance aircraft/helicopters, laser rangefinders and meteorological stations, to name just a few.

The Israelis used the M107 widely in the 1973 Yom Kippur war and intend to keep it in service. Firing the special 40-km (24.8-mile) plus round developed for them, the long range of the 175-mm (6.89-in) gun is ideal for Israel's special requirement.

Mk 61 105-mm Self-Propelled Howitzer

The development by the Atelier de Construction d'Issy-les-Moulineaux of the AMX-13 light tank in the late 1940s laid the basis for one of the largest families of tracked vehicles ever developed. At an early stage the French army issued a requirement for a 105-mm (4.13-mm) self-propelled howitzer, and it was decided to base the **Mk 61** equipment on a modified AMX-13 tank chassis. After trials with prototype vehicles, the equipment was placed in production at the Atelier de Construction Roanne in the late 1950s under the designation **Obusier de 105 Modèle 50 sur Affût Automoteur** for the French army. It is still available to special order from Creusot-Loire, which now builds and markets all members of the AMX-13 light tank family. In addition to being used by the French army, it has been purchased by Morocco, Israel and the Netherlands, the last having a longer 30-calibre barrel. The type has already been phased out of service with the Israeli army, having been replaced by the 155-mm (6.1-in) M109A1; in the French army it is being replaced by the 155-mm (6.1-in) GCT self-propelled weapon.

The vehicle is of all-welded steel construction that provides the crew with protection from small arms fire and shell splinters. The engine and transmission are at the front, the driver is on the left side, and the fully enclosed gun compartment is at the rear. Access hatches are provided in the roof and rear, and the commander has a cupola with periscopes for all-round observation. The suspension is of the well-proven torsion-bar type, and consists on each side of five rubber-tyred road wheels, with the drive sprocket at the front, the idler at the rear and three track-return rollers. Hydraulic shock absorbers are provided at the first and last road wheel stations. The tracks are steel, but can be fitted with rubber pads to reduce damage to the road surface.

The 105-mm (4.13-in) howitzer has a double-baffle muzzle-brake, and can be elevated from −4° 30′ to +66°; traverse is 20° left and right. Traverse and elevation are both manual. Various types of standard 105-mm (4.13-in) separate-loading ammunition can be fired, including an HE projectile weighing 16 kg (35.3 lb) to a maximum range of 15000 m (16,405 yards) and a HEAT projectile which will penetrate 350 mm (13.8 in) of armour at an incidence of 0° or 105 mm (4.13 in) of armour at 65°. A total of 56 rounds of ammunition is carried, and of these six are normally HEAT rounds. A 7.62-mm (0.3-in) or 7.5-mm (0.295-in) machine-gun is mounted externally on the roof for anti-aircraft defence, and a similar weapon is carried inside the vehicle for use in the ground role, 2,000 rounds of ammunition being carried for these weapons. The Mk 61 does not have an NBC system, and has no amphibious capability.

One of the drawbacks of the Mk 61 is the limited traverse of the ordnance.

The prototype of a similar vehicle but fitted with a turret that could be traversed through 360° was built but not placed in production, although a few were purchased for trials purposes by Switzerland. By the time the turret version was ready most countries had already decided to replace their 105-mm (4.13-in) equipment with more effective 155-mm (6.1-in) weapons, and in most cases chose the American M109. The chassis of the Mk 61 was also used for trials with the Roland surface-to-air missile system and as a minelayer, but neither of these variants entered production. A similar chassis is also used for the AMX-13 DCA twin 30-mm self-propelled anti-aircraft gun produced for the French army in the 1960s.

The Mk 61 is one of the many vehicles based on the AMX-13 light tank chassis. Obsolete by modern standards, it is still available to special order.

Specification
Crew: 5
Weight: 16500 kg (36,375 lb)
Dimensions: length 5.70 m (18 ft 8½ in); width 2.65 m (8 ft 8¼ in); height 2.70 m (8 ft 10¼ in)
Powerplant: one SOFAM 8Gxb 8-cylinder petrol engine developing 250 hp (186 kW)
Performance: maximum road speed 60 km/h (37 mph); maximum range 350 km (217 miles); gradient 60%; vertical obstacle 0.65 (2 ft 2 in); trench 1.60 m (5 ft 3 in)

Mk F3 155-mm Self-Propelled Gun

In the period immediately after World War II the standard self-propelled howitzer of the French army was the American 155-mm (6.1-in) M41 Howitzer Motor Carriage, essentially the M24 Chaffee light tank chassis fitted with a slightly modified version of the standard M114 towed howitzer. This was replaced in the 1960s by the 155-mm (6.1-in) **Mk F3** self-propelled gun, which is basically a shortened AMX-13 light tank chassis with 155-mm (6.1-in) gun mounted at the rear of the hull. The ordnance is based on the Modèle 50 towed weapon of the same calibre. In addition to being used by the French army, the Mk F3 is used by Argentina, Chile, Ecuador, Kuwait, Morocco, Qatar, Sudan, United Arab Emirates and Venezuela. It will be replaced in the late 1980s in French service by the 155-mm (6.1-in) GCT. Production of the Mk F3, along with other members of AMX-13 light tank family, was originally undertaken at the Atelier de Construction Roanne, a French government facility, but as this plant tooled up for production of the AMX-30 MBT, AMX-30 variants and the AMX-10P family, production of the whole AMX-13 family, including the Mk F3, was transferred to Creusot-Loire at Châlon-sur-Saône, where production continues today, although at a much lower rate.

The 155-mm (6.1-in) ordnance is mounted at the very rear of the chassis and can be elevated from 0° to +67°, with a traverse of 20° left and right up to an elevation of +50° and of 16° left and 30° right from +50° up to the maximum elevation. Elevation and traverse are both manual. When travelling the ordnance is held in a travel lock and

The Mk F3 is widely used in a number of Middle East and South American countries, including Argentina.

traversed 8° to the right. The 33-calibre barrel has a double-baffle muzzle-brake and a screw breech mechanism. Ammunition is of the separate-loading type, and the following can be fired: high explosive with a maximum range of just over 20000 m (21,875 yards), illuminating and smoke to a range of 17750 m (19,410 yards), and a rocket-assisted projectile to a range of 25300 m (27,670 yards). Rate of fire for the first few minutes is three rounds per minute, but when the Mk F3 is used in the sustained fire role the rate is one round a minute. Before firing commences two spades are manually released at the rear of the hull and the vehicle then reversed backwards to provide a more stable firing platform.

A major disadvantage of the Mk F3 (in addition to the total lack of protection for the gun and its crew) is that only the driver and commander can be carried in the actual vehicle. The remainder of the gun crew are carried in an AMX VCA (Véhicule Chenillé d'Ac- compagnement, or tracked support vehicle) or 6×6 truck which also carries 25 projectiles, charges and associated fuzes. The VCA can also tow an

The Mk F3 in firing position with its recoil spade down. The total lack of gun and crew protection is self-evident.

ARE 2-tonne F2 ammunition trailer which carries an additional 30 projectiles and charges.

The Mk F3 can ford to a depth of 1 m (3 ft 3 in) but has no NBC system; active or passive night-vision equipment can be installed, and all vehicles have direct and indirect sights, and a loud-speaker and cable. The basic vehicle is powered by a petrol engine, but if required this can be replaced by a General Motors Detroit Diesel 6V-53T developing 280 hp (209 kW). This produces a slightly higher road speed and, most important of all, an increased operational range from 300 to 400 km (185 to 250 miles).

Specification
Crew: 2
Weight: 17400 kg (38,360 lb)
Dimensions: length (gun forward) 6.22 m (20 ft 5 in); width 2.72 m (8 ft 11 in); height 2.085 m (6 ft 10 in)

Powerplant: one SOFAM 8Gxb 8-cylinder petrol engine developing 250 hp (186 kW)
Performance: maximum road speed 60 km/h (37 mph); maximum range 300 km (185 miles); gradient 40%; vertical obstacle 0.60 m (2 ft 0 in); trench 1.50 m (4 ft 11 in)

GCT 155-mm Self-Propelled Gun
FRANCE

For many years the standard self-propelled weapons of the French army have been the 155-mm (6.1-in) Mk F3 and the 105-mm (4.13-in) Mk 61. The former suffered a major disadvantage in that its weapon was in an unprotected mount with limited traverse and most of the gun crew had to be carried in another full-tracked vehicle that also carried the ammunition. In the late 1960s a new self-propelled gun called the **GCT** (Grande Cadence de Tir) was developed on a slightly modified AMX-30 MBT chassis. The first prototype was completed in 1972, and following trials with a pre-production batch of 10 vehicles production got under way in 1977. For a number of reasons Saudi Arabia was the first country to deploy the GCT; they ordered 51 systems plus a complete fire-control system. The French army designates the GCT the **155 AU F1**, and deploys it in regiments of 18 weapons (three batteries each with six GCTs). More recently Iraq has placed an order for 85 GCTs, and these are now being delivered. The GCT is manufactured at the Atelier de Construction Roanne with the assistance of many other GIAT establishments all over France.

As mentioned above, the chassis is similar to that of the AMX-30 MBT but with a new all-welded turret in the centre fitted with a 155-mm (6.1-in) 40-calibre barrel that has a multi-baffle muzzle-brake and a vertical sliding wedge breech block. Elevation is from −4° to +66° at a rate of 5° per second, and turret traverse is 360° at the rate of 10° per second. Turret traverse and gun elevation are hydraulic, with manual controls for emergency use.

The major feature of the GCT is the automatic loading system for a total of 42 projectiles and a similar number of cartridges carried in racks in the turret rear. Ammunition mix depends on the tactical situation, but can consist of 36 (six racks of six) HE and six (one rack of six) smoke projectiles. Access to the ammunition racks for reloading purposes is via two large turret doors in

Although meant to replace the Mk F3 in French service, the GCT was first deployed by Saudi Arabia, since when it has been adopted by Iraq and used in the Gulf War. The automatic loading system enables the GCT to fire up to eight rounds per minute.

the rear. The four-man crew can reload the GCT in 15 minutes, and if required loading can be undertaken while the weapon is being fired. The automatic loading system enables a rate of eight rounds per minute, and the gunner can select either single shots or six-round bursts, the latter taking just 45 seconds. When manual loading is used, two to three rounds per minute can be fired.

The following projectiles can be fired by the GCT: high explosive, illuminating, smoke and rocket-assisted. The last has a range of 30500 m (33,355 yards) and has been developed by Thomson-Brandt. More advanced projectiles are now under development for the GCT and the towed equivalent, the TIR, including a round carrying six anti-tank mines. The ordnance can also fire the American Cannon-Launched Guided Projectile (CLGP), although this has not yet been accepted by the French army.

A 7.62-mm (0.3-in) or 12.7-mm (0.5-in) machine-gun is mounted on the turret roof for anti-aircraft defence, and two electrically-operated smoke-dischargers are mounted on each side of the turret. Standard equipment of all vehicles includes night-vision equipment and a ventilating system, while optional equipment includes an NBC pack, muzzle velocity measuring equipment and various fire-control devices. For trials purposes the turret of the GCT has also been fitted to the

Leopard 1 MBT chassis but this combination has not so far been adopted by any country.

Specification
Crew: 4
Weight: 42000 kg (92,595 lb)
Dimensions: length (gun forward) 10.25 m (33 ft 7½ in); length (hull) 6.70 m (22 ft 0 in); width 3.15 m (10 ft 4 in); height 3.25 m (10 ft 8 in)
Powerplant: one Hispano-Suiza HS 110

The GCT is seen here with its ordnance at its maximum elevation of 66 degrees.

12-cylinder water-cooled multi-fuel engine developing 720 hp (537 kW)
Performance: maximum road speed 60 km/h (37 mph); maximum range 450 km (280 miles); gradient 60%; vertical obstacle 0.93 m (3 ft 0⅔ in); trench 1.90 m (6 ft 3 in)

M107 175-mm Self-Propelled Gun
USA

In the 1950s the standard 203-mm (8-in) self-propelled howitzer of the US Army was the M55, which had the chassis and turret of the M53 155-mm (6.1-in) self-propelled gun. The main drawbacks of both these weapons were that at a weight of about 45 tons they were too heavy for air transport and their petrol engines gave them an operating range of only 260 km (160 miles). In the mid-1950s a decision was taken to design a new family of self-propelled artillery that would share a common chassis and mount, be air-portable, and come into and be taken out of action quickly. Prototypes were built by

the Pacific Car and Foundry Company under the designations 175-mm (6.89-in) self-propelled gun **T235**, 203-mm (8-in) self-propelled howitzer T236, and 155-mm (6.1-in) self-propelled gun T245. Further development, including the replacement by diesels of the petrol engines for increased operational range, resulted in the T235 being standardized as the **M107** and the T236 as the M110. The chassis of the family was also used as the basis for a number of armoured recovery vehicles (ARVs) but in the end only the T120E1 was placed in production as the M578 light ARV; this serves with many countries

including the United States.

Production of the M107 was undertaken initially by the Pacific Car and Foundry Company, the first vehicles being completed in 1962 and the first battalion forming at Fort Sill (home of the US Field Artillery) in early 1963. At a later date production was also undertaken by FMC, and from 1965 to 1980 by Bowen-McLaughlin-York.

The US Army deployed the 175-mm (6.89-in) M107 in 12-gun battalions at corps level but in recent years all of these weapons have been converted to the 203-mm (8-in) M110.2 configuration as this has a range of just over

29000 m (31,715 yards) with a HERA (High Explosive Rocket Assist) projectile. The M107 was also exported to Greece, Iran, Israel, Italy, South Korea, the Netherlands, Spain, Turkey, the United Kingdom and West Germany; many of these countries are now also converting their M107s to the M110A2 configuration.

The chassis of the M107 is fully described in the entry for the M110. The 175-mm (6.89-in) gun has an elevation of +65° and a depression of −2° and traverse is 30° left and right. Traverse and elevation are powered, although manual controls are provided for emergency use. Only one round was ever standardized for US Army use, the HE M437A1 or M437A2 which with a charge three propellant had a maximum range of 32700 m (35,760 yards), although a special round is used by Israel with a range of some 40000 m (43,745 yards). To assist the crew in loading the 66.7-kg (147-lb) projectile, a rammer and loader assembly is mounted at the rear of the chassis. This lifts the projectile from the ground, positions in and then rams it into the chamber. The charge is then loaded and the ordnance fired. Only two projectiles and charges are carried on the M107, which has a total crew of 13, of whom five (driver, commander and three gunners) travel on the M107. The remainder are carried in the M548 tracked cargo carrier that also carries the bulk of the ammunition. Some countries use 6×6 trucks to support the M107, but often these have poor cross-country mobility compared with the M107. The M107 is normally fitted with

infra-red night-vision equipment, but does not have an NBC system. It has no amphibious capability although it can ford to a depth of 1.066 m (3 ft 6 in).

Specification
Crew: 5+8
Weight: 26168 kg (57,690 lb)
Powerplant: one Detroit Diesel Model 8V-71T diesel developing 405 hp (302 kW)
Dimensions: length (gun forward) 11.256 m (36 ft 11 in); length (hull) 5.72 m (18 ft 9 in); width 3.149 m (10 ft 4 in); height 3.679 m (12 ft 0.8 in)
Performance: maximum road speed 56 km/h (36 mph); maximum range 725 km (450 miles); gradient 60%; vertical obstacle 1.016 m (3 ft 4 in); trench 2.362 m (7 ft 9 in)

A US Army M107 in travelling order. All of these vehicles have now been converted to the M110A2 configuration by replacing the 175-mm (6.8-in) gun.

M109 155-mm Self-Propelled Howitzer

The **M109** 155-mm (6.1-in) self-propelled howitzer is the most widely used self-propelled artillery weapon in the world today. Its development can be traced back to 1952, when the requirement was issued for a new self-propelled howitzer to replace the 155-mm (6.1-in) M44. At that time the 110-mm (4.33-in) T195 self-propelled howitzer was already being designed, and it was decided to use its hull and turret as the basis for the new weapon, which would be armed with a 156-mm (6.14-in) howitzer. But in 1956 it was decided to stick to a 155-mm (6.1-in) calibre for commonality in NATO, and in 1959 the first prototype was completed under the designation T196. There were numerous problems with this equipment, and much redesign work had to be carried out to improve its reliability. At the same time a decision was taken that all future American AFVs would be powered by diesel engines for greater operating range, so the vehicle was redesignated T196E1 with such a powerplant. In 1961 this was accepted for service as the M109 self-propelled howitzer, and the first production vehicles were completed in late 1962 at the Cleveland Army Tank Plant, this facility being run by the Cadillac Motor Car Division. At a later date the plant was run by Chrysler, but in the 1970s all production of the M109 series was taken over by Bowen-McLaughlin-York (BMY), where production of the latest version continues today.

In the United States Army the M109 is issued on the scale of 54 per armoured and mechanized division (three battalions each of 18 vehicles, each battalion having three batteries of six M109s). In addition to the US Army and US Marine Corps, the M109 is used by Austria, Belgium, Canada, Denmark, Ethiopia, West Germany, Greece, Iran, Israel, Italy, Jordan, Kampuchea, Kuwait, Libya, Morocco, the Netherlands, Norway, Oman, Pakistan, Peru, Portugal, Saudi Arabia, South Korea, Spain, Switzerland, Taiwan, Tunisia, Turkey and the United Kingdom. It has been used in action in a number of conflicts in the Middle East (by Iran and Israel) and the

The basic M109 self-propelled howitzer mounting the short barrel M126 howitzer barrel. The M109 series is the most widely used of all self-propelled weapons and has seen extensive combat service throughout the world, as well as seeing constant adaptation and updating.

Far East (by the USA in Vietnam and by Kampuchea).

The hull and turret of the M109 are of all-welded aluminium construction. The driver is seated at the front on the left, with the engine compartment to his right, and the turret is at the rear. The suspension is of the well-tried torsion-bar type, and consists of seven road wheels with the drive sprocket at the front and the idler at the rear; there are no track-return rollers. Standard equipment includes infra-red driving lights and an amphibious kit enabling the vehicle to propel itself across slow-flowing rivers with its tracks.

The M109 has a 155-mm (6.1-in) howitzer M126 with an elevation of +75° and a depression of −5°. Turret traverse is 360°, and both gun elevation and turret traverse are powered, with manual controls available for emergency use. The ordnance has a large fume extractor, large muzzle-brake and a Welin-step thread type breech block. Normal rate of fire is one round per minute, but for short periods three rounds per minute can be attained. The weapon can fire a wide range of projectiles including high explosive (maximum range 14320 m/15,660 yards), illuminating, tactical nuclear, smoke, tactical CS and Agents VX or GB. A total of 28 projectiles and charges is carried. A 12.7-mm (0.5-in)

M2HB machine-gun is mounted on the commander's cupola for anti-aircraft defence, and 500 rounds are provided for this weapon.

One of the reasons that the M109 has been in production for so long is that its basic chassis has proved capable of constant updating and of accepting longer-barrelled ordnance that fires projectiles to a greater distance. The first of these improved versions became operational in 1973 as the **M109A1**. This is a standard M109 which has been fitted with a much longer barrel (increasing the normal range to more than 18,000 m/19,685 yards) and improvements to the suspension and to the elevation and traverse mechanisms. The **M109A2** is a full production version incorporating a number of further improvements, including a re-designed rammer and improved recoil mechanism, an enlarged turret bustle containing an additional 22 rounds, and numerous detail changes. First delivered in 1979, the M109A2 has been upgraded to **M109A3** standard by further product improvements.

The M109 was the subject of a much more radical improvement programme in support of the abortive US Army Divisional Artillery Support Weapon System project. The Howitzer Improvement Programme (HIP) is a re-

sult, which will see the M109 modified to a new **M109A5** standard, with advanced fire control, ordnance, ammunition and ammunition handling systems being fitted to allow the M109 to remain effective into the next century.

Specification
Crew: 6
Weight: 23786 kg (52,440 lb)
Powerplant: one Detroit Diesel Model 8V-71T diesel developing 405 bhp (302 kW)
Dimensions: length (gun forward) 6.612 m (21 ft 8¼ in); length (hull) 6.256 m (20 ft 6¼ in); width 3.295 m (10 ft 9¾ in); height 3.289 m (10 ft 9½ in)
Performance: maximum road speed 56 km/h (35 mph); maximum range 386 km (240 miles); gradient 60%; vertical obstacle 0.533 m (1 ft 9 in); trench 1.828 m (6 ft 0 in)

A US Army M110A2. This differs from previous M110 versions in having a long, muzzle-braked barrel. All of the M110 series in the US Army will eventually be fitted with a crew shelter and NBC system, to rectify the original lack of cover for the gun crew.

USA

M110 203-mm Self-Propelled Howitzer

The **M110** 203-mm (8-in) self-propelled howitzer uses the same chassis and mount as the 175-mm (6.89-in) M107 self-propelled gun and details of its development are given in the entry for the M107. The M110 entered service with the US Army Field Artillery in 1963, and is issued today on the scale of one battery of four per infantry division and one battalion of 12 for each armoured and mechanized division. Production was originally completed in the late 1960s but was resumed in the 1970s by Bowen-McLaughlin-York (BMY) and the latest models remain in current production. In addition to being used by the US Army and US Marines, the M110 is operated by Belgium, Greece, Iran, Israel, Italy, Japan, Jordan, the Netherlands, Pakistan, Saudi Arabia, South Korea, Spain, Taiwan, the United Kingdom and West Germany. This list includes those on order and in many cases, especially in Europe, the M110s are being upgraded with the aid of kits supplied by the United States.

The chassis of the M110 is of all-welded steel construction with the driver seated under armour on the front at the left, with the engine compartment to his right and the howitzer on its mount on top of the chassis at the rear. Suspension is of the torsion-bar type and consists of five large road wheels with the rearmost acting as the idler; the drive sprocket is at the front and there are no track-return rollers. The suspension can be locked when the M110 is in the firing position to provide a more stable firing platform.

The 203-mm (8-in) M2A2 howitzer was developed well before World War II and is located on the mount M158, this allowing an elevation of +65° and a depression of −2°, with traverse 30° left and right. Elevation and traverse are hydraulic, with manual controls for emergency use. The M2A2 has no muzzle brake or fume extractor and has an interrupted screw breech block. At the rear of the chassis is a rammer and loader assembly to lift the projectile from the ground, position it and ram it into the chamber. The following projectiles can be fired: high explosive (weight 92.53 kg/204 lb to a maximum range of 16800 m/18,375 yards), high explosive (carrying 104 or 195 grenades), Agents GB or VX, and tactical nuclear. Only two projectiles and charges are carried on the M110, others being provided from the M548 carrier that also transports the remainder of the crew. The complete crew of the M110 consists of 13 men, of whom five (commander, driver and three gunners) are on the actual vehicle.

One of the main drawbacks of the M110 is the complete lack of any protection for the gun crew from shell splinters, small arms fire and NBC agents. A protection kit is being developed and is expected to be fielded soon.

All American M110s have now been upgraded to **M110A1** or **M110A2** standard. The former has a longer barrel and fires an HE projectile to a maximum range of 21300 m (23,300 yards) or a HE rocket-assisted projectile to 29100 m (31,825 yards); other rounds available are Improved Conventional Munitions, Agents GB or VX. Binary or tactical nuclear. The **M110A2** is almost identical to the M110A1 but has a muzzle-brake which enables it to fire charge nine of the M118A1 propelling charge whereas the M110A1 can go only up to charge eight.

Specification
Crew: 5+8
Weight: 26536 kg (58,500 lb)
Dimensions: length (gun forward) 7.467 m (24 ft 6 in); length (hull) 5.72 m (18 ft 9 in); width 3.149 m (10 ft 4 in); height 2.93 m (9 ft 7¼ in)
Powerplant: one Detroit Diesel Model 8V-71T diesel developing 405 bhp (302 kW)
Performance: maximum road speed 56 km/h (35 mph); maximum range 725 km (450 miles); gradient 60%; vertical obstacle 1.016 m (3 ft 4 in); trench 2.362 m (7 ft 9 in)

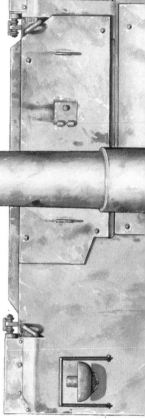

Modern Self-Propelled Guns and Howitzers

Designed to fire a wide range of nuclear, chemical, HE and improved conventional munition rounds, the versatile M110A2 has now replaced the M107 in providing long-range heavy artillery support to the US Army and Marine Corps.

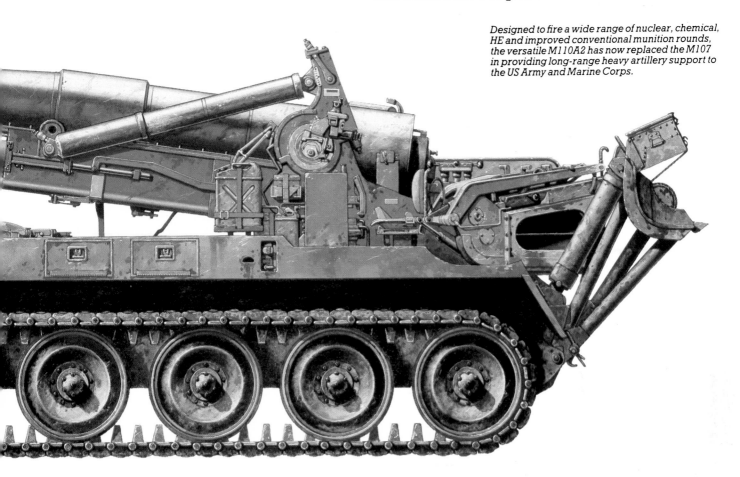

Israeli Self-Propelled Artillery

In the 1950s the Israelis used a wide range of towed artillery weapons to provide fire support for their mechanized units, but it was soon realized that such artillery could not keep up with these highly mobile forces when they deployed to the desert, where roads were nonexistent. Israel therefore purchased quantities of the American World War II **Priest** 105-mm (4.13-in) and French 105-mm (4.13-in) **Mk 61** self-propelled howitzers despite the fact that they felt, as did most members of NATO at that time, that the 155-mm (6.1-in) projectile was much more effective than the 105-mm (4.13-in) shell because of the former's greater content of high explosive.

The first self-propelled weapon of 155-mm (6.1-in) calibre to enter service with the Israeli army was the **M-50**, which was developed in France by the Etablissement d'Etudes et Fabrications d'Armement de Bourges and entered service in 1963. This system was essentially a rebuilt Sherman tank chassis with the engine moved forward to the right of the driver to enable a French 155-mm (6.1-in) Modèle 50 howitzer (which in its towed configuration was used by Israel at that time) to be mounted in an open-topped compartment at the rear of the hull. When the vehicle is deployed in action, the two doors open to each side of the hull rear revealing horizontal ammunition racks and a tailgate folded down to provide space for the crew to operate the howitzer. Additional ammunition storage space is provided under the mount, and external stowage compartments are provided in each side of the hull. The 155-mm (6.1-in) howitzer fires an HE projectile weighing 43 kg (95 lb) to a maximum range of 17600 m (19,250 yards). Maximum elevation of the howitzer is +69° but traverse is very limited. The M-50 has a crew of eight men and weighs 31000 kg (68,340 lb) fully loaded. The main drawback of the system, which was used for the first time in the 1967 Middle East War, is the lack of any overhead protection for the crew from shell splinters and small arms fire.

The M-50 was followed in Israeli service by the **L-33** (named after the length of the ordnance in calibres) which was developed in Israel by Soltam and this saw action for the first time in the 1973 Middle East War. This is based on the M4A3E8 Sherman chassis, which has Horizontal Volute Spring Suspension (HVSS) rather than the Vertical Volute Spring Suspension (VSS) of the M-50, and gives a much improved ride across country. The original petrol engine has been replaced by a Cummins diesel for a much increased operational range.

The 155-mm (6.1-in) **M-68** gun/howitzer is almost identical to the standard towed weapon and is mounted in the forward part of the superstructure with an elevation of +52°, a depression of −3° and a traverse of 30° left and right. Weapon elevation and traverse are manual. The ordnance has a single-baffle muzzle brake, fume extractor, gun travel lock and a horizontal sliding semi-automatic breech block.

To assist in maintaining a high rate of fire and in loading the ordnance at any angle of elevation, a pneumatic rammer is installed. The weapon fires an HE projectile weighing 43 kg (95 lb) to a maximum range of 21000 (22,965 yards) at maximum charge; smoke and

illuminating projectiles can also be fired. A total of 60 projectiles and charges is carried, 16 of which are for ready use. A 7.62-mm (0.3-in) machine-gun is mounted on the roof for local and anti-aircraft defence.

The hull is of all-welded steel construction and provides the crew with complete protection from small arms fire and shell splinters. Entry doors are provided on each side of the hull, and ammunition resupply doors are fitted in the hull rear; ammunition can be loaded via these doors when the weapon is still firing. The driver is seated at the front on the left with the commander to his rear; the anti-aircraft machine-gunner is in a similar position on the opposite side, and each of these crew members is provided with a roof hatch and bulletproof windows to their front and side for observation.

Unlike the earlier M-50 conversion, which entailed moving the engine forward, the L-33 has its engine at the rear, power being transmitted to the transmission at the front of the hull by a two-part propeller shaft.

As a private venture Soltam has also developed the 155-mm (6.1-in) self-propelled howitzer M72. This is a turret that weighs 14000 kg (30,865 lb) complete with ammunition and can be fitted onto a variety of tank chassis including the M60 and M48. The prototype has already been fitted onto a Centurion tank chassis for trials purposes. The prototype has a 33-calibre barrel but a 39-calibre barrel can be fitted, this allowing a 43-kg (95-lb) projectile to be fired to a range of 23500 m (25,700 yards). So far this turret system has not been adopted by the Israeli army as it already has some 400 American supplied M109A1 and M109A2 self-propelled artillery weapons in service.

Specification
Soltam L-33 155-mm Self-Propelled Gun/Howitzer
Crew: 8
Weight: 41500 kg (91,490 lb)
Dimensions: length (gun forward) 8.47 m (27 ft 9½ in); length (hull) 6.47 m (21 ft 2¾ in); width 3.50 m (11 ft 6 in);

Above: The crew of a 155-mm (6.1-in) L-33 man their vehicle during an exercise. The L-33 was first extensively used in combat during the 1973 war and Lebanon.

height 3.45 m (11 ft 3¾ in)
Powerplant: one Cummins diesel developing 460 hp (343 kW)
Performance: maximum road speed 36.8 km/h (23 mph); maximum range 260 km (162 miles); gradient 60%; vertical obstacle 0.91 m (3 ft); trench 2.30 m (7 ft 6½ in)

Below: Oldest of the self-propelled guns in Israeli service is the 155-mm (6.1-in) M-50. This entered service in 1963 and is still in service today with reserve units.

Below: The Israeli Army is the only Western nation to use 160-mm (6.3-in) self-propelled mortars. The high angle of fire proved extremely useful in the mountain fighting against Syrian troops during the 1982 invasion of Lebanon.

Type 75 155-mm Self-Propelled Howitzer

When the Japanese Ground Self-Defense force was formed in the 1950s all its artillery was of towed types and supplied by the United States. With increased mechanization taking place in the 1960s, the United States also supplied 30 105-mm (4.13-in) M52 and 10 155-mm (6.1-in) M44 self-propelled howitzers. In the later 1960s development of indigenous 105-mm (4.13-in) and 155-mm (6.1-in) self-propelled howitzers started in Japan, the former eventually being standardized as the Type 74 and the latter as the **Type 75**. Only 20 of the Type 74 were built as a decision was taken to concentrate on the more effective 155-mm (6.1-in) system.

Mitsubishi Heavy Industries are responsible for the hull and final assembly, and Japan Iron Works/Nihon Seiko for the gun and turret. The Japanese Ground Self-Defense Force expects to have 200 Type 75s in service by 1988.

In many respects the Type 75 is similar to the American M109, with the engine and transmission at the front and the fully enclosed turret at the rear. The six-man crew consists of the commander, layer, two loaders and radio operator in the turret, and the driver at the front. The hull and turret are of all-welded aluminium construction, which provides the crew with complete protection from small arms fire and shell splinters. The suspension is of the torsion-bar type, and consists of six road wheels on each side, the rearmost serving the idler; the drive sprocket is at the front, and there are no return rollers.

The 30-calibre barrel has an interrupted screw type breech block, a fume extractor and a double-baffle muzzle-brake. When the Type 75 is travelling the barrel is normally held in a travel lock mounted on the glacis plate. The ordnance has an elevation of +65° and a depression of −5°, and the turret can traverse 360°. Weapon elevation and turret traverse are hydraulic, with manual controls provided for emergency use. Before fire is opened, two spades are manually lowered to the ground at the rear of the hull to provide a more stable firing platform.

The Type 75 can fire 18 rounds in three minutes, such a rate being achieved by the use of two drum-type magazines (one on each side of the turret and containing nine projectiles each), a two-part extending loading tray and an hydraulic rammer. Once the gun has fired, it automatically returns to an angle of +6° for reloading. The breech is opened, the extending loading tray positioned, the projectile is then charge loaded with the aid of the hydraulic rammer, the breech closed, the loading tray returned to normal position and the weapon fired again. The drum magazines are rotated electrically or manually and can be reloaded from outside the vehicle via two doors/hatches in the turret rear. In action the Type 75 would probably fire 12 or 18 rounds before moving

off to a new fire position before the enemy could return fire. In addition to the 18 projectiles in the two magazines, a further 10 projectiles are carried internally as are 56 fuzes and 28 bagged charges. Mounted externally at the commander's station is a standard 12.7-mm (0.5-in) M2HB machine-gun with a shield.

Standard equipment includes infra-red night-vision lights, a fire extinguishing system, an NBC pack, a turret ventilator and a crew compartment heater. An amphibious kit was developed but not adopted, but the Type 75 can ford to a depth of 1.3 m (4 ft 3 in) without preparation.

The Type 75 self-propelled howitzer is essentially a Japanese-designed and built counterpart to the American M109.

Specification
Crew: 6
Weight: 25300 kg (55,775 lb)
Dimensions: length (gun forward) 7.79 m (25 ft 6⅔ in); length (hull) 6.64 m (21 ft 9½ in); width 3.09 m (10 ft 1¾ in); height (without MG) 2.545 m (8 ft 4 in)
Powerplant: one Mitsubishi 6-cylinder diesel developing 450 hp (336 kW)
Performance: maximum road speed 47 km/h (29 mph); range 300 km (185 miles); gradient 60%; vertical obstacle 0.70 m (2 ft 3 in); trench 2.50 m (8 ft 2½ in)

Palmaria 155-mm Self-Propelled Howitzer

The **Palmaria** 155-mm (6.1-in) self-propelled howitzer has been developed by OTO Melara specifically for the export market, and shares many common components with the OF-40 MBT which is already in service with Dubai. The first prototype was completed in 1981, and production vehicles were completed in the following year. The type has so far been ordered by Libya (200), Argentina (25 turrets only) and Nigeria (25).

The layout of the Palmaria (named after an Italian island) is similar to that of a tank with the driver at the front of the hull, turret in the centre and the engine and transmission at the rear. The major difference between the chassis of the Palmaria and that of the OF-40 MBT is that the former has thinner armour and is powered by a V-8 diesel developing 750 hp (559 kW) whereas the OF-40 has a V-10 diesel developing 830 hp (619 kW).

The 155-mm (6.1-in) 41-calibre barrel is fitted with a fume extractor and a multi-baffle muzzle-brake. The turret has 360° traverse and the ordnance can be elevated from −4° to +70° hydraulically, with manual controls for emergency use. An unusual feature of the Palmaria is the installation of an auxiliary power unit to provide power for the turret, thus conserving fuel for the main engine. The Palmaria is available with a normal manual loading system or a semi-automatic loading system. With the latter, a three-round burst can be fired in 30 seconds and then one round every 15 seconds can

Specifically developed to export, the Palmaria has now been bought by Libya, Nigeria and Oman. An additional 25 turrets were supplied to Argentina for fitting on the TAM tank chassis.

be maintained until the 23 ready-use projectiles have been fired; a further seven projectiles are stowed elsewhere in the hull. Once the ordnance has fired, it automatically returns to an elevation of +2°, the breech opens, the projectile is loaded with power assistance, the charge is loaded manually, the breech is closed and the ordnance can be fired again.

A complete range of ammunition has been developed for the Palmaria by Simmel: the range consists of four different rounds, each of which weighs 45.5 kg (100 lb). The high explosive, smoke and illuminating projectiles have a range of 24000 m (26,245 yards), and the rocket-assisted projectile has a range of 30000 m (32,800 yards). The extra range of the RAP has a penalty, however, inasmuch as it is achieved only at the expense of HE content, which is 8 kg (17.6 lb) compared with 11.7 kg (25.8 lb) in the normal projectile.

A 7.62-mm (0.3-in) machine-gun is mounted at the commander's station on the right side of the turret roof, and four electrically-operated smoke dischargers can be fitted to each side of the

turret if required.

A wide range of optional equipment can be fitted, including passive night-vision equipment and an NBC system. Standard equipment on all vehicles includes a hull escape hatch, bilge pumps and an automatic fire-extinguishing system. Track skirts help to keep down dust when the vehicle is travelling across country.

One of the prototypes of the OTO Melara Palmaria, based on the chassis of the OF-40 MBT but fitted with a smaller diesel engine.

Specification
Crew: 5
Weight: 46000 kg (101,410 lb)
Dimensions: length (gun forward) 11.474 m (37 ft 7¾ in); length (hull) 7.40 m (24 ft 3⅓ in); width 2.35 m (7 ft 8½ in); height (without MG) 2.874 m (9 ft 5¼ in)
Powerplant: 8-cylinder diesel developing 750 hp (559 kW)
Performance: maximum road speed 60 km/h (37 mph); maximum range 400 km (250 miles); gradient 60%; vertical obstacle 1.00 m (3 ft 3 in); trench 3.00 m (9 ft 10 in)

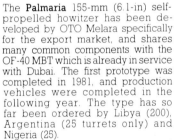

Abbot 105-mm Self-Propelled Gun

After the end of World War II the standard self-propelled gun of the British Royal Artillery was the 25-pounder Sexton, which was designed and built in Canada. Prototypes of various self-propelled guns were built on a modified Centurion tank chassis, including one with a 25-pounder gun and the other with a 140-mm (5.5-in) gun. By the 1950s these calibres were not standard within NATO, which was standardizing on 105-mm (4.13-in) and 155-mm (6.1-in) rounds. To meet the Royal Artillery's immediate requirements for SP weapons of the latter calibre, quantities of American M44 self-propelled howitzers were supplied while development concentrated in England on the 105-mm (4.13-in) self-propelled gun which used the engine, transmission and suspension of the FV432 series of APC. Vickers of Elswick was awarded a contract to build 12 prototypes, of which six were powered by a petrol engine and six by a diesel engine. Following trials with these prototypes the company was awarded a production contract, series vehicles being built between 1964 and 1967. In the British army the **FV433 Abbot** 105-mm (4.13-in) self-propelled gun is used by the Royal Artillery in regiments of three batteries, each battery having eight Abbots. The Abbot is deployed in West Germany with the British Army of the Rhine, while a few serve with the Royal School of Artillery at Larkhill, Wiltshire, and at the British Army Training Area in Suffield, Canada. The **Value Engineered Abbot**, which is the basic vehicle without such luxuries as flotation screen, powered traverse, NBC system and night-vision equipment, was produced for India although the British army also has a few.

The hull and turret of the Abbot are of all-welded steel which provides the four-man crew with complete protection from small arms fire and shell splinters. The driver is seated at the front on the left, with the engine to his right. The turret is mounted at the very rear of the hull, with the commander and gunner on the right and the loader

Used in the Field Regiments of the Royal Artillery, the Abbot is supported by the amphibious 6×6 Alvis Stalwart High Mobility Load Carrier with prepacked ammunition pallets, and is capable of operating in an NBC environment.

on the left. In addition to the commander's cupola and loader's roof hatches a large door is provided in the hull rear which is also used for ammunition supply. The Abbot is fitted with an NBC system, infra-red driving lights and, when originally introduced into the British army, with a flotation screen; the last has now been removed.

The main armament consists of the L13A1 Royal Ordnance 105-mm gun, (which also forms the basis for the 115-mm Mark 8 gun which arms many of the Royal Navy's combat ships), a 7.62-mm (0.3-in) Bren light machine-gun at the commander's station for use in the anti-aircraft role, and one bank of three electrically-operated smoke dischargers on each side of the turret. The 105-mm (4.13-in) gun has a double-baffle muzzle-brake, a fume-extractor and a semi-automatic breech. Traverse is powered through 360°, while elevation is manual from −5° to +70°. The gun has a maximum range of 17000 m (18,600 yards) and fires the following types of separate-loading ammunition: HE, HESH, SH/PRACT, smoke (three types) and illuminating. A total of 40 projectiles is carried.

The Abbot's ammunition is also used in the combat-proven Royal Ordnance 105-mm light gun, which was itself developed from the L13A1 ordnance of the Abbot.

Replacement of the Abbot by the

155-mm (6.1-in) M109A2 has started recently, but it is expected that the Abbot will not be retired from the Royal Artillery until the late 1980s.

Specification
Crew: 4
Weight: 16556 kg (36,500 lb)
Dimensions: length (gun forward) 5.84 m (19 ft 2 in); length (hull) 5.709 m (18 ft 8¾ in); width 2.641 m (8 ft 8 in); height (without armament) 2.489 m (8 ft 2 in)

Powerplant: one Rolls-Royce 6-cylinder diesel developing 240 hp (179 kW)
Performance: maximum road speed 47.5 km/h (30 mph); maximum range 390 km (240 miles); gradient 60%; vertical obstacle 0.609 m (2 ft 0 in); trench 2.057 m (6 ft 9 in)

Eventually to be replaced in the late 1980s by the M109A2 155-mm (6.1-in) gun, the Abbot is no longer fitted with a flotation screen.

Bandkanon 1A 155-mm Self-Propelled Gun

For many years Bofors has been well known for its expertise in the design, development and production of guns and their associated ammunition systems for both army and naval applications. This work was put to good use in the development of the **Bandkanon 1A** 155-mm (6.1-in) self-propelled gun for the Swedish army. The first prototype was completed in 1960, and after extensive trials and some modifications the equipment was placed in production from 1966 to 1968. The Bandkanon 1A has the distinction of being the first fully automatic self-propelled gun to enter service with any army. It is also the heaviest and slowest, factors which make the equipment very difficult to conceal and of limited mobility.

The hull and turret are of all-welded steel construction that varies from 10 mm (0.4 in) to 20 mm (0.8 in) in thickness. The vehicle uses many automotive components of the Bofors S-tank, including the powerpack and

Although the first fully automatic self-propelled gun, the Bandkanon 1A was only procured in small quantities by the Swedish army because of size and lack of mobility.

suspension. The engine and transmission are at the front of the hull, with the driver seated to the immediate front of the turret. Suspension is of the hydro-pneumatic type and consists of six road wheels, with the drive sprocket at the front and the last road wheel acting as the idler. To provide a more stable firing platform the suspension can be locked.

The turret is mounted at the rear of

the hull, and is in two parts with the 155-mm (6.1-in) ordnance mounted between them. In the left part are the commander, gun layer and radio operator, while in the right part are the loader and 7.62-mm (0.3-in) anti-aircraft machine gunner. Turret traverse is manual, 15° left and right when the ordnance is above 0° in elevation, reducing to 15° left and 4° right when the ordnance is below 0°. Elevation is

electric from +2° to +38°, and manual from −3° to +40°.

The 155-mm (6.1-in) ordnance has a pepperpot muzzle-brake, no fume-extractor and a semi-automatic wedge breech block that opens downwards. An unusual feature of the ordnance is that it has a replaceable liner. When travelling, the ordnance is held in position by a lock pivoted at the front of the hull.

The ammunition is fed from a 14-round clip carried externally in an armoured magazine at the rear of the hull. This clip consists of seven compartments, each of which contain two rounds of ammunition, these being fed to the breech by a loading tray before being rammed into the breech by a rammer. The loading tray and rammer are operated by springs that are cocked by the run-out of the gun. The first round has to be manually loaded but after this the sequence is fully automatic and the gunner can select single shots or fully automatic. The empty cartridge cases are ejected from the breech to the rear. Once the clip of ammunition has been expended a fresh clip is brought up by truck, the ordnance is elevated to +38°, covers on the magazine are opened vertically, a hoist on the upper part of the turret slides along the slide bar before picking up the clip and placing it in the magazine, the doors are then closed and the hoist is returned to travelling position. Fire can then be resumed. This whole sequence takes just two

The Bandkanon 1A prepares to fire. The unique 14-round armoured magazine is at the rear of the hull; once expended it can be reloaded in less than two minutes from a resupply truck.

minutes.

The 155-mm (6.1-in) projectile has a range of 25600 (28,000 yards). For some time it has been reported that a rocket-assisted projectile is under development that will have a range of about 30000 m (32,800 yards).

Specification
Crew: 5
Weight: 53000 kg (116,845 lb)
Dimensions: length (gun forward) 11.00 m (36 ft 1 in); length (hull) 6.55 m (21 ft 6 in); width 3.37 m (11 ft 0⅔ in); height (including AA MG) 3.85 m (12 ft 7½ in)
Powerplant: one Rolls-Royce diesel developing 240 hp (179 kW) and Boeing gas turbine developing 300 shp (224 kW)
Performance: maximum road speed

28 km/h (17.4 mph); maximum range 230 km (143 miles); gradient 60%;

vertical obstacle 0.95 m (3 ft 1½ in); trench 2.00 m (6 ft 6¾ in)

CZECHOSLOVAKIA
DANA 152-mm Self-Propelled Howitzer

The Czech 152-mm (6-in) **DANA** is the first wheeled self-propelled howitzer to enter service in modern times, although full details and its exact role are still uncertain. Wheeled self-propelled artillery systems have a number of advantages over their more common tracked counterparts. Firstly, they are cheaper and easier to manufacture and to maintain and, secondly, they have a much greater strategic mobility as almost without exception wheeled armoured vehicles are much faster than their tracked counterparts and have a greater operational range. More recently South Africa has developed the 6×6 G6 155-mm (6.1-in) self-propelled howitzer, but this has yet to enter production.

It is almost certain that the DANA, which was first observed during a military parade held in 1980, is based on the 8×8 Tatra 815 truck, which probably has the best off-road performance of any truck in existence. The crew compartment is at the front, the fully enclosed turret in the centre and the armoured engine compartment at the rear. The armour is of all-welded steel and provides the crew with complete protection from small arms fire and shell splinters. It is believed that the crew normally travel in the front compartment, entering the turret only when coming into action.

The engine is coupled to a manual gearbox with 10 forward and two reverse gears, which in turn transmits power to a two-speed transfer box, so giving a total of 20 forward and four reverse gears. Steering is power-assisted on the front four wheels, and a central tyre-pressure regulation system allows the driver to adjust the tyre pressure to suit the type of ground being crossed.

Before firing commences three hydraulically-operated stabilizers (one at the rear of the hull under the engine compartment and one on each side between the second and third axles) are lowered to the ground for extra stability.

The turret has a limited traverse of between 30° and 40° left and right, and

Right: Only Czechoslovakia among the Warsaw Pact armies uses the DANA wheeled gun. The DANA is based on the 8×8 Tatra 815 high mobility truck chassis.

Below: The DANA is a cheaper but more roadworthy alternative to the tracked self-propelled guns now entering the Warsaw Pact inventories.

it is believed that the ordnance is based on that installed in the the Soviet M1973 self-propelled tracked howitzer, although the Czech weapon is longer and does not have a fume-extractor. The Czech Skoda works have a long history of successful artillery design and production, and it is quite possible that the ordnance has been designed and built there to fire Soviet ammunition. A hydraulic crane is fitted on the roof and it is believed that this is used to hoist ammunition into the turret, or perhaps forms part of an automatic or semi-automatic loading system. It is believed that the ordnance has a depression of −3° and an elevation of +60° for a maximum range of between 15000 and 20000 m (16,405 and 21,870 yards). The maximum rate of fire for a short period is four to five rounds per minute, reducing to one round per minute in the sustained-fire role. About 40 projectiles and charges are carried.

The DANA can ford to a depth of about 1.4 m (4 ft 7 in) but has no amphibious or NBC capability. The only export sales of the DANA to date are the 48 acquired by Libya.

Specification (provisional)
Crew: 4 to 5
Weight: 23000 kg (50,705 lb)
Dimensions: length gun forward 10.5 m (34 ft 5 in); length hull 9 m (29 ft 6 in); width 2.8 m (9 ft 2 in); height 2.6 m (8 ft 6 in)
Powerplant: V-12 diesel developing 345 hp (257 kW)
Performance: maximum road speed 80 km/h (49.71 mph); maximum range 600 km (372.83 miles); gradient 60%; vertical obstacle 1.5 m (4 ft 11 in); trench 1.4 m (4 ft 7 in)

M1973 152-mm Self-Propelled Gun/Howitzer

The **M1973** 152-mm (6-in) self-propelled gun/howitzer is known as the 2S3 in the Soviet Union, and is issued on the scale of 18 per tank division and a similar number per motorized rifle division. The equipment is also known to be used by East Germany, Iraq and Libya. Its chassis is a shortened version of that used for the SA-4 'Ganef' surface-to-air missile system and GMZ armoured minelayer, which have both been in service with the Soviet Union for many years.

The M1973 has three compartments, that for the driver at the front, that for the engine to its right and that for the turret at the rear, the last being slightly forward of the very rear as it has such a large overhang. The torsion-bar suspension consists of six road wheels, with a distinct gap between the first and second and the third and fourth road wheels; the drive sprocket is at the front with the idler at the rear, and there are four track-return rollers.

The commander's cupola is on the roof of the turret, on the left side, and this is fitted with a 7.62-mm (0.3-in) machine-gun for local and anti-aircraft defence. This is the only hatch in the roof, but there is also a hatch in the right side of the turret. In the hull rear is a large hatch that opens downwards, and on each side of this is one circular hatch. These, and the two square openings in the turret rear, are believed to be used for the rapid loading

Known as the SO-152 Akatsiya (Acacia) in Soviet army service, this vehicle forms the basis for a standard chassis design used for other purposes, including the SA-4 'Ganef' launcher and the GMZ minelayer.

of projectiles and fuses.

The ordnance is based on the 152-mm (6-in) D-20 gun/howitzer but with a bore evacuator, which helps stop fumes from entering the crew compartment when the breech is opened, to the rear of the double-baffle muzzle-brake. The ordnance fires an HE projectile weighing 43.5 kg (95.9 lb) to a maximum range of 18500 m (20,230 yards). Other projectiles that can be fired include HEAT (this will penetrate 300 mm/11.8 in of armour at 1000 m/1,095 yards), HE extended range (with a claimed range of 24000 m/26,245 yards), HE RAP (with a claimed range of 37000 m/40,465 yards), illuminating, smoke and 2-kiloton tactical nuclear. A total of 40 projectiles and charges is carried, and maximum rate of fire is four rounds per minute. The ordnance has an elevation of +60° and a depression of −4°; turret traverse is 360°.

Unlike the 122-mm (4.8-in) M1974 self-propelled howitzer, the M1973 does not have amphibious capability, although it can ford to a depth of 1.5 m (4 ft 11 in). The M1973 is fitted with an NBC system, and with night-vision equipment for the commander and driver.

In recent years the Soviet Union has developed and placed in production at least three new weapons, a 152-mm (6-in) self-propelled gun, a 203-mm (8-in) self-propelled howitzer and a 240-mm (9.45-in) self-propelled mortar. It is believed that the last is probably an updated version of the 240-mm (9.45-in) M240 towed weapon which fires a chemical, high explosive fragmentation or nuclear projectile to a maximum range of 9700 m (10,610 yards). Photographs of the 152-mm (6-in) gun were released by the United States in 1982 and showed a chassis similar to that of

the M1973 but with the ordnance in an unprotected mount on the top rear of the chassis. The ordnance is not fitted with a fume extractor, and when travelling is clamped in position. Located at the rear of the hull is a large spade.

Specification
Crew: 6
Weight: 25000 kg (55,115 lb)
Dimensions: length (gun forward) 8.40 m (27 ft 6⅔ in); length (hull) 7.80 m (25 ft 7 in); width 3.20 m (10 ft 6 in); height 2.80 m (9 ft 2¼ in)
Powerplant: one V-12 diesel developing 520 hp (388 kW)
Performance: maximum road speed 55 km/h (34 mph); maximum range 300 km (186 miles); gradient 60%; vertical obstacle 1.10 m (3 ft 7 in); trench 2.50 m (8 ft 2½ in)

M1974 122-mm Self-Propelled Howitzer

In the period after World War II the Soviet Union placed its main emphasis on the continuing development of towed artillery whereas NATO emphasized self-propelled weapons. Although the latter are much more expensive to build, maintain and operate they do have many advantages over their towed counterparts, including increased cross-country mobility, full armour protection for the crew and ammunition, the possibility of an NBC system, and a reduction in the time necessary for the equipment to be brought into and taken out of action. The Soviet Union did continue to develop specialized tank destroyers such as the ASU-57 and ASU-85, but it was not until 1974 that the first 122-mm (4.8-in) self-propelled howitzer made its appearance on a parade in Poland, although it had doubtless already entered service with the Soviet Union by this date. NATO calls this 122-mm (4.8-in) self-propelled howitzer the **M1974**, this being the year when it was first seen, while the Soviet designation is 2S1. The system is also used by Algeria, Angola, Czechoslovakia, Ethiopia, East Germany, Hungary, Iraq, Libya, Syria and Yugoslavia, and licensed production may well take place in Czechoslovakia and/or Poland. In the Soviet army the M1974 is employed on the scale of 36 per motorized rifle division and 72 per tank division.

The layout of the M1974 is similar to that of the American M109 with the engine, transmission and driver at the front and the fully enclosed turret at the rear. The suspension is adjustable, and consists of seven road wheels with the drive sprocket at the front and the idler at the rear; there are no track-return rollers. For normal use 400-mm (15.75-

The M1974 has the Soviet designation SO-122 Gvozdika (Carnation) and is fully amphibious, unlike the SO-152. The chassis is also used for the TT-LB (or ACRV in NATO circles), a mine-clearing vehicle, and for a new chemical warfare reconnaissance vehicle.

in) wide tracks are fitted, but when operating in the snow or swampy areas 670-mm (26.4-in) wide tracks are fitted to reduce the vehicle's ground pressure as much as possible. Standard equipment includes an NBC system and a full suite of night-vision equipment for the driver and commander. The M1974 is fully amphibious, being propelled in the water by its tracks at a speed of 4.5 km/h (2.8 mph).

The turret is fitted with a modified version of the standard 122-mm (4.8-in) D-30 towed howitzer, which has an elevation of +70° and depression of −3°; turret traverse is 360°. Turret traverse and weapon elevation are electric, with manual control for emergency use. The ordnance has a double-baffle muzzle-brake, a fume-extractor and a semi-automatic vertical sliding breech block; an ordnance travel lock is mounted on top of the hull. The howitzer fires an HE projectile weighing 21.72 kg (47.9 lb) to a maximum range of 15300 m (16,730 yards), and can also fire chemical, illuminating, smoke and HEAT-FS projectiles. The last is used to engage tanks and will penetrate 460 mm (18.1 in) of armour at an incidence of 0° at a range of 1000 m (1,095 yards). It is also re-

ported that an HE RAP is available, and that this has a maximum range of 21900 m (23,950 yards). A normal ammunition load consists of 40 projectiles: 32 HE, six smoke and two HEAT-FS. It is believed that a power rammer is fitted to permit a higher rate of fire (five rounds per minute) and also to enable the ordnance to be loaded at any angle of elevation.

The chassis of the M1974 is also used for a number of armoured command and reconnaissance vehicles (ACRVs) fitted with the 'Big Fred' artillery/mortar-locating radar, and for a specialized mine-clearing vehicle. The latter is similar in concept to the British Giant Viper.

Specification
Crew: 4
Weight: 16000 kg (35,275 lb)
Dimensions: length 7.30 m (23 ft 11½ in); width 2.85 m (9 ft 4 in); height 2.40 m (7 ft 10½ in)
Powerplant: one YaMZ-238V V-8 water-cooled diesel developing 240 hp (179 kW)
Performance: maximum road speed 60 km/h (37 mph); maximum range 500 km (310 miles); gradient 60%; vertical obstacle 1.10 m (3 ft 7 in); trench 3.00 m (9 ft 10 in)

Two of the 90 SO-122 guns currently credited with being in service with the Hungarian army.

203-mm M1975 self-propelled gun

Apart from self-propelled anti-tank guns such as the ASU-57 and ASU-85 developed specifically for use by the airborne forces, the Soviet army in the post-war period has relied on artillery towed by full-tracked prime movers or by 6×6 trucks to provide fire support for its mechanized units.

The various Middle East conflicts clearly showed, however, that towed artillery cannot hope to keep up with mechanized forces moving at speed across country, tanks and troop carriers in these wars often outrunning their support artillery.

In the early 1970s the Soviets thus introduced two self-propelled artillery pieces into service, the 122-mm (4.8-in) 2S1 (called the M1974 in NATO) self-propelled howitzer and the 152-mm (5.98-in) 2S3 (called the M1973 in NATO) self-propelled gun/howitzer. Although these vehicles have different hulls they are very similar in layout to the US 155-mm (6.1-in) M109 series of weapons, which has been in service for over 25 years.

Since then the Soviets have introduced at least three other new self-propelled artillery pieces. The 2S5 152-mm self-propelled gun was first seen in the late 1970s and is believed to consist of the chassis of the GMZ minelayer with a long-barrelled 152-mm weapons mounted at the rear. No protection is provided for the crew against shell fragments. The ordnance is believed to fire a standard HE projectile to a range of 27000 m (29,530 yards) or a rocket-assisted projectile to a range of perhaps 37000 m (40,465 yards). It also has a nuclear capability.

In the mid-1970s the Soviet Army introduced a 203-mm (8-in) self-propelled howitzer which has been given the NATO designation M1975 (Soviet designation SO-203) in the usual absence of any official Soviet designation. The M1975 is believed to be employed at front level, and has the distinction of being the largest armoured vehicle in service at the present time.

The fully enclosed armoured cab is at the front of the vehicle, with the engine to the rear. The weapon itself is mounted at the very rear of the hull, and when travelling is held in position by a lock above the cab roof. Before the weapon can be fired a large hydraulically-operated blade is lowered at the rear of the hull to provide a more stable firing platform, and mounted on the right side of the chassis is a hydraulic loading system to help lift the heavy projectiles and charges into the breech.

It is probable that a few rounds of ready-use ammunition are carried on the actual vehicle, though the main supply of ammunition and most of the gun crew are carried in another tracked and armoured supporting vehicle.

Like the 2S5, the M1975 suffers from one major disadvantage: there is no protection for the gun crew when the vehicle is in action.

No firm details of the types of ammunition fired by the M1975 are yet available, but it is likely that the weapon has both nuclear and conventional capabilities, and it is generally comparable to the American M110/M110A1/M110A2 self-propelled howitzers that have been in service for many years.

Also introduced in the mid-1970s was a 240-mm (9.45-in) self-propelled mortar which has also been called the M1975 (this being the year it was first seen by Western intelligence). Like the 203-mm M1975 self-propelled gun, it has yet to make a public appearance and no firm details are available.

Since the early 1970s the Soviets have been manufacturing an expanding range of self-propelled artillery which now includes the massive M1975 203-mm SO-203, the world's largest AFV. It is assumed to fire nuclear as well as conventional ammunition.

Specification (provisional)
M1975
Weights: empty 37000 kg (81,570 lb); loaded 40000 kg (88,183 lb)
Powerplant: one diesel developing 450 hp (336 kW)
Dimensions: length, with gun 12.80 m (42 ft 0 in) and hull 10.50 m (34 ft 5.4 in); width 3.50 m (11 ft 5.8 in); height 3.50 m (11 ft 5.8 in)

A US Department of Defense impression of the Soviet M1975 203-mm self-propelled gun firing. The equipment's Soviet designation is SO 203.

G6 155-mm self-propelled howitzer

In 1975 South Africa carried out a number of operations against SWAPO guerrillas across the Namibia/Angola border. The SADF were shocked by the ease with which their opponents' Soviet made artillery outranged their own World War II vintage equipment. A lesson was learned from the experience and a South African self requirement emerged which saw the development (from an original design by SRC of Quebec) of the highly effective G5 155-mm towed howitzer, one of the most advanced artillery pieces in the world.

A related project initiated by SRC was a wheeled self-propelled gun, and when SRC went out of business Armscor, the South African state arms manufacturing company continued with development. South Africa's unique operational conditions, especially the vast distances traversed far from base facilities, makes tracked SP artillery prohibitively expensive so a wheeled self-propelled weapon was of great interest.

Armscor produced their first prototype of the **G6 Renoster (Rhino)** in 1981. It is a large six-wheeler, travelling on massive tyres coupled to a central tyre pressure system which gives the G6 remarkable cross-country ability. Production models may be offered with 6×4 or even 6×2 options. The driver sits forward in his own compartment separated from the rest of the crew by the engine. The turret is mounted directly onto the hull (there is no basket). It houses the remaining four crew members, who are the commander and the layer, or gunner, to the left of the breech, and the loader and

the ammunition handler on the right side. The racks on the rear wall of the fighting compartment hold 47 projectiles, 52 propellant charges, and also primers and fuzes. The commander has access to a 12.7-mm roof mounted MG through a roof hatch. Unusually, the turret is fitted with three weapon ports, as used in the Ratel MICV, for close in defence.

The main armament is a version of the 155-mm (6.1-in) 45 calibre howitzer used in the G5. It fires the same standard ammunition to the exceptional unassisted range of 30,000 m (32,800 yards) and with a special base bleed shell can hit targets at least 40,000 m (43,750 yards) in the thin atmosphere of the African plateau.

The first production models of the G6 appeared in 1987. They are more heavily armoured than the prototypes, the steel being designed to provide protection from 23-mm cannon fire. Despite the fact that it is one of the heaviest wheeled combat vehicles ever to enter service, the excellent cross-country ability and superb ordnance of the G6 make it an extremely potent weapon.

Specification
Crew: 5/6
Combat weight: 47000 kg (103,263b)
Powerplant: air cooled diesel delivering 525 hp (392 kW)
Dimensions: length, gun forwards 10,4 m (34.12 ft); width 3.3 m (10.8 ft); height to turret top 3.2 m (10.5 ft)
Performance: maximum road speed 85 km/h; maximum road range 600 km (373 miles); fording 0.8 m (2.62 ft);

vertical obstacle 0.45 m (1.48 ft); trench 1 m (3.28 ft); gradient 50 per cent

In spite (or possibly because) of the United Nations arms embargo, South Africa has developed an arms industry of considerable sophistication. Artillery pieces such as the G6 Renoster are as good as any in the world, and make the Republic the most powerful state in the region.

122-mm SP122 self-propelled howitzer

Until the recent introduction of the US M109A2 155-mm (6.1-in) self-propelled howitzer, virtually all Egyptian artillery was towed, most of this having been supplied by the USSR and including large numbers of excellent 122-mm (4.8-in) D-30s, whose ammunition Egypt has been making for some years. More recently Egypt has started to produce the D-30 for both the home and export markets.

The Egyptian army decided that it wanted a self-propelled version of the D-30 more advanced than the Syrian version, which was essentially an old T-34/85 tank with its turret replaced by a D-30 firing over the rear engine decking; no protection is provided for the gun crew from small arms fire and shell splinters.

In 1984 it was announced that BMY of the USA and Royal Ordnance of the UK had each been awarded contracts to design and build a self-propelled version of the D-30 which would eventually be made in Egypt. The prototypes made their first official appearance at a defence exhibition in Cairo late in 1984.

The BMY entry in this competition consists essentially of a M109 chassis with a new fixed superstructure at the rear: in the forward part of this is the D-30 howitzer, which has an elevation of +70° a depression of −5° and a traverse of 30° left and right. Some 85 rounds of 122-mm ammunition are carried, of which five are normally HEAT (High Explosive Anti-Tank). Mounted on the roof is a 12.7-mm (0.5-in) M2 HB

machine-gun, for which 500 rounds of ammunition are carried.

Rather than use an existing chassis Royal Ordnance Leeds designed a new vehicle from scratch of all welded steel construction rather than aluminium as used in the BMY entry. The reason for this was that steel is easier to weld than aluminium, and Egypt already has extensive experience in using this material in other armoured vehicle programmes.

The layout of the Royal Ordnance D-30 self-propelled howitzer is similar to the BMY type, but is much more compact. The driver is at the front left with engine to his right and the gun compartment at rear. Weapon elevation, depression and traverse are identical to the BMY vehicle, and 80 projectiles and charges are carried. A 12.7-mm M2 HB machine-gun is carried on the roof for anti-aircraft defence.

The Perkins diesel engine is coupled to a fully automatic Self-Changing Gears six-speed transmission. Some parts of the suspension are also used in the Royal Ordnance Nottingham Combat Engineer Tractor already in service with the British and Indian armies.

Egypt has been manufacturing the Soviet D-30 122-mm gun for some years, and invited Royal Ordnance and BMY in the USA to produce a self-propelled version. Royal Ordnance have designed a completely new chassis, which may also be used for a whole family of AFVs.

Royal Ordnance Leeds expects that SP122 will be the first of a complete family of light tracked vehicles using the same basic chassis, the other vehicles including a command post with extensive communications equipment, a recovery vehicle, an ambulance and an ammunition carrier.

Specification (provisional)
SP122
Crew: 5
Weights: empty 17500 kg (38,580 lb); loaded 20000 kg (44,092 lb)
Powerplant: one Perkins TV8.540 eight-cylinder diesel developing 300 hp (224 kW)
Dimensions: length 7.70 m (25 ft 3 in); width 2.82 m (9 ft 3 in); height 2.69 m (8 ft 10 in)
Performance: maximum road speed 55 km/h (34 mph); range 300 km (186 miles); fording 1.0 m (3 ft 3 in); vertical obstacle 0.75 m (2 ft 6 in); trench 2.2 m (7 ft 3 in); gradient 60 per cent; side slope 30 per cent

Modern Towed Artillery

Towed artillery has been superseded in many of the highly mechanized armies of the 1980s. In spite of this, development of the towed gun/howitzer has proceeded rapidly, and with good reason; recent conflicts such as Angola, Grenada and the Falklands have shown that there is still a need for 105-mm and 155-mm howitzers that can quickly be deployed from one area to another by aircraft or helicopter.

A Westland/Aérospatiale Puma helicopter of the Royal Air Force with a Royal Ordnance Factory Nottingham 105-mm (4.13-in) Light Gun slung underneath. The 105-mm Light Gun was extensively used by the Royal Artillery in the Falkland campaign.

Although many European and Middle East armies have replaced much of their towed artillery with self-propelled guns and howitzers, the towed weapon still has an important part in most armies. While mechanized infantry and armoured divisions require tracked artillery weapons, as only these systems can keep up with the main formations while moving across country, there are still, even in the United States, a number of basic infantry divisions that rely on trucks to transport much of their personnel. For this type of unit, and for reserve units, towed 155-mm (6.1-in) systems such as the American M198, Swedish FH-77A, French TR and British/West German/Italian FH-70 have been developed and recently deployed. All but the M198 have an auxiliary power unit (APU) which enables the weapon to propel itself locally across country or around the battery position. The artillery piece with an APU is by no means a new concept, the Soviets having had the 85-mm (3.35-in) SD-44 auxiliary-propelled field gun in service for many years. In some cases the APU can also help to bring the weapon into action, as well as assisting with ammunition handling. Towed weapons are also much cheaper to procure, maintain and operate than their self-propelled counterparts.

In recent years a number of countries outside the major powers, such as Argentina, Austria, Israel and South Africa have developed 155-mm (6.1-in) artillery systems. Sometimes these weapons are based in part or whole on European designs, while in other cases the weapon and its associated ammunition is of wholly local design.

While most of the recent Western systems are of 155-mm (6.1-in) calibre, the British ROF Light Gun and the OTO Melara Model 56 pack howitzer, both in 105-mm (4.13-in) calibre, are still in production and widely used for airborne, commando, marine and alpine units, the 155-mm (6.1-in) systems often being too heavy for deployment in the terrain encountered by such units. Although the Model 56 has a short range by modern standards, it is one of the few weapons that can be dismantled for transportation by pack animal across mountainous terrain.

It should not be forgotten that the gun or howitzer is only part of the weapon system, as the whole object of the weapon is to put the ammunition onto the target so as to cause the maximum possible amount of damage. To achieve this end, the ammunition must be effective, the crew well trained, an adequate towing vehicle supplied and, of course, a fire-control system employed.

American field artillery gunners prepare to load their 105-mm (4.1-in) M102 light howitzer during operations in Grenada in 1983. The M102 was originally developed in response to an urgent need in Vietnam. It replaced the M101 in US Army service, but is itself to be replaced by the M119 variant of the Royal Ordnance Light Gun in the Airborne and new Light Divisions.

CITEFA Model 77 155-mm howitzer

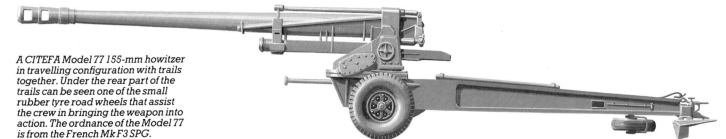

A CITEFA Model 77 155-mm howitzer in travelling configuration with trails together. Under the rear part of the trails can be seen one of the small rubber tyre road wheels that assist the crew in bringing the weapon into action. The ordnance of the Model 77 is from the French Mk F3 SPG.

Some years ago Argentina purchased a number of members of the AMX-13 family of light tracked vehicles from France as well as undertaking the assembly of a quantity of vehicles. These included the AMX-13 light tank with a 90-mm (3.54-in) gun, the AMX VCI armoured personnel carrier, and the 155-mm (6.1-in) Mk F3 self-propelled gun. At that time the standard 155-mm (6.1-in) towed howitzer of the Argentine army was the American M114, which dated back to World War II and had a maximum range of 14600 m (15,965 yards). To replace the M114 the Instituto de Investigaciones Cientificas y Tecnicas de las Fuerzas Armadas (CITEFA) designed a new bottom carriage that would take the complete top carriage (barrel, cradle, recoil system and equilibrators) of the Mk F3 self-propelled gun. After trials this was accepted for service with the Argentine army under the designation **155-mm Howitzer L33 X1415 CITEFA Model 77**, L33 referring to the length of the ordnance in calibres and Model 77 to the year of acceptance. A later model, the **Model 81**, differs in minor details and also has a barrel of Argentine rather than French manufacture. Together with the OTO Melara 105-mm (4.13-in) Model 56 pack howitzer the Model 77 was deployed to the Falklands, and all of these equipments were subsequently captured by the British, some of them being shipped to the UK for trial and display purposes.

The barrel of the Model 77 is 5.115 m (16 ft 9.4 in) long, and is provided with a double-baffle muzzle brake and a screw breech mechanism. The top carriage is of welded steel construction and contains the traverse mechanism and elevating brackets. The former is mounted inside the lower part

and forming the connection with the cradle trunnion attachment and the bottom carriage. The bottom carriage is of the split-trail type, and is also of welded construction. Each trail leg is provided with a small rubber-tyred road wheel to assist in bringing the weapon into and out of action, and at the end of each trail is a spade. When the equipment is in the firing position the carriage wheels are raised clear of the ground, support then being provided by a circular steel base attached to the carriage by a ball socket; the latter feature helps to compensate for rough ground. When the equipment is being towed, the support is raised, giving ground clearance of 0.3 m (12 in). Maximum rate of fire is four rounds per minute, and sustained rate one round per minute. The equipment fires an HE projectile weighing 43 kg (94.8 lb) with a maximum muzzle velocity of 765 m (2,510 ft) per second to a maximum range of 22000 m (24,060 yards); there are also illuminating and smoke projectiles. According to the manufacturer a rocket-assisted projectile is available, but as far as is known such a projectile was not used in the Falklands campaign.

Specification
Model 77 howitzer
Calibre: 155 mm (6.1 in)
Weight: travelling 8000 kg (17,637 lb)
Dimensions: length, travelling 10.15 m (33 ft 3.6 in); width, travelling 2.67 m (8 ft 9 in); height, travelling 2.20 m (7 ft 2.6 in)
Elevation: +67°/−0°
Traverse: total 70°
Maximum range: with normal ammunition 22000 m (24,060 yards) and with rocket-assisted projectile 23300 m (25,480 yards)

A CITEFA Model 77 155-mm howitzer in the firing position with ordnance at maximum elevation. Each trail is fitted with its spade, but as the weapon has yet to be fired they are not bedded in. The Model 77 was used against the British forces during the 1982 Falklands campaign.

GHN-45 155-mm gun/howitzer

In the 1970s PRB of Belgium, a well-known manufacturer of ammunition, and Space Research Corporation of Canada jointly established a company called SRC International with its headquarters in Brussels. This company developed a gun howitzer called the **GC 45**, of which 12 were subsequently ordered by the Royal Thai Marines, as well as a conversion kit for the standard 155-mm (6.1-in) M114 howitzer. The first two weapons were built in Canada while the remaining 10 were built in Canada but assembled in Austria by Voest-Alpine. Further de-

A NORICUM GHN-45 155-mm gun/howitzer in the travelling position with ordnance locked over trails. This Austrian-produced weapon is in service with the Jordanian army, and some may have found their way to Iraq and seen recent use.

velopment by Voest-Alpine resulted in the **GHN-45** 155-mm (6.1-in) gun/howitzer, of which 200 were ordered by Jordan. Production of these weapons started in 1981, the first weapons being delivered during the following year. A number have been passed on to Iraq for use in the Gulf War. The original Thai weapons have been in use on the Kampuchean border. Now being marketed by NORICUM, the GHN-45 has been sold in small numbers to the Austrian Army, and is to be made under licence by ENGESA of Brazil. It has been demonstrated and tested in several countries, including India and Malaysia.

The basic version of the GHN-45 is normally towed by a standard 10-tonne (6×6) truck if required. More recently a model fitted with an auxiliary power unit on the front of the carriage has been developed. This enables the weapon to propel itself on roads at a maximum speed of 35 km/h (22 mph), and the 80-litre (17.6-Imp gal) fuel tank provides a range of 150 km (93 miles). In normal practice the system is moved from one firing position to another by a truck with the ordnance traversed over the trails and locked in position to reduce its overall length, the APU then being used for final positioning and for bringing the weapon into and out of action more quickly.

The GHN-45 has a standard 45-calibre barrel fitted with a triple-baffle muzzle brake, and can fire a standard US M107 high explosive projectile to a maximum range of 17800 m (19,465 yards) or an M101 projectile to a maximum range of 24000 m (26,245 yards).

With the Extended-Range Full Bore (ERFB) projectile manufactured by PRB, a range of 30000 m (32,810 yards) can be achieved, while the ERFB projectile with base bleed goes out to 39000 m (42,650 yards).

The ERFB projectile, developed from the earlier extended-range sub-bore and extended-range sub-calibre projectiles, is longer and more streamlined than a conventional projectile, and therefore has reduced aerodynamic drag and thus increased range. The ERFB base bleed is the basic projectile with a different boat tail containing the base bleed unit, which reduces drag at the rear of the projectile, which thus decelerates more slowly, so increasing range. The basic HE ERFB projectile weighs 45.54 kg (100.4 lb), of which 8.62 kg (19 lb) is the Composi-

tion B explosive. Other projectiles include smoke, illuminating, smoke base-ejection and a cargo round which carries 13kg (28.7lb) of M42 grenades.

Specification
GHN-45 gun/howitzer
Calibre: 155 mm (6.1 in)
Weight: 8900 kg (19,621 lb)
Dimensions: length, travelling 9.068 m (29 ft 9 in); width, travelling 2.48 m (8 ft 1.6 in); height, travelling 2.089 m (6 ft 10.25 in)
Elevation: +72°/−5°
Traverse: total 70°
Maximum range: with ERFB ammunition 30000 m (32,810 yards) and with base-bleed ammunition 39000 m (42,650 yards)

FRANCE
Modèle 50 155-mm howitzer

For the last 30 years the **modèle 50** 155-mm (6.1-in) howitzer has been the standard towed howitzer of the French army, and has also been made under licence by Bofors of Sweden for the Swedish army under the designation **15.5-cm Field Howitzer Fr.** In the French army it will soon be replaced by the new 155-mm (6.1-in) TR towed gun, which has an integral auxiliary power unit and a much longer range, while in the Swedish army it is being replaced by the Bofors 155-mm (6.1-in) FH-77A. The modèle 50 howitzer, which is also called the **OB-155-50 BF** by the French army, was also exported to the Lebanon (where some were captured from the PLO during the fighting of the summer of 1982), Israel, Switzerland and Morocco.

The barrel of the modèle 50 is 4.41 (14 ft 5.6 in) long, and has an unusual multi-baffle muzzle brake, hydro-pneumatic recoil system that varies with elevation, and a screw breech mechanism. The carriage is of the split-trail type with two rubber-tyred road wheels located on each side of the forward part of the carriage. When being towed by a truck the ordnance is locked to the trails by a locking device which is situated in the rear part of the cradle. To enable the equipment to be towed at high speeds on roads, the modèle 50 has a brake system operated by compressed air from the towing vehicle.

When in the firing position the forward part of the carriage is supported by a circular pivot plate underneath and by the ends of each trail.

The modèle 50 is operated by an 11-man crew, and in the French army is normally towed by a Berliet GBU 15 (6+6) truck, which also carries the crew and ammunition. Ammunition is of the separate-loading type, the HE projectile weighing 43 kg (94.8 lb) and having a maximum muzzle velocity of 650m (2,135ft) per second to give a range of 18000 m (19,685 yards). Illuminating and smoke projectiles can also be fired. More recently Brandt has developed a rocket-assisted HE projectile with a maximum range of 23300 m (25,480 yards). Maximum rate of fire is between three and four rounds per minute.

To meet the requirements of the Israeli army, the French Etablissement d'Etudes et Fabrications d'Armement de Bourges fitted the modèle 50 howitzer to a much modified Sherman chassis, and this entered service with the Israeli army in 1963 as the 155-mm (6.1-in) self-propelled howitzer **Model 50** (or **M-50**). The modifications to the chassis were extensive, and included moving the engine to the front of the vehicle on the right side with the driver being located to its left. The 155-mm (6.1-in) howitzer is mounted at the rear of the hull in an open-topped compartment, over which a tarpaulin cover can be fitted in wet weather. Stowage boxes are provided externally above the tracks. When the vehicle is in the firing position the rear of the hull folds down and doors open on each side to reveal ammunition stowage. Loaded weight of the M-50 is 31 tonnes, and the crew consists of eight men including the driver. Several of these systems were captured by the Egyptians in the heavy fighting around Suez in the 1973 Middle East War.

Specification
modèle 50 howitzer
Calibre: 155 m (6.1 in)
Weight: travelling 9000 kg (19,841 lb) and firing 8100 kg (17,857 lb)
Dimensions: length, travelling 7.80 m (25 ft 7.1 in); width, travelling 2.75 m (9 ft 0 in); height, travelling 2.50 m (8 ft 2.4 in)
Elevation: +69°/−4°
Traverse: total 80°
Maximum range: with standard round 18000 m (19,685 yards) and with rocket-assisted projectile 23300 m (25,480 yards)

This Modèle 50 155-mm howitzer, captured by the Israeli army during the 1982 invasion of Lebanon, clearly shows the turntable in the raised position under the carriage. The weapon is still used by France, Morocco, Sweden and Switzerland.

TR 155-mm gun

While the United Kingdom, Italy and West Germany elected to develop a 155-mm (6.1-in) towed howitzer first (FH-70) and then a self-propelled model (SP-70), France decided to do the reverse. The 155-mm (6.1-in) GCT self-propelled gun on an AMX-30 MBT chassis entered production for Saudi Arabia in 1977, first production vehicles being completed during the following year, but the type was not formally adopted by the French army until 1979. Since then it has also been ordered by Iraq.

The prototype of the **TR** 155-mm (6.1-in) towed gun was shown for the first time at Satory in 1979 and following trials with eight pre-production models the first of 79 French army weapons (down from an original requirement of 180 systems) was delivered in 1984.

The TR towed gun has a barrel 6.20 m (20 ft 4.1 in) long, a double-baffle muzzle brake, a hydropneumatic recoil system and horizontal-wedge breech mechanism. The carriage is of the split trail type, with an auxiliary power unit located on the forward part. The 39-hp (29-kW) engine drives three hydraulic pumps, one for each of the main road wheels and the third to provide power for elevation, traverse, raising the suspension, trail wheel jacks and projectile-loading mechanism. The APU enables the weapon to propel itself around the battery position or on the road at a maximum speed of 8 km/h (5 mph). When being towed or travelling under its own power, the TR has its barrel traversed 180° and locked in position over the closed trails. The projectile-loading system makes possible firing rates of three rounds in the first 18 seconds, six rounds per minute for the first two minutes, and 120 rounds per hour thereafter. On any future battlefield in Europe such a weapon would have to be redeployed in a very short time as its position would soon be determined by the enemy, resulting in counterbattery fire.

The TR can fire several types of ammunition: the older modèle 56/59 HE projectile to a range of 19250 m (21,050 yards), the more recent Cr TA 68 HE projectile weighing 43.2 kg (95.25 lb) to a range of 24000 m (26,245 yards), the 155-mm (6.1-in) illuminating projectile (providing 800000 candelas of light) to a range of 21500 m (23,515 yards), a smoke incendiary projectile to a range of 21300 m (23,295 yards), and a Brandt rocket-assisted projectile to a range of 30500 m (33,355 yards). GIAT has recently announced that it is developing three new projectiles for the TR and GCT. The first of these is the so-called cargo round, which carries six anti-tank mines dispensed over the target; each of these weighs 0.55 kg (1.2 lb) and will penetrate 50 mm (1.47 in) of armour steel. The HE base-bleed round is called the HE BB, has a maximum range of 29500 m (32,260 yards) and weighs 43.5 kg (95.9 lb) of which 10 kg (22.05 lb) is high explosive. The last is the rocket-assisted projectile, which has a range of 33000 m (36,090 yards).

The TR has an eight-man crew, and will be towed by the new TRM 10 000 (6×6) 10-tonne truck, which also carries 48 projectiles, charges and fuses.

Specification
TR gun
Calibre: 155 mm (6.1 in)
Weight: travelling and firing 10650 kg (23,479 lb)
Dimensions: length, travelling 8.25 m (27 ft 0.8 in); width, travelling 3.09 m (10 ft 1.65 in); height, firing 1.65 m (5 ft 5 in)
Elevation: +65°/−5°
Traverse: total 65°
Maximum range: with standard projectile 24000 m (26,245 yards) and with rocket-assisted projectile 33000 m (36,090 yards)

Above: One of the prototypes of the new French TR 155-mm gun in the firing position. The French army is to take delivery of 79 of these systems to replace the 155-mm Modèle 50 howitzer, which has been in service for some 30 years. Like most modern weapons of this type it is fitted with an auxiliary power unit.

Below: A TR 155-mm gun from the front, showing the auxiliary power unit on the front of the carriage. This not only provides the power required to propel the weapon around on its own, but also to bring the weapon into and out of action as well as running the projectile loading mechanism.

Soltam M-68 155-mm gun/howitzer

The only manufacturer of towed artillery in Israel is Soltam, which is believed to have close links with the Finnish company Tampella. The Soltam **M-68** 155-mm (6.1-in) gun/howitzer was developed as a private venture in the late 1960s, the first prototype being completed in 1968 and the first production models following two years later.

The ordnance of the M-68 is 5.18 m (17 ft 0 in) long and fitted with a single-baffle muzzle brake, fume extractor and a horizontal breech mechanism. The recoil system is below the barrel and the counter recoil system above, the pneumatic equilibrators being located on the sides of the barrel. When travelling, the top carriage is traversed to the rear so that the ordnance is over the closed trails. The carriage is of the split-trail type. Two rubber-tyred road wheels are mounted on a bogie on each side; each wheel is fitted with a hydraulic brake, and a maximum towing speed of 100 km/h (62 mph) is thus possible. When in the firing position the carriage is supported by a screw type firing jack. Four spades are carried, one of these being attached to the end of each trail for firing when the weapon is brought into action. The other two are carried to enable the

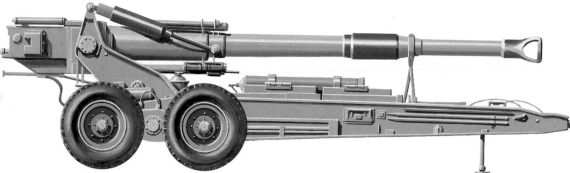

Above: The Soltam M-68 155-mm gun/howitzer in the travelling position with ordnance traversed to rear and locked in position over trails. The Israeli army uses this weapon mounted on a rebuilt Sherman tank chassis in the self-propelled role.

Right: The Soltam M-68 155-mm gun/howitzer in travelling configuration, being towed by a truck. More recently the company has developed a new long-barrelled howitzer.

155-mm Artillery Fire Control

In recent years many armies have not only introduced new types of towed and self-propelled weapons, but also complete artillery fire-control systems that make the maximum possible use of the artillery available. This is of considerable importance within NATO, whose forces are outnumbered by a factor of three to one in artillery systems. In the past, forward observers on the ground or air observation post (AOP) aircraft radioed the position of the target to the battery commander (or higher command authority), and once the target was engaged would watch the fall of shot and then correct aim. All this took time and often wasted valuable ammunition. This basic method of fire and correction is still employed, but a number of sophisticated devices are also now standard.

Today the forward observer is often mounted in a full-tracked armoured vehicle fitted with a land navigation system so that the observer can quickly determine his own position. He also has powerful binoculars, night observation equipment and a laser rangefinder; with the last he can determine the range to the target within just a few metres. The vehicle is also fitted with extensive communications equipment to relay this information to battery headquarters for immediate action. Not all forward observers are provided with armoured vehicles, however, many having jeeps in which the forward observer is provided with a hand-held laser rangefinder (the British use the Norwegian Simrad LP7) and a rapid-burst radio. With the latter the forward observer can enter all target information, which is then stored and sent in a very short burst of radio transmission, so making detection almost impossible.

In the past most NATO artillery regiments (towed and self-propelled) normally comprised three batteries each of six guns, but the trend is now to eight-gun batteries. A typical British army 105-mm (4.13-in) Light Gun battery has a headquarters battery and three EMI Cymbeline mortar-locating radars, three batteries each with six guns, and a light aid detachment (LAD). Each battery can be split into two troops each of three guns, each of the latter being towed by 1-tonne Land Rover. At battery headquarters is a Marconi Space and Defence Systems Field Artillery Computer Equipment (FACE). In the light regiments (with 105-mm/4.13-in guns) this is mounted in a long-wheelbase Land Rover, while in the self-propelled regiments a FV432 is used. FACE, which entered service in the early 1960s and is used by many other armies (including those of Australia, Canada and Egypt), can be used both in the survey and fire-calculation roles. In the latter role information such as a gun and target position, type of ammunition to be used (e.g. smoke or high explosive), muzzle velocity of each weapon, weather data (from AMETS), temperature and charge are entered; the computer then calculates the elevation and traverse of the gun to get the projectile onto the target; and this information is then passed to each gun by word of mouth, radio or the Artillery Weapons Data Transmission System (AWDATS), one of which can be positioned alongside each gun.

The British army also uses the Artillery Meteorological System (AMETS) at artillery division level. This equipment obtains information on atmospheric conditions, which is then passed down to the battery. With the increasing range of artillery weapons AMETS plays a vital role. For example, there may be little or no wind at the battery itself, but 20 km (12.4 miles) away at the target there could be a wind of 15 km/h (9.3 mph) or more, and this would obviously have an effect on the projectile.

A long-wheelbase Land Rover of the British Royal Artillery fitted with the Marconi Space and Defence System Field Artillery Computer Equipment (FACE), which is issued on the scale of one per command post.

The EMI Cymbeline radar is in service in two models, a trailer-mounted system towed by a long-wheelbase Land Rover and a self-propelled version mounted on the FV432 armoured personnel carrier. Cymbeline has a maximum range of 20 km (12.4 miles) and can determine the position of the enemy mortar in less than 30 seconds. The US Army has recently fielded the Firefinder system, a division normally having two AN/TPQ-36 mortar-locating radars and one larger AN/TPQ-37 artillery-locating radar, both developed by the Hughes Aircraft Company, Ground Systems Division. The AN/TPQ-36 is towed by a Gama Goat and can detect both artillery and mortars, whose exact position is plotted on a roller-type map display. The AN/TPQ-36 has also been ordered by a number of other countries including Jordan, Saudi Arabia, Thailand and Australia, and in 1983 was deployed to the Lebanon by the United States in an effort to pinpoint hostile mortars and artillery systems.

eight-man crew to change direction and open fire again without taking out the original spdes.

The M-68 fires a standard NATO HE projectile weighing 43.7 kg (96.3 lb) to a maximum range of 21000 (22,965 yards), as well as smoke and illuminating projectiles. The weapon can also fire Soltam-designed projectiles with a higher muzzle velocity (820 m/2,690 ft per second compared with 725 m/ 2,380 ft per second) to a maximum range of 23500 m (25,700 yards).

The Soltam M-68 is no longer in volume production, although it could be placed back in production if sufficient numbers were ordered. The latest Soltam 155-mm (6.1-in) weapon is the **M-71** howitzer, which uses the same carriage, breech and recoil system as the M-68 but is fitted with a longer 39-calibre barrel. Mounted on the M-71 is a rammer powered by a compressed air cylinder on the right trail, this enabling the weapon to be loaded at all angles of elevation and so making possible a short-period fire rate of four rounds per minute. The M-71 is known to be in service with the Israeli army, and fires an HE projectile to a maximum range of 23500 m (25,700 yards). For trials purposes one M-71

has been fitted with an auxiliary power unit on the left trail and an ammunition-handling crane on the right trail, with elevation increased from 52° to 70°. The APU enables the weapon, called the **Model 839P**, to propel itself on roads at a maximum speed of 17 km/h (10.6 mph), sufficient fuel being carried for a range of at least 70 km (43.5 miles)

Other users of Soltam 155-mm pieces include Singapore, Thailand, and four undisclosed countries. The Israeli L33 self-propelled howitzer uses the M-68 ordnance, and a prototype Centurion based vehicle has been built using the M-71 gun/howitzer.

Specification
Soltam M-68 gun/howitzer
Calibre: 155 mm (6.1 in)
Weight: travelling 9500 kg (20,944 lb) and firing 8500 kg (18,739 lb)
Dimensions: length, travelling 7.20 m (23 ft 7.5 in); width, travelling 2.58 m (8 ft 5.6 in); height, travelling 2.00 m (6 ft 6.75 in)
Elevation: +52°/−5°
Traverse: total 90°
Maximum range: 21000 m (22,965 yards)

Israeli 155-mm M-68 gun/howitzer in the firing position with trails firmly staked to the ground. The split trail carriage is unusual in that it has a total of four rubber-tyred road wheels, each of which has a hydraulic brake operated from the towing vehicle.

OTO Melara modello 56 105-mm pack howitzer

The mountainous terrain of northern Italy is defended by five Alpine brigades, and these and the sole Italian airborne brigade required a 105-mm (4.13-in) howitzer that could be disassembled for easy transportation across the mountains and when assembled be light enough to be airdropped or carried slung underneath a helicopter. To meet this requirement the Italian armaments manufacturer OTO Melara at La Spezia designed a weapon that became known as the **modello 56** 105-mm (4.13-in) pack howitzer. This entered production in 1957, and was soon adopted by many countries all over the world. By 1984 some 2,400 weapons had been delivered, and the type has seen combat use in many areas. The British used it in the South Yemen and during the Borneo confrontation, while the Argentines used it in the Falklands campaign of 1982. By today's standards the modello 56 howitzer has a short range, and in the British Royal Artillery it has already been replaced by the Royal Ordnance Factory 105-mm (4.13-in) Light Gun, which has a maximum range of 17000 m (18590 yards) compared with only 10575 m (11,565 yards) for the modello 56, which is much lighter, however.

The modello 56 has a very short barrel with a multi-baffle muzzle brake, a hydraulic buffer and helical recuperator, and a vertical sliding wedge breech block. The carriage is of the split-trail type and fitted with rubber tyres for high-speed towing. An unusual feature of the modello 56 is that its wheels can be fitted in two different positions: in the normal field position the wheels are overslung, the weapon then having an elevation of +65° and a depression of −5°, and a total traverse of 36° (18° left and right); but for the anti-tank role the wheels are underslung and the weapon has an elevation of +25° and a depression of −5°, total traverse remaining 36°. The main advantage of having the wheels underslung is that the height is reduced from 1.93 m to 1.55 m (6 ft 4 in to 5 ft 1 in), so making the weapon much easier to conceal, a valuable asset in the anti-tank role.

The modello 56 can be dismantled into 11 sections for transport across rough country, and in peacetime the shield is often removed to save weight. The weapon is manned by a seven-man crew, and can be towed by a long-wheelbase Land Rover or similar vehicle. It can also be carried slung under a Bell UH-1 or Westland Wessex helicopter.

Another advantage of the modello 56 is that it fires the same ammunition as the American M101 or M102 105-mm (4.13-in) towed guns, and this ammunition is manufactured all over the world. Types of ammunition fired include an HE projectile weighing 21.06 kg (46.4 lb) with a maximum muzzle velocity of 472 m (1,550 ft) per second, as well as smoke, illuminating and HEAT (High Explosive Anti-Tank). The last weighs 16.7 kg (36.8 lb) and will penetrate 102 mm (4 in) of armour.

A Royal Artillery unit attached to the Royal Marine Commandos carry 105-mm pack howitzers in Norway. The normal towing vehicle is the Swedish Bv 202, which was successfully used in the Falklands towing the more modern 105-mm Light Gun.

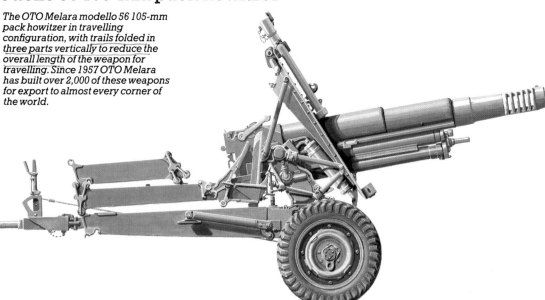

The OTO Melara modello 56 105-mm pack howitzer in travelling configuration, with trails folded in three parts vertically to reduce the overall length of the weapon for travelling. Since 1957 OTO Melara has built over 2,000 of these weapons for export to almost every corner of the world.

Specification
OTO Melara modello 56 howitzer
Calibre: 105 mm (4.13 in)
Weight: travelling 1290 kg (2,844 lb)
Dimensions: length, travelling 3.65 m (11 ft 11.7 in); width, travelling 1.50 m (4 ft 11 in); height, travelling 1.93 m (6 ft 4 in)
Elevation: +65°/−5°
Traverse: total 36°
Maximum range: 10575 m (11,565 yards)

Right: OTO Melara modello 56 105-mm pack howitzer of the Canadian Armed Forces, with its shield removed to reduce its weight. This photograph clearly shows the axle arrangement that allows the overall height to be dramatically reduced when being used in the anti-tank role.

155-mm FH-70 in the firing position with ordnance horizontal. This weapon is now in service with West Germany, Italy, the UK and Saudi Arabia.

In 1968 a Memorandum of Understanding (MoU) was signed between the UK and West Germany for the joint development of a 155-mm (6.1-in) howitzer which would replace the 140-mm (5.5-in) gun for the former and the 155-mm (6.1-in) M114 howitzer for the latter. The main requirements of this weapon included a high rate of fire with a burst fire capability, increased range and lethality together with a new family of ammunition, high mobility and a minimum of effort for deployment. The UK was team leader for this weapon, which became known as the **FH-70**, while West Germany became team leader for the self-propelled equivalent, SP-70, which was cancelled in late 1986. Nineteen prototypes of the FH-70 were built, and in 1970 Italy joined the project as a full partner. In 1976 the FH-70 was accepted for service, the first production weapons being completed in 1978. Three production lines were established, one in the UK (Vickers Shipbuilding and Engineering Limited), one in West Germany (Rheinmetall) and one in Italy (OTO Melara). The UK ordered 71 equipments, West Germany 216 and Italy 164. The weapon has recently entered service with Saudi Arabia, and will be made under licence in Japan.

The barrel of the FH-70 is 6.022 m (19 ft 9 in) long, and has a double-baffle muzzle brake and a semi-automatic wedge-type breech mechanism. The carriage of the FH-70 is of the split-trail type, with an auxiliary power unit mounted on the forward part. This enables the FH-70 to propel itself on roads and across country at a maximum speed of 16 km/h (10 mph). In addition the APU provides power for steering, and for raising and lowering the main and trail wheels. When travelling, the ordnance is traversed to the rear and locked in position over the closed trails. To achieve the requirement for a burst-fire capability a semi-automatic loading system is fitted, and this operates at all angles of elevation. The loading system includes a loading tray that presents the projectile to the chamber. A burst rate of three rounds in 13 seconds can be achieved, while the normal rate of fire is six rounds per minute.

The FH-70 fires three main types of ammunition: HE with a weight of 43.5 kg (95.9 lb) smoke (base ejection), and illuminating. The last provides one million candelas for one minute. The FH-70 can also fire the Martin Marietta Cannon-Launched Guided Projectile (CLGP), although this has yet to be adopted by any European member of NATO, and the US M549A1 rocket-assisted projectile, which has a range of 30000 m (32,810 yards).

The FH-70 has an eight-man crew, with each country having a different towing vehicle: West Germany uses the MAN (6×6) 7-tonne truck, Italy the

Above: 155-mm FH-70s of the British Royal Artillery on the ranges. This weapon fires a high explosive projectile to a maximum range of 24000 m (26,245 yards), although a rocket assisted projectile can also be fired with a longer range.

Right: 155-mm FH-70 firing at high angle during trials in Sardinia some years ago. The UK was project leader for the FH-70, while West Germany was project leader for the SP-70. Each of the three producing countries use different towing vehicles.

FIAT 66066 TM (6×6) truck, and the UK the Foden Medium Mobility Vehicle (6×6), which shares many common automotive components with the Low Mobility range of vehicles used in large numbers by the British army.

Specification
FH-70 field howitzer
Calibre: 155 mm (6.1 in)
Weight: travelling and firing 9300 kg (20,503 lb)
Dimensions: length, travelling 9.80 m (32 ft 1.8 in); width, travelling 2.204 m (7 ft 2.75 in); height, travelling 2.56 m (8 ft 4.8 in)
Elevation: +70°/−5°
Traverse: total 56°
Maximum range: with standard round 24000 m (26,245 yards) and with rocket-assisted projectile 30000 m (32,810 yards)

105-mm Light Gun

In 1959 the Royal Artillery adopted the Italian OTO Melara 105-mm (4.13-in) pack howitzer as its standard weapon for employment with airborne and air-portable units, and this subsequently gave excellent service in such places as Aden and Borneo. The weapon's main drawback from the British point of view was its relatively short range of 10575 m (11,565 yards). So in 1965 the Royal Artillery issued a requirement for a replacement weapon with a longer range, ability to be towed across country at high speed and a more stable firing platform. Design work began at the Royal Armament Research and Development Establishment in 1966, and after the construction of prototypes, field tests and the resultant modifications the **105-mm Light Gun** was accepted for service in 1973. The first production weapons were completed at Royal Ordnance Factory Nottingham in 1974. In the Royal Artillery the weapon is issued on the scale of 18 guns per regiment, each battery having six guns. It is in service with regular units based in the UK (including those earmarked for rapid out-of-area deployment), Belize and Gibraltar, and also equips a number of Territorial artillery units. Overseas sales have been made to Botswana, Brunei, Eire, Kenya, Malawi, Moroco, Oman, and the United Arab Emirates. Australia is licence-producing a version of the Light Gun known as the **Hamel** Gun. Regular units will receive it from 1988, and reserves from 1990. New Zealand ordered 24 Australian guns for delivery from 1986. When in use with the British army the weapon is towed by a

1-tonne Land Rover. This is no longer produced, however, and the Light Gun can be towed by a number of other tracked and wheeled vehicles, including the Swedish Bv 202 all-terrain vehicle. The Light Gun can also be slung under a helicopter such as an Aérospatiale Puma, while the smaller Westland Wessex can take it in two loads.

Two types of barrel can be fitted. The standard barrel is the L19A1, which fires the Abbott range of ammunition out to 17200 m (18,810 yards), and there is also the shorter L20A1 barrel, which fires the standard American M1 series of ammunition out to 11000 m (12,030 yards). Many countries keep the Light Gun with the short barrel for training purposes as the ammunition is much cheaper and available from a variety of manufacturers in almost every corner of the world.

The ordnance (barrel) of the Light Gun is fitted with a double-baffle muzzle brake, a hydropneumatic recoil system and a vertical sliding breech mechanism. Traverse is limited to 5.5° left and right, but when the Light Gun is positioned on its turntable, which is normally carried over the bow-type trails, it can be quickly traversed through 360° to be laid onto a new target. When travelling, the ordnance is normally traversed over the trails to make it more compact.

The ammunition fired by the Light Gun is identical to that fired by the Abbott 105-mm (4.13-in) self-propelled gun, is manufactured by the Royal Ordnance Factories, and includes HE (projectile weight 16.1 kg/35.5 lb), HE squash head (for engaging tanks and other targets), squash head practice and smoke (three colours).

After a series of intensive trials with the 9th Infantry Division, the US Army decided to adopt the Light Gun as a non-developmental item (in other words, an off the shelf purchase) in early 1986. Type-classified as the **M119**, the American version will have the shorter L20A1 barrel firing a new series of ammunition currently being developed in addition to the standard M1 series. The total US Army requirement is for more than 540 units, to be

manufactured in the USA. These will replace the M102 currently in service with Airborne and Air Assault divisions, and will equip the new light divisions being formed for the 1990s.

India has also produced a 105-mm light gun, the **Light Field Gun Mark 2**. It is virtually identical to the Royal Ordnance Light Gun, as like the British weapon it has been developed from the ordnance of the Abbott 105-mm self-propelled gun which is used by the Indian army.

The Light Gun proved to be a highly effective weapon in the Falklands campaign of 1982, and since then a number of Light Guns have been permanently retained as part of the islands' garrison.

The Royal Ordnance Factory's 105-mm Light Gun fires at maximum elevation during demonstrations at the Royal School of Artillery at Larkhill, Wiltshire. The 105-mm Light Gun has now replaced the Model 56 Pack Howitzer in the Royal Artillery, and not only has a longer range but also fires the same highly lethal range of ammunition as the Abbott 105-mm self-propelled gun used by the British and Indian armies.

Specification
105-mm Light Gun
Calibre: 105 mm (4.13-in)
Weight: firing and travelling 1858 kg (4,096 lb)
Dimensions: length, travelling (gun over trail) 4.876 m (16 ft 0 in); width, travelling 1.778 m (5 ft 10 in); height, travelling (gun over trail) 1.371 m (4 ft 6 in)
Elevation: +70°/−5.5°
Traverse: total 11° or on turntable 360°
Maximum range: 17200 m (18,810 yards)

Below: Royal Ordnance Factory Nottingham 105-mm Light Gun in the firing position. This weapon has now replaced the 105-mm Pack Howitzer in the light regiments of the Royal Artillery and is deployed in the UK, Belize and with Gibraltar Regiment. Over 400 have now been built for both the home and export markets, and it has the longest range of any weapon of its type in the world today.

Royal Ordnance 105-mm Light Gun cutaway drawing

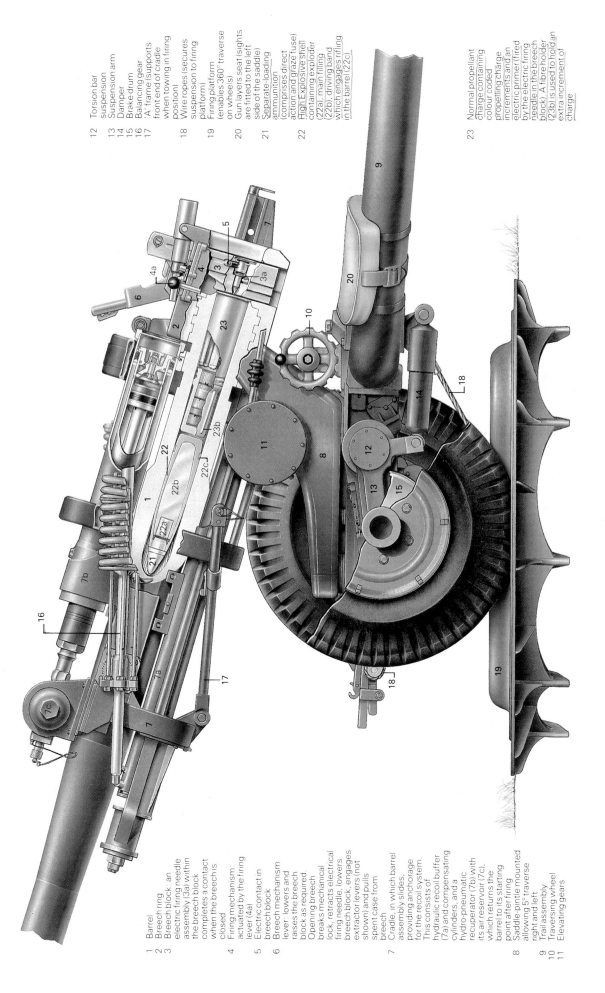

1 Barrel
2 Breech ring
3 Breech block: an electric firing needle assembly (3a) within the breech block completes a contact when the breech is closed
4 Firing mechanism: actuated by the firing lever (4a)
5 Electric contact in breech block
6 Breech mechanism lever: lowers and raises the breech block as required
Opening breech breaks mechanical lock, retracts electrical firing needle, lowers breech block, engages extractor levers (not shown) and pulls spent case from breech
7 Cradle, in which barrel assembly slides, providing anchorage for the recoil system. This consists of hydraulic recoil buffer (7a) and compensating cylinders, and a hydro-pneumatic recuperator (7b) with its air reservoir (7c), which returns the barrel to its starting point after firing
8 Saddle-pintle mounted allowing 5° traverse right and left
9 Trail assembly
10 Traversing wheel
11 Elevating gears

12 Torsion bar suspension
13 Suspension arm
14 Damper
15 Brake drum
16 Balancing gear
17 'A' frame (supports front end of cradle when towing in firing position)
18 Wire ropes (secures suspension to firing platform)
19 Firing platform (enables 360° traverse on wheels)
20 Gun layers seat (sights are fitted to the left side of the saddle)
21 Separate-loading ammunition (comprises direct action and graze fuse)
22 High Explosive shell containing exploder (22a), main filling (22b), driving band which engages rifling in the barrel (22c)
23 Normal propellant charge containing colour coded propelling charge increments and an electric primer (fired by the electric firing needle in the breech block). A fibre holder (23b) is used to hold an extra increment of charge

137

G5 155-mm gun/howitzer

ARMSCOR G5 155-mm gun/howitzer in the travelling position, with ordnance locked in position over the forward part of the carriage on which is mounted the auxiliary power unit. This enables the G5 to be quickly brought into action in the field by its eight-man crew.

For 30 years after the Second World War, the artillery mainstays of the South African army were the British 5.5-in (140-mm) Medium Gun and the famous 25-Pdr Field Gun. It was something of a shock during operations into Angola in 1975, to find them outranged by modern Soviet supplied guns, and by a considerable margin. This led to the development of a number of new weapon systems, of indigenous manufacture due to an anti-apartheid arms embargo. Foremost among them was the **G5 155-mm Gun/Howitzer**, an artillery piece as good as any in the world, which has proved highly effective in action. It has mainly been used in the Operational Area of the Angola/Namibia border but has reportedly been sold to Iraq for use in the Gulf War.

The G5 owes much to the Canadian Space Research Corporation GC 45 155-mm (6.1-in) weapon, of which 12 are in service with the Thai marines, but so many additional features have been incorporated into the G5 that this now bears little resemblance to the original Canadian weapon.

The G5 has a 45-calibre barrel fitted with a single-baffle muzzle brake and an interrupted-thread breech mechanism. To the rear of the breech is a pneumatically-operated rammer to ram projectiles into the chamber at all angles of elevation; this is powered by an air bottle mounted on the right trail. The bagged charges are loaded by hand. On the forward part of the split trail carriage is the auxiliary power unit, which consists of a 68-hp (51-kW) diesel engine. In addition to providing power to the main driving wheels, the APU also supplies power for raising and lowering the circular firing platform under the carriage, for opening and closing the trails, and for

raising and lowering the trail wheels. To reduce the overall length of the G5 for travelling, the ordnance is normally traversed through 180° and locked in position over the trails. The ordnance has a total traverse of 84° at up to 15° of elevation, and 65° above 15° of elevation. Maximum rate of fire over a 15 minute period is three rounds per minute, with two rounds per minute possible in the sustained fire role. The weapon is operated by an eight-man crew, and is normally towed by a South African-built SAMIL 100 (6×6) 10-tonne truck which carries the crew, projectiles, charges and fuses.

The G5 can fire five types of ammunition, also manufactured in South Africa by ARMSCOR. The standard HE projectile weighs 45.5 kg (100.3 lb) and is of the Extended-Range Full Bore (ERFB) type. The HE

base-bleed (HE BB) type is slightly heavier because of the base-bleed attachment, but has a range of 37000 m (40,465 yards) at sea level, though greater ranges are attained when the G5 is fired at higher altitude. The other three projectiles are illuminating, smoke and white phosphorus. To operate with the G5 South Africa has developed a complete fire-control system including a muzzle-velocity measuring device, AS 80 artillery fire-control system with a 16-bit mini-computer, S700 meteorological ground station and a complete range of communications equipment. South Africa has also developed a 155-mm (6.1-in) self-propelled howitzer (6×6) called the **G6**, which has an ordnance based on the G5 and uses the same ammunition, but this has yet to enter production.

Three G5 155-mm gun/howitzers of the South African army in the firing position. The G5 is normally towed by a SAMIL 100 (6×6) 10-tonne truck that also carries the gun crew and its ammunition. The G5 has an exceptionally long range.

Specification
G5 gun/howitzer
Calibre: 155 mm (6.1 in)
Weight: travelling 13500 kg (29,762 lb)
Dimensions: length, travelling 9.10 m (29 ft 10.25 in); width, travelling 2.50 m (8 ft 2.4 in); height, travelling 2.30 m (7 ft 6.55 in)
Elevation: +73°/−3°
Traverse: total 84° (see text)
Maximum range: with standard ammunition 30000 m (32,810 yards) and with base-bleed projectile 37000 m (40,465 yards)

Bofors FH-77A 155-mm field howitzer

In the late 1960s the Swedish army carried out a series of studies to determine its future artillery requirements, and finally decided to develop a new 155-mm (6.1-in) towed weapon that would have superior cross-country performance, a high rate of fire, good range and fire more effective ammunition. At that time Bofors was building the 155-mm (6.1-in) Bandkanon 1A self-propelled gun, which is fully armoured and has a high rate of fire as it is fitted with an automatic loader for 16 rounds of ready-use ammunition. Its main drawback, however, was and is its size and weight (53 tonnes), which limit its

movement in certain parts of Sweden as well as making it difficult to conceal.

Bofors was awarded the development contract for the new towed weapon, which subsequently became known as the **FH-77A** 155-mm (6.1-in) field howitzer, for which the first orders were placed by the Swedish army in 1975.

The FH-77A has a barrel 5.89 m (19 ft 3.9 in) long and fitted with a pepperpot muzzle brake and a vertical sliding breech mechanism. The split-trail carriage has an auxiliary power unit mounted on the front, enabling the FH-77A to propel itself on roads and across

country. The equipment is normally towed by a Saab-Scania SBAT 111S (6×6) truck, which also carries ammunition in pallets and the six man crew consisting of commander, gunner, two ammunition handlers, loader and crane handler. When the truck and the FH-77A encounter very rough country the main wheels of the howitzer can be engaged from the cab of the truck, so giving an 8×6 combination and a maximum speed of 8 km/h (5 mph). When this speed is exceeded the main wheels of the FH-77A are disengaged. Elevation and traverse of the FH-77A is hydraulic, though manual

controls are provided for emergency use. Mounted on the right side of FH-77A is the loading tray, on which clips of three projectiles can be placed. A typical firing sequence is that the cartridge case is placed on the loading tray followed by the projectile, which is fed from the loading table. When the projectile has slipped down into the neck of the cartridge case the projectile and charge are rammed, the breech is closed and the weapon is fired. Using this method three rounds can be fired in six to eight seconds. In the sustained-fire role six rounds can be fired every other minute for 20

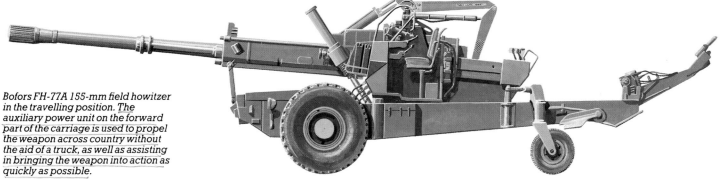

Bofors FH-77A 155-mm field howitzer in the travelling position. The auxiliary power unit on the forward part of the carriage is used to propel the weapon across country without the aid of a truck, as well as assisting in bringing the weapon into action as quickly as possible.

minutes.

The Bofors-developed M/77 projectile weighs 42.4 kg (93.5 lb), has a muzzle velocity of 774 m (2,540 ft) per second and goes out to a maximum range of 22000 m (24,060 yards). It is believed that Bofors is currently developing a base-bleed projectile which will have a maximum range of between 27000 and 30000 m (29,530 and 32,810 yards). For the export market Bofors has developed the **FH-77B** with a slightly longer barrel, increased elevation of +70°, mechanized loading system and a number of other major improvements. The FH-77B has already been ordered by Nigeria and Zimbabwe, and is the subject of one of the largest export orders for Swedish armaments in history, when India ordered 400 units (with more possibly built under licence) together with all support equipment.

Specification
Bofors FH-77A field howitzer
Calibre: 155 mm (6.1 in)
Weight: travelling 11500 kg (25,353 lb)
Dimensions: length, travelling 11.60 m (38 ft 0.7 in); width, travelling 2.64 m (8 ft 8 in); height, travelling 2.75 m (9 ft 0.25 in)
Elevation: +50°/+3°
Traverse: total 50°
Maximum range: 20000 m (21,870 yards)

Bofors FH-77A 155-mm field howitzer in the firing position with two ammunition members preparing to load charges. The first three projectiles can be fired in between six and eight seconds, with the loading tray on the right side of the carriage holding the three projectiles. The more recent FH-77B is now in production for Nigeria.

USA
M102 105-mm howitzer

For many years the standard 105-mm (4.13-in) howitzer of the US Army was the M1, which was developed in the 1930s and finally standardized as the M2 in 1940. A total of 10,202 such weapons had been built by the time production ended in 1953. In the post-war period the weapon was re-designated the M101. The main drawback of the M101, which in 1948 was still in use in some 60 countries, was its weight of 2030 to 2258 kg (4,475 to 4,978 lb) depending on the model, and the lack of all-round traverse.

In 1955 a requirement was issued for a new 105-mm (4.13-in) howitzer which would fire the same range of ammunition and yet be lighter than the M101. Rock Island Arsenal designed a new weapon under the designation **XM102**, the first prototype being completed in 1962. Following trials the weapon was classified as standard A in the following year, and designated **M102**. First production M102s were completed in January 1964 and several months later the weapon was deployed to South Vietnam. After so short a development period problems were inevitably encountered with early M102s, but these were soon rectified. The M102 is issued on the scale of 18 per battalion, each battery having six weapons. Today the M102 is used mainly by airborne and airmobile divisions, to whom weight rather than range is important. The M102 is also used by Brazil, Saudi Arabia, Kampuchea, South Korea and Vietnam.

The M102 consists of four main components, namely the M137 cannon, M37 recoil system, M31 carriage, and the fire-control equipment. The M137

cannon has a vertical sliding-wedge breech mechanism, but is not fitted with a muzzle brake. The recoil system is hydropneumatic and variable, so eliminating the need for a recoil pit. The most unusual feature of the M102 is the two-wheel box-type carriage, which is constructed of aluminium. When the weapon is deployed in the firing position, a circular baseplate is lowered to the ground under the forward part of the base and the two rubber-tyred road wheels are lifted clear of the ground. A roller located at the rear of the trial assembly allows the complete carriage to be traversed through 360°. This proved to be of considerable use in Vietnam, where M102s had to engage targets in different directions at

very short notice, situated as they were on hill-top fire-bases providing support to a number of widely dispersed units.

The M1 range of ammunition fired by the M102 includes chemical and anti-personnel (flechette and HE/grenade carriers) rounds in addition to the usual HE, illuminating, smoke and training rounds.

The M102 is to be replaced in front-line service with US Army Airborne, Air Assault and the new Light Divisions by the British M119 Light Gun, but the M102s will themselves replace remaining M101 howitzers in the Army and National Guard.

Specification
M102 howitzer
Calibre: 105 mm (4.13 in)
Weight: firing and travelling 1496 kg (3,300 lb)
Dimensions: length, travelling 5.182 m (17 ft 0 in); width, travelling 1.964 m (6 ft 5.25 in); height, travelling 1.594 m (5 ft 2.75 in)
Elevation: +75°/−5°
Traverse: total 360°
Maximum range: with M1 ammunition 11500 m (12,575 yards) or with M548 HERA 15100 m (16,515 yards)

An M102 105-mm light howitzer of the American 82nd Airborne Division in action during the invasion of Grenada in 1983.

M198 155-mm howitzer

M198 155-mm howitzer in one of its two travelling configurations. This is now the standard 155-mm howitzer of the US Army and Marines, and replaces the old 155-mm M114.

For many years the standard 155-mm (6.1-in) towed howitzer of the US Army was the M114, which was developed in the 1930s and standardized as the M1 in 1941. By the end of World War II some 6,000 had been built, and in the post-war period the weapon was redesignated M114. Like the 105-mm (4.13-in) M101 towed howitzer, the M114 suffered the major drawback of having a limited range and traverse. Following the issue of a formal requirement for a new 155-mm (6.1-in) howitzer, Rock Island Arsenal started design work in 1968, its first development prototype being completed two years later. A total of 10 prototypes was built under the designation **XM198**, and after trials and the usual modifications it was adopted as the 155-mm (6.1-in) howitzer **M198**. Production started at Rock Island Arsenal in 1978, with the first battalion of 18 M198s forming at Fort Bragg in the following year. Each battalion has three batteries each with six M198s.

In addition to being used by the US Army and US Marine Corps, the M198 has also been ordered by Australia (36 to replace the British 140-mm/5.5-in gun) and a number of other countries, notably in the Middle East. In the US Army and US Marine Corps the M198 is towed by a 5-ton (6×6) truck which also carries the ammunition and 11-man crew, although the weapon can be towed by a variety of other tracked and wheeled vehicles. It is airportable, and can be carried slung underneath Boeing Vertol CH-47 and Sikorsky CH-53 helicopters. The M198 is normally issued to US infantry, airborne and air assault divisions, while the mechanized infantry and armoured divisions have the 155-mm (6.1-in) M109 self-propelled howitzer. The M198 was first used operationally by the US Marines in the Lebanon in 1983.

Main components of the M198 are the carriage, recoil system, fire-control equipment, and cannon (or ordnance, as the British prefer to call it). The carriage is of the split-trail type and fitted with a two-position rigid suspension. When the weapon is in the firing position, a firing platform is lowered to the ground under the forward part of the carriage and the wheels are raised clear of the ground. The cradle has the elevation and traverse system, while the top carriage has the assembly cradle, equilibrators and recoil guides. The recoil mechanism is of the hydropneumatic type with a variable recoil length. The M199 cannon has a double-baffle muzzle brake, thermal warning device and a screw-type breech mechanism. Fire-control equipment includes an M137 panoramic telescope, two elevation quadrants and an M138 elbow telescope.

When in the travelling position the ordnance is normally traversed to the rear and locked in position over the trails. Unlike the new French 155-mm (6.1-in) towed guns, British/West German/Italian FH-70 and the Swedish FH-77A, the M198 does not have an auxiliary power unit to enable it to be moved under its own power.

Ammunition is of the separate-loading type and includes Agent, anti-tank (carrying mines), Cannon-Launched Guided Projectile, high explosive, high explosive with various types of grenade including dual-purpose and anti-personnel, rocket assisted projectile, illumination, smoke, and tactical nuclear.

Specification
M198 howitzer
Calibre: 155 mm (6.1 in)
Weight: travelling 7076 kg (15,600 lb)
Dimensions: length, travelling 12.396 m (40 ft 8 in); width, travelling 2.794 m (9 ft 2 in); height, travelling 3.023 m (9 ft 11 in)
Elevation: +72°/−5°
Traverse: total 45°
Maximum range: with M107 projectile 18150 m (19,850 yards) and with rocket-assisted projectile 30000 m (32,810 yards)

M198 155-mm howitzer in static fire position, with sand bags providing some form of protection. This weapon was first used in combat during the recent fighting in Lebanon. It is also used by a number of other countries.

D-30 122-mm howitzer

The **D-30** 122-mm (4.8-in) howitzer was designed by the F.F. Petrov design bureau at Artillery Plant Number 9 at Sverdlovsk as the replacement for the 122-mm (4.8-in) M1938 (M-30) howitzer which had been introduced into the Soviet army shortly before World War II. The D-30 entered service with the Soviet army in the early 1960s and has a number of significant advantages over the weapon it replaced, including a range of 15400 compared with 11800 m (16,840 compared with 12,905 yards) and a traverse of 360° compared with 49°. In addition to being used by the Soviet army, the weapon is in service with well over 30 countries, and has seen widespread use in the Middle East, Africa and the Far East. The more recent 122-mm (4.8-in) M-1974 self-propelled howitzer has an ordnance based on the D-30. Another SP mounting was evolved some years ago, when Syria was short of self-propelled artillery and installed a number of D-30 ordnances on obsolete T-34/85 tank chassis. Under contract to the Egyptian government the Royal Ordnance Factory Leeds (where the Chieftain, Challenger and Khalid tanks are built) is fitting the D-30 howitzer onto the chassis of the Combat Engineer Tractor for the Egyptian army.

In the Soviet army the D-30 is issued on the scale of 36 per tank division (one artillery regiment with two battalions of 18 weapons, each battalion having three batteries of six D-30s), and each motorized rifle division has 72 D-30s (each motorized rifle regiment having a battalion of 18 D-30s and the artillery regiment two 18-gun battalions). More recently it is believed that the Soviets, like some members of NATO, are increasing the number of guns in the battery from six to eight: each battalion would thus now have 24 instead of 18 D-30s.

The D-30 has a 4.875-m (16-ft) barrel fitted with a multi-baffle muzzle brake and a semi-automatic vertical sliding-wedge breech mechanism, the recoil system being mounted over the ordnance. The weapon is towed muzzle first, the three trails being clamped in position under the ordnance. On arrival at the pre-determined firing position the crew must first unlock the barrel travel lock, which then folds back onto the central trail. The firing jack under

Three Soviet D-30 122-mm howitzers in the firing position. For many years the D-30 was the backbone of Soviet artillery regiments, but is now being replaced by the 122-mm M-1974 self-propelled howitzer. It has been supplied to almost every country receiving Soviet aid.

A D-30 122-mm howitzer in the firing position with trails staked to the ground. One of the features of this weapon is that it can be quickly traversed through 360° without repositioning the carriage.

the carriage is then lowered to the ground, so raising the wheels well clear of the ground, and the outer trails are each spread through 120°. The firing jack is then raised until the ends of each trail are on the ground to provide a stable firing platform, the ends of the trails being staked to the ground. The D-30 is provided with a small shield, and is normally towed by a ZIL-157 or Ural-375D (6×6) truck, or by an

MT-LB multi-purpose tracked vehicle.
The D-30 fires case-type separate-loading ammunition including FRAG-HE, HEAT-FS (which will penetrate some 460 mm/18.1 in of armour), chemical, smoke and illuminating. More recently a rocket-assisted projectile has been introduced with a maximum range of 21000 m (22,965 yards).

China produces a direct copy of the D-30.

Specification
D-30 howitzer
Calibre: 121.92 mm (4.8 in)
Weight: travelling 3210 kg (7,077 lb) and firing 3150 kg (6,944 lb)
Dimensions: length, travelling 5.40 m

(17 ft 8.6 in); width, travelling 1.95 m (6 ft 4.75 in); height, travelling 1.66 m (5 ft 5.35 in)
Elevation: +70°/−7°
Traverse: 360°
Maximum range: with HE Projectile 15400 m (16,840 yards) and with HE rocket-assisted projectile 21000 m (22,965 yards)

M-46 130-mm field gun

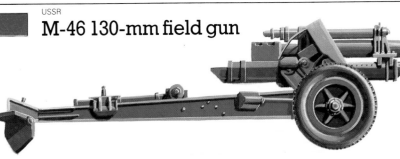

This M-46 130-mm field gun shows its long barrel with the pepperpot muzzle brake. It has been in service for some 30 years, and has a long range that has only recently been matched by the introduction of Western artillery weapons that fire a rocket-assisted projectile (RAP).

The M-46 130-mm (5.1-in) field gun is believed to be a development of a naval weapon, and was first seen in public during the 1954 May Day parade. For this reason the M-46 is sometimes designated M-1954. Although developed over 30 years ago, it still remains a highly effective weapon with its exceptional range. The weapon has been used in combat in both the Middle East and Vietnam, and in the latter conflict only the American 175-mm (6.89-in) M107 self-propelled gun (with a range of 32700 m/35,760 yards) could outrange the M-46.

In addition to being used by the Soviet Union, the M-46 is operated by more than 30 countries around the world. The Indians have taken the weapon off its normal carriage and installed it on the chassis of the Vickers Mk 1 main battle tank, which is built under the name of the Vijayanta as a self-propelled gun. There is also reason to believe that the Soviets have fitted the ordnance of the M-46 to a main battle tank chassis for use in the tank destroyer role. In the Soviet army the M-46 is deployed in the artillery regiment of an army, which includes two battalions each with 18 M-46s (three batteries each with six weapons). The artillery regiment also has an HQ and service battery, a target-acquisition battery and a battalion of 18 152-mm (6-in) D-20 gun/howitzers. The artillery division, deployed at front (army group) level also includes two regiments each with 54 M-46s, each regiment having three battalions of 18 weapons. The Chinese have a different model of the M-46 cal-

led the **Type 59** 130-mm (5.1-in) field gun.

The M-64 has a barrel 7.60 m (24 ft 11.2 in) long, fitted with a very distinctive pepperpot muzzle brake and a horizontal sliding-wedge breech mechanism. The recoil system consists of a hydraulic buffer below the barrel and a hydropneumatic recuperator above the barrel. To reduce the overall length of the M-46 when travelling, the barrel is withdrawn out of battery to the rear and locked in position between the spades. The carriage is of the split-trail type and is provided with a two-wheel limber at the rear. For travelling the two spades are removed and carried on the tops of the trails. The M-46 has a nine-man crew, takes

four minutes to bring into action, and can be towed by a variety of vehicles including the AT-S, ATS-59 and M1972 unarmoured artillery tractors as well as the AT-P armoured tracked artillery tractor.

The ammunition fired by the M-46 is of the separate-loading type and includes FRAG-HE (fragmentation high-explosive) and APC-5 (armoured piercing capped tracer). The former weighs 33.4 kg (73.63 lb), of which 4.63 kg (10.2 lb) is the bursting charge; maximum muzzle velocity is 1050 m (3,445 ft) per second. The APC-T projectile also has a maximum muzzle velocity of 1050 m (3,445 ft) per second and will penetrate 230 mm (9.05 in) of armour at a range of 1000 m (1,095

yards). Other types of projectile available include illuminating and smoke, and a rocket-assisted projectile was introduced in the late 1960s. The RAP was first used by Syria during the 1973 Middle East war.

Specification
M-46 field gun
Calibre: 130 mm (5.12 in)
Weight: travelling 8450 kg (18,629 lb) and firing 7700 kg (16,975 lb)
Dimensions: length, travelling 11.73 m (38 ft 5.8 in); width, travelling 2.45 m (8 ft 0.5 in); height, travelling 2.55 m (8 ft 4.4 in)
Elevation: +45°/−2.5°
Traverse: total 50°
Maximum range: 27150 m (29,690 yards)

A battery of Soviet M-46 130-mm guns are camouflaged during training. When travelling the barrel is withdrawn out of battery to the rear to reduce its overall length and a two wheel dolly attached. It is deployed in battalions of 18 guns.

S-23 180-mm gun

For some 30 years this weapon has been able to outrange virtually all NATO towed and self-propelled artillery weapons. It was first seen in public during a 1955 Moscow parade, and for many years was known as the 203-mm (8-in) **M-1955** gun/howitzer in the West. It is believed to have entered service several years before 1955 and to be a development of a naval weapon. During the Middle East war of 1973 a number of these weapons were captured by Israel and then taken back to Israel for detailed evaluation by intelligence personnel. It was then discovered that the actual calibre of the weapon was 180 mm (7.09 in) and that its correct Soviet designation is **S-23**. In the Soviet army the S-23 is issued on the scale of 12 weapons in the heavy artillery brigade of every artillery division. More recent information has shown that the artillery division in the Soviet Union no longer has S-23s and now consists of a headquarters, anti-tank regiment with 36 T-12 or T-12A towed anti-tank guns, multiple rocket-launcher brigade with four battalions of BM-27 (8×8) multiple rocket-launchers (total of 72 launchers), target-acquisition battalion, signal company, motor transport battalion, two regiments of 130-mm (5.1-in) M-46 field guns (total of 108 equipments) and two regiments of 152-mm (6-in) D-20 gun/howitzers or the new M-1973 self-propelled gun/howitzer (total of 108 equipments).

The S-23 is known to be in service with a number of other countries including Egypt, India and Syria, and unconfirmed reports have added Cuba, Ethiopia, North Korea, Libya, Mongolia and Somalia. The weapon is normally towed by an AT-T heavy tracked artillery tractor, which also carries the 16-man crew and a small quantity of

ammunition.

The S-23 has a barrel some 8.8 m (28 ft 10.46 in) long with a pepperpot muzzle brake, the recoil system under the barrel and a screw breech mechanism. To reduce the overall length of the weapon for travelling the barrel can be withdrawn out of battery to the rear and linked to the trails. The carriage is of the split-trail type, with two twin rubber-tyred road wheel units at the front and a two-wheel dolly at the rear.

The S-23 fires a bag-type variable-charge separate-loading HE projectile designated OF-43 (weighing some 84.09 kg/185.4 lb with a maximum muzzle velocity of 790 m/2,590 ft per second) as well as a G-572 concrete-piercing projectile (weighing 97.7 kg/215.4 lb) and a 0.2-kiloton tactical nuclear projectile. After the weapon had been in service for some time an HE rocket-assisted projectile was introduced: with a muzzle velocity of 850 m (2,790 ft) per second this has a maximum range of 43800 m (47,900 yards) compared with 30400 m (33,245 yards) for the original projectile. Because of the heavy weight of the projectile the S-23 has a relatively slow rate of fire (one round per minute), dropping to one round every two minutes in the sustained fire role.

Specification
S-23 gun
Calibre: 180 mm (7.09 in)

S-23 180-mm gun in travelling configuration with the dolly attached to the rear. For many years this was thought to be a 203-mm weapon, but examination of weapons captured by Israel showed that it was in fact 180 mm in calibre.

Weight: in action 21450 kg (47,288 lb)
Dimensions: length, travelling 10.485 m (34 ft 4.8 in); width, travelling 2.996 m (9 ft 9.95 in); height, travelling 2.621 m (8 ft 7.2 in)
Elevation: +50°/−2°
Traverse: 44°
Maximum range: with HE projectile 30400 m (33,245 yards) and with rocket-assisted projectile 43,800 m (47,900 yards)

M-56 105-mm howitzer

With the German surrender in Yugoslavia at the end of World War II, large quantities of German artillery were abandoned and much of this was taken over by the Yugoslav army. Even today, some 40 years later, numbers of German 88-mm (3.46-in) guns are still in service in the coastal-defence role, while the 105-mm (4.13-in) towed M18, M18M and M18/40 howitzers are known to be used by reserve units. In the immediate post-war period the United States supplied Yugoslavia with considerable amounts of towed artillery, including 155-mm (6.1-in) M114 and 105-mm (4.13-in) M101 howitzers, and 155-mm (6.1-in) M59 'Long Tom' guns. These remain in service today, as does a copy of the M114 called the M-65. More recently Yugoslavia has designed and built two weapons to meet her own requirements, these being the 105-mm (4.13-in) howitzer **M-56** and a 76-mm (3-in) mountain gun M-46, the latter developed to meet the specific requirements of Yugoslav mountain units.

The M-56 has a barrel 3.48 m (11 ft 5 in) long with a multi-baffle muzzle brake, a hydraulic recoil buffer and hydropneumatic recuperator above and below the barrel, and a horizontal sliding-wedge breech mechanism. The carriage is of the split-trail type, with a spade attached to each end of the pole-type trail. The M-56 has a split

shield that slopes to the rear and sides. Some carriages have been observed with American type road wheels and tyres similar to that fitted to the M101, which allows the weapon to be towed up to 70 km/h (43.5 mph), while others have wheels with solid tyres similar to that fitted to the German 105-mm (4.13-in) howitzers of World War II. When the latter are fitted the weapon cannot be towed at high speed.

Fire-control equipment consists of a panoramic telescope with a magnification of ×4, a direct-fire anti-tank telescope with a magnification of ×2, and a gunner's quadrant.

Ammunition is of the semi-fixed type (e.g. projectile and a cartridge case containing the bagged charge). The following projectiles can be fired at a maximum rate of 16 rounds per minute for a short period: HE projectile weighing 15 kg (33.1 lb) with a muzzle velocity of 570 m (1,870 ft) per second, smoke projectile weighing 15.8 kg (34.8 lb), armour-piercing tracer, and high explosive squash head tracer (HESH-T). The HESH-T projectile weighs 10 kg (22.05 lb), and when it hits an enemy armoured vehicle the 2.2 kg (4.85 lb) of explosive flattens itself against the armour before exploding, when it can penetrate up to 100 mm (3.9 in) of armour plate at an angle of 30°.

An unusual feature of the M-56 is that

in an emergency it can be fired before the trails are spread, although in this case total traverse is limited to 16° and elevation to +16°. The M-56 has a crew of 11 men and is normally towed by a TAM 1500 (4×4) truck. It is used by Burma, Cyprus, El Salvador (where it is towed by the US supplied M35 6×6 truck), Iran and Indonesia in addition to the Yugoslav army.

Specification
M-56 howitzer
Calibre: 105 mm (4.13 in)
Weight: travelling 2100 kg (4,630 lb) and firing 2060 kg (4,541 lb)

Dimensions: length, travelling 6.17 m (20 ft 3 in); width, travelling 2.15 m (7 ft 0.66 in); height, travelling 1.56 m (5 ft 1.4 in)
Elevation: +68°/−12°
Traverse: total 52°
Maximum range: 13000 m (14,215 yards)

A Yugoslav M-56 105-mm howitzer in its travelling configuration. This particular model has wheels with solid rubber tyres similar to those fitted to German 105-mm howitzers also used by the Yugoslav army since World War II.

Modern Multiple Rocket Launchers

European members of NATO will shortly follow the US Army in purchasing the Vought Multiple Launch Rocket System. But, despite its ultra-modern appearance, the MLRS is no more effective than its truck-mounted Soviet equivalent, and is far more expensive.

The Soviet Union introduced the multiple rocket launcher (MRL) during World War II, and remains the world leader in their production and use. MRLs can produce a devastating concentration of fire; the shock effect alone has produced dramatic results in recent wars in Africa, and the MRL is also the ideal delivery system for smoke and chemical munitions.

Today the major exponent of the multiple rocket launcher (MRL) is still the USSR, which first introduced this weapon system onto the battlefield during World War II under the name 'Katyusha'. Basically an offensive weapon, the MRL is able to create tremendous concentrations of firepower in a short space of time, thus enhancing its surprise effect against any target engaged. The Soviets treat MRLs rather as a supplement to tube artillery because their rate of fire is low and the rockets they use are comparatively more expensive than shells. However, MRLs can put down heavy concentrations of smoke and chemical warfare agents, and it is this ability to deliver almost instantaneous high levels that puts them in a category above other systems, especially when blood agents such as hydrogen cyanide are concerned. During several of the wars in southern and central Africa it has been the shock effect of a salvo of rockets with all the attendant noise rather than the actual physical damage that has caused poorly trained troops to run away.

Surprisingly it is only recently that the West, and in particular the USA, has realized the importance of the MRL in modern warfare; but instead of learning direct from the Soviets their use of such weapons, most of the NATO nations which are due to deploy the joint American-European system known as the Multiple Launch Rocket System will, in fact, use it in place of conventional artillery pieces instead of as a supplement to them. Other countries happily have learnt the distinction and are bringing such systems into service with their armies. Perhaps the most noteworthy of these are Egypt, Israel, South Africa and Brazil, which are all now producing their own MRL designs. The last country has its newly designed ASTROS II system in service with the Iraqi army on the battlefields of the still seething Gulf War, while Israel has tested her designs against Syria during the 1982 'Peace for Galilee' invasion of Lebanon.

The launch signature of the Brazilian SS-60 is considerable; thus the firing platform will stay back from the forward line of troops in order to conceal itself by taking full advantage of the SS-60's 60-km (37.5-mile) range.

Light Artillery Rocket System (LARS)

The 110-mm (4.33-in) Light Artillery Rocket System (LARS) was developed in the mid-1960s and accepted into West German army service in 1969. It is issued on the scale of one battery of eight launchers per army division, each battery also having two 4×4 truck-mounted Fieldguard fire-control systems and a resupply vehicle with 144 rockets. Following upgrading to the LARS II standard, each launcher is now mounted on the rear of a 7000-kg (15,432-lb) MAN 6×6 truck chassis and consists of two side-by-side banks of 18 launcher tubes. The fin-stabilized solid propellant rockets can all be fired within 17.5 seconds, manual reloading taking approximately 15 minutes. The minimum and maximum ranges are 6 km (3.73 miles) and 14 km (8.7 miles) respectively. There are seven types of warhead that can be fitted to the rocket, these including the DM-711 mine dispenser with five parachute-retarded AT-2 anti-tank mines, the DM-21 HE-fragmentation, and the DM-701 mine dispenser with eight AT-1 anti-tank mines. A total of 209 LARS II launchers is in service with the West German army at present, and these are likely to be relegated to reserve units as the MLRS is phased into service during the late 1980s and early 1990s.

The West German army's 110-mm (4.33-in) Light Artillery Rocket System has recently been upgraded from LARS I to LARS II standard. The programme included a new fire-control system, additional rocket types and an increase in mobility by fitting the launcher to a MAN 6×6 truck chassis.

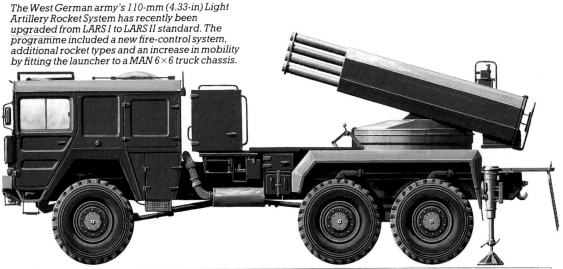

Specification
LARS II
Combat weight: 17480 kg (38,537 lb)
Crew: 3
Chassis: 7000 kg (15,432 lb) MAN 6×6 truck
Calibre: 110 mm (4.33 in)
No. of launcher tubes: 36
Rocket length: not known
Rocket weight: not known
Warhead types: HE-fragmentation, submunition, smoke, practice, radar target
Warhead weights: not known

Called the Artillerie Raketenwerfer 110SF by the West German army, the system is issued on the scale of one battery per division, each battery having two Swiss Contraves Fieldguard radar fire control systems on a 4×4 truck chassis and a resupply vehicle with 144 rockets.

BM-21 multiple rocket-launcher

The 122-mm (4.8-in) BM-21 MRL entered service in the early 1960s and has since become the standard MRL of the Warsaw Pact and most Soviet-supplied client states. Variants of the system have also been manufactured in China (the 40-round Type 81 MRL), Egypt (a straight 40-round copy and modified 21- and 30-round systems, together with the Sakr-18 and Sakr-30 systems), India (the 40-round LRAR system) and Romania (a 21-round launcher on a Bucegi SR-114 lorry chassis). In the Warsaw Pact the BM-21 is found on both the Ural-375D 6×6 truck and, more recently, the ZIL-131 truck in a modified 36-round version identified as the M1976 by NATO. There is also a 12-round launcher mounted on a small 4×4 vehicle, the M1975, which is in service with Soviet airborne troops as a replacement for the older towed 140-mm (5.5-in) MRLs. During the 1982 Israeli invasion of Lebanon the Israeli army came across a 30-round BM-21

The standard Warsaw Pact Multiple Rocket Launcher is the 122-mm (4.8-in) BM-21, with a 40-round launcher mounted on the rear of a Ural-375 6×6 truck chassis. Several countries have copied the system, while others have built their own versions.

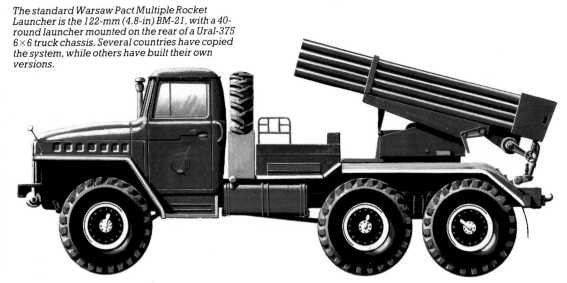

variant mounted on the rear platform of a Japanese Isuzu 6×6 truck which is identical in most respects to the Egyptian 30-round system mounted on the same chassis but is actually manufactured in North Korea under the designation **BM-11**.

The BM-21 is normally found in battalions of 18 integrated into the divisional artillery regiment, but a number of Category 1 motorized rifle divisions also have regimental batteries of six BM-21s or M1976s in service. The 122-mm rocket can be fitted with a smoke, HE-fragmentation, incendiary or chemical warhead, and the launcher can be filled with mixed loads if required. Most of the BM-21 variants have now been used in combat throughout the world, the latest Soviet systems having been blooded in Afghanistan against the guerrillas there. A number of local guerrilla forces such as the PLO have also taken

parts of the BM-21 launcher to produce home-built systems for use in their internal conflicts. The PLO MRLs saw considerable use in the battles in and around Beirut from 1982 onwards.

Specification
BM-21
Combat weight: 11500 kg (25,353 lb)
Crew: 6
Chassis: Ural-375D 6×6 truck
Calibre: 122 mm (4.8 in)
No. of launcher tubes: 40
Length of rocket: standard 3.23 m (10.6 ft), and short 1.91 m (6.3 ft)
Weight of rocket: standard 77 kg (169.75 lb), and short 45.8 kg (100.97 lb)
Warhead types: HE-fragmentation, incendiary, smoke, chemical
Warhead weight: 19.4 kg (42.77 lb)
Maximum range: standard 20.38 km (12.66 miles), and short 11 km (6.84 miles)

The BM-21 is seen in a Moscow parade with several 200-mm (7.87-in) four-round BMD-20 multiple rocket systems in front. In recent years the Soviets have also produced 36-round and 12-round MRL, code-named M1976 and M1975 respectively by NATO, based on the BM-21 system.

USSR

BM-24 multiple rocket-launcher

Introduced into service during the early 1950s, the 240-mm (9.45-in) **BM-24** MRL has now been replaced in front-line service by either the 122-mm (4.8-in) BM-21 or the 220-mm (8.66-in) BM-27 systems, and is now usually found in Soviet second-line units and the strategic reserve stockpile for issue during wartime to mobilized divisions. The BM-24 has been widely exported and has seen widespread use with the Arab armies in the Middle East against Israel.

The system was originally mounted on the rear of the 2500-kg (5,512-lb) ZIL-151 6×6 truck, but is now to be found on the ZIL-157 truck chassis. The launcher consists of two rows of six tubular frame rails with two stabilizer jacks and armoured window shutters that need to be lowered for firing. Israel was so impressed by the system when it was used against its forces that it adopted captured BM-24s as one of the Israeli army's standard MRL systems. A new rocket was manufactured for the launcher, and the equipments were grouped into independent MRL artillery battalions which were used in combat during the 1973 'Yom Kippur' and 1982 'Peace for Galilee' wars. The new Israeli Military Industries rocket is 1.29 m (4.23 ft) long and weighs

The 12-round 240-mm (9.45-in) BM-24 Multiple Rocket Launcher entered service with the Soviet army in the early 1950s and is now found only in training units and the strategic war reserve for mobilization units.

110.5 kg (243.6 lb) with a 48.3 kg (106.5-lb) HE-fragmentation warhead of superior performance to that of the original Soviet type. The maximum range is slightly less than that of the Soviet rocket at 10.7 km (6.65 miles).

The Soviets also mounted a 12-round 240-mm launcher on the rear of an AT-S medium artillery tractor under the designation **BM-24T** for use by

armoured units, but as far as it is known this is no longer in service, the tractors having been converted back to their original use.

Specification
BM-24
Combat weight: 9200 kg (20,283 lb)
Crew: 6

Chassis: 2500-kg (5,512-lb) ZIL-157 6×6 truck
Calibre: 240 mm (9.45 in)
No. of launcher rails: 12
Length of rocket: 1.18 m (3.87 ft)
Weight of rocket: 112..5 kg (248 lb)
Warhead types: HE-fragmentation, smoke, chemical
Warhead weight: 46.9 kg (103.4 lb)
Maximum range: 11 km (6.84 miles)

Following the 1967 war between the Arabs and the Israelis, the latter came into possession of large numbers of BM-24s as war booty. These were promptly refurbished and issued to independent MRL battalions of the Israeli army, who used them against the Arabs in 1973 and in Lebanon in 1982.

The adoption of the BM-24 into Israeli army service resulted in Israel Military Industries manufacturing a new rocket for the system that has greater lethality than the original Soviet model, although maximum range of the rocket has been marginally reduced.

BM-27 multiple rocket-launcher

The 16-round 220-mm (8.66-in) BM-27 MRL entered the active inventory of the Soviet army in the mid-1970s and is found in selected Category 1 motorized rifle and tank division artillery regiment rocket-launcher battalions, and at battalion strength in the combined arms army artillery brigades. In the tank army the artillery brigade has been replaced by an MRL regiment of three battalions with 72 BM-27s, while at front level the system has been integrated into the rocket-launcher brigade of the artillery division. The BM-27 is designed to provide chemical, HE and submunition (including anti-personnel, incendiary and minelet) supporting fire to first-echelon manoeuvre units during offensive and defensive operations. The launcher comprises one layer of four tubes on two layers of six tubes, and is carried on the rear platform of a ZIL-135 8×8 truck chassis. A rapid-reload system allows a second ZIL-135 carrying 16 reload rounds to transfer its load within five minutes. For firing four stabilizer jacks have to be lowered, two at the rear and one on each side of the vehicle. It is believed that the system has also been exported in limited numbers to Syria for combat evaluation against Israel.

Specification
BM-27
Combat weight: 22750 kg (50,155 lb)
Crew: 6
Chassis: ZIL-135 8×8 truck
Calibre: 220 mm (8.66 in)
No. of launcher tubes: 16

Length of rocket: 4.8 m (15.75 ft)
Weight of rocket: 360 kg (793.7 lb)
Warhead types: HE-fragmentation, chemical, submunition
Warhead weights: not known
Maximum range: 40 km (24.85 miles)

The most recent Soviet rocket-launcher system to enter service is the 220-mm (8.66-in) 16-round BM-27 mounted on the rear of the ZIL-135 8×8 truck chassis. In operational characteristics it is very similar to the American MLRS.

Brazilian multiple rocket-launcher systems

Since the early 1960s the Brazilians have been developing MRL systems both for the home and export markets. The first was the **FGT-108RA1** which is currently used by the Brazilian army, Brazilian marines and Iraq. It utilizes a single-stage solid-propellant 108-mm (4.25-in) calibre rocket fired from a 16-round launcher which is mounted either on the back of a light 4×4 vehicle or, more normally, on a two-wheeled trailer. The crew consists of four and a battery of these weapons has four launchers.

The X2A1 trailer used for the FGT-108 was also the basis for the next system, the 36-round **SBAT-70** launcher. This fires a modified version of the standard 70-mm (2.76-in) Avibras folding-fin aircraft rocket which can be fitted with one of seven different types of warhead. Although not operational with the Brazilian army the SBAT-70 has been produced for several unidentified export customers.

Avibras also adapted its 127-mm (5-in) calibre air-to-surface rocket in the same way to produce the **SBAT-127** system for export. This utilizes a 12-rail launcher for either trailer or vehicle mounting, but has the choice of only two different-weight HE-fragmentation warheads. The maximum range is achieved at a launcher elevation of 47°.

These systems were followed by two experimental research rockets, the **FGT X-20** and **FGT X-40** to improve long-range rocket technology. These were followed in the early 1980s by a request to Avibras from a foreign country, believed to be Iraq, to design a mobile MRL system. With the aid of Brazilian army inputs this resulted in the **Astros II** modular mobile MRL system mounted on identical 10000-kg (22,046-lb) Tectran 6×6 truck chassis. The three variants are the 32-round **SS-30**, the 16-round **SS-40** and the four-round **SS-60**, which differ only in the size and weight of the rockets they fire.

The X-40 is the largest of the Brazilian rockets, and is fired from the XLF-40 version of the X1A1/X1A2 series light tank. Although at one time thought to be an operational system, it is now known to be used in armament research trials.

The 70-mm (2.76-in) SBAT-70 36-tube trailer-mounted rocket-launcher system is based on the standard Avibras folding-fin aircraft rocket, and is currently being offered on the export market.

A typical battery is believed to comprise from four to eight launchers with optional radar fire-control vehicles. The crew consists of three men, with reloading undertaken from other trucks using module rocket pods. Iraq ordered 60 batteries of the Astros II and is already using the system in combat against Iran. Libya is also believed to have ordered a few batteries, while the Brazilian army is known to be interested.

Specifications

FGT-108
Combat weight: 802 kg (1,768 lb)
Crew: 4
Chassis: X2A1 trailer
Calibre: 108 mm (4.25 in)
No. of rocket tubes: 16
Rocket length: 0.97 m (3.18 ft)
Rocket weight: 17 kg (37.5 lb)
Warhead type: HE-fragmentation
Warhead weight: 3 kg (6.6 lb)
Maximum range: 7 km (4.35 miles)

SBAT-70
Combat weight: 1000 kg (2,205 lb)
Crew: 4
Chassis: X2A1 trailer
Calibre: 70 mm (2.76 in)
No. of rocket tubes: 36
Rocket length: not known
Rocket weight: 9 kg (19.84 lb)
Warhead types: HEAT, HE-
fragmentation, HE-anti-tank/anti-
personnel, anti-personnel flechette,
smoke, practice
Warhead weight: 4 kg (8.8 lb)
Maximum range: 7.5 km (4.66 miles)

SBAT-127
Combat weight: not known
Crew: 4
Chassis: trailer or vehicle
Calibre: 127 mm (5 in)
No. of launcher rails: 12
Rocket length: not known
Rocket weights: 48/61 kg (105.8 lb/
134.5 lb)
Warhead type: HE-fragmentation
Warhead weights: 22/35 kg (48.5/
77.2 lb)
Maximum ranges: 14 km/12.5 km (8.7/
7.77 miles)

Astros II
Rocket: SS-30
Crew: 3
Chassis: 10000-kg (22,046-lb) Tectran
6×6 truck
Calibre: 127 mm (5 in)
No. of launch tubes: 32
Rocket length: 3.9 m (12.8 ft)
Rocket weight: 68 kg (149.9 lb)
Maximum range: 30 km (18.64 miles)
Warhead types: HE

Rocket: SS-40
Crew: 3
Chassis: 10000-kg (22,046-lb) Tectran
6×6 truck
Calibre: 180 mm (7.09 in)
No. of launch tubes: 16
Rocket length: 4.2 m (13.78 ft)
Rocket weight: 152 kg (335.1 lb)
Maximum range: 35 km (21.75 miles)
Warhead types: HE, submunition

Rocket: SS-60
Crew: 3
Chassis: 10000-kg (22,046-lb) Tectran
6×6 truck
Calibre: 300 mm (11.81 in)
No. of launch tubes: 4
Rocket length: 5.6 m (18.37 ft)
Rocket weight: 595 kg (1,311.7 lb)
Maximum range: 60 km (37.28 miles)
Warhead types: HE, submunition

The fire control system for the Astros II modular multiple rocket system can be the Swiss Contraves Fieldguard J-band radar, with a 300-m (328-yd) to 20000-m (21,870-yd) range. It is used to plot rocket trajectories and hence calculate the impact point.

Above: The relative sizes of the 127-mm (5-in) SS-30, the 180-mm (7.09-in) SS-40 and 300-mm (11.81-in) SS-60 artillery rockets can be seen here. The two larger rockets have cluster munition warheads with dual effect anti-armour anti-personnel bomblets.

Below: This is the Tectran 6×6 truck chassis launcher for the SS-30 rocket. The modular design can be clearly seen, with the four eight-round launch tube containers located within the firing platform on the truck's rear deck.

Above: Smallest of the Astros II artillery rockets fired from the Tectran 6×6 truck launcher is the 127-mm (5-in) calibre SS-30, which has a range of 30 km (18.75 miles). A total of 32 launch tubes are fitted to this configuration of the launcher.

IMI multiple rocket launcher

Work on the Israeli 290-mm (11.42-in) medium artillery rocket began in 1965 and the system entered service in the 1970s as a four-round frame launcher mounted on a Sherman tank chassis. Used in combat during the 1982 'Peace for Galilee' Israeli invasion of Lebanon, this **Israel Military Industries MRL** is now being mounted on converted Centurion MBT chassis in a new four-round tube launcher arrangement. The Centurion has a crew of four, who take cover within the vehicle for firings. A full salvo takes less than 10 seconds to be fired, the launch vehicle then moving to a prearranged location for reloading from a supply truck. The reloads are first lowered to the ground and placed on a special frame by the truck's crane. The Centurion then positions itself and hydraulically lifts the frame to the same height as the launch tubes and slides the rockets into the tubes. This entire operation takes only 10 minutes, the Centurion operations being controlled by only one man. The warhead used is of the HE-fragmentation type although submunition types are known to have been developed and used in combat against Syrian air-defence systems.

Specification
IMI MRL
Combat weight: 50800 kg (111,995 lb)
Crew: 4
Chassis: Centurion MBT
Calibre: 290 mm (11.42 in)
No. of launcher tubes: 4
Rocket length: 5.45 m (17.88 ft)
Rocket weight: 600 kg (1,322.8 lb)
Warhead types: HE-fragmentation, submunition
Warhead weight: 320 kg (705.5 lb)
Maximum range: 25 km (15.5 miles)

The original version of the Israel Military Industries 290-mm (11.42-in) Medium Artillery Rocket System is seen mounted on a Sherman tank chassis in a four-round frame rack. The current version employs cylindrical counter-launcher tubes on a Centurion MBT chassis.

Valkiri multiple rocket-launcher

Development of the 127-mm (5-in) **Valkiri** started in 1977 as a counter to the Soviet 122-mm (4.8-in) BM-21 MRLs and other long-range artillery pieces in service with neighbouring African countries. The first systems entered service in late 1981 with the South African army, and are deployed with artillery regiments in batteries of eight launchers that are tasked either to work on their own or with more conventional tube artillery to attack area targets such as guerrilla camps, troop or artillery concentrations, and soft-skinned vehicle convoys. The system consists of a 24-round launcher mounted on the rear hull of a 4×4 SAMIL truck chassis with overhead canopy rails so as to make it appear to be just a normal truck when travelling. A second 5-ton truck with 48 reload rounds is assigned to each Valkiri. The full load of 24 rounds can be fired in 24 seconds, reloading taking about 10 minutes. The solid-propellant rocket is fitted with an HE-fragmentation warhead filled with some 3,500 steel balls to give a lethal area of some 1500 m² (16,146 sq ft). The range can be varied from a minimum of 8 km (5 miles) to a maximum of 22 km (13.67 miles) depending upon which spoiler rings are fitted to the rocket body.

Above: The highly mobile Valkiri is ideally suited for the South African mechanized cross-border raids against SWAPO guerrilla bases and Angolan army units deep within Angola itself.

Below: Overhead canopy rails are fitted to the Valkiri launcher in order to camouflage the vehicle to appear as a normal South African Army SAMIL 20 4×4 light truck. With the canopy down it is almost impossible to tell the difference.

The launch signature of the Valkiri is minimal. This helps the system to avoid counter-battery fire from the long-range Soviet-supplied artillery pieces belonging to surrounding African states and guerrilla forces.

Specification
Valkiri
Combat weight: 6440 kg (14,198 lb)
Crew: 2
Chassis: 2200-kg (4,850-lb) SAMIL 20 4×4 truck
Calibre: 127 mm (5 in)
No. of launcher tubes: 24
Rocket length: 2.68 m (8.79 ft)
Rocket weight: not known
Warhead type: HE-fragmentation
Warhead weight: not known
Maximum range: 22 km (13.67 miles)

Initiated as a feasibility study in 1976, the concept definition phase of the **General Support Rocket System (GSRS)** was contracted to five different firms. After evaluation of these, Boeing Aerospace and Vought Corporation (now LTV Aerospace and Defence Company) were asked to compete in the follow-on validation stage. At the same time the system was directed towards a standard NATO weapon design. The trials were held in 1979 and early 1980, with the result that Vought was chosen as the winner. In the same year the GSRS title was changed to the definitive **Multiple Launch Rocket System (MLRS)**.

The first production battery of Self-Propelled Launcher Loaders (SPLL), based on the M2 IFV chassis, was delivered to the US Army in 1982, with the final inventory total due to be 333 by the early 1990s. The European nations that have decided to procure the MLRS are the UK (67 SPLLs), West Germany (202 SPLLs), France (56 SPLLs), and Italy (20 SPLLs), with the Netherlands indicating a requirement for 30 SPLLs for procurement when funding permits. Most of the European systems will be built in Europe by a consortium of companies.

Each SPLL carries 12 rockets in two six-round pods, and can be self-loaded from a resupply vehicle within 10 minutes. Four warheads have or are in the process of being developed for the single-stage solid-propellant rocket. These are the basic Phase I submunition model with a range of about 30 km (18.6 miles) carrying 644 M77 dual-purpose shaped-charge blast-fragmentation bomblets each weighing 0.23 kg (0.51 lb) and capable of piercing some 100 mm (3.94 in) of armour plate; the Phase II mine-dispenser model, with 28 AT-2 parachute-retarded anti-tank mines de-

veloped by West Germany, allowing a rocket range of 40 km (24.9 miles); the Phase III submunition model with six individual active-radar terminally-guided shaped-charge free-fall weapons allowing a rocket range of 42 km (26.1 miles); and a US only chemical warhead containing approximately 41.7 kg (92 lb) of binary nerve gas chemical agents.

Further studies are being carried out to see if lightweight three- or six-round rocket pods based on the MLRS design can be mounted on more mobile chassis types for use by the new US Army lightweight divisions.

Specification
MLRS
Combat weight: 25191 kg (55,536 lb)
Crew: 3
Chassis: M2 IFV
Calibre: 227 mm (8.94 in)
Rocket length: 3.94 m (12.93 ft)
Rocket weight: 308 kg (679 lb)
Warhead types: submunition, chemical
Warhead weights: not known
Maximum ranges: see text

Designed for all-terrain mobility, the Self-Propelled Launcher-Loader (SPLL) is fitted with two pods of six 227-mm (8.94-in) calibre rockets, which can be rapidly replaced.

A Multiple Launch Rocket System (MLRS) vehicle fires one of its 227-mm (8.94-in) rockets. Based on the M2 Infantry Fighting Vehicle chassis, the MLRS has already been ordered by the American, French, Italian, West German and British armies, to replace or supplement current tube artillery.

Vought Multiple Rocket Launch System

Above: A typical MLRS battery will contain an M577 Armoured Command Post and a number of Oshkosh Heavy Expanded Mobility Tactical Trucks (HEMTT) with Heavy Expanded Mobility Ammunition Trailers (HEMAT) that each carry four reload six-round rocket pods for the launchers.

Right and below: Air transportable in C-130, C-141 and C-5 transport aircraft, together with its support vehicles, the MLRS is currently being issued to the new-style 'heavy' armoured and mechanized divisions of the US Army under the 'Division '86' plan on the scale of one battery each with three firing platoons of three MLRS, and two batteries each with six M110 203-mm (8-in) self-propelled howitzers in a single mixed artillery battalion. A total of 333 Self-Propelled Launcher-Loaders (SPLLs) with 362,832 tactical and 27,648 training rockets, together with 480 resupply vehicles, are due to be procured by 1990.

Egyptian multiple rocket-launchers

The Egyptian arms industry produces copies of the Soviet 132-mm (5.2-in) rocket for the army's elderly BM-13-16 Soviet systems and 122-mm (4.8-in) rockets for its BM-21 systems. It has also reverse-engineered the latter to produce a new 30-round launcher mounted on a Japanese 2500-kg (5,512-lb) Isuzu 6×6 truck chassis as well as the more usual 40-round version on a Soviet 3500-kg (7,716-lb) ZIL truck. The former is very similar in appearance to the North Korean BM-11 variant of the BM-21, which is mounted on the same chassis.

In addition to the reverse-engineered models two new systems have also been designed and built for the Egyptian army. These are the 122-mm calibre **Sakr-18** and the 122-mm calibre **Sakr-30** MRLs. The former has a range of 18 km (11.18 miles) and is built in 21-round, 30-round and 40-round versions mounted on lorry chassis types. It utilizes a 3.25-m (10.66-ft) long, 67-kg (147.7-lb) weight rocket fitted with a 21-kg (46.3-lb) submunition warhead containing either 28 anti-personnel or 21 anti-tank bomblets.

The Sakr-30 has a range of 30 km (18.64 miles) and fires three types of rocket which vary in length from 2.5 m (8.2 ft) to 3.16 m (10.37 ft). The longest weighs 63 kg (138.9 lb) and carries a 24.5 kg (54-lb) warhead which delivers five anti-tank mines. The medium-length round at 3.1 m (10.17 ft) weighs 61.5 kg (135.6 lb) and carries a sub-munition-dispensing 23-kg (50.7-lb) warhead with either 28 anti-tank or 35 anti-personnel bomblets as payload. The anti-tank bomblet is the same as that used in the SAKR-18, and can pierce over 80 mm (3.15 in) of armour, while the anti-personnel bomblets of both systems are lethal to a radius of 15 m (49.2 ft) from the point of detonation. The smallest round weighs 56.5 kg (124.6 lb) and has a basic 17.5-kg (38.6-lb) HE-fragmentation warhead. The increased range over the BM-21 and SAKR-18 systems has been achieved by using an improved lightweight rocket motor and case coupled with a new composite bonded star-grain propellant instead of the standard Soviet double-base grained

The Egyptians use locally-made 12-round rocket launchers on the rear of Walid 4×4 APCs to fire 80-mm (3.15-in) D-3000 smokescreen rockets to hide major troop and armour attacks.

propellant used in the shorter-range systems.

For infantry and anti-guerrilla use the 12-round 80-mm (3.15-in) **VAP** light vehicle-mounted MRL has been produced. This is mounted on a pedestal which is fitted in the rear of a 4×4 jeep-type vehicle and is fired by remote control. The 1.5-m (4.92 ft) long 12-kg (26.5-lb) fin-stabilized rocket can be fitted with either a HE-fragmentation or an illuminating warhead. The maximum range is 8 km (5 miles).

There is also a specialized system for laying down smoke screens. This can be found either as a 12-round rectangular frame launcher in the rear of a Walid 4×4 wheeled APC or as quadruple box-like launchers mounted on each side of a T-62 MBT turret. The

Right: An Egyptian army VAP-80 light vehicle mounted 80-mm (3.15-in) rocket launcher system with the 12-round launcher elevated to the firing position. The 12-kg (26.6-lb) rocket has a range of 8 km (5 miles).

rocket fired in both cases is the 80-mm (3.15-in) calibre 1.51 m (4.95 ft) long D-3000 which can form a smoke screen that lasts up to 15 minutes. A full 12-round salvo from a Walid can form a 1000-m (3,281-ft) long smoke screen of sufficient thickness and duration to cover most activities.

Below: Walid APCs of the Egyptian army parade through Cairo carrying 12-round rocket launchers. These can fire a salvo of smoke rockets to create a smokescreen up to 1000 m (1,094 yards) long, which can last 15 minutes in favourable wind conditions.

Type 63 and Type 81 107-mm multiple rocket-launchers

Developed in the late 1950s as the replacement for the 102-mm (4.02-in) six-round Type 50 MRL, the 107-mm (4.21-in) system is issued on the scale of 18 launchers per Chinese infantry division.

The basic **Type 63** 12-round launcher has three rows of four barrels and is mounted on a rubber-tyred split-pole trailer carriage. For firing the wheels are removed and the launcher is supported by two legs at the front and the two trails at the rear, the latter being fitted with spades. A lighter model is used by the Chinese airborne and mountain infantry units, and this can be dismantled into loads for carriage by men or horses.

To increase mobility the launcher can also be mounted on the rear of a 4×4 truck fitted with an enlarged cab to accommodate the crew of four and 12 reload rounds. The launcher can either be remote-fired from the vehicle or dismounted for use on its normal towing carriage. This variant is known as the **Type 81**.

The 107-mm systems have seen extensive combat service throughout the world, the Chinese having used them against the Vietnamese, the Vietnamese against the Americans, Chinese and Kampucheans, the Ira-

Right: The 107-mm (4.21-in) 12-round Type 63 rocket launcher is in widespread use with the People's Liberation Army. The rocket can also be fired on its own and is currently being used by the Afghanistan Mujahideen guerrillas to bombard both Soviet and Afghan army bases and airfields

nians against the Iraqis, and the Palestinians against the Israelis and Shi'ites, to name but a few. Both HE and incendiary rounds have been used.

**Specification
Type 63**

Combat weight: 602 kg (1,327 lb)
Crew: 4
Chassis: two-wheeled trailer
Calibre: 107 mm (4.21 in)
No. of launcher tubes: 12
Rocket length: 0.84 m (2.76 ft)
Rocket weight: 18.8 kg (41.45 lb)

Above: Type 81 is the Chinese designation for a Type 63 12-round MRL mounted on a 4×4 truck with an enlarged cab which accommodates the crew and 12 reloads.

Warhead types: HE-fragmentation, incendiary
Warhead weights: 8.33 kg (18.36 lb) and 7.54 kg (16.62 lb)
Maximum ranges: 8.5 km (5.28 miles) and 7.9 km (4.9 miles)

Type 63 and Type 70 130-mm multiple rocket-launchers

The Chinese have indigenously designed and built two types of 19-tube 130-mm (5.12-in) calibre MRL systems, the **Type 63** mounted on the rear platform of the 2500-kg (5,511-lb) NJ-230 4×4 truck in two variants, and the **Type 70** mounted on the top of the Type YM531 tracked APC, to replace elderly Soviet systems. The major difference in the truck-mounted variants is that the second has a covered crew cabin. All three types are grouped into batteries of six launchers, the truck-mounted systems serving in the artillery's MRL regiments and the APC systems serving in the armoured divisions. The launch tubes are arranged in two rows, with a top one of 10 over a lower row of nine. Both systems are in production and have seen combat use with the Chinese and Vietnamese armies during their short border war in 1979. The North Korean army is also known to have the truck-mounted system in service, and may well be building it under licence in North Korean state arsenals as part of that country's arms-building programme.

**Specification
Type 70**

Combat weight: 13400 kg (29,542 lb)
Crew: 6
Chassis: Type YW531 tracked APC
Calibre: 130 mm (5.12 in)
No. of launch tubes: 19
Rocket length: 1.05 m (3.45 ft)
Rocket weight: 32.8 kg (72.3 lb)
Warhead type: HE-fragmentation
Warhead weight: 14.7 kg (32.4 lb)
Maximum range: 10.37 km (6.44 miles)

The Type 70 Multiple Rocket System is of 130-mm (5.12-in) calibre and is the tracked vehicle-mounted version of the Type 63 system. The vehicle used is the Type YW531 APC.

Below: The Type 70 carries 19 130-mm (5.12-in) rocket tubes on a YM531 APC chassis, and saw action in 1979 during the border clashes with Vietnam. North Korea has adopted the truck-mounted system, the Type 63.

Above: A six-launcher battery of Type 70 130-mm (5.12-in) MRLs opens fire during a People's Liberation Army exercise. The Type 70 MRLs serve with armoured divisions, and the truck-mounted models with the infantry.

Type 67 multiple rocket-launcher

Developed in 1965 by a division of the Nissan Motor Company Ltd, the 307-mm (12.09-in) Type 67 MRL entered service with the Japanese Ground Self-Defence Force in 1968. The system consists of a 4000-kg (8,818-lb) Hino 6×6 truck chassis fitted with two launch rails for the Type 68 rocket. Another Hino 6×6 truck acts as the resupply vehicle and carries six reload rounds, which are transferred to the launcher by a hydraulic crane. Before firing three truck stabilizers have to be lowered to the ground, one on each side of the vehicle and one at the rear. The Type 67 is used by artillery units and some 50 in-service systems complement the similar number of 15-km (9.3-mile) 130-mm (5.12-in) 30-round Type 75 MRLs mounted on a derivative of the Type 73 tracked APC

which are used by the mechanized and armoured brigades. More modern systems to eventually replace the Type 67 and Type 75 are already under investigation, with the former likely to be mounted on a tracked chassis to improve mobility over rough terrain.

Specification
Type 67 MRL
Combat weight: not known
Crew: 4-6
Chassis: 4000 kg (8,818-lb) Hino 6×6 truck
Calibre: 307 mm (12.09 in)
No. of launch rails: 2
Rocket length: 4.5 m (14.76 ft)
Rocket weight: 573 kg (1,263 lb)
Warhead type: HE-fragmentation
Warhead weight: not known
Maximum range: 28 km (17.4 miles)

A Type 67 rocket launcher is seen in travelling order with two Type 68 rockets in position on the launch rails. Another Hino 6×6 truck fitted with a hydraulic crane and carrying six reload rounds is used to resupply the vehicle.

Right: The two Type 68 307-mm (12.09-in) solid fuel rockets are seen on the launch rails of a Hino 6×6 truck-mounted Type 67 launcher of the Japanese Ground Self-Defence Force. The rocket has a range of 28 km (17.4 miles) and is fitted with an HE warhead.

RM-70 multiple rocket-launcher

First seen during 1972, the 122-mm (4.8-in) calibre **RM-70** MRL is an armoured version of the Czech Tatra 813 8×8 truck with the Soviet 40-round BM-21 launcher and a reload pack of 40 rounds mounted to the rear of the cab for rapid reloading. The vehicle is fitted with a central tyre pressure-regulation system (to allow adjustment to suite the type of terrain being cros-

sed) and, if required, a BZT dozer blade for preparing its own fire positions and clearing obstacles. The scale of issue of the RM-70 is one battalion of 18 launchers in three batteries per Czech army tank and motorized rifle division. The RM-70 is also known to be in service with the East German and Libyan armies and, it is believed, with selected Category 1 divisions of

the Soviet army.

Two types of fin-stabilized rocket are fired, a short round with a range of 11 km (6.84 miles) and the standard long round with a range of 20.38 km (12.66 miles). It is also possible to fire the short round with an additional motor to increase the range to 17 km (10.56 miles). However, this version together with the short one are more

likely to be encountered in the single-tube launcher used by guerrilla forces throughout the world.

Specification
RM-70
Combat weight: 33700 kg (74,296 lb)
Crew: 6
Chassis: 7900-kg (17,417-lb) Tatra 813 8×8 truck

Calibre: 122 mm (4.8-in)
No. of launcher tubes: 40
Rocket lengths: standard 3.23 m
(10.6 ft), and short 1.91 m (6.27 ft)
Rocket weights: standard 77 kg
(169.75 lb), and short 45.8 kg
(100.97 lb)
Warhead types: HE-fragmentation,
incendiary, smoke, chemical
Warhead weight: 19.4 kg (42.77 lb)
Maximum ranges: standard 20.38 km
(12.66 miles), and short 11 km (6.84
miles)

*The Czechoslovakian army has
adopted its own version of the
standard Soviet 122-mm (4.8-in)
multiple rocket launcher system
known as the RM-70, the major
difference being that the new version
has a complete 40-round reload pack
of rockets to speed up reloading.*

YUGOSLAVIA

Yugoslav multiple rocket-launchers

The Yugoslav army uses two types of
128-mm (5.04-in) MRL, the 32-round
towed **M-63 Plaman** and the truck-
mounted 32-round **YMRL-32 Oganj**.
The former was developed in the late
1950s and early 1960s, and is mounted
on a split-trail carriage. It fires the 8.6-
km (5.34-mile) range spin-stabilized
M-63 rocket, which is 0.81 m (2.66 ft)
long, weighs 23.1 kg (50.93 lb) and has
a 7.6-kg (16.75-lb) HE-fragmentation
warhead. An improved version with a
wider carriage has also been built,
while both 16-round and 8-round
variants are available for export on
carriages or vehicle mounts if required.

The YMRL-32 (a NATO designation
in the absence of the official Yugoslav
designation) was developed in the
early 1970s and is based on the
FAP 2220BDS 6×4 truck fitted with a
32-round launcher and a reload pack
of 32 rounds on the rear platform. The
rocket fired by this system is of a newer type, 2.6 m (8.53 ft) long, 65 kg
(143.3 lb) in weight with a maximum
range of 20 km (12.43 miles) and an
HE-fragmentation warhead weighing
20 kg (44 lb). Reloading of the tubes

takes approximately two minutes
when using the reload pack.

The M-63 is normally found in battalions of three batteries, each with four
launchers, while the YMRL-32 is found
in batteries of six vehicles. It is believed that both systems have been
exported, but the only known user outside Yugoslavia is Cyprus, which has a
few YMRL-32 systems.

Specification
M-63
Combat weight: 2134 kg (4,705 lb)
Crew: 3-5
Chassis: two-wheeled trailer
Calibre: 128 mm (5.04 in)
No. of launcher tubes: 32
Length of rocket: 0.81 m (2.66 ft)
Weight of rocket: 23.1 kg (50.93 lb)
Warhead type: HE-fragmentation
Warhead weight: 7.6 kg (16.75 lb)
Maximum range: 8.6 km (5.34 miles)

YMRL-32
Combat weight: (estimated) 13000 kg
(28,660 lb)
Crew: 6
Chassis: 10000-kg (22,046-lb) FAP
2020BS 6×6 truck

Calibre: 128 mm (5.04 in)
No. of launcher tubes: 32
Length of rocket: 2.6 m (8.53 ft)
Weight of rocket: 65 kg (143.3 lb)
Warhead type: HE-fragmentation
Warhead weight: 20 kg (44 lb)
Maximum range: 20 km (12.43 miles)

*The 128-mm (5.04-in) M-63 Plaman
multiple rocket launcher is used in
battalions of three batteries, each
with four launchers, to support
Yugoslavian infantry units.*

*Although supplied with many weapons by the Soviet Union, Yugoslavia chose
to develop the YMRL 32 Oganji 128-mm (5.04-in) multiple rocket launcher on
the FAP 2220BDS 6×4 truck chassis as its standard self-propelled system. It is
used by the army's armoured and mechanized units.*

Surface-to-air Missiles

Land forces are extremely vulnerable to air attack, and anti-aircraft systems are perhaps the single most important element in an army's equipment. Guns and surface-to-air missiles share this prime role, but the missiles are the more glamorous element of the partnership

A surface-to-air missile hitting a drone aircraft. The introduction of SAMs on a large scale has made air forces adopt new tactics to enable them to carry out their assigned mission. Most countries have a combination of gun and missile air defence systems, although some, for example the UK, rely only on missiles.

During World War II anti-aircraft guns were used on a large scale to provide defence against air attack for both armies in the field and fixed strategic targets such as ports, airfields, factories and other key centres. In the case of the Allies, low-level air defence was provided by weapons such as 20-mm cannon and the 40-mm gun, while high-level defence was provided by the British 94-mm (3.7-in) and US 90-mm (3.54-in) guns. As the war went on radar fire-control systems and proximity fuses were introduced by the Allies to increase the effectiveness of such weapons to a marked degree, especially against targets such as the V-1 flying bomb. The Germans faced even greater problems as Allied bombers took to flying higher and the number of weapons that could effectively engage them thus declined. From 1944 the Germans put considerable effort into the design of surface-to-air missiles (SAMs) but by the end of the war none of these had been deployed and much of their work was then taken over by the United States and the Soviet Union.

Flying at low level, aircraft must now run the gauntlet of both gun and missile systems, a combination which has proved to be most effective in the Middle East and Vietnam. Most armies today prefer a mix of guns and missiles although some, such as the British, rely on missiles alone (Blowpipe and Rapier). Some systems are highly mobile and are deployed well forward, for example the Roland 2 and Chaparral, while others are semi-mobile and need some preparation before they can be brought into action, for example the HAWK and towed Rapier.

In the West, the only SAM to be developed in recent years that can be used against both high- and low-flying aircraft is the US Patriot, which will replace the HAWK and the Nike-Hercules in US Army service. Development of this system started in 1965 but it was 1983 before the first battalion was formed, and since originally conceived the system has increased considerably in cost, and consequently it is not expected that many of the countries who now operate HAWK will be able to afford to replace it with Patriot.

Of all the countries in the world, the Soviet Union has by far put the most effort into the development and production of air-defence missile systems, many of which have been used operationally in the Middle East, Africa and the Far East. In some cases these systems have proved to be highly effective while in others, for example in the Lebanon in the summer of 1982, they have been totally ineffective. More often than not improper employment and poor operator training, rather than the design of the equipment, can be blamed.

Recent years have also seen the employment of man-portable missiles, such as the SA-7 and Redeye, on a large scale, and these have proved to be highly effective in the hands of guerrilla and terrorist organizations, and they have not infrequently been used to shoot down civilian aircraft. More recent man-portable systems such as the Stinger and Blowpipe are even more effective.

Mobile air defence weapons must be highly portable, tough and able to cope with climatic extremes. The BAe Dynamics Rapier system has proved itself in operation from the searing heat of Oman to the icy cold of the Falklands.

Crotale surface-to-air missile system

In the early 1960s the South African government placed a contract with the French company of Thomson-Houston, which later became Thomson-CSF, for the development of a mobile all-weather SAM system. This became known as the **Cactus**, Thomson-CSF being responsible for the overall system, radar and electronics, and Engins Matra for the **R.440** missile as it had considerable experience in the development and production of air-to-air missiles. The first batteries were delivered to South Africa in 1971 with final deliveries in 1973. Since then the **Crotale**, this being its French name, has been ordered by Chile, Egypt, Libya, Pakistan, Saudi Arabia and the United Arab Emirates. Further development of the Crotale has resulted in the Shahine, SICA which is in service with Saudi Arabia. There is also a naval version of the Crotale.

A typical Crotale battery consists of one acquisition and two or three firing units, each of the latter having four missiles in the ready-to-launch position. Both units are based on a fully armoured 4×4 chassis whose wheels are raised off the ground by hydraulic jacks when the vehicle is in the operating position. An unusual feature of the vehicle is that it is electrically propelled.

The acquisition unit carries out target surveillance, identification and designation and is fitted with a large radar with a maximum detection range of about 18 km (11.2 miles). It also has a real-time digital computer, display consoles, data links and is capable of handling up to 12 targets simultaneously.

A target engagement takes place as follows. The acquisition unit first locates the aircraft and, if this is confirmed as hostile, allocates it to one of the firing units, target information being transmitted via a data link. The radar on the firing unit can track one target and guide two missiles at the same time, there being a slight gap in launching. The firing unit also has the command transmitter, infra-red gathering system, digital computer, digital data link and a TV/optical tracking system for use in an ECM environment. Once the four missiles have been launched new missiles in the transport/launching containers have to be loaded with the aid of a crane. Four missiles can be loaded in about two minutes by a well trained crew.

The R.440 missile is 2.89 m (9 ft 5.75 in) long, 15.0 cm (5.9 in) in diameter and 54.0 cm (21.25 in) in span, and weighs 85 kg (187 lb) of which 15 kg (33 lb) is accounted for by the HE warhead, which is of the fragmentation type to cause as much damage to the target as possible. The warhead is detonated by a proximity fuse which is not armed until after the missile is launched. The single-stage solid-propellant rocket motor gives the missile a top speed of about Mach 2.3. The effective range of the system depends on the speed of the target, but against an aircraft flying at a speed of Mach 1.2 a maximum range of 8500 m (9,295 yards) can be achieved with a maximum altitude of 3000 m (9,845 ft). Against slower aircraft and helicopters, the range is significantly greater.

The Crotale is normally used (for example by South Africa, Saudi Arabia and the French air force) for the defence of air bases and other strategic targets. Once halted, the Crotale/Cactus system takes about five minutes to become fully operational. Information from the acquisition unit can be passed to the firing unit by cable (maximum length of 800 m/875 yards) or a data link (maximum range 3000 m/3,280 yards).

Specification
Matra R.440
Dimensions: length 2.89 m (9 ft 5 in); diameter 15 cm (5.9 in); span 54 cm (21.25 in)
Launch weight: 85 kg (187.4 lb)
Performance: speed Mach 2.3; maximum ceiling 3000 m (9842 ft); maximum range 12000 m (7.5 miles) against a 200 m/sec (450 mph) target

Crotale missile being launched during trials in France. The missile itself is manufactured by Engins Matra with the overall system and electronics being the responsibility of Thomson-CSF. It was originally developed to meet the requirements of South Africa but has since been adopted by many other countries. Further development has resulted in the Shahine, SICA which has been produced specifically for Saudi Arabia.

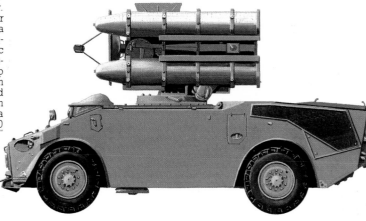

Each Crotale launcher has four missiles. Three firing units are coupled to one acquisition unit to form a battery.

Shahine, SICA surface-to-air missile system

The **Shahine, SICA** low-altitude SAM system was developed from 1975 specifically to meet the requirements of Saudi Arabia and is a logical development of the earlier Crotale. Prime contractor is the Electronics Systems Division of Thomson-CSF, which is responsible for the radars, electronics and systems integration; Engins Matra is responsible for the missiles. Following successful trials with prototype systems, production started in 1979, the first systems being delivered to Saudi Arabia in 1982 and final deliveries being made in 1983. A total of 36 systems were delivered as were 53 AMX-30 DCA self-propelled 30-mm anti-aircraft guns to provide close in protection, especially when missiles are being reloaded.

The Shahine consists of a firing unit and an acquisition unit, each mounted on a modified AMX-30 MBT chassis which offers complete armour protection for the crew and electronics inside the vehicle as well as having much improved cross-country performance than the original Crotale wheeled system.

The acquisition unit has a large pulse-Doppler surveillance radar with a range of some 18 km (11.2 miles) with a digital receiver for the MTI (moving target indication) function. The automatic information processing and threat evaluation system allows up to 40 targets to be registered on the computer and no less than 18 actual targets to be handled. One acquisition unit can control up to four firing units.

The firing unit has six missiles in the ready-to-launch position (the basic Crotale has four); once these missiles have been launched replacement missiles in travelling/launch containers are loaded from a vehicle with the aid of a crane. Between the missiles is a triple-channel fire-control radar that can simultaneously guide two missiles to a target. The radar tracks the missile and sends out guidance commands, acquisition of the missile during the early part of the flight being via an infra-red receiver sensitive to the wavelength of the missile exhaust. Another feature of this system is that a

TV system is integrated into the turret and this assumes target- and missile-tracking functions and also ensures a full back-up mode in case of enemy jamming.

The missile used by the Shahine is the **Matra R.460**, a longer and heavier version of the Matra R.440 used in the Crotale system, its SNPE double-stage rocket motor giving a burn of 4.5 seconds (compared with 2.5 seconds in the Crotale system) to produce a maximum speed of about Mach 2.

A major advantage of the Shahine over the original Crotale is that the firing units and acquisition unit can deploy over a much wider area as they do not have to stop and be coupled together by cables before target engagement. This is possible as the Shahine units are fitted with an automatic data transmission and reciprocal microwave system. Twelve batteries of an improved Shanine were ordered in 1984, having increased acquisition range and better altitude capacity.

Specification
Matra R.460
Dimensions: length 3.15 m (10 ft 4 in); diameter 15.6 cm (6.14 in); span 59.0 cm (23.23 in)
Launch weight: 100 kg (220 lb)
Performance: maximum ceiling 6100 m (19,685 ft); maximum range 11000 to 13500 m (12,030 to 14,765 yards)

FRANCE/WEST GERMANY
Roland surface-to-air missile system

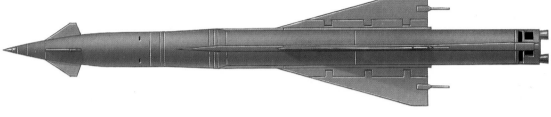

In the early 1960s Aérospatiale of France and Messerschmitt-Bölkow-Blohm of West Germany, working as Euromissile, began the development of a mobile low-altitude surface-to-air missile system which eventually became known as the **Roland**. France was responsible for the Roland clear-weather version while West Germany was design leader for the **Roland 2** all-weather version. As the Roland 2 is the current production model the description relates to this model. In the West German army Roland is based on the chassis of the Marder MICV while France uses an AMX-30 MBT chassis and the United States the M109 self-propelled howitzer chassis.

A typical target engagement of the Roland 2 takes place as follows. The pulse-Doppler radar, mounted on top of the turret rotating at 60 rpm, detects aircraft and helicopters at a range of between 15 and 18 km (9.3 and 11.2 miles). The target is then interrogated by the vehicle's own IFF system and, if confirmed as hostile, acquired and tracked. In normal engagements tracking is carried out by the tracking radar mounted on the forward part of the turret, but if enemy countermeasures are active an optical sight can also be used. In the radar mode the tracking radar has two channels, one of which tracks the target and the other the missile. The radar is slaved to follow the target by misalignment. Once a missile has been launched an infrared localizer on the antenna of the tracking radar is used to capture the missile between 500 and 700 m (545 and 765 yards) after launch as by this time the missile has entered the pencil of the tracking radar. Missile deviation is calculated from the angular deviation between target/antenna and antenna/missile, this information being supplied to the on-board computer which calculates the required guidance commands which are then passed onto the missile via a radio command link. The missile receives the commands which are then converted into jet-deflection orders. With Roland it is possible for the operator to switch from the optical to the radar mode after the missile has been launched. The optical method is used whenever possible as it is more accurate, especially in an ECM environment.

The two-stage solid-propellant missile is 2.40 m (7 ft 10.5 in) long, with span and diameter of 50.0 and 16.0 cm (19.7 and 6.3 in respectively), and has a cruising speed of about Mach 1.6. Launch weight is 63 kg (139 lb), and the missile is provided with a high explosive warhead that is detonated either by impact or an electromagnetic (radar-type) proximity fuse.

In the case of the Marder and AMX-30 chassis versions of Roland, two missiles are mounted in the ready-to-launch position, an additional eight missiles being carried inside the vehicle for automatic loading from two rotary-type magazines each holding four rounds.

In 1985, Euromissile estimated that 604 fire units had been ordered or sold, with 24,300 individual missiles. Roland is in service with Argentina, Brazil, France, Iraq, West Germany, Spain, the USA, and Venezuela. Roland has also been offered as an interim component of the US Army's Forward Area Air Defense System (FAADS).

Specification
Roland 2
Dimensions: length 2.4 m (7 ft 10½ in); diameter 16 cm (6.3 in); span 50 cm (19.7 in)
Launch weight: 63 kg (139 lb)
Performance: speed Mach 1.5; range 6000 m (3.73 miles); radar detection range 16 km (9.95 miles); minimum interception range about 500 m (1640 ft); minimum interception height under 20 m (65.6 ft)

A West German army Roland SAM system, on Thyssen Henschel Marder chassis with two missiles in ready-to-launch position and eight missiles in reserve.

UK
Bloodhound Mk 2 surface-to-air missile system

The original **Bloodhound Mk 1** SAM system was developed from the late 1940s (to meet the requirements of the Royal Air Force) by the Bristol Aeroplane company (now British Aerospace Dynamics) and Ferranti, the first units becoming operational in 1958. Further development resulted in the much more effective **Bloodhound Mk 2**, which entered service in 1964. This was deployed by the RAF in the United Kingdom, West Germany and Singapore but by early 1983 those in West Germany had been redeployed to the United Kingdom and those in Singapore had been handed over to the Singapore Air Defence Command. The weapon is also used by Switzerland under the designation **BL-84** and was also used by Sweden as the **RB 68**,

but these were recently withdrawn from service. The British army had a very similar missile system called the **Thunderbird**, but this has now been withdrawn from service without replacement, so leaving the army without any high-level air-defence system.

A typical Bloodhound missile section consists of four missiles on their individual launchers, target illuminating radar (TIR) and a launch control post (LCP). Two TIRs were developed, the air-transportable Ferranti Firelight and the semitransportable Ferranti Scorpion, the latter having a much longer range.

A Bloodhound target engagement takes place as follows. A target is first detected by surveillance radar, which may be part of the Bloodhound system or part of an overall air-defence system which would decide which particular weapon system would engage the target. Basic target information is then supplied to the TIR, which searches for the target, then tracks and illuminates it. At the same time the TIR

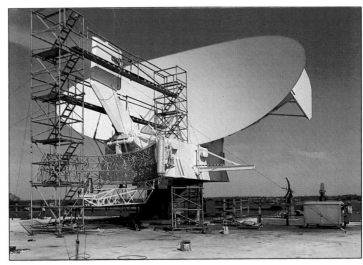

transmits this information to the launch control post. A computer in the latter then determines the optimum conditions for target engagement. When the target is within range a missile is launched, the receiver in the nose of the missile detecting and homing onto radiation reflected by the target. The warhead of the missile, which is in fact well to the rear of the nose, is high explosive and fitted with a proximity fuse developed by Thorn EMI.

The missile itself is launched by four solid-propellant boosters, which are mounted externally to take the missile to supersonic speed when the two Thor ramjets take over and the boos-

Bloodhound SAMs on their launchers at an RAF base. All these missiles have now been withdrawn from West Germany and concentrated along the east coast of England; no official announcement has so far been made concerning their replacement.

ters fall away. The ramjets are mounted above and below the missile and give Bloodhound an exceptional range of some 80 km (50 miles) and a maximum speed of some 3860 km/h (2,400 mph). The control surfaces of the missile consist of two moving wings to provide the necessary manoeuvres and cruciform fixed tailplanes to pro-

The RAF also uses the Marconi Type 82 series radar for surveillance purposes with the Bloodhound SAM. In the background is a Plessey HF 200 height-finding radar. The Bloodhound is also used by Switzerland and Singapore.

vide pitch stability. The missile manoeuvres by means of twist and steer in the same way as a bird in flight: the wings are moved differentially so as to roll the missile into the vector direction in which the manoeuvre is required, and then moved in concert to pitch the missile in that direction to complete the manoeuvre.

For ease of repair, most of the guidance system is on printed circuit cards, which enables replacement of faulty cards to be carried out very quickly, so returning the missile to an operational status without undue delay.

Specification
Bloodhound Mk 2
Dimensions: length 7.75 m (25 ft 5 in); diameter 54.6 cm (21.5 in); wing span 2.83 m (9 ft 3½ in)
Weight: 2300 kg (5,070 lb)
Performance: operating altitude 100 to 23010 m (325 to 75.500 ft); range over 80 km (50 miles)

Blowpipe man-portable surface-to-air missile system

The **Blowpipe** missile was developed by the Missile Systems Division of Short Brothers to meet a British army requirement for a man-portable SAM missile system that could shoot down an attacking aircraft before it released its weapons. Other man-portable missiles, such as the American Stinger and the Soviet SA-7 home onto the exhaust of the attacking aircraft and can often only engage the attackers after they have released their weapons.

The Blowpipe system consists of two main components: the missile within its launching canister and the aiming unit. In the missile itself the forward part contains the guidance equipment, the HE warhead is in the centre and the rear part houses the rocket motors. There are four delta-shaped aerofoils on the nose for aerodynamic control and four at the tail to provide ballistic stability. The nose section of the missile is free to rotate independently of the main body, it being attached to the latter by a low-friction bearing. The missile is factory-sealed in a lightweight container which acts as a recoilless launcher. The container houses the firing sequence unit, thermal battery to power the aiming unit, guidance aerials and electrical connections. When the missile is fired the front cap of the container is blown off by gas pressure while the laminated rear closure is ejected at launch.

The aiming unit is a self-contained firing and control pack with a pistol grip on the right side. The aiming unit contains a radio transmitter, auto-

gathering device, monocular sight and, if required an interrogator (IFF) system. The controls include a trigger, thumb-controlled joystick and switches for fuse option, auto-gather and guidance command frequency change.

Before use the aiming unit is clipped onto the canister containing the missile. The target is obtained visually in the monocular sight, which has a graticule to assist the operator in both range estimation and allowance for cross winds. The safety catch is then released and the trigger squeezed. The latter activates a generator which supplies firing current to the thermal batteries in the missile and canister. The missile is launched from the canister by a first-stage motor. Once the Blowpipe is a safe distance from the operator the second-stage motor ignites to accelerate the missile to supersonic (Mach 1.5) speed, the missile then cruising as a fully controlled dart. The Blowpipe is then automatically gathered into the centre of the operator's field of vision. He then guides the weapon onto the target by radio command produced by movements of the thumb-controlled joystick. The high explosive warhead is detonated by impact or a proximity fuse. Once the target has been destroyed the oper-

ator unclips the empty canister and replaces it with a fresh unit; he is then ready to commence another target engagement.

Shorts have adapted Blowpipe for firing from a number of mobile platforms, including the Shorland armoured vehicle.

Blowpipe serves with at least 12 countries, including Argentina, Canada, Chile, Ecuador, Malawi, Nigeria, Oman, Portugal, Thailand and the United Kingdom. It was used in the Falklands, shooting down an MB.339 at Goose Green, and has been used to considerable effect by the Mujahideen of Afghanistan.

A Shorts Blowpipe man-portable missile leaves its launcher tube.

Specification
Blowpipe
Dimensions: length of missile 1.39 m (4 ft 6.7 in); length of canister 1.40 m (4 ft 7.1 in); diameter of missile 7.60 cm (3 in); span 27.5 cm (10.8 in)
Weights: complete system 21.9 kg (48.3 lb); missile and canister 13 kg (28.7 lb); missile 11 kg (24.5 lb)
Performance: effective ceiling 2000 m (6,560 ft); effective range about 3 to 4 km (1.86 to 2.5 miles)

Javelin man-portable surface-to-air missile system

Javelin is the successor to the highly successful Blowpipe produced by the Missile Systems division of Short Brothers in Belfast. The system was developed from Blowpipe, and uses a similar missile with four delta shaped control-surfaces near the nose and cruciform stabilizing fins at the tail but with a revised blast/fragmentation warhead and a more powerful two-stage rocket motor. Where Javelin differs most from Blowpipe is in the adoption of SACLOS (semi-automatic command to line-of-sight) guidance. With SACLOS all the aimer has to do is keep the target centred on the graticule seen through the aiming unit and the guidance system will automatically transmit flight corrections by radio-link. This does away with the thumb-controlled joy-stick with which the Blowpipe user manually controls his missile.

The factory sealed container/launcher used to house the Javelin missile looks very much like that of Blowpipe, but the reusable clip-on aiming unit is different. It contains a solid-state video camera connected to a microprocessor which turns the camera's signals into flight correction data for onward transmission to the missile.

In its basic form, Javelin is fired from the shoulder like Blowpipe, Stinger or the SA-7. However, up to three individual launcher/containers can be pedestal mounted on a **Lightweight Multiple Launcher (LML)**. This gives a single Javelin aiming unit a multi-target capability. The **LML(N)** is a similar unit for naval use and the **LML(V)** has been suggested for mounting on APCs or similar vehicles. The basic LML tripod can also be used from the cargo-bed of trucks.

Javelin has demonstrated that it is a very efficient infantry air-defence system. It is now in service with the Royal Marines and with the British army,

Above: A Javelin missile is launched from its container. Very similar in appearance to the preceding Blowpipe, it is much more capable.

Right: A Javelin team is ready to fire. The aiming unit automatically provides missile course corrections if it is kept on target.

where it is supplementing the Blowpipes of the Royal Artillery Light Air Defence regiments.

Very little physical data has been released as yet, but it is known that the missile is 1.4 m (4 ft 7.1 in) long, is supersonic and has a range in excess of 4,000 m (4,374 yards).

Starstreak high-velocity surface-to-air missile system

In the early 1980s, the British army formulated a requirement for a new high-velocity missile system which would provide enhanced low-level air-defence capability for the Royal Artillery. The original intention was to develop a Mach 4+ missile that would require a minimum of in-flight guidance and which would be able to handle targets such as close support aircraft and hovering helicopters fitted with long-range anti-tank weapons. Short Brothers and British Aerospace were each awarded £3m project definition contracts by the Ministry of Defence. In June 1986 Short Brothers were awarded the full development contract for their **Starstreak** system, while BAe have continued to work on their system, known as Thunderbolt, for the export market.

Starstreak is a high velocity missile fired from a factory-sealed container/launcher. Fired from its tube by an initial rocket motor, it continues on its way powered by a sustainer motor. This propels what might be called the 'carrier body', as the missile ejects three or more small metal darts when approaching the target. These then fly on under their own impetus to impact with the target (although it is unclear as yet if the sub-munitions have their own terminal guidance). Such clusters of

high-velocity darts would do considerable damage to the thin skins of attack helicopters and close support aircraft, especially if as seems likely the projectiles are to be made of tungsten or similar dense material.

Starstreak will be fired from a number of different types of platforms. The first to be developed will be an eight-round multiple launcher turret fitted to an Alvis Stormer APC. Up to twelve reloads will be carried inside the vehicle, and the gunner's surveillance, tracking and firing controls will be in a cupola ahead of the missile launcher. Starstreak will also be fired from lightweight multiple mounts similar to those used with Javelin, and like Javelin it will also be fired as a single portable launcher from the shoulder using a clip-on aiming unit.

Stormer mounted Starstreak is due to enter service with the British army by the end of the 1980s.

A model of an Alvis Stormer equipped with Starstreak. This will be the first version of the hyper-velocity system to enter service.

Rapier surface-to-air missile system

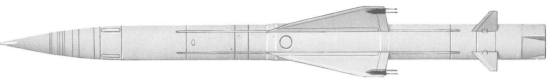

The **Rapier** low-level air defence missile system was developed by the British Aircraft Corporation (now British Aerospace) to meet the requirements of the British army and Royal Air Force for a mobile SAM system to replace the 40-mm Bofors guns then in service. Development started in the early 1960s, and the first production units were completed in 1971.

The basic clear-weather Rapier system consists of a fire unit, optical tracker and a generator. The former has four missiles in the ready-to-launch position, surveillance radar, IFF system, command transmitter and computer. The system is transported into action by two long wheelbase Land Rovers, one towing the missile launcher with its four missiles, generator, tracker and some reload missiles, and the second a trailer carrying additional missiles.

A typical target engagement takes place as follows. The target is first detected by the surveillance radar mounted on top of the launcher and is then automatically interrogated by the IFF system. If the target is friendly no action is taken but if hostile the tracker operator is alerted. The operator then acquires the target in his optical sight and tracks it using a joystick control. The computer informs the operator when the target is within range, and a Rapier missile is then launched. Once the missile has been launched the operator continues to track the target using the joystick. A TV camera in the tracker, collimated to the tracking sight, watches the flares mounted in the tail of the missile and so measures deviation from the sightline. The measurement is then fed to the computer which issues orders to the command transmitter for transmission to the missile. The missile itself is fitted with a high explosive warhead with an impact fuse. Once the four missiles have been launched new missiles can be quickly loaded by hand.

To give the system an all-weather capability Marconi Space and Defence Systems have developed the trailer-mounted DN181 Blindfire radar which can also be towed by a Land Rover or similar vehicle. In the **Blindfire Rapier** system the operator does not have to track the missile, this being fully automatic.

Early in 1983 the British army took delivery of the first of 62 **Tracked Rapier** systems. This was originally developed to meet the requirements of the Imperial Iranian Army but this contract was cancelled with the fall of the Shah. The Tracked Rapier consists of a modified M548 tracked cargo chassis, which itself is a member of the M113 family of vehicles, with a fully armoured cab. On the rear is a Rapier launcher with eight missiles (four on each side) in the ready-to-launch position, with additional missiles carried in reserve. The optical tracker is located in the cab and projects through the roof. In the future the Royal Artillery will have a mixture of towed and tracked Rapier systems.

Other variants include **Rapier Laserfire,** and **Rapier Darkfire.** Laserfire is a palletized system which can be used from the ground or any load carrier able to take 3 tonne payloads. It has an automatic laser tracker and designator in place of the optical control system, and a four missile launcher unit. Darkfire has improved radar, ECM, and an infra-red/TV optical tracker allowing the six-missile firing unit to fire at night or on smoke obscured battlefields.

Rapier 2000 will be the standard British Army system from the mid 1990s. The three elements of the firing unit will include separate tracking and launch radars, and an eight-round launch platform incorporating an optical acquisition system and an IR tracker. The missiles will be proximity fused to handle small targets such as cruise missiles.

Rapier has been sold to at least 14 nations, from Abu Dhabi to Zambia and is under consideration as an 'off-the-shelf' buy for the US Army's Forward Area Air Defense programme. It has seen action with Iran in the Gulf War and most notably in the South Atlantic during the Falklands campaign.

Specification
Rapier
Dimensions: length 2.24 m (7 ft 4.2 in); diameter 13.30 cm (5.25 in); span 38.10 cm (15 in)
Launch weight: 42.6 kg (94 lb)
Performance: maximum ceiling 3000+ m (9,845+ ft); maximum range 6500+ m (7,100+ yards)

Above: One of the prototypes of the Tracked Rapier launching a missile during trials in the UK. The Royal Artillery will deploy a mix of towed and Tracked Rapiers in the British Army of the Rhine. The first system was delivered late in 1982.

Right: Tracked Rapier has eight missiles in ready-to-launch position, compared to the four of the basic towed version. Here the launchers are elevated with tracking antenna raised.

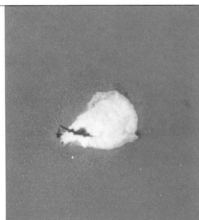

A Meteor target drone meets a fiery death as a highly effective Rapier missile strikes home.

RBS 70 man-portable surface-to-air missile system

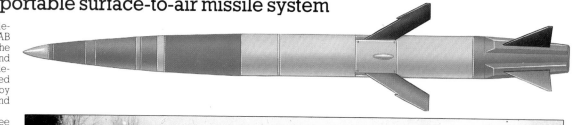

The **RBS 70** SAM system was developed from the late 1960s by AB Bofors to meet the requirements of the Swedish army, although Switzerland did contribute some funds to its development. In addition to being used by Sweden it is now also used by Bahrain, Eire, Norway, Singapore and the United Arab Emirates.

The RBS 70 system consists of three main components, namely the stand, sight and missile in its launch tube, each of which can be transported by one man. The complete system can be assembled in about 30 seconds. If required the RBS 70 system can also be fitted with an IFF system; this has been developed for the Swedish army by SATT Elektronic AB.

The missile is an optical beam rider. The sight generates a modulated laser beam which coincides with the line of sight. Before firing, the operator aims coarsely the line of sight at the target with the whole sight. The missile is then launched from its container and comes into the guidance beam, which it follows until it hits the target. So all the operator has to do is to keep the sight on the target through the engagement, using a thumb lever to control the gyro-stabilized optics.

The missile is launched from the transport/launch tube by means of a booster which burns out in the tube and is then jettisoned. Once the missile has left the tube the fins and control surfaces are extended. The sustainer motor is ignited when the missile is a safe distance from the operator, and this accelerates the missile to supersonic speed. Once the sustainer motor has burned out the missile continues in free flight.

The pre-fragmented warhead contains a large number of heavy metal balls and is detonated either by a direct hit or by means of a proximity fuse when it passes close to the target. It can also be self-destructed by the operator simply by switching off the guidance beam.

The stand consists of a vertical tube, three legs which are folded up for transport, and the operator's seat. There are contacts on the central tube for the electrical connection of the sight, missile, IFF equipment, target data receiver and the operator's headset. The sight consists of the guidance beam transmitter (with zoom optics) and an aiming telescope, all compo-

nents being specially protected against rough handling.

The RBS 70 can also be used in conjunction with a central search radar which provides target information for a number of missile systems. The Swedish army uses the PS 70/R, or Giraffe, developed by L. M. Ericsson, although other radars can be used, for example the Dutch HSA Reporter. The PS 70/R is mounted on a container which is carried on a cross-country truck; the antenna is mounted on a folding mast which gives the former a height of 12 m (39 ft 4.5 in) above the ground. Each firing unit is then provided with a target data receiver so that it can re-

ceive target information (speed and direction) from the radar, the data being transmitted either by radio or land line.

Bofors has also developed a vehicle-mounted system of the RBS 70 which can be fitted on the rear of a Land Rover (4×4) or similar vehicle, and another version for installation on armoured vehicles such as the M113, under the respective designations **RBS 70 VL** and **RBS 70 ARMAD**. Other proposed variants include the **RBS 70 SLM** naval version, and an helicopter launched air-to-air version.

Bofors RBS 70 SAM being launched from a Land Rover, just one of the many launch platforms for this versatile missile system.

Specification
RBS 70 man-portable surface-to-air missile system
Dimensions: length 1.32 m (4 ft 4 in); diameter 10.6 cm (4.17 in); span 32.0 cm (12.6 in)
Weights: missile in container 24 kg (52.9 lb); stand 23.5 kg (51.8 lb); sight 35 kg (77.2 lb)
Performance: maximum ceiling 3000 m (9,845 ft); maximum range 5000 m (5,470 yards)

SA-4 'Ganef' surface-to-air missile system

The **SA-4 'Ganef'** (this being the American designation) medium-to-high altitude SAM system was developed in the late 1950s and was first seen in public during a parade held in Red Square, Moscow, in 1964. The only known operators apart from the Soviet Union are Czechoslovakia, East Germany and Poland. Several units were deployed to Egypt, but these were returned to the Soviet Union before the outbreak of the 1973 Middle East conflict.

The SA-4 system is organized into special brigades each of three battalions, each of the latter having three 'Ganef' batteries and eight ZSU-23-4 self-propelled anti-aircraft guns for close defence. Each battery has three SA-4 tracked launchers, plus one each of the 'Pat Hand' and 'Thin Skin' radars.

Known as Krug in the Soviet army, this is an SA-4 'Ganef' surface-to-air missile launcher in its travelling mode. The chassis is also used for the GMZ armoured minelayer and an SPG.

The SA-4 system is normally deployed well to the rear of the forward edge of the battle area, and forms an integral part of the Soviet concept of air defence in depth by a combination of gun and missile systems to cover all ranges and altitudes. The SA-4 system is believed to have a maximum horizontal range of 72 km (44.75 miles) and a

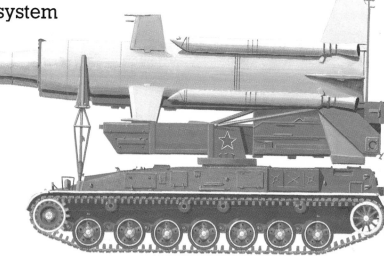

minimum horizontal range of 8 km (5 miles), the minimum effective engagement altitude being 1100 m (3,610 ft) and maximum altitude being 24000 m (78,740 ft).

The 'Ganef' transporter/launcher is a fully tracked vehicle based on the chassis of the GMZ armoured minelayer, and this was subsequently adopted for the 152-mm M1973 self-propelled howitzer. Mounted on top of the vehicle is a hydraulically operated turntable carrying the two missiles, the left missile being carried slightly higher than the right one. Before the missiles can be launched they have to be released from their travelling locks, and the coverings over their inlets and nozzles have to be removed.

The missile itself weighs about 1800 kg (3,968 lb) and is fitted with an HE warhead detonated by a proximity fuse. The missile has a length of 9.0 m (29 ft 6.3 in), a diameter of 80.0 cm (31.5 in) and a span of 2.6 m (8 ft 6.4 in). It is launched by four solid-propellant booster rockets mounted externally around the body of the missiles, but once the integral ramjet sustainer ignites these fall away, the missile accelerating to Mach 2.5.

A typical target engagement takes place as follows. The 'Long Track' radar, which is mounted on a modified AT-T heavy artillery tractor, first detects the target and passes target information to the SA-4 battery (it can also pass target information to an SA-6 'Gainful' battery). The 'Pat Hand' fire-control and command guidance radar at the battery then takes over and acquires the target. Once the target is within range, with altitude confirmed by the 'Thin Skin' radar, a 'Ganef' missile is launched and guided to the target by command guidance with

semi-active terminal homing for the final stage. Mounted on one of the tail fins of the missile is a continuous-wave radar transponder beacon which enables the missile to be tracked in flight by the 'Pat Hand' radar.

Once the two missiles have been launched new missiles are loaded with the aid of a crane. A Ural-375 (6×6) 4-tonne truck carries one missile, which is so long that it protrudes over the cap of the vehicle. The 'Ganef' system apparently cannot achieve high rates of fire, as according to American sources the battery has only four reload vehicles, each carrying only one missile.

More recently improved missiles have been produced that are more effective at lower altitudes. There are unconfirmed reports that the 'Ganef' has a secondary surface-to-surface capability.

Specification
SA-4 'Ganef'
Dimensions: length 8.8 m (28.87 ft); diameter 0.9 m (2.95 ft); tailspan 2.6 m

(8.53 ft); wing span 2.3 m (7.54 ft)
Launch weight: about 1800 kg (3968 lb)
Performance: speed Mach 2.5; range 72 km (44.74 miles); minimum engagement height 1100 m (3600 ft); ceiling 24000 m (78,740 ft)

Right: The SA-4 'Ganef' SAM system is used by Bulgaria, Czechoslovakia, East Germany, Poland and the USSR. It was also deployed to Egypt but withdrawn before the 1973 Middle East war. In wartime a fourth launcher is issued to each battery.

Below: SA-4 'Ganef' missiles being prepared for action shortly after coming to a halt. Before launching the intakes are uncovered, travel lock lowered to front of hull and target information received from the command post some way away.

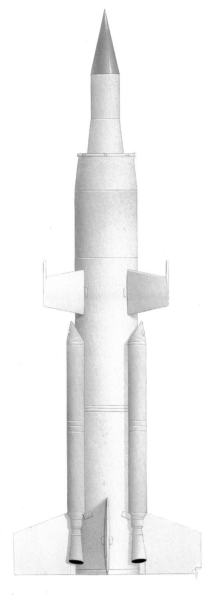

SA-6 'Gainful' surface-to-air missile system

The **SA-6**, which has been given the NATO reporting name 'Gainful', was first seen in Moscow in 1967 and was first used in action by the Egyptian and Syrian armies during the 1973 Middle East war. The SA-6 was one of the most successful air-defence systems of the campaign and forced Israeli aircraft to fly very low, where they could be engaged by SA-7 man-portable SAMs and the 23-mm ZSU-23-4 self-propelled anti-aircraft gun. The 'Gainful' has been exported on a large scale and in addition to the USSR it is also used by Algeria, Angola, Bulgaria, Cuba, Czechoslovakia, East Germany, Egypt, Ethiopia, Finland, Guinea-Bissau, Guyana, Hungary, India, Iraq, Kuwait, Libya, Mali, Mozambique, Peru, Poland, Romania, Somalia, Syria, Tanzania, Vietnam, Yemen Arab Republic (North Yemen), Yugoslavia and Zambia.

In the Soviet army SA-6s are deployed in regiments, each of these having a regimental HQ with one 'Thin Skin' height-finding and two 'Long Track' surveillance radars and five SA-6 batteries. Each SA-6 battery has one 'Straight Flush' fire-control radar vehicle, four SA-6 launchers and two ZIL-131 (6×6) missile resupply trucks, each carrying three missiles which are loaded with the aid of a crane.

The chassis of the SA-6 system is based on that of the ZSU-23-4, with the crew compartment at the front, the

missile-launcher in the centre, and the engine and transmission at the rear. Standard equipment includes an NBC system and night-vision equipment, but the system has no amphibious capability.

The three missiles are carried on a turntable that can be traversed through 360° and provide the missiles with an elevation of about +85°. For travelling the launcher is normally horizontal and traversed to the rear. The SA-6 missile itself is about 6.20 m (20 ft 4 in) long, 33.5 cm (13.2 in) in diameter and 1.52 m (5 ft 0 in) across the tail; the missile has a launch weight of about 550 kg (1,213 lb), of which the warhead weighs about 80 kg (176 lb). The missile's propulsion system consists of an integral ram/rocket, the latter being used to launch the missile. When a speed of about Mach 1.5 has been achieved the ramjet takes over and then increases speed to a maximum of Mach 2.8. The original version has a maximum range of about 22000 m (24,060 yards), and an en-

gagement altitude envelope between 100 to 9000 m (330 to 29,530 ft).

A target engagement takes place as follows. The 'Long Track' radar first detects the target and passes target information such as bearing, altitude and range to the SA-6 battery, where the 'Straight Flush' radar takes over. This is based on a similar chassis to that used by the SA-6 and carries out limited search, low-altitude detection/acquisition, target tracking and illumination, missile radar command guidance and secondary radar missile tracking functions. The 'Straight Flush' locates the target and, if this is confirmed as hostile, locks onto it using its tracking and illumination radars. Once this has been accomplished the radar changes to the continuous-wave mode and a missile is launched. The missile receives and transmits information back to the 'Straight Flush' radar, and terminal homing is of the semi-active radar type. The warhead is fitted with a radar proximity fuse as well as an impact fuse, and so does not have to

score a direct hit in order to destroy the target.

The basic SA-6 system is now some 20 years old and improved models have recently started to enter service, although the type's replacement could be on hand in the form of the SA-11. The Israelis captured many examples of this system in the 1973 Middle East war and were soon able to devise countermeasures to enable their aircraft to survive over the battlefield, and this information plus a number of complete SA-6 systems were supplied to the United States.

Specification
SA-6 'Gainful'
Dimensions: length 6.2 m (20 ft 4 in); diameter 33.5 m (13.2 in); span 1.52 m (5 ft 0 in)
Launch weight: about 550 kg (1212 lb)
Performance: speed Mach 2.8; maximum range 22-30 km (13.67 to 18.67 miles); range at low level about 60 km (37.34 miles); maximum ceiling up to 18000 m (59,000 ft) according to model

SA-6 'Gainful' surface-to-air missile

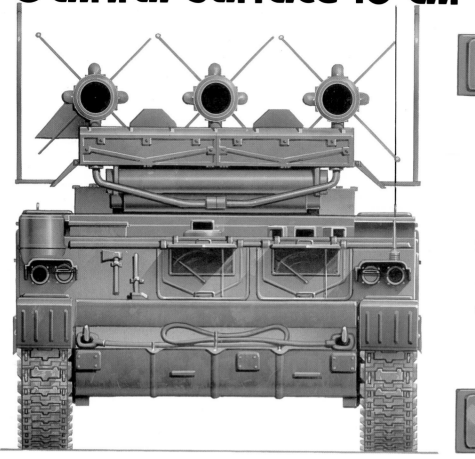

The SA-6 'Gainful' SAM system, known in the Soviet army as Kub. Used for the first time by the Egyptian and Syrian forces during the 1973 Yom Kippur war in the Middle East, it proved to be highly effective against the Israeli air force and prevented them from providing effective close air support during the early part of the campaign. Two additional launchers will be issued to each battery on mobilization for war.

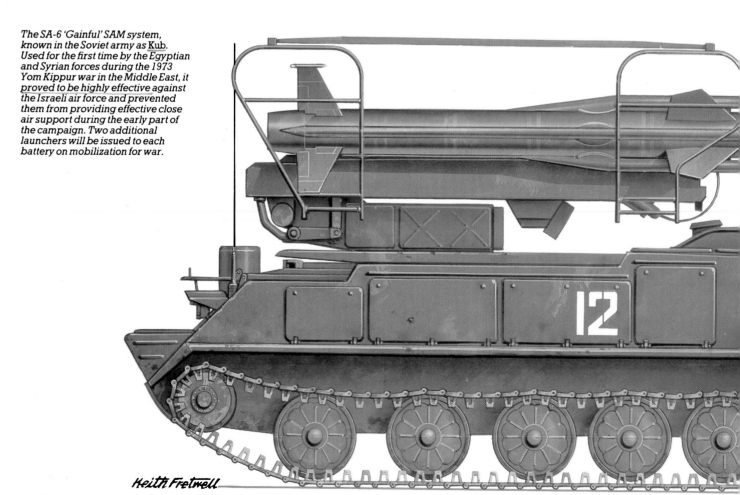

Keith Fretwell

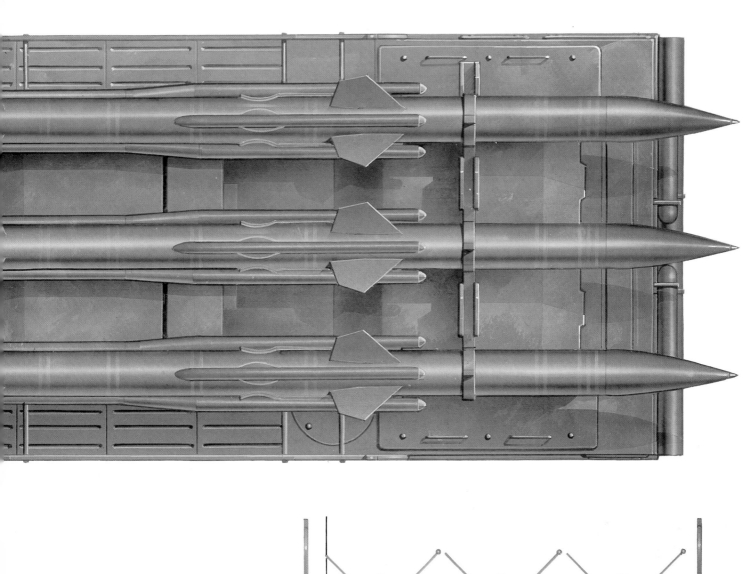

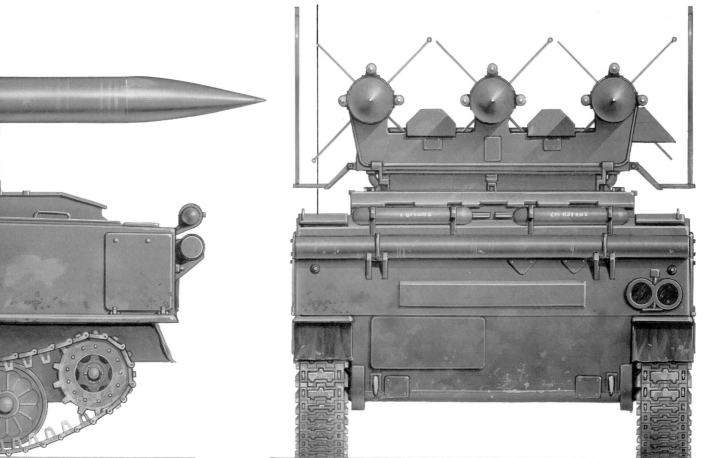

SA-2 'Guideline'

Unlike the SA-1, the **SA-2 'Guideline'** seems to have been designed from the outset as a mobile system, although as such it is very bulky and the complete system weighs over 100 tons. It first entered service in about 1956, and since that time has been used in combat more than any other SAM, and has seen continuous updating and improvement.

Like many other systems of the 1950s, 'Guideline' appears to have been designed to counter fast high-flying aircraft. Just how high flying was not known, until in 1960 an American Lockheed U-2 reconnaissance aircraft piloted by Francis Gary Powers was brought down from what the CIA, which operated the aircraft, had thought was a safe height. The shocking fact that the missile was capable of shooting down aircraft at the highest altitude forced drastic evolution upon the development of air tactics.

Originally the missile was a shapely design with cruciform rectangular nose surfaces, much larger cropped delta wings towards the tail and small powered control fins mounted at the rear; all these surfaces were indexed in line. The nitric acid/kerosene-powered missile was boosted by a tandem-mounted solid-propellant first stage, which was itself fitted with large delta wings. Later models featured delta nose surfaces, and a model first seen in 1967 had a large white-painted nosecone thought to cover a nuclear warhead in place of the original HE type.

The 'Guideline' is radio command-guided. Each SA-2 battery of six single launchers is linked to a 'Spoon Rest' early warning radar and the regimental level 'Side Net' height-finding radar. These systems acquire and identify targets, and transmit the information to the battery's own 'Fan Song' radar, usually by radio or landline. 'Fan Song' is capable of tracking

up to six targets at a time, and in all versions can track-while-scan (tracking targets and passing data to the fire-control computer while simultaneously scanning and trying to acquire new targets). Once launched, the SA-2 is powered by its solid-fuel booster away from the battery, where the liquid-fuel sustainer cuts in. Control signals are transmitted along a narrow line-of-sight UHF radio beam, which must be picked up by the missile within six seconds or it will go ballistic and lose any chance of hitting the target.

The SA-2 eventually shot down six U-2s (one each over the USSR and Cuba, and four over China). The type first saw major combat use in 1965, being fired by India in the war against Pakistan, reducing the efficiency of Pakistani air attacks although only one aircraft was damaged by an SA-2. In the same year North Vietnam launched the first of more than 9,000 missiles against the might of the USA. Initially fairly accurate, the SA-2 was gradually reduced in effectiveness by US countermeasures. The weapon nevertheless remained a threat, although in December 1972, when faced with the kind of target it had been designed to destroy (when the Boeing B-52s bombing Hanoi during 'Linebacker II' were ordered to fly straight bomb runs) the SA-2 achieved only about 2 per cent success.

The other major war zone which has seen extensive use of SA-2s is the Middle East, where the Egyptians were even less successful than the North Vietnamese. This may have been due to the fact that Israel deployed smaller, faster low-flying aircraft, which are not what the 'Guideline' was designed to engage. It was during the 1967 war, when Israeli ground forces captured a number of SA-2 sites, that it was learned that the Soviet designation for the system was **V75SM**, the missile itself (in the captured version)

being known as the **V750 VK**. Incidentally, the ease with which the Israelis evaded the SA-2s fired at them during the 'Six Day War' and the 'War of Attrition' led to a sense of false security about Soviet SAMs before the 'Yom Kippur War', when the much more advanced SA-6 proved a nasty shock.

Combat experience during the SA-2's long lifetime has seen modifications to the fusing guidance and warhead, the addition of radar (those used in the 'Yom Kippur' War of 1973 were reported to have been fitted with terminal guidance), and, above all, enhancement of ECCM. The SA-2 remains in service in diminishing numbers with the USSR, and has been supplied to most Soviet client states as well as to China, Albania and Egypt.

Specification
SA-2 'Guideline'
Type: medium/long-range land-based semi-mobile SAM
Dimensions: length 10.80 m (35 ft 5.2 in) but varying in some subtypes; diameter (missile) 500 mm (19.69 in) and (booster) 660 mm (25.98 in); span (missile) 1.70 m (5 ft 6.9 in) and (booster) 2.20 m (7 ft 2.6 in)

An SA-2 (V 750 as it is known to the Soviets) of the PVO (Air Defence of the Homeland) is launched during an exercise in the early 1960s. It was an SA-2 which ended the era of the high-flying bomber when the Lockheed U-2 spyplane flown by Gary Powers was shot down in 1960.

Launch weight: 2300 kg (5,071 lb)
Performance: operating range 35-50 km (21.75-31.1 miles) according to subtype; maximum speed at burn-out Mach 3-3.5; operating altitude limits 1500 m (4,920 ft) in later models to 28000 m (91,865 ft)
Warhead: 130-kg (286-lb) HE with proximity (and/or radio command or impact) fuse

Certainly the surface-to-air missile to have seen most action, the SA-2 'Guideline' has been in Soviet service since the late 1950s. It is nominally a mobile system, although compared to modern types that mobility is distinctly ponderous.

USSR
SA-3 'Goa'

Essentially a medium-altitude partner to the SA-2 'Guideline', the **SA-3** 'Goa' is one of the same generation, being introduced in 1961. Considerably smaller than 'Guideline', the 'Goa' is more manoeuvrable, but in early models used a similar radio command-guidance system, and shared the larger missile's vulnerability to electronic countermeasures. Like the SA-2, the 'Goa' uses a solid-fuel booster, but the second stage sustainer is also of the solid type, unlike the liquid-propellant sustainer of the earlier missile.

SA-3 missiles are normally carried in pairs on their launch rails on the back of the same ZIL-157 tractors used to tow the much larger SA-1 and SA-2 trailers. When used for base defence, the 'Goa' is fired from a power-rotated twin launcher at an elevation of 75°. More recently, the SA-3 has been seen on triple launchers in Yugoslavia, and a quad launcher has been introduced to the air-defence forces of the Warsaw Pact.

Although technically a mobile system, the SA-3 is somewhat cumbersome in comparison with more recent systems, but the Soviet tendency to retain in service systems that work reasonably well has seen the 'Goa' transferred from the army to the air-defence forces, by whom the type is used for short-range defence of airfields.

The radar systems associated with the 'Goa' include 'Flat Face' early warning and target-acquisition radar, which has a range of some 250 km (155 miles), and the 85-km (53-mile) range 'Low Blow' target-tracking and missile-guidance radar, which can track up to six targets at once and guide up to two missiles to each target. 'Low Blow' is optimized for target detection at low level, and is reported to be able to pick targets out of ground clutter. Later

models may have optical tracking equipment fitted to the radar system for use in intensive ECM environments. The missile itself is radio command-guided, but may have been fitted with semi-active radar homing for guidance in the terminal phase of the attack.

The SA-3 first saw action during the 'War of Attrition' in the Middle East, but Israeli countermeasures developed to deal with the SA-2 were found to be effective against the smaller missile. Nevertheless the 'SA-3' was the most numerous Arab SAM of the 1973 'Yom Kippur' war, although it was overshadowed by the much more effective SA-6 'Gainful'. It has been supplied to most Soviet client states, as well as to countries such as Peru, Uganda and India. The 'Goa' has also been taken to sea by the Soviet navy as the **SA-N-1**, and in this form has become one of the principal anti-aircraft defences of the Soviet fleet.

Specification
SA-3 'Goa'
Type: medium-range land-based semi-mobile SAM
Dimensions: length 6.70 m (21 ft 11.8 in); diameter (missile) 450 mm (17.72 in) and (booster) 600 mm (23.62 in); span (missile) 1.22 m (4 ft 0.3 in) and (booster) 1.50 m (4 ft 11.1 in)
Launch weight: 636 kg (1,402 lb)
Performance: operating range 18-30 km (11.2-18.6 miles) according to model; speed at burn-out Mach 3.5; operating altitude limits 1500-13000+ m (4,920-42,650+ ft)
Warhead: 60-kg (132-lb) HE with proximity fuse

Above: SA-3 'Goa' has been used in both mobile and static versions, the former being less common today as more modern systems enter service. In the airfield defence role, 'Goa' is mounted on a powered twin launcher which can elevate to 75° and which is fixed in place.

More recently, SA-3s have been fitted to quadruple launchers in the various air defences of the nations of the Warsaw Pact. In common with most Soviet systems, 'Goa' has been the subject of continuous updating, to make an essentially crude system suitable for the modern battlefield.

SA-7 'Grail' man-portable surface-to-air missile system

The **SA-7 'Grail'** man-portable SAM was developed in the early 1960s and is similar in concept to the US Redeye missile. It was first used in combat in the 1967 Middle East war, and has been issued to every member of the Warsaw Pact, most countries that have received Soviet aid and many guerrilla factions around the world. It is operated by a two-man team consisting of the gunner, who carries a gripstock and one missile in a canvas bag, and an assistant gunner who carries an additional missile.

The SA-7 system consists of the missile in its launcher, thermal battery and a reusable gripstock. The missile itself has an infra-red seeker head, two canard fins at the front and four spring loaded tail fins that stabilize the missile in flight. The gripstock assembly is attached to the underside of the forward part of the launcher, and contains the trigger mechanism, safety switch, locking pin and an audible alarm. The circular thermal battery is attached to the forward part of the gripstock assembly by a key slot which contains four locking pins.

A typical target engagement takes place as follows. Once the operator has sighted a target he removes the end cap of the launch tube and points the launcher at the target. The trigger

has two stages of operation, the first stage switching on the thermal battery. When the missile has picked up sufficient infra-red radiation from the target an audible warning is given and a light also comes on. The trigger is then pulled right back and the missile is ejected from the launcher by a motor which burns out before the tail of the missile has left the launcher. A rocket booster then accelerates the missile to Mach 1.5 and the sustainer takes over. The infra-red seeker then homes onto the exhaust of the aircraft or helicopter. The missile is fitted with a direct-action and graze fuse, and therefore has to hit the target in order to detonate. The warhead contains RDX/AP explosive but from all accounts this will damage the aircraft rather than destroy it. If the missile has not hit its target after a period of 15 seconds or a range of about 6.5 km (4.04 miles) it will self-destruct. There are many accounts of

Israeli aircraft, especially McDonnell Douglas A-4s, that returned with damaged tailpipes. Fresh missiles are delivered to the unit in wooden boxes which contain two missiles and four thermal batteries.

The SA-7 has a maximum speed of 1600 km/h (994 mph) and a maximum range and altitude of about 3.2 km (2 miles), while the later-production **SA-7B** has a maximum speed of 1930 km/h (1,200 mph) and a maximum altitude of about 4800 m (15,750 ft). When originally introduced the system was not fitted with an IFF system and the crew had therefore to make a positive identification before launching a missile, but later models were fitted with an IFF system. The SA-7B has a 28-pin connector between the gripstock and the launcher whereas the original model has a 24-pin connector.

The SA-7 missile has many limitations including its infra-red seeker

which tends to make it chase the aircraft, its relatively low speed and altitude, its limited manoeuvrability, its somewhat protracted warming-up period and its lack of an IFF system.

The SA-7 is being replaced in Soviet service by the **SA-14 'Gremlin'**. This looks like it's predecessor, but has greatly increased manoeuvrability and is thought to have all-aspect targetting ability.

Specification
SA-7 'Grail'
Dimensions: length of missile 1.30 m (4 ft 3.2 in); diameter about 7.0 cm (2.75 in); length of launcher 1.346 m (4 ft 5 in)
Weights: launcher 10.6 kg (23.4 lb); missile 9.2 kg (20.3 lb)
Performance: effective altitude between 45 and 1500 m (150 and 4,920 ft); range 3.2 km (2 miles)

SA-8 'Gecko' surface-to-air missile system

The **SA-8 'Gecko'** low-altitude surface-to-air missile system was first deployed in the early 1970s, and was first seen in public during a parade held in Red Square, Moscow, during 1975. Unlike earlier Soviet self-propelled air-defence missile systems, the SA-8 'Gecko' is completely self-contained in that it has its own tracking and surveillance radars and so can therefore operate on its own. In the Soviet army it is now rapidly replacing the 57-mm S-60 towed anti-aircraft gun, each division having five batteries each with four SA-8s and four missile resupply vehicles. At HQ level there is one 'Thin Skin' height-finding and two 'Long Track' surveillance radars for command and control. Used by over a dozen countries, the SA-8 had its operational debut in the Bekaa valley in 1982, Syrian systems being roughly handled by Israel.

The system is mounted on a 6×6 chassis which is believed to be a development of the ZIL-167 vehicle; this is fully amphibious, being propelled in the water by two waterjets at the rear of the hull. Steering is on the front and rear axles and a central tyre-pressure regulation system allows the driver to adjust the tyre pressures to suit the type of ground being crossed. The crew compartment, which is provided with an NBC system, is at the front of the hull, with the missile system in the centre, and the engine and transmission at the rear.

The missile system can be traversed through 360° and has two missiles in the ready-to-launch position per side at the rear, surveillance radar with a range of 30 km (18.6 miles) on top (when travelling this can be lowered horizontally to the rear), and the missile guidance group at the front. The last consists of the large central tracking radar with a smaller missile-guidance radar and a command-link

Left: The first version of the SA-8 'Gecko' (called Romb in the Soviet army) had four missiles in the ready-to-launch position but the current production version has six missiles in launch/transport containers. It was first used in combat by Syria in mid-1982. On mobilization a further two launchers are issued to each battery.

horn for missile-gathering on each side. Mounted above each missile guidance radar is a low-light-level television/optical assistance system, which is believed to be used for tracking in conditions of either low visibility or heavy electronic countermeasures. Why the system has two tracking and two guidance radars is not completely clear, but it is probably to allow a salvo of two missiles to be launched at a target, with a gap between launchings, to give a higher kill probability. The missiles are believed to have infra-red and semi-active seekers.

The missile has a launch weight of 190 kg (419 lb) and is 3.20 m (10 ft 6 in)

long, 21.0 cm (8.25 in) in diameter and 64.0 cm (25.2 in) in span. The solid-propellant single-stage rocket motor produces a maximum speed of Mach 2. Minimum and maximum target engagement altitudes are 50 m (165 ft) and 13000 m (42,650 ft), and maximum slant range is about 12 km (7.5 miles).

More recently an improved version of the SA-8 has been seen, and this has been given the Western designation **SA-8B**. This has six missiles in the ready-to-launch position, and these, which are possibly longer and have increased capabilities, are carried in fully enclosed containers. The latter provide the missile with increased en-

vironmental protection as well as giving the missile protection against rough handling in the field. The SA-8 launcher system has no integral reload capability.

Specification
SA-8 'Gecko'
Dimensions: length 3.2 m (10 ft 6 in); diameter 21.0 cm (8.25 in); span 64 cm (25.2 in)
Launch weight: 190 kg (419 lb)
Performance: speed Mach 2; range 12 km (7.5 miles); minimum engagement height 50 m (164 ft); maximum ceiling 13000 m (42,650 ft)

SA-9 'Gaskin' surface-to-air missile system

USSR

The **SA-9 'Gaskin'** low-altitude SAM system was developed in the 1960s and was first seen in public in the 1970s. It is deployed in the Soviet Army on the scale of 16 systems per division, with each regiment, be they tank or motorized rifle, having four systems. In addition to being used by the Soviet Union the SA-9 is also used by many other countries including Algeria, Egypt, East Germany, Hungary, India, Iraq, Libya, Poland, South Yemen, Syria, Vietnam and Yugoslavia. The first known operational use of the SA-9 system was in Lebanon in May 1981 when an SA-8 battery manned by Libyans engaged Israeli aircraft. The battery was subsequently destroyed by the Israeli air force without loss. The type has also been used operationally by Iraq against Iranian aircraft during the recent conflict.

The SA-9 'Gaskin' system is essentially the BRDM-2 (4×4) reconnaissance vehicle with its one-man machine-gun turret removed and replaced by a new power-operated turret. In the forward part of this is a seat for the operator, who is provided with a large transparent window to his front. To the rear of the operator is a pedestal and on each side of this are two missiles in their ready-to-launch containers. When the vehicle is travelling, the launcher and its associated missiles lie horizontally along the top of the hull. Once the four missiles have been launched the empty canisters have to be removed, and new missiles in their

containers are then loaded manually by the crew from outside the vehicle. As far as it is known the SA-9 retains the amphibious characteristics of the BRDM-2 and is fitted with two belly wheels between the front and rear axles, allowing it to cross trenches with ease.

It is believed that the missile is a further development of the SA-7 man-portable missile but fitted with a more powerful rocket motor for increased performance and a longer range. It is probable that target engagement is similar to that of the SA-7 but with two missiles launched at each target (with gap of five seconds) for a higher kill probability. The missile's infra-red seeker is set to operate against different target intensities in order to defeat flare-type decoys launched by the target aircraft.

The missile itself is carried and launched from a container that protects it during handling, and is about 1.829 m (6 ft 0 in) long, 11.0 cm (4.33 in) in diameter and 30.0 cm (11.8 in) in span. It has an effective range of 8000 m (8,750 yards) and a maximum engagement altitude of 4000 m (13,125 ft). The missile is believed to weigh about 30 kg (66 lb) and to have a maximum speed of more than Mach 1.5.

The SA-9 'Gaskin' has a number of major drawbacks in that it is a clear-weather system only and the gunner must traverse his turret continuously on the look out for targets, although initial target information such as direc-

tion, speed and altitude are probably provided from a central command post. The rate of fire is slow as the missiles have to be reloaded manually. For some years there have been unconfirmed reports that the SA-9 is being fitted with the 'Gun Dish' radar (as fitted to the ZSU-23-4 self-propelled anti-aircraft gun system) to give the system an all-weather capability. This radar, which is probably mounted above the turret, carries out target-acquisition and tracking functions to a maximum range of about 20 km (12.4 miles).

Because of its limitations the SA-9 is now being replaced by the SA-13 system, which has its own radars and carries four missiles in the ready-to-launch position.

An SA-9 'Gaskin' system, based on the BRDM-2 (4×4) amphibious scout car, parades through Red Square, Moscow.

Specification
SA-9 'Gaskin' launcher system
Crew: 3
Weight: 8000 kg (17,635 lb)
Dimensions: length 5.75 m (18 ft 10.4 in); width 2.35 m (7 ft 8.5 in); height (travelling) 2.35 m (7 ft 8.5 in)
Powerplant: one GAZ-41 V-8 water-cooled petrol engine developing 140 hp (104 kW)
Performance: maximum road speed 100 km/h (62 mph); maximum range 750 km (466 miles); fording amphibious; gradient 60 per cent; vertical obstacle 0.4 m (15.75 in); trench 1.25 m (4 ft 1 in)

SA-11 'Gadfly' surface-to-air missile system

USSR

The **SA-11** is the replacement for the SA-6 'Gainful' SAM system, which has now been in service for almost 20 years. The chassis is similar to that of the SA-6 but carries four missiles on a turntable that can be traversed

through 360°. A second vehicle based on a similar chassis carries acquisition, guidance and tracking radars that provide information on the target's height, bearing and range. The missile, according to American sources, is ab-

out 5 m (16 ft 5 in) long and has a maximum effective altitude of 14000 m (45,930 ft) and a minimum altitude of less than 100 m (330 ft). Minimum range is about 3 km (1.86 miles) and maximum range is around 30 km (18.6

miles). It is very similar to the US Navy's Standard SM-1 missile, and is probably related to the naval SA-N-7 missile. It is deployed at divisional level, and has been supplied to Syria.

SA-13 'Gopher' surface-to-air missile system

USSR

The **SA-13** (an American designation in the absence of any known Soviet designation) was developed in the late 1970s and was first seen in the Group of Soviet Forces Germany (GSFG) in the spring of 1980. It is the replacement for the SA-9 Gaskin system on the BRDM-2 (4×4) chassis, and is issued on the scale of 16 systems per tank and motorized rifle division. Early in 1983 sever-

al SA-13 SAM systems were seen deployed around Kabul airport in Afghanistan.

The SA-13 is based on the chassis of the MT-LB multi-purpose tracked vehicle and has four missiles in the ready-to-launch position. The missiles are in containers of a type similar to those of the SA-9, and a version with six launch containers has also been

observed. Between the two banks of two missiles is a range-only radar, though passive radar emission detectors are also mounted. Most sources state that the seeker on the missile is cryogenically cooled and operates on two frequency bands. The latter factor gives a higher degree of resistance to infra-red countermeasures such as flares dropped or ejected from aircraft

and helicopters. Effective engagement altitude are a minimum of 50 m (165 ft) and a maximum of 10000 m (32,810 ft), and a slant range of 8 km (5 miles) is claimed. As far as it is known the SA-13 has no rapid reload system, although there is sufficient space inside of the vehicle to carry at least one complete reload of missiles. The system is believed to be in service with Syria.

M48 Chaparral surface-to-air missile system

USA

The **M48 Chaparral** low-level self-propelled SAM system was developed some 20 years ago to meet an urgent US Army requirement. It consists essentially of a modified M548 tracked carrier, which is a member of the M113 family, with a missile launch station mounted on the rear. The latter consists of the base structure and turret with its four Chaparral missiles in the ready-to-launch position. The Chaparral is basically the Sidewinder air-to-air infra-red homing missile modified for the surface-to-air role. In the US Army a composite anti-aircraft battalion has 24 Chaparral SAM systems and 24 M163 20-mm Vulcan self-propelled anti-aircraft gun systems,

early warning for the battalion being provided by a number of truck-mounted AN/MPQ-49 Forward Area Alerting Radars.

The original missile used with the system was the **MIM-72A** which weighed 85 kg (187 lb) of which 11.2 kg (24.7 lb) was explosive; this

was replaced in production in the late 1970s by the much-improved **MIM-72C** which is slightly heavier at 86.3 kg (190 lb) but has a more powerful HE blast fragmentation warhead, new proximity fuse and a new seeker.

When travelling the launcher is normally covered by a tarpaulin cover

over metal frames, which can quickly be removed and stowed at the front of the vehicle. Reserve missiles are carried below and to each side of the launcher, and are reloaded manually.

The basic Chaparral is a day system, and a typical target engagement would take place as follows. The target

169

aircraft would first be detected visually or by the AN/MPQ-49 radar. The gunner, who is seated under a transparent dome in the centre of the launcher, with two missiles to each side of his position, then acquires the target and continues tracking it using his power controls. Turret traverse is 360°, and the missiles on their launcher arms can be elevated to +90° and depressed to −5°. When the target is within the infra-red sensing range of the missile an audio tone is given in the gunner's headset. The missile is then launched and the gunner can then start tracking another target or keep tracking the original target in case the missile does not hit it. Once the missile is launched it homes onto the hot exhaust of the target and the proximity fuse means that a direct hit is not required in order to destroy a hostile aircraft. The Chaparral system can engage targets flying at an altitude of between 350 and 3050 m (1,000 and 10,000 ft) and has a maximum range of 6000 m (6,560 yards).

The Chaparral was to have been replaced in the US Army by the Roland surface-to-air missile system manufactured in the United States by Boeing and Hughes Aircraft, but production of the Roland system was terminated in 1983 after only 27 systems, these being issued to the Texas National Guard. To keep the Chaparral system effective as the US Army's forward area low-

Chaparral SAM system in travelling configuration. If required the bows stowed on the front of the vehicle can be fitted over the missiles, which then makes the system difficult to detect from the basic M548 carrier.

level defence well into the 1990s, an intensive modernization pogramme has been established. Improvements already fielded include an improved infra-red guidance system using Rosette Scan Seeker technology (giving Chaparral forward engagement capability), a new smokeless motor, improved IFF systems, and a FLIR thermal-imaging system mounted on the launcher (allowing adverse weath-

er and limited night operations).

The US Army has a requirement for 632 self-propelled Chaparral systems, with procurement of the improved missile expected to reach 1,200 units per year by 1990. The system is used by Egypt, Israel, Morocco, Taiwan (who are also the sole users of Sea Chaparral) and Tunisia.

Specification
M48 Chaparral
Dimensions: length 2.91 m (9.54 ft); diameter 13 cm (5.12 in); span 64 cm (25.19 in)
Launch weight: 84 kg (185.18 lb)
Performance: speed, supersonic; range 6 km (3.72 miles); minimum engagement height 350 m (1,150 ft); maximum ceiling 3050 m (10,000 ft)

MIM-104 Patriot surface-to-air missile system

The **MIM-104 Patriot** tactical air-defence system has been developed from 1965 to meet the requirements of the US Army for a missile system to replace both the HAWK and Nike-Hercules. Prime contractor is the Raytheon Corporation, the principal sub-contractors being Martin-Marietta Aerospace for the missile airframe and launcher, and the Hazeltine Corporation for the IFF interrogator. First test launches took place in 1970 but for a variety of reasons, including both cost and design problems, limited production of the system was not authorized for some time, and the first operational Patriot battalion was not fielded until early 1983.

A typical Patriot fire unit consists of the radar set, engagement control system, electric powerplant, up to eight four-missile launch stations, and a number of supporting vehicles and pieces of equipment.

The AN/MPQ-53 radar set is a multi-function phased-array unit that provides for all of the functions of airspace surveillance, target detection and track, and support of missile guidance. The combination of computer control and phased-array technology permits the time-sharing of functions so that the performance workload of this radar is equal to that of the nine different radars used by present-day systems. The radar is on a semi-trailer that is towed by a standard 5-ton (6×6) truck.

The AN/MSQ-104 engagement station is installed in a container carried on the rear of a standard M816 (6×6) long wheelbase truck, and houses the system's two operators, the weapons control computer and two tactical display consoles. The software-controlled computer exercizes authority over all tactical operations from

radar scheduling, weapon assignment, missile launch and intercept assessment. Several operating modes are available, including computer-aided manual mode, semi-automatic and full automatic, with the operator always retaining full override capability of computer decisions.

The M901 launch station is mounted on a semi-trailer which has its own generator and is also towed by a 5-ton 6×6 truck. Each of the four missiles is sealed into a canister which serves both as travelling and launcher tube. In a tactical situation the launchers are widely dispersed and communicate with the engagement control station via secure radio data links.

The missile itself is delivered to the unit as a certified round requiring no maintenance in the field. From the nose, the missile consists of the radome, semi-active radar (plus command) terminal guidance, high explosive warhead, propulsion system and control actuator section at the very rear. The missile has a five-year storage life and according to the manufacturer its high-g tail control outmanoeuvres any manned aircraft. The missile is powered by a single-stage solid-propellant Thiokol TX-486 motor which gives a maximum speed of Mach 3.

In 1979 the USA together with Belgium, Denmark, France, Germany, Greece and the Netherlands signed a

memorandum of understanding to study the most practical and economic ways for the European countries to procure the Patriot system. The system will be fully operational by the end of the 1980s, its high performance, powerful warhead and unique Track Via Missile (TVM, with a data downlink to upgrade the information in the digital computer in the engagement control station) guidance aspect ensuring the ability of the US Army to deal with targets of all altitudes, as well as providing a limited anti-missile capability.

A Patriot SAM is launched from its canister during early trials. In the US Army this SAM will replace the HAWK and Nike Hercules and is expected to be made under licence in Europe.

Specification
MIM-104 Patriot
Dimensions: length 5.18 m (17 ft 0 in); diameter 40.6 cm (16 in); wing span 91.4 cm (36 in)
Launch weight: about 998 kg (2,200 lb)
Performance: maximum ceiling 24000 m (78,750 ft); range 60 km (37.3 miles)

MIM-23B Improved HAWK surface-to-air missile system

Above: Raytheon HAWK missile being launched. The HAWK is the most widely used SAM in the West and is also being built under licence by a European consortium headed by France and West Germany. Since being introduced in 1960 it has been constantly updated to enable it to remain an effective weapon system. The latest model is called the Improved HAWK.

The **HAWK** (Homing All the Way Killer) was developed by Raytheon to meet the requirements of the US Army. The first guided launch took place in June 1956 when a HAWK successfully shot down a QF-80 drone aircraft. The first US Army **MIM-23A HAWK** battalion was activated in August 1960, and since then the type has been purchased by some 20 countries and is also being built under licence in Europe and Japan. Since it was first introduced the HAWK has been constantly updated to meet the changing threat. The type was first used operationally in the 1973 Middle East war when Israeli HAWKs were credited with the destruction of at least 20 Egyptian and Syrian aircraft.

The latest model is the **MIM-23B Improved Hawk**, and this has a new guidance package, a larger and more effective warhead, improved motor propellant, and many smaller changes to the fire-control system. Mainte-

nance has also been much improved as electronics have not only become much smaller but also much more reliable since the missile was developed in the 1950s. The Improved HAWK entered service with the US Army in the 1970s, and most HAWK users are now bringing their older systems up to the improved standard.

Today an Improved HAWK battery consists of the Pulse Acquisition Radar, a new Continuous-Wave Acquisition Radar, the Range Only Radar, the Battery Control Centre, the high-power Continuous-Wave Illuminator, three launchers each with three missiles, plus tracked missile loaders/transporters. The launchers are mounted on a two-wheeled carriage that can be towed by a 2½-ton (6×6) truck or similar vehicles. A self-propelled version of the HAWK mounted on a modified M548 tracked carrier chassis designated the **M727 SP HAWK** was developed, but this was only used by

Israel and the United States, and is no longer in service with the former.

A typical Improved HAWK target engagement takes place as follows. The PAR and CWAR (the latter concerned with low-altitude threats) sweep the HAWK battery's area of defence, and when a target is detected and confirmed as hostile its position is relayed to the CWI radar. The latter illuminates the target with electromagnetic energy which is reflected back to the guidance system of the missile. The HAWK missile tracks the target by following the reflected electromagnetic energy. The missile itself is fitted with a high explosive blast-fragmentation warhead, and is powered by a dual-thrust solid-propellant motor.

A recent introduction into the US Army MIM-23B force is the Northrop-developed Tracking Adjunct System (TAS). This is a passive sensor system which tracks targets picked up by the

Improved HAWK radar and displays them on a television monitor. This increases the survivability of the HAWK battery as it enables operations to be carried out with a reduction of signals detectable by an enemy. It also permits the operator to discriminate between targets close together or near the horizon.

The nearest Soviet system to the Improved HAWK is the SA-6 'Gainful'; this is more mobile than the American system but it has a shorter operational range. In the US Army HAWK is to be replaced by the Raytheon Patriot.

Specification
MIM-23B Improved HAWK
Dimensions: length 5.12 m (16 ft 9½ in); diameter 35.6 cm (14 in); wing span 1.22 m (48 in)
Launch weight: 626 kg (1,380 lb)
Performance: effective ceiling 30 to 11580 m (100 to over 38,000 ft); range 40 km (25 miles)

FIM-92A Stinger man-portable surface-to-air missile system

The **Stinger** man-portable surface-to-air missile system, officially designated **FIM-92A**, was developed to meet the requirements of the US Army and US Marine Corps by the Pomona Division of General Dynamics, who had developed the earlier Redeye.

Main improvements over the Redeye may be summarized as an all-aspect engagement capability (it being possible for the operator to engage the aircraft while it is flying towards him), an IFF system, improved range and manoeuvrability, and much improved re-

sistance to enemy countermeasures. The Stinger can intercept and destroy hovering helicopters and high-speed manoeuvring targets. It became operational with the US Army in Germany during 1981, and with the 82nd Airborne Division in the continental USA

during 1982. It has also been ordered by Japan and will be built under licence in Europe.

A typical target engagement takes place as follows. The operator visually acquires the target and aligns this with the open sight on the launcher. He then

Surface-to-air missiles

General Dynamics (Pomona Division) Stinger missile just coming out of its launcher tube. In September 1983 it was announced that this missile would be manufactured under licence in Europe for some NATO countries.

its type in the world, to identify the aircraft positively. If it is confirmed as hostile he actuates the missile functions and the missile is then launched and homes onto the enemy aircraft without any further action by the operator. The gripstock is then detached from the empty launcher, which is discarded to permit a fresh launcher/missile to be attached to the gripstock for the engagement of another target.

The missile has an HE warhead, electronic control system and a dual-thrust rocket motor, in which an ejector motor launches the Stinger before the flight motor boosts the missile to its Mach 2+ cruising speed once clear of the launcher. The Stinger uses a passive infra-red seeker and proportional navigation guidance.

For ease of transport the missile (in its launcher complete with gripstock, IFF system and battery coolant units) comes in a compact aluminium container which can be easily transported on the back of vehicles or in aircraft and helicopters without damage to the contents.

Stinger is in service with or has been ordered by Chad, Italy, Japan, the Netherlands, Saudi Arabia, Turkey, the UK (with whom it saw limited use in the Falklands) and West Germany. Stingers supplied to the Mujahideen of Afghanistan have proved very effective against Soviet and government aircraft and helicopters.

Stinger is to be superseded in US service by **Stinger-POST** (Passive Optical Seeker Technique). This has

an advanced electro-optical seeker which can more effectively isolate targets from backgrounds, a useful characteristic for coping with very low flying targets. Included in the system will be a re-programmable micro-processor, which will allow the system to be up-graded in the future without costly retrofits. Production of at least 6,000 missiles per year is expected through to 1992.

Stinger has become an important component of the US Army's Forward Area Air Defense programme. Pedestal mounted Stinger is a multiple launcher mounted on the HMMWV Hummer utility vehicle, as is Boeing's private venture **Avenger**. Stinger has been used in a number of proposed gun/missile air defence combinations, and an air-to-air Stinger has been studied for use with a number of battlefield helicopters.

Specification
FIM-92A Stinger
Dimensions: length 1.52 m (5 ft 0 in); diameter 7.0 cm (2.75 in); span 9.14 cm (3.6 in)
Weights: missile 10.1 kg (22.3 lb); missile and launcher 13.6 kg (30 lb); complete system 15.1 kg (33.3 lb)
Performance: maximum ceiling 4800 m (15,750 ft); maximum range 5 km (3.1 miles)

Tan-SAM surface-to-air missile system

The **Tan-SAM** short range surface-to-air missile system has been developed by Toshiba from the mid-1960s as a replacement for the wide range of anti-aircraft guns at present used by the Japanese Ground Self-Defense Force, most of which date back to World War II. As a result of the usual shortage of funds, development of the Tan-SAM has been very slow, technical tests being carried out between 1972 and 1977 and operational tests in 1978 and 1979. Late in 1980 the weapon was finally standardized as the **Type 81** short-range SAM system, the first production units being delivered in 1982.

In the Japanese Ground Self-Defense Force the Tan-SAM will be deployed at division level, with each division allocated four sets, each of the latter comprising one fire-control vehicle and two launchers each mounted on an unarmoured Type 73 Truck (6×6), a type widely used by the Japanese Ground Self-Defense Force. The system will also be deployed by the Japanese Air Self-Defense Force for the defence of air bases.

The three main components of the system are the missile, the launcher and the fire-control system. The missile is powered by a single-stage solid-propellant rocket motor, which accelerates it to a maximum speed of about Mach 2.4. A major drawback is

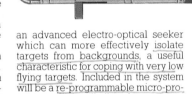

Tan-SAM is transported and launched from an unarmoured (6×6) truck and entered service with the Japanese Ground Self-Defense Force in 1982.

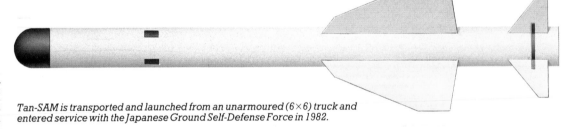

that the rocket emits a considerable amount of smoke, which could lead to the launcher being detected and subsequently destroyed. The missile has an HE warhead and an infra-red passive homing/inflight lock-on guidance system; and in the centre of the missile are four wings, the four control fins being located at the rear.

The launcher is mounted on the rear of the Type 73 truck and once the four missiles have been launched new missiles are loaded hydraulically, although they have to be unpacked from the transit cases by hand. The launcher is stabilized by hydraulically operated legs.

The fire-control system consists of a phased-array search radar and a fire-control computer plus three cathode-ray tubes (CRTs) on which target information is displayed. The radar antenna rotates 10 times per minute

and sweeps through 360° in azimuth and 15° in elevation. In the sector-search mode it sweeps 110° in azimuth and 20° in elevation. The radar, which has an IFF system, has a range of 30 km (18.6 miles) and can handle a number of targets at the same time. The fire-control system has a four-man crew consisting of the commander, radar operator and two launch operators. To the rear of the cab is a generator.

Once the vehicles have halted it takes about 30 minutes for the system to become operational as the two launch vehicles have to be connected with the FCS; the vehicles can be up to 1000 m (1,095 yards) apart. Once operational the radar starts to search for targets with information (range, altitude and bearings) displayed on the CRT. The target is then selected by the commander and tracked by the radar. When the target is within range a mis-

sile is launched. For the first part of its flight the missile flies under command of the autopilot, but then the infra-red seeker takes over and locks onto the target until it is destroyed. A Tan-SAM battery can handle up to four targets at once.

One of the major drawbacks of this system is the poor mobility of the Type 73 truck, the complete lack of any armour protection for the system and its crew, and the relatively low rate of fire.

Specification
Tan-SAM surface-to-air missile system
Dimensions: length 2.70 m (8 ft 10.3 in); diameter 16.0 cm (6.3 in); span 60.0 cm (23.6 in)
Launch weight: 100 kg (220 lb)
Performance: maximum ceiling (estimated) 3000 m (3,280 yards); maximum range (estimated) 7000 m (7,655 yards)

Modern Self-Propelled Anti-Aircraft Guns

A battery of ZSU-23-4 'Zhilka' self-propelled AA guns parades in Moscow. These hard hitting systems have been amongst the most effective battlefield weapons of the last twenty years.

The rise in tactical air power has added a new dimension to the modern battlefield. Aircraft can now deliver sophisticated, accurate weaponry in high-speed, low-level attacks, and defences have had to evolve to meet the threat. To most armies that means missile defences, but an important component in overall battlefield air defence is provided by gun systems.

To many people the term 'mechanized forces' means just tanks and armoured personnel carriers/mechanized infantry combat vehicles. While these are numerically the most important, without the support of engineers, self-propelled artillery, air-defence systems, army aviation and other supporting arms they cannot survive on the high-intensity battlefield of today. Armies approach the air-defence element of their forces in quite different fashions, some (the British, for example) relying only on surface-to-air missiles (SAMs), while others (the Americans, Soviets and West Germans, for example) have a mix of guns and missiles.

Guns and missiles are complementary, the missile taking care of the longer ranges and the guns providing close-in defence. The USSR has by far the most 'in-depth' array of air-defence weapons ever seen, and many of these have been used operationally in Africa, Middle East and the Far East in recent years. In addition close-in defence can be provided by man-portable missiles such as the SA-7 and Stinger, by machine-guns mounted on top of vehicles from tanks down to trucks, and even by the individual soldier firing a rifle or machine-gun into the air, the whole object of the exercise being to put as much fire into the air as possible. While the chances of an infantryman hitting a fast and low-flying aircraft are fairly remote, it does give him a sense of purpose in hitting back at the enemy.

Some of the self-propelled anti-aircraft gun systems described here are clear-weather systems only, while others can engage targets under a variety of weather conditions. In many parts of the world clear-weather systems are more than adequate to deal with the air threat, especially if potential enemies lack all-weather aircraft. Often the more complicated systems, although more effective, are not only more expensive to procure but difficult to operate and to maintain, especially in underdeveloped parts of the world.

On the alert for intruding aircraft, the six barrels of an American Vulcan 20-mm cannon nose hungrily skyward. Seen here on exercise in Korea, the Vulcan has been in service with the US Army since the late 1960s.

Chinese self-propelled AA guns

The Soviet Union supplied China with considerable amounts of military equipment in the 1950s and 1960s before the breaking-off of relations between the two countries. To meet its needs for a self-propelled anti-aircraft gun system China used the T-34 series tank chassis with its turret replaced by a new open-topped turret armed with twin 37-mm anti-aircraft guns; this gun was already in service with the Chinese army, mounted on a four-wheeled carriage. The chassis of the **Type 63** is identical to that of the tank with the driver at the front left and bow machine-gunner to his right, though it is probable that the bow machine-gun was removed. The turret is in the centre of the hull with the engine and transmission at the rear. The Christie-type suspension has five dual rubber-tyred road wheels, with drive sprocket at the rear and idler at the front.

The twin 37-mm cannon are recoil-operated and have a cyclic rate of fire of 160 to 189 rounds per minute, but practical rate of fire per barrel is 80 rounds a minute. Weapon elevation and turret traverse are manual, which would be a major tactical drawback in the engagement of aircraft flying at low level and high speed. Only optical sights are fitted, with no provision at all for radar fire-control. The ammunition is fed to each weapon in clips of five rounds, some ready-use ammunition being stowed inside the turret with the bulk of the ammunition stowed externally in panniers on each side of the hull. Two basic types of ammunition are fired, FRAG-T (fragmentation tracer) being used against aerial targets and AP-T (armour-piercing tracer) being used against armoured targets such as light tanks. Both projectiles have a muzzle velocity of 880 m (2,887 ft) per second, and the AP-T round will penetrate 37 mm (1.46 in) of armour at a range of 1000 m (1,095 yards) or 46 mm (1.81 in) of armour at a range of 500 m (547 yards), penetration being better at shorter ranges because of the projectile's higher velocity. Effective anti-aircraft range is 3000 m (3,280 yards), although maximum vertical range is 6700 m (21,980 ft).

The **Type 80** self-propelled AA system is now in production as a replacement for the Type 63. It is a hybrid, mounting a copy of the Soviet ZSU-57-2 turret and armed with twin Type 59 cannon. These are copies of the Soviet

S-60, and have a combined cyclic rate of fire of up to 240 rounds per minute. The Type 80 has a fully enclosed five-man turret which is electro-mechanically driven. There is a basic fire-control computer, but lack of radar or optical devices make the Type 80 little more than a simple fair-weather system.

Specification
Type 80
Crew: 6
Weight: 31000 kg (68,342 lb)
Powerplant: V-12 diesel developing 580 hp (432 kW)
Dimensions: length with guns forward 8.42 m (27.62 ft); width with side skirts 3.307 m (10.85 ft); travelling height 2.748 m (9.02 ft)
Performance: maximum road speed 50 km/h (31 mph); maximum road range 440 km (273 miles); fording 1.4 m (4.6 ft); gradient 60 per cent; vertical obstacle 0.8 m (2.62 ft); trench 2.7 m (8.86 ft)

Specification
Type 63
Crew: 6
Weight: 32000 kg (70,547 lb)
Dimensions: length (guns forward) 6.432 m (21.1 ft); length (hull) 7.53 m 24.7 ft); height (turret top) 2.995 m

(9.83 ft)
Powerplant: one V-12 water-cooled diesel developing 500 hp (373 kW)
Performance: maximum road speed 55 km/h (34 mph); maximum range (road) 300 km (186 miles); gradient 60 per cent; vertical obstacle 0.73 m (2 ft 5 in); trench 2.5 m (8 ft 2 in)

The Type 63 is a weapon of limited capability. Mounted onto an unmodified T-34 tank hull, the open turret has no provision for radar fire control, and the optically sighted weapons are elevated and traversed manually.

This Type 63 was supplied to the Viet Cong, from whom it was captured by the US Forces during the Vietnam war.

BTR-152A twin 14.5-mm self-propelled AA gun

While the ZSU-57-2 twin 57-mm SPAAG was the first purpose-built weapon of its type to be introduced into the Soviet army in large numbers during the post-war period, the **BTR-152A** (6×6) and BTR-40A (4×4) entered service some years before. In both cases these were essentially armoured personnel carrier chassis with the normally-towed twin 14.5-mm (0.57-in) KPV heavy machine-guns turret-mounted in the troop compartment at hull rear. The turret is designated the ZPTU-2 and can be traversed through 360°, the weapons being able to elevate −5° to +80°. The KPV machine-gun is also fitted in a number of Soviet armoured vehicles including the BRDM-2 (4×4) amphibious scout car and the BTR-60PB and BTR-70

(8×8) armoured personnel carriers. It was also installed as the co-axial and anti-aircraft weapon of the T-10M heavy tank, which is no longer in front-line service with the Soviet Union. There are also three versions of the towed KPV heavy anti-aircraft machine-gun: the ZPU-1 (single), ZPU-2 (twin) and ZPU-4 (quadruple). In the Warsaw Pact most of the towed ZPUs have been replaced by the 23-mm ZU-23 anti-aircraft gun, and the BTR-152A and BTR-40A each remain in front line service only outside the Soviet Union.

The KPV heavy machine-gun has a

The BTR-152A has been used operationally in Vietnam and the Middle East in both AA and fire support roles.

cyclic rate of fire of 600 round per minute per barrel, but its practical rate of fire is 150 rounds per minute per barrel. The method of operation is gas-assisted short recoil. The barrel is air-cooled, is fitted with a flash eliminator and a handle for carrying out quick changes, and is chromium-plated internally to reduce barrel wear. Two types of ammunition, API and HEI-T, are fired. The armour piercing incendiary round is used mainly against armoured vehicles and will penetrate 32 mm (1.29 in) of armour at a range of 500 m (547 yards). The high explosive

incendiary-tracer (HEI-T) round is used against aircraft. Only optical sights are fitted, there being no provision for radar fire-control. This limits the system's capability to clear-weather operations only. The lack of power traverse and elevation also limits the system's capability to engage fast-moving targets at low level.

In addition to being used in its originally-designed anti-aircraft role in the Middle East and Vietnam, the system has also been used in the ground fire-support role, in which its high rate of fire has proved most useful. During the

fighting in the Lebanon in the summer of 1982 the Israeli army captured a number of BTR-152 APCs with the more effective twin 23-mm ZU-23 cannon mounted in the rear, but as far as is known this was a local modification.

One of the more interesting local modifications carried out by Egypt on the BTR-152 was the installation of the Czech quadruple 12.7-mm (0.5-in) M53 machine-gun mounting in the rear of the vehicle. The weapons have a lower cyclic rate of fire than the KPV and also a shorter effective range.

Specification
BTR-152A
Crew: 4
Weight: 9600 kg (21,164 lb)
Dimensions: length 6.83 m (22 ft 5 in); width 2.32 m (7 ft 7 in); height (overall) 2.80 m (9 ft 2 in)
Powerplant: one ZIL-123 6-cylinder petrol engine developing 110 hp (82 kW)
Performance: maximum road speed 65 km/h (40 mph); maximum range 780 km (485 miles); gradient 55 per cent; vertical obstacle 0.60 m (2 ft); trench 0.69 m (2 ft 3 in)

USSR
ZSU-57-2 twin 57-mm self-propelled AA gun

The **ZSU-57-2** was the first post-war Soviet self-propelled anti-aircraft gun to be introduced on a large scale and was first seen in public during November 1957. The chassis of the ZSU-57-2 is essentially a lightened version of the

The first purpose-built self-propelled AA gun to be introduced into the Soviet inventory, the ZSU-57-2 is in wide use with Soviet-supplied forces, although no longer in front-line Soviet use.

T-54 MBT with thinner armour protection and one road wheel less on each side, though the length of track on the ground remains identical. The guns fire the same ammunition and have the same performance as the widely used towed 57-mm S-60 anti-aircraft gun. In the ZSU-57-2 designation ZSU means that the equipment is a self-propelled anti-aircraft gun system, 57 is for the calibre of the weapons (57-mm) and 2 is for the number of guns. The system was widely deployed by the Soviet Union but has now been replaced in all front line units by the ZSU-23-4 self-propelled anti-aircraft gun system. It is still used by Algeria, Angola, Bulgaria, Cuba, East Germany, Egypt, Ethiopia, Finland, Hungary, Iran, Iraq, North Korea, Poland, Romania, Syria and Yugoslavia. In 1982 the Syrian army made extensive use of the ZSU-57-2 in the ground-support role during fighting in the Lebanon.

The chassis is of all-welded steel construction, with the driver at the front left, the other five crew members in the open-topped turret in the centre of the hull, and the engine and transmission at the rear. Suspension is of the torsion-bar type with the drive sprocket at the rear and the idler at the front; there are four road wheels but no track-return rollers. As the ZSU-57-2 is lighter than the T-54 tank on which it is based it has a higher power-to-weight ratio of 18.56 hp/tonne and a lower ground pressure. To extend its operating range to 595 km (370 miles), long-range fuel tanks can be fitted to the rear of the hull.

The twin 57-mm cannon are power-operated from −5° to +85° at 20° per second, with turret traverse through 360° at a speed of 30° per second; manual controls are provided for emergency use.

Each gun has a cyclic rate of fire of 105 to 120 rounds per minute, though the practical rate of fire is 70 rounds per minute. Ammunition is fed to each weapon in clips of four rounds, the empty cartridge cases and clips being deposited onto a conveyor belt under the weapon. This runs to the turret rear and drops the empty cartridge cases and clips into the large wire basket mounted externally at the turret rear.

The following types of fixed ammunition can be fired: FRAG-T (fragmentation-tracer) and APC-T (armour piercing capped-tracer). The former is used mainly against aerial targets while the latter, which will penetrate 96 mm (3.7 in) of armour at a range of 1000 m (1,094 yards), is used against ground targets such as tanks and APCs. Effective anti-aircraft range is 4000 m (4,375 yards) with maximum vertical range 8800 m (28,870 ft). Maximum horizontal range is 12000 m (13,125 yards), although fire control would be a major problem at such long ranges.

Specification
ZSU-57-2
Crew: 6
Weight: 28100 kg (61,949 lb)
Dimensions: length 8.48 m (27 ft 10 in); length (hull) 6.22 m (20 ft 5 in); width 3.27 m (10 ft 9 in); height 2.75 m (9 ft)

Powerplant: one Model V-54 V-12 diesel developing 520 hp (388 kW)
Performance: maximum road speed 50 km/h (31 mph); maximum range 420 km (260 miles); gradient 60 per cent; vertical obstacle 0.80 m (2 ft 7 in); trench 2.70 m (8 ft 10 in)

In the ground support role the ZSU-57-2 (as used by Syria in Lebanon) has proved extremely potent.

ZSU-23-4 quadruple 23-mm self-propelled AA gun

The **ZSU-23-4** was developed in the 1960s as the replacement for the 57-mm ZSU-57-2 self-propelled anti-aircraft gun system. Although the ZSU-23-4's 23-mm cannon has a shorter range than the earlier weapon, the system is much more effective as it has a radar fire-control system and a much higher rate of fire. Since being introduced into the Soviet army on a large scale it has also been exported to almost every country that has received Soviet military equipment, including Afghanistan, Algeria, Angola, Bulgaria, Cuba, Czechoslovakia, East Germany, Egypt, Ethiopia, Hungary, India, Iran, Iraq, Jordan, Libya, Mozambique, Nigeria, North Korea, North Yemen, Peru, Poland, Romania, Somalia, South Yemen, Syria, Vietnam and Yugoslavia. In addition to seeing extensive action during the conflict in Vietnam, the ZSU-23-4 also proved to be one of the most effective systems during the 1973 Middle East war: Soviet-supplied missiles such as the SA-6 'Gainful' forced Israeli aircraft to fly at low altitude, where they encountered the ZSU-23-4 and the SA-7 man-portable missiles. In the Soviet army, who call the system the Shilka, the ZSU-23-4 is issued on the scale of 16 systems per division and normally operates in pairs.

The chassis of the ZSU-23-4 is very similar to that of the SA-6 'Gainful' SAM system, and uses automotive components of the PT-76 amphibious light tank family. It is of all-welded steel construction with a maximum thickness of 15 mm (0.6 in) at the front and 10 mm (0.4 in) over the remainder of the vehicle including the turret, and this provides protection only against small arms fire and shell splinters. The driver is seated at the front of the hull on the left, with the turret in the centre, and engine and transmission at the rear. Suspension is of the torsion-bar type and consists of six single rubber-tyred road wheels with the drive sprocket at the rear and idler at the front. A gas turbine is installed in the rear to provide power for the turret and other systems while the main engine is not running.

The commander, search radar operator/gunner and rangefinding number are all seated in the large flat turret. Main armament consists of four AZP-23 23-mm gas-operated cannon with a cyclic rate of fire of 800 to 1000 rounds per minute per barrel. These weapons have an elevation of +85° and a depression of −4° in a turret

Seeing extensive operational use in Vietnam and the Middle East, the ZSU-23-4 (called 'Shilka' in Soviet service) proved one of the most effective air defence weapons of the 1970s. The four-barrelled weapon can provide radar-directed fire in bursts of up to 50 rounds at a time.

capable of traversing through 360°. Turret traverse and weapon elevation are powered, manual controls being provided for emergency use. The gunner can select 3/5-, 5/10- or 50-round bursts, and the cannon have an effective anti-aircraft range of 2500 m (2,735 yards) and a similar range in the ground-target role. Each cannon is provided with 500 rounds of ready-use ammunition; the two types normally fired are API-T (armoured-piercing incendiary-tracer) and HEI-T (high explosive incendiary-tracer). The ZSU-23-4 is fitted with a fire-control system that includes a radar scanner mounted on the turret rear, sights and a fire-control computer. Targets can be engaged while the vehicle is travelling across country, but where possible the ZSU-23-4 would stop to provide a more stable firing platform.

Specification
ZSU-23-4
Crew: 4
Weight: 19000 kg (41,888 lb)
Dimensions: length 6.54 m (21 ft 5 in); width 2.95 m (9 ft 8 in); height (without radar) 2.25 m (7 ft 4 in)
Powerplant: one V-6R diesel developing 280 hp (210 kW)
Performance: maximum road speed 44 km/h (27 mph); maximum road range 260 km (162 miles); gradient 60 per cent; vertical obstacle 1.10 m (3 ft 7 in); trench 2.80 m (9 ft 2 in)

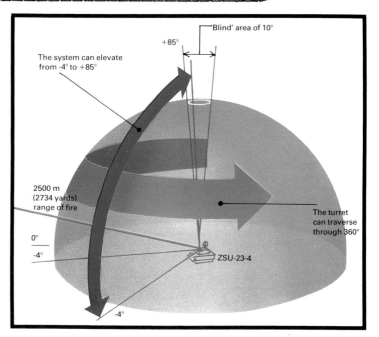

'Blind' area of 10°
The system can elevate from -4° to +85°
+85°
2500 m (2734 yards) range of fire
0°
-4°
The turret can traverse through 360°
ZSU-23-4
-4°

The ZSU-23-4 can throw up a wall of impenetrable fire covering a hemisphere of 2500 m (2,734 yards) around itself. Its radar can pick up targets 20 km (12 miles) out, and its computer automatically bears the guns onto the hapless intruder. Able to quickly traverse through 360° and elevate from −4° to +85°, the system can kill anything that enters its zone.

ZSU-23-4s are seen in Egyptian service prior to the 1973 war with Israel. In combination with the SA-6 'Gainful' missile system, the guns wrought havoc for a time amongst Israeli ground attack aircraft.

Soviet 'Shilkas' on the move, with armament and radar systems at the ready. The Soviet army normally operates the weapons in pairs, with some 16 systems being the normal complement per division.

M42 twin 40-mm self-propelled AA gun

Based on the M41 light tank, the M42 was first produced in 1951. Essentially a clear-weather weapon, being optically sighted, the open M42 turret offers little protection to the crew. It still equips units of the National Guard.

During the latter half of World War II the United States developed a series of tracked vehicles (the Light Combat Team) which included the M24 Chaffee light tank, M37 105-mm (4.13-in) howitzer motor carriage, M41 155-mm (6.1-in) howitzer motor carriage and M19 twin 40-mm self-propelled anti-aircraft gun system. After the end of the war a new family of light vehicles was developed, this including a light tank called the M41 (or Walker Bulldog) while the anti-aircraft gun system, which had the same automotive components but a different hull, was called the **M42**, or more commonly the **Duster**. The turret of the M42 is the same as that of the earlier M19, though in the former it is mounted in the centre of the hull and in the latter at the rear of the hull. The M42, whose development designation was **T141**, was in production from 1951 to 1956 and about 3,700 equipments were built, the majority by the Cadillac Motor Car Division of the General Motors Corporation at the Cleveland Tank Plant. Late production equipments were called the **M42A1**, the major difference being the fuel injection system for the engine. One of the main drawbacks of the M42, along with other members of this family, was its use of a petrol engine, which resulted in a very short operating range. Today the M42 is still used by the US Army National Guard (eight battalions), as well as by Austria, Greece, Japan, Jordan, Lebanon, Saudi Arabia, Taiwan, Thailand, Turkey and Venezuela. It was used successfully in Vietnam by both the US and South Vietnamese armies, although its primary role was in the ground-support fire role rather than the air-defence role for which it was originally designed.

The hull and turret of the M42 are of all-welded steel construction, with the commander and driver seated in the front of the vehicle, turret with other four crew members located in the centre, and the engine and transmission installed at the rear. Suspension is of the well-tried torsion-bar type, and consists of five dual rubber-tyred road wheels, with the drive sprocket at the rear and idler at the front; there are three track-return rollers.

Right: M42A1 vehicles wait on the range firing line at Dina Beach in the Panama Canal Zone. By 1967, when the photograph was taken, the Dusters were nearing the end of their front-line service, although still being used operationally in Vietnam.

The turret and weapons are power-operated; the turret can be traversed through 360° at 40° per second, and the guns can be elevated from −3° to +85° at a speed of 25° per second. Manual controls are provided for emergency use. A total of 480 rounds of ammunition is carried, and the guns have a practical rate of fire of 120 rounds per minute per barrel with an effective anti-aircraft range of 5000 m (5,470 yards). The gunner can select single shots or full automatic fire, and four types of ammunition carried are AP-T, HE-T, HEI-T and TP-T. A 7.62-mm (0.3-in) M60 or M1919A4 machine-gun is mounted externally on left rear of turret for local defence, and 1,750 rounds of ammunition are carried for this weapon.

The M42 is essentially a clear-weather weapon as its fire-control system consists of an M38 computing sight, M24c reflex sight and a speed ring sight. Efforts were made to fit a radar fire-control system, but this idea was eventually dropped.

Specification
M42
Crew: 6
Weight: 22452 kg (49,497 lb)
Dimensions: length (guns forward) 6.356 m (20 ft 10 in); length (hull) 5.819 m (19 ft 1 in); width 3.225 m (10 ft 7 in); height 2.847 m (9 ft 4 in)
Powerplant: one Continental AOS-895-3 6-cylinder air-cooled petrol engine developing 500 bhp (373 kW)
Performance: maximum road speed 72.4 km/h (45 mph); maximum range 161 km (100 miles); gradient 60 per cent; vertical obstacle 0.711 m (2 ft 4 in); trench 1.829 m (6 ft)

M163 Vulcan 20-mm self-propelled AA gun

In the early 1960s Rock Island Arsenal developed two 20-mm Vulcan air-defence systems. The self-propelled model was based on a modified M113 APC chassis and was designated the **XM163** (the chassis being the XM741) while the towed model was the XM167. These were subsequently accepted for service as the **M163** and **M167** respectively. The former was produced by the General Electric Company of Burlington, Vermont, and was soon deployed to South Vietnam where it was widely used in the ground fire-support role. In the US Army the M163 is deployed in composite battalions, each of which has two batteries each with 12 Chaparral SAM launchers and two batteries each with 12 M163s. The towed M167 is used mainly by the air-mobile and air-assault divisions. In addition to the United States, the M163 is also used by Ecuador, Portugal, Israel, Morocco, North Yemen, South Korea and Tunisia. In the regular US Army the M163 was to be replaced by the ill-fated DI-

VAD (Sergeant York) 40-mm gun system, but with the cancellation of that programme the Vulcan will have to soldier on into the 1990s.

The M163 consists of a standard M113 chassis on top of which has been mounted an electrically-operated turret fitted with a 20-mm six-barrelled M61 series cannon, a US Navy Mk 20 lead-computing sight, and an EMTECH range-only radar located on the right side of the turret. The turret can be traversed through 360° at a speed of 60° per second and the gun elevated from −5° to +80° at 45° per second. Manual controls are provided in case of power failure. The 20-mm cannon, which is a development of the weapon originally designed for the Lockheed F-104 Starfighter in the

Standard anti-aircraft gun in US Army service, the Vulcan is available in tracked self-propelled (M163) and wheeled towed (M167) forms.

M163 Vulcan 20-mm self-propelled AA gun (continued)

1950s and still fitted in aircraft such as the General Dynamics F-16, has two rates of fire in this application, 1,000 and 3,000 rounds per minute. The former is normally used for engagement of ground targets, while the higher rate of fire is used against aerial targets. The gunner can select 10-, 30-, 60- or 100-round bursts, and 1,100 rounds of ready-use ammunition are carried, with a further 1,000 rounds in reserve. Ammunition types that can be fired include APT (armour piercing tracer), TP (target practice), HEI (high explosive incendiary), TPT (target practice tracer) and HEI-T (high explosive incendiary-tracer). All have a muzzle velocity of 1030 m (3,380 ft) per second. Maximum effective range in the anti-aircraft role is 1600 m (1,750 yards) and in the ground role 3000 m (3,280 yards). A typical target engagement is described in the entry for the Vulcan Commando air-defence system, which has been developed specifically for the export market.

PIVADS or the **Product Improved Vulcan Air Defence System** has a stabilized 'director' sight, improved electronics making use of digitalized microprocessors, computerized fire control and much improved servos and turret drives. A private venture by Lockheed electronics, PIVADS has been ordered by the US Army as the **M163A2** and the **M167A2**

Specification
M163
Crew: 4
Weight: 12310 kg (27,139 lb)
Dimensions: length 4.86 m (15 ft 11 in); width 2.85 m (9 ft 4 in); height (overall) 2.736 m (8 ft 11 in); height (hull top) 1.83 m (6 ft 0 in)

Powerplant: one Detroit Diesel 6V-53 6-cylinder diesel developing 215 bhp (160 kW)
Performance: maximum road speed 67 km/h (42 mph); maximum range 483 km (300 miles); gradient 60 per cent; vertical obstacle 0.61 m (2 ft 0 in); trench 1.68 m (5 ft 6 in)

Above: The M163 consists of a 20-mm Gatling-type cannon mounted upon an M113 APC chassis.

Below: The gunner can select rates of fire of 1,000 or 3,000 rounds per minute for use with ground or airborne targets, and he can select bursts of 10, 30, 60 or 100 rounds.

Commando Vulcan 20-mm self-propelled AA gun

USA

While the M163 self-propelled Vulcan air-defence system on the standard M113 chassis satisfied the needs of the US Army, it did not meet the requirements of the Saudi Arabian National Guard (SANG) which operates a huge fleet of Cadillac Gage V-150 (4×4) armoured cars in a variety of versions. As it would create logistical, operational and training problems to integrate a tracked vehicle into a wheeled armoured battalion, General Electric and Cadillac Gage developed a special version of the V-150 to meet the SANG requirements and this **Commando Vulcan** system is now in service. It consists of a standard V-150 (4×4) chassis fitted with the same turret, weapon and associated controls as the M163, which makes training and the provision of spares an easy matter. The vehicle has a four-man crew consisting of the commander, gunner, radio operator and driver. The chassis has been fitted with three hydraulic jacks, one at the front and one on each side of the hull at the rear, which can be lowered to the ground from within the safety of the vehicle to provide a more stable firing platform.

A typical target engagement of the Commando Vulcan or tracked M163 Vulcan air-defence system is as follows. The gunner first observes the target visually, or the system may be tied into a radar that alerts the gunner to the approximate heading and alti-

tude of the target. The gunner then acquires the target in his sight and starts to track the target using the Navy Mk 20 gyro lead-computering gunsight. The I-band pulse-Doppler radar mounted on the right side of the turret is servoed to the optical line of sight and provides target range and range rate data to the sight generator. With other information the sight automatically computes the future position of the target and then adds super-elevation required to hit the target. When the target is within range a green light appears in the sight optics, this informing the gunner not only that the radar has acquired the target and is performing its functions but also that the target is within the effective range of the 20-mm cannon, so avoiding the waste of valuable ammunition. When fitted with the Vulcan cannon the system retains its amphibious capability and is propelled in the water by its wheels at a speed of about 4.8 km/h (3 mph).

Another SPAAG developed specifically for the export market was the **Eagle** twin 35-mm system developed in the 1970s to meet the requirements of the Imperial Iranian army for a highly mobile anti-aircraft gun system that would defend strategic targets such as factories and oil installations. It basically consists of a modified M548 tracked carrier fitted with an unmanned twin-gun turret on the hull rear. This has 280

rounds of ready-use ammunition, and the guns each have a cyclic rate of fire of 575 rounds per minute. With the fall of the Shah of Iran the contract was cancelled, although the system is still being offered by ARES for export.

Specification
Crew: 4
Weight: 10206 kg (22,500 lb)
Dimensions: length 5.689 m (18 ft 8in); width 2.26 m (7 ft 5 in); height (overall) 3.302 m (10 ft 10 in)

The Commando Vulcan consists of an M163 gun, turret and fire control system mounted on a standard Cadillac Gage V-150 Commando armoured car chassis.

Powerplant: one Cummins V-8 diesel developing 202 bhp (150 kW)
Performance: maximum road speed 88.54 km/h (55 mph); maximum road range 640 km (400 miles); gradient 60 per cent; vertical obstacle 0.914 m (3 ft 0 in); trench not applicable

---

Panhard M3 VDA twin 20-mm self-propelled AA gun

FRANCE

The Panhard AML (4×4) light armoured car has been one of the most successful vehicles of its type designed since World War II. To operate with this vehicle Panhard also developed a 4×4 armoured personnel carrier that uses 95 per cent of the automotive components (for example the engine, transmission and suspension) of the original armoured car. This vehicle, called the M3, has also proved to be highly successful and since production started in the early 1970s over 1,500 have been built for export to more than 30 countries. The anti-aircraft member of the M3 family is the **M3 VDA** (Véhicule de Défense Antiaérienne) and entered production in 1975.

The VDA is a standard M3 APC on top of which has been mounted a turret with twin 20-mm anti-aircraft cannon. The turret itself was designed by Hispano-Suiza with Galileo of Italy providing the sight, Oerlikon the 20-mm cannon and Electronique Serge Dassault the radar; the last is the prime contractor for the turret before it is delivered to Panhard for installation on the chassis. The M3 VDA is known to be in service with the Ivory Coast, Niger and Abu Dhabi, and the turret can also be fitted without difficulty to other tracked and wheeled chassis such as the Renault VAB (6×6), Simbas (6×6), Panhard ERC (6×6) and Engesa EE-11 Urutu (6×6) wheeled vehicles, and on the Alvis Spartan, Steyr and, most recently, AMX-13 VCI full-tracked vehicles.

The M3 VDA has a crew of three with the commander at the front, gunner in the turret (in the centre of the hull) and the commander at the rear. The turret has full powered traverse through 360° at a speed of 60° per

second, with the guns capable of elevation from −5° to +85° at a speed of 90° per second. Mounted on the turret rear is a radar scanner that rotates at a speed of 40 rpm; this carries out both surveillance and tracking functions, and can track up to four targets, information being relayed to a screen at the commander's position. The gunner has a P56T sight with magnifications of ×5 and ×12 for engaging aerial targets, a ground sight and six periscopes for all-round observation. The 20-mm cannon are mounted externally, one on each side of the turret, the gunner having the option of selecting either or both cannon. The gunner can also select single shots, bursts or full automatic fire. Two cyclic rates of fire are available, 200 or 1,000 rounds per minute. The latter is used for the anti-aircraft role. Each cannon is provided with 300 rounds of ready-use ammunition, and additional ammunition can be carried in the hull. A 7.62-mm (0.3-in) machine-gun is normally fitted for local protection, and two electrically-operated smoke dischargers are mounted on each side of the turret firing forwards. To provide a steadier firing platform, four stabilizers are lowered to the ground hydraulically before the equipment starts firing, although in an emergency the guns can be fired at the lower cyclic rate of fire without the stabilizers in position.

Specification
M3 VDA
Crew: 3
Weight: 7200 kg (15,873 lb)
Dimensions: length 4.45 m (14 ft 7 in); width 2.40 m (7 ft 11 in); height (excluding radar) 2.995 m (9 ft 11 in)
Powerplant: one Panhard Model 4 HD 4-cylinder air-cooled petrol engine

Above: The M3 VDA is a version of the successful Panhard M3 APC, armed with twin Oerlikon 20-mm cannon.

Below: Four stabilizers are lowered automatically before firing, although the guns can be fired at a low cyclic rate without them.

developing 90 hp (67 kW)
Performance: maximum road speed 90 km/h (56 mph); maximum range 1000 km (621 miles); gradient 60 per

cent; vertical obstacle 0.30 m (12 in); trench 0.80 m (2 ft 7 in) with one channel or 3.10 m (10 ft 2 in) with four channels

AMX-13 DCA twin 30-mm self-propelled AA gun

In the 1950s prototypes of a number of self-propelled anti-aircraft gun systems were designed and built to meet the requirements of the French army, but was not until the late 1960s that one of these was considered sufficiently developed to enter production. This was designated **AMX-13 DCA** (Défense Contre Avions) and was essentially an AMX-13 chassis fitted with a cast steel turret mounted on the hull at the rear. Prime contractor for the turret was SAMM, with CGT (now Thomson-CSF) responsible for the radar and its associated electronics, and with Hispano-Suiza of Switzerland (now taken over by Oerlikon-Bührle) responsible for the weapons and ammunition. Sixty AMX-13 DCA equipments were built for the French army, with final deliveries in 1969. In 1987 the AMX-13 DCA remains the only self-propelled anti-aircraft gun system in service with the French army. More recently the French army was to have received the VADAR twin 20-mm system on a VAB wheeled chassis, but this was cancelled on economy grounds several years ago.

Main armament of the AMX-13 DCA consists of twin HSS-831A 30-mm cannon with an elevation of +85° and a depression of −5° in a turret capable of traversing through 360°. Maximum rate of powered elevation is 45° per second, and of powered traverse 80° per second. Each cannon has 300 rounds of ready-use ammunition and the gunner can select single shots, 5- or 15-round bursts, or full automatic fire. The empty cartridge cases are ejected from the turret together with the links. In the anti-aircraft role the weapons have a maximum effective range of 3500 m (3828 yards), and also possess a very useful secondary capability against ground targets.

Mounted at the turret rear is the Oeil Noir 1 (black eye 1) radar scanner, which can be retracted into the turret bustle when not required. Although the cannon are normally aimed with the radar system and the anti-aircraft sights, sights are also provided for the engagement of ground targets. Mounted on each side of the turret is a bank of three electrically-operated smoke dischargers.

In the 1960s this DCA turret was also fitted to the chassis of the AMX-30 MBT, but the combination was not adopted by the French army as it was already ordering the Roland SAM system on the AMX-30 chassis. To provide close-in defence to its Thomson-CSF/MATRA Shahine mobile surface-to-air missile systems, Saudi Arabia ordered 53 examples of a more up-to-date version of this turret on the AMX-30 chassis, and by 1984 all of these equipments had been delivered. This is called the **AMX-30 SA**, and its turret is fitted with the more powerful Thomson-CSF Oeil Vert (green eye) radar as well as improved electronics. Thomson-CSF has also developed with SAMM the SABRE turret, which has for trials purposes already been installed on a number of other chassis such as the Chieftain MBT, Marder MICV and Steyr-Daimler-Puch APC. This also has twin 30-mm cannon but a different fire-control system.

Specification
AMX-13 DCA
Crew: 3
Weight: 17200 kg (37,919 lb)

Entering service with the French army in 1969, the AMX-13 DCA comprises a twin 30-mm Hispano (now Oerlikon) gun system mounted on an AMX-13 chassis with an Oeil Noir 1 (black eye 1) radar scanner mounted at the rear of the turret. A total of 60 AMX-13 DCAs were delivered to the French army.

Dimensions: length 5.40 m (17 ft 9 in); width 2.50 m (8 ft 2 in); height (radar up) 3.80 m (12 ft 6 in); height (radar down) 3.00 m (9 ft 10 in)
Powerplant: one SOFAM Model 8Gxb 8-cylinder water-cooled petrol engine developing 250 hp (186 kW)
Performance: maximum road speed 60 km/h (37 mph); maximum range 300 km (186 miles); gradient 60 per cent; vertical obstacle 0.65 m (2 ft 2 in); trench 1.70 m (5 ft 7 in)

Below: Pursuing a line of development from the original DCA turret through the Saudi AMX-30 SA and the Dragon, Thomson-CSF have developed the SABRE. The twin 30-mm system has been mounted for trials purposes onto a Steyr APC, but has also been tested on the Chieftain MBT and the Marder.

Above: As a private venture, the DCA turret was mounted onto an AMX-30 MBT chassis, but found no buyers. A version with an improved turret was sold to Saudi Arabia, and by 1984 the last of 53 examples ordered had been delivered.

Dragon twin 30-mm self-propelled AA gun

Given the ever increasing cost of defence equipment, there has been an increasing trend since the 1960s, especially in Europe, for the co-operative development of weapon systems. For example, the 155-mm (6.1-in) FH-70 howitzer has been developed by West Germany, Italy and the United Kingdom, with production undertaken in all three countries. Private-venture development has also taken place along similar lines as in the case of the **Dragon** twin 30-mm SPAAG. The chassis has been developed by Thyssen-Henschel while the turret and its associated fire-control system have been developed by the Electronics Systems Division of Thomson-CSF. The chassis is similar to that of the Marder MICV and TAM medium tank, and is of all-welded steel construction which provides the crew with protection from small arms fire and shell splinters. The driver is seated at the front left with the engine to his right, the turret is in the centre and the reserve ammunition supply is at the rear of the hull. The Dragon retains the power-operated ramp in the hull rear allowing quick access to the reserve ammunition supply. The torsion-bar suspension consists of six dual rubber-tyred road wheels, with the drive sprocket at the front, and the idler at the rear; there are three track-return rollers. The upper part of the track is covered by a rubber skirt that helps to keep the dust down. Like the TAM tank, the Dragon can be fitted with additional fuel tanks at the rear of the hull to increase operating range from 600 km (373 miles) to 1000 km (621 miles).

The all-welded steel turret is in the centre of the hull, with the commander seated on the left and the gunner on the right. Mounted at the rear of the turret is the Oeil Vert (green eye) radar that carries out both tracking and surveillance functions; when not re-

quired the radar can be retracted into the turret bustle. Both the commander and gunner are provided with a sight for engaging ground targets, as well as periscopes for observation purposes.

The turret has full powered traverse through 360° at a speed of 35° per second, and the twin 30-mm cannon can be elevated from −8° to +85° at a speed of 30° per second. Turret traverse and weapon elevation are hydraulic, with manual controls for emergency use. The gunner can select bursts of one to five rounds, or a burst of 15 rounds. The weapons have a maximum effective range of 3000 m (3,280 yards), and can also be used against ground targets. In the latter role SAPHEI (semi-armour-piercing

high explosive incendiary) ammunition would be used to penetrate the thin armour of APCs before exploding inside the vehicle.

The Dragon SPAAG has yet to enter production and has been developed specifically for the export market. Further development of the turret by Thomson-CSF has resulted in the SABRE turret which has already been fitted for trials purposes onto the British Chieftain MBT and Austrian Steyr APC chassis; it is also being proposed for the French AMX-10RC (6×6) armoured car.

Specification
Dragon
Crew: 3

Mounted on a Marder-type chassis, the new Dragon system is equipped with the Oeil Vert (green eye) radar used on the Saudi AMX-30.

Weight: 31000 kg (68,342 lb)
Dimensions: length 6.775 m (22 ft 3 in); width 3.12 m (10 ft 3 in); height (radar up) 4.195 m (13 ft 11 in)
Powerplant: one MTU 6-cylinder supercharged diesel developing 720 hp (536 kW)
Performance: maximum road speed 72 km/h (45 mph); maximum range 600 km (373 miles); gradient 65 per cent; vertical obstacle 1.00 m (3 ft 3 in); trench 2.50 m (8 ft 2 in)

Gepard twin 35-mm self-propelled AA gun

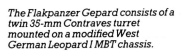

When the West German army was formed in the 1950s it was supplied with some 500 M42 twin 40-mm self-propelled anti-aircraft gun systems by the United States. The M42 had quite a good range but lacked any kind of onboard fire-control system. From the late 1960s various projects were initiated for the development of a new SPAAG, but these all came to nothing. In 1966 contracts were issued for the development of a SPAAG based on the chassis of the Leopard 1 MBT which had recently entered production for the West Germany army, and after the completion of systems with twin 30-mm and twin 35-mm cannon the latter was selected for full-scale development. The prime contractor for the twin 35-mm system was Contraves of Switzerland and after the construction of additional prototypes this system was selected for service with the West German army as the **Flakpanzer Gepard**. The first production vehicle was completed in 1976 and

The Flakpanzer Gepard consists of a twin 35-mm Contraves turret mounted on a modified West German Leopard I MBT chassis.

final deliveries were made in 1970. Some 420 Gepards were built for the West German army, 55 for the Belgian army and 95 for the Dutch army. The last differed from the Belgian and West German vehicles in that the turret was fitted with a Dutch Hollandse Signaalapparaten surveillance and tracking radar with moving-target indication and other minor differences. The turret can also be installed on other chassis such as the Swiss Pz 68 MBT and Italian OTO Melara OF-40, and more recently Saudi Arabia has expressed an interest in acquiring up to 100 of a modernized version of this turret fitted to the chassis of the Leopard 2 MBT.

The chassis of the Gepard is similar to that of the Leopard 1 but with thinner armour protection for the hull. The driver is at the front of the hull on the right, with the auxiliary power unit to his left; the turret is in the centre; and the engine and transmission are at the rear. Suspension is of the torsion-bar type, and consists of seven dual rubber-tyred road wheels, with the idler at front and the drive sprocket at the rear; there are two track-return rollers. The search radar is mounted at the turret rear and can be folded down if required, while the tracking radar is on the front of the turret. Mounted externally on each side of the turret is a 35-mm Oerlikon KDA cannon with a cyclic rate of fire of 550 rounds per minute. This weapon is provided with 310 rounds of ready-use anti-aircraft ammunition and 20 rounds of APDS-T (armour piercing discarding sabot-tracer) for the engagement of ground

targets. In addition to the APDS-T ammunition, HEI (high explosive incendiary), HEI-T (high explosive incendiary-tracer), practice and SAPHEI-T (semi-armour-piercing high explosive incendiary tracer) ammunition is available. In addition to the tracking and surveillance radars the Gepard has a comprehensive fire-control system, onboard land navigation system, sights for engaging both aerial and ground targets, and an NBC system. Some of the West German Gepards have been fitted with a Sie-

mens laser rangefinder.

Specification
Gepard
Crew: 3
Weight: 47300 kg (104,278 lb)
Dimensions: length (guns forward) 7.73 m (25 ft 4 in); length (hull) 6.85 m (22 ft 6 in); width 3.37 m (11 ft 1 in); height (radar elevated) 4.03 m (13 ft 3 in); height (periscopes) 3.01 m (9 ft 11 in)
Powerplant: one MTU MB 838 Ca M500 V-10 diesel developing 830 hp

Gepard is equipped with both tracking and surveillance radars, and onboard equipment includes computerized fire control and navigation equipment and an NBC system.

(619 kW)
Performance: maximum road speed 65 km/h (40 mph); maximum road range 550 km (342 miles); gradient 60 per cent; vertical obstacle 1.15 m (3 ft 9 in); trench 3.00 m (9 ft 10 in)

Wildcat twin 35-mm self-propelled AA gun

Krauss-Maffei of Munich built all of the Gepard twin 35-mm self-propelled anti-aircraft guns on a modified Leopard 1 chassis delivered to the Belgian, West German and Dutch armies. The company realized, however, that although this was a highly effective system for European armies it was too heavy, complicated and expensive for many countries overseas. With this in mind a decision was made to develop a complete family of self-propelled anti-aircraft gun systems that would be able to meet the requirements of almost every customer. Given Krauss-Maffei's experience with the Transportpanzer 1 (6×6) cross-country vehicle, already in production for the West German army, a decision was taken to use automotive components of this vehicle in a new hull which could be fitted with a turret armed with twin 30-mm cannon. Five different fire-control options are available, these ranging from the **V1** clear-weather system with optical tracking to the **V3** with radar target-detection and automatic target-tracking, up to the **V5** with an all-weather fire-control system and automatic target-tracking, The first prototype was the **V3**, with optical periscope and a search radar together with a TV-tracker/laser rangefinder and automatic target tracking. The second turret was completed to **V4** standard, and has been installed on a MOWAG Shark 8×8 chassis. This has a FLIR/laser rangefinder in place of the TV tracker giving adverse weather and day/night capability.

The basic layout of the **Wildcat**, as the system is designated, is the same in all versions, with the driver and radio operator/gunner in the front, turret in the centre, and engine and transmission at the rear. The suspension consists of axles with coil springs and hydraulic shock absorbers to provide good cross-country ride. Steering is power-assisted on the front four wheels, and run-flat tyres can be fitted.

The turret is fitted with two externally-mounted 30-mm Mauser Mk 30-F cannon (one on each side), each with

250 rounds of ready-use ammunition. This cannon has a cyclic rate of fire of 800 rounds per minute and can fire three types of ammunition, namely APDS (armour-piercing discarding sabot), HEI (high explosive incendiary) and TP (target practice).

A typical target engagement could take place as follows. The radar operator/gunner monitors his radar scope on a constant basis, and once an aircraft has been spotted by the radar and appeared on his scope, the operator must then determine whether or not it is hostile. If the target is confirmed by IFF as hostile the periscope traverses onto the target's bearing and then searches for the target in elevation. The laser rangefinder then starts to feed information to the computer, whereupon the turret and guns are trained on the target, the cannon opening fire as soon as the target is in range. At the same time the computer is being

Wildcat is based on a 6 × 6 cross-country chassis mounting a turret with twin Mauser 30-mm cannon. Modular design gives five alternative fire control systems, ranging from clear weather to all-weather automatic.

updated with new information should a second burst be required to destroy the target. In addition to use in the anti-aircraft/anti-helicopter role with a range of about 3000 m (3,280 yards), the weapons can also be used to engage ground targets. A more recent concept, called the **V6**, is to replace the twin 30-mm cannon by short-range missiles such as the American General Dynamics Stinger or British Shorts Blowpipe/Javelin.

Specification
Wildcat
Crew: 3
Weight: 18500 kg (40,785 lb)
Dimensions: length 6.88 m (22 ft 7 in); width 2.98 m (9 ft 9 in); height (radar down) 2.74 m (9 ft 0 in)
Powerplant: one Mercedes-Benz turbocharged 8-cylinder diesel developing 320 hp (239 kW)
Performance: maximum road speed 80 km/h (50 mph); maximum range 600 km (373 km); gradient 60 per cent

Wildcat is designed as an alternative to the capable but extremely costly systems such as Gepard, and is available with a range of capabilities. The automotive components are derived from the Transportpanzer.

SWITZERLAND

GDF-DO3 twin 35-mm self-propelled AA gun

For many years the Swiss-based company Oerlikon-Bührle, with subsidiaries in Italy and the United Kingdom, has produced the world's largest range of towed anti-aircraft guns including the highly successful GDF series of 35-mm weapons, of which more than 1,500 have been manufactured. It also designed the armament and weapons used in the West German Gepard twin 35-mm anti-aircraft gun system. The company also realized that there was a requirement for a highly mobile twin 35-mm system to defend rear-area targets such as airports, command centres and factories, and that such a system would not need to be based on a MBT chassis as was the Gepard, The **GDF-DO3 Escorter 35** has been developed to fill that requirement. The mechanical component of the Escorter is based on the four-wheel drive, all-wheel steering HYKA cross country truck. This has very large tyres for maximum rough terrain mobility and has a notably small turning circle. In addition to rear area protection duties, the Escorter is being offered for protection of motorized combat units during deployment and for protection of units on the march. The GDF-CO3 was a tracked system using the same armament but based on a derivative of the widely used M548 Cargo Carrier but which did not reach the prototype stage. The Contraves (Italy) search radar has a maximum range of some 23 km (14 miles). For most applications a customer would probably order one vehicle fitted with the radar to every three without the radar, the former then supplying target information to the others.

All versions are fitted with a power-operated turret armed with twin 35-mm KDF cannon and 430 rounds of ready-use ammunition. Each cannon has a cyclic rate of fire of 600 rounds per minute. Effective range of the 35-mm cannon is about 3500 m (3,830 yards), and types of ammunition that can be fired include HEI (high explosive incendiary), HEI-T (high explosive incendiary-tracer), SAPHEI-T (semi-armour-piercing high explosive incendiary-tracer), APDS-T (armour-piercing discarding sabot-tracer) and

Above: *Developed for the task of defending rear area targets such as airports, factories, ports and command centres, the GDF-DO3 has twin 35-mm KDF cannon mounted on the HYKA cross-country truck chassis, and is equipped with laser rangefinder and a Contraves (Italy) search radar.*

practice. The APDS-T round is used against ground targets such as light tanks and armoured personnel carriers, and will penetrate 40 mm (1.6 in) of armour at an angle of 60° at a range of 1000 m (1,094 yards).

In both systems the crew compartment is at the front of the vehicle with the turret at the rear, and has a three-man crew consisting of vehicle commander, gunner and driver.

Specification
Crew: 3
Combat weight: 24,000 kg (52,910 lb)
Dimensions: length 8.745 m (28 ft 8.4 in); width 2.98 m (9 ft 9.3 in); height (with radar up) 3.934 m (12 ft 10.8 in)
Powerplant: diesel developing 450 hp (335 kW)
Performance: maximum road speed 120 km/h (75 mph); road range 600 km (373 miles); fording 1 m (3 ft 3 in)

The GDF-DO3 is much more mobile than comparable tracked systems, and much less expensive to operate.

Development has now been completed, and the Escorter awaits production.

M53/59 twin 30-mm self-propelled AA gun

Dating from the 1950s, the M53/59 is a clear weather system. Four of the crew sit in the armoured cab, with the twin 30-mm mount operating hydraulically. No infra-red night vision lights are carried, nor is there any NBC protection.

It is widely believed that the Soviet Union forces its Warsaw Pact countries either to purchase Soviet equipment or manufacture it under licence. In fact some of the Warsaw Pact countries have their own flourishing defence industries, one such being Czechoslovakia, which has recently developed a 152-mm (6-in) self-propelled gun on an 8×8 Tatra truck chassis. In the 1950s Czechoslovakia developed and placed in production the **M53/59** twin 30-mm self-propelled anti-aircraft gun system, and this is known to be in service with Libya and Yugoslavia in addition to the Czech army itself. In some Czech units, however, the M53/59 has already been replaced by the ZSU-23-4 SPAAG which is a much more effective system.

The M53/59 was used by the Czech army in place of the Soviet ZSU-57-2 SPAAG, and consists essentially of the Praga V3S (6×6) 3-tonne truck chassis fitted with an armoured cab and a twin M53 30-mm anti-aircraft gun system at the rear.

The engine is at the front of the vehicle and provided with full armour protection from shell splinters and small arms fire. The cab is to the immediate rear of the engine, with the driver seated on the left and the commander on the right; the latter has a hemispherical Plexiglas cupola in the cab roof for all-round observation. Both crew members are provided with side door and vision slits while for their immediate front is a windscreen covered by an armoured shutter in combat. To the rear of the commander and driver are the two ammunition members, who sit facing the rear.

The twin 30-mm mount has hydraulic power traverse through 360°; the weapons elevate from −10° to +85°. Cyclic rate of fire is 450 to 500 rounds

per gun per minute, while the practical rate of fire (conditioned by ammunition resupply) is 150 rounds per minute per gun. The basic towed 30-mm M53 is fed with clips of 10 rounds whereas the M53/59 has a 50-round vertical magazine for each gas-operated cannon. It is estimated that between 600 and 800 rounds of 30-mm ammunition of two types (API and HEI) are carried. The API (armour-piercing incendiary) projectile will penetrate 55 mm (2.16 in) of armour at a range of 500 m (546 yards) and is used mainly against vehicles, while the HEI (high explosive incendiary) round is used against aerial targets. Both have a muzzle velocity of 1000 m (3,280 ft) per second. Effective anti-aircraft range of the system is estimated to be 3000 m (3,280 yards) and maximum vertical range is 6300 m (20,670 ft).

Apart from its obvious drawback of being a clear-weather anti-aircraft system, the M53/59 also lacks cross-country mobility when operating with

full-tracked vehicles such as tanks and armoured personnel carriers, and has neither NBC protection nor infra-red night-vision lights. An unusual feature of the M53/59 is that the complete mount can be removed from the chassis and placed on the ground.

Specification
M53/59
Crew: 6
Weight: 10300 kg (22,707 lb)
Dimensions: length 6.92 m (22 ft 8 in); width 2.35 m (7 ft 9 in); height (without magazines) 2.585 m (8 ft 6 in)

The age of the M53/59 is displayed by the lack of protection for the gunners, and its lack of cross-country mobility would hamper operations with tracked vehicles.

Powerplant: one Tatra T 912-2 6-cylinder diesel developing 110 hp (82 kW)
Performance: maximum road speed 60 km/h (37 mph); maximum range 500 km (311 miles); gradient 60 per cent; vertical obstacle 0.46 m (1 ft 6 in); trench 0.69 m (2 ft 3 in)

OTOMATIC 76-mm self-propelled AA gun

The **OTOMATIC 76-mm 76/62** self-propelled anti-aircraft/anti-helicopter system has been developed by OTO Melara of La Spezia as a private venture specifically for the export market. It consists basically of a modified OF-40 MBT chassis fitted with a new all-welded turret armed with a 76-mm (3-in) automatic gun that is a direct development of the naval weapon of the same calibre and used by many navies around the world and also manufactured in Japan, Spain and the USA. The unique feature of the OTOMATIC compared with the many other systems on the market today is that it is designed specifically to engage and destroy attack helicopters before they themselves can release their missiles at the tank. Most self-propelled anti-aircraft/helicopter systems are in the 30-mm to 40-mm cannon bracket and have a maximum effective range of between 3000 and 4000 m (3,280 and 4,375 yards), and can therefore just about engage attack helicopters before they launch their deadly missiles. New generations of air-launched missiles are now under advanced development or even entering service (an example is the American Hellfire) which have an even longer range as well as a fire-and-forget capability. Once these are in service in significant numbers the attack helicopter will be able to stand off and attack tank formations

without any danger of being destroyed by smaller-calibre self-propelled anti-aircraft gun systems.

The 76-mm (3-in) gun of the OTOMATIC is mounted in a turret with powered traverse, and the weapon has maximum elevation of +60° and a depression of −5°. Some 100 rounds of fixed ammunition are carried, of which 70 rounds are in the turret and the remaining 30 in the chassis; 25 of these rounds are in the automatic loading system for immediate use. For the engagement of aerial targets the weapon would fire high explosive or pre-formed fragmentation projectiles with either a point detonating or proximity fuse, while for the engagement of ground targets an APFSDS (armour-piercing discarding sabot) projectile is fired. According to the company, targets can be destroyed at a maximum range of at least 6000 m (6,560 yards), a six-round burst being considered sufficient for most targets. A comprehensive fire-control system is installed, and includes a search radar mounted on the rear of the turret and a tracking radar on the turret roof, both of which can be retracted if required. Mounted on each side of the turret is a bank of three electrically-operated smoke dischargers, while a 7.62-mm (0.3-in) machine-gun can be mounted on the turret roof for local protection. The first of two prototypes is now

being tested. Major sub-contractors are SMA, which is supplying the search and tracking radars, and Galileo, which is supplying the optronic and all-weather fire-control system.

Specification
OTOMATIC
Crew: 4
Weight: 46000 kg (101,411 lb)
Dimensions: length (gun forward) 9.635 m (31 ft 7 in); length (hull) 7.265 m (23 ft 10 in); width 3.35 m (11 ft 0 in); height (turret top) 3.152 m (10 ft 4 in)

A private venture by OTO-Melara, the OTOMATIC 76-mm self-propelled gun is designed to counter the threat of new-generation armoured helicopters with longer-ranged guided weapons.

Powerplant: one four-stroke supercharged diesel developing 1000 hp (746 kW)
Performance: maximum road speed 60 km/h (37 mph); maximum range (road) 500 km (311 miles); gradient 60 per cent; vertical obstacle 1.15 m (3 ft 9 in); trench 3.00 m (9 ft 10 in)

Modern Towed Anti-Aircraft Weapons

Cheaper, easier to maintain and more flexible than their self-propelled counterparts, towed anti-aircraft guns nonetheless employ sophisticated tracking and fire control systems, making them a serious threat to ground attack aircraft.

The Oerlikon 35-mm GDF system is used by over 20 countries. Recent operators include the RAF, which has formed a unit to use the Oerlikons captured in the Falklands. Argentine Oerlikons shot down four Harriers and at least two of their own aircraft during the conflict.

Since aircraft first appeared over the battlefield, anti-aircraft weapons have been developed and employed in an effort to stop them. During World War II a variety of anti-aircraft guns ranging in calibre from 12.7-mm machine-guns up to 120-mm guns were employed by the major powers in an effort to combat air attacks. By the end of the war bombers were flying higher and faster, and it was realized that anti-aircraft guns, even with proximity-fused ammunition and complex radar fire-control systems, were incapable of stopping them.

The major powers, namely the UK, USA and USSR, soon started to develop surface-to-air missiles such as the Bloodhound, Nike-Hercules and SA-2 'Guideline' which could successfully intercept aircraft flying very fast and very high. This forced the aircraft to adopt new tactics and fly very low to escape the surface-to-air missiles and radar systems.

Most countries today employ a mix of guns and missiles to defend their forward units. In the major powers these are normally self-propelled weapons such as the Soviet 23-mm ZSU-23-4 or the West German twin 35-mm Gepard. Many countries do, however, use towed anti-aircraft

guns on a large scale as these are not only much cheaper than their self-propelled counterparts but are easier to maintain and operate. In most cases, moreover, they can be rapidly transported by aircraft or helicopter to where they are most needed. Towed anti-aircraft guns are also widely used to defend static areas such as supply dumps, airfields and command centres. In these cases they are often integrated into an overall air-defence system.

The Middle East campaigns of 1973, the Vietnam conflict and more recently the Falklands campaign have proved that the light anti-aircraft gun is a real complement to missiles: not only has it a quicker reaction time in many situations, but it is also highly effective in the ground-to-ground role.

The Rheinmetall 20-mm anti-aircraft gun is fitted with the Italian Galileo P56 computing sight. The gunner uses a joystick to elevate and traverse the guns and an analogue computer calculates the lead angles necessary to hit the target aircraft.

20-mm FK 20-2 light anti-aircraft gun

The 20-mm **FK 20-2** light anti-aircraft gun mounting was developed to meet the rather special requirements of the Norwegian armed forces and certain units of the West German army. The Rheinmetall twin 20-mm light anti-aircraft gun is widely used by the West German army, but its weight of 2160 kg (4,762 lb) is too great to permit the type's use by airborne and mountain units. The FK 20-2 weighs only 620 kg (1,367 lb) in its travelling configuration and can be quickly disassembled to allow transport by pack animals.

Companies involved in the design and development of the FK 20-2 included A/S Kongsberg Vappenfabrikk of Norway, Rheinmetall of West Germany, Hispano-Suiza of Switzerland (since taken over by Oerlikon-Bührle) and Kern, the last responsible for the sight.

The FK 20-2 is fitted with the Rheinmetall 20-mm MK 20 Rh 202 cannon as installed in the twin 20-mm mount used by the West German army and air force. The gunner can fire either single shots or bursts, the cannon having a cyclic rate of fire of 1,000 rounds per minute. A total of 160 rounds of ready-use ammunition is provided; of these, 150 are normally anti-aircraft ammunition and the remaining 10 armour-piercing for the engagement of armoured vehicles. On each side of the cannon is a box of 75 rounds of ammunition (high explosive incendiary/HEI or high explosive incendiary-tracer/HEI-T), while above the cannon is a box of 10 rounds of armour-piercing discarding sabot-tracer (APDS-T). Traverse and elevation are manual via two hand wheels, which

The 20-mm FK 20-2 anti-aircraft gun is a joint development between Norway and West Germany and uses the same 20-mm MK 20 Rh 202

cannon as the twin 20-mm Rheinmetall system used by the West German army and air force.

have the optical sight mounted between them. The latter has a magnification of ×1.5 for engaging aerial targets and ×5 for engaging ground targets. The sight has two eyepieces: the upper one is used when the gunner is seated while the lower one is used when the gunner is engaging ground targets from the much safer prone position. To the front of the gunner is a small shield, but in peace this is often removed to save weight.

The system is normally mounted on a two-wheeled carriage that can be towed by any light 4×4 cross-country vehicle, which also carries the three-man crew and a supply of ready-use ammunition.

In the firing position the weapon is supported on three outriggers, one at

the rear and one on each side. The FK 20-2 is a clear-weather system only with no capability for radar control. Other anti-aircraft systems used by the Norwegian army include the American 12.7-mm (0.5-in) quadruple machine-gun, Bofors RBS-70 surface-to-air missile system and Bofors 40-mm L/60 and L/70 towed anti-aircraft guns.

The 20-mm Rheinmetall MK 20 Rh 202 cannon is also used by the Norwegian army, installed in a one-man Swedish turret mounted on M113 armoured personnel carriers.

Specification
FK 20-2
Calibre: 20 mm (0.79 in)
Weights: travelling 620 kg (1,367 lb); firing 440 kg (970 lb)

This 20-mm FK 20-2 anti-aircraft gun in the firing position clearly shows the two magazines, one each side of the barrel holding 75 rounds of ready-use ammunition. The gunner has a dual sight which enables him to track both aerial and ground targets easily.

Dimensions: length travelling 4.00 m (13 ft 1.5 in); width travelling 1.86 m (6 ft 1.2 in); height travelling 2.20 m (7 ft 2.6 in)
Elevation: +83°/−8°
Traverse: 360°
Ranges: maximum horizontal 6000 m (6,562 yards); maximum vertical 4500 m (14,764 ft); effective vertical 2000 m (6,562 ft)
Crew: 3 (1 on mount)

Breda 30-mm and 40-mm anti-aircraft guns

For many years the Breda company of Brescia has been involved in the design and production of a wide range of weapons for both naval and ground forces. One of its most important naval weapons is the Compact Twin 40-mm L/70 Type 70 Naval Mount, which is already in service with over 20 navies and used in conjunction with an Orion radar to provide a close-defence system against both aircraft and air- or sea-launched anti-ship missiles. The company realized that this weapon also had an army application for the defence of high-value targets such as airfields, command posts, oil installations and so on. The 40-mm **Breda 40L70** mount is now in service with Venezuela, which already has the original naval installation in service on board its six 'Lupo' class frigates. The 40L70 cannot be used alone as it has no fire-control system, but a wide range of fire-control systems is available from a number of manufacturers, a typical equipment being the Dutch Hollandse Signaalapparaten Flycatcher. When used in conjunction with the Flycatcher the complete system is known as the **Guardian**. A typical fire unit consists of two 40-mm 40L70s, one Flycatcher fire-control system, and generators.

The twin 40-mm 40L70 mount is essentially the standard naval turret installed on a four-wheeled carriage. In the firing position the system is supported on six jacks that are adjustable to suit the different ground conditions; one jack is located at each end of the carriage, and the other four are placed

Italian Breda 40L70 Field Mounting is essentially a naval anti-aircraft and anti-missile system, installed on a four-wheeled carriage for army use. Venezuela has recently taken delivery of 18 40L70 Field Mountings, which it uses in conjunction with the Dutch HSA Flycatcher radar.

two on each side on outriggers.

Turret traverse and weapon elevation are electric at a maximum traverse speed of 90° per second. The mount has two 40-mm 70-calibre Bofors guns which have a cyclic rate of fire of 300 rounds per barrel per minute. Ammunition is identical to that used in the famous Bofors L/70 anti-aircraft gun and includes proximity-fused pre-fragmented high explosive (PFHE),

high-capacity high explosive (HCHE), high explosive-tracer (HE-T), armour-piercing capped-tracer (APC-T) and target practice. To engage aerial targets such as helicopters, aircraft and missiles the PFHE round would be used as it produces over 2,400 fragments of which some 600 are tungsten pellets, which can penetrate 14 mm (0.55 in) of aluminium.

A total of 444 rounds of 40-mm

ammunition (in clips of four rounds) is provided under the turret, and the empty cartridge cases are ejected outside the forward part of the turret. When firing the turret is unmanned, being controlled by the operator in the fire-control centre.

For many years Breda has been producing the Bofors 40-mm L/70 anti-aircraft gun under licence, including the towed system. To increase the rate of fire of the latter weapon Breda has designed an automatic feeding device which increases cyclic rate of fire from 240 to 300 rounds per minute, with a total of 144 rounds carried for ready use.

More recently Breda has developed to the prototype stage a twin 30-mm towed anti-aircraft gun which uses the West German 30-mm Mauser Model F gun, which has a cyclic rate of fire of 800 rounds per gun per minute. Each barrel has 250 rounds of ready-use ammunition. The system is fitted with the Italian Galileo P75D optronic fire-control system and an on-carriage power unit.

Specification
Breda 40-mm 40L70
Calibre: 40 mm (1.57 in)
Weights: travelling without

ammunition 9900 kg (21,826 lb); travelling with ammunition 10966 kg (24,176 lb)
Dimensions: length travelling 8.05 m (26 ft 4.9 in); width travelling 3.20 m (10 ft 6 in); height travelling 3.65 m (11 ft 11.7 in)
Elevation: +85°/−13°
Traverse: 360°
Ranges: maximum horizontal 12500 m (13,670 yards); maximum vertical 8700 m (28,543 ft); effective vertical 4000 m (13,123 ft)

The Breda Twin 30-mm AA gun can carry 500 rounds on the mount. The two Mauser Model F cannon have been designed to fire a number of types of ammunition including HEI, API, and APDS for use against light armour.

ISRAEL
20-mm TCM-20 light anti-aircraft gun

This TCM-20 twin 20-mm light anti-aircraft gun in the firing position has jacks lowered to the ground to provide a more stable firing platform. This system is essentially the old American M55 with its four 12.7-mm (0.50-calibre) M2 HB machine-guns replaced by two 20-mm cannon.

For some years Israel used the old American M55 trailer-mounted 12.7-mm (0.5-in) quadruple light anti-aircraft gun system, but they realized that it had a very short range. The RAMPTA Structures and Systems Division of Israel Aircraft Industries then modernized the system as the 20-mm **TCM-20** to meet the requirements of the Israeli Air Defence Command and, following trials with prototype systems, the type was accepted for service in time to be used in combat during the 1970 'War of Attrition', when it is claimed to have shot down 10 aircraft in 10 engagements. It was also used during the Yom Kippur War, when it is credited with shooting down some 60 per cent of enemy aircraft downed by air defences, the remaining 40 per cent being shot down by other anti-aircraft guns and HAWK surface-to-air missiles. In the 1982 invasion of the Lebanon the TCM-20 was used not only to shoot down Syrian aircraft and helicopters but also in urban fighting and to engage ground targets. The TCM-20 was offered on the export market at an early date and is now in service with at least six countries apart from Israel.

The TCM-20 is the M55 with the four 12.7-mm M2 HB Browning heavy machine-guns replaced by two Hispano-Suiza HS 404 cannon with a cyclic rate of fire of 650 to 700 rounds per minute, but a practical rate of fire of 150 rounds per minute. Each barrel has a quick-change drum magazine that holds 60 rounds of ready-use ammunition. The gunner aims the cannon with an M18 reflex sight. Turret traverse and weapon elevation are electric, with onboard power provided by two 12-volt batteries mounted at the rear of the carriage; the batteries are kept charged by an auxiliary power unit. In the firing position the wheels are normally removed and the carriage is supported on three levelling jacks.

The basic model is normally towed by any 4×4 light vehicle, although Israel also has in service a self-propelled model based on the M3 series halftrack. There is no provision for all-weather fire control, although warning of the exact direction of approach by enemy aircraft can be given by an Israeli-designed EL/M 2106 point-defence alerting radar.

More recently RAMPTA Structures

and Systems has developed a new system called the **TCM Mk 3**, which appears to be similar in concept to the original TCM but can be fitted with a variety of different weapons in the 20-mm to 25-mm class, the example shown in 1983 being fitted with 23-mm cannon as used in the Soviet ZU-23 towed anti-aircraft gun system. In addition to the same M18 optical sight as installed on the original TCM-20, the TCM Mk 3 is being offered with a Starlight sight with a magnification of ×4 for night operations and a fire-control system that includes a laser rangefinder and computerized sight.

Specification
TCM-20
Calibre: 20 mm (0.79 in)
Weights: travelling 1350 kg (2,976 lb)
Dimensions: length travelling 3.27 m (10 ft 8.7 in); width travelling 1.70 m (5 ft 6.9 in); height travelling 1.63 m (5 ft 4.2 in)
Elevation: +90°/−10°
Traverse: 360°
Ranges: maximum horizontal 5700 m (6,234 yards); maximum vertical 4500 m (14,764 ft); effective vertical 1200 m (3,937 ft)
Crew: 4

At present there are two versions of the Israeli TCM-20 twin 20 mm anti-aircraft gun system: towed and self-propelled, with the latter being mounted on the rear of an M3 halftracked vehicle. The system was used for the first time during the so-called War of Attrition in 1970.

20-mm Tarasque light anti-aircraft gun

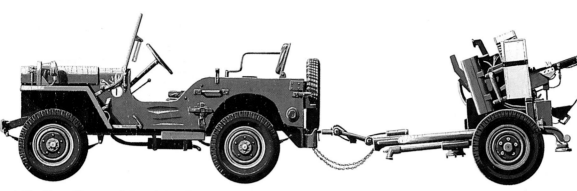

One of the features of the French 20-mm Tarasque light anti-aircraft gun is that it can be towed by a light vehicle such as the M201 (4×4). The 20-mm M693 cannon has dual feed, so enabling the gunner to change from one type of ammunition to another to engage different types of target.

The 20-mm **Tarasque** light anti-aircraft gun entered service with the French army several years ago under the designation **Type 53 T2**. It is armed with the 20-mm M693 cannon (the standard weapon of its type in the French army), which is also installed in the AMX-10P mechanized infantry combat vehicle and the AMX-30 main battle tank.

The Tarasque light anti-aircraft gun is carried on a two-wheeled carriage that can be towed by a light 4×4 vehicle such as the M201 or Land Rover. The weapon can be brought into action by two men in about 15 seconds: on arrival at the selected firing position the locking pin retaining the rear foot is removed and the mount slewed through 90° to place the other two feet in contact with the ground; the carriage is then removed and the mount supported on the three feet.

Only one man is required to operate the Tarasque gun, the other two men acting as ammunition handlers or aircraft spotters. The gunner is seated on the left side of the mount and moves in elevation with the 20-mm cannon. Elevation and traverse are hydraulic, though manual controls are provided for emergency use. Maximum traverse speed is 40° per second and maximum elevation speed is 80° per second.

The 20-mm M693 is a dual-feed cannon and has a cyclic rate of fire of 740 rounds per minute. The gunner fires the cannon by pressing down his right foot, and can fire single aimed shots or bursts. A total of 140 rounds of ready-use ammunition is carried, of which 100 are normally high explosive (HE) or high explosive incendiary (HEI) for engaging aerial targets, and 40 of

armour-piercing discarding sabot (APDS) for engaging armoured targets. The latter round will penetrate 20 mm (0.79 in) of armour at an incidence of 0° at a range of 1000 m (1,094 yards).

The gunner has an anti-aircraft sight with a magnification of ×1 and a ground-to-ground sight with a magnification of ×5.

The Tarasque can also be installed, less its carriage, in the rear of cross-country vehicles such as the TRM 2000 4×4 truck; this gives the weapon greater cross-country mobility as well as enabling it to open fire as soon as the vehicle comes to a halt.

The French air force uses the twin 20-mm **Cerbère** light anti-aircraft gun to provide close protection for the Crotale surface-to-air missile systems protecting its air bases. The Cerbère, also known as the **Type 76 T2**, is essentially the West German Rheinmetall twin 20-mm light anti-aircraft gun with its original MK 20 Rh 202 cannon replaced by the French GIAT M693 cannon. Currently being tested for use with the Cerbère is the DALDO target indicator helmet: in this system the gun commander, situated away from the Cerbère, constantly scans the sky for a target. Once a hostile target has been selected the commander presses a button and the Cerbère mount is automatically laid onto the target in elevation and traverse, thus saving valuable seconds in target acquisition.

More recently GIAT has developed a twin 20-mm light anti-aircraft gun system as a private venture. Designated **Type 53 T4** this weighs 2500 kg (5,512 lb), and is thus much heavier

The GIAT 20-mm Tarasque light anti-aircraft gun can also be carried in the rear of trucks such as this Renault TRM 2000 (4×4) for greater cross- *country mobility. This gun is now in wide-scale use with the French army and is also offered for export, as are most French weapons today.*

than the Cerbère or Tarasque. It has hydraulic elevation and traverse, and 150 rounds of ready-use ammunition for each of the 20-mm cannon.

Specification
Tarasque
Calibre: 20 mm (0.79 in)
Weights: travelling with ammunition 840 kg (1,852 lb); firing with ammunition 660 kg (1,455 lb)

Dimensions: length travelling 4.15 m (13 ft 7.4 in); width travelling 1.90 m (6 ft 2.8 in); height travelling 1.70 m (5 ft 6.9 in)
Elevation: +83°/–8°
Traverse: 360°
Ranges: maximum horizontal 6000 m (6562 yards); maximum vertical 4500 m (14,764 ft); effective vertical 2000 m (6,562 ft)
Crew: 3 (1 on mount)

20-mm M55A2 light anti-aircraft gun

In recent years the Yugoslav defence industry has designed and placed in production a number of 20-mm light anti-aircraft guns, all of which use the same basic Hispano-Suiza 20-mm HSS-804 70-calibre barrel which is produced under licence in Yugoslavia.

The **20/1 mm M75** is the most unsophisticated weapon in the family, and has a single barrel with the gunner sitting on a seat at the rear of the mount. Elevation and traverse are manual, and the gunner aims the cannon at aircraft targets by means of an M73 reflex sight while a sight with a magnification of ×3.8 is used to engage ground targets. The cannon is normally fed from a drum holding 60 rounds of ammunition, but there is also a box type magazine that holds 10 rounds of ammunition; the latter is normally used for API, API-T and AP-T, while the

drum magazine is used for the anti-aircraft rounds (HEI and HEI-T). The ammunition used by this gun is identical to that used in other weapons of this family.

The **20/3 mm M55A4 B1** has a carriage and sighting system similar to that of the Oerlikon-Bührle GAI-DO1 light anti-aircraft gun, and each of the three barrels has a 60-round drum magazine. The gunner sits on a seat at the rear of the mount, and power for the hydraulic elevation and traverse system is provided by a Wankel engine mounted under the gunner's seat. Maximum traverse and elevation rates are 80° per second.

Sighting is effected by an Italian Galileo P56 sight with a magnification of ×1 for use against aircraft and ×4 for use against ground targets. Each of the 20-mm cannon has a cyclic rate of fire

of 700 rounds per minute, and the gunner fires the cannon by depressing a foot pedal. For transportation the mount is carried on a small two-wheel carriage, which in the firing position is supported on four outriggers.

The **20/3 mm M55A2** is very similar to the M55A4 B1 system, but has a different sight and manual elevation and traverse. The gunner is seated at the rear and has two handwheels (one for elevation and one for traverse), and fires the cannon by pressing a foot pedal. The gunner is provided with a sight for target tracking, but has to insert key data (for example target range and speed) manually to ensure a hit.

All of these 20-mm cannon are basically clear-weather systems with no provision for radar fire control. They are also offered for export, and sales

have been made to a number of countries including Cyprus and Mozambique.

Specification
M55A2
Calibre: 20 mm (0.79 in)
Weights: travelling (with ammunition) 1100 kg (2,425 lb); firing (without ammunition) 970 kg (2,138 lb)
Dimensions: length travelling 4.30 m (14 ft 1.3 in); width travelling 1.27 m (4 ft 2 in); height travelling 1.47 m (4 ft 9.9 in)
Elevation: +83°/–5°
Traverse: 360°
Ranges: maximum horizontal 5500 m (6,015 yards); effective horizontal 2500 m (2,734 yards); maximum vertical 4000 m (13,123 ft); effective vertical 2000 m (6,562 ft)
Crew: 6 (1 on mount)

30-mm M53 light anti-aircraft gun

Czechoslovakia had an excellent gun-making capability well before World War II, and this was subsequently taken over by the Germans. After the end of the war Czechoslovakia continued to design and build weapons such as the 30-mm **M53** light anti-aircraft gun, which it still uses in place of the Soviet 23-mm ZU-23. The Czech weapon is heavier and has a slower rate of fire, but it does have a more effective range than the ZU-23. In addition to being used by Czechoslovakia, it is also used by Cuba, Romania, Vietnam and Yugoslavia. There is also a self-propelled model called the **M53/ 59**, which is mounted on a modified and armoured Praga V3S 6×6 truck chassis. An unusual feature of the M53/ 59 is that the twin 30-mm weapons can be removed from the vehicle and placed on the ground for ease of concealment while the truck is driven away and camouflaged. The M53/59 is fed from vertical magazines holding 50 rounds, while the M53 is fed horizontally in 10-round clips.

The M53 system is mounted on a four-wheeled carriage, no shield being provided for the four man crew. To provide a more stable firing platform in action, the wheels are raised off the ground and the carriage is supported by four jacks, one on each side on outriggers and one at each end.

The weapons are gas-operated, each having a cyclic rate of fire of 450 to 500 rounds per minute though the practical rate of fire is only 100 rounds per minute. Ammunition is fed to each barrel in clips, and two types of ammunition are available, both having a muzzle velocity of 1000 m (3,281 ft) per second: these are high explosive incendiary (HEI) and armour-piercing incendiary (API) for use against armoured vehicles. The latter round will penetrate 55 mm (2.17 in) of armour at a range of 500 m (547 yards).

The main drawback of the M53 light anti-aircraft gun is that, like the Soviet ZU-23, it is limited to clear-weather operations as there is no provision for radar or off-carriage fire-control.

Czechoslovakia developed two other anti-aircraft weapons in the period after World War II, although as far as it is known neither remains in front line service with the Czech forces. These are the 12.7-mm (0.5-in) M53 quadruple anti-aircraft machine-gun, and a 57-mm anti-aircraft gun. The M53 is a two-wheeled carriage fitted with four Soviet DShKM machine-guns, each fed from a drum holding 50 rounds of ammunition. This weapon has an effective anti-aircraft range of 1000 m (1,094 yards) and is normally towed by a GA-69 4×4 truck which also carries its crew and a small amount of ready-use ammunition. The 57-mm anti-aircraft gun was used by the Czech army in place of the Soviet 57-mm S-60 and has a higher rate of fire, being fed with three- rather than four-round clips of ammunition. It is reported that this weapon was exported to a few countries including Cuba, Guinea and Mali.

Specification
M53
Calibre: 30 mm (1.18 in)
Weights: travelling 2100 kg (4,630 lb); firing 1750 kg (3,858 lb)
Dimensions: length travelling 7.587 m (24 ft 10.7 in); width travelling 1.758 m (5 ft 9.2 in); height travelling 1.575 m (5 ft 2 in)
Elevation: +85°/–10°
Traverse: 360°
Ranges: maximum horizontal 9700 m (10,608 yards); maximum vertical 6300 m (20,669 ft); effective vertical 3000 m (9,843 ft)
Crew: 4

Twin 30-mm M53 weapons are towed by a Praga V3S 6×6 truck. Ammunition is fed to each of the 30-mm barrels in clips of 10 rounds, with practical rate of fire being 100 rounds per barrel per minute. The M53 has no radar system, so is limited in its engagements.

The Czech twin 30-mm M53 light anti-aircraft gun is used here to defend a 'Bar Lock' air defence radar installation against air attack. In addition to this towed model there is also a self-propelled version called the M53/59, mounted on a 6×6 Praga V3S armoured truck chassis.

23-mm ZU-23 light anti-aircraft gun

For many years after the end of World War II the standard light anti-aircraft gun of the Soviet army was the ZPU series of 14.5-mm (0.57-in) weapons using the Vladimirov KPV heavy machine-gun, which even today is installed in turrets mounted on a number of Soviet armoured vehicles including the BRDM-2, BTR-60PB and OT-64. There are three basic models of the ZPU, the ZPU-1, ZPU-2 and ZPU-4, the numeral referring to the number of barrels. Although withdrawn from front-line service with the Soviet army some years ago, the ZPU series remains in service with about 40 countries around the world.

In the 1960s the ZPU series was replaced in the Soviet army by the **ZU-23** twin 23-mm towed anti-aircraft gun system, which is no longer in front-line Soviet use, so far as is known, having been replaced by surface-to-air missiles. At divisional level the last users were the airborne or airborne rifle divisions which each had a total of 24 systems, four in each of the three airborne rifle regiments and 12 in the divisional artillery element. The weapon is still used by some 20 countries, however, and was even encountered by United States forces during their invasion of Grenada in October 1983, when ZU-23 and ZPU series light anti-aircraft guns downed a number of

American helicopters. In Afghanistan the Soviets have mounted a number of ZU-23s on the rear of trucks to provide suppressive ground-to-ground fire when convoys are attacked by guerrillas.

The ZU-23 is normally towed by a light vehicle such as the 4×4 GAZ-69,

the Soviet equivalent of the Land Rover. The carriage has two rubber-tyred road wheels: in the firing position these wheels are raised off the ground and the carriage is supported on three screw-type levelling jacks. Each of the 23-mm barrels is provided with a flash suppressor, and a handle is mounted

A Soviet-built 23-mm ZU-23 light anti-aircraft gun of the East German army is seen in the firing position, showing the box of 50 rounds of ready-use ammunition for each barrel. The ZU-23 has been seen in Afghanistan mounted on the rear of cross-country trucks

on top of each barrel to enable it to be changed quickly. Each barrel has a box of 50 rounds of ready-use ammunition, and though a cyclic rate of fire of 800 to 1,000 rounds per minute is possible, the practical rate of fire is 200 rounds per minute. Two types of fixed ammunition are fired by the ZU-23: armour-piercing incendiary-tracer (API-T) and high explosive incendiary-tracer (HEI-T), the former being used to engage armoured vehicles and the latter to engage aircraft. Both projectiles have a muzzle velocity of 970 m (3,182 ft) per second, and the API-T projectile will penetrate 25 mm (0.98 in) of armour at a range of 500 m (547 yards). The mounting has no provision for off-carriage fire control. The 23-mm cannon of the ZU-23 are also used in the famous 23-mm ZSU-23-4 self-propelled anti-aircraft gun system, although in this application the weapons are water-cooled to enable a higher rate of fire to be achieved.

More recently Egypt has been testing two versions of the M113 armoured personnel carrier with twin 23-mm anti-aircraft guns mounted on the roof, while Israel has captured a number of BTR-152 6×6 armoured personnel carriers from the PLO with a ZU-23 mounted in the rear.

Specification
ZU-23
Calibre: 23 mm (0.91 in)
Weights: 950 kg (2,094 lb)
Dimensions: length travelling 4.57 m (15 ft 0 in); width travelling 1.83 m (6 ft 0 in); height travelling 1.87 m (6 ft 1.6 in)
Elevation: +90°/–10°
Traverse: 360°
Ranges: maximum horizontal 7000 m (7,655 yards); maximum vertical 5100 m (16,732 ft); effective vertical 2500 m (8,202 ft)
Crew: 5

Although no longer in large-scale use with the Soviet Union the twin 23-mm ZU-23 light anti-aircraft gun system is still highly effective, and a number were used against American forces during the invasion of Grenada.

57-mm S-60 anti-aircraft gun

The 57-mm (2.24-in) S-60 anti-aircraft gun entered service with the Soviet army after the end of World War II as the replacement for the 37-mm M1939 light anti-aircraft gun; this was the Soviet equivalent of the famous Bofors 40-mm L/60 weapon used in large numbers by the American and British armies during the war. Until very recently each tank division and motorized rifle division in the Soviet army had an anti-aircraft regiment equipped with the S-60. Each regiment had four batteries each with six guns, each battery having two three-gun platoons. Each battery had a SON-9/SON-9A 'Fire Can' fire-control radar, while at regimental HQ were two 'Flat Face' target-acquisition radars. More recently the 'Flap Wheel' radar has been used with the S-60 system.

The S-60 is still used by some 30 countries, especially in Africa, the Middle East and the Far East, and features in the inventory of most Warsaw Pact countries. In the Soviet army it has been replaced in many front-line units by the SA-8 'Gecko' surface-to-air missile (SAM), which in addition to being a much more effective all-weather system can be ready for action within seconds. China has built a model of the S-60 under the designation **Type 59**, while the ZSU-57-2 self-propelled anti-aircraft gun system uses the same ammunition as the S-60.

The S-60 can be towed by a variety of vehicles including 6×6 trucks such as the Ural-375D or the AT-L light tracked artillery tractors. The weapon can engage anti-aircraft targets with its wheels in contact with the ground, but it is much more accurate with its wheels raised off the ground and the carriage supported by four screw jacks, one on each side on outriggers and one at each end. Optical sights are fitted for the engagement of both ground and aerial targets. Four modes of operation are available: firstly, manual with the crew operating handwheels for elevation and traverse; secondly, power-assisted with the handwheels operated by the crews but assisted by a servo motor; thirdly, remotely-controlled by a Puazo series director and zero indicator; and fourthly, fully automatic and remotely-

controlled by a director and zero indicator, plus radar. In each case ammunition is loaded in four-round clips by ammunition feeders, one clip being in the feed tray to the left of the breech and another clip on the mount itself. Three types of fixed ammunition can be fired by the S-60, all of which have a muzzle velocity of 1000 m (3,281 ft) per second: two types of fragmentation tracer (FRAG-T) and armour-piercing capped-tracers (APC-T). The latter will penetrate 96 mm (3.78 in) of armour at a range of 1000 m (1,094 yards). The S-60 has a cyclic rate of fire of 105 to 120 rounds per minute and a practical rate of fire of 70 rounds per minute.

Specification
S-60
Calibre: 57 mm (2.24 in)
Weights: travelling 4660 kg (10,274 lb); firing 4500 kg (9,921 lb)
Dimensions: length travelling 8.50 m (27 ft 10.6 in); width travelling 2.054 m (6 ft 8.9 in); height travelling 2.37 m (7 ft

Right: The 57-mm S-60 anti-aircraft gun is highly effective when used together with the PUAZO-6/60 director and the SON-9/SON-9A radar, which is called 'Fire Can' by NATO. In 1985 Iraq was using the S-60 together with a low-light-level television system to engage Iranian aircraft.

9.3 in)
Elevation: +85°/–4°
Traverse: 360°
Ranges: maximum horizontal 12000 m (13,123 yards); maximum vertical 8800 m (28,871 ft); effective vertical with optical sights 4000 m (13,123 ft); effective vertical with off-carriage control 6000 m (19,685 ft)
Crew: 8

For many years the 57-mm S-60 was one of the standard towed anti-aircraft guns of the Soviet army and was issued on the scale of 24 guns per division. This S-60 is of the Egyptian army and is in the travelling position, being towed by a 6×6 truck. In the Soviet army its replacement is the SA-8.

100-mm KS-19 anti-aircraft gun

One of the standard anti-aircraft guns of the Soviet army during World War II was the 85-mm (3.35-in) M1939, replaced in production by the M1944 which had a longer barrel and fired ammunition with higher muzzle velocity for increased range. In 1985 the M1939 and M1944 are still used by almost 20 countries, although in the Warsaw Pact they have been replaced by surface-to-air missiles. After the end of the war the Soviet Union introduced two new towed anti-aircraft guns, the 100-mm (3.94-in) **KS-19** and the 130-mm (5.12-in) KS-30; by 1985 neither of these remained in front-line service with the Soviet Union, although some 20 countries still use the KS-19 and two or three the much heavier KS-30. China has built the KS-19 under the designation **Type 59**.

The KS-19 is normally towed by an AT-S medium or AT-T heavy full-tracked artillery tractor, which also carries the 15-man crew and a small quantity of ready-use ammunition. The weapon is mounted on a two-axle carriage, and in the firing position the axles are raised off the ground and the carriage is supported by four screw jacks, one on each side on outriggers and one at each end of the carriage. When travelling the mount is traversed to the rear and the barrel is held in position by a lock.

The KS-19 fires ammunition of the fixed type which is loaded in single rounds from the left; to increase its rate of fire, the weapon is fitted with a single-round loading tray, automatic fuse

The Soviet 100-mm KS-19 anti-aircraft gun was introduced some 40 years ago, but in Warsaw Pact countries has long been replaced in front-line service by missiles such as the SA-2 'Guideline'. The KS-19 is, however, still in widespread use in both the Middle and Far East.

setter and a power rammer. A well-trained crew can achieve a maximum rate of fire of 15 rounds per minute. Like most heavy-calibre anti-aircraft weapons, the KS-19 was designed as a dual-role (anti-aircraft and anti-tank) gun. Three types of ammunition, all with a muzzle velocity of 900 m (2,953 ft) per second, are available for the anti-aircraft role: high explosive, high explosive fragmentation and fragmentation. Two rounds are available for the anti-tank role: AP-T (armour-piercing tracer) and APC-T (armour-piercing capped tracer); the first of these has a muzzle velocity of 1,000 m (3,281 ft) per second and can penetrate 185 mm (7.28 in) of armour at a

range of 1000 m (1,094 yards).

Anti-aircraft targets can be engaged with the sights installed on the KS-19, but better results are obtained with the PUAZO-6/19 director and the SON-9/SON-9A (NATO reporting name 'Fire Can') fire-control radar system. In most countries the KS-19 is used to defend strategic rather than tactical targets, and the weapon can be tied into an overall air-defence system. Lighter anti-aircraft guns, such as the 57-mm S-60, are used by field armies as they are easier to move about. The KS-19 has been used in action during the Korean War, the many wars in the Middle East, and also by North Vietnam against American aircraft.

Specification
KS-19

Calibre: 100 mm (3.94 in)
Weight: travelling 9550 kg (21,054 lb)
Dimensions: length travelling 9.45 m (31 ft 0 in); width travelling 2.35 m (7 ft 8.5 in); height travelling 2.201 m (7 ft 2.7 in)
Elevation: +85°/-3°
Traverse: 360°
Ranges: maximum horizontal 21000 m (22,966 yards); maximum vertical with time fuse 12700 m (41,667 ft); maximum vertical with proximity fuse 15000 m (49,213 ft); effective vertical 13700 m (44,948 ft)
Crew: 15

12.7-mm M55 light anti-aircraft gun

The 12.7-mm (0.5-in) **M55** quadruple anti-aircraft gun system was developed in World War II by the Kimberly-Clark Corporation, and by the time production was completed in 1953 some 10,000 systems had been built. In addition to being used during World War II the M55 was used by the United States forces in Korea and South Vietnam. In the latter conflict it was used in the ground fire-support role to break up mass attacks by Viet Cong on American supply bases and camps. Some M55 systems were also put on the rear of trucks and armour plated for use in the convoy escort role. In the US Army the M55 was replaced from the late 1960s by the 20-mm M167 Vulcan towed anti-aircraft gun system, but it is still used by almost 20 countries all over the world. More recently Israel has developed from the M55 the TCM-20 anti-aircraft gun system which has two 20-mm cannon in place of the four 12.7-mm (0.5-in) machine-guns of the original. The Brazilian company LYSAM has carried out a modernization of the M55 for the Brazilian army and has also fitted two 20-mm cannon in place of the four 12.7-mm machine-guns.

The M55 system consists essentially of two parts, the **M45C** mount and the **M20** trailer. The former is an armoured mount with a seat for the gunner and also contains an integral electric power unit which in turn is run from two 6-volt batteries. Mounted on each side of the mount are two 12.7-mm M2 HB machine-guns, each of which is fed from a belt containing 210 rounds of ready-use ammunition. The machine-guns are fully automatic and have a

cyclic rate of fire of 450 to 550 rounds per barrel per minute, though the practical rate of fire is 150 rounds per barrel per minute. Types of ammunition that can be fired by the M2 machine-guns include armour-piercing (AP), armour-piercing incendiary (API), armour-piercing incendiary-tracer (API-T), incendiary, standard ball and training.

Turret traverse and weapon elevation are electric at a rate of 60° per second, the gunner using a pair of control handles which also accommodate the triggers. The weapons continue to fire as long as there is sufficient ammunition left and the triggers are depressed. The M55 is a clear-weather system only, and the gunner has a standard M18 reflex sight to his front that projects a graticule image on an inclined glass plate. The graticule image consists of four concentric circles, each corresponding to various aircraft speeds, and three dots on a vertical line in the centre of the field of view that are used to determine line of sight and compensate for gravity pull on the projectile.

The M20 two-wheeled trailer can be towed by a light vehicle but not at speeds above 16 km/h (10 mph), and for this reason the M55 is normally carried in the rear of a 6×6 truck such as the American M35. The weapon can be fired from the truck or unloaded onto the ground with the aid of two channels, one of which is carried on each side of the truck. On the ground the M55 is supported by three jacks (one at the front and two at the rear) and the small road wheels are removed.

During World War II two self-propelled models of the M55 were built, and some of these still remain in service in South America and elsewhere. The M16 was based on the M3 halftrack, while the M17 was based on the M5 halftrack.

An American M55 quad 12.7-mm (0.50-calibre) anti-aircraft gun system is shown mounted in the rear of an M35 (6×6) truck. In addition to being used for the anti-aircraft role, it has also been used in the ground fire support role.

Specification
M55

Calibre: 12.7 mm (0.5 in)
Weights: travelling 1338 kg (2,950 lb); firing 975 kg (2,150 lb)
Dimensions: length travelling 2.89 m (9 ft 5.8 in); width travelling 2.09 m (6 ft 10.3 in); height travelling 1.606 m (5 ft 3.2 in)
Elevation: +90°/-10°
Traverse: 360°
Ranges: effective horizontal 1500 m (1,640 yards); effective vertical 1000 m (3,281 ft)
Crew: 4

20-mm Vulcan light anti-aircraft gun

In the early 1960s the General Electric Company developed two anti-aircraft gun systems to meet the requirements of the US Army. Both of these used the same 20-mm cannon developed from the M61 series installed in high-speed fighter aircraft such as the Lockheed F-104 Starfighter. After trials with both systems at Fort Bliss, Texas (home of US Army air defence), both weapons were accepted for service. The self-propelled system, mounted on a modified M113 series armoured personnel carrier chassis, is called the M163 and was the replacement for the 40-mm M42 Duster self-propelled anti-aircraft gun. The towed model, called the **M167**, was the replacement for the 12.7-mm (0.5-in) M55 quadruple machine-gun system developed in World War II.

The M167 is still in front-line service with the US Army, where it is employed with airborne and airmobile divisions. Each of these formations has one air-defence battalion with a battalion headquarters and four batteries. Each of the latter has a battery headquarters and three firing platoons each with four M167 systems.

The M167 low-level air-defence system consists of a two-wheeled carriage on which is mounted an electrically-powered turret containing the 20-mm **M168 Vulcan** cannon, the linked-feed ammunition system, and the fire controls.

The M168 Vulcan cannon has six barrels and two rates of fire, 1,000 and 3,000 rounds per minute. The slower rate is normally used against ground targets, while the higher rate is reserved for aerial targets. To conserve ammunition, the gunner can select bursts of 10, 30, 60 or 100 rounds from the total of 300 or 500 ready-use rounds provided.

Turret traverse and weapon elevation are electric, recharging being carried out by a generator installed on the forward part of the carriage. Turret traverse rate is 60° per second and weapon elevation rate is 45° per second.

The fire-control system on the M167 consists of a range-only radar on the right side of the mount, a sight current generator and a gyro lead-computing sight.

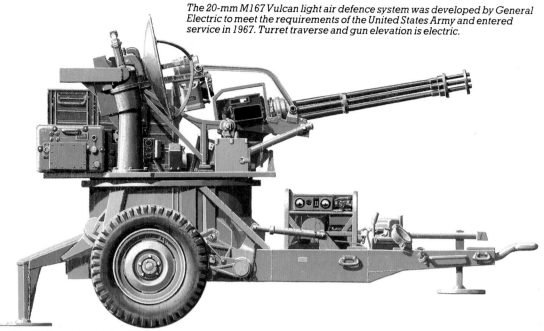

The 20-mm M167 Vulcan light air defence system was developed by General Electric to meet the requirements of the United States Army and entered service in 1967. Turret traverse and gun elevation is electric.

The US Army is acquiring 285 towed and self-propelled **Product Improved Vulcan Air Defence Systems** or **PIVADS**, as the M163A2 and the towed **M167A2**. The fire-control system has been considerably improved to take the Vulcan into the 1990s. A Vulcan/Stinger hybrid Gun/Missile system is also under development.

The M167 is normally towed by an M715 4×4 light truck and can also be slung under a helicopter. In addition to being used by the US Army, the M167 is also used by a number of other countries including Belgium, Ecuador, Israel, Jordan, Morocco, North Yemen, Saudi Arabia, Somalia, South Korea and Sudan.

Specification
Vulcan
Calibre: 20 mm (0.79 in)
Weights: travelling 1588 kg (3,501 lb); firing 1565 kg (3,450 lb)
Dimensions: length travelling 4.906 m (16 ft 1.1 in); width travelling 1.98 m (6 ft 6 in); height travelling 2.038 m (6 ft 8.2 in)

Elevation: +80°/–5°
Traverse: 360°
Ranges: maximum horizontal 6000 m (6,562 yards); effective horizontal 2200 m (2,406 yards); maximum vertical 4500 m (14,764 ft); effective vertical 1200 m (3,937 ft)
Crew: 4-5 (1 on mount)

It is generally accepted that the 20-mm Vulcan anti-aircraft gun system has very limited capabilities. The towed M163 will probably be replaced by a 25-mm gun or a new system combining a 25-mm gun and the Stinger missile.

Rheinmetall 20-mm twin light anti-aircraft gun

The **Rheinmetall 20-mm** light anti-aircraft gun was developed to meet the requirements of the West German ministry of defence by the Rheinmetall company of Düsseldorf. The mount is armed with two examples of the MK 20 Rh 202 20-mm cannon which is the standard weapon in its class in the West German army: it is also installed in the Marder mechanized infantry combat vehicle in a two-man power-operated turret; it arms the Wiesel light airportable armoured vehicle which has recently been ordered into production for West German airborne units; and it is fitted in a two-man turret on the Luchs 8×8 amphibious armoured car. The cannon is also installed on a single mount for various naval applications, and the Italians have installed the cannon in the FIAT/OTO Melara 6616 4×4 armoured car.

This 20-mm twin light anti-aircraft gun system is carried on a two-wheel

trailer that can be towed by a light vehicle such as a Mercedes-Benz Unimog 4×4 truck. The gunner is seated at the rear of the mount and aims the twin cannon using an Italian Galileo P56 computing sight which has an optical sight with a magnification of ×5, an electronic analogue computer for calculating the lead angles required to hit aerial targets, a joystick for elevation and traverse, and a panel for inserting target information.

A West German Rheinmetall twin 20-mm light anti-aircraft gun is seen in the firing position, showing the gunner's seat at the rear with the Italian Galileo P56 sight to his immediate front.

Rheinmetall 20-mm twin light anti-aircraft gun (continued)

Elevation and traverse are hydraulic, maximum traverse speed being 80° per second and maximum elevation speed 48° per second, power for these functions being obtained from an air-cooled two-stroke petrol engine mounted under the gunner's seat.

The cannon are gas-operated and fully automatic, the gunner firing them via a foot-operated pedal that is fitted with a safety device. The gunner can select either single shots or full automatic with either barrel or both together. The cannon have a cyclic rate of fire of 2,000 rounds per barrel per minute and each cannon is provided with an ammunition box containing 270 rounds of fixed ammunition, another 10 rounds being in the flexible feed system that connects the ammunition boxes with the gun. Types of ammunition that can be fired include armour-piercing discarding sabot-tracer (APDS-T), armour-piercing incendiary-tracer (API-T), high explosive incendiary (HEI), high explosive incendiary-tracer (HEI-T), and various

training rounds. The APDS-T has a muzzle velocity of 1150 m (3,773 ft) per second.

Nearly 1,500 of these fair weather systems have been sold to Argentina (who used them in the defence of Port Stanley), Chile, Greece, Indonesia, Portugal and Turkey in addition to West Germany. The French Cerbère system uses the same mount with French M693(F2) 20-mm cannon.

To meet the requirements of the Norwegian armed forces, Hispano-Suiza and A/S Kongsberg Vappenfabrikk designed and built a single-mount anti-aircraft gun called the **FK 20-2** which uses the same 20-mm cannon as the Rheinmetall twin 20-mm mount. This is used by the West German and Norwegian armies. In the future all of the 20-mm cannon of West Germany are expected to be replaced by the Mauser Model E 25-mm cannon, which was selected over the Rheinmetall Rh 205 25-mm cannon several years ago.

The Rheinmetall 20-mm MK 20 Rh 202 cannon is used in this twin anti-aircraft gun mount, the Marder MICV and the Luchs (8×8) reconnaissance vehicle. All of these guns will probably be replaced by the new Mauser Model E cannon, with longer range and improved ammunition.

Specification
Rheinmetall 20-mm mounting
Calibre: 20 mm (0.79 in)
Weights: travelling 2160 kg (4,762 lb); firing 1640 kg (3,616 lb)
Dimensions: length travelling 5.035 m (16 ft 6.2 in); width travelling 2.36 m (7 ft 8.9 in); height travelling 2.075 m (6 ft 9.7 in)
Elevation: +81.6°/–3.5°
Traverse: 360°
Ranges: maximum horizontal 6000 m (6,562 yards); maximum vertical 4500 m (14,764 ft); effective vertical 2000 m (6,562 ft)
Crew: 4-5 (but only 1 on mount)

Oerlikon 20-mm GAI-BO1 light anti-aircraft gun

The Oerlikon-Bührle 20-mm **GAI-BO1** light anti-aircraft gun was originally called the **10 ILa/5TG**, the 5TG standing for the actual cannon, which was subsequently called the KAB-001.

For many years Oerlikon-Bührle, now called Machine Tool Works Oerlikon-Bührle and based in Zurich, was in competition with Hispano-Suiza which also built an extensive range of light anti-aircraft weapons and their associated ammunition. In 1972 Hispano-Suiza was taken over by Oerlikon-Bührle and some of the former's weapons were subsequently integrated into the Oerlikon range. The HS-666A twin 20-mm weapon became the GAI-DO1, the 20-mm HS-639-B 3.1 became the GAI-CO1, the HS-639-B 4.1 became the GAI-CO3 while the HS-639-B5 became the GAI-CO4. By 1984 all of these had been phased out of production although they remained in service with many countries; for example, the GAI-CO1 is used by both Chile and South Africa.

The GAI-BO1 is the lightest of Oerlikon-Bührle's extensive range of anti-aircraft weaponry currently in production. It is in the inventory of several countries, including Austria, South Africa, Spain and Switzerland. To provide greater mobility some countries have fitted the weapon in the rear of cross-country vehicles; for example, Austria has the weapon on the rear of the Steyr 6×6 vehicle with ready-use ammunition carried to the rear of the cab. The main drawback of systems such as the GAI-BO1 is that they rely on manual controls for elevation and traverse and therefore some operators find it difficult to track high-speed aircraft; no provision is made for radar fire control. Such systems do offer the advantage of being very light and can be disassembled into smaller parts for transportation in rough terrain where heavier weapons cannot be employed.

For travelling the GAI-BO1 is carried on a small two-wheeled carriage towed behind a light truck. The weapon can be brought into action in about 20 seconds, and is then supported on its outriggers.

For many years the 20-mm GAI-BO1 has been the lightest in the extensive range of light anti-aircraft guns built by Oerlikon-Bührle. Traverse and elevation is manual, and drums of 20 or 50 rounds of ammunition can be fitted or a box holding just eight rounds.

An Oerlikon-Bührle 20-mm GAI-BO1 anti-aircraft gun is seen in the firing position. A key feature of this weapon is its very light weight, and it can be brought into action by its two-man crew in about 20 seconds.

The 20-mm cannon has a cyclic rate of fire of 1,000 rounds per minute, and the gunner can select either single shot or full automatic fire. Three types of magazine are available for this weapon: 50- and 30-round drums, and an eight-round box. The former two are normally used for anti-aircraft ammunition while the latter is for armour-piercing ammunition. The following types of ammunition can be fired by this cannon: armour-piercing-tracer (AP-T), high explosive incendiary-tracer (HEI-T), high explosive incendiary (HEI), semi-armour-piercing high explosive incendiary-tracer (SAPHEI-T), semi-armour-piercing high explosive incendiary (SAPHEI), and training.

The cannon is elevated by the gunner turning a handle, while traverse is obtained using the gunner's feet. An unusual feature of this weapon is that the gunner can also engage ground targets from the prone position; in this mode traverse is limited to 60° and elevation from –5° to +25°.

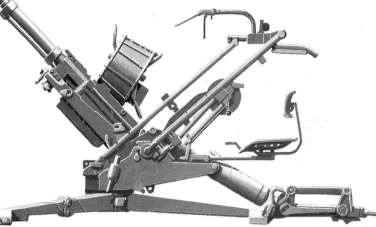

Specification
GAI-BO1
Calibre: 20 mm (0.79 in)
Weights: travelling 547 kg (1,206 lb); firing 405 kg (893 lb)
Dimensions: length travelling 3.85 m (12 ft 7.6 in); width travelling 1.55 m (5 ft 1 in); height travelling 2.50 m (8 ft 2.4 in)

Elevation: +85°/–5°
Traverse: 360°
Ranges: maximum horizontal 5700 m (6,234 yards); effective 2200 m (2,406 yards); maximum vertical 4500 m (14,764 ft); effective vertical 1500 m (4,921 ft)
Crew: 3 (1 on mount)

Oerlikon 20-mm GAI-DO1 light anti-aircraft gun

The Oerlikon-Bürhle twin 20-mm **GAI-DO1** light anti-aircraft gun was originally designed and built by Hispano-Suiza under the designation **HS-666A**, and was the most sophisticated 20-mm weapon in the company's range. The main advantages of the GAI-DO1 over the other 20-mm light anti-aircraft guns manufactured by the company were powered elevation and traverse, a new sight, and two rather than one 20-mm cannon.

The system is fitted with two 20-mm KAD series cannon with a cyclic rate of fire of 1,000 rounds per minute per barrel. Each barrel is provided with a box magazine that holds 120 rounds of fixed ammunition. The gunner can select either single shots, rapid single shot, bursts or full automatic fire. The ammunition fired by the GAI-DO1 is identical to that of the GAI-BO1.

The gunner is provided with a shield, and mounted under the gunner's seat is the Wankel engine which provides hydraulic power for cannon elevation and mount traverse, maximum elevation speed being 48° per second and maximum traverse speed 80° per second. As with all powered anti-aircraft guns, manual controls are provided for emergency use. The gunner also has an Italian Galileo P56 sight which is identical to that installed on the Rheinmetall twin 20-mm light anti-aircraft gun used by the West German armed forces. This allows the gunner to engage ground and aerial targets with a high hit probability.

In the firing configuration the GAI-DO1 is supported on three adjustable feet, and for transportation it is carried on a two-wheeled carriage towed by a light truck. From its travelling position the weapon can be brought into action by its crew in less than one minute.

The basic GAI-DO1 light anti-aircraft gun is a clear-weather system, and therefore limited to daylight use; in conditions of low cloud its effectiveness is much reduced. It is no longer in production, but it is known to be in service with Guatemala as well as with the armed forces of several undisclosed countries.

Oerlikon-Bürhle did offer a 25-mm anti-aircraft gun called the **GBI-AO1** with a single 25-mm KBA series cannon on a one-man mount with manual elevation and traverse. A feature of this weapon was that the dual-feed cannon was provided with two boxes of ammunition each containing 40 rounds, one holding armour-piercing discarding sabot-tracer (APDS-T) ammunition for engaging light armoured vehicles, and the other with high explosive incendiary-tracer (HEI-T) for engaging aerial targets. This weapon is no longer offered and is not known to have entered service in any quantity. In its place Oerlikon-Bürhle is now offering the much improved Diana twin 25-mm light anti-aircraft gun.

This Oerlikon-Bührle twin 20-mm GAI-DO1 light anti-aircraft gun in the firing position shows the Wankel engine under the gunner's seat. This is a clear-weather system, although a radar such as the Contraves LPD-20 could be used to provide early warning to a number of guns.

Specification
GAI-DO1
Calibre: 20 mm (0.79 in)
Weights: travelling with ammunition 1800 kg (3,968 lb); firing with ammunition 1330 kg (2,932 lb)
Dimensions: length travelling 4.59 m (15 ft 0.7 in); width travelling 1.86 m (6 ft 1.2 in); height travelling 2.34 m (7 ft 8.1 in)
Elevation: +81°/–3°
Traverse: 360°
Ranges: maximum horizontal 5700 m (6,234 yards); effective horizontal 2200 m (2,406 yards); maximum vertical 4500 m (14,764 ft); effective vertical 1500 m (4,921 ft)
Crew: 5 (1 on mount)

An Oerlikon-Bührle 20-mm GAI-DO1 twin light anti-aircraft gun in firing position. Mounted each side of the 20-mm cannon is a box of 120 rounds of ready-use ammunition. The gunner aims the weapon using an Italian Galileo P56 sight and an aiming unit containing a computer.

Oerlikon 25-mm Diana light anti-aircraft gun

The Swiss company Oerlikon-Bürhle manufactures a wide range of 20-mm and 35-mm towed anti-aircraft gun systems, but some years ago realized that there was a gap between the most sophisticated 20-mm system (the twin GAI-DO1) and the twin 35-mm GDF series. To bridge this gap the company has developed the twin 25-mm **Diana** light anti-aircraft gun system, which has the company designation of the **GBF** series.

The Diana weighs only 2100 kg (4,630 lb) complete with ammunition, enabling it to be transported quickly by helicopters such as the Aérospatiale Puma or Sikorsky/Westland Sea King to where it is needed. The system is normally towed behind a light vehicle on its two-wheeled carriage. In the firing position the wheels are raised off the ground and the carriage is supported on three hydraulic jacks (one at the front and two at the rear) which can be adjusted to suit varying ground conditions.

So far two versions of the Diana are being offered, the **GBF-AOA** and the **GBF-BOB**. The first of these is armed with twin 25-mm KBA cannon, which is already used by four NATO countries installed in armoured vehicles and has a cyclic rate of fire of 570 rounds per barrel per minute. The 25-mm KBA fires five different types of ammunition: high explosive incendiary-tracer (HEI-T), semi-armour-piercing high explosive incendiary shell with tracer (SAPHEI-T), target practice with tracer (TP-T), armour-piercing discarding sabot-tracer (APDS-T), and armour-piercing practice-tracer (APP-T). The HEI-T is used to engage aerial targets while the APDS-T round is used against ground targets and will penetrate 25 mm (0.98 in) of armour at an angle of 30° at a range of 2000 m (2,187 yards). The GBF-AOA is fitted with the Italian P75 Galileo sight.

The GBF-BOB has the Oerlikon KBB cannon, which is also used on the Sea Zenith naval anti-missile defence system. The KBB has a longer barrel than the KBA, and fires ammunition with a

This Oerlikon-Bührle Diana twin 25-mm light anti-aircraft gun system in the firing position shows the wheels raised clear of the ground. Each cannon has a dual-feed system enabling the gunner to switch from one type of ammunition to another to engage either ground or air targets.

Oerlikon 25-mm Diana light anti-aircraft gun (continued)

higher muzzle velocity and therefore greater target penetration. The GBF-BOB also has the Contraves Gun King sight which was first installed on the 35-mm GDF series of anti-aircraft guns. This features an optical sight with a magnification of ×5 and a 12° field of view, night sight, laser rangefinder with a range of 5000 m (5,468 yards) to an accuracy of ±5 m (5.46 yards), and a digital computer. Both the GBF-AOA and GBF-BOB have powered elevation and traverse to allow high-speed targets to be tracked: maximum traverse speed is 80° per second and maximum elevation speed is 48° per second.

The Diana can also be used in conjunction with the Contraves Sky Guard trailer-mounted fire-control system (originally designed for use with the Oerlikon GDF twin 35-mm cannon), which carries out both target surveillance and tracking. The Contraves Alerter radar can provide the gunner with the range and speed of the approaching target so the weapons are already laid in the general direction of the target as it appears.

As of early 1985 four prototypes of the Diana had been built with a turret suitable for installation on armoured vehicles.

The Oerlikon-Bührle Diana twin 25-mm light anti-aircraft gun has been introduced by the company to bridge the gap between its 20-mm and 35-mm weapons. Diana can be quickly brought into action and has a rapid elevation and traverse, thanks to its on-board auxiliary power unit.

Specification
Diana
Calibre: 25 mm (0.98 in)
Weights: without ammunition 1725 kg (3,803 lb); with ammunition 2100 kg (4,630 lb)

Dimensions: length travelling 4.295 m (14 ft 1.1 in); width travelling 2.10 m (6 ft 10.7 in); height travelling 2.13 m (6 ft 11.9 in)
Elevation: +85°/−5°
Traverse: 360°

Ranges: maximum horizontal 6000 m (6,562 yards); effective horizontal 3000 m (3,281 yards); maximum vertical 5000 m (16,404 ft); effective vertical 2500 m (8,202 ft)
Crew: 4-5 (1 on mount)

Oerlikon 35-mm GDF anti-aircraft gun

In the late 1950s the Swiss company Oerlikon-Bührle developed a twin 35-mm towed anti-aircraft gun called the **1ZLA/353**, which today is more commonly known as the **GDF** series. Since this entered production in the early 1960s over 1,600 weapons have been built for sale to at least 20 countries. Known operators of the GDF series include Argentina, Austria, Brazil, Cameroun, Finland, Greece, Japan, South Africa, Spain and Switzerland. Early in 1985 it was announced that the British Royal Air Force Regiment was to form a new air-defence squadron equipped with the GDF twin 35-mm system to protect the Nimrod AEW base at Waddington, Lincolnshire. These GDF anti-aircraft guns were captured during 1982 in the Falklands, where they had been used by Argentina to defend Port Stanley airfield in conjunction with Rheinmetall twin 20-mm light anti-aircraft guns and Euromissile Roland surface-to-air missiles. It is believed that the Argentine GDFs shot down four British Aerospace Harrier aircraft and at least two Argentine aircraft as well.

The GDF twin 35-mm anti-aircraft gun system is mounted on a four-wheeled carriage. In the firing position the wheels are raised clear of the ground and supported on four jacks, one at each end and one on each side on outriggers. Weapon elevation and traverse are electro-hydraulic, traverse speed being a maximum of 112° per second and elevation a maximum of 56° per second.

Since its introduction the GDF has been constantly modernized and many of these modifications are now available in kit form to enable purchasers of older weapons to bring them up to the latest production standard. The GDF-005 is the most recent model, which features a Contraves 'Gun King' computerized optronic sighting system, a fully automatic reloader and

Twin 35-mm GDF anti-aircraft gun in travelling mode. When in firing position the carriage is raised clear of the ground and supported on four outriggers. This system is most effective when used with a fire control system such as the Swiss Contraves Skyguard.

more ammunition.

The GDF series is armed with twin 35-mm KDB automatic cannon which have a cyclic rate of fire of 550 rounds per barrel per minute. The barrels are each fitted with a muzzle brake, and can be fitted with muzzle velocity-measuring equipment which feeds information to the fire-control system. A total of 112 rounds of ready-use ammunition is carried, with a further 126 rounds held in reserve on the mount. Each barrel has 56 rounds of ready-use ammunition in clips of seven rounds. Ammunition fired is of the fixed type and includes high explosive incendiary-tracer (HEI-T), high explosive incendiary (HEI), semi-armour-piercing high explosive incendiary-tracer (SAPHEI-T) and practice rounds.

The basic GDF is a clear-weather system only, but most countries prefer to use it in conjunction with a fire-control system. This was originally the Contraves Super Fledermaus, but this has been replaced in production by the much more effective Contraves Skyguard system. A typical GDF bat-

tery consists of two GDF twin 35-mm anti-aircraft guns, two generators and a single Skyguard fire-control system.

Specification
GDF
Calibre: 35 mm (1.38 in)
Weights: travelling (with ammunition) 6700 kg (14,771 lb); travelling (without ammunition) 6300 kg (13,889 lb)
Dimensions: length travelling 7.80 m (25 ft 7.1 in); width travelling 2.26 m (7 ft 5 in); height travelling 2.60 m (8 ft 6.4 in)
Elevation: +92°/−5°

Although designed primarily for use in the anti-aircraft role, the Oerlikon-Bührle twin 35-mm GDF anti-aircraft gun system is also highly effective in the ground role, and was thus used by the Argentine army against the British in the 1982 Falklands conflict.

Traverse: 360°
Ranges: maximum horizontal 9500 m (10,389 yards); maximum vertical 6000 m (19,685 ft); effective vertical 4000 m (13,123 ft)
Crew: 3 (on mount)

40-mm Bofors L/70 anti-aircraft gun

Over 50 years ago the Bofors company developed a 40-mm towed anti-aircraft gun which within a few years became world famous. This had a 60-calibre barrel (resulting in the standard appellation Bofors 40 mm L/60) and had a cyclic rate of fire of 120 rounds per minute. This weapon was widely used during World War II and was manufactured under licence in many countries including the USA (as the M1), the UK (the Mk 1), Hungary, Italy and Poland. Even in 1985 the weapon remains in front-line service with more than 10 countries.

After the end of World War II a much-improved 40-mm light anti-aircraft gun was developed by Bofors, and this entered service in 1951 as the 40-mm Bofors L/70. In addition to having a longer 70-calibre barrel, the new weapon had a rate of fire increased to 300 rounds per minute (cyclic). This higher fire rate was achieved by ramming the new round during run-out and ejecting the empty cartridge cases forward of the mount towards the end of recoil. Initially two models of the Bofors 40-mm L/70 were offered, these being designated the **Bofors L/70 Model A** and **Bofors L/70 Model B**. The Model A relied on an external source for power while the Model B had its own generator mounted towards the front of the carriage.

The basic Bofors L/70 has a six-man crew, of whom four are on the carriage at all times: the elevation and traverse layers are seated one on each side of the mount, while two ammunition feeders are placed one on each side at the

The Swedish Bofors 40-mm L/70 anti-aircraft gun is shown in the travelling position. This is the Model B with an auxiliary power unit mounted on the rear of the carriage, enabling the weapon to be run without any external power source and to be brought into action much faster.

rear. Ammunition is fed to the weapon in clips of four rounds and an ammunition tray above the weapon can hold 26 rounds of ready-use ammunition. At the rear of the mount, one on each side, are ready-use racks that hold 96 rounds of ammunition.

Weapon elevation and mount traverse are electro-hydraulic, with manual controls for emergency use. Maximum elevation speed is 45° per second and maximum traverse speed is 85° per second.

Ammunition development is a continuous process at Bofors, and today five basic rounds are available for the Bofors L/70 anti-aircraft gun in its land and numerous naval applications. All ammunition fired by the gun is of the fixed type. The five types are pre-fragmented high explosive (PFHE), high-capacity high explosive (HCHE),

high explosive-tracer (HE-T), armour-piercing capped-tracer (APC-T), and training. Additional details of the Bofors L/70 ammunition and its associated fire-control systems are given elsewhere.

In the firing position the wheels are raised clear of the ground and the carriage is supported on four jacks, one at each end of the carriage and one on each side on outriggers.

The Bofors L/70 has been made under licence in a number of countries including the UK, Italy, Spain, India, West Germany and the Netherlands. It is normally towed by a 4×4 or 6×6 truck, which also carries the crew and supply of ready-use ammunition. In some countries, for example the UK and West Germany, the Bofors L/70 has now been replaced by missiles such as Rapier or Roland. Neverthe-

less, with an up-to-date fire-control system, the Bofors L/70 remains a highly effective weapon system.

Specification
Bofors L/70
Calibre: 40 mm (1.57 in)
Weights: travelling (with generator) 5150 kg (11,354 lb); travelling (without generator) 4800 kg (10,582 lb)
Dimensions: length travelling 7.29 m (23 ft 11 in); width travelling 2.25 m (7 ft 4.6 in); height travelling 2.349 m (7 ft 8.5 in)
Elevation: +90°/-4°
Traverse: 360°
Ranges: maximum horizontal 12500 m (13,670 yards); maximum vertical 8700 m (28,543 ft); effective vertical 4000 m (13,123 ft)
Crew: 6 (4 on mount)

Below: This Bofors L/70 Model A of the Austrian army has had a muzzle velocity measuring device fitted for testing purposes. The Model A relies on an external power source for operations, but otherwise differs little from other versions and fires the same wide range of ammunition.

Right: The Bofors BOFI (Bofors Optronic Fire-control Instrument) all-weather gun system is a Model B L/70 to which has been added a pulse-Doppler automatic acquisition and tracking radar, an optronic tracker and a laser rangefinder. A fair-weather system is available without the radar.

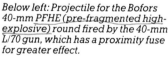

Below left: Projectile for the Bofors 40-mm PFHE (pre-fragmented high-explosive) round fired by the 40-mm L/70 gun, which has a proximity fuse for greater effect.

Below: Cross-section of the new Bofors 40-mm PFHE (pre-fragmented high-explosive) round, with the fuse on the right and high-explosive content on left.

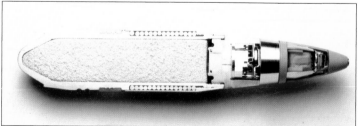

Anti-Tank Missiles

Today, as in the past, the tank remains a dominant force on the battlefield. It is being challenged, however, by a new generation of weapons which range from man-portable systems to those carried by armoured vehicles and assault helicopters.

Modern anti-tank weapons are divided into three basic categories. Heavy anti-tank weapons (HAWs) are designed to engage enemy armour well away from the defensive location, and are typified by such systems as TOW and 'Sagger'. Medium anti-tank weapons (MAWs) can engage targets out to about 1000 m (1,095 yards) from the defensive position, and are typified by the Carl Gustav and Folgore. Light anti-tank weapons (LAWs) are usually simple one-shot throw-away systems, such as the LAW80, that are used to engage close-range targets.

In terms of operational use, MAWs and LAWs have seen extensive service from World War II onwards, whilst HAWs, which are almost all anti-tank guided weapons (ATGW), have only recently come of age.

The 1973 Yom Kippur War saw the first extensive use of the ATGW, initial press reports after the war indicating that these weapons had finally vanquished the tank as the primary battlefield weapon. However, the constructive technical evaluations which followed showed that it was in fact the tank gun which scored the highest success rate, both the ATW and the LAW being classed as only moderately successful. This was in complete contrast with the relatively poor showing of the ATGW in the

The M151 Jeep and Bell UH-1B mounted TOW systems first saw combat in the Vietnam War during the 1972 North Vietnamese invasion of the South. The two helicopter systems deployed recorded 73 hits out of their first 89 missiles fired, destroying at least 26 tanks. TOW can also be fired from ground mounts, or as here from vehicles such as the M151 Jeep.

1956 Sinai campaign, the 1967 Six-Day War and the 1971 Indo-Pakistan conflict. The 1972 North Vietnamese invasion of South Vietnam saw the first uses of ATGWs in South East Asia, in the forms of the AT-3 'Sagger' and then the TOW, the latter initially being used in the helicopter-borne role with startling success. Further proof of the potency of the helicopter/ATGW pairing has come since then in both the continuing Gulf War and the 1982 'Peace for Galilee' invasion of Lebanon by Israel. High confidence in such systems is demonstrated today by the high proportion of resources that both NATO and the Warsaw Pact are investing in these developments, whilst other more exotic weapons are being researched.

A British Aerospace Swingfire explodes against the thick hide of a Conqueror heavy tank. Conventional armour is no longer proof against the modern warhead, and such a strike would almost certainly disable the vehicle.

BAe Swingfire

Swingfire is the standard long-range ATGW of the British army, and is used from tracked vehicles. In its Beeswing guise the missile is produced under licence by Egypt to replace the obsolete Soviet AT-1 'Snapper' missile.

The **BAe Swingfire** is the British army's long-range wire-guided ATGW, and was designed originally for use on vehicles operating with armoured units. Allocated to the Royal Artillery, the Swingfire is mounted on the Striker (five with five reloads) and the FV438 (two with 14 reloads) armoured vehicles. Both can engage targets in either the direct or separated-fire modes. In the latter the controller can site himself up to 100 m (110 yards) from the launch point and up to 23 m (75 ft) higher, with the target up to 20° above or below the horizontal axis and up to 45° to each side of the concealed launcher's bearing. The Swingfire has now been adapted to fit on almost any vehicle and, in the **Beeswing** version, can be used from a removable crew-served launcher assembly. Once fired the missile is automatically gathered into the control sight's field of view, after which the operator flies the missile to the target by a joystick control. The warhead is able to defeat the armour of all known battle tanks. To improve the missile's combat capabilities a thermal-imaging sight has been developed for night engagements, and micro-miniaturized electronics have been introduced to increase reliability and maintainability. The Beeswing is currently being licence-built in Egypt, which is also supplying Sudan with the system. Current operators of the Swingfire system are Belgium, Egypt, Kenya, Sudan and the UK.

Specification
Swingfire
Type: anti-tank missile
Dimensions: length 1.07 m (3 ft 6 in); diameter 17.0 cm (6.7in); span 37.3 cm (14.7in)
Launch weight: 27 kg (60 lb)
Propulsion: two-stage solid-propellant booster/sustainer rocket
Performance: range 150-4000 m (165-4,375 yards)
Warhead: 7-kg (15.4-lb) hollow-charge HE
Armour penetration: 800 mm (31.5 in) or more

A British army FV438 fires a Swingfire ATGW from its roof-mounted missile launcher rack assembly. The 4000-m (4,375-yard) range missile has a 7-kg (15.4-lb) hollow charge warhead capable of defeating the armour of all current main battle tanks.

Hunting LAW80

The one-shot disposable **Hunting LAW80** weapon is under development by Hunting Engineering Ltd to replace the British army's Carl Gustav MAW and M72 LAW systems. The LAW80 will be capable of disabling all the armoured vehicle types likely to be encountered on the battlefield in the next decade or so, from all angles of attack (including head on through the frontal armour plate). This requirement makes the weapon more expensive in terms of size, weight and cost than contemporary LAW systems. The launcher will be issued as a round of ammunition, and will be equipped with an integral 9-mm 5-round spotting rifle attachment to ensure a very high first-round hit probability. To fire the 4-kg (8.8-lb) round the launcher's two protective end caps are discarded, the projectile tube extended to its fullest extent, and the weapon armed and cocked. The firer then uses the spotting rifle and, if he decides not to shoot, can close the blast shield to make the weapon safe until the next action. The LAW80 will also be issued to the Royal Marines and the RAF Regiment. But though designed to replace the Carl Gustav, the LAW80 will not be able to give the same service as it is unable to function as an infantry support weapon in firing HE, smoke and illuminating rounds. In this respect the army might well be advised to reconsider its options and retain the Carl Gustav at higher unit levels.

Specification
LAW80
Type: anti-tank rocket-launcher
Dimensions: length 1.0 m (3 ft 3.4 in) folded and 1.5 m (4 ft 11.1 in) extended; calibre 9.4 cm (3.7 in)
Weight: 9.5 kg (20.9 lb)
Performance: range 500 m (545 yards)
Ammunition: advanced-design 4-kg (8.8-lb) hollow-charge rocket
Armour penetration: estimated at 600 mm (23.62 in) or more

Bofors Bantam

The **Bofors Bantam** is a small first-generation one-man portable manual command to line of sight wire-guided missile produced by AB Bofors. The missile container holds both the missile and a 20-m (66-ft) control cable which connects the missile to the control unit, which can take up to three missiles. Distribution boxes can be connected to each of the cables to boost this number to 18. To bring the Bantam into action the container is placed on the ground and the control unit is connected (if necessary extra cable can be used to displace the operator by up to 120 m/130 yards from the missile site). The operator then selects from between one and four of the tracking flares carried on the missile (according to the prevailing conditions of visibility) and launches the

The ground-launched version of the AB Bofors Bantam ATGW emerges from its container-launcher box under power from the booster. After 40 m (130 ft) of wire is reeled out, a micro-switch ignites the sustainer motor.

Bofors Bantam (continued)

Right: The Swedish Bantam was one of the first generation wire-guided ATGWs, and was produced in large numbers until 1978 for the armies of Sweden and Switzerland. It is one of the smallest and lightest of the ATGWs and introduced into service the GRP airframe with folding wings.

The Bantam can also be used from fixed-wing light aircraft, or helicopters such as the Swedish army Agusta-Bell AB.204 Huey seen here. The Swedes are already supplementing this old missile with quantities of the modern American TOW.

Bantam. The sustainer and flare are ignited after 40 m (130 ft) of guidance wire has been reeled out and the booster section has burnt out. The warhead is armed after 230 m (250 yards) and the operator manually guides the missile to the target. Only two countries, Sweden and Switzerland, adopted the Bantam, in 1963 and 1967 respectively, in a variety of launching modes including one from light fixed-wing aircraft. Production finished in the 1970s, and although the missile is considered to be obsolete it is still found in some numbers with those countries.

Specification
Bantam
Type: anti-tank missile
Dimensions: length 0.85 m (2 ft 9.46 in); diameter 11.0 cm (4.33 in); span 40.0 cm (15.75 in)
Launch weight: including the container 11.5 kg (25.35 lb)
Propulsion: two-stage solid-propellant booster/sustainer rocket
Performance: range 300-2000 m (330-2,190 yards)
Warhead: 1.9-kg (4.2-lb) hollow-charge HE
Armour penetration: 500 mm (19.68 in) or more

 SWEDEN
FFV Ordnance Carl Gustav

Right: The Carl Gustav is normally fired by a two-man crew, one acting as the gunner and the other as the loader. A well-trained team can fire about six rounds per minute at moving or stationary armoured vehicles out to 400-500 m (437-547 yards) distance.

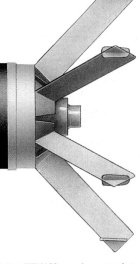

The 84-mm (3.31-in) calibre M2 Carl Gustav is seen here with the HEAT and HE rounds that it fires, together with the canisters in which they are carried.

The 84-mm (3.31-in) calibre **FFV Ordnance Carl Gustav** recoilless gun is intended for use by the infantry as a medium anti-armour weapon. It is normally crewed by two men, one acting as the firer and the other as the loader and ammunition carrier. A well-trained crew can sustain a rate of fire of six rounds per minute. The weapon is breech-loaded and can be fired from the shoulder, from the prone position, from the edge of a trench or from a mount on an APC. The usual sighting system on the **Carl Gustav M2** model is a ×2 telescope with a 17° field of view. The M2 can effectively engage a stationary armoured vehicle at 500-m (545-yard) range with the FFV551 HEAT round, and a moving target at ranges up to 400 m (435 yards) with a penetration of 400 mm (15.75 in). It is also a useful infantry support weapon in that it can fire the 3.1-kg (6.8-lb) spin-stabilized FFV545 illuminating round to 2300 m (2,515 yards), the 3.1-

kg (6.8-lb) FFV469 smoke round to 1300 m (1,420 yards) and the 3.1-kg (6.8-lb) FFV441 HE shrapnel round to an effective range of 1000 m (1,095 yards).

An improved version with a better sight, the **Carl Gustav M2-550**, has also been produced to fill the gap between close-range weapons and the ATGW. This uses a higher-velocity rocket-assisted HEAT round, the FFV551, which has a maximum effective engagement range of 700 m (765 yards) with the same armour-penetration capability as the FFV551 round, and can also fire the rounds mentioned above. A new 3.2-kg (7.1-lb) dual-purpose HE/HEAT FFV502 projectile is also under development for the Carl Gustav series, this being designed for use against light armoured vehicles (out to 250 m/275 yards with 200-mm/7.87 in armour penetration or more) as well as unprotected targets to 1000 m

(1,095 yards). In order to defeat the new composite-armour tanks, production is about to start of the FFV597 two-piece over-calibre rocket-assisted fin-stabilized HEAT round with a stand-off probe fuse to give optimum penetration effect. The FFV597 consists of a 4-kg (8.8-lb) warhead section, which is inserted into the muzzle of the gun, and a 3-kg (6.6-lb) propulsion cartridge which is loaded as normal. The 5.8-kg (12.8-lb) projectile has a range in excess of 300 m (330 yards) and can penetrate over 900 mm (35.43 in) of frontal armour.

A lightweight version of the standard weapon, the **Carl Gustav M3**, entered production in 1984 and is able to fire all the existing types of ammunition. The Carl Gustav has seen extensive combat use throughout the world, including use with the British forces on the Falklands in 1982. The basic Carl Gustav M2 is used by Australia, Austria, Canada, Denmark, Eire, Ghana, the Netherlands, Norway, Sweden, the United Arab Emirates, UK, East Germany and several other countries; the Carl Gustav M2-550 is operated by Japan, Sweden and other countries; and the Carl Gustav M3 is used only by Sweden.

Specification
Carl Gustav
Type: anti-tank rocket-launcher
Dimensions: length 1.13 m (3 ft 8.5 in); calibre 8.4 cm (3.31 in)
Weight: M2 14.2 kg (31.3 lb), M2-550 15 kg (33.1 lb) and M3 8 kg (17.6 lb)
Performance: range see text
Ammunition: see text
Armour penetration: see text

FRANCE
Aérospatiale SS.11

Originally developed by Nord-Aviation, the **Aérospatiale SS.11** started life in 1953 as the **Type 5210** and entered service with the French army in 1956. Apart from its normal ground- or vehicle-launched role, it can also be launched from a helicopter or ship. It is a manually-guided line-of-sight weapon, the operator acquiring the target by means of a telescopic sight. As soon as the missile enters his field of view after launch the operator commands it to his line of sight via a joystick control and wires, and then flies it to the target using tracking flares mounted on the rear of the missile for visual reference. From 1962 a modified **SS.11B1** variant was produced with transistorized firing equipment. This weapon can be fitted with a variety of warheads including the Type 140AC anti-tank, the Type 140AP02 semi-armour-piercing delay-action anti-personnel, and the Type 140AP59 anti-personnel fragmentation. Production ceased at the beginning of the 1980s after some 179,000 rounds of the SS.11 family had been built for more than 20 countries. A modified SS.11 derivative with a much improved semi-automatic guidance system, the Harpon, was

First developed in the 1950s, the SS.11 family has seen action in over a dozen conflicts, including the 1982 Falklands war and the current Gulf War.

produced in some numbers for the French, West German and Saudi Arabian armies from 1967 onwards. The missile family has seen action in numerous conflicts over the years and was used most recently from British army Westland Scout helicopters against Argentine ground positions during the recapture of the Falklands in 1982. It is also seeing regular use in the Gulf War with both the Iraqis and the Iranians. Current operators of the SS.11 are Argentina, France, India, Iran, Iraq, Italy, Tunisia, Turkey, UK, Venezuela and a number of undisclosed customers. As far as is known, the only current possessor of the Harpon type is India.

France used the SS.11 when it was amongst the earliest missiles to arm helicopters for the anti-tank role, as exemplified by the Aérospatiale Gazelle III in action here.

Produced in large numbers since 1956, the SS.11 has served in many armies on a wide variety of vehicles. This triple launcher was photographed in Portugal.

Specification
SS.11B1
Type: anti-tank missile
Dimensions: length 1.20 m (3 ft 11.25 in); diameter 16.40 cm (6.46 in); span 50.00 cm (19.7 in)
Launch weight: 29.9 kg (65.9 lb)
Propulsion: two-stage solid-propellant rocket
Performance: range 500-3000 m (545-3,280 yards)
Warhead: see text
Armour penetration: Type 140AC 600 mm (23.62 in) and Type 140AP02 10 mm (0.4 in)

FRANCE/WEST GERMANY
Euromissile HOT

The **Euromissile HOT** is the heavyweight spin-stabilized tube-launched wire-guided counterpart to the MILAN for use from dug-out positions, vehicles and helicopters. Planned as the direct replacement for the SS.11, the HOT has automatic command to line of sight guidance with an IR tracking system. All the operator has to do is to keep his optical tracking sight on the target to ensure a hit. This guidance system allows a very rapid gathering of the missile to the line of sight after launch, thus enabling a very

The long-range HOT is designed to be fired from vehicles, helicopters and fixed positions against tanks, infantry combat vehicles and APC targets. To ensure its lethality

against the new generation of Soviet laminate armour, an improved hollow-charge warhead is under development.

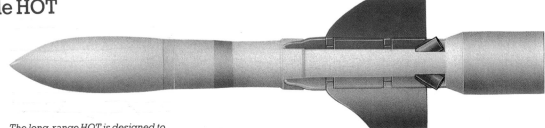

good short-range engagement envelope. Vehicles which have been fitted with the system include the M113 APC (two launchers with 11 reloads), the AMX-10P APC (four launchers with 16-20 reloads), the Panhard M3 APC (four launcher with 14 reloads), the Saviem VAB armoured vehicle (four launchers with eight reloads) and the Raketenjagdpanzer tank destroyer 3 (one launcher with 8 reloads). The helicopter types that have been fitted include the MBB PAH1 (six rounds), the Aérospatiale SA 341 and SA 342L Gazelle (four or six rounds), the Aérospatiale SA 361H Dauphin (eight rounds) and the Westland Lynx (eight rounds). The large hollow-charge warhead is detonated by distortion of the

A West German army Jagdpanzer Jaguar 1 tank destroyer fires a Euromissile HOT ATGW. The 316 Jaguars were rebuilt from Jagdpanzer Rakete vehicles equipped with two launchers for the less capable SS.11 ATGW during the period 1978-83.

nose skin to allow incidence attacks of up to 65°. The warhead is said to be capable of penetrating the armour of all known battle tanks in frontal attacks. The Syrians used HOT against the Israelis in the 1982 'Peace for Galilee' war from Gazelle helicopters on up to 100 occasions, and credit the system with destroying a sizable number of Israeli tanks and APCs. The Iraqis also

use it against the Iranians in the Gulf War from both vehicle and helicopter platforms. Euromissile, the manufacturer, states that as at early 1984 14 countries have ordered 52,907 missiles. Current operators of the HOT missile are Egypt, France, Iraq, Kuwait, Libya, Saudi Arabia, Spain, Syria, West Germany and five undisclosed countries.

Specification
HOT
Type: anti-tank missile
Dimensions: length 1.275 m (4 ft 2.2 in); diameter 16.5 cm (6.5 in); span 31.2 cm (12.28 in)
Launch weight: missile 23.5 kg (51.8 lb)

The Panhard 4×4 VCR APC, armed with the Euromissile Mephisto launcher system for the HOT long range ATGW. The UTM800 HOT turret variant of the 6×6 Panhard VCR/TT has already seen combat with the Iraqi army during the Gulf War.

and missile in launch tube 32 kg (70.55 lb)
Propulsion: solid-propellant booster/ sustainer rocket
Performance: range 75-4250 m (82-4,650 yards)
Warhead: 6-kg (13.2-lb) hollow-charge HE
Armour penetration: 800 mm (31.5 in) or more

FRANCE/WEST GERMANY
Euromissile MILAN

The **Euromissile MILAN** is an advanced wire-guided second-generation man-portable spin-stabilized ATGW, and started life in 1962 as a design study between Nord-Aviation and Messerschmitt-Bölkow. It incorporates a semi-automatic guidance technique that requires the operator only to maintain the cross hairs of his guidance unit sight on the target during the engagement. The system comprises a launch-and-control unit and a missile in a container-launcher tube, which is mounted on the launcher/controller just before firing. The whole system can then be mounted on a tripod for ground launch or on a pivot for vehicle launch. Since it attained operational status the MILAN has had a night-firing capability developed for it in the form of the MIRA thermal imaging device for the French, West German and British armies. This consists of a 7-kg (15.4-lb) imaging sight which is mounted on the firing post to allow the detection of targets at over 3000 m (3,280 yards)

The MILAN has already seen combat service in a number of conflicts including Chad, where one was used to knock out a Panhard ERC armoured car that had been captured by the Libyan-backed rebels.

Above: The MILAN was used extensively in the 1982 Falklands war by the British army and Royal Marines, who fired several hundred

against well-prepared bunkers and emplacements in the hills and mountains barring the way to Port Stanley.

and their engagement at about 1500 m (1,640 yards). Once the missile has been launched, the forces inherent in the system throw the used container-launcher (which has been automatically disconnected) backwards from the firing post for reloading. The missile is automatically tracked in flight by an IR unit in the control unit, which monitors the radiation output from the tail-mounted flares on the missile. A programme is currently under way to improve the warhead's effectiveness by at least 25 per cent at close range against the new types of laminated armour protecting Soviet tanks. By early 1984 30 countries had bought a total of 164,576 missiles. Although a relatively new system, the MILAN has seen combat in Chad against the Libyans, in the Gulf War and in the Falklands with the UK against Argentina. In the last conflict it gained a reputation as a capable but somewhat expensive 'bunker basher'. The MILAN is used by Algeria, Belgium, Cameroun, Chad, Chile, Egypt, Eire, France, Greece, India, Iraq, Israel, Iran, Kenya, Lebanon, Libya, Morocco, Senegambia, Soma-lia, Spain, Syria, Tunisia, UK, West Germany and five other countries.

Specification
Type: anti-tank missile
Dimensions: length 0.769 m (2 ft 6.28 in); diameter 9.0 cm (3.54 in); span 26.5 cm (10.43 in)
Launch weight: missile 6.65 kg (14.66 lb) and complete launcher outfit (with control unit, launcher tube and tripod) 16.5 kg (36.38 lb)
Propulsion: solid-propellant booster/sustainer rocket
Performance: range 25-2000 m (27-2,190 yards)
Warhead: 2.98-kg (6.57-lb) hollow-charge HE
Armour penetration: 650 mm (25.6 in) or more

The man-portable Euromissile MILAN, mounted on the rear of a West German army Faun Kraka 4×2 light vehicle. The MILAN-equipped Kraka with six reload missiles has replaced the 106-mm recoilless rifle vehicles of the same type.

WEST GERMANY

MBB Cobra and Mamba

The **MBB Cobra** started life in 1957 as a project by Bölkow GmbH, and went into service three years later in an initial 1600-m (1,750-yard) range form with the West German army. Since then some 170,000 or more rounds have been produced in both this form and the 2000-m (2,185-yard) range definitive **BO 810 Cobra 2000** version for the armed forces of 18 countries. A first-generation ATGW, the Cobra is a one man line-of-sight wire-guided missile that is set up by being placed on the ground in a suitable space, with its nose preferably pointing in the required direction. The operator can deploy up to eight missiles in this fashion, the missiles being connected via 20-m (66-ft) cables to a junction box and thus to his control unit, which may itself be deployed up to a further 50 m (165 ft) away. The operator uses the controller to select and fire the round that is in the best position to engage the target. Once launched, the missile is given a vertical boost to rise into the air, where the limited-duration sustainer takes over. The operator then rapidly gathers the missile into his line of sight and flies the missile to the target with the aid of a joystick and tail-mounted flares.

In 1972 MBB announced a successor to the Cobra 2000 known as the **Mamba**. Of the same general appearance, this weapon system has a new and improved controller that can be attached to up to 12 missiles, and a new propulsion unit which allows jet lift throughout the flight at a higher maximum speed to give a shorter flight time. The Mamba is still in production and has replaced the Cobra in a number of armies with the added bonus that it can be fired from a five-round missile-launch frame mounted on a vehicle. The Cobra was used in combat during the Indo-Pakistan War of 1971 and by Israel against the Arabs in 1973. Current operators of the Cobra include Argentina, Brazil (licence-built), Denmark, Greece, Israel, Italy (licence-built), Pakistan (licence-built), Spain, Turkey (licence-built), West Germany

Above: The first post-war German ATGW missile, the Cobra, achieved operational status with the West German army in 1960. Since then it has been superseded by the Mamba depicted here.

Below: Argentina took supplies of Cobras to the Falklands in their 1982 invasion, although none saw any use. Left-over stores were destroyed in controlled explosions.

(in store) and eight undisclosed countries. The Mamba is used by Chile and an unknown number of other countries.

Specification
Cobra
Type: anti-tank missile
Dimensions: length 0.95 m (3 ft 1.4 in); diameter 10.0 cm (3.93 in); span 48.0 cm (1 ft 6.6 in)
Launch weight: 10.3 kg (22.7 lb)
Propulsion: solid-propellant booster/sustainer rocket
Performance: range 400-2000 m (435-2,190 yards)
Warhead: 2.7-kg (5.95-lb) hollow-charge HE or anti-tank shrapnel
Armour penetration: hollow charge 500 mm (19.69 in) and shrapnel 350 mm (13.78 in)

Specification
Mamba
Type: anti-tank missile
Dimensions: length 0.955 m (3 ft 1.6 in); diameter 12.0 cm (4.72 in); span 40.0 cm (1 ft 3.75 in)
Launch weight: 11.2 kg (24.7 lb)
Propulsion: solid-propellant booster/sustainer rocket
Performance: range 300-2000 m (330-2,190 yards)
Warhead: 2.7-kg (5.95-lb) hollow-charge HE
Armour penetration: 500 m (19.69 in)

The Cobra ATGW was used in combat during the 1965 Indo-Pakistan war, with limited results. Despite this the missile is used by a number of armies in conjunction with other systems as a very useful man-portable unit.

Above: A Cobra sectioned to show the major internal subsystems. The booster rocket used to launch the missile can be seen between the lower pair of wings, its nozzle deflected downwards to give the sudden initial jump into the air on firing.

USA
Hughes BGM-71 TOW

The **Hughes BGM-71 TOW** (Tube-launched Optically-tracked Wire-guided) heavy anti-tank missile for helicopter- or vehicle-launch application entered the design phase in 1962, the first guided firings taking place in 1968. Two years later TOW entered service, and by the summer of 1972 had seen its first combat firings when it was used against North Vietnamese tank units. During the 1973 Yom Kippur War the Israelis had it delivered as part of the arms lift by the USA, and by 1984 the missile had been used in many conflicts all over the world. On the strength of its operational success the TOW has become the West's most numerous ATGW with over 350,000 units so far produced for more than 25 countries. As in most contemporary systems, all the operator has to do is keep the cross hairs of his optical sight on the target, an IR sensor tracking the signal from the missile to permit the calculation of correction commands which are automatically sent via the guidance wire link. In order to improve the lethality of the warhead of infantry units' TOW missiles, a two-stage upgrade programme was adopted; the first phase was marked by the procurement of a warhead of 127-mm (5-in) diameter fitted with a telescopic nose probe fuse that pops out when the missile is in flight to give an optimum stand-off penetration

The TOW is now a standard Western ATGW system and has been produced in four versions: the basic TOW as shown, the enhanced-range TOW, the Improved TOW and the TOW 2.

capability, the missile fitted with this warhead being known as the **Improved TOW**; the second stage saw the introduction of the **TOW 2** missile, which has a 152-mm (6-in) diameter warhead fitted with telescopic nose probe, improved digital guidance and a new propulsion system. All these improvements are also being retrofitted to the helicopter and armoured vehicle TOW launcher systems. The TOW version sometimes described as the **Extended-Range TOW** is the basic TOW variant that entered production from 1976 onwards with increased range capablities. The TOW missile is very widely used, typical operators being Bahrain, Canada, Denmark,

Egypt, Finland, Greece, Iran, Israel, Italy, Japan, Jordan, Kenya, Kuwait, Lebanon, Luxembourg, Morocco, the Netherlands, North Yemen, Norway, Oman, Pakistan, Portugal, Saudi Arabia, South Korea, Taiwan, Thailand, Turkey, United Arab Emirates, UK, USA and West Germany. Israel has developed a laser-guided version of TOW.

Specification
TOW
Type: anti-tank missile
Dimensions: length 1.174 m (3 ft 10.2 in) for basic model, 1.555 m (5 ft 1.2 in) for Improved TOW with probe, and 1.714 m (5 ft 7.5 in) for TOW 2 with probe; diameter 15.2 cm (6 in); span

34.3 cm (13.5 in)
Launch weight: 22.5 kg (49.6 lb) for basic model, 25.7 kg (56.65 lb) for Improved TOW, and 28.1 kg (61.95 lb) for TOW 2
Propulsion: two-stage solid-propellant rocket
Performance: range 65-3000 m (70-3,280 yards) for pre-1976 models, and 65-3750 m (70-4,100 yards) for post-1976 models
Warhead: 3.9-kg (8.6-lb) shaped-charge HE for basic and Improved TOW models, and 5.9-kg (13-lb) shaped-charge HE for TOW 2 model
Armour penetration: 600 mm (23.62 in) for basic model, 700 mm (27.56 in) for Improved TOW, and 800 mm (31.5 in) or more for TOW 2

McDonnell Douglas M47 Dragon

Above: Dragon has been supplied to a number of nations and is currently being used in combat by Iran against Iraq in the Gulf War. Propulsion is by 60 small rocket sustainers which fire in pairs and control attitude.

Right: The Dragon Medium Anti-tank/Assault Weapon is a tube-launched, optically tracked wire-guided missile operated by one man, who normally sits with his legs extended forward and the launcher resting on his shoulder, with the forward end of the smooth-bore glass fibre tube supported by a stand.

The manpack nature of Dragon is ideal for infantry units, as they can literally carry it on their backs around the battlefield. Further improvements to the missile to increase its range and lethality are under investigation in order to counter the current Soviet armour plate laminate types.

The **McDonnell Douglas M47 Dragon** (or **Medium Anti-tank/Assault Weapon**) was conceived in 1966 when an engineering development contract was awarded to the then McDonnell Aircraft Corporation. In 1972 the go-ahead was given to the follow-on McDonnell Douglas Corporation (MDC) for the first part of a multi-year procurement programme. From Fiscal Year 1975 onwards the procurement

was established initially on a two-source basis from MDC and Raytheon, though from 1975 the latter became sole source, with MDC as prime contractor. The Dragon is a one-man tube-launched optically-tracked wire-guided anti-tank weapon, with the front of the smooth-bore fibreglass tube supported on a stand and the firer normally seated with his legs extended forward with the mid-section of the tube resting on his shoulder. Once the missile has been fired the operator has no other task than keeping his cross hairs centred on the target. The missile is tracked in flight by a sensor that monitors the output from an infra-red transmitter on the missile's tail, and the displacement of this from the line of sight is measured. Any corrective commands are then sent via the wire.

Recently a 4.5-kg (9.9-lb) thermal-imaging sight has been put into production to give the missile a night-firing capability. Further improvements to achieve longer range, shorter flight time and greater warhead penetration are under investigation. Since its initial deployment, the Dragon has seen combat use with the Iranians, Moroccans and Israelis. The Dragon system is widely used, amongst the known operators being Iran, Israel, Jordan, Morocco, the Netherlands, North Yemen, Saudi Arabia, Spain, Switzerland, Thailand and the USA.

Specification
M47 Dragon
Type: anti-tank missile

Dimensions: length 0.744 m (2 ft 5.3 in); diameter 12.7 cm (5 in); span 33.0 cm (13 in)
Launch weight: missile 6.2 kg (13.66 lb) and whole system 13.8 kg (30.4 lb)
Propulsion: solid-propellant rocket after gas launch
Performance: range 75-1000 m (82-1,095 yards)
Warhead: 2.45-kg (5.4-lb) shaped-charge HE
Armour penetration: 600 mm (23.62 in)

The considerable debris and blast created by Dragon firing is evident in this photograph. Once fired, the fibreglass launcher is discarded and the tracking unit is clipped to a new launcher with its sealed-in missile.

ADATS

SWITZERLAND

The **Air Defence Anti-Tank System (ADATS)** has been developed from 1979 by Oerlikon-Bührle specifically as a private venture for the export market. Prime contractor for the missile is Martin Marietta of the USA. By 1983 three prototypes of ADATS had been completed, two mounted on the chassis of the well known FMC M113A2 full-tracked armoured personnel carrier and the third ready for installation on a variety of tracked and wheeled chassis. In 1986, ADATS was selected by Canada as winner of the Canadian Forces LLAD (low-level air-defence) competition for the 1990s. As such, the anti-tank role will be secondary, although more capable than most other systems.

The main part of the system is a power-operated turret that can be traversed through 360°, with the operator seated under cover between two banks of four missiles in launch containers. The latter can be elevated to +85° and depressed to −5°. The surveillance radar is mounted on the rear of the turret, the FLIR, TV tracker, laser rangefinder and missile guidance laser all being mounted in the forward part of the turret.

A typical aircraft target engagement would take place as follows. The airborne target is first detected by the Contraves Italiana surveillance radar (mounted on the turret rear), this being capable of detecting targets up to a maximum height of 5000 m (16,405 ft) and out to a maximum range of 20 km (12.4 miles). The radar first detects the target which, if confirmed as hostile, appears on the radar operator's PPI (plan position indicator) display. The radar operator is seated within the vehicle. The turret is then automatically traversed in bearing and search is initiated by the gunner to bring the target into the field of view of the FLIR or TV camera, the choice between the two sensors depending on the weather conditions at the time of the engagement; TV is used only in fair conditions. The sensor selected then locks onto the target and commences tracking. The target range is measured by the laser rangefinder to ensure that a missile is not launched if the target is not within range. Once the target is within range a missile is launched, riding along the missile-guidance radar beam until it impacts with the target.

The missile is carried in a launch/transport container which weighs 65 kg (143 lb) complete with missile. The latter has a Mach 3+ performance on its smokeless propellant motor, no wings and four control fins. It is fitted with a hollow-charge (HEAT) warhead that weighs 12 kg (26 lb) and gives a good fragmentation effect against aircraft. According to Oerlikon the missile's warhead will also penetrate over 900 mm (35.4 in) of armour. Two fuses are fitted, an impact type for ground targets and an electro-optical proximity type for aircraft targets. Engagement of ground targets is similar to that of aerial targets except that the target

is first detected by FLIR or TV tracker with the laser rangefinder being used to determine target range. When being used against ground targets minimum and maximum ranges are 500 and 6000 m (545 and 6,560 yards) respectively.

Specification
ADATS missile
Length: 2.05 m (6 ft 8.7 in)
Diameter: 15.2 cm (5.98 in)
Launch weight: 51 kg (112 lb)
Range: 8000 m (8,750 yards)
Altitude: 5000 m (16,405 ft)

Above: One of the two M113A2 ADATS prototypes launches a missile. The minimum and maximum ranges for an anti-tank engagement are 500 m (547 yards) and 6000 m (6562 yards) respectively.

Having to cope with airborne targets (at greater distances than is usual on the ground) means that the ADATS missile is considerably larger than usual ATGWs. This allows the engagement range to increase to some 6000 m (6562 yards), or nearly twice that of TOW.

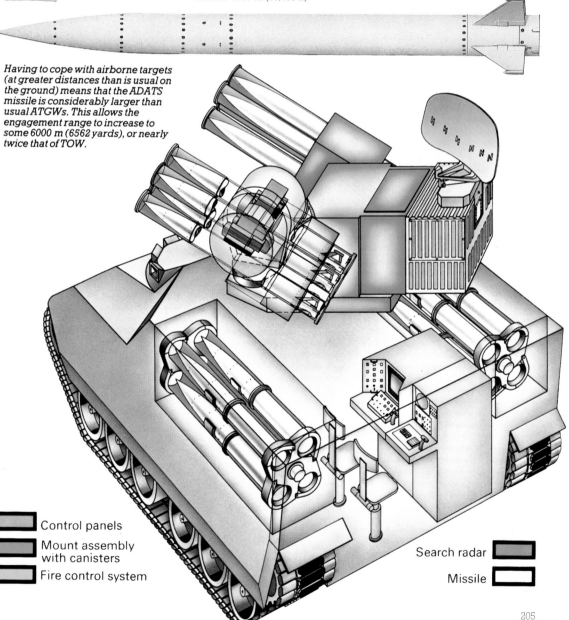

Designed as a dual role air defence/anti-tank missile system, ADATS consists of a 360° traversable turret with surveillance devices and eight ready-to-fire missile container-launchers that can be mounted on a variety of wheeled or tracked vehicles, such as the M113APC.

- Control panels
- Mount assembly with canisters
- Fire control system
- Search radar
- Missile

Breda Folgore

The **Breda Folgore** is a modern recoilless anti-tank rocket-launcher under advanced development by Breda Meccanica Bresciana for use in the shoulder-, tripod- or vehicle-mounted roles to a maximum range of 1000 m (1,095 yards) without too much effort in interchanging the systems. For the shoulder role it is normally operated by a two-man team, but can if required be used by one man only. A special lightweight optical sighting device and a bipod are used. In the case of the tripod mounting a larger optronic sight is provided in order to enable the aimer to estimate within a few seconds the target's range, speed and angle of elevation. The vehicle mounting is normally external to a small turret on a reconnaissance vehicle or APC with either of the sights mentioned above. The ammunition is the same in all three systems, and comprises a fin-stabilized hollow-charge rocket with a simple low pressure recoilless launching cartridge that both fires the rocket clear of the tube and brings it up to a speed sufficient for its own double-base propellant motor to ignite and sustain the forward motion. The fusing utilizes an electrical double-safety system that is initially operated when the projectile attains a fixed acceleration rate and secondly when it strikes the target, thus considerably reducing the possibility of a premature explosion. The Folgore is currently undergoing final field trials and it is not known yet whether the weapon has been adopted by any nation.

Specification
Folgore
Type: anti-tank rocket-launcher
Dimensions: length 1.85 m (6 ft 0.83 in); calibre 8.0 cm (3.15 in)
Weight: shoulder model 17 kg (37.5 lb) and tripod model 27 kg (59.5 lb)
Performance: effective range 50-700 m (55-765 yards)
Ammunition: 3-kg (6.6-lb) hollow-charge rocket with 2.2-kg (4.85-lb) ejection round
Armour penetration: not known

The Folgore shoulder-launch variant has an optical sighting device and is effective out to 700 m (766 yards).

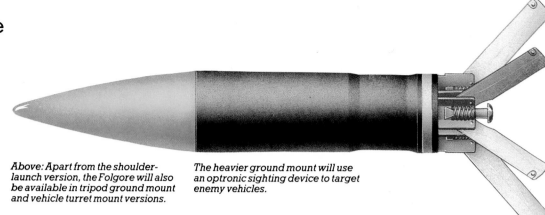

Above: Apart from the shoulder-launch version, the Folgore will also be available in tripod ground mount and vehicle turret mount versions.

The heavier ground mount will use an optronic sighting device to target enemy vehicles.

AT-2 'Swatter'

The **AT-2 'Swatter'** was the second of the Soviet first-generation ATGWs to be identified. It is a manually-guided command to line of sight vehicle- and helicopter-mounted system known to the Soviets as the **PTUR-62 'Falanga'**. It is unusual among ATGWs in having a UHF radio command guidance link with three possible frequencies for ECCM purposes. It is at its most effective when launched directly at the target but can, if required, be switched from one target to another as long as the new one is within the field of fire. The missile arms itself when it reaches 500 m (545 yards) from the launcher. In a later **'Swatter-B'** version the maximum range was increased from the 3000 m (3,280 yards) of the original **'Swatter-A'** to 3500 m (3,830 yards). A **'Swatter-C'** version is now used on the Mil Mi-24 'Hind-A' and 'Hind-D' gunship helicopters (four rounds), with semi-automatic command to line of sight guidance and a further increase in maximum range to 4000 m (4,375 yards). All three versions are used on BRDM-1 and BRDM-2 scout car conversions in quadruple mounts. The 'Swatter' is now being replaced by more modern systems, and as far as it is known has never been used in combat, although 'Hind A' and 'Hind-D' helicopters have been seen carrying the type in Afghanistan. Countries that use the 'Swatter' are Bulgaria, Cuba, Czechoslovakia, East Germany, Egypt, Hungary, Libya, Poland, Romania, South Yemen, Syria and the USSR.

Specification
AT-2 'Swatter'
Type: anti-tank missile
Dimensions: length 1.14 m (3 ft 8.88 in); diameter 13.2 cm (5.2 in); span 66.0 cm (26.0 in)
Launch weight: 'Swatter-A' 26.5 kg (58.4 lb), 'Swatter-B' 29.5 kg (65 lb) and 'Swatter-C' 32.5 kg (71.65 lb)
Propulsion: solid-propellant rocket
Performance: range 'Swatter-A' 500-3000 m (545-3,280 yards), 'Swatter-B' 500-3500 m (545-3,830 yards) and 'Swatter-C' 250-4000 m (275-4,375 yards)

The AT-2 'Swatter' was the second of the Soviet first-generation ATGWs to be named by NATO. It is currently used on the Mil Mi-24 'Hind-D' assault helicopter in the 'Swatter-C' variant with a semi-active command to a line-of-sight guidance system, out to a maximum effective range of some 4000 m (4,375 yards).

Warhead: hollow-charge HE
Armour penetration: 'Swatter-A' 480 mm (18.9 in) and 'Swatter-B/C' 510 mm (20.08 in)

AT-3 'Sagger'

The **AT-3 'Sagger'** is known to the Soviets as the **PTUR-64 'Malatyuka'**, and until recently was their standard domestic and export ATGW. It was produced in three versions, the optically-tracked manually wire-guided **Sagger-A'**, the **'Sagger-B'** which came into service in late 1973 and has an improved propulsion motor to make it 25 per cent faster, and the **'Sagger-C'** which is the 'Sagger-B' with semi-automatic guidance that entered service in the late 1970s. The 'Sagger' is used in a number of ways, that most often encountered being the three-man team carrying two rounds and the control unit. The 'Sagger' is also used on sextuple launchers on the BRDM-1 (with no reloads) and the BRDM-2 (with eight reloads) tank destroyers. Single-rail launchers are fitted to the BMP-1 and BMD infantry combat vehicles (with four reloads each) for self-defence. The missile, believed to be the 'Sagger-B' and 'Sagger-C' versions, is also carried on the Mil Mi-2 'Hoplite', Mi-8 'Hip' and Mi-24 'Hind' helicopters of the Warsaw Pact and allies, whilst the Yugoslavs have mated it to the Aérospatiale SA 342 Gazelle and their indigenous BOV-1 armoured vehicle on sextuple launcher (with six reloads). Other vehicle mounts include a modified East German BTR-40 APC and the Czech OT-64 APC. The missile has seen extensive combat service with many nations. The Arabs used it against the Israelis in the War of Attrition, the 1973 Yom Kippur War and the 1982 'Peace for Galilee' campaign. The North Vietnamese have used it against the South Vietnamese, Americans and Chinese in Indo-China, and the Iraqis have deployed the weapon extensively against Iranian targets in the Gulf War from the ground, vehicles and

Probably the best-known of the Soviet ATGWs is the AT-3 'Sagger', which gained notoriety during the 1973 Yom Kippur War when the Egyptians fired several thousand

'Hind-D' helicopters. Although not given the missile before their ideological split with the Soviets, the Chinese have since copied the type, and the Taiwanese have used it as the basis of their **Kun Wu** ATGW. The AT-3 'Sagger' is widely employed, known operators being Algeria, Angola, Bulgaria, China (unlicensed copy), Cuba, Czechoslovakia, East Germany, Egypt, Ethiopia, Hungary, India, Iraq, Israel, Libya, Mozambique, North Korea, Poland, Romania, South Yemen, Syria, Taiwan (unlicensed copy), USSR, Vietnam and Yugoslavia.

Specification
AT-3 'Sagger'
Type: anti-tank missile
Dimensions: length 0.883 m (2 ft 10.76 in); diameter 11.9 cm (4.69 in); span not known
Launch weight: 11.29 kg (24.9 lb)
Propulsion: two-stage solid-propellant rocket
Performance: range 300-3000 m (330-3,280 yards)
Warhead: 3-kg (6.6-lb) hollow-charge HE
Armour penetration: 410 mm (16.14 in) or more

against the Israeli Armoured Corps, with what turned out to be moderate success when compared to other anti-tank systems.

Above: A Soviet army AT-3 'Sagger-B' mounted on the launcher rail above the 73-mm gun of a BMP-1 infantry combat vehicle.

Below: A three-man infantry 'Sagger' team can deploy four missiles, checked and ready to fire, in between 12 and 15 minutes.

AT-4 'Spigot'

In the late 1970s persistent reports circulated about a new Soviet second-generation man-portable tripod-mounted ATGW with semi-automatic command to line of sight guidance. By 1980 the first photographs had appeared of the NATO-designated **AT-4 'Spigot'** system, which is believed to be called **'Faggot'** by the Soviets. The fact that in general appearance and operation the weapon is very similar to the Euromissile MILAN is more than coincidental, recent reports from the USA suggesting that the 'Spigot' is based on technology gained by spying and on the examination of actual specimens gained from third parties friendly to the Soviets. The main outward differ-

ences are that the AT-4's sight is smaller and that the guidance computer and goniometer are located in a box below the launch rail. By 1984 all of the most trusted Warsaw Pact allies had been issued with the 'Spigot' to replace the 'Sagger' in the manpack role, the three-man team now carrying four rounds, sight and a tripod mount. More recently the 'Spigot' has been seen in East Germany on BRDM-2/'Spandrel' vehicles on the two outermost (of five) launcher positions to give the vehicle a new missile load of six AT-5 'Spandrel' and eight 'Spigot' missiles. It has also been seen on some BMP-1 and BMD armoured vehicles replacing the 'Sagger' system; the same reload capacity is assumed. The 'Spigot' underwent its

baptism of fire with the Syrians in 1982 against the Israelis, and several samples were said to have been captured. The AT-4 'Spigot' system is used by Czechoslovakia, East Germany, Hungary, Poland, Syria, USSR and several other countries.

Specification
AT-4 'Spigot'
Type: anti-tank missile
Dimensions: not known
Launch weight: total system 40 kg (88.2 lb)
Propulsion: solid-propellant rocket
Performance: range 25-2000 m (27-2,190 yards)
Warhead: shaped charge HE
Armour penetration: 600 m (23.62 in) or more

The AT-4 looks enough like the Euromissile MILAN system that it could easily be a copy.

AT-5 'Spandrel'

The **AT-5 'Spandrel'** is a second-generation Soviet ATGW equivalent to the Euromissile HOT, and generally seen on BRDM-2 vehicles, on which the type is mounted in a quintuple launcher-tube assembly with a separate optical day and night tracking system on the vehicle's roof. A further five rounds are carried inside the vehicle as reloads. The BRDM-2 is replacing the older BRDM tank destroyer vehicles in the anti-tank companies of the Soviet units facing NATO and in Category 1 divisions within the USSR on a one-for-one basis. The missile is also to be found on the 30-mm gun-equipped BMP-2 as a roof installation in place of the 'Sagger' rail over the gun; a similar reload capacity is assumed. As far as it

can be ascertained, the Soviets have not yet exported or used the missile in combat. Further applications of the 'Spandrel' are expected over the next year or so.

Specification
AT-5 'Spandrel'
Type: anti-tank missile
Dimensions: length 1.30 m (4 ft 3.2 in); diameter 15.5 cm (6.1 in); span not known
Launch weight: 12 kg (26.45 lb)
Propulsion: solid-propellant rocket
Performance: range 100-4000 m (110-4,375 yards)
Warhead: hollow-charge HE
Armour penetration: 750 mm (29.53 in) or more

A close-up of the BRDM-2's quintuple launcher arrangement for the AT-5. The 'Spandrel' is very similar to

Euromissile's HOT in operation, and may be based on stolen technology.

AT-6 'Spiral'

The tube-launched **AT-6 'Spiral'** is believed to be the first third-generation Soviet ATGW. At present it is only deployed on the Mil Mi-24 'Hind-E' assault helicopter (four rounds) but its presence on the new Mi-28 'Havoc' attack helicopter as its standard ATGW payload is expected soon. Much conjecture has arisen over its guidance system, laser homing with a fire-and-forget capability being the most favoured suggestion. Recently, however, informed sources in the USA have indicated that the weapon has a much-improved radio command guidance unit with considerably enhanced ECCM capability than its predecessor, the AT-2 'Swatter'. This

would explain the apparent absence of a laser designator on the 'Hind-E'. No country other than the Soviet Union has fielded the AT-6, which indicates the importance of this missile in the Soviets' anti-armour force.

Specification
AT-6 'Spiral'
Type: anti-tank missile
Dimensions: length about 1.8 m (5 ft 10.86 in); diameter about 14.0 cm (5.5 in); span not known
Launch weight: 32 kg (70.55 lb)
Propulsion: dual-thrust solid-propellant rocket
Performance: range 100-7000 m (110-7,655 yards)

Warhead: 8-kg (17.6-lb) hollow-charge HE
Armour penetration: 800 mm (31.5 in) or more

The AT-6 'Spiral' anti-tank missile equips Mil Mi-24 'Hind' helicopters of the Soviet forces. As yet, the sophisticated weapon has not been exported even to Warsaw Pact nations.

RPG-7 family

The **RPG-7V** is the standard man-portable short-range anti-tank weapon of the Warsaw Pact and its allies. It is similar to the earlier RPG-2 in having a calibre of 40 mm (1.57 in), but its anti-tank rocket diameter is 85 mm (3.35 in) instead of 82 mm (3.23 in). The firer screws the cylinder containing the propellant into the warhead and then inserts the complete round into the muzzle of the launcher. The warhead nosecap is then removed and the safety pin extracted. A pull on the launcher's trigger then fires the round, which is reasonably accurate when there is no cross wind; if there is such a wind, the round becomes very erratic. The length of the launcher and noise are also significant operational problems. In 1968 a folding version of the RPG-7 was seen, this subsequently

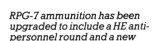

RPG-7 ammunition has been upgraded to include a HE anti-personnel round and a new

being designated the **RPG-7D**, which is intended specifically for use by the airborne troops. The standard projectile is the 2.25-kg (4.96-lb) PGF-7 anti-tank round, which was supplemented in the late 1970s by the OG-7 anti-personnel fragmentation round and by the ballistically improved and penetration-superior PG-7M anti-tank round. A more modern rocket-

improved HEAT rocket. Ironically, it is the RPG-7 which is causing heavy losses to the Soviets in Afghanistan.

launcher, tentatively identified as the **RPG-16**, has also been seen in service with the Soviet army in Europe and Afghanistan. This is believed to rectify most of the problems found with the RPG-7. The RPG series has seen widespread combat service throughout the world with both regular and irregular troops, and has turned up in Northern Ireland in the hands of IRA terrorists.

Specification
RPG-7
Type: anti-tank rocket-launcher
Dimensions: length 0.99 m (3 ft 2.98 in); calibre 4.0 cm (1.57 in)
Weight: 7 kg (15.43 lb)
Performance: range 300 m (330 yards) against a moving target and 500 m (545 yards) against a stationary target
Ammunition: see text
Armour penetration: PG-7 round 320 mm (12.6 in) and PG-7M round 400 mm (15.75 in) or more

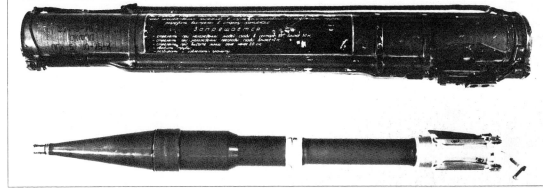

The latest Soviet infantry anti-tank weapon is the RPG-18, a very light missile launcher not unlike the American M72 LAW. Unlikely to be of use against tanks except at suicidally close range, the RPG-18 would be much more effective against light armour and soft skinned vehicles.

A Soviet infantryman operating in support of tanks aims his RPG-7. The RPG-7 is an effective weapon which has seen action in numerous wars since 1962 when it was introduced. In Afghanistan, the RPG-7 has been seen with high-explosive anti-personnel warheads in place of the standard HEAT rocket.

Modern Combat Pistols

Pistols remain in widespread military service, despite their limited range and the increasing handiness of sub-machine guns. In the USA their design is a matter of national pride but, surprisingly, the Italian firm of Beretta won the competition to supply a new pistol for the US Army.

Two Portuguese soldiers demonstrate that carrying a side-arm is still no guarantee of personal safety. Given their lack of range and accuracy, pistols often serve as much in a symbolic as in a practical role; nevertheless, manufacturers strive to improve their design with larger magazines and more reliable safety devices.

For many years military prophets have forecast the demise of the military pistol in both automatic and revolver forms. Such prophets have a case: in an era dominated by the ever-increasing firepower of assault rifles and machine-guns it would appear that this weapon no longer has a viable combat role and indeed, when the operational requirement is considered objectively, it is difficult to find one. Yet the pistol continues to flourish.

The short answer to the question of why this should be the case is that although there is no longer an operational field requirement for the pistol, there are still many other roles it can cover. Many military personnel, even in the front line, are unable by the very nature of their duties to carry any other weapon. Personnel in this category include tank crew, signallers, commanders and many others who would have to venture into battle areas unarmed unless they carried a pistol.

Thus the military pistol survives and continues to be produced in as wide a variety of forms and shapes as ever. As will be seen in this study the revolver continues to make its presence felt, although many of the potent Magnum rounds (rounds with a particularly heavy propellant load) have yet to have any marked effect on the front-line combat scene, for reasons that will be unfolded in the various entries. The automatic pistol continues to make use of all the technological innovations that arrive, and while it would seem that the whole spectrum of changes that could be effected to the automatic were made long ago, a short perusal of the contents of these pages will reveal that changes are still possible.

Most of them involve the ever-increasing use of a safety mechanism to prevent the pistol firing when dropped or other mischances of this type. Modern trigger mechanisms can now be called upon to control limited bursts of fully automatic fire (usually three rounds) as a means of converting ordinary automatic pistols into powerful close-range weapons. Weight can be saved by using light alloys or plastics to replace steel components, and so on.

The importance that the pistol still possesses can be gauged from the great interest and investment in the American military pistol trials held over the last few years. The US armed forces have made a considerable allocation of defence capital to ensure they have a pistol suitable for their requirements into the next century. If the Americans are thinking in such terms it is certain that others are too, so it seems that the military pistol will be with us for some time to come.

The Browning High-power is one of the world's most widely used pistols; today it is in service with over 50 countries. Its 13-round magazine capacity gives the weapon a bulky butt grip which does not detract from the handiness of the gun. Introduced by Fabrique Nationale in 1935, it remains one of the most successful pistol designs ever produced.

FRANCE
French automatic pistols

The most important of the post-war French automatic pistols has been the **mle 1950 MAS** which was manufactured at both St Etienne and Chatellerault. It is no longer in production, but is still a standard pistol of the French armed forces and it has also been sold to many ex-French colonial forces.

The MAS uses a standard swinging-link locking mechanism and a virtually standard trigger system with all the usual safeties. The trigger mechanism uses an external hammer and the hammer can be lowered without firing if the safety catch is set to 'Safe'. When the pistol is in the firing condition a red dot appears next to the safety catch. Nine rounds can be loaded into the box magazine. All in all the MAS is a fairly straightforward pistol with few frills or items of particular note.

Another post-war French automatic pistol is the **Model D MAB**. Unlike the MAS, which fires the 9-mm (0.354-in) Parabellum cartridge, the Model D MAB fires either the 7.65-mm (0.301-in) or 9-mm Short (also known as 0.380-in Auto). These less powerful rounds are used as the Model D MAB was originally designed for police use where more powerful ammunition such as the 9-mm Parabellum is not normally needed. Some military sales of the Model D MAB have been made, however, as it is a handy little pistol with good accuracy. It has no external

hammer, and this allows the weapon to be carried in a pocket without any danger of the hammer catching in clothing.

The current French service pistol is the **PA 15 MAB**, firing 9-mm Parabellum rounds. Unusually, the PA 15 has a delayed blowback action, the slide being locked on firing until the pressure in the chamber drops to a safe level. The PA 15 is in production for the French armed forces, while the Model D is used by the police.

The 9-mm PA15 MAB is the current service pistol of the French army, in production at Manufacture d'Armes Automatiques in Bayonne. The bulky grip of this delayed blowback design holds up to 15 Parabellum rounds.

Specification
MAS
Calibre: 9 mm (0.354 in)
Weights: empty 0.86 kg (1.896 lb); loaded 1.04 kg (2.3 lb)
Lengths: overall 195 mm (7.677 in); barrel 112 mm (4.4 in)
Muzzle velocity: 354 m (1,161 ft) per second
Magazine capacity: 9 rounds

Model D MAB
Calibre: 7.65 mm (0.301 in)
Weights: empty 0.725 kg (1.6 lb); loaded 0.825 kg (1.82 lb)
Lengths: overall 176 mm (6.93 in); barrel 103 mm (4.05 in)
Muzzle velocity: 365 m (1,197 ft) per second
Magazine capacity: 9 rounds

The post-war 9-mm Model 1950 MAS self-loading pistol (made by Chatellerault as the MAC) used the basic M1911 Colt mechanism with modifications to its safety mechanism. It remains in French service.

SWITZERLAND
SIG-Sauer P220

For very many years the Schweizerische Industrie-Gesellscahft (SIG) has been producing excellent weapons at its Neuhausen Rhinefalls factory, but has always been restricted by the strict Swiss laws governing military exports from making any significant overseas sales. By joining up with the West German J P Sauer und Sohn concern, SIG was able to transfer production to West Germany and gain access to more markets, and thus SIG-Sauer was formed.

One of the first military pistols developed by the new firm was the **SIG-Sauer P220**, a mechanically-locked single- or double-action automatic pistol. When dealing with the P220 it is difficult to avoid superlatives, for this is a truly magnificent pistol in many ways. Its standards of manufacture and finish are superb, despite the extensive use of metal stampings and an aluminium frame to keep down weight and cost. The pistol handles very well, being one of those weapons that immediately feels right as soon as it is picked up. It is accurate, and the overall design is such that it is difficult for dirt or dust to find its way into the interior and cause stoppages. Despite this the pistol is easy to strip and maintain, and has all the usual pistol safeties.

One design feature of the P220 is that it can be supplied in any one of four calibres. These are the usual 9-mm (0.354-in) Parabellum, 7.65-mm (0.301-in) Parabellum, 0.45-in ACP (11.27-mm, ACP standing for Automatic Colt Pistol) and 0.38-in Super (9-mm) not to be confused with 9-mm Parabellum. It is possible to convert any pistol from one calibre to another and kits can be provided to convert any pistol to fire 0.22-in Long Rifle (5.59-mm) for training purposes. Using 9-mm Parabellum the magazine holds nine rounds, but when firing 0.45-in ACP only seven rounds can be accommodated.

The excellence of the P220 has rewarded SIG-Sauer with a stream of orders. To date well over 100,000 have been produced, one of the largest orders coming from the Swiss government who ordered a batch of 35,000 weapons. The P220 is now in service with the Swiss army, which knows it as the 9-mm **Pistole 75**, a designation which sometimes provides the P220 with the name **Model 75**.

There is a later version of the P220 known as the **P225** which is slightly smaller and chambered only for the 9-mm Parabellum cartridge. This version has been selected for Swiss and West German police use as the **P6**.

Specification
Pistole 75
Calibre: 9 mm (0.354 in)
Weight: empty 0.83 kg (1.83 lb)
Lengths: overall 198 mm (7.8 in); barrel 112 mm (4.4 in)
Muzzle velocity: 345 m (1,132 ft) per second
Magazine capacity: 9 rounds

The magnificent SIG-Sauer P220 resulted from a collaborative venture between the Swiss SIG company and JP Sauer und Sohn to produce a pistol for export, unfettered by Swiss government restrictions. It is available in 0.45 ACP, 9-mm Parabellum, 7.65-mm Parabellum and even .22 LR.

IMI Desert Eagle

The automatic pistol produced by Israel Military Industries and known as the **IMI Desert Eagle** was originally an American design proposed by M.R.I. Limited of Minneapolis, Minnesota. The basic concept has been developed in Israel to the point where the Desert Eagle is an extremely advanced and powerful weapon.

The Desert Eagle can be converted to fire either the 0.357-in Magnum (9-mm) cartridge or the even more powerful 0.44-in Magnum (10.92-mm) round; the latter cartridge is one of the most powerful pistol rounds available. All that is required to convert the pistol from one calibre to the other is the replacement of a few parts. To ensure complete safety when using these large rounds the Desert Eagle uses a rotating bolt for a maximum locking action. The safety catch can be engaged by either the right or left hand, and when in position on 'Safe' the hammer is disconnected from the trigger and the firing pin is immobilized.

The pistol uses a 152-mm (6-in) barrel as standard, but this basic barrel is interchangeable with barrels 203 mm (8 in), 254 mm (10 in), and 356 mm (14 in) long. The extended barrels are intended for long-range target shooting and may be used with a telescopic sight fitted to a mounting on top of the receiver. No special tools are required to change the barrels.

Several other options are available for the Desert Eagle. The trigger can be made adjustable and several different types of fixed sight can be fitted. The trigger guard is shaped to be used with a two-handed grip, although special grips can be fitted if required. The normal construction is of high quality

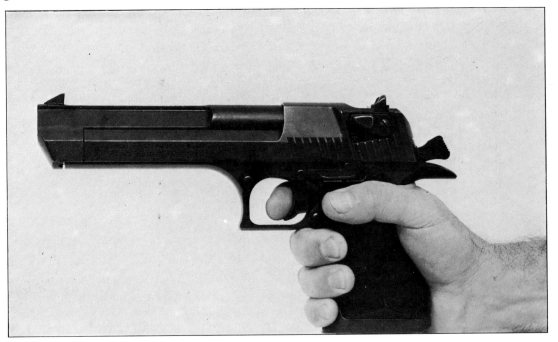

steels, but an aluminium frame can be supplied.

To date the Desert Eagle has been marketed with the civilian target shooter or enthusiast in mind, but it could also make a very powerful military or police weapon. However, most military authorities usually frown upon the use of Magnum cartridges as they are really too powerful for general military or police use and require a great deal of careful training for their best capabi-

lities to be realised. Thus pistols such as the Desert Eagle seem destined to remain in the hands of special police units and enthusiast who simply want the best and most powerful hand-guns available.

Specification
Desert Eagle
Calibre: 0.357 in or 0.44 in Magnum
Weight: empty 1.701 kg (3.75 lb)
Lengths: overall with 6-in barrel

IMI have entered the pistol field with the 'Desert Eagle', an automatic chambered for the ever-popular 0.357 Magnum cartridge. Military interest remains speculative.

260 mm (10.25 in); barrel 152.4 m (6 in)
Muzzle velocity: 0.357 Magnum 436 m (1,430 ft) per second; 0.44 Magnum 448 m (1,470 ft) per second
Magazine capacity: 0.357 Magnum 9 rounds; 0.44 Magnum 7 rounds

Beretta Model 1951

Pietro Beretta SpA has been making high-quality automatic pistols at Brescia for decades, and as over the years it has made its mark on pistol development in a number of ways it came as something of a surprise when in 1951 Beretta developed a pistol that did away with the company's former use of a simple blowback mechanism in favour of a locked breech. In this system the breech and barrel are locked together for an instant after firing until they are unlocked by contact with the frame after a short recoil movement.

This pistol became known as the **Beretta Model 1951**, and it was also known at one time as the **Model 951** or **'Brigadier'**. It retained the usual Beretta trademark of an open-topped slide, but early hopes that this slide could be made from aluminium did not materialize and most production models use an all-steel unit. The first examples of the Model 1951 did not appear until 1957 as a result mainly of attempts to develop a satisfactory light slide. In more recent years the aluminium slide has become available as an option.

As always on Beretta weapons, the standard of finish of the Model 1951 was excellent and the pistol proved to be rugged and reliable. It was not long before overseas sales were made, and the Model 1951 became the standard service pistol of Israel and Egypt. In fact a production line was established in Egypt to manufacture the Model 1951: that was during the 1960s, and the Model 1951 is known in Egypt as the

Helwan. The Model 1951 is also used in Nigeria and some other countries. The Italian armed forces also use large numbers of this pistol.

The Model 1951 continues to use the basic Beretta layout, despite the adoption of the locked breech system. The recoil rod and spring are still located under the largely open barrel, and the well-sloped butt holds the box magazine containing eight rounds. A very hard type of black nylon-based plastic

is used for the butt grips. There is an external hammer and the safety catch engages the sear when in use. Both rear and fore sights are adjustable on most versions of the Model 1951.

Specification
Model 1951
Calibre: 9 mm (0.354 in)
Weight: empty 0.87 kg (1.918 lb)
Lengths: overall 203.2 mm (8 in); barrel 114.2 mm (4.5 in)

The Beretta Model 1951 is the standard pistol of the Italian armed forces and has been exported to a number of countries, including Israel and Egypt. This is an example manufactured in Egypt, where the locally produced model is called the Helwan.

Muzzle velocity: 350 m (1,148 ft) per second
Magazine capacity: 8 rounds

Beretta 9-mm Model 92 series

During 1976 Beretta placed in production two new families of automatic pistols, the Model 81 which used a blow-back operating system and was chambered for calibres such as 7.65 mm (0.301 in), and the much larger **Beretta Model 92** which fires the usual 9-mm (0.354-in) Parabellum cartridge and accordingly uses a short recoil system very like that used on the earlier Mod-

el 1951. Since its introduction the Model 92 series has grown into a considerable range of weapons and it also seems certain to be one of Beretta's most successful designs for one of its variants, the **Model 92F**, has been selected as the US armed force's new standard automatic pistol.

Starting from the basic Model 92, the **Model 92 S** has a revised safety catch

on the slide rather than below it as on the basic Model 92. This allows the hammer to be lowered onto a loaded chamber with complete safety as the firing pin is taken out of line with the hammer. The **Model 92 SB** is essentially similar to the Model 92 S, but the slide-mounted safety catch can be applied from each side of the slide. The **Model 92 SB-C** is a more compact and handier version of the Model 92 SB.

The **Model 92F** was a development of the Model 92 SB for the US Army pistol contest, which it won. The main changes from the Model 92 SB are a revised trigger guard outline to suit a two-handed grip (much favoured by the military), an extended magazine base, revised grips and a lanyard ring. The bore is chrome-plated and the exterior is coated in a Teflon-type material to resist wear and act as a non-glare surface.

Following on from the Model 92F there is a **Model 92F Compact** along the same lines as the Model 92 SB-C but using the features of the Model 92F, and also produced along the same lines is the **Model 92 SB-C Type M** which has an eight-round magazine instead of the 15-round magazine used on all the models mentioned above. To cap all these variants there are also two more models based on the Model 92 series but in a smaller calibre. They are the **Model 98** and **Model 99**, both in

7.65-mm calibre and based on the Model 92 SB-C and Model 92 SB-C Type M respectively.

This array of Model 92 pistols should be enough to satisfy just about every military or police requirement likely to arise. The selection of the Model 92F for the American armed forces has already led to a number of orders from other sources, including one from a police force in the UK, and more such orders can be expected. The original Model 92 is now no longer in production, but the Model 92 S still is and all the other variants are available. Apart from the American order various forms of the Model 92 are in service with the Italian armed forces and some of the 'compact' versions are used by various police forces in Italy and elsewhere.

Specification
Model 92F
Calibre: 9 mm (0.354 in)
Weight: loaded 1.145 kg (2.524 lb)
Lengths: overall 217 mm (8.54 in); barrel 125 mm (4.92 in)
Muzzle velocity: about 390 m (1,280 ft) per second
Magazine capacity: 15 rounds

Used extensively by the Italian armed forces, the Beretta Model 92 forms part of the equipment of the Italian army's 'Folgore' parachute brigade. Based at Pisa, the brigade incorporates a parachute battalion of the Carabinieri (who function as military police and as an internal security force).

Introduced in 1976, the Model 92 has proved a logical successor to the Model 1951. This has a frame-mounted safety catch (later models have the catch on the slide).

Beretta 9-mm Model 93R

With the **Beretta Model 93R** one is back in that no-man's land between true machine pistols and selective-fire pistols, for the Model 93R is another modern pistol design intended to fire three-round bursts. Derived from the Beretta Model 92, the Model 93R can be handled and fired as a normal automatic pistol, but when the three-round burst mode is selected the firer has to use both hands to hold the pistol reasonably steady during the burst. To do this Beretta has designed a simple and compact grip system on which the right hand carries out its normal function of operating the trigger and grasping the butt. For the left hand a small forehand grip is folded down from in front of the elongated trigger guard. The left thumb is inserted into the front of the trigger guard and the rest of the

fingers grasp the forehand grip. For additional assistance in holding the pistol steady during firing the end of the protruding barrel is equipped with a muzzle brake that also acts as a flash hider.

To provide even more firing stability it is possible to fix a metal folding stock to the butt. When not in use this can be carried in a special holster, and when mounted on the pistol can be extended to two lengths to suit the firer.

Two types of box magazine can be used with the Model 93F, one holding 15 rounds and the other holding 20. The usual 9-mm (0.354-in) Parabellum cartridge is used.

The design detail incorporated into the Model 93R is considerable and one item that will no doubt be seen on future designs is the use of the foregrip in

front of the trigger guard. This is so arranged tht the two-handed grip derived from its use is much steadier than the usual two-handed grip with both hands wrapped around what is often a bulky pistol butt. Using this foregrip it is quite possible to provide reasonably accurate burst fire as both hands are 'spaced' to produce a longer holding base and yet are close enough to prevent either hand wavering. It is possible to fire bursts without using the metal extending stock, but for really accurate fire (even with single shots) its use is recommended.

Early teething troubles with the Model 93R, largely centred on the relatively complex three-round burst mechanism, are being overcome for service use and the type is now in production. Even so, maintenance of the

burst mechanism is a job for a qualified armourer. The Model 93R is in service with Italian Special Forces, and is thought to have been acquired by similar units in a number of other countries.

Specification
Model 93R
Calibre: 9 mm (0.354 in)
Weights: loaded with 15-round magazine 1.12 kg (2.47 lb); loaded with 20-round magazine 1.17 kg (2.58 lb)
Lengths: pistol 240 mm (9.45 in); barrel 156 mm (6.14 in)
Muzzle velocity: 375 m (1,230 ft) per second
Magazine capacity: 15 or 29 rounds

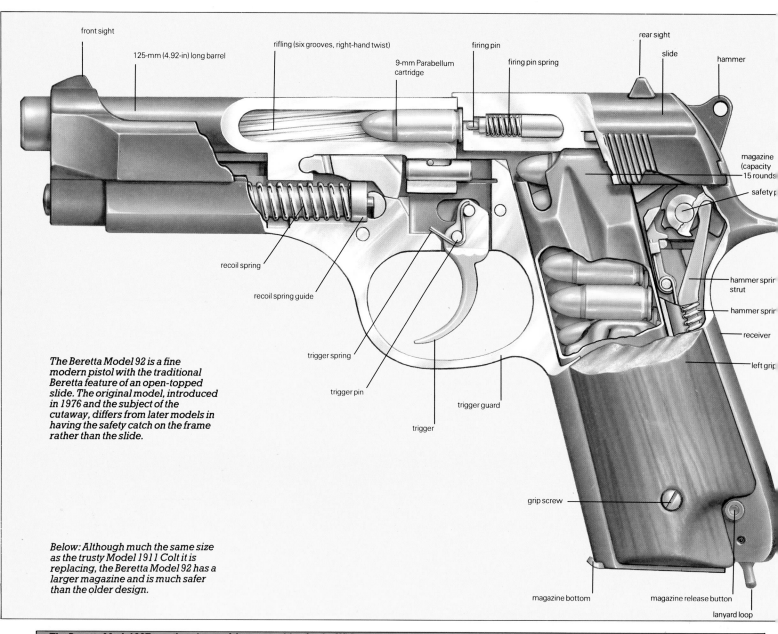

front sight

125-mm (4.92-in) long barrel

rifling (six grooves, right-hand twist)

9-mm Parabellum cartridge

firing pin

firing pin spring

rear sight

slide

hammer

magazine (capacity 15 rounds

safety

recoil spring

recoil spring guide

trigger spring

trigger pin

trigger

trigger guard

hammer spri strut

hammer spri

receiver

left grip

grip screw

magazine bottom

magazine release button

lanyard loop

The Beretta Model 92 is a fine modern pistol with the traditional Beretta feature of an open-topped slide. The original model, introduced in 1976 and the subject of the cutaway, differs from later models in having the safety catch on the frame rather than the slide.

Below: Although much the same size as the trusty Model 1911 Colt it is replacing, the Beretta Model 92 has a larger magazine and is much safer than the older design.

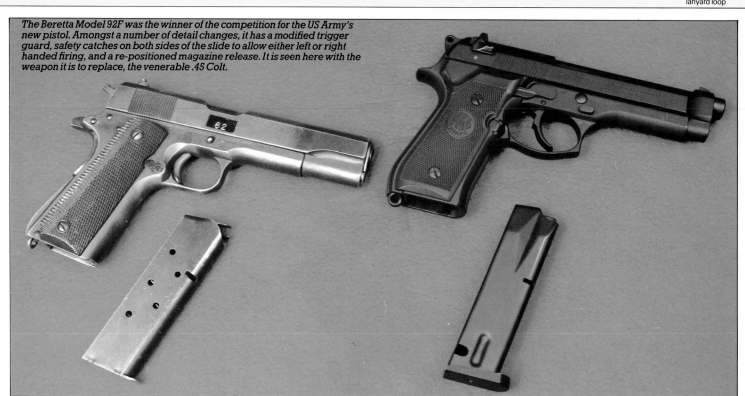

The Beretta Model 92F was the winner of the competition for the US Army's new pistol. Amongst a number of detail changes, it has a modified trigger guard, safety catches on both sides of the slide to allow either left or right handed firing, and a re-positioned magazine release. It is seen here with the weapon it is to replace, the venerable .45 Colt.

9-mm FN High-power

The **Browning High-power** pistols were first designed in 1925 by J.M. Browning, the famous weapons designer, but they are still in production and service to this day. The main producer is still the Belgian Fabrique Nationale (FN) of Herstal, although spares are being made in Canada following World War II production in that country.

FN now makes several variants of the High-power in addition to the basic military version. All use the same basic Browning short recoil method of operation, and can easily be recognized as coming from the same stable. One variant is the **High-power Mk 2**, which can be regarded as an updated version of the original with more modern finish and grip shape but still unchanged inside. There are also three versions of the standard military model.

The basic military model is now known to FN as the **BDA-9S**. The smaller **BDA-9M** uses the same frame as the BDA-9S but it is combined with a shorter slide and barrel, also used on the compact version of the family, the **BDA-9C**. The BDA-9C is a very small pistol for its calibre, and has a much shortened butt holding only seven rounds instead of the usual 14 of the other models. It is intended to be a 'pocket pistol' for use by plain clothes police units and for specialist roles such as VIP protection.

In recent years other versions of the High-power have appeared, some with specially-lightened slides to reduce weight and some with components made from light alloys, again to reduce weight. All these versions fire the 9-mm (0.354-in) Parabellum cartridge and all have found ready buyers, even in a world market sated with more modern pistol designs.

One factor that has consistently sold the FN High-power pistols has been the series' extreme robustness. The pistols are capable of accepting very hard use and will fire under the most adverse conditions, always providing that (as with any weapon) they are properly maintained and are loaded with decent ammunition. The High-power can be a bit awkward to handle as on all but the BDA-9C Compact

Above: Many of the great J.M. Browning's designs have proven exceptionally long-lived, with the Browning High-power pistol being no exception. This example has an advanced 'red spot' sighting device, and custom non-slip grips.

model the butt is rather wide to accommodate the double-stack box magazine. However, this has not prevented the High-power being used as a target pistol by some enthusiasts.

Specification
FN High-power
Calibre: 9 mm (0.354 in)
Lengths: overall 200 mm (7.874 in); barrel 118 mm (4.645 in)
Weights: empty 0.882 kg (1.944 lb); loaded 1.04 kg (2.29 lb)
Muzzle velocity: 350 m (1,148 ft) per second
Magazine capacity: 14 rounds →13

Above: Developed from the High-power to provide a genuine pocket pistol capable of firing full-power rounds, the Browning Compact has a very short butt, although the shortened slide is less obvious.

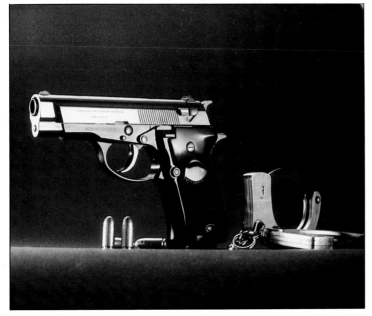

Left: Latest development from FN is the 7.65-mm or 9-mm short DA 140. Years of experience with the High-power and a collaboration with Beretta of Italy have produced a light, effective pistol.

Above: The 'Grande Puissance' remains in production after 45 years, and is in use in 55 countries. It was the first of the large-capacity pistols, and remains one of the most popular.

Smith and Wesson revolvers

Smith and Wesson has been making revolvers for well over 100 years, and during that time it has produced just about every type of revolver it is possible to make. Among the company's prolific output have been many military revolvers, but today Smith and Wesson do not make any revolver specifically for military use. This does not prevent many armed forces from using Smith and Wesson revolvers for many roles, but from the outset it has to be said that it is unlikely that any armed forces are likely to use Smith and Wesson revolvers in a front-line capacity. Instead they are to be found with military and security police and other such military agencies.

The most striking of all the Smith and Wesson range are the mighty Magnums. First introduced in 1955, the **No. 29 0.44-in Magnum** was for many years the most potent production handgun made. It was followed in 1964 by the hardly less powerful **No. 57 0.41-in.** A Magnum is a considerable handful, requiring experience or special training to make the best use of it's hard-hitting power. For that reason, Magnums will only be found in the hands of troops who need weapons of this type and who can be effectively trained in their use, such as MPs or security guards.

But to most observers of the pistol scene Smith and Wesson means 0.38-in (9-mm) revolvers. There are many of these still on the Smith and Wesson marketing lists, a typical example being the **No. 38 Bodyguard.** This small snub-nosed revolver has a shrouded hammer to allow it to be concealed on the person without too much danger, but a stud over the hidden hammer

allows the pistol to be cocked for single-action shooting. The cylinder holds only five rounds, and the No. 38 uses an aluminium body; the otherwise similar No. 49 uses an all-steel body.

Pistols such as the No. 38 and No. 49 are not likely to be used in front-line combat, but they can still be found on the inventories of many armed forces. Pilots carry them (or pistols very similar to them) on missions over enemy territory, and the weapons are often issued to military personnel operating in plain clothes in areas where the local population is hostile to their presence. It seems that there will always be a need for weapons such as the small Smith and Wesson revolvers.

Specification
No. 38 Bodyguard
Calibre: 0.38 in (9 mm)
Weight: 0.411 kg (0.9 lb)
Lengths: overall 165 mm (6.5 in); barrel 51 mm (2 in)
Muzzle velocity: 260 m (853 ft) per second
Chamber capacity: 5 rounds

Smith and Wesson 0.38-in (9-mm) revolvers are in common use with police and military forces worldwide. The typical snub-nosed, double-action weapon (top) is most widely seen, but the more specialized No. 38 Bodyguard has no external hammer and can be brought rapidly into action from a pocket or holster without danger of snagging.

Colt revolvers

To many the very name Colt means revolvers since it was the Colt's Firearms Company that produced the first successful commercial revolvers, including the famous single-action Colts such as the 'Peacemaker', the gun enshrined in the legends of the Old West. Gradually Colt moved away from producing revolvers (to leave the field open to others, as it was to learn to its cost) and concentrated on automatics. But Colt still continued to make some revolver designs apart from its various well-known and attractive commemorative models.

The modern Colt military revolvers are now all double-action designs, and although most models are produced with police use in mind many are still used by various military agencies in the USA and elsewhere. Many are used by military police units who can obtain the special training needed to handle the powerful Magnum rounds now in use. Thus although many present-day Colt revolvers have names such as **Trooper, Lawman, Police Positive** and so on, they may well be used in military hands.

One particular Colt revolver that comes into this category is the **Python.** First introduced in 1955, this weapon has a shrouded barrel with a distinctive appearance and is chambered for one cartridge only, the 0.357-in Magnum (9-mm). The Python is a very powerful weapon, but to absorb some of the effects of the heavy cartridge load it has to be constructed in an equally heavy fashion. It is thus very

heavy (1.16 kg/2.56 lb) but this weight makes the revolver a very steady weapon to aim and fire, and also makes it very strong, so strong in fact that it can withstand the very worst rigours of a long military life. The Python is available in two barrel lengths, 102 mm (4 in) and 152 mm (6 in).

One advantage of the revolver is its capacity to remain in operation after harsh treatment. Powerful weapons such as the Colt Python would be extremely valuable to a Central American guerrilla, with guns, rounds and spares provided in many cases by interested parties in the USA.

Colt revolvers (continued)

Another Colt revolver is the Trooper. Although no longer available, the Trooper first appeared in 1953, again in a variety of barrel lengths and in various calibres, most of them tending to the heavy side, and with many ending up in military use, although mostly in security rather than combat roles. The Trooper has now been replaced by the **Lawman Mark III**, which is produced only in 0.357-in Magnum and with barrels as short as 51 mm (2 in). Again, many of these are in military use all over the world.

Specification
Lawman Mark III
Calibre: 0.357-in Magnum (9-mm)
Weight: 1.022 kg (2.253 lb)
Lengths: overall 235 mm (9.25 in); barrel 2 or 4 in (51 or 102 mm)
Muzzle velocity: about 436 m (1,430 ft) per second
Chamber capacity: 6 rounds

Colt revolvers are available in a number of calibres, with the .357 Magnum round (actually of 9-mm calibre) being used in the powerful Lawman Mk III. The Colt Cobra (bottom) is similar to the Python, but is chambered for the 0.38 Special round instead of the Magnum.

Ruger revolvers

The armaments concern of Sturm, Ruger and Company Inc. of Southport, Connecticut, produced its first pistol, an automatic, in 1949 and thereafter has never looked back. The company owe a great deal of its success to the astute observation that there was still a large market for single-action revolvers in the USA but that Colt, the obvious choice for such a weapon, was no longer interested in making them. Sturm, Ruger and Co. decided to fill the gap and has been making revolvers (among other types of weapon) ever since.

Before simply copying the old Colt designs, William B. Ruger decided to examine the fundamental design aspects of the revolver in all its forms and soon came up with what was a very modern version of a weapon that had been around for nearly a century. New types of steel and other materials (especially springs) were introduced and the manufacture was gradually developed into a modular system where components could be added or subtracted to form any particular model. The point has now been reached where Sturm, Ruger and Co. produces a very wide range of modern revolvers to meet just about any requirement, military or civil.

Ruger revolvers are today produced in various barrel lengths and in varying finishes, including stainless steel. The revolvers are also available in a wide range of calibres from 0.38-in Special (9-mm) up to the Magnums, although the Magnums are not usually selected for ordinary military use. Typical of the service revolvers currently on offer is the **Service-Six** chambered for either the 0.38 Special or 0.357-in Magnum (again 9-mm) cartridges. The Service-Six can be fitted with either a 70-mm (2.75-in) or 102-mm (4-in) barrel, while the generally similar **Security-Six**, intended for police use, can have even longer bar-

rels. The trigger actions of both are single- and double-action. Some Ruger revolvers fire rimless 9-mm Parabellum ammunition, so for loading these rounds special 'half moon' clips, each holding three rounds, have to be used.

One particular Ruger revolver caused quite a stir when it was first introduced in 1955. This was the famous **Ruger Blackhawk** that could fire the very powerful 0.44-in Magnum (10.92-mm) round, making the Blackhawk one of the most powerful revolvers obtainable. This was too much of a handful for most users, so the Blackhawk range has now been extended to include other less potent cartridges and it is still in great demand by many pistol enthusiasts.

Specification
0.38-in Service-Six
Calibre: 0.38-in Special (9 mm)

Above: Ruger's Speed-Six is known to the US Army as the GS-32N. It is made in two versions: one for 0.357 Magnum/0.38 Special and one for 9-mm Parabellum. The 9-mm is rimless so three round half-moon clips are used to ensure ejection.

Weight: 0.935 kg (2.06 lb)
Lengths: overall 235 mm (9.25 in); barrel 102 mm (4 in)
Muzzle velocity: 260 m (853 ft) per second
Chamber capacity: 6 rounds

Most Ruger pistols in US military use are in the hands of military police or security forces. These roles require familiarity with and training in handling powerful handguns so that the capability of Magnum or Special calibre pistols is not wasted.

217

Colt M1911 and M1911A1

Above: For the last 70 or more years, the M1911 Colt has proved a trusty weapon. These Marines are searching a Japanese bunker in the Pacific in 1943.

The **Colt M1911** vies with the Browning HP as being one of the most successful pistol designs ever produced, for it has been manufactured in millions and is in widespread service all over the world some 70 years after it was first accepted for service in 1911. The design had its origins well before then, however, for the weapon was based on a **Colt Browning Model 1900** design. This weapon was taken as the basis for a new service pistol required by the US Army to fire a new 11.43-mm (0.45-in) cartridge deemed necessary, as the then-standard calibre of 9.65 mm (0.38 in) was considered by many to be too light to stop a charging enemy. The result was a series of trials in 1907, and in 1911 the **Pistol, Automatic, Caliber .45, M1911** was accepted. Production was at first slow, but by 1917 was well enough under way to equip in part the rapid expansion of the US Army for its new role in France.

As the result of that battle experience it was decided to make some production changes to the basic design and from these came the **M1911A1**. The changes were not extensive, and were confined to such items as the grip safety configuration, the hammer spur outline and the mainspring housing. Overall the design and operation changed only little. The basic method of operation remained the same, and this mechanism is one of the strongest ever made. Whereas many contemporary pistol designs employed a receiver stop to arrest the backwards progress of the receiver slide the M1911 had a locking system that also produced a more positive stop. The barrel had lugs machined into its outer surface that

fitted into corresponding lugs on the slide. When the pistol was fired the barrel and slide moved backwards a short distance with these lugs still engaged. At the end of this distance the barrel progress was arrested by a swinging link which swung round to pull the barrel lugs out of the receiver slide, which was then free to move farther and so eject the spent case and restart the loading cycle. This robust system, allied with a positive applied safety and a grip safety, make the M1911 and M1911A1 very safe weapons under service conditions. But

the pistol is a bit of a handful to handle and fire correctly, and a good deal of training is required to use it to full effect.

The M1911 and M1911A1 have both been manufactured by numerous companies other than Colt Firearms and have been widely copied direct in many parts of the world, not always to very high levels of manufacture.

Specification
Colt M1911A1
Calibre: 0.45 in
Weight: 1.36 kg (3 lb)

This pistol is the M1911 (the M1911A1 had several detail changes) and it is still the standard US Army service pistol after over 70 years in service. Firing an 0.45-in ball cartridge, it is still a powerful man-stopper, but is a bit of a handful to fire and requires training to use to its full potential.

Lengths: overall 219 mm (8.6 in); barrel 128 mm (5.03 in)
Muzzle velocity: 252 m (825 ft) per second
Magazine: 7-round box

Heckler & Koch pistols

Since the early 1950s Heckler & Koch GmbH of Oberndorf-Neckar has been one of the major European small-arms manufacturers, and although best known for its range of rifles and sub-machine guns the firm has also produced a range of advanced automatic pistol designs.

One of the first of these was the **Heckler & Koch HK4** intended as a small pistol firing a variety of light ammunition varying from 9-mm Short (0.380-in), through 7.65-mm (0.301-in) to 6.35-mm (0.25-in) and even 0.22-in Long Rifle (5.59-mm). All that has to be done to change the ammunition fired is the replacement of the barrel, the springs and the magazine. The HK4 is no longer in production.

The much larger **P7 K3** pistol uses 9-mm Parabellum ammunition and is one of the West German 'super safety' pistols with various built-in safety features to meet police requirements. It uses a prominent grip safety to prevent firing if the pistol is dropped accidentally and the same grip safety also acts as a cocking device for complete one-handed operation. Locking is carried out using a gas-operated delayed-blowback method similar to that used on the Steyr GB pistol and the German Volkspistole of World War II. The P7 K3, adopted by the West German army is a simple blowback variant, without the gas delay. The **P7M13** is a version with a 13-round magazine. The P7 series is used by armed and police forces worldwide, and has also had

considerable commercial success.

By contrast a third Heckler & Koch pistol, the **P9S**, uses a small version of the roller and block delay locking device used on the Heckler & Koch G3 assault rifle. This system uses the recoil forces to force the bolt-body to the rear but at the same time two rollers are forced into barrel extensions to prevent further movement until the pressure on the bolt body has dropped to a safe level. This safe locking system allows the 9-mm Parabellum cartridge to be fired from a relatively light pistol, and to add to the locking safety there are numerous others including the usual feature that allows the pistol to be carried safely with a round already in

the chamber; this safety can be released by operating a small cocking lever. The P9S has been sold to many armed and police forces worldwide.

Specification
HK4
Calibre: 9 mm Short*
Weight: loaded 0.6 kg (1.32 lb)
Lengths: overall 157 mm (6.18 in); barrel 85 mm (3.35 in)
Muzzle velocity: 299 m (981 ft) per second
Magazine capacity: 7 or 8 rounds*
(* also other smaller calibres, all using an 8-round magazine)

P9S
Calibre: 9 mm (0.354 in)
Weight: loaded 1.065 kg (2.348 lb)
Lengths: overall 192 mm (7.56 in); barrel 102 mm (4.015 in)
Muzzle velocity: 351 m (1,152 ft) per second
Magazine capacity: 9 rounds

P7 K3
Calibre: 9 mm (0.354 in)
Weight: loaded 0.95 kg (2.09 lb)
Lengths: overall 171 mm (6.73 in); barrel 105 mm (4.13 in)
Muzzle velocity: 351 m (1,152 ft) per second
Magazine capacity: 8 or 13 rounds

Above: Conceived as a military pistol, the Heckler & Koch P9 is unusual in that it employs a version of the roller and block delayed-locking system (as used in the well-known Heckler & Koch family of rifles).

Below: Of rugged and simple construction, the Heckler & Koch P7 (PSP) self-loading pistol has been adopted as standard by the West German police and army. It has been designed as a police pistol.

An increasingly important element in any nation's armed forces is that of counter-terrorist warfare. Many nations have formed paramilitary units within the police forces; amongst the most effective of such groups is West Germany's GSG-9, ostensibly a branch of the Border Police.

Heckler & Koch 9-mm VP70M

The 9-mm (0.354-in) **Heckler & Koch VP70M** is a rather unusual pistol that at one time might have been placed in the machine pistol category, but for various reasons it cannot be called that for it has only a limited automatic-fire capability. A true machine pistol can fire in fully automatic mode, but the VP70M can fire only three-round bursts and then only when the carrying holster is attached to the butt to form a shoulder stock.

As a conventional pistol the VP70M uses a blowback action allied to an unusual trigger design. It uses a double-action mechanism and requires a pronounced first pressure when pulled back. Further pressure causes the trigger bar to slip off a spring-loaded firing pin to fire the loaded cartridge. There is thus no additional safety catch as it requires a definite pressure to fire the weapon.

Much of the receiver is made from hard plastics and there are only four moving parts, a number that has been kept to a minimum, for when the pistol is firing three-round bursts the cyclic rate of fire is equivalent to 2,200 rounds per minute which sets up considerable internal forces. The three-round bursts can only be fired when the holster/shoulder stock is fitted as the selector for the burst mode is in the holster. The stock engages in grooves on the pistol receiver and butt, and to take full advantage of the burst mode the magazine holds 18 rounds. Single shots can still be selected when the stock is attached.

A special version of the VP70M known as the **VP70Z** was produced. This version did not have the holster/

shoulder stock capability and could not be used to fire bursts. It was produced for civilian sales only.

The VP70M caused quite a stir when it first appeared, and sales were made to several police and armed forces in Asia and Africa. But both the VP70M and VP70Z are now no longer manufactured. The VP70M in particular was viewed with deep suspicion by security forces in several European nations who had visions of these pistols falling

into the wrong hands, but for all that the design features of the VP70M are almost certain to reappear in future pistols.

Specification
VP70M
Calibre: 9 mm (0.354 in)
Weights: empty 0.823 kg (1.814 lb); pistol loaded 1.14 kg (2.5 lb); pistol and stock loaded 1.6 kg (3.53 lb)
Lengths: pistol 204 mm (8.03 in); barrel

Heckler and Koch's VP70 represents one of the most successful compromises between handling and rate of fire.

116 m (4.57 in); pistol and stock 545 mm (21.45 in)
Muzzle velocity: 360 m (1,181 ft) per second
Magazine capacity: 18 rounds
Rate of fire: 3-round burst (cyclic) 2,200 rpm

Walther P1 and P5

One of the most widely-admired and respected pistol designs that emerged from World War II was the 9-mm (0.354-in) **Walther Pistole 38**, or **P38**. This is still in production to this day at the Carl Walther Waffenfabrik at Ulm, but is now known as the **Walther P1**, though versions produced for civilian sales are still marked as the P38.

The main change in the P1 from the wartime version is that the modern weapon uses a lighter frame rather than the all-steel frame of World War II. Otherwise the only differences are the markings. The P1 remains an excellent combat pistol and it is still used by the West German armed forces and by those of a number of other nations,

including Portugal and Chile.

The **Walther P5** is a much more modern design that was originally produced to meet a West German police specification that called for a double-action trigger mechanism combined with a high standard of safety. The resultant weapon emerged as a very compact and neat design with the required double action but with no less than four inherent safety features. The first is that the firing pin is kept out of line with the hammer unless the trig-

Walther's P5 pistol has been adopted by several European police forces, and has been built to a very high safety specification.

ger is physically pulled. Another is that even if the hammer is released by any other means than the trigger the firing pin will not be struck. The hammer itself has a safety notch to form the third safety feature, and to top it all the pistol will not fire unless the slide is fully closed with the barrel locked to it.

Getting all these safeties into a pistol as small as the P5 has been a major design accomplishment, but the P5 is an easy weapon to use and fire, and as far as the user is concerned there are no extra features to worry about. The P5 is easy to aim and shoot, and its smooth lines ensure that it is unlikely to be caught on clothing when being handled. It continues to use the same

well-tried 9-mm Parabellum ammunition as the P1 and many other pistols. To date some West German regional police forces have adopted the P5 and it has been adopted as the standard police pistol for the Netherlands police force.

Specification
P1
Calibre: 9 mm (0.354 in)
Weight: loaded 0.96 kg (2.11 lb)
Lengths: overall 218 mm (8.58 in);

The Walther P1 is still produced commercially as the P38. This is the P38K, or short version of the pistol.

Walther P1 and P5 (continued)

barrel 124 mm (4.88 in)
Muzzle velocity: 350 m (1,148 ft) per second
Magazine capacity: 8 rounds

P5
Calibre: 9 mm (0.354 in)
Weight: loaded 0.885 kg (1,95 lb)
Lengths: overall 180 mm (7.09 in); barrel 90 mm (3.54 in)
Muzzle velocity: 350 m (1,148 ft) per second
Magazine capacity: 8 rounds

Weapons fitted with suppressors are much in demand for clandestine purposes. This version of the P1, known as the P4, was among a batch seized by Customs to forestall an attempt to export them illegally to Libya.

GERMANY
Walther PP and PPK

The **Walther PP** was first produced in 1929 and was marketed as a police weapon (PP standing for Polizei Pistole), and during the 1930s it was adopted by uniformed police forces throughout Europe and elsewhere. It was a light and handy design with few frills and a clean outline but was intended for holster carriage. Plain clothes police were catered for by another model, the **Walter PPK** (K standing for *kurz*, or short). This was basically the PP reduced in overall size to enable it to be carried conveniently in a pocket or under a jacket.

Although intended as civilian police weapons, both the PP and the PPK were adopted as military police weapons and after 1939 both were kept in production for service use. Each model was widely used by the Luftwaffe, and was often carried by the many German police organizations. Both were also widely used by staff officers as personal weapons. Both types could also be encountered in a range of calibres, the two main calibres being 9 mm short and 7.65 mm, but versions were produced in 5.56 mm (0.22 LR) and 6.35 mm. All these variants operated on a straightforward blowback principle, and more than adequate safety arrangements were incorporated. One of these safeties was later widely copied, and involved placing a block in the way of the firing pin when it moved forward, this block only being removed when the trigger was given a definite pull. Another innovation was the provision of a signal pin above the hammer which protruded when a round was

actually in the chamber to provide a positive 'loaded' indication when necessary. This feature was omitted from wartime production, in which the general standard of finish was lower. Production resumed soon after 1945 in such countries as France and Turkey. Hungary also adopted the type for a while but production is now once more by the Walther concern at Ulm. Production is still mainly for police duties but purely commercial sales are common to pistol shooters who appreciate the many fine points of the basic design.

One small item of interest regarding the PP centres on the fact that it is now a little-known and rarely seen pistol used by the British armed forces as the

XL47E1. The weapon is used for undercover operations where civilian clothing has to be worn and it is often issued to soldiers of the Ulster Defence Regiment for personal protection when off duty.

The Walther PP pistol was, and still is, one of the best small pistol designs ever produced. In German service it was used by various police organizations and by Luftwaffe aircrew.

Specification
Walther PP
Cartridge: 9 mm short (0.38 ACP), 7.65 mm (0.32 ACP), 6.35 mm (0.25 ACP), 0.22 LR
Length overall: 173 mm (6.8 in)
Length of barrel: 99 mm (3.9 in)
Weight: 0.682 kg (1.5 lb)
Muzzle velocity: 290 m (950 ft) per second
Magazine: 8-round box

Specification
Walther PPK
Cartridge: 9 mm short (0.38 ACP), 7.65 mm (0.32 ACP), 6.35 mm (0.25 ACP), 0.22 LR
Length overall: 155 mm (6.1 in)
Length of barrel: 86 mm (3.39 in)
Weight: 0.568 kg (1.25 lb)
Muzzle velocity: 280 m (920 ft) per second
Magazine: 7-round box

Tokarev TT-33

The first Tokarev automatic pistol to see extensive service was the **TT-30**, but not many of these pistols had been produced before a modified design known as the **TT-33** was introduced in 1933. This pistol was then adopted as the standard pistol of the Red Army to replace the Nagant revolvers that had served so well for many years. In the event the TT-33 never did replace the Nagant entirely until well after 1945, mainly because the revolver proved so reliable and sturdy under the rough active service conditions of the various fronts.

The TT-33 was basically a Soviet version of the Colt-Browning pistols, and used the swinging-link system of operation employed on the American M1911. However, the ever practical Soviet designers made several slight alterations that made the mechanism easier to produce and easier to maintain under field conditions, and production even went to the length of machining the vulnerable magazine feed lips into the main receiver to prevent damage and subsequent misfeeds. The result was a practical and sturdy weapon that was well able to absorb a surprising amount of hard use.

By 1945 the TT-33 had virtually replaced the Nagant revolver in service and as Soviet influence spread over Europe and elsewhere so did TT-33 production. Thus the TT-33 may be found in a variety of basically similar forms, one of which is the Chinese **Type 51**. The Poles also produced the TT-33 for their own use and for export to East Germany and to Czechoslovakia. The Yugoslavs still have the TT-33 in production and are still actively marketing the design as the **M65**. North Korea has its own variant in the form of the **M68**. The most drastic producer of the TT-33 is Hungary, which rejigged the design in several respects and recalibred it for the 9-mm Parabellum cartridge. The result was known as the **Tikagypt** and was exported to Egypt, where it is still used by the local police forces.

The Tokarev TT-33 was a sturdy and hard-wearing pistol that was used throughout World War II, but it never entirely replaced the Nagant.

Above: The Soviet Tokarev TT-33 in action in a well-posed propaganda photograph dating from about 1944. The officer is leading a section of assault infantry and has his pistol on the end of the usual lanyard. Snipers on all sides came to recognize these 'pistol wavers' as prime targets.

The TT-33 is now no longer used by the Soviet armed forces, who use the Markarov automatic pistol, but the TT-33 will be around for a long while yet. Despite the introduction of the Makarov many second-line and militia units within the Warsaw Pact are still issued with the TT-33 and as the type's overall standard of design and construction was sound there seems to be no reason why they should be replaced for many years.

Right: A Red Army military policeman, for whom the Tokarev TT-33 would have been the primary weapon. Military policemen of all nations still carry the pistol as the nature of their duties often precludes the use of any type of larger weapon, and they have no actual combat role.

Specification
TT-33
Cartridge: 7.62 mm Type P (M30)
Length overall: 196 mm (7.72 in)
Length of barrel: 116 mm (4.57 in)
Weight: 0.83 kg (1.83 lb)
Muzzle velocity: 420 m (1,380 ft) per second
Magazine: 8-round box

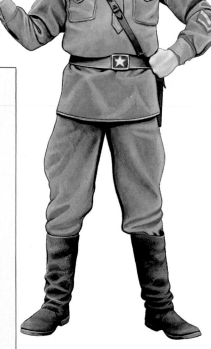

Avtomaticheskiy Pistolet Stechkina (APS)

The pistol known to the West as the **Stechkin** and to the Soviet bloc as the **APS** fell into the category known as machine pistols. Although it resembled a conventional automatic pistol it had a fire-selection mechanism that allowed it to fire fully automatically, i.e. in bursts. Machine pistols were much in vogue in the year before World War II, but operational experience soon showed them to be somewhat less than effective other than at extremely short ranges: they were also very wasteful of ammunition. This waste was caused by the fact that as soon as the trigger was pulled the recoil forces forced up the muzzle away from the target.

It was therefore something of a surprise when the Soviets produced the APS during the decade after World War II. It seems that the APS was intended more as a police than a military weapon, but many were used by Warsaw Pact front-line forces. The APS had a magazine holding only 20 rounds, a factor which limited any burst that might be fired. The round used was the then-standard Soviet 9-mm (0.354-in) automatic type used with Soviet sub-machine guns. These were really too powerful for the APS's blowback system and made the violent recoil of the weapon even more pronounced. In an attempt to control the recoil the Soviet designers intended the pistol to be used with a bulky wooden holster acting as a shoulder butt. This holster was almost identical to the old 'broomhandle' Mauser component, which no doubt acted as the starting point for the whole APS design, but the butt was bulky and awkward to use, even if it did allow aimed fire up to 200 m (219 yards) and contain the pistol's cleaning tools and equipment.

The APS had a relatively short career in Soviet terms. It was issued throughout the Warsaw Pact armed forces, but it was never liked and was gradually relegated from front-line use to second-line duties. Today it is still around, but usually in the hands of border guards and other such paramilitary forces. Many have found their way into the hands of terrorists/freedom-fighters who are often attracted by the APS's volume of fire rather than its combat efficiency.

Specification
APS
Calibre: 9 mm (0.354 in)
Weights: empty 1.03 kg (2.27 lb); empty with stock 1.58 kg (3.48 lb)
Lengths: overall 225 mm (8.86 in); barrel 127 mm (5 in)
Muzzle velocity: 340 m (1,115 ft) per second
Rate of fire: (cyclic) 750 rpm
Feed: 20-round box

9-mm Makarov

The **Makarov** automatic pistol was developed in the USSR during the late 1950s and was first noticed by various Western intelligence agencies during the early 1960s. In design terms it is an enlarged version of the German Walther PP, a pistol first introduced in 1929 and ever since acknowledged to be one of the best of its type. However, the Makarov uses a different 9-mm (0.354-in) cartridge to any other in use, for it is intermediate in power between the 9-mm Parabellum and the 9-mm Short. This allows the Makarov to use a straightforward blowback operating mechanism without the complications that would be needed with a more powerful cartridge. The Makarov cartridge appears to have been based on a World War II design known as the Ultra which was not accepted for German war-time service, but which attracted some attention in the West for a while. The Ultra has not been produced in the West in any form, but the Soviets took to it and also use the Makarov round in the Stechkin machine pistol.

The Soviets know the Makarov as the **PM (Pistole Makarov)**. As well as being used by the Soviet armed forces the Makarov is also used by virtually all other Warsaw Pact forces and by a great many of the Eastern bloc police forces as well. It is a sound, rugged and simple weapon that can be relied upon to operate even under severe conditions. Most accounts state that the pistol is rather awkward to handle as the butt is rather thick, but this is presumably no problem for Eastern bloc soldiers, many of whom have to wear heavy gloves during most of the year.

The Makarov has been manufactured outside the USSR. One of the largest producers is China, where it is known as the **Type 59** and from where it is being offered for export in opposition to the Soviets who often hand out Makarovs as part of their military aid packages. The East Germans produce a pistol almost identical to the Makarov known as the **Pistole M**, while the Poles turn out yet another Makarov 'look-alike' known as the **P-64**. The special Makarov ammunition is also manufactured in all three of these countries.

Below: The Makarov is a straightforward blowback pistol apparently derived from the pre-war Walther PP and PPK designs.

Specification
Makarov
Calibre: 9 mm (0.354 in)
Weight: empty 0.663 kg (1.46 lb)
Lengths: overall 160 mm (6.3 in); barrel 91 mm (3.58 in)
Muzzle velocity: 315 m (1,033 ft) per second
Magazine capacity: 8 rounds

An officer of the Soviet Naval Infantry prepares to fire his Makarov 9-mm pistol. The Naval Infantry is small in comparison with most Soviet arms, but for its size is regarded as one of the most effective fighting forces possessed by the Soviet Union.

Enfield No. 2 Mk 1 and Webley Mk 4

During World War I the standard British service revolver was one variant or other of the Webley 0.455-in (11.56-mm) pistol. These were very effective pistols, but their weight and bulk made them very difficult to handle correctly without a great deal of training and constant practice, two commodities that were in short supply at the time. After 1919 the British army decided that a smaller pistol firing a heavy 0.38-in (9.65-mm) bullet would be just as effective as the larger-calibre weapon but would be easier to handle and would require less training. So Webley and Scott, which up to that time had been pistol manufacturers of a virtually official status for the British armed forces, took its 0.455-in (11.56-mm) revolver, scaled it down and offered the result to the military.

To the chagrin of Webley and Scott, the military simply took the design, made a few minor alterations and then placed the result in production as an 'official' government design to be produced at the Royal Small Arms Factory at Enfield Lock in Middlesex. This procedure took time, for Webley and Scott offered its design in 1923 and Enfield Lock took over the design in 1926. Webley and Scott was somewhat nonplussed at the course of events but proceeded to make its 0.38-in (9.65-mm) revolver, known as the **Webley Mk 4** which sold all over the world with limited success.

The Enfield Lock product became the **Pistol, Revolver, No.' 2 Mk 1** and was duly issued for service. Once in service it proved sound and effective enough, but mechanical progress meant that large numbers of these pistols were issued to tank crews and other mechanized personnel, who made the unfortunate discovery that the long hammer spur had a tendency to catch onto the many internal fittings of tanks and other vehicles with what could be nasty results. This led to a redesign in which the Enfield pistol had the hammer spur removed altogether and the trigger mechanism lightened to enable the weapon to be fired double-action only. This revolver became the **No. 2 Mk 1***, and existing Mk 1s were modified to the new standard. The double action made the pistol very difficult to use accurately at all except minimal range, but that did not seem to matter too much at the time.

Webley and Scott re-entered the scene during World War II, when supplies of the Enfield pistols were too slow to meet the ever-expanding demand. Thus the Webley Mk 4 was ordered to eke out supplies, and Webley and Scott went on to supply thousands of its design to the British army after all. Unfortunately, although the two pistols were virtually identical in appearance there were enough minor differences between them to prevent interchangeability of parts.

Both pistols saw extensive use between 1939 and 1945, and although the Enfield revolvers (there was a **No. 2**

The Webley Mk 4 revolver was used as the basis for the Enfield No. 2 Mk 1 but was passed over in favour of the government-sponsored development. In time the call for more revolvers was so great that the Mk 4 was placed in production for the British armed forces and used alongside the Enfield pistols.

Mk 1** which embodied wartime production expedients) were the official standard pistols, the Webley Mk 4 was just as widely used among British and Commonwealth armed forces. Both remained in service until the 1960s and both are still to be encountered as service pistols in various parts of the world.

Specification
Revolver No. 2 Mk 1*
Cartridge: 0.380 SAA ball (9.65 mm)
Length overall: 260 mm (10.25 in)
Length of barrel: 127 mm (5 in)
Weight: 0.767 (1.7 lb)
Muzzle velocity: 183 m (600 ft) per second
Chamber capacity: 6 rounds

Specification
Webley Mk 4
Cartridge: 0.380 SAA ball (9.65 mm)
Length overall: 267 mm (10.5 in)
Length of barrel: 127 mm (5 in)
Weight: 0.767 (1.7 lb)
Muzzle velocity: 183 m (600 ft) per second
Chamber capacity: 6 rounds

Above: The Enfield No. 2 Mk 1 revolver was that most widely used by all the British and Commonwealth armed forces. Firing an 0.38-in (9.65-mm) ball cartridge, it was an efficient combat pistol but lacked any finesse or frills; yet it was able to withstand the many knocks of service life.*

Below: An airborne soldier stands guard on a house in Holland during Operation 'Market Garden'. The pistol is an Enfield No. 2 Mk 1 with the hammer removed to prevent snagging on clothing or within the close confines of vehicles or aircraft. They were issued to airborne soldiers such as glider pilots.*

Modern Sub-Machine Guns

South Africa is one of the many nations to use the Israeli UZI. First seeing major service in the 1956 Arab-Israeli conflict, the UZI is one of the most successful post-war sub-machine gun designs.

Evolved through necessity in the confined spaces of the trenches during World War I, the sub-machine gun has found a useful place in modern armed forces. Small, cheap and easily concealed, it is an ideal weapon for facing the urban terrors of the latter half of the 20th century.

Ever since the assault rifle became a viable weapon during the latter stages of World War II the pundits have been saying that the sub-machine gun's day was over. The trouble is that no one seems to have told the designers of small arms or the men who use sub-machine guns. Today the numbers of sub-machine guns on the market are as high as ever, and more seem to appear each year. The modern sub-machine guns described in this part are but a few of the more important types currently in use. There are many more types around, some of them having been in service since World War II, but most of the types described are of a much more sophisticated form. All manner of detail design features have been introduced to differentiate them from the hasty tube and sheet metal designs of World War II, although the same basic manufacturing principles are often used. Today there is more time to apply better finishes and construction methods, but while costs may have risen somewhat since World War II the modern sub-machine gun is still a relatively cheap weapon. Perhaps it is this that ensures the longevity of the type.

But it cannot be cost alone that maintains the sub-machine gun in use all over the world. Despite the many advantages that the assault rifle has

to offer, it is still a complex and lengthy weapon that is nowhere near as effective in close-quarter fighting as the sub-machine gun. Despite the increases in weapon power achieved in recent years, many combats still take place at close ranges and here the sub-machine gun is still as effective as it was when it was produced to 'sweep trenches of the enemy' during World War I. The short and handy sub-machine gun still reigns supreme in such circumstances.

Today the sub-machine gun is carried by one new operator, the policeman or the member of a security organization. The growth of national and international terrorism in recent years has meant that the agencies set against it have to be armed as effectively as their highly organized and well-armed opponents. Thus the sub-machine gun has entered a new and dangerous era, and it may be many years (if ever) before the weapon is no longer used in this relatively new and but dreadfully public cockpit.

Outside the Washington Hilton, 30 March 1981, President Reagan has just been shot; his assailant is buried under a swarm of police and secret service men. Prominent is the Israeli-made UZI sub-machine gun, carried by the agent in the foreground.

ARGENTINA
9-mm PA3-DM

The Argentine **PA3-DM** is a typical example of modern sub-machine gun design in two respects; one is the use of the forward-mounted 'wrap-around' breech block and the other the ability of a relatively unsophisticated engineering industry to produce modern and viable weapons.

The 'wrap-around' bolt is now a virtual fixture on many modern sub-machine guns, for it provides two important functions. One is that the breech block is to a large extent forward of the chamber when the cartridge is fired, so providing extra mass for the recoil to overcome, thereby providing an increase in locking efficiency for what is otherwise a relatively effective but inefficient blowback system. The other advantage is that by placing much of the breech block around the barrel the weapon length can be much reduced, making the overall design shorter and handier for carriage and stowage. Nearly all these 'wrap-around' designs, and the PA3-DM is no exception, use the pistol grip as the magazine housing, and this has the advantage of allowing rapid aiming, for by holding the weapon with the 'master' hand, one-handed firing is possible as though the weapon is a pistol.

The first weapon to use this 'wrap-around' feature was the Czech vz 23 series, and it has appeared on many subsequent weapons. The Argentine design closely follows the Czech original in overall construction, for it relies on the use of simple stampings and has as its receiver housing nothing more than a section of steel tubing. The PA3-DM has its cocking handle on the left-hand side well forward so that it can be operated by either hand, and a hand grip is provided forward of the metal pistol group assembly. The PA3-DM may be found in two forms: one has a fixed plastic butt, while the other has a wire-form butt which telescopes forward on each side of the receiver. This latter is a direct copy of the wire butt used on the American M3 sub-machine gun. On both versions the barrel screws onto the front of the tubular receiver and the barrel can be adapted to mount a device for launching grenades.

The PA3-DM was used during the Falkland Islands campaign of 1982, though not in very great numbers. Some 'trophies' were returned to the United Kingdom and may be found in some regimental museums, but otherwise it is not a weapon that is likely to be encountered outside Argentina, where it is issued to the armed forces.

The PA3-DM is manufactured by the Fabrica Militar de Armas 'Domingo Matheu' at Rosario, from which the 'DM' of the designation is derived. It is only the latest model in a long string of sub-machine guns that have been designed and produced in Argentina since the period just after World War II. Many of these sub-machine guns were orthodox designs with little of note to mention, and not all of them reached the full production stage. Some were direct copies of successful designs elsewhere: for example, the **PAM 2** dating from the early 1950s was nothing more than a direct copy of the

Captured by British forces on the Falklands during the South Atlantic conflict, the PA3-DM exemplifies the modern sub-machine gun, being simply designed and easy to manufacture.

US M3A1 calibred in 9 mm (0.354 in). Some of the other designs, such as the **MEMS** series and the **Halcon** guns, were more adventurous designs that made little impact outside Argentina.

Specification
PA3-DM (fixed-butt version)
Calibre: 9 mm (0.354 in) Parabellum
Weight: loaded 3.9 kg (8.6 lb)
Length: 700 mm (27.56 in)
Length of barrel: 290 mm (11.4 in)
Muzzle velocity: 400 m (1,312 ft) per second
Cyclic rate of fire: 650 rpm
Magazine: 25-round box

UK
9-mm L2A3 Sterling

The sub-machine gun that is now almost universally known as the **Sterling** entered British Army use in 1955 although an earlier form, known as the **Patchett**, underwent troop trials during the latter stages of World War II. It was intended that the Patchett would replace the Sten gun, but in the event the Sten lasted until well into the 1960s.

The British army model is designated the **L2A3** and equates to the **Sterling Mk 4** produced commercially by the Sterling Armament Company of Dagenham, Essex. This weapon is one of the major export successes of the post-war years, for to date it has been sold to over 90 countries and it is still in production in several forms. The basic service model is of simple design with the usual tubular receiver and a folding metal butt stock, but where the Sterling differs from many other designs is that it uses a curved box magazine that protrudes to the left. This arrangement has proved to be efficient in use and presents no problems. It has certainly created no problems for the army in India where the type is produced under licence, or in Canada where the design is produced as the C1 with some slight modifications.

The Sterling is a simple blowback weapon with a heavy bolt, but this bolt incorporates one of the best features of the design in that it has raised and inclined splines that help to remove any internal dust or dirt and push it out of the way. This enables the Sterling to be used under the worst possible conditions. The usual magazine holds 34 rounds, but a 10-round magazine is available along with a string of accessories including a bayonet. The weapon can be fitted with any number of night vision devices or sighting systems, although these are not widely used.

Several variants of the Sterling exist. One is a silenced version known to the British army as the **L34A1**. This uses a fixed silencer system allied to a special barrel that allows the firing gases to leak through the sides of the barrel into a rotary baffle silencer that is remarkably efficient and almost silent in use. There is also a whole range of what are known as paratrooper's pistols that use only the pistol group and the receiver allied to a short magazine and a very short barrel. These are available in single-shot or machine pistol versions. Several types of finish are produced, including what must be that for the most luxurious of sub-machine guns, for one version is literally gold-plated. These have been produced for various potentates in the Middle East who use them for their personal bodyguards and to impress visitors; both silenced and normal versions have been produced with gold plating. Chromium-plated versions have also been made.

Right: The Sterling saw considerable service in Malaya and Borneo, where the inherent inaccuracy of the sub-machine gun proved no handicap.

Below: The Sterling is seen on exercise in the UK, at Bassingbourn. It is being replaced by the new Enfield Individual Weapon.

Machine Pistols

The virtues of the sub-machine gun in close-quarter combat soon led designers to attempt to turn the contemporary self-loading (or automatic) pistol into a fully automatic weapon.

Almost as soon as the automatic pistol was first produced designers were tempted into allowing their progeny to fire in fully automatic bursts. The conventional automatic pistol simply fires a round, re-cocks itself and loads another round ready to fire on the repeated pull of a trigger. By simply keeping the trigger mechanism out of the way it was (and is) easy to allow the pistol to produce burst fire, but the designers soon learned that this was not a course to be undertaken lightly.

The pistol cartridge is weak compared with a rifle cartridge, but can still produce considerable recoil forces. If such cartridges are fired in rapid succession they can soon overcome the mass of a light hand-held pistol and force the muzzle to rise or jump about erratically. In either case aimed fire becomes almost impossible. Moreover, the bolts of most pistols are light, and this allows full automatic fire to be very rapid indeed, to the extent that the limited ammunition capacity of most pistols will be used in less than a second. These two limitations have made the machine pistol something of a rarity among combat weapons, but the machine pistol has nonetheless turned up throughout small arms development.

The first of the machine pistols to be used on any large scale were the Mausers. Derived from the C/96 pistols, the *Schnellfeuer* (quick fire) pistols became very popular at one time. They must be judged as among the more successful of the type, for the old C/96 'broomhandle' pistols had the bulk and weight to overcome, partially at least, some of the recoil forces while the box magazines in front of the trigger guard had the space potential to accommodate long magazines. But outside Germany and to a lesser extent Spain these Mauser machine pistols never caught on to any great extent in Europe. In the Far East, however, it was a different story. The Chinese took to the Mausers with a will and were soon turning out their own locally-produced copies that varied in materials and manufacturing standards from the excellent to the vile. The Chinese found the machine pistol to be just the sort of weapon that struck fear into an opponent, and the war lords who ruled in China between the world wars found them ideal for keeping their subjects under control. The Chinese even discovered the way to use the machine pistol's muzzle jump to good effect: they simply turned their Mausers onto one side as they fired so that, instead of spraying bullets at the sky, the machine pistol produced a wide fan of lethal projectiles that could cover a wide horizontal arc. This simple expedient has been little used elsewhere, but in the Far East this ploy was standard practice.

During World War II the machine pistol underwent a brief flurry of revival but the advantages of the sub-machine gun proved to be too many for the relatively expensive machine pistol, and few were made. From time to time interest was revived, but it was not until after World War II that service examples were seen in any numbers. These were intended for use by the crews of armoured or 'B' vehicles who did not normally require a rifle, or who did not have the space to carry one on their normal duties. For such personnel the machine pistol seemed attractive and thus the Czech Skorpion, the Polish wz 63 and the Soviet Stechkin came upon the scene. The Stechkin may be regarded as an update of the old Mauser pistols. It has even revived the practice of using a wooden holster that doubles as a butt stock, and it retains all the old problems of muzzle climb during burst fire. At least the Skorpion and the wz 63 have bulk and some degree of compensation built into their designs.

Above: The Heckler und Koch VP70 is an ingenious modern attempt to produce a controllable machine pistol. Automatic fire is only possible when the holster/stock is fitted, allowing three-round bursts. The burst facility allows reasonable aimed automatic fire.

Below: To convert a blowback pistol to full automatic, all that is required is some means of interrupting the trigger mechanism. This home-made conversion of a Government Model Colt was captured from the IRA in Ulster. Note the extended magazine.

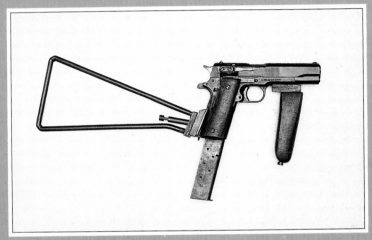

Despite the problems with the machine pistol listed above, it would be as well to list its advantages. The machine pistol can have a considerable shock effect in confined areas where any sudden spray of automatic fire will hit a target. Even the knowledge that a sudden burst of fire might be imminent can be enough for the owner of such a weapon to control local events, and it is this latter fact that makes the machine pistol attractive to many police and security forces. Even so, many sub-machine guns are now small and handy enough to rival the facilities of the machine pistol, the Mini-UZI and the Ingram designs being cases in point. But no doubt the machine pistol will continue to surface in the future.

The Sterling in all its forms has proved to be a very reliable and sturdy weapon. With many armies, including the British army, the weapon is used to arm second-line personnel who do not have to carry the normal service rifle and on vehicles it can easily be folded away to take up very little stowage space. With the British army the L2A3 will be gradually be replaced by the new 5.56-mm (0.219-in) Individual Weapon (IW) starting in the near future, but the large numbers of Sterlings still around the world mean that it will be a widely used type for many years to come.

Specification
L2A3
Calibre: 9 mm (0.354 in) Parabellum
Weight: loaded 3.47 kg (7.65 lb)
Length: with stock extended 690 mm (27.16 in) and with stock folded 483 mm (19 in)
Length of barrel: 198 mm (7.8 in)
Muzzle velocity: 390 m (1,280 ft) per second
Cyclic rate of fire: 550 rpm
Magazine: 10- or 34-round

Replacing the ubiquitous Sten in British army service, the Sterling L2A3 9-mm sub-machine gun has been sold in over 90 countries, and has proved effective and reliable under the most extreme of weather conditions, ranging from Arctic cold to jungle heat and humidity.

9-mm F1

During World War II a Lieutenant Owen invented the sub-machine gun that still bears his name, and this weapon was used by Australian soldiers during World War II and for many years after it. One of the most recognizable features of the **Owen** sub-machine gun was the vertical magazine, a feature with no particular merit or demerit but one that the Australians found very much to their liking. Thus when the Australian army began searching for a new design to replace the old and worn Owens, it was not averse to choosing a design with an overhead vertical magazine.

Before selecting the design now known as the **F1**, the Australians investigated a number of experimental weapons that rejoiced in such names as 'Kokoda' and the 'MCEM'. Some of these experimental designs had some advanced features but were generally regarded as not being 'soldier-proof' enough to suit Australian conditions. But in 1962 a design known as the **X3** was selected for production, and this became the F1. The predilections of the Australian military were very evident, for the F1 has a vertical magazine but in order to allow a certain amount of interchangeability with other weapons the magazine is now curved and identical to that of the British Sterling and the Canadian C1.

This interchangeability factor is also evident in several other features of the F1. The pistol grip is the same as that used on the L1A1 7.62-mm (0.3-in) NATO rifle, and the bayonet is another Sterling component. In fact it is tempting to regard the F1 as an Australian Sterling but there are too many differences to support such a claim. The F1 uses a simple 'straight-through' design with the butt fixed in line with the tubular receiver, and the pistol group is arranged differently from that of the Sterling. The overhead magazine does produce one difficulty, namely sighting. In action deliberate aiming is not common but has to be taken into account, so a form of offset sighting system had to be introduced. On the F1 this is done simply by using an offset leaf sight (folding down onto the tubular receiver) allied with a fixed offset foresight. The F1 does have one rather unusual safety built into the design

which is not common but yet is simple and effective: on a short-barrelled weapon it is often too easy to place the forward grip over the muzzle or too close to it for safety, but on the F1 a simple sling swivel bracket prevents the hand from getting too close to the muzzle.

The F1 has some other simple but effective design features. One is the cocking handle, which exactly duplicates the position and action of its counterpart on the L1A1 standard service rifle in use with the Australian forces; this handle has a cover which prevents dirt and debris getting into the action, though if enough dirt does get into the action to prevent the bolt closing the cocking handle can be latched to the bolt for the firer to force it closed in an emergency.

For all its many attributes the F1 has yet to be bought outside Australia and some of its associated territories. No longer in production, the F1 may well be replaced by a carbine version of the Steyr AUG, which has been adopted as the new Australian assault rifle.

Specification
F1
Calibre: 9 mm (0.354 in) Parabellum
Weight: loaded 4.3 kg (9.48 lb) with bayonet
Length: 714 mm (28.1 in)
Length of barrel: 213 mm (8.386 in)
Muzzle velocity: 366 m (1,200 ft) per second
Cyclic rate of fire: 600-640 rpm
Magazine: 34-round curved box

Above: Replacing the extremely popular Owen sub-machine gun in Australian service, the F1 retains the uniquely Australian feature of a vertical top-loading magazine. The F1 is otherwise similar to the Sterling.

Below: Simple and effective, the F1 in its prototype X3 form performed extremely well in the Mekong Delta during the Vietnam War. Modern construction made it almost 1 kg (2.2-lb) lighter than its World War II ancestor.

9-mm Model 45

The 9-mm **Model 45** was produced originally by the Karl Gustav Stads Gevärsfaktori (now part of the FFV consortium) at Eskilstuna, and is thus widely known as the Carl Gustav sub-machine gun. The Model 45 is an entirely orthodox design with no frills, and uses a simple tubular receiver and barrel cover with a simple folding butt hinged onto the pistol grip assembly. The usual blowback operating principle is employed, and overall there is little that is remarkable about the Model 45.

But there is one interesting point regarding the Model 45, and that is the magazine. On many sub-machine guns the magazine is usually one of the most trouble-prone components, for the magazine relies upon simple spring pressure to push the rounds towards the receiver, whence they are fed into the firing system. It is all too easy for rounds to become misaligned or

forced together and the result is then a misfeed or jam, and these can happen at inopportune moments in combat. On the original Model 45 the magazine used was that once used on the pre-war Suomi Model 37-39, a 50-round magazine that was then considered to be one of the best in use anywhere. But in 1948 a new magazine was introduced that held 36 rounds in twin rows that were carefully tapered into a single row by the use of a wedge cross-section. This new magazine proved to be remarkably reliable and trouble-free in use, and was soon being widely copied elsewhere. Production Model 45s were soon being offered with a revised magazine housing to accommodate both the Suomi magazine and the new wedge-shaped magazine, and this version was known as the **Model 45/B**. Later production models made provision for the wedge-shaped magazine only.

The Model 45 and Model 45/B became one of Sweden's few major export weapons. Numbers were sold to Denmark and some other nations such as Eire. Egypt produced the Model 45/B as the **'Port Said'** under licence. Copies have also been produced in Indonesia. Perhaps the oddest service use of the Model 45/B was in Vietnam. Numbers of these weapons were obtained by the American CIA and converted in the United States to take a special barrel allied to a silencer. These were used in action in Vietnam by the US Special Forces on undercov-

The 9-mm Model 45 is generally known as the Carl Gustav, after its manufacturer. Conventional in design and operation, it has been in production since 1945 and has been exported widely, although in varying numbers.

er missions. According to most reports the silencers were not particularly effective and they were not retained in use for long.

Numerous accessories have been produced for the Model 45, one of the oddest being a special muzzle attachment that doubles as a blank firing device or a short-range target training device. The attachment is used together with special plastic bullets which are shredded into pieces as they leave the muzzle for safety. These bullets generate enough gas pressure to operate the mechanism and if required enough pressure is available to project a steel ball from the attachment itself. This reusable steel ball can thus be used for short-range target practice.

Specification
Model 45/B
Calibre: 9 mm (0.354 in) M39B Parabellum
Weight: loaded 4.2 kg (9.25 lb)
Length: with stock extended 808 mm (31.8 in) and with stock folded 551 mm (21.7 in)
Length of barrel: 213 mm (8.385 in)
Muzzle velocity: 365 m (1,198 ft) per second
Cyclic rate of fire: 550-600 rpm
Magazine: 36-round box

Used by many countries, including Egypt (in the 1967 war with Israel) and the USA (in a silenced version by special forces in Vietnam), the Carl Gustav remains in large-scale service with the Swedish forces.

FRANCE
9-mm MAT 49

Immediately after 1945 the French armed forces were armed with a variety of sub-machine guns, some of them dating from before the war and others were coming from the United States and the United Kingdom. While the weapons were serviceable enough, the range of ammunition calibres and types was considered to be too wide, and after a selection process it was decided to standardize on the 9-mm Parabellum round for future developments. A new sub-machine gun of French origins was requested, and three arsenals responded with new designs. That of the Manufacture d'Armes de Tulle (hence MAT) was selected, and the weapon went into production in 1949.

The **MAT 49** is still in widespread service, for it is a very well made weapon. Although it uses the now-commonplace method of fabricating parts and assemblies from stampings, those in the MAT 49 were made from heavy-duty steels and are thus very strong and capable of absorbing a great deal of hard use. The design uses the blowback principle but in place of what is now described as a 'wrap-around' breech block to reduce the

length of the receiver the MAT 49 has an arrangement in which a sizable portion of the breech block enters the barrel chamber to have much the same effect. No other design uses this feature, and there is another aspect of the MAT 49 which is typically French. This is the magazine housing, which can be folded forward with the magazine inserted to reduce the bulk of the weapon for stowage and transport. This feature is a carry-over from the pre-war MAS 38, and was considered so effective by the French army that it was retained in the MAT 49: a catch is depressed and the magazine housing (with a loaded magazine in place) is folded forward to lie under the barrel, while to use the weapon again the magazine is simply pulled back into place so that the housing acts as a foregrip. This foregrip is made all the more important by the fact that the MAT 49 can be fired on automatic only, so a firm grip is needed to keep the weapon under control when fired.

Considerable pains are taken on the MAT 49 to keep out dust and dirt, which is another historical carry-over from previous times as the MAT 49 was intended for use in the deserts of North

Africa. Even when the magazine is in the forward position a flap moves into position to keep out foreign matter. If repairs or cleaning are required the weapon can be easily stripped without tools. In action a grip safety locks both the trigger mechanism and any possible forward movement of the bolt.

Overall the MAT 49 is a sturdy and foolproof weapon. It is still used by the French armed forces and by various of the French police and paramilitary units. It has also been sold abroad to many of the ex-French colonies and wherever French interests prevail. There is a chance that the recent introduction of the 5.56-mm (0.219-in) FA MAS rifle to the French army may reduce the numbers in service, but there are enough operators left to ensure that the MAT 49 will remain around for a long time to come.

Specification
MAT 49
Calibre: 9 mm (0.354 in) Parabellum
Weight: loaded 4.17 kg (9.19 lb)
Length: with butt extended 720 mm (28.34 in) and with butt closed 460 mm (18.1 in)
Length of barrel: 228 mm (8.97 in)
Muzzle velocity: 390 m (1,280 ft) per second
Cyclic rate of fire: 600 rpm
Magazine: 20- or 32-round box

Above: Entering French service in 1949, the 9-mm MAT 49 is an extremely rugged design, made from heavy-gauge steel stampings. The pistol grip/magazine housing hinges forward for stowage and transport.

Right: Designed with colonial service in mind, the MAT 49 was used extensively in Indo-China, as well as with the paratroops so notably involved in the bloody conflict in Algeria. It stood such stern tests successfully.

9-mm UZI

Once Israel had fought its War of Independence in 1948 the new nation had some breathing space in which to arm itself for any future conflict. Submachine guns were high on the list of priorities, for the new Israeli army was then equipped with all manner of old weapons varying from Sten guns to Czech weapons. The Czech weapons attracted the close attention of one Lieutenant Uziel Gail, for they had the advantage that their breech blocks or bolts were 'wrapped around' the barrel, so placing the mass of the bolt well forward around the barrel on firing and allowing a short weapon to have a relatively long barrel. The Czech weapons concerned were of the vz 23 series, and using these Gail was able to design and develop his own design that was more suitable to the manufac-

turing methods then available in relatively undeveloped Israel. He came up with a weapon that is now universally known as the **UZI** after its designer.

The UZI is made largely from simple pressings held in place by spot welds or other welding. The main body is made from a single sheet of heavy gauge sheet steel with grooves pressed into the sides to take any dust, dirt or sand that might get into the works. This simple feature makes the UZI capable of operation under even the most arduous conditions, a fact that has been proved on many occasions. The overall cross-section of the main body is rectangular with the barrel secured to the body by a large nut just behind the muzzle. The trigger group is situated centrally, and the box magazine is inserted through the pistol grip, which

makes reloading very easy in the dark for 'hand will naturally find hand'. The normal combat magazine holds 32 rounds, but a common practice is to join two magazines together using a cross-over clip or even tape to allow rapid changing. A grip safety is incorporated into the pistol grip.

The UZI is now virtually one of the symbols of Israeli military prowess, but Israel is not the only nation to use the type. The West Germans also use the UZI, which they know as the **MP2**; this model was produced under licence by FN in Belgium. Numerous other nations also use the UZI. It is part of legend that the President of the United States is always accompanied by bodyguards carrying UZIs in specially fitted brief cases, and many other security agencies and police forces

use the UZI.

The UZI may be encountered with either a sturdy fixed wooden butt stock or a metal stock that can be folded forward under the main body with the butt plate still available to assist in steadying automatic fire. The UZI can be used to fire single-shot by use of a change lever just above the pistol butt.

Specification
UZI (with wooden stock)
Calibre: 9 mm (0.354 in) Parabellum
Weight: loaded with 32-round magazine 4.1 kg (9 lb)
Length: 650 mm (25.59 in)
Length of barrel: 260 mm (10.24 in)
Muzzle velocity: 400 m (1,312 ft) per second
Cyclic rate of fire: 600 rpm
Magazine: 25- or 32-round box

Right: The UZI (with wooden stock) and the Mini-UZI. The Mini-UZI is just 36-cm (14-in) long with its stock folded, making for easy concealment under ordinary clothing. The UZI is a design of great simplicity and is famous for reliability in awkward conditions.

Below: This Israeli carries the UZI fitted with metal folding stock. In addition to a grip safety, the UZI features a ratchet on the cocking handle to prevent accidental firing if the user's hand slips off the handle after the breech block has passed behind a round.

9-mm Mini-UZI

The **Mini-UZI** has been developed by Israel Military Industries from the full-scale UZI and differs from the original only in dimensions and weights. A few modifications have been introduced to the basic design, but these are only superficial while the operating system of the original has been retained unchanged.

The Mini-UZI has been developed as a weapon suitable for concealment by police and security personnel. This prompted an overall decrease in dimensions, and to improve this concealment a smaller 20-round magazine has been introduced, although the Mini-UZI can still use the existing 25- and 32-round magazines if required. The UZI parentage is immediately apparent but one change that can be noted is that the normal folding metal butt has been replaced by a single-strut butt stock that folds along the right-hand side of the body. When folded the butt plate acts as a rudimentary foregrip, but the normal foregrip is a plastic section just forward of the trigger group.

To date the Mini-UZI has been marketed as suitable for police and secur-

ity agencies but it is bound to attract the attentions of various military organizations for special missions. It would make an ideal commando-type weapon where light weight is required, and it must be stressed that although the Mini-UZI is a scaled-down version of the original it still uses the potent 9-mm (0.354-in) × 19 Parabellum round. As the weapon is lighter than the full-size version its breech block is lighter too, and this provides a cyclic rate of fire of 950 rounds per minute, which is much higher than on the original.

The Mini-UZI is being marketed in the United States carried in a specially-fitted brief case together with spare magazines and a small cleaning and spares kit. It has already been suggested that some form of silencer could be fitted to the muzzle.

There are also some UZIs other than the standard version and the Mini-UZI. One is the semi-automatic **Carbine UZI** which has been produced to conform with the legal requirements of some American states that require non-automatic weapons only to be held by their inhabitants. In order to prevent

the rapid conversion of semi-automatic versions of automatic weapons they call for such semi-automatic versions to have barrels at least 406 mm (16 in) long. Thus the standard UZI may be seen with a long barrel protruding from the body and this denotes that the weapon can be fired single-shot only.

Another UZI variant that has only recently been introduced is the UZI pistol. Although really outside the scope of this survey it is still recognizable as an UZI. It can be fired single-shot only and there is no form of butt stock.

Specification
UZI
Calibre: 9 mm (0.354 in) Parabellum
Weight: loaded with 20-round magazine 3.11 kg (6.85 lb)
Length: with stock extended 600 mm (23.62 in) and with stock folded 360 mm (14.17 in)
Length of barrel: 197 mm (7.75 in)
Muzzle velocity: 352 m (1,155 ft) per second
Cyclic rate of fire: 950 rpm
Magazine: 20-, 25- or 32-round box

Heckler und Koch MP5

Since World War II the West German concern of Heckler und Koch has become one of Europe's largest and most important small-arms manufacturers with its success based soundly on the production of its G3 rifle, which has become a standard NATO weapon and is in use all over the world. Working from the G3 and employing its highly efficient breech-locking mechanism, the company has also produced the **Heckler und Koch MP5**, which may thus be regarded as the sub-machine gun version of the G3.

In appearance the MP5 looks very similar to the G3 although it is of course much shorter. It fires the usual 9-mm (0.354-in) × 19 Parabellum cartridge, and although this is relatively low-powered compared with the 7.62-mm (0.3-in) rifle cartridge the MP5 uses the same roller and inclined ramp locking mechanism as the G3. The complexity of this system is more than offset by its increased safety, and by the ability of the MP5 to be fired very accurately as it can fire from a closed bolt, i.e. the breech block is in the forward position when the trigger is pulled so there is no forward-moving mass to disturb the aim as there is with other sub-machine guns. The resemblance to the G3 is maintained by the use of many G3 components on the MP5.

There are six main versions of the MP5. The **MP5A2** has a fixed butt stock while the **MP5A3** has a metal strut stock that can be slid forward to reduce its length. There are no fewer than three differing versions of the **MP5 SD**, which is a silenced version of the basic model for use in special or anti-terrorist warfare. The **MP5 SD1** does not have a butt stock at all; the **MP5 SD2** has a fixed butt as on the MP5A2; and the **MP5 SD3** has the sliding metal butt stock used on the MP5A3. Then there is the **MP5K** which is a very short version of the basic MP5, only 325 mm (12.8 in) long and recognizable by a small foregrip under the almost non-existent muzzle. The **MP5K A1** is a special version of this variant with no protrusions so that it can be carried under clothing or in a special holster.

In all its forms the MP5 has proved to be an excellent and reliable sub-machine gun. It is in use with some of the various West German police agencies and border guards, and numbers have been purchased by Swiss police and the Netherlands armed forces. It is known to be one of the weapons most favoured by the British SAS for close-quarter combat.

Unfortunately some MP5s have fallen into the wrong hands, usually by theft from weapon stores. The MP5 was the main weapon of the Baader-Meinhoff gang and many similar groups are known to have used the MP5 at one time or another. The MP5 has been described by one counter-insurgency authority as 'the most efficient terrorist weapon now in production', and it will no doubt feature in many future terrorist or 'freedom fighter' outrages. This future use might well involve various forms of night sight, for the MP5 has been demonstrated on numerous occasions with such devices, along with other sighting devices such as telescopic sights and other rapid-aiming systems.

Top: The MP5A3 is fitted with a sliding metal strut stock which can allow a considerable reduction in overall length, from 660 mm (26 in) to 490 mm (19.3 in).

Above: The MP5A2 is fitted with fixed plastic butt stock. After 1978 the MP5 was fitted with a curved magazine to improve cartridge feed.

Below: The MP5 SD3 is a silenced version of the MP5A3, all parts except barrel and silencer being the same. It is used by several military and police forces around the world.

Right: The extremely short MP5K was introduced for use by special police and anti-terrorist squads, where weapon concealment may be essential.

Specification
MP5A2
Calibre: 9 mm (0.354 in) Parabellum
Weight: loaded 2.97 kg (6.55 lb)
Length: 680 mm (26.77 in)
Length of barrel: 225 mm (8.86 in)
Muzzle velocity: 330 m (1,083 ft) per second
Cyclic rate of fire: 800 rpm
Magazine: 15- or 30-round box

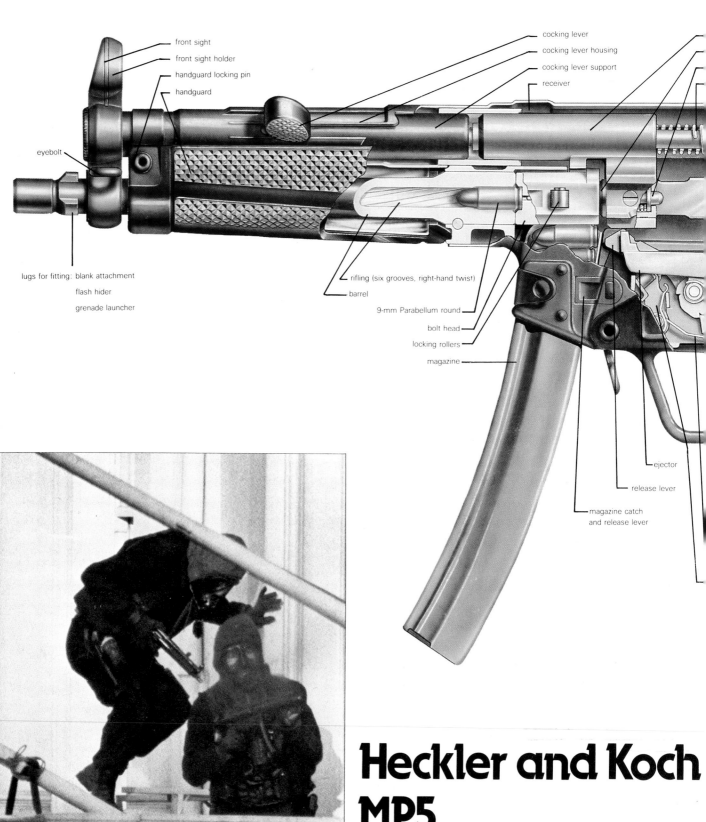

front sight

front sight holder

handguard locking pin

handguard

eyebolt

cocking lever

cocking lever housing

cocking lever support

receiver

lugs for fitting: blank attachment

flash hider

grenade launcher

rifling (six grooves, right-hand twist)

barrel

9-mm Parabellum round

bolt head

locking rollers

magazine

ejector

release lever

magazine catch
and release lever

Heckler and Koch MP5

The MP5 came to public notice in dramatic fashion during the 1980 siege of the Iranian Embassy in London. The SAS chose the 'Hockler' (as they have christened the weapon) because it is amongst the most accurate of sub-machine guns.

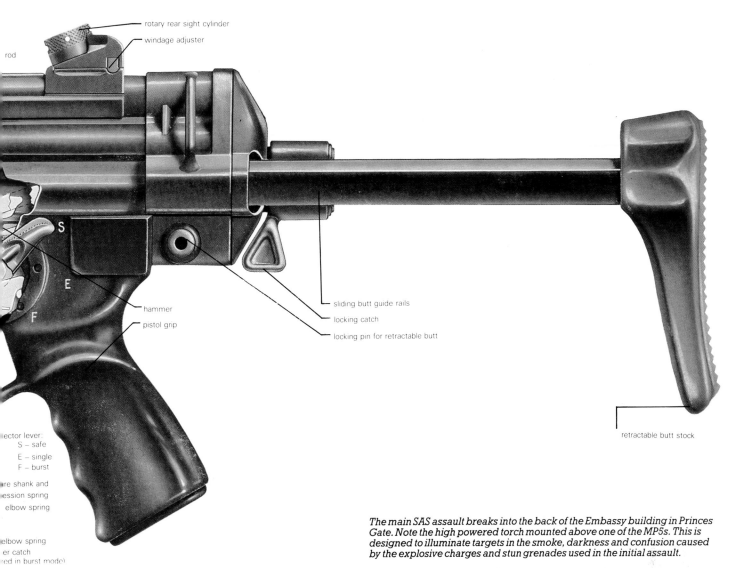

rotary rear sight cylinder

windage adjuster

rod

hammer

pistol grip

S

E

F

sliding butt guide rails

locking catch

locking pin for retractable butt

retractable butt stock

ector lever:
  S – safe
  E – single
  F – burst

re shank and
ession spring

elbow spring

elbow spring
er catch
ed in burst mode)

The main SAS assault breaks into the back of the Embassy building in Princes Gate. Note the high powered torch mounted above one of the MP5s. This is designed to illuminate targets in the smoke, darkness and confusion caused by the explosive charges and stun grenades used in the initial assault.

Walther MP-K and MP-L

Walther has for long been in the forefront of small arms design and development, but the end of World War II saw most of its facilities taken over by the new East German government, so for many years the company was unable to re-enter its chosen market. But by the early 1960s Walther was back in business, and in 1963 introduced its 9-mm (0.354-in) **Walther MP-K** and **MP-L** sub-machine guns.

The MP-K and MP-L (MP standing for *Maschinenpistole*, K for *kurz* or short, and L for *lange* or long) differ only in their barrel length. They are both well-made sub-machine guns constructed in the usual manner from steel stampings, and both use the same blowback operating principle. The butt stock is a skeleton tube arrangement, and when not in use this can be folded along the right-hand side of the receiver. The box magazine is inserted into a housing under the receiver and just forward of the trigger

group. This magazine is wedge-shaped in cross-section and contains 32 rounds. As one would expect with Walther products, the overall standard of manufacture is excellent.

From the side both models present a rather deep silhouette. This is because the main mass of the breech block is mounted over the barrel and guided throughout its backward and forward travel on a guide rod. Normally the bolt handle does not move with the breech block, but if required it can be latched into the block in order to clear a stoppage. There are all manner of small detail points on these two weapons. One is that when the stock is folded forward the butt portion can be used as a forward grip. Another is the rear sight, which is normally fixed for use at 100 m (109 yards) using conventional rear and fore sights. But for use in low visibility conditions the upper portion of the sight becomes an open rear sight and is used in conjunction with

the top of the fore sight protector. There is a fire selector switch just behind the trigger, allowing rapid and easy selection of 'safe', single shot or full automatic.

The first Walther MP-Ks and MP-Ls were sold to the West German navy and to some German police forces. Since then more have been sold to Brazil, Colombia, the Mexican navy and Venezuela. The types are no longer in production, but both are still being offered for sale by Walther and could be placed back in production within a short time. Some accessories have been offered with these guns. At one point the MP-K was offered with a screw-on silencer, but this was apparently not long developed and there appear to have been few takers. All weapons have provision for sling swivels and these are so arranged that the sling can be used to stabilize the gun when firing bursts.

Specification
MP-K
Calibre: 9 mm (0.354 in)
Weight: loaded 3.425 kg (7.55 lb)
Length: with stock open 653 mm (25.7 in) and with stock folded 368 mm (14.49 in)
Length of barrel: 171 mm (6.73 in)
Muzzle velocity: 356 m (1,168 ft) per second
Cyclic rate of fire: 550 rpm
Magazine: 32-round box

Specification
MP-L
Calibre: 9 mm (0.354 in)
Weight: loaded 3.625 kg (7.99 lb)
Length: with stock open 737 mm (29 in) and with stock folded 455 mm (17.9 in)
Length of barrel: 257 mm (10.12 in)
Muzzle velocity: 396 m (1,299 ft) per second
Cyclic rate of fire: 550 rpm
Magazine: 32-round box

7.62-mm Type 64

The Chinese **Type 64** is one of the most unusual sub-machine guns in service today, for it has been designed and produced from the outset as a silenced weapon. During World War II several types of machine-gun were fitted with various types of suppressor for special missions (such as behind-the-lines and commando-type operations), but no country went to the extent of producing a special weapon for these roles. For reasons best known to themselves the Communist Chinese have done so.

The Type 64 fires the standard Soviet 7.62-mm (0.3-in) × 25 pistol round, but the use of a Maxim-type silencer arrangement makes this round effective only at short ranges. To make matters more complicated the Chinese use this pistol round fitted with a special bullet known as the Type P, which is slightly heavier than the normal bullet and is thus slightly more effective. As silenced weapons go the Type 64 has been tested to the point where it seems to be effective enough, but the time and trouble involved in the design and production of such a special weapon and cartridge seem wasteful to many Western experts.

The Type 64 is a mixture of various design features mainly lifted from other weapons. The basic overall design and bolt action resemble those of the Soviet PPS-43 of World War II, while the trigger mechanism is taken from the Bren Gun, many of which were used in China during and after World War II. The folding stock also comes from the Soviet PPS-43, while the silencer uses the well-established principles introduced by Hiram Maxim who was at one time as well known for his silencer designs as he was for his machine-guns. The barrel extends along only part of the silencer, and the last part of the barrel is perforated by a

The Type 64 uses a selective fire trigger mechanism derived from that of the Bren gun and a bolt action taken from the Type 43 – the Chinese copy of the Soviet PPS-43.

series of holes; the propellant gases exhaust through these and the muzzle into a series of baffles that continue until the muzzle of the silencer proper. This silencer also acts as a flash suppressor.

The exact operational role of this weapon with the ChiCom forces is not known with exactitude. The few examples seen in the West came mainly

from Vietnam and similar Far East origins, and it is doubtful if the Type 64 was kept in production for very long or even if it was produced in any quantity. It remains an enigma.

Specification
Type 64
Calibre: 7.62 mm (0.3 in) × 25 Type P
Weight: empty 3.4 kg (7.495 lb)
Length: with stock extended 843 mm (33.19 in)
Length of barrel: 244 mm (9.6 in)
Muzzle velocity: about 313 m (1,027 ft) per second
Cyclic rate of fire: uncertain
Magazine: 20- or 30-round box

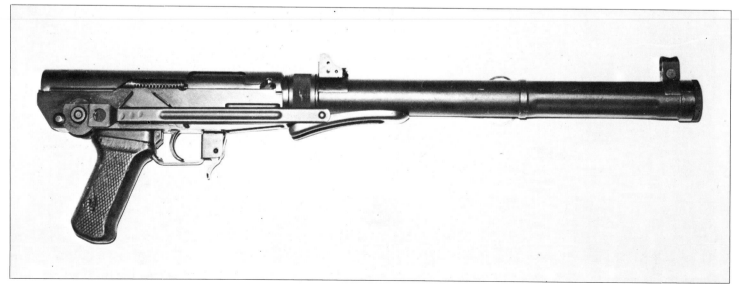

CZECHOSLOVAKIA
Model 61 Skorpion

The Czech **Model 61 Skorpion** lies in that small-arms no-man's-land where a weapon that is neither a pistol nor a true sub-machine gun is described as a 'machine pistol': it is small enough to be carried and fired as a pistol, but it fires fully automatically when required. It has the advantages and disadvantages of both types of weapon and is perhaps below par as both a pistol and a sub-machine gun, but it is now one of the

The Model 61 Skorpion is a favourite weapon of the Palestine Liberation Organization, its small size making for easy concealment.

most feared of all 'underground' weapons, despite the fact that it was originally intended to be a standard service weapon for the Czech armed forces.

The Skorpion was designed for use by tank crews, signallers and other personnel who have no normal need for anything larger than a pistol. But since a pistol is essentially a short-range weapon, the introduction of a fully automatic feature provided this small weapon with a considerable short-range firepower potential. The Skorpion resembles a pistol, though the magazine is not in the butt but forward of the trigger assembly, and a folding wire butt is provided for aimed fire. The overall appearance is short and chunky, and the weapon is small enough to be carried in a rather over-sized belt holster. When fired on full automatic the weapon has a cyclic rate of about 840 rounds per minute, which

Above right: Stock fully extended, the Type 61 can shoot with reasonable accuracy at up to 200 m (220 yards). It uses a simple blowback operation, but the empty case is ejected directly upwards

makes it a formidable weapon at short ranges, but this benefit is offset by two considerations. One is that using any machine pistol on full automatic makes the weapon almost impossible to aim accurately: the muzzle forces cause the muzzle to climb and judder to such an extent that it is virtually impossible to hold the weapon still for more than an instant. The other consideration is that the Skorpion uses magazines with only 10- or 20-round capacity, and on automatic either would soon be exhausted. But while the Skorpion fires it sprays bullets in an alarming swathe and this makes it a formidable close-quarter weapon.

The Skorpion operates on the blow-back principle. Single shots can be selected, and aiming is assisted by use of the folding wire butt. The basic

Model 61 Skorpion fires the American 0.32-in (actual 7.65-mm) cartridge, making it the only Warsaw Pact weapon to use this round, but the **Model 63** uses the 9-mm short (0.38-in) round and the **Model 68** the 9-mm (0.354-in) Parabellum. A silenced version of the Model 61 is available.

Apart from the Czech armed forces, the Skorpion has also been sold to some African nations, but its main impact has been in the hands of guerrillas and 'freedom fighters'. The firepower impact of the Skorpion is considerable at short ranges, which suits the requirements of assassination and terror squads, so the type is now much favoured by such groups. With them it has turned up in many parts of the world from Central America to the Middle East.

Specification
Model 61 Skorpion
Calibre: 0.32 in (actual 7.65 mm)
Weight: loaded 2 kg (4.4 lb)
Length: with butt extended 513 mm (20.2 in) and with butt folded 269 mm (10.6 in)

Length of barrel: 112 mm (4.4 in)
Muzzle velocity: 317 m (1,040 ft) per second
Cyclic rate of fire: 840 rpm
Magazine: 10- or 20-round box

POLAND
9-mm wz 63 (PM-63)

The 9-mm **wz 63** (*wzor*, or model) is also known as the **PM-63**, and is one of those weapons that falls into the category of machine pistol. Although only slightly larger than an orthodox pistol, it can be fired fully automatic at a cyclic rate of 600 rounds per minute. It was designed by Piotr Wilniewicz, who led a design team to produce a weapon for those elements of the Polish forces who are unable to carry a conventional weapon during their combat duties. The wz 63 is thus used by Polish tank crews, signallers and other troops such as truck drivers.

The wz 63 is rather long for a conventional pistol and is fitted with a butt that can be folded forward to lie under the barrel. When folded forward the butt either lies under the forward grip, or the butt plate can be folded down to act as a forward grip. This forward grip is essential to hold the weapon steady on automatic fire, for the wz 63 suffers from the usual difficulty of rapid and erratic muzzle movement mainly caused by the cyclic rate of fire. Some of this muzzle movement is compensated by a simple fixture on the end of

the barrel which is little more than an open trough angled upwards at a slight angle to push the barrel downwards. In practice this device appears to be of marginal value. Accurate single-shot aiming is possible, but even when using the butt any deliberate aim is likely to be disturbed by the bolt moving forward as the trigger is pulled since, like most other blowback-operated weapons, the wz 63 operates from an open bolt. However its effective range using the stock extended into the shoulder is stated to be 200m (220 yards); on automatic the range is much less.

The wz 63 may be used with either a 25- or a 40-round magazine, although some references also mention a 15-

Although classed as a machine pistol, the wz 63 is more complex than the Skorpion and it would require a firm hand indeed to fire 9-mm × 18 cartridges on full automatic. It is perhaps no accident that the handbook only shows it deployed for two-handed use.

round magazine. It is normally issued together with a special holster and a pouch holding three magazines and a cleaning kit.

The round fired by the wz 63 is the 9-mm (0.354-in) × 18 Makarov cartridge, which differs in several ways from the usual 9-mm (0.354-in) × 19 Parabellum round. It provides the wz 63 with a considerable striking capability at short combat ranges but as

stated before the ability of any machine pistol to remain on target for more than a fleeting second is unlikely. Instead the wz 63 produces a 'spray' effect which can be of considerable value in combat, but even this effect is reduced by the magazine capacity.

The wz 63 is still used by the Polish troops for which it was designed, and the type is now extensively used by Polish police and security units. Out-

side Poland the wz 63 appears to be little used, though numbers of these weapons have turned up in the Middle East and have been observed by several of the organizations involved in the civil war in Lebanon. The Chinese produce a copy of the wz 63.

Specification
wz 63
Calibre: 9 mm (0.354 in) Makarov

Weight: with empty 32-round magazine 1.8 kg (3.97 lb)
Length: with stock retracted 333 mm (13.1 in)
Length of barrel: 152 mm (6 in)
Muzzle velocity: 323 m (1,060 ft) per second
Cyclic rate of fire: 600 rpm
Magazine: 25- or 40-round box; also references to 15-round box

---

USA
Ingram Model 10

There have been few weapons in recent years that have 'enjoyed' the attentions of the Press and Hollywood to such an extent as that lavished on the Ingram sub-machine guns. Gordon B. Ingram had designed a whole string of sub-machine guns before he produced his **Ingram Model 10**, which was originally intended to be used with the Sionics Company suppressor. First produced during the mid-1960s, the little Ingram Model 10 soon attracted a great deal of public attention because of its rate of fire, supposedly high enough to 'saw a body in half', coupled with the highly efficient sound suppressor. Hollywood and television films added their dramatic commentaries and the Ingram Model 10 soon became as widely known as the old Thompson sub-machine guns of the 1920s.

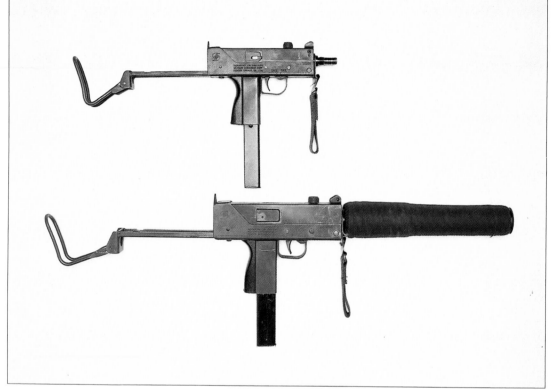

The Ingram Model 11 (top) is chambered for 9-mm Short (.380 ACP), while the Model 10 (below), fitted with a suppressor, can be chambered for either 9-mm Parabellum or .45 ACP. Both are relatively well balanced due to the bolt enveloping the breech.

The Ingram Model 10 is indeed a remarkable little weapon. It is constructed from sheet metal but manufactured to a very high standard and is extremely robust. This has to be, for it fires at a cyclic rate of over 1,000 rounds per minute, yet control of the weapon is still relatively easy thanks to the good balance imparted by the centrally-placed pistol group through which the box magazine is inserted. Most versions have a folding metal butt

Its efficient suppressor makes the Ingram a handy weapon for the Special Forces. By reducing the escaping gas to subsonic speed and eliminating flash, the position of the firer can remain a mystery to the target, until it is too late.

but this may be removed, and many weapons not fitted with the long tubular suppressor use a forward webbing hand-strap as a rudimentary foregrip. The muzzle on most models is threaded to accommodate the suppressor, and when fitted this is covered with a heat-resistant canvas or plastic webbing to allow it to be used as a forward grip. The cocking handle is on top of the slab-sided receiver and when turned through 90° acts as a safety lock. As this handle is slotted for sighting purposes the firer can soon notice if this safety is applied, and there is a normal trigger safety as well.

The Model 10 may be encountered chambered for either the well-known 11.43-mm (0.45-in) cartridge or the more usual 9-mm (0.354-in) Parabellum. The latter round may also be used on the smaller **Model 11** which is normally chambered for the less powerful 9-mm Short (.380 ACP). In all these calibres the Ingram is a dreadfully efficient weapon and not surprisingly it has been sold widely to customers ranging from paramilitary forces to bodyguard and security agencies. Military sales on any large scale have been few but several nations have acquired numbers for 'testing and evaluation'. The British SAS is known to have obtained a small quantity for test-

ing. Sales have not been encouraged by the fact that the ownership and manufacturing rights have changed hands several times, but both the Model 10 and Model 11 are now back in production and selling well. In order to keep sales rolling several variants have been made. Versions firing single-shot only and without the folding butt are available, and at one point a long-barrelled version was produced, though only in limited numbers as the type did not find a ready market.

In the meantime Ingrams will be found in countries as diverse as Yugoslavia, Israel and Argentina. Many have been sold to the Central and South American nations.

Specification
Model 10 (0.45-in model)
Calibre: 11.43 mm (0.45 in)
Weight: loaded with 30-round magazine 3.818 kg (8.4 lb)
Length: with stock extended 548 mm (21.575 in) and with stock folded 269 mm (10.59 in)
Length of barrel: 146 mm (5.75 in)
Length of suppressor: 291 mm (11.46 in)
Muzzle velocity: 280 m (918 ft) per second
Cyclic rate of fire: 1,145 rpm
Magazine: 30-round box

9-mm Beretta Model 12

During World War II the Beretta sub-machine guns were among the most highly-prized of all war trophies, and many remained for many years after the war in service with both military and paramilitary formations. The last of the 'war-time' Beretta variants was produced in 1949, and in 1958 an entirely new Beretta design was introduced. This owed nothing to previous designs and for the first time Beretta adopted the tubular receiver and stamped component construction that had for long been employed by many other manufacturers. The new design was the **Beretta Model 12**, but although it looked simple it was still a Beretta product, as was revealed by the overall high standard of finish and by its quality manufacture.

The Model 12 had an orthodox construction down to the 'wrap-around' bolt that was by then commonplace. This allowed it to be a short and handy weapon that as usual could be fitted with either a folding metal stock or a fixed wooden stock.

The Model 12 was sold extensively

The men of the Italian Parachute Brigade are mainly equipped with the BM59 rifle, but the Beretta 12S is better suited for close-range work. The 12S is designed to operate in harsh environments, having grooves along the sides of the receiver which catch any debris entering the weapon.

to such nations as Libya and Saudi Arabia, but only in small numbers to the Italian armed forces, who purchased the type for use only by special units. However, Beretta was able to negotiate licence production of the Model 12 in Indonesia and Brazil for local sales and export.

Beretta then decided to develop the basic design one stage further and produced the **Model 12S**. This is now the current Beretta sub-machine gun and production of the Model 12 has now ceased. Externally the Model 12S looks very like the Model 12 but there are some detail differences. One is the epoxy-resin finish, making the metal resistant to corrosion and wear. The fire selector mechanism on the Model 12 was of the 'push through' type, operated by pushing a button from either side of the receiver just over the pistol grip, but the Type 12S has a conventional single-lever mechanism with a safety that locks both the trigger and the grip safety. The folding butt, when fitted, now has a more positive lock for both the open and the closed positions, and some changes have been made to the sights. One laudable feature that has been carried over from the original Model 12 is the retention of the raised grooves that run along each side of the tubular receiver. These grooves act as catchers for any dirt or debris that find their way into the interior, and enable the Model 12S to operate under really muddy and arduous conditions.

To date the Model 12S has been

A dramatic break from pre-war Beretta designs, the Model 12 and 12S use heavy sheet metal stampings

to form the magazine housing and receiver, but retain the elegant simplicity associated with Beretta.

purchased by the Italian armed forces in small numbers, and more were sold to Tunisia. Once again Beretta has been able to negotiate licence production and the Model 12S is now

being offered by FN of Herstal, Belgium, as part of its small arms range. Incidentally, the Model 12 was one of the favoured weapons of 'Carlos', the international terrorist.

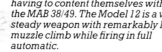

The 12S can be distinguished from the earlier Model 12 by the single lever fire selector and safety. The white 'S' is for safe, the red 'I' for semi automatic and the 'R' for full automatic.

Specification
Model 12S (metal stock version)
Calibre: 9 mm (0.354 in) Parabellum
Weight: loaded with 32-round magazine 3.81 kg (8.4 lb)
Length: with stock extended 660 mm (26 in) and with stock folded 418 mm (16.45 in)
Length of barrel: 200 mm (7.87 in)
Muzzle velocity: 381 m (1,250 ft) per second
Cyclic rate of fire: 500-550 rpm
Magazine: 20-, 32- or 40-round box

Right: Although widely exported, the Model 12 is only issued to Special Troops of the Italian army, the rest having to content themselves with the MAB 38/49. The Model 12 is a very steady weapon with remarkably low muzzle climb while firing in full automatic.

Modern Assault Rifles

Since the turn of the century, and largely as a result of experience gained during colonial wars, conventional military thinking held that the infantry rifle must be accurate at long range. Strangely, the relatively short-range fighting in the trenches of World War I made little impact upon prevailing opinion. As a result of the lessons of the first years of World War II, however, a radical re-appraisal of infantry doctrine was required.

A typical Vietnam situation, with the soldier in the foreground keeping his M16A1 well clear of the water. He is wearing bandoliers of 7.62-mm ammunition for the section M60 machine-gun. In such conditions the light weight and handiness of the modern assault rifle came to the fore.

The modern assault rifle had its roots in the novel art of combat analysis (carried out by the German army after 1939) coupled with ammunition development carried out by the German concern of Polte. The combat analysis revealed that most infantry combats took place at ranges well below 400 m (435 yards), yet the standard infantry rifle of the day was designed to perform at ranges up to over 1000 m (1,095 yards). The short-range combat did not need such a powerful cartridge as the existing rifles so the Polte ammunition developments were studied to reveal a potential cartridge that would be efficient at the short range. The resultant cartridge produced such low recoil forces that automatic fire from a hand-held rifle was possible, and from this the modern assault rifle was born.

The modern assault rifle uses a cartridge that is adequate for infantry combat at ranges up to about 400 m (435 yards) but no more. Most of these cartridges are smaller and lighter than conventional rifle cartridges, and can thus be fired in fully automatic bursts to provide a considerable increase in fire power over single-shot weapons but yet can be used for aimed single-shot fire when required. Since the recoil forces are usually relatively low the construction of the assault rifle need not be very robust, with consequent benefits in light weight and simple mass production methods. For all that some modern assault rifles are very well manufactured and are very robust, though others follow the sheet steel and stampings approach adopted by many of the later sub-machine gun designs.

Tactically the assault rifle has had a considerable impact. A single infantry fire section can now produce fire power that would have been inconceivable only a few years ago and this had led to the fire saturation tactics often employed to neutralize enemy positions and movement. Thus the early promise of lighter ammunition loads for the laden foot soldier has been replaced by extra numerical loads of cartridge carried on the person. But now a relatively small number of men can lay down defensive fire to halt an attack yet advance rapidly firing bursts of automatic fire to overcome opposition; in both cases the expenditure of ammunition can be considerable. In irregular or guerrilla hands the assault rifle is a formidable weapon capable of spraying fire over a lethal radius in a very short time and then vanishing, for the assault rifle is a relatively small weapon.

The assault rifle has largely replaced the sub-machine gun, for the two provide the same product (automatic fire at short ranges for close-quarter combat) yet the assault rifle can also provide useful fire at ranges up to 400 m (435 yards).

British infantry with their L1A1s 'de-bus' from their FV432 armoured personnel carrier. They usually 'de-bus' about 400 m from the enemy position.

AUSTRIA
Steyr 5.56-mm AUG

The **Steyr AUG** (Armee Universal Gewehr, or army universal rifle or gun) is one of the most striking in appearance of all the modern assault rifles and it may almost be said to have a 'Star Wars' look about it. It is a 'bull-pup' design weapon, with the trigger group forward of the magazine, which makes it a short and compact weapon. The thoroughly modern appearance is enhanced by the liberal use of nylonite and other non-metallic materials in the construction. The only metal parts are the barrel and the receiver with the internal mechanism; even the receiver is an aluminium casting. All the materials are very high quality of their kind but the non-use of metal has been carried even as far as the magazine which is clear plastic so that the soldier can see at a glance how many rounds the magazine contains.

The Steyr AUG has been designed to be not only an assault rifle, for by varying the barrel length and the fittings on top of the receiver it can be easily produced as a carbine, or a specialist sniper, or a night-action rifle, or even a form of light machine-gun. By changing the fittings on the receiver the AUG can be fitted with a wide range of night sights or sighting telescopes, but the usual sight is a simple optical telescope with a graticule calibrated for normal combat ranges. Stripping the AUG for cleaning is rapid and simple, and cleaning is facilitated by the use of a chromed barrel interior.

Production of the AUG began in 1978, and since that date the Steyr production line has been kept busy supplying the Austrian army, various Middle East states and some South American armed forces. Production is still well under way with no signs of the market weakening, and the AUG seems set for a long future. It has been ordered by Australia (who will also undertake licence manufacture) and has been sold to New Zealand.

Specification
Steyr AUG (assault rifle version)
Calibre: 5.56 mm (0.22 in)
Length: 790 mm (31.1 in)
Length of barrel: 508 mm (20.0 in)
Weight loaded: 4.09 kg (9.02 lb)
Magazine: 30-round box
Rate of fire, cyclic: 650 rpm

Above: The standard Steyr 5.56-mm AUG showing the overall 'bull-pup' layout and the optical sight over the receiver. The weapon has a 40-mm MECAR rifle grenade over the muzzle, which can be fired using normal ammunition to a range of about 100 m; HE, smoke and other grenades can be used.

Right: A Steyr 5.56-mm AUG in use by an Austrian soldier. Note the slender barrel with the flash-suppressor/grenade launcher, and how the folding foregrip is easy to hold and use to 'point' the weapon. The ×1 optical sight can be replaced by night sights or image intensifiers for use in poor light.

FRANCE

FA MAS

For some years before and just after World War II the French armaments industry lagged behind the rest of the world in small-arms design, but with the **FA MAS** assault rifle it has made up that leeway with a vengeance. The FA MAS is a thoroughly modern and effective little rifle, and yet another example of the overall compactness that can be achieved by using the unorthodox 'bull-pup' layout with the trigger group in front of the magazine. Even using this design the FA MAS is very short and handy, and must be one of the smallest in-service assault rifle designs of all.

The FA MAS has now been accepted as the standard service rifle for the French armed forces and this alone will keep the weapon coming off the production lines at St Etienne for at least the next 10 years. The first ex- amples were issued to some paratroop and specialist units, and the type was used by French troops in Chad and the Lebanon in 1983. The FA MAS is easy to spot, for in appearance it is quite unlike any other assault rifle. It fires the American M193 5.56-mm cartridge and has over the top of the receiver a long handle that doubles as the rear- and fore-sight base. The butt is prominent and chunky, and from the front protrudes a short length of barrel with a grenade-launching attachment.

The French 5.56-mm FA MAS rifle, one of the smallest and most compact of the modern assault rifles. The magazine has been removed, but note that the carrying handle contains the sights and that the cocking lever is just underneath; note also the folded bipod legs.

FA MAS (continued)

There is provision for a small bayonet and bipod legs are provided as standard. The fire selector has three positions: single-shot, automatic and three-round burst. The mechanism to control this last feature is housed in the butt along with the rest of the rather complex trigger mechanism. The operation is a delayed blow-back system. Use is made of plastics where possible and no particular attention is paid to detail finish: for instance, the steel barrel is not chromed.

Despite its unusual appearance the FA MAS is comfortable to handle and fire, and presents no particular problems in use. Attention has been given to such features as grenade sights and generally easy sighting. In service the weapon has proved to be easy to handle, and training costs have been reduced by the introduction of a version that uses a small sparklet gas cylinder to propel inert pellets for target training; this version is identical to the full service version in every other respect. The shape of the weapon has led to it's being nicknamed 'Le Clarion' (the Bugle) by French soldiers.

The French have offered the FA MAS for export at various defence exhibitions but the production programme for the French armed forces is such that it may be some years before significant numbers appear in service with other nations. Expected to be in the queue are the various ex-French colonies who still look to France for equipment and training.

Specification
Calibre: 5.56 mm (0.22 in)
Length: 757 mm (29.80 in)
Length of barrel: 488 mm (19.21 in)
Weight loaded: 4.025 kg (8.87 lb)
Magazine: 25-round box
Rate of fire, cyclic: 900-1,000 rpm
Muzzle velocity: 960 m (3,150 ft) per second

Nicknamed 'Le Clarion' (the Bugle) by French soldiers (for obvious reasons) the FA MAS is a thoroughly modern and compact assault rifle with a very high rate of fire.

FRANCE

Fusil Mitrailleur Modèle 49 (MAS 49)

The **Fusil Mitrailleur Modèle 49 (MAS 49)** was one of the first semi-automatic rifles to enter service, and although resembling the bolt-action MAS 36, and indeed using the same two-piece stock, it was not merely an automatic version of the MAS 36 but a completely new design. At over 4.5 kg (10 lb) it is no lightweight, but its strength proved invaluable in the campaigns in Indo-China and Algeria.

The MAS 49 is a gas-operated weapon, but uses no cylinder or piston; instead, some of the propellant gas is deflected into a tube and conducted to the bolt carrier where it expands, forcing the carrier back. This type of system is generally eschewed by gun designers because it can produce excessive fouling, but the MAS 49 has not suffered unduly. The breech is locked in the same simple manner as on the FN mle 49, namely by tilting the breech block. Unusually, the MAS 49 has an integral grenade launcher, with a sight fitted on the left hand side.

The MAS 49 was modified in 1956 to produce the **MAS 49/56** which is still in service with units of the French army although it will eventually be completely replaced by the FA MAS. The MAS 49/56 is easily distinguished from the earlier weapon; the wooden forestock is much shorter and the barrel has a combined muzzle-brake/grenade-launcher with raised foresight. The length of the whole weapon was reduced by 90 mm and that of the barrel by 60 mm. The French obstinately stuck with the 7.5 mm ×54 M 1929 cartridge, although a few MAS 49/56s were experimentally modified to fire standard NATO 7.62 mm. Armour-piercing ammunition was produced, but has proved very unkind to barrels.

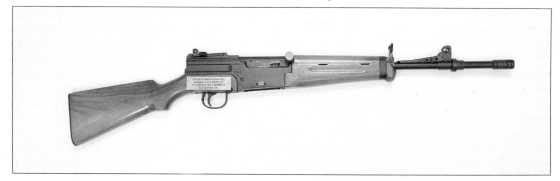

Above: This MAS 49/56 was presented to the Weapons Museum at the School of Infantry, Warminster. The MAS 49/56 gas-operated self-loading rifle has served the French army for nearly 30 years, although it is now being replaced by the FA MAS.

Right: Legionnaires of the 2nd REP are seen armed with (left) a MAT-49 sub-machine gun and (right) a MAS-49/56 self-loading rifle, which can be used as a grenade launcher. The MAS 49/56 fires the French 7.5-mm ×54 cartridge. An armour-piercing round is available as well as standard ball and tracer.

Specification
Fusil Mitrailleur Modèle 49
Calibre: 7.5 mm (0.295 in)
Lengths: overall 1010 mm (39.76); barrel 521 mm (20.51 in)
Weights: (without magazine) 3.9 kg (8.6 lb); (loaded) 4.34 kg (9.52 lb)
Magazine: 10-round box
Muzzle velocity: 817 m (2,680 ft) per second.

FN FAL and L1A1

Produced by the Belgian concern of Fabrique Nationale, or FN, the rifle now known as the **Fusil Automatique Legère** (FAL, or light automatic rifle) was originally produced in 1948. At that time the prototypes fired the German 7.92-mm×33 *kurz* (short) cartridge but later attempts at NATO ammunition standardization meant that the FAL was eventually chambered for the standard 7.62-mm×51 cartridge. As such it has since been widely adopted, not only throughout NATO but in many other nations, and has even been licence-produced by nations as diverse as South Africa and Mexico. Many of these overseas production models differ in detail from the original FAL but the overall appearance is the same.

The FAL is a sturdy weapon which uses many of the manufacturing methods of a bygone era. High-grade materials are used throughout, and extensive use is made of machining and fine tolerances. The action is gas-operated, using a gas regulation system that taps off propellant gases from above the barrel to operate a piston that pushes back the bolt action for unlocking the breech. The unlocking system has a delay action built in for increased safety. Automatic fire is possible on most models by use of a selector mechanism located near the trigger group.

FAL models are many and various. Most have solid wooden or nylonite butts and other furniture but some models, usually issued to airborne forces, have folding butts that are far sturdier than many other folding butts in use. Overall, sturdiness is a feature of the FAL, for the high manufacturing standards have resulted in a weapon well able to withstand the rigours of service life.

One production version of the FAL that deserves further mention is the British version, known by its service designation **L1A1**. The L1A1 was adopted by the British armed forces only after a lengthy series of trials and modifications that resulted in the elimination of the automatic fire feature, the L1A1 thus firing single-shot only. There are some other differences as well, but the L1A1 itself has been adopted by many other nations, including India where the type is still in production. The Australians also adopted the type and even produced a shorter version, the **L1A1-F1**, to suit the stature of the New Guinea troops.

Both the FAL and the L1A1 are equipped to fire rifle grenades, but these grenades are now little used. Bayonets can also be fitted and some versions of the FAL have heavy barrels and bipods to enable them to be used as light machine-guns. Night sights are another optional fitting.

Although the 7.62-mm FAL is still in production, the trend is now towards a 5.56-mm version and a new model in this calibre is now in production as the **FNC**.

Specification
Calibre: 7.62 mm (0.3 in)
Length: 1143 mm (45.0 in)
Length of barrel: 554 mm (21.81 in)
Weight loaded: 5 kg (11.0 lb)
Magazine: 20-round box
Rate of fire: 30-40 rpm (single shot) or 650-700 rpm (FAL, cyclic)
Muzzle velocity: 838 m (2,750 ft) per second

Top: A British L1A1, the standard British infantry weapon; centre: the FN FAL with a shortened barrel; bottom: an Argentinian FN FAL with folding butt.

Australian infantrymen with their locally-produced version of the British L1A1; these rifles were produced at Lithgow in New South Wales.

The FNC is the Belgian company's current assault rifle chambered for the 5.56-mm NATO round. It can take the standard US M16 magazines, which are also interchangeable with those of the FN Minimi LMG.

5.56-mm Individual Weapon

UK

The British army has been trying on and off to adopt a new small-calibre rifle cartridge since before 1914. For various reasons, both military and political, it has been unable to do so until comparatively recently. In the years after 1945 it did attempt to adopt a rifle known as the EM-2 which used a 7.11-mm (0.280-in) cartridge, but the adoption by NATO of the 7.62-mm×51 cartridge scotched that idea.

During the early 1970s another attempt to produce a new calibre was made. This time various researches indicated that a 4.85-mm projectile allied to the case of the American 5.56-mm round would be an ideal choice and a new weapon, the **Individual Weapon XL65E5**, was produced and demonstrated.

The Individual Weapon (IW) seemed to be an ideal rifle for the British army, but once again the British were foiled in their project. NATO decided that any new cartridge would have to be the standard round for all the NATO nations, and each nation had its 'pet' cartridge and weapon project. The result was one of the most exhaustive series of small-arms trials ever carried out over a series of years. Although the 4.85-mm round and the IW performed very well it soon became obvious that the extensive production facilities already set up to churn out the M193 5.56-mm round would be the final factor in the choice of 'winner'. The outcome was the selection of a Belgian round, the 5.56-mm SS109, and this marked the end of the 4.85-mm IW.

Nevertheless, the positive qualities of the basic concept led to the Individual Weapon design being adapted to the new NATO standard round. The **5.56 m Enfield L85A1 (Individual Weapon)** is the assault rifle member of a family of small arms known as the **SA 80**. Other weapons include the **L86A1 Light Support Weapon** and the manually-operated single-shot **Enfield Ensign** cadet and training rifle.

The SA 80 has been designed from the outset as a fighting rifle. The compact 'bullpup' layout is suitable for handling and use within confined spaces such as armoured personnel carriers and helicopters, while remaining easy to fire and handle and accurate at modern battle ranges. It is largely made from pressed and welded steel, with furniture of high strength nylon. The magazine is currently that used by the American M16 rifle, but is prone to stoppages. A custom design is being produced to overcome the problem. The muzzle has a bayonet mount and a grenade launcher/flash suppressor.

The SA 80 is the first British infantry rifle to enter service capable of fully automatic fire, and is one of the first generation of front line weapons to have an optical sight as standard, the SUSAT×4 sight enhancing performance in low light conditions. The first SA 80s were issued to British Army units late in 1985.

The Individual Weapon is one of a number of weapons in the SA 80 family. The 5.56-mm Light Support Weapon (seen here with the radio operator) shares many components with the rifle, and uses the same ammunition and magazines.

Above: This is the original 4.85-mm XL65E3 Individual Weapon, from which the present 5.56-mm SA 80 has been developed. It differs from the current model in several ways, especially the shape of the forestock, and the magazine is now a slightly curved M16A1 item. Note the large optical sight, known as a SUSAT.

An SA 80 is worked out on the ranges. Troops who have switched to the Individual Weapon are delighted with its ease of handling and the improvement in accuracy over their old, almost worn out L1A1 SLRs

Specification
L85A1 Individual Weapon
Calibre: 5.56 mm NATO
Length: 785 mm (30.9 in)
Length of barrel: 518 mm (20.4 in)

Weight, loaded, with sight: 4.98 kg (10.98 lb)
Magazine: 30-round box

Rate of fire, cyclic: 650-800 rpm
Muzzle velocity: 940 m (3,084 ft) per second

242

M14 rifle

The rifle that was eventually to be the standard American service rifle for most of the late 1950s and 1960s had a simple origin but a most convoluted development period. When the American military planners virtually imposed their 7.62-mm (0.30-in) cartridge upon their NATO partners, they had to find their own rifle to fire it, and quickly. For various reasons it was decided simply to update the existing M1 Garand rifle design to fire the new ammunition and to add a selective-fire mechanism. Unfortunately these innovations proved to be less than simple to achieve, for the development period from M1 had to progress through a number of intermediate 'T' trials models. Eventually, in 1957, it was announced that a model known as the **T44** had been approved for production as the **M14** (a planned heavy-barrel version, the **M15**, did not materialize) and the assembly lines began to hum, involving four different manufacturing centres at one time.

The M14 was basically an M1 Garand updated to take a new 20-round box magazine and a selective-fire mechanism. The M14 was a long and rather heavy weapon that was very well made, involving a great deal of machining and handling during manufacture at a time when other weapon designers were moving away from such methods. But the Americans could afford it and the soldiers liked the weapon. In service there were few problems, but the selective-fire system that had caused so much development time was usually altered so that automatic fire could not be produced: the US Army had soon discovered that prolonged bursts overheated the barrel and that ammunition was in any event wasted firing non-productive bursts.

Production of the basic M14 ceased in 1964, by which time 1,380,346 had been made. In 1968 a new version, the **M14A1**, was introduced. This had a pistol grip, a bipod and some other changes and it was designed for use as a squad fire-support weapon producing automatic bursts, but the bursts had to be short as the barrel could not be changed when hot. Also produced as variants were experimental folding-butt versions and a sniper model, the **M21**.

The M14 is still in use with the US armed forces, although by now most are with units such as the National Guard and other reserve formations. As the M14s were replaced by M16s many were passed to nations such as Israel where they remained in combat service until replaced by Galils. Even now many civilian guards carrying M14s can be seen around Israel, guarding schools and bus stations.

Specification
M14
Calibre: 7.62 mm (0.30 in)

Length: overall 1.12 m (44 in); barrel 559 mm (22 in)
Weight: 3.88 kg (8.55 lb)
Magazine: 20-round box
Rate of fire: (cyclic, M14A1) 700-750 rpm
Muzzle velocity: 853 m (2,798 ft) per second

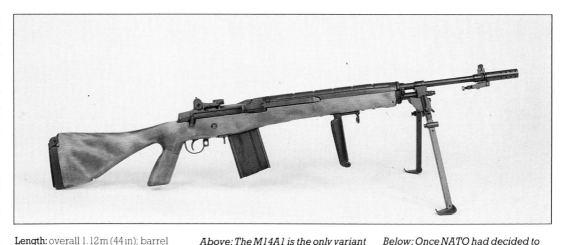

Above: The M14A1 is the only variant of the M14 to be adopted in any numbers. The rifle is fitted with a straight-line stock, pistol- and foregrips and mounted on a bipod. It looks and feels like a light machine-gun but is hardly suited to the role, as it has no facility for barrel change.

Below: Once NATO had decided to adopt a standard rifle cartridge, the USA needed a weapon to fire it. Most other nations opted for the versions of the Belgian FN, but the 'not invented here' syndrome reared its head and the US Army received the M14 – basically a modernized M1.

Rebel Philippine soldiers open fire on government forces defending a TV station during the last days of the Marcos regime. Note the spent case ejecting from the M14; this weapon has been supplied to other American allies in the Far East, including Taiwan and South Korea.

Modern Assault Rifles

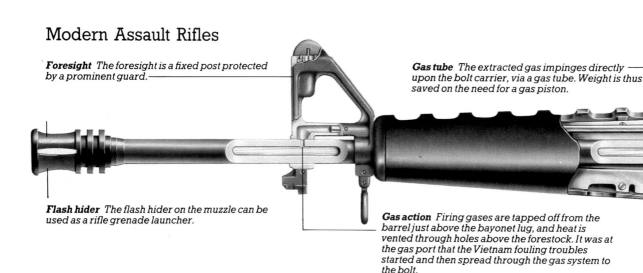

Foresight *The foresight is a fixed post protected by a prominent guard.*

Gas tube *The extracted gas impinges directly upon the bolt carrier, via a gas tube. Weight is thus saved on the need for a gas piston.*

Flash hider *The flash hider on the muzzle can be used as a rifle grenade launcher.*

Gas action *Firing gases are tapped off from the barrel just above the bayonet lug, and heat is vented through holes above the forestock. It was at the gas port that the Vietnam fouling troubles started and then spread through the gas system to the bolt.*

Hammer *The M16A1 lug bolt action which cams in the receiver w cleaned the bolt will s*

USA
M16 and M16A1

Unlike so many rifles of its type, the rifle that is now the **M16A1** was a commercial design. It was a product of the prolific designer Eugene Stoner and first emerged as a product of the Armalite concern as its **AR-10** during the mid-1950s. The AR-10 used 7.62-mm ammunition, and with the advent of the 5.56-mm Fireball cartridge the AR-10 was redesigned to suit the new calibre. The result was the **Armalite AR-15.**

The AR-15 was submitted for a competition to decide the new standard rifle for the US armed forces. But before the competition was decided, commercial sales had already started: the British army took a batch of 10,000, making it one of the first customers to purchase significant quantities of the new design, and the US Air Force made another purchase soon afterwards. That was in 1961, and soon after this the AR-15 was selected by the US Army to become its new standard rifle as the **M16**. Production was then switched to the Colt Firearms Company, which took out a production and sales contract with Armalite. Since then Colt has kept its production contract, but somehow the name 'Armalite' still clings to the rifle that is now the M16A1.

The M16 became the M16A1 in 1966 with the addition of a bolt closure device fitted as the result of experiences in Vietnam. Since then the M16A1 can perhaps be regarded as the AK-47 of the Western world, for it has been produced in hundreds of thousands and has been widely issued and sold to nations all around the world. Numerous developments have been produced and tried, ranging from the usual light machine-gun variant with a heavy barrel and a bipod, down- to short-barrel versions for special forces; there has even been a submachine gun variant. For all these changes the current M16A1 looks much like the first AR-15. Over the years there have been some changes as the rifling has been modified and more use is now made of internal chroming to aid cleaning.

A new version of the M16 has been introduced following the adoption of the Belgian SS109 cartridge as a NATO standard. The **M16A2**, in full production for the US Marine Corps and the US Army, is similar in appearance to previous models but differs in a number of significant details. The barrel is

rifled to match the new bullet, and is heavier for greater stiffness and accuracy in combat conditions. The furniture (hand-guard, pistol grip and butt) is made from stronger plastic. The handguard is now round, and a new muzzle suppressor is more effective at countering flash and muzzle climb. Improved sights have been fitted, with windage and elevation adjustments on the rearsight allowing shooters to make use of the greater range and accuracy of the new standard round to ranges of 800 m (875 yd). The M16A2 can be supplied with semi-automatic and full-auto or semi-automatic and three-round burst firing options. The 30-round magazine is now standard, the earlier 20-round magazine rarely being seen, and grenade launchers such as the M203 can still be fitted. Overall length of the M16A2 is now 1000 mm (39.37 in), and weight has risen to 3.4 kg (7.5 lb).

The M16A1 is a gas-operated weapon that uses the almost universally adopted locking system of the rotary bolt. A carrying handle over the receiver also acts as the rear-sight base, and nylonite is used for all the furniture. Although lending itself to mass production the M16A1 does not have the tinny appearance of many of its contemporaries, and has all the feel and finish of a high-quality weapon. In service it has become the carrier for a number of accessories which range from a blank adaptor to a special 40-mm grenade launcher mounted under

Above: Top: the original M16, recognized by the absence of the bolt-assist plunger of the M16A1 which is located above the trigger group. Below: the Colt Commando, a carbine version of the M16 and used in trials in Vietnam, where it was not a great success.

the forestock (the M203).

The M16 has been in production for a quarter of a century, and seems set to remain so for many years to come. It is made under licence in Korea, the Philippines and Singapore, and has also been copied by a number of countries. The Chinese make a weapon called the CQ 5.56 mm Automatic Rifle which apart from having a curved pistol grip is virtually identical to the M16. It is being marketed at a fraction of the cost of the original rifle. Taiwan has used the M16 as the basis for their Type 65 rifle, and the SAR 80 of Singapore also uses a number of M16 parts.

The M16 is used by US forces and the armed forces of a dozen other nations. The British army use it in Belize, and British special forces saw action with the M16 in the Falklands. It has been acquired by many police forces, and is available commercially in semi-automatic form.

Above: M16A1 fitted with a 40-mm M203 grenade launcher under the barrel. This launcher can propel small spin-stabilized grenades to a range of about 350 m. Some of these grenades can be seen alongside the launcher and can be produced in a wide range of offensive loads, including HE and CS.

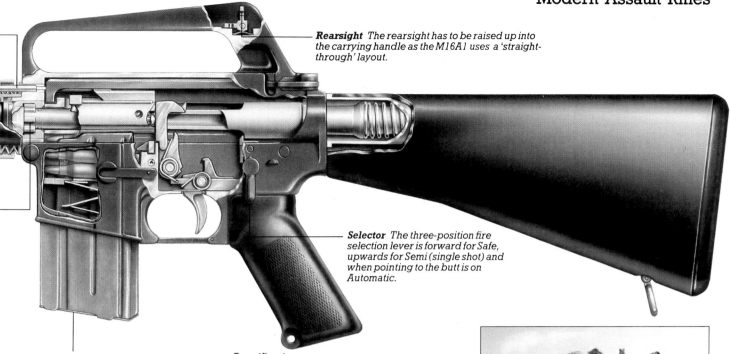

Rearsight The rearsight has to be raised up into the carrying handle as the M16A1 uses a 'straight-through' layout.

Selector The three-position fire selection lever is forward for Safe, upwards for Semi (single shot) and when pointing to the butt is on Automatic.

Magazine 20- or 30-round magazines may be used and metal and nylonite types are in use.

Specification
M16A1
Calibre: 5.56 mm (0.22 in)
Length: 990 mm (38.98 in)
Length of barrel: 508 mm (20.0 in)
Weight loaded: 3.64 kg (8.02 lb)
Magazine: 30-round box
Rate of fire, cyclic: 700-950 rpm
Muzzle velocity: 1000 m (3,280 ft) per second

Below: Near Duc Pho City, Vietnam, June 1967. American soldiers patrol to find North Vietnamese units and both are carrying M16s. The soldier in the foreground has 7.62-mm ammunition belts for the section M60.

On the ranges with an M16A1. This photograph clearly shows the early type of flash hider, which has now been replaced by a revised design with a cruciform notch along the centre to improve its performance.

This M16A1 is fitted with an AN/PVS-2 Starlight night-sighting telescope, which uses an internal image intensifier to amplify available light so that the user can aim at targets in what appears to be complete darkness to the naked eye.

An M203 40-mm grenade launcher is fitted onto the forestock of an M16A1. The M203 uses its own sleeve to clip over the forestock, and once in place the launcher uses its own trigger system separate from that of the M16A1.

Ruger Mini-14

When it was first produced in 1973, the **Ruger Mini-14** marked a significant turn away from the mass production methods introduced during World War II towards the fine finish and attention to detail that was formerly the hallmark of the gunsmith's art. The Mini-14 is an unashamed example of how guns used to be made before the steel stamping and the die-cast alloy came upon the scene.

From a design viewpoint the Ruger Mini-14 is a 5.56-mm version of the 7.62-mm (0.30-in) Garand M1 service rifle of World War II. By adopting the Garand action Ruger has managed to combine a sound and well-engineered design with the ammunition of a new technology. When this is allied to craftsmanship and a deliberate appeal to those who look for that something extra in a weapon the result is a remarkable little rifle.

In appearance the Mini-14 has the characteristics of a previous age. The materials used are all high quality and in an age where plastics have now taken over the furniture is all manufactured from high-grade walnut. But visual appeal has not been allowed to take precedence over functional safety, for the Mini-14 has been carefully engineered to prevent dust and debris entering the action. But some degree of eye appeal has been allowed to affect the finish, for the weapon has been carefully blued all over, and there is even a stainless steel version that sells very well in the Middle East.

The Mini-14 has not yet been adopted by any major armed forces but it has been sold to such establishments as police forces, personal bodyguard units and to many special forces who prefer a well-engineered and balanced weapon to the usual 'tinny' modern products. To suit the requirements of some armed forces Ruger has now developed a special version that should appeal to many soldiers. This is the **Mini-14/20GB**. Police forces have been catered for by the introduction of the **Ruger AC-556** with glassfibre furni-

ture, and another innovation is the **AC-556F** with a folding stock and a shorter barrel. The two AC-556 designs can be used to fire on full automatic for bursts, whereas the normal Mini-14 is a single-shot weapon only.

Specification
Mini-14
Calibre: 5.56 mm (0.22 in)
Length: 946 mm (37.24 in)
Length of barrel: 470 mm (18.50 in)
Weight loaded: 3.1 kg (6.83 lb) with 20-round magazine
Magazine: 10-, 20- or 30-round box
Rate of fire, cyclic: 40 rpm
Muzzle velocity: 1005 m (3,300 ft) per second

Top: The attractive lines of the Ruger Mini-14 seen fitted with a 10-round box magazine. The bottom weapon is the Ruger AC-556F, which is intended for service as a purely military assault carbine. It has a folding metal butt and is seen here fitted with a 30-round box magazine.

Armalite AR-18

Once the Armalite concern had cleared its design desks of the AR-15 with production under way by Colt Firearms of the M16/M16A1 series, it decided to look to the future for new products. With the 5.56-mm round well established, Armalite decided that what was needed was a simple weapon that could fire the cartridge. While the AR-15 was a sound weapon it was not easy to produce without sophisticated machine tools, and throughout much of the world these machine tools were not available. Thus the need for a weapon which could be simply produced by Third World nations was recognized, and a drastic revision of the AR-15 design was undertaken.

The result was the **AR-18**, which is very basically an AR-15 adapted for manufacture by the now-familiar production expedients of pressed steel, plastics and castings. For all these expedients the AR-18 is a sound design that is easy to produce, maintain and use. In general appearance and layout it is similar to the AR-15 but the stamped steel receiver gives it a bulkier outline. The plastic butt is designed to fold alongside the receiver

for stowage or firing from the hip.

Once the AR-18 design was complete Armalite attempted to find purchasers, but with the AK-47 and the M16A1 flooding the world markets there were few takers. An arrangement to produce the AR-18 in Japan fell through and for some years the design was in abeyance. Then the Sterling Armaments Company of the United Kingdom took out a licence, undertaking some production and at one time moving production to Singapore. Some sales were then made locally but what was more important was that the local

defence industry took the design as the basis for its own weapon designs, the AR-18 now living on disguised in many forms and under various labels.

Specification
Calibre: 5.56 mm (0.22 in)
Length: 940 mm (37.00 in) with stock extended or 737 mm (29.00 in) with stock folded
Weight loaded: 3.48 kg (7.67 lb) with 20-round magazine
Magazine: 20-, 30- and 40-round box
Rate of fire, cyclic: 800 rpm

This AR-18 was originally manufactured in Japan but was captured from the IRA in Belfast. It is the standard production model with a butt that can be folded along the right-hand side of the receiver. The cocking handle can be seen poking upwards above the magazine.

Muzzle velocity: 1000 m (3,280 ft) per second

vz.58

At first sight the Czech **vz.58** assault rifle looks very like the Soviet AK-47, but this resemblance is deceptive for the two designs are different mechanically. The vz.58 is a gas-operated weapon but the unlocking mechanism uses a pivoted locking piece in place of the rotating bolt of the AK-47 family. The trigger mechanism is also different and employs flat springs rather than coil springs. The overall result is an entirely different mechanism. Exactly why the Czechs felt it necessary to produce their own design in view of the availability of the AK-47 adopted by all other Warsaw Pact nations is uncertain, but one fact that has resulted from this 'go it alone' stance has been that the vz.58 has been sold on the open arms market with a facility that would not have been possible with the AK-47.

The vz.58 is very well made, with the receiver machined from solid metal.

Early versions used a wooden butt, with plastic for such items as the pistol grip and the forestock. More recent versions have used a form of plastic into which wooden chips and shavings have been compressed resulting in a characteristic appearance. Three basic models have been produced, one with a conventional butt, one with a folding butt and a version with the receiver fitted to take a variety of night sights. The last version may also be fitted with a light bipod and a prominent flash hider over the muzzle.

The facility with which the Czechs can market the vz.58 is such that the type can be purchased commercially 'over the counter' in many countries, but has still been used by armed forces as disparate as the Viet Cong and the IRA. One great attraction of the vz.58 is the price. Although this varies according to the quantity involved it is still relatively low compared with

many other weapons. The Czechs are very willing to supply the 7.62 mm×39 ammunition as well, again at a very attractive price.

Specification
Calibre: 7.62 mm (0.3 in)
Length: 820 mm (32.28 in)
Length of barrel: 401 mm (15.79 in)
Weight loaded: 3.82 kg (8.42 lb)
Magazine: 30-round box
Rate of fire, cyclic: 800 rpm
Muzzle velocity: 710 m (2,330 ft) per second

Seen here carried by a young Czech tank crewman, the vz.58, also shown below, differs internally from the otherwise ubiquitous Kalashnikov. Also different is the compressed plastic/woodchip mixture which forms the butt and foregrip.

Samozaryadnyi Karabin Simonova (SKS)

The semi-automatic rifle known as the **SKS** was actually devised during World War II, but was not placed in production until some time afterwards. The designer was Sergei Simonov, who was responsible for many important Soviet small arms, but with the SKS Simonov decided to play things safe and stick to a relatively uninspired design.

The SKS was the first weapon designed to use the new Soviet 7.62-mm (0.30-in) cartridge derived from the German 7.92-mm (0.312-in) *kurz* round. The SKS used a gas-operated mechanism with a simple tipping bolt locking system. So conservative was the overall design that the SKS even outwardly resembled a conventional bolt-action rifle, complete with extensive wooden furniture. A fixed folding bayonet was fitted under the muzzle and the box magazine could hardly be seen: it held only 10 rounds and was fixed to the receiver. Loading was by chargers or insertion of single rounds; to unload, the magazine was hinged downwards, allowing the rounds to fall free. In typical Soviet fashion the SKS was very strongly built, so strong that many Western observers derided it as being far too heavy for the relatively light cartridge it fired. Despite this the SKS was well able to withstand the many knocks and rough treatment likely to be encountered during service use, and the SKS was the standard

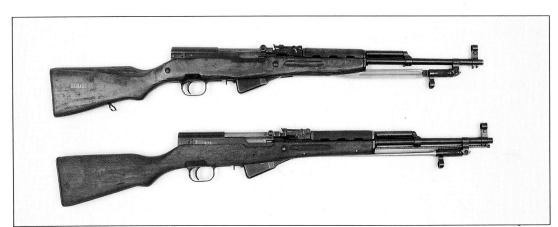

rifle of the Warsaw Pact nations for years until the AK-47 and AKM arrived in sufficient numbers.

The SKS is no longer in Warsaw Pact service other than as a ceremonial weapon for parades or 'honour guards'. However, it may still be encountered elsewhere as enormous numbers were produced, not only in the USSR but in East Germany and Yugoslavia where it was known as the **m/59**. The communist Chinese still produce a slightly revised version of the SKS known as the **Type 56**, and they are currently offering this version for export. Exactly what success they are

having is difficult to determine in an arms market where the AK-47 and its derivatives are all the vogue.

With so many SKS rifles produced it is not surprising that many remain in use throughout the Middle and Far East. Many were encountered by US and South Vietnamese forces during the Vietnam conflict, and from there many have passed into irregular hands. Being simple and robust weapons they are easy to use after a minimum of training and the SKS will be around for many years to come.

The SKS carbine was designed during World War II and produced in vast numbers after the war. The top rifle is a Chinese copy, the Type 56.

Specification
SKS

Calibre: 7.62 mm (0.30 in)
Weight: empty 3.85 kg (8.49 lb)
Lengths: overall 1021 mm (40.2 in) barrel 521 mm (20.5 in)
Muzzle velocity: 735 m (2,411 ft) per second
Magazine: 20-round box

AK-47 and AKM

The **AK-47** must be rated as one of the most successful and widely-used of any type of small arm ever produced. Both it and its successor, the **AKM**, are now used all over the world by forces regular and irregular, and both types are still in production in one form or another in many countries.

The first AK-47 was designed around a short 7.62-mm calibre cartridge that owed much to the introduction of the German 7.92-mm *kurz* round. The Red Army was often on the receiving end of the German assault rifle family (the MP 43, MP 44 and StuG 44) and asked for their own counter. The result was the 7.62-mm×39 cartridge and the AK-47. The designer was Mikhail Kalashnikov and his design is often referred to by his surname. The first examples were issued for service during 1946 and the weapon gradually became the standard weapon of the Warsaw Pact forces. The production lines were huge and the numbers that rolled off them were vast, but such was the demand that most Warsaw Pact nations set up their own production facilities. From this sprang the large numbers of AK-47 sub-variants that continue to delight the gun research buff to this day.

The basic AK-47 is a sound and well-made weapon that carried over few of the mass production expedients employed by its German wartime equivalents. The AK-47 receiver is machined and good-quality steel is used throughout with wooden furniture as standard; the result is a weapon that can absorb any amount of hard use and mishandling. As there are few moving parts and stripping is very simple, maintenance is also simple and can be accomplished with even a minimum of training.

Before long different production versions of the basic AK-47 emerged, even within the Soviet Union, and a version with a folding steel butt was produced. All these different versions used the same mechanism, a simple rotary bolt that was cammed into corresponding grooves in the receiver by bolt cams. Operation is by gas tapped from the barrel via a gas port.

AK-47s were produced in China, Poland and East Germany and the basic design was copied by several designers abroad, including those of the Finnish **Valmet M60** and **M62**.

For all its huge success and accept-

ance, it was finally admitted during the late 1950s that production of the AK-47 was too involved in manufacturing facilities. A redesign produced the AKM, which outwardly resembles the earlier design but is generally revised to facilitate production. The most obvious external change is to the receiver, which is formed from a steel stamping in place of the former machined equivalent, but internally the locking system has been revised to make it more simple. There are numerous other differences but the overall changes are in manufacturing methods.

The AKM did not immediately take the place of the AK-47 but acted more as a supplement to numbers. The other Warsaw Pact production lines gradually switched to the AKM, some nations (such as Hungary) even going so far as to modify the basic design to

produce their own version, which often differs in many ways from the original (the Hungarian **AKM-63** even looks different but retains the basic mechanism of the AKM). A version with a folding steel butt is known as the **AKMS**.

The AKM is still being produced, and the AK-47 and AKM will remain in service until well into the next century, if not beyond. This longevity must be partially attributed to widespread availability and the numbers produced but the basic fact is that the AK-47 and AKM are both sound and tough weapons that are easy to use and simple to maintain.

Specification
AK-47
Calibre: 7.62 mm (0.3 in)
Length: 869 mm (34.21 in)
Length of barrel: 414 mm (16.30 in)
Weight loaded: 5.13 kg (11.31 lb)
Magazine: 30-round box
Rate of fire, cyclic: 600 rpm
Muzzle velocity: 710 m (2,330 ft) per second

Top: AK-47 with folding metal butt; centre: AKM identifiable by muzzle brake attachment and hand-grip on forestock, and bottom: Chinese Type 56 from Zimbabwe, the Chinese version of the AK-47 with its own integral bayonet seen folded under the forestock.

Specification
AKM
Calibre: 7.62 mm (0.3 in)
Length: 876 mm (34.49 in)
Length of barrel: 414 mm (16.30 in)
Weight loaded: 3.98 kg (8.77 lb)
Magazine: 30-round box
Rate of fire, cyclic: 600 rpm
Muzzle velocity: 710 m (2,330 ft) per second

Egyptian troops during the Yom Kippur War of 1973. Their weapons are AKMs with the characteristic angled muzzle attachments and the handgrip grooved into the forestock. The AKM is now the standard Egyptian service rifle.

The AK-47 has been manufactured throughout the Warsaw Pact countries, and this East German infantryman would be armed with the MPiKM version, made in the DDR.

The Soviet Union was surprisingly slow in following the Western adoption of small-calibre cartridges for its future weapon designs. Perhaps the huge numbers of AK-47s and AKMs already in service made such a change a low priority, so it was not until the early 1970s that any intimation of a new Warsaw Pact cartridge was given. In time it emerged that the new cartridge had a calibre of 5.45-mm×39 and the first examples of a new weapon to fire it were noted. In time the weapon emerged as the **AK-74**, which is now in full-scale production to meet the requirements of the Red Army; in time it can be expected that the AK-74 will be issued to other Warsaw Pact armed forces.

The AK-74 is nothing more than an AKM revised to suit the new cartridge. It is almost identical to the AKM in appearance, weight and overall dimensions. Some changes, such as a plastic magazine, have been introduced and there is a prominent muzzle brake. There are versions with the usual wooden stock and with a folding metal stock.

One matter relating to the AK-74 that deserves special mention is the bullet used. To gain maximum effect from the 5.45-mm calibre bullet the designers have adopted a design that is very effective but outlawed by international convention, for the steel-cored projectile has a hollow tip and the centre of gravity far to the rear. This has the effect that when the bullet strikes a target the nose deforms, allowing the weight towards the rear to maintain the forward impetus and so tumble the bullet. In this way the small-calibre bullet can have an effect on a target far in excess of its cross-sectional area. Some high-velocity projectiles can display this nasty effect but on some, such as the M193 5.56-mm cartridge, it is an unintended by-product. On the Soviet 5.45-mm the effect has been deliberately designed into the projectile. International conventions have for many years outlawed such 'Dum-Dum' bullets and its various progeny, but to date no corresponding strictures appear to have been forthcoming regarding the 5.45-mm bullet.

Specification (provisional)
Calibre: 5.45 mm (0.215 in)
Length: 930 mm (36.61 in)
Length of barrel: 400 mm (15.75 in)
Weight unloaded: 3.6 kg (7.94 lb)
Magazine: 30-round box
Rate of fire: 650 rpm
Muzzle velocity: 900 m (2,953 ft) per second

Right: An AK-74 (top), with an AK-47 for comparison beneath. The AK-74 has a skeleton butt, but note the prominent muzzle brake and the brown plastic magazine. Note also the size difference between the 5.45-mm cartridges (top) and the 7.62-mm×39 cartridges.

The AK-74 is now in wide use in the Soviet armies, and has seen service in Afghanistan, where this example was captured. It is to all intents and purposes a small calibre AKM, with many parts seeming identical.

Soviet paratroopers, wearing their traditional blue and white striped undershirts, rush into the attack with their AK-74 rifles well to the fore.

5.45mm AKR

The fighting in Afghanistan has been used by the Soviet Union to test a number of weapons and weapon systems in combat conditions. The capture of examples of these by the Mujahideen often provides western analysts with their first chance to examine new equipment, and has been the source of several surprises. One such surprise was the appearance of a carbine version of the AK-74 assault rifle.

The **AKR**, as the carbine is called, is in fact so short that it could quite easily be classed as a sub-machine gun, and is almost certainly used in a similar manner (for the arming of vehicle and helicopter crews or personnel working in confined spaces). The few examples to have reached the West to date have been subject to thorough examination.

The AKR fires the full-power 5.45×39.5mm Soviet rifle round, and exhibits a number of interesting features and modifications as a result. Naturally the gas pistons, springs and similar parts have been reduced in length, although otherwise they remain much the same as in the parent rifle. The receiver cover is unlike other AK series weapons in that it is fixed to the body, hinging forward on opening rather than lifting right off as has been the case previously. Perhaps the main item of interest is the unusual muzzle attachment. The cylinder fitted to the short barrel forms an expansion chamber, allowing propellent gases to expand before the bullet they are propelling leaves the muzzle. This reduces pressure within the gas-operation system considerably, removing the need to greatly strengthen and modify the gas-piston and springs which would otherwise be necessary. It probably serves a second function in association with the bell-shaped flash-hider at the muzzle in reducing the flash and vicious kick which firing full power rounds through such a short barrel would cause. Even so, the rate of fire is greater than in the full size rifle, and by all accounts the AKR is still quite a handful in action making it useful at short ranges only.

The sights are much simpler than on other AKs, being reduced to a simple mount hinged at one end. Flipping it over gives the firer a choice of two 'U' shaped notches marked for 200 and 400 metres. The AKR can take standard AK-74 magazines, but the short barrel leaves them more exposed and vulnerable to damage. A special magazine has been developed which has extra strengthening ribs moulded into the concave forward edge. The skeleton butt folds to the left alongside the receiver.

Specification (provisional)
Calibre: 5.45mm Soviet
Length: butt folded 420mm (16.5in); butt extended 675mm (26.57in)
Length of barrel: 200mm (7.87in)
Weight: not known
Magazine: 30-round box
Rate of fire: approx 800 rpm
Muzzle velocity: approx 800m (2,624ft) per second

The AKR short assault rifle/sub-machine gun fires the standard Soviet 5.45×39.5mm assault rifle cartridge. Combined with a very short barrel such a powerful round inevitably leads to enormous muzzle flash and blast, making the weapon quite a handful in inexperienced hands. The designers have eased the problem somewhat with the adoption of an expansion chamber and conical flash hider at the muzzle.

Valmet m/60 and m/62 assault rifles

Although not a member of the Warsaw Pact, because of its proximity to the USSR Finland inevitably has to go along with the Soviet way of doing things in some matters. So it was when the Finnish army decided to adopt a new service rifle in the late 1950s: not surprisingly it opted for the Soviet AK-47 assault rifle and its ammunition, and the country negotiated a manufacturing licence for both. Once the AK-47 design was in their hands, the ever-active Finnish small-arms designers at Valmet decided to make a few changes and the result was the **Valmet m/60**.

The AK-47 origins can be discerned in the m/60, but the energetic re-working by the Finns resulted in a much

The m/62 has different sights to those fitted on the AK-47 and introduced a three-pronged flash eliminator, but the selector lever and safety catch are exactly the same as on the Soviet weapon. In addition to serving with the Finnish army, the m/62 has been bought by Qatar.

better all-round weapon. For a start the m/60 used no wood whatever in its construction, the wooden furniture of the AK-47 being replaced by plastics or metal tubing. The tubular butt of the m/60 was not only easier to produce, it was also more robust and it carried the cleaning tools and equipment. The pistol grip and forestock were cast from hard plastic, while the trigger was left virtually unguarded to allow gloves to be worn when firing, an important point considering Finnish winter conditions.

Other changes from the AK-47 included slightly altered sights, a three-pronged flash hider at the muzzle and a revised bayonet mounting bracket to accommodate the Finnish bayonet, which could also be used as a fighting knife. Internally the AK-47 mechanism was left virtually unchanged apart from a few manufacturing expedients, and the curved magazine and its housing were also left untouched to allow AK-47 magazines to be used.

The m/62 has minor improvements, which include a more solid trigger guard, and is the version adopted by the Finnish Defence Forces. A semi-automatic version is available commercially. The m/76 is the current model, aimed at export markets and available with wooden and folding butt stocks in addition to the tubular type. The m/76 is available in both 7.62 mm Soviet and 5.56 mm (NATO calibres. It has been sold to Qatar and to Indonesia.

The Valmet is an excellent adaptation of the original AK design, well suited for operations in Finland's tough winter climate.

Specification
m/62
Calibre: 7.62 mm (0.30 in)
Weights: empty 3.5 kg (7.7 lb); loaded 4.7 kg (10.36 lb)
Lengths: overall 914 mm (36 in); barrel 420 mm (16.54 in)
Muzzle velocity: 719 m (2,359 ft) per second
Rate of fire: (cyclic) 650 rpm
Magazine: 30-round box

The m/62 is the Finnish variant of the Soviet AK-47. It uses no wood in its construction and has a tubular butt which, apart from being easy to manufacture, has the added bonus of being able to carry the cleaning tools and equipment.

 ISRAEL/SOUTH AFRICA
Galil and R4

In the 1960s, the Israel Defence Forces were equipped with the well-tried FN FAL rifle. Following the Six Day War of 1967, it was decided that a rifle more suited to Israeli requirements should be adopted, and that it should fire the then quite new 5.56 mm×45 cartridge as used in the American M16. A stringent series of trials were carried out, mostly in the desert, involving a number of weapons including the M16, the Soviet AK-47 (many of which had been captured in the war), and the Stoner rifle being made in the Netherlands.

It was the **Galil** assault rifle, designed by Yaacov Lior and Israel Galili which came closest to meeting the requirements, however, and in 1972 the Galil was officially adopted. The Galil has often been called a copy of the AK-47, and it is true that the Israelis were impressed with the AK-47s they were confronted with in 1967. It is also true that the first prototypes of the Galil used the body of the Finnish Valmet m/62, itself a copy of the AK. Nevertheless, although the action is copied from the AK, the adoption of the NATO 5.56 mm round means that many of the working parts differ from those of the Soviet weapon.

The Galil assault rifle has been produced in both 5.56-mm and 7.62-mm calibres, and is now one of the most widely used weapons issued to the various Israeli armed forces. It is produced in three forms: one is known as the **Galil ARM**, which has a bipod and a carrying handle and is the all-purpose weapon; another is the **Galil AR**, which lacks the bipod and handle; and the third is the **Galil SAR**, which has a shorter barrel and no bipod or carrying handle. All three having folding stocks. The bipod on the ARM can be used as a barbed wire cutter, and all three versions have a bottle cap opener fitted as standard to prevent soldiers using other parts of the weapon as bottle openers (eg the magazine lips). A fixture over the muzzle acts as a rifle grenade launcher.

In its full ARM version the Galil can be used as a form of light machine-gun and 35- and 50-round magazines are

produced; there is also a special 10-round magazine used to contain the special cartridges for launching rifle grenades. As usual a bayonet can be fitted.

The Galil has proved to be very effective in action and has attracted a great deal of overseas attention. Some have been exported and the design has also been copied – the Swedish 5.56-mm **FFV 890C** is obviously based on the Galil. One nation that negotiated licence production was South Africa, and its version is the **R4**, now the standard rifle for the front-line units of the South African defence forces. The R4 is produced in 5.56-mm calibre and differs in some details from the original, the changes resulting mainly from operational experience in the South African and Namibian bush. The R4 has been strengthened to withstand long hard use on operations far from any armoury, and the butt has been lengthened because South African soldiers tend to be larger than the average Israeli. The rifling is slightly different, and certain parts have been modified for ease of manufacture.

Specification
Galil 5.56-mm ARM
Calibre: 5.56 mm (0.22 in)
Length: 979 mm (38.54 in)
Length of barrel: 460 mm (18.1 in)
Weight loaded: 4.62 kg (10.19 lb) with 35-round magazine
Magazine: 35- or 50-round boxes
Rate of fire, cyclic: 650 rpm
Muzzle velocity: 980 m (3,215 ft) per second

Israeli Galil SAR (short assault rifle) with the metal stock folded forward to reduce the length. This version cannot be used to fire rifle grenades and does not have the bipod fitted to the longer models. It can be found calibrated for 5.56-mm and 7.62-mm ammunition.

Length of barrel: 533 mm (20.98 in)
Weight loaded: 4.67 kg (10.30 lb)
Magazine: 20-round box
Rate of fire, cyclic: 650 rpm
Muzzle velocity: 850 m (2,790 ft) per second

Specification
Galil 7.62-mm ARM
Calibre: 7.62 mm (0.3 in)
Length: 1050 mm (41.34 in)

South Africa has adopted a modified form of the Galil as the new standard weapon of the Defence Forces: the R4 has been strengthened to withstand the rigours of the bush. The bipod is fitted as standard.

Heckler und Koch G3

The **Heckler und Koch G3** assault rifle is a development of the CETME design and was adopted by the West German Bundeswehr during 1959. In many ways it has proved to be one of the most successful of all the post-war German weapon designs and it is still in production not only in West Germany but in numerous other countries which have produced their own weapons under licence.

Although the makers would not like it to be said, the Heckler und Koch G3 is the nearest that designers have come to the use-and-throw-away rifle. Despite the cost the G3 is a weapon designed from the outset for mass production using as much simple machinery as is possible. On the basis of the CETME design Heckler und Koch have developed the design so that plastics and pressed steel are used wherever possible. The ex-CETME locking roller system is retained to provide a form of delayed blow-back when firing.

There is a general resemblance to the FN FAL in the G3 but there are many differences. The G3 is a whole generation ahead of the FN FAL, and this is reflected not only in the general construction and materials but also in the development of a whole family of variants based on the basic G3. There are carbine versions, some with barrels so short they could qualify as sub-machine guns, sniper variants, light machine-gun versions with bipods and heavy barrels and so on. There is also a version for use with airborne or other such troops: this is the **G3A4**, which has a butt that telescopes onto either side of the receiver.

For all its overall simplicity the G3 has some unusual features. One is the bolt, which is so designed that it locks with the bulk of its mass forward and over the chamber to act as an extra mass to move when unlocking. Stripping is very simple and there are only a very few moving parts. With very few changes the basic G3 can be produced with a calibre of 5.56 mm and this version is already in production as the **Heckler und Koch HK 33**.

Along with the FN FAL, the G3 has been one of the most widely used

Western weapons in the last twenty years. In service with nearly 50 armies, the G3 is licence built in more than a dozen nations (including the UK, which builds the G3 for export and not for the use of the British army). It was used by the Rhodesian army before the establishment of Zimbabwe, and large numbers originally supplied to Iran under the Shah have found their way onto the arms markets of the world since the Islamic revolution. The HK 33 has also been exported, largely to South East Asian countries, and similar weapons (such as the **HK 53**, an even smaller gun sized between the rifle and the MP5 sub-machine gun) have been ac-

quired by a number of special military and police units.

Specification
Heckler und Koch G3A3
Calibre: 7.62 mm (0.3 in)
Length: 1025 mm (40.35 in)
Length of barrel: 450 mm (17.72 in)
Weight loaded: 5.025 kg (11.08 lb)
Magazine: 20-round box
Rate of fire, cyclic: 500-600 rpm
Muzzle velocity: 780-800 m (2,560-2,625 ft) per second

The Heckler und Koch G3 is one of the most successful of postwar western rifles. Ultimately descending from the pioneering Sturmgewehr 44 via the Spanish CETME, the G3 was the first of a large family of small arms.

Using the same basic layout as the G3, this 5.56-mm version is known as the HK 33. It can take 20- or 40-round magazines and exists in several versions, including a special sniper's rifle and a version with a telescopic folding butt. Most versions can fire rifle grenades.

Heckler und Koch G11

The revolutionary **Heckler und Koch G11** assault rifle could well be the first example of the small arms of the 21st century.

In 1967, a NATO feasibility study was set up to look into caseless small arms ammunition. It was recognized that much of the weight of ammunition was taken up by the cartridge case, and the extraction system took up a large part of the internal working parts of current weapons. Eliminating the cartridge case would allow more ammunition to be carried, and greatly simplify construction of small arms.

Although NATO interest waned when problems of cook-off (premature ignition of ammunition in a hot firing chamber), adequate sealing of the firing chamber (done in a conventional weapon by the expansion of the brass cartridge case) and handling of the uncased rounds seemed insoluble, the German government continued with the programme. After several years

Dynamit Nobel succeeded in producing a caseless round using a new propellant which can meet the Bundeswehr's strict requirements. Latest versions of the round look nothing like old-style bullets, with a rectangular block of propellant (less than half the length of a conventional cartridge) having a 4.7mm calibre bullet firmly embedded deep within it.

The rifle to handle this unconventional round is necessarily very different from earlier types. The smooth outer casing enclosing the entire rifle is of carbon-fibre and has a combination sight/carrying handle above and a pistol grip and trigger beneath. The selector lever is just above the trigger, where it can easily be reached by the firing hand, and behind the trigger is the large circular 'cocking handle'. The only holes in the rifle are the muzzle and a port through which misfires can be ejected.

The sealed, 50-round magazine is

slipped into the rifle from the front, lying along the top of the barrel. The rounds are fed vertically downwards into a cylinder which lines up with the barrel for firing and rotates back to pick up the next round. When fired, the entire mechanism, barrel and magazine recoils within the outer casing.

The G11 can fire both semi-automatic and full automatic, but has a unique three-round burst mechanism. This operates at the extremely fast cyclic rate of 2,000 rounds per minute, ensuring that the three rounds can be fired before the recoil from the first shot has reached the end of it's travel. This means that all of the burst follows the same trajectory with none of the muzzle climb normally associated with automatic fire.

After many years of effort, the G11 is in final development, with the first German army technical trials taking place in 1986. Many people are dubious ab-

out caseless ammunition, but if all problems are overcome, Heckler & Koch will have given the Bundeswehr a head start into the next century with the G11.

Specification
Calibre: 4.7mm (0.185 in)
Length: 750 mm (29.53 in)
Barrel length: 540 mm (21.26 in)
Weight with 50 rounds: 3.95 kg (8.7 lb)
Magazine: 50-round sealed strip
Rate of fire: 600 rpm (cyclic, automatic) or 2,000 rpm (cyclic, three-round burst)
Practical battlefield range: 300 m (328 yds)

CETME Modelo 58 assault rifle

The **CETME Modelo 58** has a long history stretching back to the German Sturmgewehr 45 (StG 45) of World War II. This was an attempt by Mauser designers to produce a low-cost assault rifle that incorporated a novel action using a system of rollers and cams to lock the bolt at the instant of firing. After the Allied victory the nucleus of the StG 45 design team moved to Spain, via France, and established a new design team under the aegis of the Centro de Estudios Tecnicos de Materiales Especiales (CETME), just outside Madrid.

With CETME the roller locking system was gradually perfected at a leisurely pace. The resultant assault rifle looked nothing like the StG 45 starting point but the original low-cost manufacturing target was met. The assault rifle produced by CETME was made from low-grade steels and much of it was stamped and shaped using sheet steel. An automatic-fire capability was featured, and in overall terms the weapon was simple and basic.

It was 1956 before the first sales were made, to West Germany. This involved a batch of only 400 rifles, but the Germans decided that some modifications to the rifles were needed to meet their requirements and by a series of licence agreements (between a CETME licence production offshoot in the Netherlands and Heckler & Koch) the CETME rifle ended as the Heckler & Koch G3, though the Spanish appear to have gained little from the deal.

In 1958 the Spanish army decided to adopt the CETME rifle in a form known as the **Modelo B**, and this became the Modelo 58. The Modelo 58 fired a special cartridge outwardly identical to the standard NATO 7.62-mm (0.30-in)

Above: The core of the Mauser team which designed the German Sturmgewehr 45 decamped to Spain after the war and developed a new assault rifle based on its layout. It is made of low-grade steel and is built with the emphasis on cheapness and reliability rather than looks.

cartridge but using a lighter bullet and propellant charge. This made the rifle much easier to fire (as a result of reduced recoil) but also made the cartridge non-standard as far as other NATO cartridge users were concerned. In 1964 the Spanish adopted the NATO cartridge in place of their own less powerful product and rifles adapted or produced to fire the NATO round became the **Modelo C**.

The Modelo 58 has since been produced in a number of versions, some with bipods, some with semi-automatic mechanisms and others with folding butts, and there has even been a sniper version fitted with a telescopic sight. The latest version is the **Modelo L** chambered in 5.56 mm (0.219 in), but the basic Model 58 is still available from CETME.

Specification
Modelo C
Calibre: 7.62 mm (0.30 in)
Weight: 4.49 kg (9.9 lb)
Lengths: overall 1.016 m (40 in); barrel 450 mm (17.7 in)
Muzzle velocity: 780 m (2,559 ft) per second
Rate of fire: (cyclic) 600 rpm
Magazine: 20-round box

The Spanish army adopted the CETME as its standard rifle in 1958, initially buying the Modelo B, chambered for a unique, light, 7.62 mm round. In 1964 Spain decided to adopt the more powerful 7.62-mm NATO cartridge, and CETME modified their design accordingly to make the Modelo 58 C.

SAR 80 assault rifle

The island state of Singapore has built up a sizeable and capable defence industry in a very short time, largely under the banner of the state owned Chartered Industries of Singapore, or CIS. One of the company's first projects was the licence production of a batch of Colt M16 rifles. These were issued to the local armed forces, but were rather expensive and not robust enough for hard use. In 1976 CIS were asked to come up with something better, and they turned to the Sterling Armaments company of the United Kingdom for help in designing a suitable weapon.

Sterling's design was simple, reliable and rugged. In 1980, after extensive troop trials and a number of detail improvements it was put into production as the **SAR 80**. The SAR 80 is a gas operated rifle of 5.56 mm calibre which makes extensive use of sheet metal pressings in its manufacture. In addition, some 40 per cent of the parts used are available commercially on the open market, contributing to the weapon's notable economy of manufacture. The gas operation mechanism is identical to that of the M16 series, offering both automatic and semi-automatic fire and the 20- or 30-round magazines are M16 components.

The SAR 80 field-strips very easily, and is simple to maintain. The solid butt can be folded forwards to lie alongside the receiver, and the result-

ing shortened weapon is easy to handle at close quarters or in confined spaces. The straight line assembly of barrel, breech-block and butt-stock also adds to controllability, especially in full automatic fire. The flash suppressor, virtually the same as on the M16, also acts as a grenade launcher and bayonet mount. The foresight has a luminous insert for use at night.

The SAR 80 can mount the usual range of accessories, including telescopic and night sights and a blank-firing attachment. A light bipod can be fitted, less for use as a light machine gun than as a means of steadying the aim. Even though the gas system is designed to cause the minimum of fouling, the gas-regulator can be adjusted by hand to enable the SAR 80 to be used when fouling or clogging does occur.

The SAR 80 has proved much more suitable for use by the Singapore armed forces than the M16, although the American rifle remains in service. CIS are mounting an active marketing effort, offering a variant of the SAR 80 able to fire the new NATO standard round. The simplicity of operation and ease of maintenance is being stressed to a number of potential buyers likely to be put off by more sophisticated weapons, and export sales are expected soon.

Specification
Calibre: 5.56 mm (0.22 in)
Weight: 3.7 kg (8.16 lb) unloaded
Length: 970 mm (38.19 in)
Barrel length: 459 mm (18 in)
Magazine: 20- or 30-round box
Muzzle velocity: 970 m (3,182 ft) per second
Rate of fire: (cyclic) 600-800 rpm

The SAR 80 has similar performance characteristics to the American M16 series. It is sturdy, reliable, and is simply constructed using the most economic of construction techniques.

Modern Sniping Rifles

The <u>concealing face netting</u> used by this Yugoslav army sniper is standard equipment for most snipers. In use here is an M76 rifle, noticeable by its long barrel, fitted with a standard ×4 magnification telescopic sight. The gas system tubing over the barrel betrays the weapon's AKM origins although the Yugoslavs have introduced many features of their own.

Since the introduction of accurate long-range firearms to the battlefield, the sniper, or sharpshooter as he used to be called, <u>has had an influence upon the conduct of war out of all proportion to the numbers involved in his deadly trade.</u> In that time his weapon has evolved enormously.

The modern sniping rifle is a remarkable piece of equipment that embodies all the finer points of the gun designer's, gun maker's and ammunition specialist's skills. Although it is very often based on an existing design it is usually manufactured to high degrees of precision to ensure that its user, the sniper, secures the all-important <u>first-round hit</u> on the target every time.

Sniping rifles fall into two general categories. The <u>first</u> has already been mentioned: the conversion of the existing weapon, usually a standard service rifle. These very often do not look all that different from the originals and can often be handled and used in much the same manner. The <u>second</u> category is very different, for its members are the specially designed rifles that often appear not to be rifles at all but some form of 'space-age' weaponry. There are several examples of the latter in this study and they will be easily discerned. They seem to be (and often are) marvels of the gun maker's art, but they are rarely weapons that the sniper will want to use on the battlefield. All sniper's rifles require special care and handling, but some of the more recent examples show every mark of being laboratory test tools rather than practical weapons.

Most of the current crop of sniper's rifles are included in this study. They include stalwarts such as the Soviet SVD and British L42A1, magnificent tools for the job such as the US Marines' M40A1 and the superlative Mauser SP 66. No doubt less readily acceptable to the sniper in the front line are designs such as the Walther WA2000 and the decidedly odd-looking Iver Johnson rifles. <u>But one thing all these rifles have in common is that they are extremely accurate, and in the hands of the right man they are lethal.</u>

The Israelis have eschewed the radical approach which has produced such over-complex and unwieldy weapons as the Walther WA 2000 in favour of the studied development of their existing service rifle into the Galil Sniper.

FR-F1 and FR-F2

When the French army required a sniper's rifle to replace the varied selection of weapons which it had used since World War II, it decided that the easiest design course to follow was to modify its existing service rifle, the 7.5-mm (0.295-in) modèle 1936. This rifle had the dubious distinction of being one of the very last bolt-action rifles to be accepted as a standard service weapon by any of the major European powers, but it was not regarded as a very good design, even at the time, and was used mainly because of its French origins. Using this weapon as a starting point the resultant sniper's rifle, the mle FR-F1, emerged as not particularly innovative.

The number of modifications involved in converting the modèle 1936 into the FR-F1 meant that very little of the original remained; it was just about discernible that the modèle 1936 had been used as the origin, but that was all. The main change was the introduction of a bipod, the addition of a pistol grip for the trigger, a longer barrel with a long flash hider, and a telescopic sight. The butt was provided with a

In this photograph the French sniper is using the telescopic sight of his FR-F1 as an observation aid, resting the barrel on a tree branch. He would never fire the weapon from such a stance, for accuracy would be minimal.

cheek rest and the bolt action considerably altered.

Even with all these alterations the mle FR-F1 was not an immediate international success. For a start, the rifle fired the old French 7.5-mm standard cartridge at a time when other nations were changing to the new 7.62-mm (0.3-in) NATO round. This change to the new cartridge was so pronounced that eventually the French had to convert to it as well, and later-production mle FR-F1s were chambered for 7.62-mm ammunition; many of the older 7.5-mm rifles are still in use, however. The modèle 1936 bolt action was also retained, albeit in a much altered form. Even though the action is slightly awkward, the care put into the making of the F1 has resulted in a weapon of considerable precision that has been

used by successful French army shooting teams.

The mle FR-F1 has now been replaced by the mle FR-F2. Basically this is much the same as the earlier weapon, but the long barrel is now encased in a thick black nylonite sleeve to reduce the heat haze from the barrel that might interfere with the performance of some night sights. The bipod has also been altered and relocated so that it is now secured directly to the barrel. The forestock has been changed from all-wood to all-metal, covered in a plastic coating. The mle

FR-F2 has only been in production for a limited period so it is still too early to determine how it will fare in international esteem.

Specification
FR-F1
Calibre: 7.5 mm (0.295 in) or 7.62 mm (0.3 in)
Lengths: overall 1138 mm (44.8 in); barrel 552 mm (21.73 in)
Weight: empty 5.42 kg (11.95 kg)
Muzzle velocity: 852 m (2,795 ft) per second
Magazine capacity: 10 rounds

Rifle 7.62-mm L42A1

The Lee-Enfield rifle has had a long career with the British army reaching back to the 1890s, and throughout that time the basic Lee-Enfield manual bolt mechanism has remained little changed. It is still in service with the army to this day in the form of the **Rifle 7.62-mm L42A1**. These weapons are used only for sniping, and are conversions of 0.303-in (7.7-mm) No. 4 Mk 1(T) or Mk 1*(T) rifles, as used during World War II. The conversions involved new barrels, a new magazine, some changes to the trigger mechanism and fixed sights, and alterations to the forestock. The World War II No. 32 Mk 3 telescopic sight (renamed the L1A1) and its mounting over the receiver have been retained, and the result has for long been a good, rugged and serviceable sniping rifle, used not only by the army but also by the Royal Marines.

In modern terms the L42A1 is very much the product of a previous generation, but it can still give excellent first-shot results at ranges over 800 m

(875 yards), although this depends very much on the skill of the firer and the type of ammunition used. Normally the ammunition is selected from special 'Green Spot' high-accuracy ammunition produced at the Royal Ordnance facility at Radway Green. The rifle itself is also the subject of a great deal of care, calibration and attention. When not in use it is stowed (and transported) in a special wooden chest that contains not only the rifle but the optical sight, cleaning gear, firing sling and perhaps a few spares such as extra magazines: the L42A1 retains the 10-round magazine of the 0.303-in version but with a revised outline to

accommodate the new rimless ammunition. The often-overlooked weapon record books are also kept in the chest.

The L42A1 is not the only 7.62-mm Lee-Enfield rifle still around. A special match-shooting version known as the **L39A1** is still retained for competitive use, and there are two other models, the **Envoy** and the **Enforcer**. The former may be regarded as a civilian match version of the L39A1, while the Enforcer is a custom-built variant of the L42A1 with a heavier barrel and revised butt outline, produced specifically for police use. The L39A1 and Envoy are not normally fitted with

optical sights but the basic information relating to the L42A1 applies to the three variants.

The L42A1 is now due to be replaced by a new sniper's rifle, a 7.62-mm design from Accuracy International.

Specification
L42A1
Calibre: 7.62 mm (0.3 in)
Lengths: overall 1181 mm (46.5 in); barrel 699 mm (27.5 in)
Weight: 4.43 kg (9.76 lb)
Muzzle velocity: 838 m (2,750 ft) per second
Magazine capacity: 10 rounds

The L42A1 rifle is a 7.62-mm (0.30-in) conversion of an earlier 0.303-in (7.70-mm) Lee-Enfield rifle, and it has served the British Army well over the years. It was used by the Army and the Royal Marines during the Falklands war, usually in the form shown here with the weapon covered in camouflage scrim netting.

Below: Changes to the old No. 4 Lee-Enfield rifle for the 7.62-mm (0.30-in) sniping role involved a new heavy barrel, a new 10-round box magazine, and cutting back the forestock over the barrel. A cheek rest was added to the butt and the rifle was virtually rebuilt. Changes were also made to the trigger, and a scope mount was added.

Parker-Hale Model 82

UK

The Parker-Hale Model 82 was selected by the Canadian Armed Forces as their sniper rifle, and is seen here in winter camouflage. It uses a Mauser-type bolt action and is fitted with a four-round box magazine.

Parker-Hale Limited of Birmingham has for many years been manufacturing match rifles and their associated sights, and also produces sniping rifles. The company's best-known product to date is the 7.62-mm (0.3-in) **Parker-Hale Model 82**, also known as the **Parker-Hale 1200TX**. The Model 82 has been accepted for military and police service by several nations.

In appearance and design terms the Model 82 is an entirely conventional sniping weapon. It uses a manual bolt action very similar to that used on the classic Mauser 98 rifle, allied to a heavy free-floating barrel; the barrel weighs 1.98 kg (4.365 lb) and is manufactured from chrome molybdenum steel. An integral four-round magazine is provided. The trigger mechanism is an entirely self-contained unit that can be adjusted as required.

The Model 82 is available in a number of forms to suit any particular customer requirements. Thus an adjustable cheek pad may be provided if wanted, and the butt lengths can be altered by adding or taking away butt pads of various thicknesses. The sights too are subject to several variations, but the Model 82 is one weapon that is normally supplied with 'iron' match-type sights. If an optical sight is fitted the rear-sights have to be removed to allow the same mounting block to be used. The forward mounting block is machined into the receiver. Various types of 'iron' foresight or optical night sights can be fitted.

The Australian army uses the Model 82 fitted with a Kahles Helia ZF 69 telescopic sight. The Canadian army uses a version of the Model 82/1200TX altered to meet local requirements; this service knows the Model 82 as the Rifle 7.62-mm C3. New Zealand also uses the Model 82.

Parker-Hale produces a special training version of the Model 82 known as the **Model 83**. This single-shot rifle is fitted with match sights only and there is no provision for a telescopic sight. It has been accepted by the British Ministry of Defence as the **Cadet Training Rifle L81A1**.

The Model 82 has now been updated to the **Model 85**. This has a revised butt outline compared with the Model 82, a 10-round box magazine and a bipod (optional on the Model 82) is fitted as standard. This weapon was one of the rifles competitively tested by the British army to determine its new sniper rifle, a competition won by Accuracy International.

Specification
Model 82
Calibre: 7.62 mm (0.3 in)
Lengths: 1162 mm (45.75 in); barrel 660 mm (25.98 in)
Weight: unloaded 4.8 kg (10.58 lb)
Muzzle velocity: about 840 m (2,756 ft) per second
Magazine capacity: 4 rounds

Below: In service with the armed forces of Australia, New Zealand and Canada, the Parker-Hale model 82 is intended to hit point targets at up to 400 m in good light, or up to the maximum range of any sights fitted.

Mauser SP 66 and SP 86

WEST GERMANY

The Mauser-Werke at Oberndorf in West Germany has a long and distinguished history of design and production of bolt-action rifles, their forward locking system developed at the end of the last century being used to this day by manufacturers throughout the world. Mauser stopped making overtly military bolt-action rifles after 1945, but their sporting rifles maintained the Mauser tradition. Many of them utilized the Mauser 'short-action' bolt and receiver which relocated the bolt handle to the front of the bolt.

On most rifles this would be of little account, but on a specialist sniper rifle it means that the firer can operate the bolt action without having to move his head out of the way as the bolt itself can be made relatively short; it also means the barrel can be made correspon-

This version of the SP 66, known as the Model 86 SR, is equipped with a set of target sights and a bipod for super-accurate competition shooting; the service version is basically the same weapon fitted with a telescopic sight but without the bipod.

dingly longer for enhanced accuracy. This has been done on a custom-built Mauser-Werke sniper's rifle known as the **Mauser SP 66**. The revised bolt action is but one instance of the care lavished on this weapon, for it also has a heavy barrel, a butt with a carefully contoured thumb aperture, provision for adjustable cheek and butt pads, and a special muzzle attachment. This last is so designed that on firing the great bulk of the resultant flash is directed out of the firer's vision, and it also acts as a muzzle brake to reduce recoil. Reducing both these factors enables a user to fire second and subsequent shots more rapidly.

The standard of finish and careful design throughout the production of the SP 66 is very high. Even such details as roughening all surfaces likely to be handled to prevent slipping have been carried out with meticulous care, and the trigger is extra wide to allow it to be used when gloves have to be worn.

The sights have been selected with equal attention. There are no fixed sights and the standard telescopic sight is a Zeiss-Divari ZA with zoom capability of from ×1.5 to ×6. Night sights can be fitted, though it is recommended that the manufacturer selects and calibrates them to an exact match for the rifle on which they are used. As is usual with such rifles the ammunition

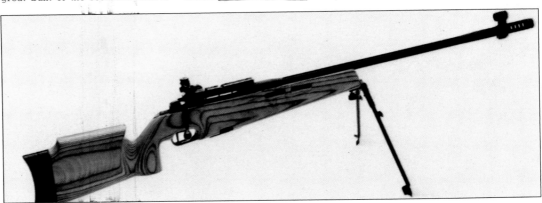

256

fired from the SP 66 is taken from carefully-selected batches of 7.62-mm (0.3-in) NATO rounds produced specifically for use by snipers.

The highly successful SP 66 has been joined in the Mauser range by the brand new **SP 86** which fires the same .308 Winchester (the sporting and target version of 7.62mm NATO) ammunition. The SP 86 has a traditional Mauser bolt and first became available in 1987.

Specification
SP 66
Calibre: 7.62 mm (0.3 in)
Lengths: overall not divulged; barrel 680 mm (26.77 in)
Weight: not divulged
Muzzle velocity: about 860 m (2,821 ft) per second
Magazine capacity: 3 rounds

This Mauser SP 86 is fitted with a night vision device. It is recommended that the manufacturer selects and calibrates the sights of each individual weapon.

Long-range accuracy depends on good ammunition, and Mauser select theirs from batches of NATO 7.62-mm cartridges. This Mauser is fitted with a laser rangefinder.

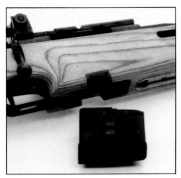

A close-up of the double-row, detachable nine-round magazine of the Mauser SP 86, one of the improvements incorporated into this development of the SP 66.

WEST GERMANY

Walther WA2000

With the **Walther WA2000** it would appear that small-arms design is already in the 'Star Wars' era, for this weapon has an appearance all of its own. The rifle was designed from the outset for the sniping role and the Walther approach has been to put aside all known small-arms design precepts and start from scratch after analysing the requirements.

The most important part of any rifle design is the barrel, for it alone imparts the required degree of accuracy. Walther decided to clamp the barrel at the front and rear to ensure that the torque imparted by a bullet passing through the bore would not lift the barrel away from the intended point of aim. The barrel is also fluted longitudi-

nally over its entire length. This not only provides more cooling area but also reduces the vibrations imparted on firing, vibrations that can also cause a bullet to stray. The designers also decided to go for a gas-operated mechanism to reduce the need for bolt manipulation between shots, and to reduce recoil effects to a minimum the barrel is in direct line with the shoulder so that the muzzle will not be thrown upwards after every shot.

Thus the strange outline of the WA2000 begins to make sense, but there is more to come for the WA2000 is a 'bullpup' design with the gas-operated bolt mechanism behind the trigger group. Such an arrangement makes the overall design that much

shorter and easier to handle without reducing the barrel length. It does mean that the ejection port is close to the firer, so special left- and right-hand versions have to be produced.

The overall standard of finish of the WA2000 is all that one would expect. The butt pad and cheek rests are adjustable, and there is a carefully-shaped pistol grip for added aiming stability. The normal telescopic sight is a Schmidt und Bender ×2.5 to ×10 zoom, but other types can be fitted.

Walther has decided that the best round for the sniping role is now the .300 (7.62-mm) Winchester Magnum cartridge, but while the WA2000 is chambered for this round others such as the 7.62-mm (0.3-in) NATO or much-

favoured 7.5-mm (0.295-in) Swiss cartridge can be accommodated with the required alterations to the bolt and rifling.

Specification
WA2000
Calibre: see text
Lengths: overall 905 mm (35.63 in); barrel 650 mm (25.59 in)
Weights: empty, no sights 6.95 kg (15.32 lb); loaded, with sight, 8.31 kg (18.32 lb)
Magazine capacity: 6 rounds

Supplied with a Schmidt & Bender telescopic sight, the remarkable Walther WA2000 fires the 0.30-in Winchester magnum cartridge.

Heckler und Koch sniper rifles

Heckler & Koch G3 SG/1 Rifle

front sight

flash suppressor

operating handle

operating handle support

barrel

locki

bipod (closed)

7.62-mm round

The range of Heckler und Koch rifles has now become so large that a weapon suitable for just about any application can apparently be selected from the array. Sniper's rifles have not been neglected but generally speaking most of these specialized weapons are little more than standard designs produced with a little extra care, a few accessories and a mounting for a telescopic sight. This does not detract from their serviceability or efficiency, many of them being more suitable for field conditions than other designs that have been produced with emphasis on supreme accuracy rather than serviceability. Typical of these Heckler & Koch sniper weapons are the 7.62-mm (0.3-in) **H&K G3 A3ZF** and **G3 SG/1** pro-

duced for the West German police. The latter model has a light bipod.

Good as these weapons are they are basically only 'breathed on' versions of standard weapons originally designed with mass production rather than specialization in mind. Accordingly Heckler und Koch has turned its attentions to production of a special design known as the **PSG 1** that continues to use the basic Heckler und Koch rotary lock mechanism but allied to a semi-automatic system and a precision heavy barrel with a polygonal-rifled bore. G3 influence can still be seen in the outlines of the receiver and in the 5- or 20-round magazine housing (it is also possible to load single rounds manually), but the rest is all-new. Forward of

the magazine housing is a new forestock and the long barrel, while the butt has been reconfigured to the widely-used all-adjustable form.

The PSG 1 uses a ×6 telescopic sight adjustable up to 600 m (656 yards). It has been stated that the weapon is extremely accurate. These claims are difficult to confirm independently as the weapon is still in the development stage with the military and paramilitary police market in mind. It is even possible that the final form of the PSG 1 will alter, the stamped receiver body perhaps being replaced with something purpose-built to ensure that the sight mounting is more rigid. For special purposes there has been mention of a precision aiming tripod for this

weapon, but its form is still u announced. It may well emerge th this tripod will be an adaptation of o of the Heckler und Koch machine-gu mountings; the butt used on the PSG is a much-modified HK 21 machin gun component.

Specification
PSG 1
Calibre: 7.62 mm (0.3 in)
Lengths: overall 1208 mm (47.56 in); barrel 650 mm (25.59 in)
Weight: less magazine 8.1 kg (17.85 l
Muzzle velocity: about 860 m (2,821 ft per second
Magazine capacity: 5 or 20 rounds

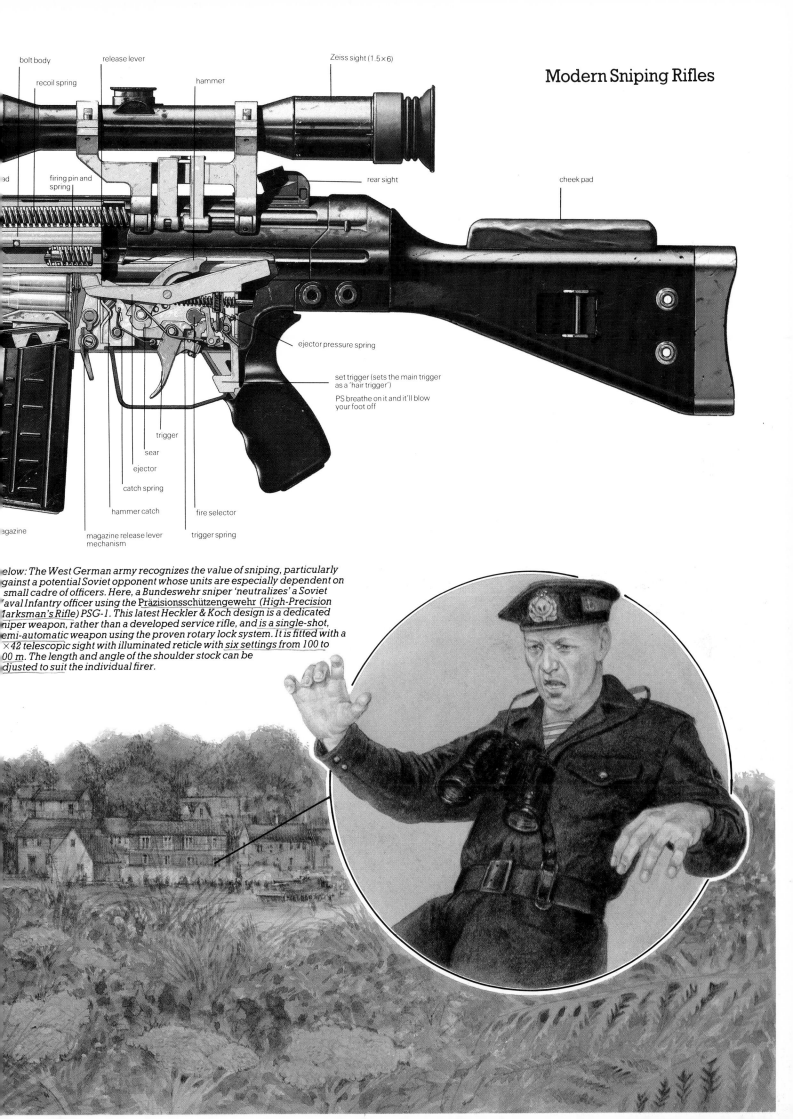

bolt body
release lever
recoil spring
hammer
Zeiss sight (1.5×6)

firing pin and spring
rear sight
cheek pad

ejector pressure spring

set trigger (sets the main trigger as a 'hair trigger')

PS breathe on it and it'll blow your foot off

trigger

sear

ejector

catch spring

hammer catch
fire selector

magazine

magazine release lever mechanism
trigger spring

Modern Sniping Rifles

below: The West German army recognizes the value of sniping, particularly against a potential Soviet opponent whose units are especially dependent on small cadre of officers. Here, a Bundeswehr sniper 'neutralizes' a Soviet Naval Infantry officer using the Präzisionsschützengewehr (High-Precision Marksman's Rifle) PSG-1. This latest Heckler & Koch design is a dedicated sniper weapon, rather than a developed service rifle, and is a single-shot, semi-automatic weapon using the proven rotary lock system. It is fitted with a ×42 telescopic sight with illuminated reticle with six settings from 100 to 00 m. The length and angle of the shoulder stock can be adjusted to suit the individual firer.

SVD

Anyone who reads accounts of the Great Patriotic War (World War II to the rest of the world) cannot but help note the emphasis given to sniping by the Soviet army. That emphasis remains undiminished, and to carry out the sniping role the Soviets have developed what is widely regarded as one of the best sniper's rifles around today; this is the **SVD**, sometimes known as the **Dragunov**.

The SVD (Samozariyadnyia Vintokvka Dragunova) first appeared in 1963, and ever since has been one of the most prized of infantry trophies. It is a semi-automatic weapon that uses the same operating principles as the AK-47 assault rifle but allied to a revised gas-operated system. Unlike the AK-47, which uses the short 7.62-mm (0.3-in)×39 cartridge, the SVD fires the older 7.62-mm×54R rimmed cartridge originally introduced during the 1890s for the Mosin-Nagant rifles. This remains a good round for the sniping role, and as it is still used on some Soviet machine-guns availability is no problem.

The SVD has a long barrel, but the weapon is so balanced that it handles well and recoil is not excessive. If the long barrel is not a decisive recognition point then the cut-away butt certainly is. The weapon is normally fired using a sling rather than the bipod favoured elsewhere, and to assist aiming a PSO-1 telescopic sight is provided. This is secured to the left-hand side of the receiver and has a magnification of ×4. The PSO-1 has an unusual feature in that it incorporates an infra-red detector element to enable it to be used as a passive night sight, althought it is normally used in conjunction with an independent infra-red target-illumination source. Basic combat sights are fitted for use if the optical sight becomes defective.

Perhaps the oddest feature for a sniper rifle is that the SVD is provided with a bayonet, the rationale for this remaining uncertain. A 10-round box magazine is fitted.

Tests have demonstrated that the SVD can fire accurately to ranges of well over 800 m (875 yards). It is a pleasant weapon to handle and fire, despite the lengthy barrel. SVDs have been provided to many Warsaw Pact and other nations and it has been used in Afghanistan, some ending in the hands of the guerrillas, who are certainly no newcomers to sniping. The Chinese produce a direct copy of the SVD and offer this version for export, quoting an effective range of 1000 m (1,094 yards).

Specification
SVD
Calibre: 7.62 mm (0.3 in)
Lengths: overall less bayonet 1225 mm (48.23 in); barrel 547 mm (21.53 in)
Weight: complete, unloaded 4.385 kg (9.677 lb)
Muzzle velocity: 830 m (2,723 ft) per second
Magazine capacity: 10 rounds

The Soviets have always given snipers a great deal of prominence in the field and have always provided them with good weapons. The current Dragunov SVD, although long and bulky, is a reliable weapon although not as accurate as, say, the L42. It uses a modified AK-47 gas-operated semi-automatic action allied to a large magazine.

Right: The Dragunov uses a bolt system similar to that of the AK-47 and its derivatives, but it is modified to suit the different characteristics of the rimmed 7.62 mm ×54 cartridge originally produced in 1908 for the Moisin-Nagant rifle.

The Dragunov has an excellent sight which displays a graduated range-finding scale, based on the height of the average man. By fitting the target into the grid, the firer gets an accurate idea of the range and aims accordingly. Simple, but effective.

China produces a direct copy of the SVD and is now offering it for export with various extras including this bayonet/wire-cutter.

ISRAEL
Galil Sniping Rifle

Ever since Israel was formed in 1948 the role of the sniper within the Israeli armed forces has been an important one, but over the years snipers have usually been equipped with an array of weapons from all around the world. At one point attempts were made to produce sniper rifles locally, so for a period Israeli army snipers used an indigenous 7.62-mm (0.3-in) design known as the **M26**. This was virtually a hand-made weapon using design features from both the Soviet AKM and Belgian FAL rifles. But for various reasons the M26 was deemed not fully satisfactory, so work began on a sniping rifle based on the Israel Military Industries 7.62-mm Galil assault rifle, the standard Israeli service rifle.

The resultant **Galil Sniping Rifle** bears a resemblance to the original but it is virtually a new weapon. Almost every component has been redesigned and manufactured to very close tolerances. A new heavy barrel is fitted, as is an adjustable bipod. The solid butt (which can be folded forward to reduce carrying and stowage bulk) has an adjustable butt pad and cheek rest, while a Nimrod ×6 telescopic sight is mounted on a bracket offset to the left of the receiver. The mechanism is now single-shot only, the original Galil 20-round magazine being retained. The barrel is fitted with a muzzle brake/compensator to reduce recoil and barrel jump on firing. A silencer can be fitted to the muzzle, but subsonic ammunition must then be used. As would be expected, various night sights can be fitted.

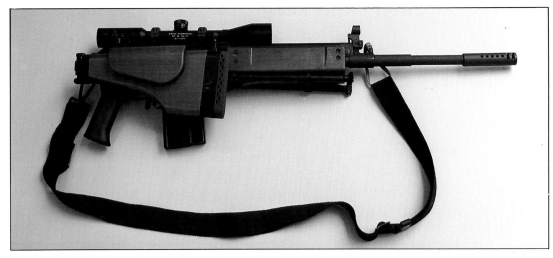

The Galil Sniping Rifle is now in production and has been offered for export. It is a very serviceable weapon that is far more suitable for the rigours of military life than many of the current crop of super-accuracy models. Despite its basic design approach it can still place groupings of less than 300 mm (11.8 in) at a range of 600 m (656 yards), which is more than adequate for most sniping purposes. Careful selection of the ammunition and use of the bipod ensures even better performances.

The Galil Sniping Rifle retains its 'iron' combat sights. When not in use the rifle is kept in a special case together with the telescopic sight, optical filters to reduce sun glare when using optical sights, a carrying and firing sling, two magazines and the all-important cleaning kit.

Specification
Galil Sniping Rifle
Calibre: 7.62 mm (0.3 in)
Lengths: overall 1115 mm (43.9 in); barrel 508 mm (20 in)
Weights: rifle only 6.4 kg (14.1 lb); complete 8.02 kg (17.68 lb)
Muzzle velocity: 815 m (2,674 ft) per second
Magazine capacity: 20 rounds

The design of the Galil Sniping Rifle was shaped by the IDF's extensive battlefield experience, and it is perhaps not surprising that the gun is built more for reliability in combat than exceptional accuracy in ideal conditions.

The semi-automatic Galil is a gas-operated weapon with a rotating bolt and a 20-round magazine. It fires standard NATO 7.62 mm ×51 and is built to hit the head at 300 m, half-body at 600 m and full figure at 800-900 m.

BELGIUM

FN Model 30-11

Fabrique Nationale (FN) has for long kept an astute eye on the arms market from its Herstal headquarters, so when it noted an increased demand over recent years for highly accurate rifles for use against point targets the company came up with the **FN Model 30-11**. At first sight the Model 30-11 appears to be a highly conventional design. And so it is, though in order to make the weapon as accurate as possible it has been designed and manufactured with great care to obtain the best possible results.

The Model 30-11 fires carefully selected 7.62-mm (0.3-in) NATO ammunition. The manual bolt action is the frequently used Mauser forward-locking action but manufactured using a very high standard of craftsmanship. The same can be said of the heavy barrel which is connected to the receiver with great care. A five-round

The Belgian FN Model 30-11 rifle was originally produced for police and para-military use, but many are in military hands. The example seen here is fitted with target sights. The odd butt shape is due to the degree of individual adjustment that can be incorporated.

box magazine is used, but normally single rounds only are loaded by hand direct into the chamber. The butt is adjustable in two planes (up and down/forward and back) to suit the individual user's comfort. Swivels are provided for a shooting sling, and there is provision for mounting a bipod under the forestock; the same bipod is used on the FN MAG machine-gun.

This bipod is recommended for use when the Model 30-11 is employed with any of the larger sighting devices that can be fitted. Unlike many other sniper rifles the Model 30-11 can be used with precision-adjustable match-type 'iron' sights, but there is also a wide range of telescopic sights available. For use at night or in poor visibility conditions image intensifier or thermal imaging sights can be used. The sights selected are normally kept in a special protective carrying case together with the rifle when they are being transported or stored.

The Model 30-11 is used by the Belgian army, although most have been issued to Belgian paramilitary police units. Some sales have been made to other nations, but only in small numbers, for the degree of care lavished

on producing the Model 30-11 means that the weapon is not cheap. This has apparently prevented the usual appearance of high-class target-shooting versions for commercial sales, although anyone fortunate enough to obtain a standard Model 30-11 with 'iron' sights will find themselves the owner of a superlative match rifle.

Specification
Model 30-11
Calibre: 7.62 mm (0.3 in)
Lengths: overall 1117 mm (43.97 in); barrel 502 mm (19.76 in)
Weight: rifle only 4.85 kg (10.69 lb)
Muzzle velocity: 850 m (2,788 ft) per second
Magazine capacity: 5 rounds

The FN Model 30-11 can be fitted with a wide range of accessories. The large sight seen here is a standard NATO infra-red night vision sight, and the bipod fitted is that used on the FN MAG machine-gun. A range of other such items can be used with this weapon, which is supplied with a special carrying case.

 USA
Rifle M21

When the US armed forces made the move from the 7.62-mm (0.3-in) NATO cartridge to the smaller 5.56-mm (0.223-in) round during the late 1960s they not surprisingly decided to retain the larger calibre for the sniping role. This was for the simple reason that the smaller round had been designed from the outset to impart its best performance at ranges much shorter than the usual sniping distances. This meant the retention of the then-current sniping rifle, at the time known as the **Rifle 7.62-mm M14 National Match (Accurised)**, but now known as the **Rifle M21**.

The M21 is a special version of the 7.62-mm M14, for many years the standard US service rifle. It retains the basic appearance and mechanism of the original, but some changes were introduced at the manufacturing stage. For a start the barrels were selected so that only those with the closest manufacturing tolerances were used. These barrels were left without their usual chromium plating inside the bore, again to reduce the possibility of manufacturing inaccuracies. A new muzzle supressor was fitted and reamed to the barrel to ensure correct alignment. The trigger mechanism was assembled by hand and adjusted to provide a crisp release action, and a new walnut stock was fitted, this latter being impregnated with an epoxy resin. The gas-operated mechanism was also the subject of attention to ensure smooth operation. The fully-automatic fire mode is retained on the M21 but normally the weapon is fired on semi-automatic (single shot) only.

The main change on assembly was the fitting of a ×3 magnification telescopic sight. As well as the usual aiming cross-hairs, this uses a system of graticules that allows the user to judge accurately the range of a man-sized target and automatically set the angle of elevation. Using this sight the M21 can place 10 rounds within a 152-mm (6-in) circle at 300 m (329 yards).

One piece of equipment that can be

fitted to the M21 is a sound suppressor. This is not a silencer in the usually accepted sense of the word, but a series of baffles that reduces the velocity of the gases produced on firing to below the speed of sound. This produces a muffled report with none of the usual firing signatures, and its use makes the source of the sound (and the firer) difficult to detect.

Specification
M21
Calibre: 7.62 mm (0.3 in)
Lengths: overall 1120 mm (44.09 in); barrel 559 mm (22 in)
Weight: loaded 5.55 kg (12.24 lb)
Muzzle velocity: 853 m (2,798 ft) per second
Magazine capacity: 20 rounds

The 5.56 mm rifles common to modern armies are designed for short range fighting, so for sniping most forces retain a full power weapon. The US Army uses a special version of the M14, known as the M21.

Although many Israeli snipers use the Galil sniping rifle some still retain the American M21, the accurized version of the M14 rifle. They were observed in use during the early stages of the invasion of Lebanon, and many were used against the PLO in Beirut in August 1982.

Sniping Rifle M40A1

The US Marine Corps has always been allowed its own equipment procurement system as it has long been accepted that its particular amphibious role requires equipment to match. Thus when the selection of a new sniping rifle to replace the M1C and M1D weapons based on the M1 Garand rifles came about, this service went its own way.

For the US Marines the sniper has always had a special role, often operating in advance of other supporting units to gain information as well as acting as a long-range killer. So when they contemplated weapons such as the

When the US Marine Corps decided to select their own sniping rifle they ordered numbers of commercial Remington Model 700 rifles, some still with 'iron' sights, as seen here. These became the M40 sniping rifle and many are still in use, despite the introduction of the later M40A1, but they are used only by the Marines.

M14/M21 sniper rifles they decided they wanted something better. They could not find exactly what they wanted on the open market but the design that came closest to their requirements was a commercial rifle known as the **Remington Model 700**. This became the **M40** in 1966.

The M40 has a Mauser-type manual bolt action and a heavy barrel. It is normally fitted with a Redfield telescopic sight with a zoom magnification of from ×3 to ×9. A five-round magazine is fitted, and the M40 is an entirely conventional but high-quality design. In service with the US Marines the M40 proved to be perfectly satisfactory, but experience gained with the basic design showed them that something better could be produced. They accordingly asked the Remington Arms Company to introduce a few modifications. These included the replacement of the barrel by a new stainless steel component, the replacement of the wooden furniture by fibreglass and the introduction of a new sight. This new telescopic sight has been produced entirely to demanding US Marine specifications and employs a fixed ×10 magnification. No iron sights are fitted in addition to this optical sight.

With all these changes embodied the M40 is now the **M40A1**, and it is produced by Remington only for the US Marines. By all accounts it is one of the most accurate sniping rifles ever

The Marines adopted the Remington 700 in 1966 and have had the weapon modified to meet their requirements. The M40A1 rifle differs from the M40 in having a heavy stainless steel barrel, a fibreglass stock and a powerful telescopic sight.

produced, although exact figures are not available to confirm this assertion. The main reasons for this are the heavy stainless steel barrel and the superb optical sight. The magnification of this sight is much more than usual on such devices, but it produces a bright and clear image for the firer. All the usual windage and other adjustments can be introduced to the sight.

As always with a weapon of this type, the degree of accuracy is dependent on the skill of the user (the US Marines spend a great deal of time training their snipers) and the performance of the ammunition selected, but by all accounts the M40A1 is the rifle 'everyone else wants'.

Specification
M40A1
Calibre: 7.62 mm (0.3 in)
Lengths: overall 1117 mm (43.97 in); barrel 610 mm (24 in)
Weight: 6.57 kg (14.48 lb)
Muzzle velocity: 777 m (2,549 ft) per second
Magazine capacity: 5 rounds

Iver Johnson Model 300 Multi-Caliber Rifle

This weapon has undergone a few changes in name since it first emerged some years back from the drawing boards of the Research Armament Industries concern in Rogers, Arizona. Its full current title is the **Iver Johnson Model 300 Multi-Caliber Long-Range Rifle**, and it is marketed by Napco International Inc.

The Model 300 is another of the attempts to produce the perfect sniping rifle capable of being effective at ranges up to 1500 m (1,640 yards). On the Model 300 everything that can eliminate technical error has been incorporated, these features ranging from a fluted barrel with a counterweight beneath to reduce vibrations and whip in the free-floating barrel, to an all-adjustable butt with a cheek pad. A ×9 Leupold telescopic sight is the only means of aiming the weapon and a bipod is provided for maximum aiming stability. A manual bolt action is used.

The designers also decided to provide what they regard as the optimum cartridge for long-range sniping. This was developed from an existing Rigby hunting cartridge by Research Arma-

ment Industries and has a calibre of 8.58 mm (0.338 in). Tables supplied to demonstrate the efficiency of this cartridge show that it has a much higher muzzle velocity than most comparable rounds and a considerably higher muzzle energy, giving the bullet a flatter ballistic path over longer ranges. However, the designers also realized that the acceptance of this new cartridge might be an uphill task, so they have also produced barrel and bolt head to enable existing 7.62-mm (0.3-in) NATO cartridges to be used; the calibres can be switched from one to the other as required. This provides the Model 300 with its 'Multi-Caliber' designation.

To date the Model 300 has had a mixed reception. It has attracted much attention by its very appearance but apparently hard orders have been slow in coming. Unconfirmed reports speak of some being used by US Special Forces, but that is all. The US Marines have procured trial numbers of the **Model 500**, a much larger and heavier version of the Model 300 that fires the 12.7-mm (0.5-in) machine-gun cartridge. The ballistic limitations of

this cartridge apparently ensured that the Model 500 was not a great success with the US Marines, and one feature of the Model 500 they did not accept is the fact that on this larger version the bolt has to be removed to load every round. After a few rounds the bolt often jammed and could not be removed without force, i.e. kicking it out.

Specification
Model 300
Calibre: 8.58 mm (0.338 in) or 7.62 mm (0.3 in)

Length: barrel only, both calibres 610 mm (24 in)
Weight: 5.67 kg (12.5 lb)
Muzzle velocity: 8.58-mm 915 m (3,002 ft) per second; 7.62-mm 800 m (2,625 ft) per second
Magazine capacity: 8.58-mm 4 rounds; 7.62-mm 5 rounds

The 'space age' Iver Johnson rifles are intended for super-long range use. The Model 300 (foreground) can fire either a 7.62-mm (0.30-in) or a special 8.58-mm cartridge.

7.92-mm M76

Yugoslavia is not one of the nations that automatically springs to mind when the international arms market is considered, but it is currently one of the nations most involved in the selling of arms to the Third World. Its small-arms industry is not particularly innovative, preferring to adapt or develop existing designs rather than branch out into startling new ventures. Thus when a requirement came to replace all the elderly World War II sniping weapons still in use by the Yugoslav armed forces it was again decided to adapt an existing design, in this case the M70B1 assault rifle, the Yugoslav derivative of the Soviet AKM.

Not surprisingly the resultant weapon, the **M76** semi-automatic sniping rifle, has much in common with the Soviet SVD. The main difference is the choice of cartridge, which on the M76 is a 7.92-mm (0.312-in) type, a left-over from the German World War II standard rifle calibre. Yugoslavia still uses this cartridge for some machine-guns, so its retention for the sniping role is understandable. For marketing purposes the Yugoslavs also offer the M76 chambered for the 7.62-mm (0.3-in) NATO cartridge and the elderly Soviet 7.62-mm (0.3-in) rimmed cartridge.

Having said that, the M76 resembles the original AKM design much more than does the Soviet SVD. The M76 is a semi-automatic weapon with a long barrel but much of the original M70B1/AKM outline survives, including the solid wooden butt. The M76 uses a 10-round box magazine, and a telescopic sight with a ×4 magnification is mounted over the receiver. This sight has much in common with the Soviet

PSO-1, including the rubber eye-piece, and is stated to make the M76 effective at ranges of 800 m (875 yards) or more. A variety of night vision devices, usually passive infra-red sights, can be fitted in its place. The normal combat sights of the M70B1 are retained, but the bayonet feature of the SVD is not.

Although the M76 may be regarded as a derivative of a Soviet design there is nothing derivative in its production standards. In common with most other Yugoslav weapons, the M76 is well-made and rugged enough to withstand the hard knocks of service life. From this point of view it is a far more prac-

tical weapon than many of the 'super-accuracy' designs now likely to be encountered. The M76 is already in service with the Yugoslav armed forces, but it is difficult to determine exactly how export sales have fared.

Specification
M76
Calibre: 7.92 mm (0.312 in)
Lengths: overall 1135 mm (44.69 in); barrel 550 mm (21.65 in)
Weight: empty, complete 5.08 kg (11.2 lb)
Muzzle velocity: 720 m (2,362 ft) per second
Magazine capacity: 10 rounds

The Yugoslav M76 sniping rifle can be found chambered for 7.92-mm (0.312-in) and both Soviet and NATO 7.62-mm (0.30-in) ammunition. It is basically a specially produced variant of the Yugoslav M70 assault rifle based on the AKM and fitted with a longer barrel and an optical sight mounting.

The Yugoslav M76 semi-automatic rifle, seen here fitted with a passive optical night sight, has obvious design similarities to the Soviet Dragunov SVD. It uses a 10-round magazine and is in service with the Yugoslav armed forces.

7.62-mm SSG 69

With this Austrian rifle the designation SSG 69 stands for Scharfschüt-zengewehr 69 (sharp-shooter rifle 69), 1969 being the year of the weapon's acceptance for service by the Austrian army. It is manufactured by the Steyr-Daimler-Puch AG concern at Steyr and was, in 1969, the latest in a long line of rifles produced by the concern.

The 7.62-mm (0.3-in) SSG 69 has some unusual design features, one of them being the use of a Männlicher bolt action with a form of rear locking instead of the far more common Mauser forward-lug locking. The bolt action is now uncommon, although it has been used on other recent Steyr rifles, and is so arranged that the entire action is very strong and the chamber is well

The Steyr SSG 69 rifle is the standard Austrian army sniper's rifle, and is used by mountain troops as it is possible for a single sniper to virtually seal a mountain pass against advancing troops for long periods. The SSG 69 is robust enough to survive in such conditions and retain its accuracy.

within the receiver for added rigidity. A safety catch locks both the bolt and firing pin when engaged. The barrel is cold-forged using a machine hammering process in which the barrel rifling is hammered into the bore using a mandrel. Another odd feature is the use of the Männlicher rotary magazine, a design feature that dates back to well before World War I. This rotary magazine holds five rounds, but a more orthodox 10-round box magazine can be fitted.

The rifle stock is made of a synthetic material and is adjustable in length to suit the firer. The firer can also adjust the double-pull trigger pressure. It is also possible to make various adjustments to the standard Kahles ZF69 telescopic sight which has a magnification of ×6. Other forms of sight (including night sights) can be used on the SSG 69, the receiver having an overhead longitudinal rib that can accommodate a wide range of vision devices. 'Iron' sights are provided for emergency use only.

The SSG 69 is very accurate. Trials have shown that it is possible to fire 10-round groups no larger than 400 mm (15.75 in) at 800 m (875 yards), which is the maximum graduated range of the ZF69 sight; at shorter

ranges the groupings get much tighter.

Since the introduction of the SSG 69 Steyr has developed some more advanced sniper rifle models, but the SSG 69 remains in service with the Austrians for the simple reason that it is an excellent military sniper's rifle and far more practical than some of the more modern technical marvels now available. A target shooting version of the SSG 69 with a heavier barrel and match sights has been produced.

Specification
SSG 69
Calibre: 7.62 mm (0.3 in)
Lengths: overall 1140 mm (44.9 in); barrel 650 mm (25.6 in)
Weight: empty, with sight 4.6 kg (10.14 lb)
Muzzle velocity: 860 m (2,821 ft) per second
Magazine capacity: 5-round rotary or 10-round box

The Steyr SSG 69 rifle uses a Kahles ZF69 telescopic sight graduated up to 800 m (875 yards) – this example is not fitted with the usual 'iron' sights. The SSG 69 uses an unusual five-round rotary magazine, but can also be fitted with a 10-round box magazine.

ITALY

Beretta Sniper

When the market for high-precision sniper's rifles expanded in the 1970s, virtually every major small-arms manufacturer in Europe and elsewhere started to design weapons they thought would meet international requirements. Some of these designs have fared better than others on the market, but one that does appear to have been overlooked by many is the **Beretta Sniper** 7.62-mm (0.3-in) sniping rifle. This design appears to have been given no numerical designation and it has only recently appeared on the scene, two factors that would normally indicate that the rifle is only just out of the development stage. But there are reports that it is already in use with some Italian paramilitary police units

for internal security duties.

Compared with many of the latest 'space-age' sniper rifle designs, the Beretta offering is almost completely orthodox but well up to the usual high standards of Beretta design and finish. The Sniper uses a manual rotary bolt action allied to the usual heavy barrel, and one of its most prominent features is the large and unusually-shaped hole carved into the high-quality wooden stock that forms a prominent pistol grip for the trigger.

Despite the overall conventional design there are one or two advanced features on the Sniper. The wooden forestock conceals a forward-pointing counterweight under the free-floating barrel that acts as a damper to reduce

the barrel vibrations produced on firing. At the front end of the forestock is a location point for securing a light adjustable bipod to assist aiming. The underside of the forestock contains a slot for an adjustable forward hand stop for the firer, and this forestop can also be used as the attachment point for a firing sling if one is required. The butt and cheek pads are adjustable and the muzzle has a flash hider.

Unlike many of its modern counterparts the Beretta Sniper is fully provided with a set of all-adjustable precision match sights, even though these would not normally be used for the sniping role. Over the receiver is a standard NATO optical or night sight mounting attachment to accommodate

virtually any military sighting system. The normal telescopic sight is the widely-used Zeiss Divari Z with a zoom capability from ×1.5 to ×6, but other types can be fitted.

Specification
Beretta Sniper
Calibre: 7.62 mm (0.3 in)
Lengths: overall 1165 mm (45.87 in); barrel 586 mm (23 in)
Weights: empty 5.55 kg (12.23 lb); complete 7.2 kg (15.87 lb)
Muzzle velocity: about 865 m (2,838 ft) per second
Magazine capacity: 5 rounds

Modern Machine-Guns

An American soldier in Vietnam uses an M60 from an emplaced position, with plenty of ammunition belts ready to hand. In such belts about one round in six is tracer.

The use of automatic weapons steadily increased during World War II, and today most infantrymen carry weapons capable of burst fire. But the machine-gun remains the prime firepower component of the infantry squad, and classic designs like the Bren have lost none of their effectiveness.

The modern machine-gun is still one of the foot soldier's most powerful weapons, but it has changed much since World War I, when the machine-gun dominated the battlefields of France and elsewhere. Today's machine-gun is much lighter, more reliable and in general more flexible in its tactical applications. Most of the machine-guns here discussed are portable enough to be used in locations where it was once unthinkable that such weapons could even be carried, but they are still as lethal and efficient as they ever were.

The machine-gun is now in its second generation of development since World War II. The first generation weapons are still very much in evidence with virtually every armed force in the world, and are the post-war general-purpose machine-guns, or GPMGs. In the years after 1945 the GPMG was embraced by many as the way ahead in machine-gun design, but the soldiers in the front line discovered the hard way that the all-purpose machine-gun is as much a myth as the all-purpose truck. Thus the second generation of machine-guns is now entering service.

The second-generation weapons are more specialized than the GPMGs. The light machine-gun has made a come-back as the squad support weapon, while the heavy machine-gun has returned in the form of the post-war GPMGs retained for the heavy fire-support role. They are now in the position of either being retained indefinitely, or are slowly being replaced by the larger-calibre weapons such as the really heavy machine-guns (of 12.7mm/0.5in calibre and upwards) or the machine weapons now generally known as cannon. It is the machine-guns that are covered in this study.

At first sight the variety of modern machine-guns looks somewhat bewildering, and the types mentioned here are but a selection of what is available. More types than can be covered in these pages are around or in the wings, for machine-gun development is still very progressive. Nearly all the major nations are either attempting to gild the lily by using the existing types, or alternatively chasing the myth of the perfect design. Some of the designs mentioned here do appear to have achieved near-perfection, for how otherwise can one contemplate the longevity of the MG3 and L4A4 Bren Gun designs? Others, such as the M60, make one wonder how they have lasted so long.

The most widely-used present-day version of the World War II Bren gun is the British L4A4, a conversion to standard NATO calibre. Seen here in action with the South African Army, it is also used by the British and many of the ex-Commonwealth armies, including India.

7.62-mm FN MAG

World War II established the general-purpose machine-gun (GPMG) as a viable weapon with its ability to be fired from a light bipod in the assault role and from a heavy tripod in the defensive or sustained role. After 1945 many designers tried to produce their own version of the GPMG concept, and one of the best was produced in Belgium during the early 1950s. The company concerned was Fabrique Nationale or FN, based at Herstal, and its design became known as the **FN Mitrailleuse d'Appui Général** or **MAG**. It was not long before the MAG was adopted by many nations, and today it is one of the most widely-used of all modern machine-gun designs.

The MAG fires the standard NATO 7.62-mm (0.3-in) cartridge and uses a conventional gas-operated mechanism, in which gases tapped off from the barrel are used to drive the breech block and other components to the rear once a round has been fired. Where the FN MAG scores over many comparable designs is that the tapping-off point under the barrel incorporates a regulator device that allows the firer to control the amount of gas used and thus vary the fire rate to suit the ammunition and other variables. For the sustained-fire role the barrel can be changed easily and quickly.

In construction the MAG is very sturdy. Some use is made of steel pressings riveted together, but many components are machined from solid metal, making the weapon somewhat heavy for easy transport. But this structural strength enables the weapon to absorb all manner of rough use, and it can be used for long periods without maintenance other than changing the barrels when they get too hot. The ammunition is belt-fed, which can be awkward when the weapon has to be carried with lengths of ammunition belt left hanging from the feed and snagging on just about everything.

When used as an LMG the MAG uses a butt and simple bipod. When used as a sustained-fire weapon the butt is usually removed and the weapon is placed on a heavy tripod, usually with some form of buffering to absorb part of the recoil. However, the MAG can be adapted to a number of other mountings, and is often used as a co-axial weapon on armoured vehicles

or as a vehicle defence weapon in a ball mounting, and as an anti-aircraft weapon on a tripod or vehicle-hatch mounting. It is also used on many light naval vessels.

The MAG has been widely produced under licence. One of the better-known nations is the UK, where the MAG is known as the **L7A2**. The British introduced some modifications of their own, (and have produced the weapon for export), and there is no sign of it being replaced in the foreseeable future as far as the British armed forces are concerned. Other nations that produce the MAG for their own use in-

clude Israel, South Africa, Singapore and Argentina, and there are others. Even longer is the list of MAG users: a brief summary includes Sweden, Ireland, Greece, Canada, New Zealand, the Netherlands and so on. There is little chance of the MAG falling out of fashion, and production continues all over the world.

Specification
FN MAG
Calibre: 7.62 mm (0.3 in)
Weights: gun only 10.1 kg (22.27 lb); tripod 10.5 kg (23.15 lb); barrel 3 kg (6.6 lb)

The Belgian FN MAG is one of the most widely used of the post-World War II general-purpose machine-guns. Well made from what are usually solid metal billets machined to spec, the MAG is a very sturdy but heavy weapon that is still in production worldwide.

Lengths: gun 1260 mm (49.61 in); barrel 545 mm (21.46 in)
Muzzle velocity: 840 m (2,756 ft) per second
Rate of fire: (cyclic) 600-1000 rpm
Type of feed: 50-round belt

Below: The FN MAG is licence-produced in Israel by Israel Military Industries and is used by all branches of the Israeli armed forces.

Above: During the Falkland Islands campaign L7A1s were hastily pressed into use on improvised anti-aircraft mountings to provide some measure of defence against Argentine attacks on the shipping in San Carlos harbour.

Below: The FN MAG is fitted to the turrets of the German Leopard 2 tanks in service with the Dutch army. Pictured here in September 1984 on Exercise 'Lionheart', the MAG has been fitted with a blank firing adaptor.

FN 5.56-mm Minimi

With the turn away from the heavy NATO 7.62-mm (0.3-in) cartridge towards the smaller 5.56-mm (0.219-in) round for use by the standard rifles of most of the NATO nations (and many others), it followed that there was a need for a light machine-gun to use the new calibre. FN accordingly drew up the design of a new weapon that eventually became known as the **FN Minimi** and was first shown in 1974. The Minimi is intended for use only as a squad support weapon as there is no way that the light 5.56-mm cartridge can be used effectively for the heavy support or sustained-fire role, for it simply lacks the power to be effective at ranges much beyond 400 m (437 yards). Thus heavier-calibre weapons such as the FN MAG will still be retained for this role.

The Minimi uses some design features from the earlier FN MAG, including the quick-change barrel and the gas regulator, but a new rotary locking device is used for the breech block which is guided inside the receiver by two guide rails to ensure a smooth travel. These latter innovations have made the Minimi into a remarkably reliable weapon, and further reliability has been introduced into the ammunition feed. This is one of the Minimi's major contributions to modern light machine-gun design as it does away with the long and awkward flapping ammunition belts used on many designs and which snag on everything when carried. The Minimi uses a simple box (under the gun body) which contains the neatly-folded belt. When the weapon is fired from a bipod, the box is so arranged that it will not interfere with normal use and on the move it is out of the way of the carrier. But the Minimi goes one step further: if re-

quired, the belt feed can be replaced by a magazine feed. FN has shrewdly guessed that the American M16A1 rifle would quickly become the standard weapon in its class, and has thus made provision for the Minimi to use the M16A1's 30-round magazine. This can clip into the receiver just under the belt feed guides after the belt has been removed.

The association with the American M16A1 rifle has turned out well for FN, for the Minimi has been adopted as the US Army's squad fire-support weapon, and is now known there as the **M249 Squad Automatic Weapon, or SAW**. This version will fire the new standard NATO SS109 5.56-mm cartridge rather than the earlier M193 cartridge. The SS109 has a longer and heavier bullet than the earlier cartridge and uses a

different rifling in the barrel, but is otherwise similar to the American cartridge.

Two possible variants of the Minimi are a 'para' version which uses a shorter barrel and a sliding butt to make the weapon shorter overall, and a vehicle model with no butt at all for mounting in armoured vehicles. The Minimi itself has many ingenious detail points as well: the trigger guard may be removed to allow operation by a man wearing winter or NBC warfare gloves, the front handguard contains a cleaning kit, the ammunition feed box has a simple indicator to show how many rounds are left, and so on.

Overall the Minimi may be regarded as one of the best of the new family of 5.56-mm light machine-guns. It will be around for a very long time.

The FN Minimi has been adopted by the US Army for the Squad Automatic Weapon (SAW) as the M249. It is now entering service with the airborne divisions of the Rapid Deployment Force and with the US Marines

Specification
FN Minimi
Calibre: 5.56 mm (0.219 in)
Weights: with bipod 6.5 kg (14.33 lb); with 200 rounds 9.7 kg (21.38 lb)
Lengths: weapon 1050 mm (41.34 in); barrel 465 mm (18.31 in)
Muzzle velocity: (SS 109) 915 m (3,002 ft) per second
Rate of fire: (cyclic) 750-1000 rpm
Type of feed: 100- or 200-round belt, or 30-round box magazine

---

7.62-mm vz 59

Czech machine-gun designers can trace their progeny back to the range of highly successful machine-guns started with the vz (vzor, or model) 26 in 1926 and which resulted in the famous Bren Guns. As successor to these designs the Czechs produced a new model during the early 1950s as the **vz 52**, which may be regarded as the old design updated to use an ammunition belt-feed system. This was not the success of the earlier weapons, and is now rarely encountered other than in the hands of 'freedom fighters' and the like, and the vz 52 has been superseded by the **vz 59**.

The vz 59 is much simpler than the earlier vz 52 but follows the same general lines in appearance and operation. In fact many of the operating principles of the vz 52 have been carried over, including the gas-operated

mechanism. The ammunition feed system is also a carry-over from the vz 52, in which it was regarded by many as being the only successful feature. In this feed system the belt is carried into the receiver by guides where a cam system takes over and pushes the cartridge forward through the belt link into the weapon. This system was copied from the Soviet PK series, but on the vz 59 the belts are fed from metal boxes; for the light machine-gun role with the light barrel and designation **vz 59L**, one of these boxes can be hung from the right-hand side of the gun in a rather unbalanced fashion. The weapon may be used in the LMG role with bipod or tripod mountings.

For the heavy machine-gun role the vz 59 is fitted with a heavy barrel. In this form it is known merely as the vz 59. When fitted with a solenoid for

firing in armoured vehicles on a co-axial or similar mount it is known as the **vz 59T**. This does not exhaust the variations of the vz 59 series for, no doubt with an eye to possible sales outside Czechoslovakia, there is a version that fires standard NATO 7.62-mm (0.3-in) ammunition and known as the **vz 59N**; the vz 59 series usually fires the Soviet 7.62-mm cartridge.

One rather unusual feature of the vz 59 is the telescopic sight, which can be used with the bipod and the tripod. This optical sight may be illuminated internally for use at night and is also used for anti-aircraft fire, for which role the vz 59 is placed on top of a tubular extension to the normal tripod.

To date the vz 59 is known to have been adopted only by the Czech army, although other nations may by now have the type in use. In the past Czech

weapons have appeared wherever there is a market for small arms, and Czech weapons have thus recently turned up in the Middle East, and especially in Lebanon; some vz 52s have certainly been seen there. To date there is no record of any nation purchasing the NATO-ammunition version, but no doubt that version will turn up in some unexpected trouble spot one day.

Specification
vz 59
Calibre: 7.62 mm (0.3 in)
Weights: with bipod and light barrel 8.67 kg (19.1 lb); with tripod and heavy barrel 19.24 kg (42.42 lb)
Lengths: with light barrel 1116 mm (43.94 in); with heavy barrel 1215 mm (47.84 in); light barrel 593 mm (23.35 in); heavy barrel 693 mm (27.28 in)
Muzzle velocity: with light barrel 810 m (2,657 ft) per second, and with heavy barrel 830 m (2,723 ft) per second
Rate of fire: (cyclic) 700-800 rpm
Type of feed: 50- or 250-round belts

The Czech 7.62-mm (0.30-in) vz 59 is a development of the earlier vz 52/57, but much easier to produce. Developed with an eye to the international export market, the vz 59 has been adopted by the Czech armed forces but others crop up in various corners of the world.

5.56-mm CIS Ultimax 100

The relatively small nation of Singapore has in recent years become a major member of the international defence matériel market. Starting from virtually nothing, Singapore has rapidly built up a defence manufacturing industry and among recent products has been a light machine-gun called the **CIS Ultimax 100** or 3U-100.

The Ultimax 100 can trace its origins back to 1978. To provide a framework in which to work, the newly-formed Chartered Industries of Singapore (CIS) had obtained a licence to produce the 5.56-mm (0.219-in) Armalite AR-18 and also the Colt M16A1 rifles. Using these two weapons as a basis, CIS decided to build in some ideas of their own and the Ultimax 100 was the result. Some of the early prototypes were less than successful, but diligence and the application of some sound engineering removed the early problems, and the Ultimax 100 is now regarded as one of the best weapons in its class.

The Ultimax 100 fires the M193 5.56-mm cartridge, although there is no reason why it could not be converted to fire the new SS 109. It is a light machine-gun that is really light, for CIS was understandably keen to produce a weapon suited to the relatively light-statured personnel found in the Asian world. The result is that the Ultimax 100 handles very like an assault rifle. CIS has taken great pains to reduce recoil forces to a minimum, and has even introduced a feature it calls 'constant recoil'. With this feature the breech block does not use the back-plate of the receiver as a buffer, as is normal in many similar designs: instead a system of springs absorbs the forces and the result is a weapon that can be handled with ease and smoothness. The Ultimax 100 can be fired from the shoulder with no problems at all.

The likeness to an assault rifle is carried over to the ammunition feed. The Ultimax 100 uses a 100-round drum magazine under the body that can be changed with the same facility as a conventional box magazine. The drum magazines can be carried in a special webbing carrier. For firing on the move a forward grip is provided, and to make the weapon even handier the butt may be removed. For more accurate firing a bipod is a fixture and the barrel change is rapid and easy. If required normal M16A1 20- or 30-round box magazines can be used in place of the drum.

Already accessories for the Ultimax 100 abound. Perhaps the most unusual of them is a silencer which is used in conjunction with a special barrel. More orthodox items include a special twin mounting in which two weapons are secured on their sides with the drum magazines pointing outwards. One very unusual extra is a bayonet, a feature which few similar weapons possess. Rifle grenades can be fired from the muzzle without preparation.

To date the Ultimax 100 is available in two versions; the **Ultimax 100 Mk 2** with a fixed barrel and the **Ultimax 100 Mk 3** with the easily-changed barrel. More versions are certain, for the Ultimax 100 has a most promising future. It is already in service with the Singapore armed forces and many more nations are showing a great interest in the weapon. It is certainly one of the handiest and most attractive of the 5.56-mm light machine-guns.

The Ultimax 100 Mark 3 light machine-gun is a small and light weapon that is ideally suited for the armed forces of many South East Asian armed forces. It is light and easy to handle and after a period of development is now a reliable and efficient weapon. It is now in full-scale production in Singapore.

Specification
Ultimax 100
Calibre: 5.56 mm (0.219 in)
Weights: gun empty 4.7 kg (10.36 lb); loaded with 100-round drum 6.5 kg (14.33 lb)
Lengths: overall 1030 mm (40.55 in); barrel 508 mm (20 in)
Muzzle velocity: (M193) 990 m (3,248 ft) per second
Rate of fire: (cyclic) 400-600 rpm
Type of feed: 100-round drum, or 20- or 30-round box magazine

Below: The Ultimax 100 uses a drum magazine holding 100 5.56-mm (0.219-in) rounds. It can also use 20- or 30-round box magazines. The full 100-round drum can be filled in only 11.6 seconds, but more drums can be carried in the special carrier shown here. A bayonet can be fitted and a silencer is available.

7.62-mm PK

One very noticeable feature in Soviet small-arms design is the strange mixture of innovation and conservatism that seems to beset every generation of weapons. Despite the impact made by the then-novel 7.62-mm (0.3-in)×39 cartridge used in the AK-47 assault rifle family, Soviet machine-guns have continued to use the much more powerful 7.62-mm×54R cartridge, which retains a distinct rim at its base. This rim was originally used for extraction from the old Mosin-Nagant rifles that can be traced back to 1895, if not before, but the same round is used for the Red Army's current general-purpose machine-gun known as the **PK** series.

There are several members of the PK range. The PK is the basic gun with a heavy barrel marked by flutes along its exterior. This was first seen in 1946, and since then the **IKM** has arrived on the scene; this is an improved version of the PK that is lighter and simpler in construction. The **PKS** is a PK mounted on a tripod which can be used for anti-aircraft as well as ground fire. The **PKT** is a version for use on armoured vehicles, while the **PKM** is a PK mounted on a bipod. When the PKM is mounted on a tripod it becomes the **PKMS**. The **PKB** has the usual butt and trigger mechanism replaced by spade grips and a 'butterfly' trigger arrangement.

The PK appears to be all things to all men, and as far as the Red Army is concerned it is a true multi-role type: the PK is used in roles ranging from infantry squad support to AFV use in special mountings. All the PK machine-guns operate on the same principle, based on the Kalashnikov rotary-bolt system used in many other current Soviet weapons. The interior of the PK is populated by surprisingly few parts: there are just the bolt/breech block, a piston and a few springs. The ammunition feed makes up a few more parts, and that is about it. Thus the PK has few parts to break or jam and it is very reliable. When used in the light machine-gun role the ammunition is normally carried in a metal box slung under the gun. For tripod operation variable lengths of belt are used. In the sustained-fire role the barrel has to be changed at regular intervals even though it is chromium-plated to reduce wear (a common Soviet practice).

These PK weapons must rank among the most numerous of all modern machine-guns. They are used not only throughout the Red Army but also by many members of the Warsaw Pact. The Chinese produce a copy known as the **Type 80**. Both the PK and the Type 80 have been passed on to many nations in the third world and some are now in the hands of 'freedom fighters'.

The one odd thing regarding the PK series is the retention of the old rimmed 7.62-mm cartridge. Even the conservative British discarded their beloved 7.7-mm (0.303-in) cartridge decades ago, but the Soviets appear to be more conservative still. Thus there originated the odd alliance of the superb PK machine-gun with all its many fine points and a cartridge that was developed during the 1890s.

Specification
PK
Calibre: 7.62 mm (0.3 in)
Weights: gun empty 9 kg (19.84 lb);
tripod 7.5 kg (16.53 lb); 100-round belt
2.44 kg (5.38 lb)
Lengths: gun 1160 mm (45.67 in);
barrel 658 mm (25.91 in)
Muzzle velocity: 825 m (2,707 ft) per
second
Rate of fire: (cyclic) 690-720 rpm
Type of feed: 100-, 200- and 250-round
belts

*The Soviet 7.62-mm (0.30-in) PK
machine-gun is seen here in its light
machine-gun form as the PKM. It is a
simple and sturdy weapon with few
moving parts, and is widely used by
many Warsaw Pact armed forces and
other forces around the world.*

USSR
7.62-mm RPK

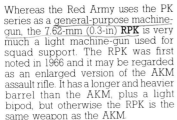

*Seen here in the hands of a Bulgarian
paratrooper, the RPK is used by
many Warsaw Pact armies as a
squad fire support weapon.
Developed from the AKM, it fires the
same 7.62-mm (0.30-in) ammunition
as the rifle but uses a larger 40-round
box magazine. The barrel cannot be
changed.*

Whereas the Red Army uses the PK
series as a general-purpose machine-
gun, the 7.62-mm (0.3-in) RPK is very
much a light machine-gun used for
squad support. The RPK was first
noted in 1966 and it may be regarded
as an enlarged version of the AKM
assault rifle. It has a longer and heavier
barrel than the AKM, plus a light
bipod, but otherwise the RPK is the
same weapon as the AKM.

This commonality of weapons
makes a great deal of sense. The AKM

fires exactly the same 7.62-mm×39
ammunition as the assault rifle, but the
commonality goes further. Some spare
parts can be interchanged between
the two weapons, and any soldier who
can use the AKM (and that means all of
them) can pick up and fire the RPK
with equal facility. If the special 75-
round drum magazine of the RPK is not
available any magazine from an AKM
can be fitted in its place. One thing the
Soviet soldier will miss if he ever has to
use the RPK in close action is that it

does not have a mounting bracket for a
bayonet.

Considering that the weapon is intended as a light machine-gun, it is
surprising that the RPK does not have
provision for changing the barrel when
it gets hot. In order to ensure the barrel
does not overheat, recruits are trained
to limit burst-firing to about 80 shots
per minute. For most tactical purposes
this will be more than adequate, but
there must be times when this fire rate
will have its disadvantages. Apart from
the 75-round drum already mentioned,
there are curved box magazines holding 30 or 40 rounds. Some RPKs have
been seen with infra-red night sights.
A copy produced by the Chinese is
known as the **Type 74**.

In recent years the Red Army has
changed its standard rifle calibre to
the new 5.45-mm (0.2146-in)×18 cartridge. For this round the AK-74 rifle
was developed, and it follows that a
new version of the RPK would follow. It
has now appeared as the **RPK-74**.
Apart from the scaling down of some
parts to suit the smaller calibre, the
RPK-74 is in overall terms identical
with the RPK.

The RPK appears to be a popular
weapon with the Red Army and the
many Warsaw Pact nations to which it
has been delivered. The type appears
to be produced in East Germany and
as far as can be determined the RPK is
still in production in the Soviet Union
(and China). It has been handed out to

some nations sympathetic to the Soviet
way of thinking, and needless to say
the RPK has found its way into the
hands of many 'freedom fighters'. RPKs
were observed during the recent
fighting in Lebanon and more have
been seen in action in Angola. Despite
its rate-of-fire limitations, the RPK will
no doubt be around for many years to
come, and the Red Army still retains
huge numbers of the type despite the
introduction of the RPK-74.

Specification
RPK
Calibre: 7.62 mm (0.3 in)
Weights: gun 5 kg (11.02 lb); 75-round
drum 2.1 kg (4.63 lb)
Lengths: gun 1035 mm (40.75 in);
barrel 591 mm (23.27 in)
Muzzle velocity: 732 m (2,402 ft) per
second
Rate of fire: (cyclic) 660 rpm and
(practical) 80 rpm
Type of feed: 75-round drum, or 30-
and 40-round box magazines

*The Soviet RPK is the standard
Warsaw Pact squad fire support
weapon. It does not have an
interchangeable barrel and so is not
capable of sustained fire. The design
may be regarded as a development
of the AKM assault rifle, and it fires
the same 7.62-mm (0.30-in)
ammunition. A Chinese version is
known as the Type 74.*

An Iraqi machine gunner takes aim with his RPK at Iranian positions from a bunker on one of the Gulf War fronts. The RPK is not really designed for operating from fixed positions as it is too light for the sustained fire role and does not have a quick change barrel. It does have the advantage of using the same ammunition as the rest of the rifle squad, and anyone familiar with the AK rifle will not find using the RPK a problem.

USSR
Ruchnoy Pulemyot Degtyarev (RPD)

Soviet designers have always been conservative in machine-gun design and when the **RPD** arrived on the scene in the early 1950s the continuation of a line through the DP, DPM and RP46 light machine-guns was very evident. However the RPD did have some innovations of its own and it has proved to be such a successful weapon that many remain in widespread use to this day.

The RPD may be regarded as the squad support weapon equivalent to the AK-47 assault rifle. It fired the same 7.62-mm (0.30-in) short cartridge and used a gas-operated mechanism that had much in common with that of the AK-47. Over the years many modifications have been made to the RPD and its mechanism to improve component life and overall accuracy, but it has always remained a typical Soviet design in that it is robust, simple and efficient.

The RPD uses a belt feed but the problem of ammunition belts flapping around to pick up dirt or snag on anything nearby has been overcome by the introduction of a drum holding a belt of 100 rounds ready to feed. The belt is held at the centre of gravity to assist carrying, but the gas-operated mechanism has a bit of a task to lift and feed a fully-loaded belt and if the belt or mechanism is dirty or even slightly damaged malfunctions can occur. Another potential problem carried over from earlier designs is that the barrel is not removable for changing when hot, and the barrel can become overheated after only a few prolonged bursts. RPD gunners therefore have to be trained to keep bursts short and not too frequent to prevent jamming. The RPD can fire on automatic only.

Although no longer in production in the USSR, the RPD was (and still is) widely issued throughout the Warsaw Pact armed forces, although no longer as a front-line weapon as it has largely been replaced by the later RPK. Elsewhere it is still in the front line and may be encountered in armies as diverse as those of Pakistan, Egypt and Angola. In China the RPD is still being produced as the **Type 56** and is being offered for export to all who will buy. There have been some takers, for the RPD is now likely to be encountered throughout the Middle East, usually in irregular hands. It has been observed in action in Lebanon and is one of the weapons used by the PLO.

Specification
RPD
Calibre: 7.62 mm (0.30 in)
Weight: gun only 7.1 kg (15.65 lb)
Length: overall 1036 mm (40.78 in); barrel 521 mm (20.5 in)
Muzzle velocity: about 700 m (2,297 ft) per second
Rate of fire: (cyclic) 700 rpm
Feed: 100-round belt

Designed in 1943 to take the new 7.62-mm × 39 cartridge, the RPD was introduced in the 1950s as the squad support weapon to complement the AK-47. The Soviets have no illusions about the standard of conscripts' rifle shooting, and have always relied on their machine-guns.

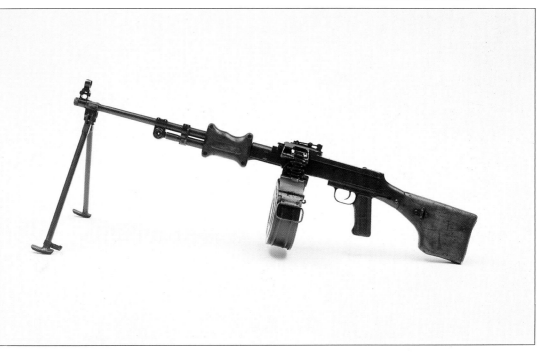

7.62-mm M60

The **M60** is a general-purpose machine-gun that can trace its origins back to the latter period of World War II, when it was known as the **T44**. The design was greatly influenced by the new German machine-gun designs: the ammunition feed is a direct lift from the MG42, and the piston and bolt assembly was copied from the revolutionary 7.92-mm (0.312-in) Fallschirmjägergewehr 42 (FG42). The T44 and its production version, the M60, made extensive use of steel stampings and plastics, and the first examples were issued for service with the US Army during the late 1950s.

These first examples were not a success. They handled badly and some of the detail design was such that changing a barrel involved taking half the weapon apart. These early difficulties were gradually eliminated, and the M60 is now as efficient a weapon as any, but many serving soldiers still profess not to like the weapon for its generally awkward handling properties. But the M60 is the US Army's first general-purpose machine-gun, and it now serves in a host of roles.

In its basic form as a squad support weapon, the M60 is fitted with a stamped steel bipod mounted just behind the muzzle. For this purpose it is carried by a small handle which is rather flimsy for the loads placed on it; moreover the point of balance of the handle is entirely wrong. Instead many soldiers prefer to use a sling, and the weapon is often fired on the move while being steadied by the sling. For the light machine-gun role the M60 is a bit hefty, but it will be replaced in the

near future by the 5.56-mm (0.219-in) M249 Minimi for the US Army. For heavier use the M60 can be mounted on a tripod or on a vehicle pedestal mount.

Some special versions of the M60 have been produced. The **M60C** is a remotely-fired version for external mounting on helicopters. The **M60D** is a pintle-mounted version with no butt for mounting in helicopter gunships and some vehicles. The **M60E2** is a much-altered variant for use as a co-axial gun on armoured vehicles.

Throughout much of its production life the M60 has been manufactured by the Saco Defense Systems Division of the Maremount Corporation, which was always aware of the shortcomings of the M60's design, especially in the light machine-gun role. Accordingly the company has now produced what

it calls the **Maremount Lightweight Machine-Gun**, which is the M60 much modified to reduce weight and improve handling. The bipod has been moved back under the receiver and a foregrip has been added. The gas-operated mechanism has been simplified, and there is now provision for a winter trigger. The result is a much lighter and handier weapon than the original, although it can now be used only for the light machine-gun role. The new weapon is currently undergoing evaluation trials by several armies.

The M60 is now in service with several armies other than the US Army. Taiwan not only uses the M60 but produces it as well. South Korea is another Asian operator, while farther south the Australian army also has the M60 in service.

The American M60 is a rather bulky and heavy weapon that is awkward to handle. First produced in the late 1940s, it underwent a protracted development programme before it entered service in the late 1950s, and has been widely used ever since. It now a reliable and efficient weapon used by several armies.

Specification
M60
Calibre: 7.62 mm (0.3 in)
Weights: gun 10.51 kg (23.17 lb); barrel 3.74 kg (8.245 lb)
Lengths: gun overall 1105 mm (43.5 in barrel 559 mm (22 in)
Muzzle velocity: 855 m (2,805 ft) per second
Rate of fire: (cyclic) 550 rpm
Type of feed: 50-round belt

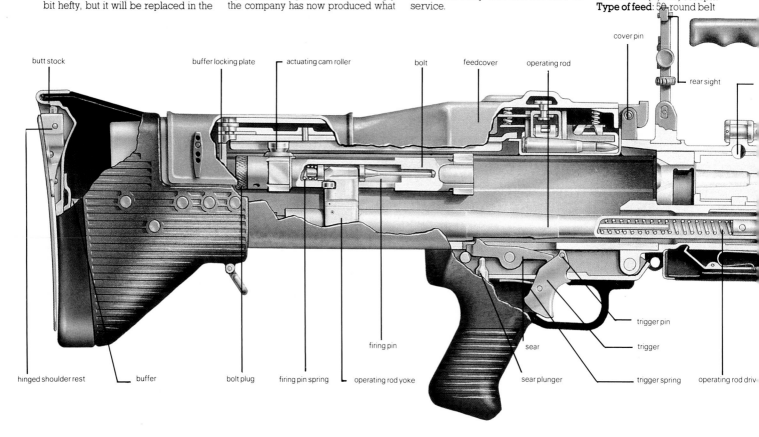

Above: An M60 light machine-gun team in action during troop exercises in South Korea, where the M60 is used not only by the US Army and Marine Corps but also by the Republic of Korea (ROK) troops. Other nations that use the M60 include Australia and Taiwan, and some have passed into guerrilla hands, including the IRA.

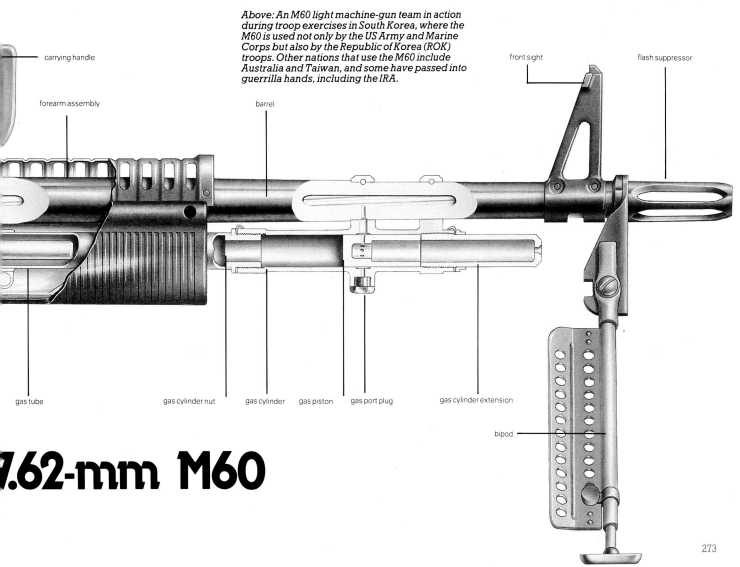

carrying handle

forearm assembly

barrel

front sight

flash suppressor

gas tube

gas cylinder nut

gas cylinder

gas piston

gas port plug

gas cylinder extension

bipod

7.62-mm M60

Browning M1919 machine-guns

USA

The **Browning M1919** series differed from the earlier M1917 series in that the original water-cooled barrel was replaced by an air-cooled barrel. This air-cooled model was originally intended for use in the many tanks the United States was going to produce, but the end of World War I led to the tank contracts being cancelled along with those for the original M1919. But the air-cooled Browning was developed into the **M1919A1**, the **M1919A2** (for use by the US Cavalry) and then the **M1919A3**. The production totals for these early models were never very high, but with the **M1919A4** the totals soared. By 1945 the production total stood at 438,971 and more have been produced since then.

The M1919A4 was produced mainly for infantry use and it proved to be a first-class heavy machine-gun capable of pouring out masses of fire and absorbing all manner of abuse and punishment. As a partner for this infantry version, a special model for use on tanks was produced as the **M1919A5**. There was also a special US Air Force model, the **M2**, for use on both fixed wing and flexible installations, and the US Navy had its own range based on the M1919A4 and known as the **AN-M2**.

Among all these types and in such a long production run there were numerous minor and major modifications and production alterations, but the basic M1919 design was retained throughout. The basic M1919 used a fabric or metal-link belt feed. The normal mount was a tripod, and of these there were many designs ranging from normal infantry tripods to large and complex anti-aircraft mountings. There were ring- and gallows-type mountings for use on all sorts of trucks from jeeps to fuel tankers, and there were numerous special mountings for all manner of small craft.

Perhaps the strangest of the M1919 variants was the **M1919A6**. This was produced as a form of light machine-gun to bolster infantry squad power, which until the introduction of the M1919A6 had to depend on the fire-power of the BAR and the rifle. The M1919A6 was a 1943 innovation: it was basically the M1919A4 fitted with an awkward-looking shoulder stock, a bipod, a carrying handle and a lighter

Above: A Browning M1919A4 machine-gun on its normal tripod and clearly showing the perforated barrel cooling jacket and the square receiver; it was produced in huge numbers and the type is still in use all over the world.

A Long Range Desert Group Jeep armed with Vickers-Berthier G.O. machine-guns and with a Browning M1919A4 mounted at the front; this gun has every appearance of being adapted from an aircraft mounting.

barrel. The result was a rather heavy light machine-gun that at least had the advantage that it could be produced quickly on existing production lines. Disadvantages were the general awkwardness of the weapon and the need to wear a mitten to change the barrel when it got hot. For all that the M1919A6 was churned out in large numbers (43,479 by the time production ended), and the troops had to put up with it, for it was better in its role than the BAR.

If there was one overall asset that was enjoyed by all the versions of the M1919 series of machine-guns it was reliability, for the types would carry on working even in conditions in which other designs (other than perhaps the Vickers) would have given up. They all used the same basic recoil method: muzzle gases push back the entire barrel and breech mechanism until a bolt accelerator continues the rearward movement to a point at which springs

return the whole mechanism to restart the process. The M1919 series (including the unlovely M1919A6) is still in widespread use, although the M1919A6 is now used by only a few South American states.

Specification
M1919A4
Calibre: 7.62 mm (0.3 in)
Length: 1041 mm (41.0 in)
Length of barrel: 610 mm (24.0 in)
Weight: 14.06 kg (31 lb)
Muzzle velocity: 854 m (2,800 ft) per

second
Rate of fire, cyclic: 400-500 rpm
Feed: 250-round belt

Specification
M1919A6
Calibre: 7.62 mm (0.3 in)
Length: 1346 mm (53.0 in)
Length of barrel: 610 mm (24.0 in)
Weight: 14.74 kg (32.5 lb)
Muzzle velocity: 854 m (2,800 ft) per second
Rate of fire, cyclic: 400-500 rpm
Feed: 250-round belt

Browning 12.7-mm (0.5-in) heavy machine-guns

USA

Ever since the first Browning 12.7-mm (0.5-in) heavy machine-gun was produced in 1921 the type has been one of the most fearsome anti-personnel weapons likely to be encountered. The projectile fired by the type is a prodigious man-stopper, and the machine-gun can also be used as an armour-defeating weapon, especially when firing armour-piercing rounds. The round is really the heart of the gun, and early attempts by Browning to produce a heavy machine-gun all foundered on the lack of a suitable cartridge.

The classic Browning machine-gun on its usual tripod. It was first placed in production in 1921 and remains so, as it is one of the best anti-personnel weapons ever developed; it also has a very useful anti-armour capability.

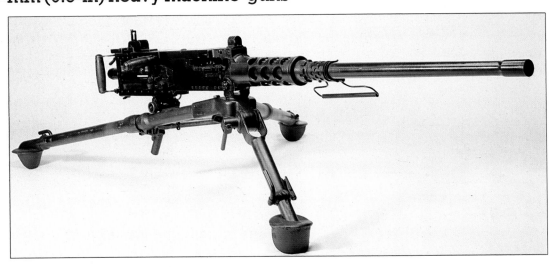

It was not until the examination of a captured German 13-mm (0.51-in) round (used in the Mauser T-Gewehr anti-tank rifle) that the solution was found, and thereafter all was well. The basic cartridge has remained essentially unchanged, although there have been numerous alternative propellants and types of projectile.

From the original **Browning M1921** heavy machine-gun evolved a whole string of variants based on what was to become known as the **M2**. On all these variants the gun mechanism remained the same, being very similar to that used on the smaller M1917 machine-gun. Where the variants differed from each other was in the type of barrel fitted and the fixtures used for mounting the gun.

One of the most numerous of the M2s has been the **M2 HB**, the suffix denoting the use of a Heavy Barrel. The HB version can be used in all manner of installations and in the past has been employed as an infantry gun, as an anti-aircraft gun and even as a fixed or trainable aircraft gun. For infantry use the M2 HB is usually mounted on a heavy tripod, but it can also be used mounted on vehicle pintles, ring mountings and pivots. Other M2 types include versions with water-cooled barrels, which were usually employed as anti-aircraft weapons, especially on US Navy vessels where during World War II they were often fixed in multiple mountings for use against low-flying attack aircraft. Single water-cooled mountings were often used to provide anti-aircraft defence for shore installations. The main change between ground-based and aircraft versions was that the aircraft model had a barrel 914 mm (36 in) long whereas the ground version had a barrel 1143 mm (45 in) long. Apart from the barrel and some mounting fixtures, any part of the M1921 and M2 machine-guns can be interchanged.

Although it is a very old design, the M2 has come back into favour with a number of armies. The British Army rushed examples back into service for the recapture of the Falklands, and a number of captured Argentine weapons have since been refurbished. Such is demand for the M2 in recent years that production has been resumed in the USA by Saco Defence and in Belgium by FN. Product improved models have quick change barrels, special low-recoil mountings, and considerably less weight to enable the M2 to be used from light aircraft and boats. New high and low impulse ranges of ammunition are being developed as are APHE and incendiary rounds.

The M2 will be around for decades to come, and there is no sign of any replacement. It must rank as one of the most successful machine-gun designs ever produced.

This anti-aircraft mounting, known as the M45 Maxson Mount, used four heavy barrelled Browning M2s.

Length of barrel: 1143 mm (45.0 in)
Weight: 38.1 kg (84 lb)
Weight of tripod: 19.96 kg (44 lb) for M3 type
Muzzle velocity: 884 m (2,900 ft) per seond
Rate of fire, cyclic: 450-575 rpm
Feed: 110-round metal-link belt

Specification
M2 HB
Calibre: 12.7 mm (0.5 in)
Length: 1654 mm (65.1 in)

SOUTH AFRICA
SS-77 light machine-gun

The South African Defence Forces have gained considerable experience of bush warfare in recent years, and have learned the hard way that the locally made or modified FN MAG and 0.30-in Browning machine-guns were not really suitable for their requirements. In the late 1970s however, the South Africans could not go out and order the weapon they wanted, due to the UN sponsored arms embargo. They had to make it themselves, and in 1977 the Lyttleton Engineering Works began to analyse examples of as many machine-gun designs as they could obtain. Copying parts from one and ideas from another, they combined several desirable features into a new design now known as the **SS 77**.

The designers wanted a general purpose machine-gun lighter than existing weapons, and the SS-77 weighs in at 9.6 kg (21.16 lb). It is a conventional gas-operated type, belt-fed and with a quick change air-cooled barrel like the FN MAG. When used as an LMG the belt is carried in a pouch secured beneath the receiver. It can deliver sustained fire from a heavy tripod, the mounting points on the SS-77 being so arranged that it can be used with a variety of existing mounts. A light bipod can be fitted, and the butt folds to reduce overall length when the gun is being carried through brush. The gas regulator has three positions allowing an increased flow of gas when the system is fouled, although it can also be used to adjust the rate of fire. The lowest position allows the least emission of gas, so enabling the SS-77 to be fired safely from within a vehicle.

While many features are taken from other designs, the SS-77 has some original points. There is a groove on the loading table which will hold ammunition belts when the loading cover is open, freeing the gunner's hand when it is most needed during loading. Similar detail innovations, particularly affecting the sights and safety mechanism, have resulted in a handy and well balanced weapon.

Although development started in 1977, it was an intermittent process which occasionally came to a halt for economic or political reasons. Full production began at the end of 1986 with the production version having a slightly revised butt outline when compared with the prototypes. All SS-77s will be issued with two tool rolls containing cleaning items and spare parts and will be available with the usual accessories such as slings and indirect-fire sights.

Specification
Calibre: 7.62 mm NATO (0.30-in)
Length: 1155 mm (45.47 in)
Barrel length: 550 mm (21.65 in)
Weight, unloaded: 9.6 kg (21.16 lb)
Muzzle velocity: 840 m (2,756 ft) per second
Rate of fire, cyclic: 600-900 rpm
Feed: 100-round belts

The SS-77 light machine-gun is typical of the South African approach to weapons manufacture in the face of the United Nations embargo. It combines useful features from a number of other guns to create a product as good as any in the world but tailored to the SADF's demanding operational requirements.

🇬🇧 7.62-mm Bren Gun

When considering modern machine-guns, it seems something of a surprise that a weapon as old as the **Bren Gun** should be included, especially as this weapon can be traced back as far as the early 1930s. But the original Bren Guns were chambered for the 7.7-mm (0.303-in) rimmed cartridge, and when the decision was made to convert to the new standard NATO 7.62-mm (0.3-in) cartridge the British armed forces still had large stockpiles of the Bren Gun to hand. It made sound commercial sense to convert them for the new calibre, and such a programme was soon put into effect at the Royal Small Arms Factory at Enfield Lock in Middlesex.

The conversion to the new calibre entailed a complete overhaul, but the task was made easier by the fact that during World War II a Canadian company produced numbers of Bren Guns in 7.92-mm (0.312-in) calibre for China. As this round was rimless, it was found that the breechblocks intended for the 'China contract' were equally suitable for the new 7.62-mm cartridge and these were used in place of the originals. A new barrel was produced with a chromium-plated interior. This not only diminished wear on the barrel but also reduced the need for the frequent barrel-changes required on World War II versions. Thus the new gun was issued with only the one barrel.

The current version of the Bren Gun used by the British Army is the L4A4. This is not used as a front-line infantry weapon, but instead is issued to the many other arms of the service who require a machine-gun. Thus the L4A4 is used by the Royal Artillery for anti-aircraft and ground-defence of its bat-teries, by the Royal Signals for the defence of its installations in the field, by units assigned for home defence, and so on. The L4A4 is also used by the Royal Air Force, and a version known as the **L4A5** is used by the Royal Navy. There is also a version known as the **L4A3** that is not often encountered as it is a conversion of the old Bren Mk 2 gun; the L4A4 is a conversion of the improved Bren Mk 3.

In all these versions the gas-operated mechanism of the original Bren Gun remains unchanged. So few are the changes involved in the change of calibre that the only points of note are that the 7.62-mm version uses a nearly-vertical magazine in place of the old curved equivalent, and the muzzle lacks the pronounced cone-shape of the old weapon.

For the anti-aircraft role the L4A4 has been fitted with some fairly sophisticated sighting arrangements. The L4A4 does not use a tripod as did the old Bren Guns, but instead it can be mounted on the roof hatches of self-propelled guns and howitzers as well as on other armoured vehicles.

So the old Bren Gun soldiers on in a new form, and there seems to be no sign of its passing from use in the foreseeable future. Many of the Commonwealth nations still use the Bren, some in its original 7.7-mm form, so although the original design may be old the weapon is still regarded as effective and in its L4A4 form the old Bren Gun is as good as many far more modern designs.

The latest version of the venerable wartime Bren Gun is the British L4A4, chambered for the NATO 7.62-mm (0.30-in) round. It has a new barrel, breech block and a new vertical 30-round box magazine and is now used by support and second-line British Army units.

Specification
L4A4
Calibre: 7.62 mm (0.3 in)
Weights: gun only 9.53 kg (21 lb); barrel 2.72 kg (6 lb)
Lengths: gun 1133 mm (44.6 in); barrel 536 mm (21.1 in)
Muzzle velocity: 823 m (2,700 ft) per second
Rate of fire: (cyclic) 500 rpm
Type of feed: 30-round box

🇬🇧 5.56-mm Light Support Weapon (LSW)

For many years the standard squad light machine-gun for the British army has been a version of the FN MAG fitted with a bipod and known as the L7A2. While this is a fine weapon, it is rather a cumbersome load and it fires a cartridge that is now generally considered too powerful for the squad-support role. With the imminent arrival of the Enfield Weapon System (or Small Arms 80, otherwise SA 80), the L7A2 is due to be replaced in the squad support role by a new weapon currently known as the **L86A1 Light Support Weapon** or LSW; the L7A2 will be retained for the sustained-fire function for some years to come.

The LSW is one half of the Enfield Weapon System, the other component being the Individual Weapon or IW, which will be the standard rifle while the LSW will become the squad-support weapon. The two new weapons have many things in common and can be easily recognized as coming from the same stable, but the LSW has a heavier barrel and a light bipod mounted well forward under the barrel. There is also a rear grip under what might be regarded as the butt to provide the firer with a better hold for sustained firing.

The term butt is rather misleading as the LSW is based on a 'bullpup' layout in which the trigger group is placed foward of the magazine. This arrangement makes the LSW more compact than a conventional weapon. Much of the LSW is steel, but the foregrip and

With the FN rifle gradually being replaced by the 5.56-mm Individual Weapon, the British Army is adopting a squad support weapon of the same calibre to replace the FN MAG general purpose machine-gun. The latter will be retained for the sustained fire role.

the pistol grip for the trigger are tough nylonite. The LSW uses the same magazine as the IW, namely a standard M16A1 30-round box.

The LSW has undergone several changes of calibre since it was first mooted. Originally it was calibred for the British experimental 4.85-mm (0.19-in) cartridge, but this was over-ruled in favour of the American M193 cartridge, which in turn was super-seded yet again in favour of the new NATO standard 5.56-mm (0.219-in) SS 109. The first production versions will be for the SS 109 round, and will also have an optical sight known as the Sight Unit Small Arms Trilux or SUSAT mounted on a bracket over the receiver. It will be possible to change this sight for some form of night sight.

Seen here in front of the GPMG is the 4.85-mm version of the Light Support Weapon, produced to complement the proposed 4.85-mm rifle. When NATO adopted the Belgian 5.56-mm round as standard, the 4.85-mm designs were abandoned despite their superior performance.

The Light Support Weapon shares many components with the 5.56-mm rifle; obvious differences are the heavy barrel, the bipod and the rear grip. The LSW uses the same magazine as the Individual Weapon, the 30-round M16A1 box.

A number of accessories are being produced for the LSW as it enters service with the British Army. A training adapter firing low-powered ammunition will be available, as will a blank-firing attachment. A multi-purpose tool is already in use for stripping and first-line repairs, and it will be possible to fit a sling for carrying. The muzzle attachment is so arranged that it is possible for rifle grenades to be fired from the muzzle, although it is not envisaged that the LSW will be used extensively for this purpose.

The LSW has undergone a protracted development period, some of the period being elongated by the change of NATO standard calibre and other considerations. This has had a beneficial side-effect in that it has entered troop service with many of the snags which hit new weapons already ironed out.

Specification
LSW
Calibre: 5.56 mm (0.219 in)
Weights: gun complete and loaded 6.88 kg (15.17 lb); gun less magazine and sight 5.6 kg (12.346 lb)

Lengths: overall 900 mm (35.43 in); barrel 646 mm (25.43 in)
Muzzle velocity: 970 m (3,182 ft) per second
Rate of fire: (cyclic) 700-850 rpm
Type of feed: 30-round box magazine

FRANCE
7.5-mm AA 52

Above: The French Foreign Legion use exactly the same weapons as the rest of the French army and so the AA 52 machine-gun, seen here in its light machine-gun form, is a familiar sight wherever the legion operates.

The machine-gun now known as the **AA 52** was designed and developed directly as a result of the Indo-China campaigns of the early 1950s. At that time the French army was equipped with a wide array of American, British and ex-German weapons, and the furnishing of support and spares for this array was too much for the army, which decided to adopt one standard general-purpose machine-gun. The result was the 7.5-mm (0.295-in) AA 52, a weapon designed from the outset for ease of production, and thus making much use of stampings and welded components.

The AA 52 is unusual among modern machine-guns in relying on a form of delayed-blowback operation, in which the force of the cartridge firing is employed to force back the breech block to the starting position, and also to power the feed mechanism. This system works very well with pistol cartridges in sub-machine guns, but using rifle cartridges in machine-guns demands something more positive if safety is to be regarded. On the AA 52 a two-part block is used: a lever device is so arranged that it holds the forward part of the block in position while the rear half starts to move to the rear; only when the lever has moved a predetermined distance does it allow the forward part of the block to move back. In order to make the spent cartridge easier to extract the chamber has

grooves that allow gas to enter between the chamber wall and the fired cartridge to prevent 'sticking', and a cartridge fired from an AA 52 can always be recognized by the fluted grooves around the case neck.

The AA 52 can be fired from a bipod or a tripod, but when a tripod is used for the sustained fire role a heavy barrel is fitted to the weapon. When used in the light machine-gun role the AA 52 is a rather clumsy weapon to carry, especially if a 50-round ammunition box is carried on the left-hand side. For this reason the box is often left off and the ammunition belt allowed to hang free. One unusual feature of the AA 52 is that for the light machine-gun role a monopod is fitted under the butt. This can be awkward at times, and another awkward point is the barrel change: the barrel can be removed readily enough, but the bipod is permanently attached to the barrel and in the light machine-gun role this can make barrel-changing very difficult, especially as the AA 52 barrels have no form of barrel plating that might reduce the temperature of the gun and barrel.

The AA 52 was originally intended to fire a 7.5-mm (0.295-in) cartridge first developed for use by the mle 1929 light machine-gun. This cartridge is powerful enough, but the switch to the NATO 7.62-mm (0.3 in) cartridge left the French army using a non-standard cartridge, and export prospects for the AA 52 were thus reduced. The basic

design has therefore been adapted to fire the NATO cartridge in a version known as the **NF-1**. Some of these have been issued to French army units, but exports have not materialized.

Overall the AA 52 is an adequate machine-gun, but it has many features (some of them regarded by some nations as inherently unsafe) that are at best undesirable. The weapon is no longer in production but is still offered for export.

Specification
AA 52
Calibre: 7.5 mm (0.295 in)
Weights: with bipod and light barrel 9.97 kg (21.98 lb); with bipod and heavy barrel 11.37 kg (25.07 lb); tripod 10.6 kg (23.37 lb)
Lengths: with butt extended (light barrel) 1145 mm (45.08 in) or (heavy barrel) 1245 mm (49.02 in); light barrel only 500 mm (19.69 in); heavy barrel only 600 mm (23.62 in)
Muzzle velocity: 840 m (2,756 ft) per second
Rate of fire: (cyclic) 700 rpm
Type of feed: 50-round belt

The French AA 52 uses a delayed blowback mechanism with a fluted chamber to ease extraction. A 7.62-mm (0.30-in) version known as the AA 7.62 NF-1 may also be encountered, but neither model is now in production. Bipod and tripod versions are in use, as are vehicle-mounted models.

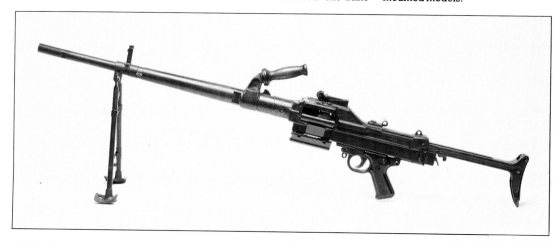

Heckler & Koch machine-guns

The West German concern Heckler & Koch, based at Oberndorf-Neckar, is among the most prolific of all modern small-arms designers, and in addition to its successful range of assault rifles and sub-machine guns it also produces a wide variety of machine-guns. It may be an oversimplification, but Heckler & Koch machine-guns are basically modified versions of the company's G-3 and associated assault rifles. They all use the same delay-roller mechanism on their breech blocks, and some of the light machine-guns are simply rifles with heavier barrels and a bipod. To confuse the issue, Heckler & Koch produce virtually every model in belt- and magazine-fed versions, and some are produced in 7.62-mm (0.3-in) NATO or 5.56-mm (0.219-in) calibres, with the added variation in the latter for the new SS 109 cartridge or the older American M193.

One of the 'base' models in the range is the 7.62-mm **HK 21A1**, a development of the earlier **HK 21** which is no longer in production. The HK 21A1 uses a belt feed and may be used as a light machine-gun on a bipod or in the sustained-fire role on a tripod. For the latter, barrel changing is incorporated. Even in this version of the Heckler & Koch range the outline of the G-3 is apparent, and this is carried over to the latest versions of the HK 21, the **HK 21E**, which has a longer sight radius and a three-round burst selection feature. The barrel is longer, and changes have been made to the ammunition feed. There is also a 5.56mm counterpart to this variant, and this is known as the **HK 23E**.

All the variants mentioned above are belt-fed weapons. There is also a magazine-fed version for every one of them: the **HK 11A1** is the magazine counterpart of the HK 21A1, while the **HK 11E** and **HK 13E** are the magazine counterparts of the HK 21E and HK 23E.

All this may sound rather confusing, but the basic factor that emerges is the ability of Heckler & Koch to produce a machine-gun suited to virtually any requirement. The belt-fed versions may be regarded as general-purpose machine-guns (although the 5.56-mm versions may really be too light for the sustained-fire role), and the magazine-fed versions as true light machine-guns. They offer a surprising amount of interchangeability of spare parts, and the magazines are usually the same as those used on their equivalent assault rifles, making the use of the automatic guns as squad support weapons even easier.

Specification
HK 21A1
Calibre: 7.62 mm (0.3 in)
Weights: gun with bipod 8.3 kg (18.3 lb); barrel 1.7 kg (3.75 lb); 100-round ammunition box 3.6 kg (7.94 lb)
Lengths: overall 1030 m (40.55 in); barrel 450 mm (17.72 in)
Muzzle velocity: 800 m (2,625 ft) per second
Rate of fire: (cyclic) 900 rpm
Type of feed: 100-round belt

The HK 21A1 is a development of the earlier HK 21. It uses a belt feed only, but the belt can be contained in a box slung under the receiver.

The Heckler & Koch HK 11 is the box magazine feed variant of the HK 21 and is a 7.62-mm (0.30-in) weapon.

The Heckler & Koch HK 13 is produced in several versions. This model accommodates a 40-round box magazine.

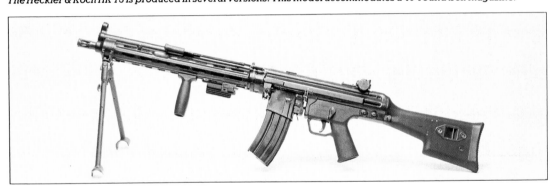

The Heckler & Koch HK 13E has a three-round burst capability as well as full automatic fire.

The Heckler & Koch HK 21 is no longer produced, but is still in use with nations such as Portugal.

WEST GERMANY
7.62 mm MG3

One of the outstanding machine-gun designs of World War II was the MG42, a weapon that introduced the advantages of mass production to an area of weapon design that had for long clung to traditional methods of construction. With the MG42, the new era of steel pressings, welds and the elimination of many machining processes was allied to an excellent design that attracted widespread respect and attention. Thus, when the Federal Republic of Germany became a member of NATO and was once more allowed a measure of weapon production for rearmament, the MG42 was one of the first designs to be resurrected.

The original MG42 had a calibre of 7.92 mm (0.312 in), but with the adoption of the standard NATO 7.62-mm (0.3-in) round the old design was reworked to accommodate the new calibre. At first stockpiled MG42s

were simply modified to this calibre with the designation **MG2**, but in parallel with this activity a production programme was under way by Rheinmetall to produce new weapons in 7.62-mm calibre. There were several variants of this production version, all having the designation **MG1**, although there were some minor changes to suit ammunition feed and so on. The current production version is the **MG3**, still manufactured by Rheinmetall.

In appearance, the war-time MG42 and the MG3 are identical apart from some minor details, few of which can be detected by the untrained eye, and there are more changes between the MG1 and MG3. Overall, however, the modern MG3 retains all the attributes of the original, and many of the mountings used with the MG3 are just adaptations or modifications of the World War II originals. Thus the MG3

can be used on a tripod that is virtually identical to the original, and the twin mounting for anti-aircraft use could still accommodate the MG42 without trouble. There are now available many mountings for the MG3.

The original MG42 was designed for ease of mass production, and this same feature makes the MG3 very suitable for manufacture in some of the less well-equipped arsenals that now abound in 'third-world' nations. The MG3 has proved to be relatively easy for such facilities and it is now licence-produced in nations such as Pakistan, Chile, Spain and Turkey; some of these nations fabricate versions of the MG1 rather than the MG3 proper. Yugoslavia also produces a version of this weapon, but the Yugoslav model is a direct copy of the MG42, still in 7.92-mm calibre and designated **SARAC M1953**.

Within NATO the MG3, or one or other of its variants, are used by the Bundeswehr, by the Italian armed forces, and by nations such as Denmark and Norway. Portugal makes the MG3 for use by the Portuguese armed forces, and is now offering the type for export. Thus from many sources the old MG42 design soldiers on. There is even talk of further development to produce a lighter version, but this is proceeding at a low priority, for the basic design of the MG3 is still as sound as it ever was, and any attempt to improve or modify the original appears to many to be an exercise about as fruitful as redesigning the wheel.

Specification
MG3
Calibre: 7.62 mm (0.3 in)
Weights: basic gun 10.5 kg (23.15 lb); bipod 0.55 kg (1.213 lb); barrel 1.8 kg (3.97 lb)
Lengths: gun with butt 1225 mm (48.23 in); gun less butt 1097 mm (43.19 in); barrel 531 mm (20.91 in)
Muzzle velocity: 820 m (2,690 ft) per second
Rate of fire: (cyclic) 700-1,300 rpm
Type of feed: 50-round belt

The West German MG3 is the modern version of the wartime MG42, and is currently rated as one of the best machine-guns of its type used by NATO. It has a high rate of fire and an easy and rapid barrel change, and can be fired from the bipod shown or from a heavy tripod for the sustained fire support role.

BRAZIL
7.62-mm Uirapuru Mekanika

Over recent decades Brazil has changed from being a defence-equipment importer to a nation that exports over 95 per cent of its defence industry's produce. The nation has undoubted talent for the defence-based industries, and in an effort to harness some of this talent to producing small arms a design team was established in the early 1960s to develop a general-purpose machine-gun. This first design team was led by a team of three experts, but while its initial designs worked they had many inherent problems. These were too numerous for the possibility of acceptance by the Brazilian army, who turned the design problem over to a private concern. This fared no better than the original team, so one of the original triumvirate took over the project on his own.

Using the facilities of a design and research establishment, this individual approach worked. Thus there emerged a design now known as the **Uirapuru Mekanika** after a Brazilian jungle bird. The Uirapuru is a general-purpose machine-gun firing standard NATO 7.62-mm (0.3-in) ammunition. It can be used as a light machine-gun with a butt and bipod, or it can be fired from a heavy tripod for the heavy machine-gun role. It can also be fitted with a solenoid for use as a co-axial weapon on armoured vehicles, and it can be adapted to firing from a number of other mounts.

In appearance the Uirapuru is a rather long, ungainly-looking weapon, especially when fitted with a butt for

the light machine-gun role. It uses a conventional gas-operated mechanism with an orthodox belt feed for the ammunition, and the barrel can be changed rapidly using a handle that also acts as a carrying handle for the weapon. The receiver of the weapon is very simple, being little more than a length of tube containing the breech block and its return spring. What appears to be a rectangular receiver is in fact the ammunition feed mechanism. The method of tapping off gas from the barrel is also simple. No gas regulating block or valve is used, the gas impinging directly onto the return mechanism. No provision appears to have been made for firing single shots.

The barrel of the Uirapuru has a large pepperpot-type muzzle brake and it is recommended that the barrel is changed after every 400 rounds have been fired. Most of the parts appear to require some machining, which should ensure a rugged construction. The Brazilian army gave its approval to the Uirapuru after lengthy trials, and the type is now being prepared for full production at a factory near Rio de Janeiro. If past Brazilian salesmanship is any guide, it will not be long before the first examples are seen outside Brazil, for if the Uirapuru can withstand the varied combat conditions that can be encountered in Brazil it will put up with virtually anything, and the simple construction certainly should keep the price of a weapon down.

Specification
Uirapuru Mekanika
Calibre: 7.62 mm (0.3 in)

The Brazilian 7.62-mm (0.30-in) Uirapuru Mekanika is the first locally-produced machine-gun design to enter production, and although it appears at first sight to be rather long it is an efficient and basically simple weapon.

Weight: with butt and bipod 13 kg (28.66 lb)
Lengths: with butt 1300 mm (51.2 in); barrel 600 mm (23.62 in)
Muzzle velocity: 850 m (2,789 ft) per second
Rate of fire: (cyclic) 650-700 rpm
Type of feed: 50-round belt

World
Armies

Glossary

Div	Division
Bde	Brigade
Regt	Regiment
Bn	Battalion
Coy	Company
Sq	Squadron
Btty	Battery
Gp	Group
Detach	Detachment
AA	Anti-Aircraft
AB	Airborne
AD	Air Defence
AFV	Armoured Fighting Vehicle
Amph	Amphibious
APC	Armoured Personnel Carrier
Armd	Armoured
Arty	Artillery
AT	Anti-Tank
ATGW	Anti-Tank Guided Weapons
Cav	Cavalry
Cdo	Commando
COIN	Counter-Insurgency
CW	Chemical Warfare
Eng	Engineer
Fd	Field
Gds	Guards
ICBM	Inter-Continental Ballistic Missile
Indep	Independant
Inf	Infantry
IRBM	Intermediate Range Ballistic Missile
Jngle	Jungle
Lt	Light
MBT	Main Battle Tank
Mech	Mechanized
Med	Medium
MICV	Mechanized Infantry Combat Vehicle
Mob	Mobile
Mot	Motorized
MP	Military Police
MRBM	Medium Range Ballistic Missile
MRL	Multiple Rocket Launcher
Mtn	Mountain
NBC	Nuclear, Biological, Chemical
Para	Paratroop/Parachute
RCL	Recoilless or unguided anti-tank rocket launcher
Recce/Recon	Reconnaissance
SAM	Surface-to-Air Missile
Sig	Signal
SP	Self Propelled
Sp.Forces	Special Forces
Spt	Support
SRBM	Short Range Ballistic Missile
SSM	Surface-to-Surface Missile
Tk	Tank
Tk Dest	Tank Destroyers
Tpt	Transport

AFGHANISTAN

Nominal strength: 45,000, mostly conscript, although desertion is common and quoted force levels must be suspect. No formal reserves, although ex-servicemen and others between 20 and 40 are liable for call-up

Para-military: 7,000 border guards, 7,000 *Sarandoy* or Interior ministry troops, 35,000 *Khad* or secret police and numerous regional and communist party militias

Army organization: 3 Corps HQ controlling 3 Armd Div, 11 Inf Div, (actually understrength Bde size), 1 Mech Inf Bde/Div, 1 Cdo Bde with 1 Cdo and 1 Para Regt, 2 Mtn Regt, 1 AA Bde

Equipment includes 450 MBT (T-34, T-54/55 and T-62); 60 light tanks (PT-76); c.600 AFV (BMP-1, BTR 40/50/60/152); 76 mm, 100 mm, 122 mm, 152 mm guns/howitzers; 50 MRL (132 mm); 82 mm, 120 mm and 160 mm mortars; 550 towed AA guns (23 mm, 23 mm SP, 37 mm, 57 mm, 85 mm, 100 mm)

ALBANIA

Strength: 31,500 including 20,000 conscripts; 155,000 reserves liable to call-up to age 56

Para-military: 5,000 internal security troops and 7,000 Frontier Guard

Army organization: 1 Tnk Bde, 4 Inf Bde, 3 Arty Regt, 6 Coastal Arty Bn

Equipment includes 190 tanks (T-34, T-54), c.100 AFV (BRDM-1, BA-64, BTR-40/50/152 and K-63); 76 mm, 76 mm SP, 85 mm, 122 mm, 130 mm and 152 mm guns and howitzers; 107 mm MRL; 120 mm and 160 mm mortars; 45 mm, 57 mm, 82 mm recoilless and 85 mm anti-tank guns; 23 mm, 57 mm, 85 mm and possibly 100 mm AA guns plus SA-2 'Guideline' SAMs

Serviceability of equipment may be doubtful due to a shortage of spares

ALGERIA

Strength: 150,000 including 70,000 conscripts; up to 150,000 reserves

Para-military: 30,000 Ministry of the Interior Gendarmerie

Army organization: 6 Military Regions controlling 2 Armd Bde, 6 Mech Bde, 8 Motorized Inf Bde, 1 Airborne/Special Forces Bde, 28 Inf Bn, 4 Para Bn, 5 Arty Bn, 5 AA Bn, 4 Engr Bn, 12 Desert Coy

Equipment includes 890 MBT (T-34, 375 T-54/55, 325 T-62, 100 T-72); 30 light tanks; 130 recce (BRDM-2); 1,350 MICV/APC (BMP-1 and BTR-50/60/152); 700 guns and howitzers (76 mm, 85 mm, 122 mm, 152 mm); 130 MRL (122 mm, 240 mm); 120 mm, 180 mm mortars; 185 anti-tank guns (100 mm SP); 82 mm, 107 mm RCL; SAGGER, Milan ATGW; 310 Lt AA (20 mm, 37 mm, 57 mm) and 190 Towed AA (85 mm, 100 mm and 130 mm); 200+ SPAAG (23 mm, 57 mm); 50 SAM (SA-6, SA-7, SA-9), Air Force has 3 AA Bdes with 85 mm, 100 mm and 130 mm guns and one SAM Regt with 30 SA-2, 20 SA-3 launchers

ANGOLA

Strength: 36,000 including perhaps 24,000 conscripts; 50,000 reserves in the People's Defence Organization

Para-military: People's Defence Organization. Other Para-military forces include 7,000 Border Guards

Army organization: 10 Military regions (some incorporating Field HQs) controlling 5 Motorized Inf Bde, 19 Inf Bde (including 2 'Guerrilla Force' Bdes made up of reservists), 4 AA Arty Bde, 10 Tank Bn and 6 Arty Bn

Equipment includes 450 tanks (T-34, T-54, T-62), c.50 Lt Tnk (PT-76); 455 AFV (BRDM-2, BTR-40/50/60/152); 460 guns and howitzers (including 76 mm, 85 mm, 100 mm, 100 mm SP, 122 mm, 130 mm, and 152 mm); 75 MRL (122 mm); 460 mortars (82 mm, 120 mm); 900 RCL (75 mm, 82 mm, 107 mm); Sagger ATGW; 350 AA guns (14.5 mm, 20 mm, 23 mm, 23 mm SP, 37 mm, 57 mm, 57 mm SP); Air Force has 5 SAM Bns with 12 SA-2, 40 SA-3, 72 SA-6, 48 SA-8 and SA-9 SAM

ARGENTINA

Strength: 100,000 including 80,000 conscripts serving one year. Reserves: 200,000 national guard and 100,000 territorial guard

Para-military: 12,000 Gendarmerie, 22,000 Federal Police

Army organization: 4 Corps controlling 2 Armd Bde, 3 Mot Inf Bde, 3 Mech Bde, 2 Inf Bde, 2 Mtn Bde, 1 Air Mob Bde, 5 AD Bn, 1 Arty Gp, 2 Jngle Bn, 1 Eng Gp

Equipment includes 300+ tanks (M4 Sherman, TAM, AMX-13); 220 Tnk Dest.; 750 AFV (Panhard ERC, AMX/VTP, TAM VTCP, M113, Panhard M3, MOWAG Roland); 200 Arty (105 mm, 155 mm, 155 mm SP); MRL (105 mm, 127 mm); 320 mortars (81 mm, 120 mm); RCL (75 mm, 90 mm, 106 mm); SS-11, Cobra, Mamba, Mathago ATGW; 20 mm, 30 mm, 35 mm, 40 mm, 90 mm AAG; Tigercat, Blowpipe, Roland SAMs

AUSTRIA

Strength: 50,000 including 25,000 conscripts serving 6 months. Reserves: 28,000 immediate, 70,000 refresher training, 970,000 with reserve commitment

Para-military: 11,250 Gendarmerie

Army organization: Full time Alert Force: 1 Mech Div, 3 Command and Spt Bn, 1 AirMob Bn, 2 Mtn Bn, 1 Gds Bn, 1 AA Bn, 1 Eng Bn, 1 Sig Bn. Regional Defence Force (Cadre): 2 Corps HQ, 2 Arty Bn, 1 SP A/T Bn, 2 AA Bn, 2 Eng Bn, 2 Sig Bn, 2 Logistic Regt, 9 Regional Commands, 30 Training Regt

Equipment includes 170 MBT (M60); 284 Tnk Dest; 450 APC (Steyr); 190 Arty (105 mm, 155 mm); 128 mm MRL; 700 Mortars (81 mm, 107 mm, 120 mm); Turret Mounted AT Guns (85 mm, 105 mm); 74 mm, 84 mm, 106 mm, LAW RCL; 20 mm, 35 mm, 40 mm SP AA guns. Air Force has 48 AA guns (20 mm, 35 mm) and extensive detection and fire control systems

American built M60 main battle tanks equip the armoured division which is the main component of the regular 'alert force' of the Austrian Army.

Australian Commandos come ashore with their collapsable canoe. They are armed with F1 sub-machine guns with their distinctive magazines.

This American built M113 armoured personnel carrier of the Belgian Army has been fitted with a MILAN anti-tank missile launcher.

AUSTRALIA

Strength: 32,600; 30,300 reserves
Organization: 1 Div HQ, 1 Armd Regt, 1 Recon Regt, 1 APC Regt, 6 Inf Bn, 1 Rifle Coy, 1 SAS Regt, 3 Med Arty Regt, 2 Fd Arty Regt, 1 Light AD Btty, 1 AD Regt, 1 Fd Eng Regt, 1 Survey Regt, 5 Sig Regt, 10 Sig Sq, 3 Tpt Sq
Equipment includes c.250 MBT (Leopard 1, Centurion, most in reserve); c.850 AFV (M113, Saracen, Ferret); c.300 Arty (105mm, 5.5in, 155mm); 84mm, 106mm RCL; Milan ATGW; Redeye, RBS 70, Rapier SAMs

BAHAMAS

496 personnel

BAHREIN

Strength: 2,700
Para-military: 2,500 Police
Army organization: 1 Inf Bn, 1 Armd Car Sqn, 1 Arty Bn
Equipment includes c.130 AFV (Ferret, Saladin, Shorland, Panhard M3, AML-90); 15 guns and howitzers (105mm, 155mm); 81mm mortars; 120mm RCL; RBS-70 SAM

BANGLADESH

Strength: 67,000
Para-military: 80,000
Army organization: 5 Inf Div HQ, 12 Inf Bde, 2 Tnk Regt, 12 Arty Regt, 7 Eng Bn
Equipment: includes 40+ tanks (Tp 59, T-54/55, M24); 65 guns/howitzers (25 Pdr, 105mm); 81mm, 120mm mortars; 106mm RCL; 57mm AT guns

BELGIUM

Strength: 62,300 including 23,700 conscripts serving 10-12 months; 50,000 reserves
Para-military: 16,000 Gendarmerie
Army organization: 1 Corps of 2 Div controlling 1 Armd Bde, 4 Mech Inf Bde, 1 Mot Inf Bde (Reserve), 2 Recce Bn, 2 Mot Inf Bn, 1 Para-Cdo Regt, 1 Tk Bn, 4 Arty Bn, 5 Eng Bn, 1 SSM Bn, 2 SAM Bn, 2 AA Bn, 4 Sig Bn
Equipment includes 320 MBT (Leopard 1); 1200 AFV (Scorpion, Scimitar, Striker, AIFV, Spartan, Sultan, M113, M75, AMX-13); 170 howitzers (155mm SP, 203mm SP); 81mm, 107mm mortar; 4 SSM (Lance); Milan ATGW; 35mm SPAAG (Gepard); HAWK, Mistral SAMs. Belgian AF controls Nike Hercules SAM Batteries

BENIN

Strength: 3,000 with 1,650 reserves. 1,100 para-military
Army organization: 3 Inf Bn, 1 Eng Bn, 1 Service Bn, 1 Armd Sqn, 1 Para-Cdo Coy, 1 Arty Btty
Equipment includes M8, M20 Armd Cars; 60mm, 81mm mortars; 4 105mm howitzers; some ex-Vietnamese MRLs

BOLIVIA

Strength: 20,000 including conscripts serving 12 months
Para-military: 5,000 including police, frontier guards and elite 'Leopardo' anti-drug unit
Army organization: 3 Corps, 9 Divisions (5 cadre), 6 Horse Cav Regt, 15 Inf Regt, 1 Palace Gd Regt, 2 Mtn Regt, 2 Mech Regt, 1 Mot Regt, 2 Ranger Bn, 1 Para Bn, 3 Arty Regt, 6 Eng Bn, 2 AT Bn
Equipment includes 120 AFV (Scorpion, Kürassier, EE-9, Commando, M113, MOWAG Roland, EE-11); 75mm, 105mm guns/howitzers; 60mm, 81mm, 107mm mortars

BOTSWANA

Strength: 5,000 plus 1,500 para-military police
Army organization: 2 Inf Bn Gps
Equipment includes 60 AFV (Shorland, Cadillac-Gage, BTR-60); 10 105mm guns; 81mm, 120mm mortars; 84mm RCL; SA-7 SAM

BRAZIL

Strength: 183,000 including 132,000 conscripts serving one year, plus 15,000 Marines
Para-military: 200,000 public security forces
Army organization: 4 Army, 8 Div Commands, 5 Lt Jungle Inf Bde, 2 Eng Bde, 1 Mixed Bde, 2 Para Bde, 1 Armd Cav Bde, 3 Armd Inf Bde, 5 Mech Cav Bde, 1 Mech Inf Bde, 11 Mot Inf Bde, 9 Fd Arty Regt, 10 AA Arty Gp. Marines have 1 Amph Div, 5 reinforcement Bn, six regional groups and one special operations group of the Internal Security Force
Equipment includes EE-T1 Osorio and MB-3 Tamoyo tanks, M4 medium tanks; 550 Lt tanks (M3A1, X-1, X-1A2, M41); 900 AFV (EE-9, M8, EE-11, M59, M113); 1,150 guns/howitzers (75mm, 105mm, 105mm SP, 155mm); 240 coastal guns (57mm, 6-in, 12-in); 108mm, 180mm MRL; 81mm, 120mm mortars; 3.5-in RCL; Cobra ATGW; 240 AA guns (35mm, 40mm, 57mm, 90mm); HAWK, Roland SAM. Marine units operate 65+ AFV (EE-9, EE-11, M113, LVTP-7); 105mm, 155mm howitzers; 108mm MRL; 81mm mortar; 89mm, 106mm RCL; 40mm AA

BRUNEI

Strength: 3,500 including 900 Gurkhas
Para-military: 1,750 Royal Brunei Police
Army organization: 3 Inf Bn, 1 Armd Recce Sqn, 1 Lt Arty Btty, 1 AD Btty, 1 Eng Troop, 1 Sig Sqn
Equipment includes 16 Lt Tank (Scorpion); 26 AFV (Sultan, AT-104); 81mm mortar; Rapier Blindfire SAM

Brazil has a significant arms industry. One of its early products was the X1A, a complete re-build of the elderly M3A1 Stuart light tank

BULGARIA

Strength: 120,000 including 70-75,000 conscripts serving 2 years plus c.500 Naval Guard; 200,000 reserves
Para-military: 16,000 border guards, 12,000 Security Police, 150,000 volunteer People's Militia, 12,000 construction troops
Army organization: 8 Mot Rifle Div, 5 Tk Bde, 3 SSM Bde, 2 SAM Regt, 4 Arty Regt, 3 AA Arty Regt, 1 Mtn Bn, 2 Recce Bn, 1 Special Cdo Coy
Equipment includes 1,800 tanks (T-34, T-54/55, T-62); 1,400 AFV (BRDM-1/2, BMP-1, BTR-50/60, OT-62, FUG-70); 1,100 guns/howitzers (85mm, 122mm, 152mm); 66 SSM (FROG, Scud); 100 MRL (122mm); 350 mortars (82mm, 120mm, 160mm); 350 AT guns (57mm, 76mm, 85mm, 100mm); Sagger, Snapper ATGW; 23mm SP, 57mm, 85mm AA guns; SA-4, SA-6, SA-7 SAMs

BURKINA FASSO

Strength: 3,900 plus reserves; 40,000 People's Militia
Para-military: 2,750 including 1,850 Gendarmerie
Army organization: 6 Inf Regt, 2 Inf Cdo Regt, 1 AB Inf Bn, 1 Armd Sqn, 6 Para Coys, 1 Arty Btty, 1 Recce Sqn, 1 Eng Bn
Equipment includes 45 AFV (Ferret, M8, AML-60/90); 105mm howitzers, 75mm RCL, 60mm and 81mm mortars

BURMA

Strength: 163,000. No formal reserves but there would be universal conscription in any emergency
Para-military: 35,000 People's Militia, 38,000 People's Police Force

Army organization: 6 Lt Inf Div HQ each with 2 or 3 Tactical Operation Commands (Bde size) totalling 16 TOCs. Each TOC has up to 10 Bn. Other units include 90-100 Inf Bn, 2 Armd Bn, 4 Arty Bn, 1 AA Btty.
Equipment includes 25 tanks (Comet); 85 AFV (Ferret, Humber armoured car); 225 guns/howitzers (76mm, 25-Pdr, 105mm, 5.5-in); 81mm, 120mm mortars; 6-Pdr, 17-Pdr AT guns; 40mm, 3.7-in AA guns

BURUNDI

Strength: 7,000 including 2,000 gendarmerie
Organization: 2 Inf Bn, 1 Para Bn, 1 Cdo Bn, 1 Armd Car Coy
Equipment includes c.40 AFV (BTR, AML-60/90); 82mm mortars; 75mm, 83mm RCL; 14.5mm AA guns

CAMEROON

Strength: 6,600
Para-military: 4,000
Army organization: 4 Inf Bn, 1 Armd Car Sqn, 1 Para Coy, 1 Arty Btty, plus Eng and Spt units
Equipment includes c.100 AFV (Ferret, M8, M20, Commando, M3 ½-track); 75mm, 105mm Fd guns; 60mm, 81mm mortars; 57mm AT guns; 57mm, 75mm, 106mm RCL; Milan ATGW; 14.5mm, 35mm, 37mm, 40mm AA

Canada's armed forces have a commitment to NATO exemplified by this Leopard tank, seen on exercise with US Army units.

Chinese Type 59 MBTs parade past portraits of Stalin and Lenin during a National Day parade in Peking. The Chinese armed forces have been greatly reduced in size in recent years, but even so the Army's modernization programme is a massive task.

CANADA
Strength: 29,000 including 16,000 mobile command; reserves 16,000
Land forces organization: 2 Bde Gps each with 1 Armd Regt, 1 Lt Arty Regt, 3 Mech Inf Bn, 1 Eng Regt, suppt units; 1 Special Service Force with 1 Armd Regt, 1 Inf Bn, 1 AB Regt, 1 Arty Regt, 1 Eng Regt, 1 Suppt unit, 2 Sig Regt; 1 Mech Bde Gp with 1 Armd Regt, 2 Mech Inf Bn, 1 Med Arty Regt, 1 Eng Regt, suppt units
Equipment includes 114 MBT (Leopard C1); 1600 AFV (Lynx, Cougar, M113, Grizzly); 250 howitzers (105 mm, 155 mm SP); 84 mm RCL; TOW ATGW; 35 mm, 40 mm AA; Blowpipe, ADATS SAMs

CENTRAL AFRICAN REPUBLIC
Strength: 2,850
Para-military: 1,500
Army organization: 1 Inf Bn, 1 Eng Coy, 1 Sig Coy, 1 Tpt Coy
Equipment includes 4 MBT (T-55); 20 AFV (Ferret, BRDM-2, BTR-152); 60 mm, 81 mm mortars; 106 mm RCL; LRAC-73 ATW

CHAD
Strength: c.9000 Government Forces
Army organization: not available
French, Zaire, Egypt and Sudan supplied equipment includes AML recce vehicles, anti-tank weapons, AA systems and small arms

CHILE
Strength: 68,000 including 20,000 conscripts serving 1 year; 5,000 Marines; 160,000 reserves
Para-military: 27,000 Carabineros
Army organization: 6 Divs controlling 18 Mot Inf Regt, 6 Mtn Regt, 10 Arty Regt, 6 Mtn Arty Gp, 3 Mech Cav Regt, 5 Mot Cav Regt, 2 AA Detach, 6 Eng Bn, 1 Ranger Bn. In addition, Inf School, Cav School, Armour School, Arty School, and Eng School are actually full-strength regiments

Equipment includes c.170 tanks (M4, AMX-30); 120 light tanks (M3, M41, AMX-13); 600+ AFV (EE-9, Piranha 6×6 and 4×4, M113, EE-11, VTP-1, VTP-2); 40+ howitzers (105 mm, 155 mm); 81 mm, 120 mm mortars; 106 mm RCL; Milan ATGW; 20 mm, 35 mm, 57 mm AA Guns; Crotale/Cactus SAM

CHINA
Strength: 2,000,000 including c.1,000,000 conscripts serving 2 to 4 years and 56,000 Marines (including 30,000 conscripts)
Para-military: 5,000,000 Armed Militia, up to 40,000,000 ordinary militia, 3,000,000 construction troops, plus border troops.
Army organization: 7 Military regions covering 27 military districts; 35 'Armies' of 2-3 Div, 3 Arty Regt, 3 Armd Regt; 110 Inf Div, 12 Mech/Armd Div, 3 AB Div, 17 Fd Arty Div, 16 AA Arty Div, 1 Mtn Div, 40 Arty Div, 50 Eng Regt, 16 Railway & Construction Div; Local/Regional Forces 65 Div, 140 Indep Inf Regt. Marines have 9 Regts with 4 Inf Bn, 3 Tank Bn, 3 Arty Bn plus support and special Recce units. Air Force has 28 AD Regt
Equipment includes 11,000+ MBT (IS-2, T-34, T-54, Tp. 59, Tp. 69, Tp. 80); 600 light tanks (PT-76/Tp. 60, Tp. 62, Tp. 63); 5,000 APC (Tp. 531, Tp. 534, Tp. 55/56/63); 20,000 guns/howitzers (85 mm, 85 mm SP, 100 mm, 100 mm SP, 122 mm, 122 mm SP, 130 mm, 152 mm, 152 mm SP); 4,500 MRL (107 mm, 122 mm, 130 mm, 132 mm, 140 mm, 284 mm); 14,000 mortars (60 mm, 82 mm, 120 mm, 160 mm); 57 mm, 76 mm AT guns; HOT, Sagger, Red Arrow-8 ATGW; 10,000 AA guns (37 mm, 57 mm, 85 mm, 100 mm); HQ-51 SPAA; HN-5 (SA-7) SAM. Air Force controls 4 ICBM, c.40 IRBM, c.100 MR/SRBM; 20,000 AA guns (57 mm, 85 mm, 100 mm); 100 HQ-2 (SA-2) SAM units

COLOMBIA

Strength: 57,000 including 28,500 conscripts serving 2 years; 70,000 reserves
Para-military: 50,000 National Police
Army organization: 11 Inf Bde, 1 Presidential Gd Bde, 1 Ranger Bn, 1 AB Bn, 1 AA Bn, 1 Mech Gp
Equipment includes 12 light tanks (M3); 300+ AFV (EE-9, M113, EE-11, M3 ½-tr); 48 howitzers (105mm); 60mm, 81mm, 105mm, 107mm mortars; 40mm AA guns; Cactus/Crotale SAM

CONGO

Strength: 8,000
Para-military: 1,000 Police, 1,400 Gendarmerie, 4,700 People's Militia
Army organization: 1 Armd Regt, 2 Inf Bn Gp, 1 Para-Cdo Bn, 1 Arty Gp, 1 Eng Bn
Equipment includes 50 MBT (T-54/55, Tp. 59); 17 light tanks (PT-76, T-62); c.100 AFV (BRDM, BTR, Panhard M3); 20+ guns/howitzers (75mm, 100mm, 122mm); 82mm, 120mm mortars; 122mm MRL; 57mm AT guns; 37mm AA guns.
Note: spares are in short supply, so general equipment serviceability is doubtful

COSTA RICA

Costa Rica has no regular army
Para-military: 6,000 Civil Guard, 3,000 reserves
Organization: 1 Presidential Gd Bn, 1 COIN Bn
Equipment includes M113 APC, 81mm mortars, 90mm RCL

CUBA

Strength: 130,000 including c.60,000 conscripts serving 3 years; 170,000 official reserves
Para-military: 15,000 state security, 3,500 frontier guards, 100,000 youth labour army, 50,000 civil defence, 1,200,000 territorial militia
Army organization: 4 Corps, 1 Armd Div, 4 Mech Inf Div, 7 Inf Div (at 60% strength), 26 AD Regts and SAM Bdes, 8 cadre Inf Div, 2 Bn Sp Forces, 1 AB Bde, 3 Fd Arty Bde, 8 Indep Inf Regt
Equipment includes 800 tanks (IS-2, T-34, T-54/55, T-62, PT-76); 700 AFV (BRDM, BMP, BMD, BTR); 1,250 guns/howitzers (76mm, 85mm, 100mm SP, 122mm, 130mm, 152mm); 122mm, 140mm, 240mm MRL; 65 SSM (FROG); 120mm mortar; 600 AT guns (57mm, 76mm, 85mm, 100mm); 57mm RCL; Snapper, Sagger ATGW; 1600 AA guns (23mm SP, 37mm, 57mm, 85mm, 100mm); SA-2, SA-3, SA-6, SA-7, SA-9 SAMs

CYPRUS

Strength: 13,000 mostly conscripts serving 26 months; 60,000 reserves
Para-military: 3,000 armed police
Army organization: 20 Inf Bn (understrength), 1 Cdo Bn, 8 Arty Bn, support
Equipment includes T-34 tanks; 260 AFV (EE-9, EE-3, Marmon Herrington, VAB, BTR-152); 120 guns/howitzers (75mm, 100mm, 105mm, 25-Pdr); 128mm MRL; 81mm, 82mm, 107mm mortars; 57mm, 89mm, 106mm RCL; Milan ATGW; 20mm, 40mm, 3.7-in AA guns; SA-7 SAM
Northern (Turkish) Cyprus has some 4,500 troops (17,000 reserves) in 7 Inf Bn and 1 Armd Coy

CZECHOSLOVAKIA

Strength: 150,000 including 100,000 conscripts serving 2 years; c.300,000 reserves
Para-military: 11,000 border troops, 120,000 People's Militia
Army organization: 5 Armd Div, 5 Mot Rifle Div, 1 AB Bde, 3 SSM Bde, 2 AT Regt, 2 Arty Bde, 2 AA Arty Bde, 5 Eng Bde. Air Force controls 3 AD Div, 6 SAM Regt
Equipment includes 3,500 MBT (T-54/55, T-72); 4,850 AFV (OT-65, BRDM, BMP, OT-62/64, OT-810); 800 guns/howitzers (100mm, 122mm, 122mm SP, 152mm, 152mm SP); 122mm, 240mm MRL; 81mm, 120mm mortars; 48 SSM (FROG/SS-21, Scud-B); 100mm AT guns; 82mm RCL; Sagger, Spigot ATGW; 23mm, 23mm SP, 57mm SP AA guns; SA-4, SA-6, SA-7, SA-8, SA-9 SAM. Air Force controls 200 SA-2/3 SAMs and 2 AD radar Regt

DENMARK

Strength: 18,000 including 6,000 conscripts serving 9 months. Reserves: 6,000 subject to immediate recall, 50,000 Field Army reserve, 20,000 Regional Defence Force, 60,000 Home Guard
Army organization: 2 Div HQ; 5 Mech Inf Bde totalling 5 Tank Bn, 10 Mech Bn, 5 Arty Bn, 5 AD Btty, 5 Eng Coy; 5 Regt Combat Teams totalling 10 Inf Bn, 5 Arty Bn, 5 AT GP, plus support units; Air Force has 1 SAM Bn
Equipment includes 250 tanks (Centurion, Leopard 1, M41); 700 APC (M113); 350 guns/howitzers (105mm, 155mm, 155mm SP, 203mm); 81mm, 120mm mortars; LAW, 84mm,106mm RCL; Cobra, TOW ATGW; 40mm AA guns; Hamlet (Redeye) SAM. Air Force controls 8 SAM Btty (Improved HAWK)

DJIBOUTI

Strength: 2,900
Para-military: 1,500 Gendarmerie
Army organization: 1 Inf Regt, 1 Armd Sq, 1 Spt Bn, 1 Cdo Bn, 1 Para Coy
Equipment includes 40+ AFV (BRDM, AML-60/90, BTR-60); 81mm, 120mm mortars; 89mm, 106mm RCL

DOMINICAN REPUBLIC

Strength: 15,000
Para-military: 10,000 Gendarmerie
Army organization: 3 Inf Bde, 1 Armd Bn, 1 Mtn Bn, 1 Para Bn, 1 Presidential Gd Bn, 2 Arty Bn, 1 AA Bn, 1 Eng Bn, 1 Armd Recce Sqn
Equipment includes 35 light tanks (AMX-13); 30 AFV (AML, Commando, M3 ½-tr); 105mm howitzers; 81mm, 120mm mortars; 106mm RCL; 40mm AA

ECUADOR

Strength: 30,000 including conscripts serving 1 year plus 1,500 Marines
Para-military: 6,000
Army organization: 5 Inf Bde, 12 Armd Cav Bde, 3 Jungle Bde, 4 Arty Bn, 3 Eng Bn, 5 Cav Gp, 3 Recce Sqn, 1 Sp Force (AB) Bde, 1 Presidential Gd Sqn, 3 AA Btty, 1 Marine Cdo Bn, 2 Marine Bn
Equipment includes 100+ light tanks (M3, M41, AMX-13); 170 AFV (AML-60, EE-9, EE-3, M113, AMX-VCI, EE-11, UR416, M3 ½-tr); 70 guns/howitzers (105mm, 155mm, 155mm SP); 81mm, 160mm mortars; 90mm, 106mm RCL; 20mm, 35mm, 40mm AA guns; Blowpipe SAM

EGYPT

Strength: 250,000 including 180,000 conscripts serving 3 years plus 80,000 Air Defence Command troops (50,000 conscripts); 300,000+ reserves
Para-military: 400,000+ Central Security Forces, National Guard, Frontier Force and Defence Security Forces
Army organization: 2 Field Armies, 4 Armd Div, 5 Mech Inf Div, 3 Inf Div, 1 Republican Gd Bde, 1 Indep Armd Bde, 3 Indep Inf Bde, 2 Air Mobile Bde, 1 Para Bde, 3 Arty Bde, 2 Heavy Mortar Bde, 7 Cdo Gp, 2 SSM Regt. Navy controls Coast Defence Units. Air Defence Command has 4 Div with 100 AA Bn, 125 SAM Bn plus Radar troops
Equipment includes 2,250 MBT (T-54/55, T-62, M60A3); 3,000 AFV (BRDM, BMP, M901-ITV, OT-62, BTR-50, Walid, Fahd, M113); 1,600 guns/howitzers (76mm, 100mm, 100mm SP, 122mm, 122mm SP, 130mm, 152mm, 152mm SP, 155mm SP); 350 MRL (80mm, 122mm, 132mm, 140mm, 240mm); 17 SSM (FROG, Scud); Coast Defence missiles (Otomat, Samlet); 400 mortars (120mm, 160mm,

240mm); 900 AT guns (57mm, 76mm, 100mm); 900 RCL (82mm, 107mm); 1,500 ATGW (Snapper, Swatter, Sagger, Swingfire, Milan, TOW); 3,500 AA guns (14.5mm, 20mm, 23mm, 23mm SP, 37mm, 40mm, 57mm, 57mm SP, 85mm, 100mm); SA-2, SA-3, SA-6, SA-7/Saqr, SA-9, Crotale, Amoun (Skyguard/Sparrow), Improved HAWK, CSA-1, Spada-Aspide SAMs

EL SALVADOR

Strength: 30-40,000 including irregular numbers of conscripts serving two years; 30,000 reserves
Para-military: 70,000 Civil Defence, 3,500 National Guard, 6,000 Police
Army organization: 6 Inf Bde, 12 Inf Regt (Cadres only), 1 Mech Cav Regt, 1 Arty Bde, 1 Eng Bn, 6 COIN Bn, 1 Para Bn, 1 AA Bn, 2 Cdo Coys
Equipment includes 12 light tanks (AMX-13); 45 AFV (M3A1, AML-90, M113, UR416); 50+ howitzers (105mm, 155mm); 81mm, 120mm mortars; LAW, 90mm RCL

EQUATORIAL GUINEA

Strength: 2,000
Para-military: 2,000 Guardia Civile
Army organization: 1 Inf Bn, support Unit, Moroccan unit seconded as Presidential Guard
Equipment includes T-34 tanks; BRDM, BTR; 81mm Mortar

ETHIOPIA

Strength: 245,000 including conscripts serving 30 months; 200,000 reserves
Para-military: 150,000 People's Militia, 10,000 People's Protection Brigades, 9,000 Mobile Police
Army organization: 20-25 Inf Div (including 3 Motorized, 4 Mtn Div), 4 Para-Cdo Bde, 30-40 Arty Bn, 30 AD Bn
Equipment includes c.1,000 MBT (M47, T-34, T-54/55, T-62, T-72); 800 AFV (BRDM-2, BMP, BTR-40, BTR-152, BTR-60, M113, Commando); 700 guns/howitzers (75mm, 105mm, 122mm, 122mm SP, 130mm, 152mm, 155mm SP); 122mm MRL; 60mm, 81mm, 82mm, 4.2-in, 120mm mortars; 100mm AT guns; Sagger ATGW; 23mm, 23mm SP, 57mm, 57mm SP AA guns; SA-2, SA-3, SA-7 SAMs

US supplied equipment is of doubtful serviceability due to lack of spares

There are 30,000+ insurgents in a dozen or more groups fighting the central government, largely armed with captured government equipment

An Egyptian infantryman is seen during a joint US/Egyptian amphibious exercise. He is armed with an RPG-7 anti-tank weapon.

FIJI

Strength: 2,000; 5,000 reserves
Para-military: 1,500 Police
Army organization: 3 Inf Bn, 1 Eng Coy
Equipment includes 4 25-Pdr gun/howitzers, 10 81mm mortars

FINLAND

Strength: 30,000 including 22,300 conscripts serving 8-11 months, 700,000 reserves of which 210,000 form the 'Rapid Action Force'
Para-military: 4,400 Frontier Guard
Army organization: 1 Armd Bde, 7 Inf Bde, 7 Indep Inf Bde, 2 Fd Arty Regt, 2 Ind Fd Arty Bn, 3 Coast Arty Bn, 4 AA Regt, 1 Indep AA Bn, 2 Eng Bn, 1 Sig Regt
Equipment includes c.100 MBT (T-54/55, T-72); 10 light tanks (PT-76); 350 AFV (BMP-1, BTR-60, BTR-152, SISU); 76mm, 100mm Coastal, 105mm, 122mm, 130mm, 150mm, 152mm, 155mm guns/howitzers; 60mm, 81mm, 120mm, 160mm mortars; 55mm, 74mm, 95mm RCL; Spigot, TOW, SS-11 ATGW; 20mm, 23mm, 30mm, 35mm, 40mm, 57mm, 57mm SP AA guns; SA-3, SA-7 SAMs

Finland is balanced between east and west, and is equipped with weapons from both power blocs. This is the Russian built BMP-1 infantry combat vehicle.

FRANCE

Strength: 305,000 including 195,000 conscripts serving 1 year, 2,500 Marines; 281,000 trained reserves (forming 27 Inf Regt on mobilization)

Para-military: 85,000 Gendarmerie

Army organization: 3 Corps; 8 Armd Div, 4 Mot Rifle Div, 5 Recon Regt, 2 Drone Regt, 3 Mot Rifle Regt, 5 Arty Regt, 7 Eng Regt, 10 Sig Regt, 2 CW Defence Regt, 3 Logistic Regt, 8 Tpt Regt, 5 SSM Regt. Force d'Action Rapide comprises 1 Air Mobile Div, 1 Lt Armd Div, 1 Alpine Div, 1 Para Div, 1 Marine Div. Berlin Sector Force has 1 Armd Regt and 1 Inf Regt. Air Force has 12 SAM Sqn

Equipment includes 1,220 MBT, (AMX-30); 1,100 light tanks (AMX-13); 5,000 AFV (AMX-10RC, ERC-90F4 Sagaie, AML-60/90, AMX-10P, AMX-13VTT, VAB); 760+ guns/howitzers (105mm, 155m̀m, 155mm SP); 44 SSM (Pluton); 550+ Mortars (120mm); 12,000 RCL (112mm); Milan, SS-11 ATGW; 800+ AA guns (20mm, 30mm, 30mm SP); 220 SAMs (HAWK, Roland). Air Force has 48 Crotale SP SAM fire units

GABON

Strength: 1,900

Para-military: 2,000 Gendarmerie and Republican Guard

Army organization: 1 Pres Gd Combined Arms Bn, 8 Inf Coys, 1 Eng Coy, 1 Para-Cdo Coy, 1 Service Coy

Equipment includes 100 AFV (EE-9, AML-90, EE-3, ERC-20, ERC-90, Commando, VXB, EE-11, VBL); 4 howitzers (105mm); 140mm MRL; 81mm, 120mm mortars; 67mm Armbrust, 120mm RCL; Milan ATGW; 23mm, 37mm, 40mm AA

GERMAN DEMOCRATIC REPUBLIC
(East Germany)

Strength: 120,000 including 71,500 conscripts serving 18 months, 330,000 reserves

Para-military: 48,000 Border Guards, 25,000 Security Troops, 8,500 Transport Police, 500,000 Worker's Militia

Army organization: 2 Tank Div, 2 Mot Rifle Div, 2 SSM Regt, 2 Arty Regt, 2 AA Arty Regt, 2 AT Bn, 1 AB Bn, 2 SAM Regt, 3 Sig Regt, 3 Eng Regt, 1 Railway Construction Regt. Air Defence Command of the Air Force controls 7 SAM Regt, 2 Radar Regt

Equipment includes c.3,000 MBT (T-54/55, T-72); 120 light tanks (PT-76); 3,500 AFV (BRDM, FUG-70, BMP-1, BMP-2, BTR-50, BTR-60/70, BTR-152, MT-LB); 600+ guns/howitzers (122mm, 122mm SP, 130mm, 152mm, 152mm SP); 125 MRL (122mm); 40 SSM (FROG, Scud, SS-21); 120mm mortars; 100mm AT guns; Sagger, Spigot ATGW; 23mm SP, 57mm, 100mm AA guns; SA-2/3 (Air Force), SA-4, SA-6, SA-7, SA-9 SAMs

Renault VAB armoured personnel carriers of the French army move en masse down the Champs Elysees in Paris during the annual Bastille day parade.

A West German Leopard 2 main battle tank is accompanied on Bundeswehr manoeuvres by a Transportpanzer APC and a JPz Jaguar tank destroyer.

GERMAN FEDERAL REPUBLIC
(West Germany)
Strength: 350,000 including 170,000 conscripts serving 15 months; 650,000 reserves
Para-military: 20,000 Border Police
Army organization: 3 Corps with 12 Div (6 Armd, 4 Armd Inf, 1 Mtn, 1 AB). 17 Armd Bde, 15 Armd Inf Bde, 1 Mtn Bde, 3 AB Bde, 2 Home Def Bde, 4 SSM Bn, 11 Div Arty Regt, numerous Eng and Spt units. Territorial Army Cadres, 5 Military Districts and 6 Home Def Bde. Air Force controls 8 SSM Sqn, 3 SAM Regt, 4 Radar Regt
Equipment includes 5,000 MBT (M48, Leopard 1, Leopard 2); 760 tank Dest. (JPz-3/4 90 mm, RPz HOT, RPzTOW); 6,000 AFV (Luchs, Marder, M113, Transportpanzer); 1,376 guns/howitzers (105 mm, 105 mm SP, 155 mm, 155 mm SP, 175 mm SP, 203 mm, 203 mm SP); 110 mm, 227 mm MLR; c.100 SSM (Pershing 1a, Lance); 120 mm mortar; 106 mm RCL; TOW, HOT, Milan ATGW; 20 mm, 35 mm SP (Gepard), 40 mm AA guns; Redeye, Roland, Nike-Hercules, HAWK, Patriot SAMs

GHANA
Strength: 10,000, 500 reserves
Para-military: 2,500 Border Guards, 5,000 People's Militia
Army organization: 2 Inf Bn, 1 Recce Bn, 3 Border Troop Bn (formerly Police units), 1 Para Bn, 1 Mortar Bn, 1 Fd Eng Bn, 1 Sig Bn

Equipment includes 75-100 AFV (Saladin, Ferret, Piranha); some 105 mm howitzers; 81 mm, 120 mm mortars; 84 mm RCL; SA-7 SAM

GREECE
Strength: 150,000+ including 110,000 conscripts serving 22 months; 350,000 reserves
Para-military: 100,000 National Guard, 30,000 Gendarmerie
Army organization: 3 Military regions controlling 4 Corps. 1 Armd Div, 1 Mech Div, 11 Inf Div, 2 Armd Bde, 1 Marine Bde, 1 Para-Cdo Div, 3 Armd Bde, 4 Armd Recce Bn, 12 Fd Arty Bn, 8 AA Arty Bn, 2 SAM Bn, 2 SSM Bn
Equipment includes 1,800 MBT (M47, M48, AMX-30, Leopard 1); 170 light tanks (M24); 2,400 AFV (M8, M20 Armd Cars, AMX-10P, Leonidas, M59, M113, M3 ½-tr); 1,400 guns/howitzers (105 mm, 105 mm SP, 155 mm, 155 mm SP, 175 mm SP, 203 mm, 203 mm SP); Honest John SSM; 81 mm, 107 mm, 120 mm mortars; 90 mm, 106 mm RCL; TOW, ITOW, SS-11, Cobra, Milan ATGW; 20 mm, 40 mm, 75 mm AA guns; Redeye, Chaparral, HAWK SAMs
National Guard equipment includes 85 tanks (M26 Med, M41 Light); 440 AFVs (M20 Recce, M2/3 ½-tr); 468 25-Pdr Gun-Howitzers; 178 75 mm Pack-howitzers, 155 mm howitzers; 60 mm, 81 mm mortars; 57 mm, 75 mm, 106 mm RCL

GUATEMALA

Strength: 20-30,000 including conscripts serving 2 years. Navy has 650 Marines. 10,000 reserves
Para-military: 9,500 National Police, 2,100 Treasury Police, up to 900,000 Militia
Army organization: 4/5 Regional Bdes. Up to 17 Inf Bn, 4 Fd Arty Gp, 1 AA Arty Bn, 1 MP Bn, 1 Presidential Gd Bde, 2 Para/Sp Forces Bn, 4 Recce Sqn, 1 Eng Bn, 1 Armd Car Bn
Equipment includes 20 light tanks (M3, M41, AMX-13); 30+ AFV (M3, M8 Armd Cars, M113, Commando); 75mm, 105mm howitzers; 81mm, 4.2-in, 120mm mortars; 106mm RCL; 40mm AA guns

GUINEA

Strength: 8,500 including 7,500 conscripts serving 2 years
Para-military: 9,200 militia
Army organization: 5 Inf Bn, 1 Armd Bn, 1 Arty Bn, 1 Eng Bn, 1 Cdo Bn, 1 Sp Force Bn, 1 AD Bn
Equipment includes 60 tanks (T-34, T-54, PT-76); 65 AFV (BRDM-1, BTR-40, BTR-50, BTR-60, BTR-152); 26 guns/howitzers (76mm, 85mm, 105mm, 122mm); 120mm mortars; 57mm AT guns; 30mm, 37mm, 57mm, 100mm AA guns; Soviet supplied SAMs

GUINEA-BISSAU

Strength: c.6,000 including conscripts
Para-military: 5,000 Militia, 2,000 Gendarmerie
Army organization: 1 Armd Sqn, 4-5 Inf Bn, 1 Eng unit, 1 Arty unit
Equipment includes 50 tanks (T-34, T-54, PT-76); 300+ AFV (BRDM-2, BTR-50, BTR-60, BTR-152); c.25 guns/howitzers (85mm, 105mm, 122mm); 82mm, 120mm mortars; 75mm, 82mm, 89mm RCL; 23mm, 37mm, 57mm AA guns; SA-7 SAM

GUYANA

Strength: 5,000
Para-military: 2,000 National Guard, 3,000 People's Militia, 4,500 National Police, 3-5,000 Guyana National Service
Army organization: 2 Inf Bn, 1 Gd Bn, 1 Arty Bn (Btty strength), support units
Equipment includes 8 APC (EE-9, Shorland); 130mm guns; 81mm, 82mm, 120mm mortars; SA-7 SAM

HAITI

Strength: 7,000
Army organization: 1 Gd Inf Bn, 21 Garrison Coys, 1 Inf Bn, 2 Arty Btty
Equipment includes 6 light tanks (M5); 10 APC (Commando, M2); 10 howitzers (75mm, 105mm); 60mm, 81mm mortars; 37mm, 57mm AT guns; 57mm, 106mm RCL; 20mm, 40mm, 57mm AA guns

HONDURAS

Strength: 15,000 including 12,000 conscripts serving 8-24 months; 50,000 reserves
Para-military: 4,500 Public Security Forces
Army organization: 3 Inf Bde each with 3 Inf Bn and 1 Arty Bn, 1 Armd Cav Regt, 3 Indep Inf Bn, 4 Arty Regt, 1 Pres Gd unit, 1 Sp Forces Bn, 1 Eng Bn
Equipment includes 17 light tanks (Scorpion, Scimitar); 72 AFV (Saladin, RBY Mk 1); 24 howitzers (105mm); 60mm, 81mm, 120mm, 160mm mortars; 51mm, 84mm, 106mm RCL; (155mm howitzers and man-portable SAMs on order)

HUNGARY

Strength: 83,000 including 50,000 conscripts serving 18 months; 130,000+ reserves
Para-military: 60,000 Worker's Militia, 16,000 Border Guards (incl 11,000 conscripts)
Army organization: 1 Tk Div, 5 Mot Rifle Div, 1 Arty Bde with 3 Arty Regt, 1 SSM Bde, 1 AA Bn, 3 SAM Regt in Divs, 1 Indep SAM Regt, 1 AB Bn. The Air Force has 3 SAM Regt
Equipment includes 1,400 MBT (T-54/55, T-72); 100 light tanks (PT-76); 2,100 AFV (BRDM-2, OT-65/FUG, BMP-1, PSZH-IV, MT-LB); 550 guns/howitzers (122mm, 122mm SP, 152mm, 152mm SP); 50 MRL (122mm); 30 SSM (FROG, Scud); 400 mortars (82mm, 120mm); 85mm, 100mm AT guns; 73mm RCL; 200 ATGW (Sagger, Spigot); 23mm, 23mm SP, 57mm, 57mm SP, 100mm AA guns; c.500 SAM (SA-4, SA-6, SA-7, SA-9). Air Force controls 120 SA-2/3 SAMs

INDIA

Strength: c.1,000,000; 250,000 reserves
Para-military: c.300,000 including Border Security Force, National Security Force, Assam Rifles
Army organization: 5 Field Armies, 8 Corps. 2 Armd Div, 1 Mech Div, 22 Inf Div, 7 Mtn Div, 7 Armd Bde, 10 Inf Bde, 1 Mtn Bde, 1 Para-Cdo Bde, 4 Army Arty Bde, 4 AD Bde, 3 Eng Bde, several indep Arty Bde. Air Force has 30 SAM Bn
Equipment includes 2,300+ MBT (T-54/55, T-62, T-72, Vijayanta); 150 light tanks (PT-76, AMX-13); 1,400 AFV (BMP-1, OT-62/64, BTR-60); c.2,000 guns/howitzers (76mm, 25-Pdr, 100mm, 105mm, 130mm, 5.5-in, 155mm); 120mm MRL; 81mm, 120mm, 160mm mortars; 57mm AT guns; 57mm, 84mm, 106mm RCL; SS-11, Sagger, Milan ATGW; 20mm, 23mm SP, 40mm, 3.7-in AA guns; SA-6, SA-7, SA-8, SA-9, Tigercat SAM. Air Force controls 280 SA-2/SA-3 SAMs

Indian mountain troops move through the rugged foothills of the Himalayas, as a transport aircraft of the Indian Air Force comes in to land at a forward air base.

INDONESIA

Strength: 215,000 plus 12,000 Marines; 36,000 reserves although cadres exist for up to 750-800,000

Para-military: 100,000 including Police Mobile Bde and over 70,000 Militia

Army organization: 10 Area Commands. 2 Inf Div, 8 Cav Bn, 63 Inf Bn, 4 AB Bn, 7 Fd Arty Bn, 6 AA Bn, 4 Construction Eng Bn, 6 Fd Eng Bn

Equipment includes 300 light tanks (AMX-13, PT-76, M3A1); 700+ AFV (Saladin, Ferret, AMX-VCI, Saracen, Commando, AMX-VTT, BTR-40/152); 100+ guns/howitzers (76mm, 105mm); 80mm, 81mm mortars; 90mm, 106mm RCL; 20mm, 40mm, 57mm AA guns; Rapier, RBS-70 SAMs

Marines use 30 PT-76, 40 MICV, 57 APC, 122mm howitzers, 140mm MRL, 40mm and 57mm AA

IRAN

The Islamic Revolution and the war with Iraq have made knowledge of numbers and organization of the Iranian forces tentative at best. Serviceability, numbers and new equipment are matters for debate

Strength: 300,000 including some 200,000 conscripts originally meant to serve 24 months. There is a similar or larger number of reserves, many on active service.

Para-military: 350,000 'Pasdaran' (Revolutionary Guards) form 8 or 9 Div (including Armd, Inf, Arty, Para) together with support units. 500,000 'Basj' (Youth Volunteers) under the control of Pasdaran are formed into c.300 sketchily armed 'Battalions', 70,000 Gendarmerie

Army organization (based on pre-war establishment): 3 Mech Div, poss 1 Armd Div, 7 Inf Div, 2 AB Bde, 1 Sp Forces Div, 5 Arty Gp, 12 SAM Bn. Air Force controls some SAM units

Equipment includes 1,000 MBT (T-54/55, Tp. 59, Tp. 62, T-72, Chieftain, M47/48, M60); 50 light tanks (Scorpion); 750 APC (BTR-50, BTR-60, M113, EE-11); 1,000 guns/howitzers (75mm, 85mm, 105mm, 122mm, 130mm, 155mm, 155mm SP, 175mm SP, 203mm SP); Scud SSM; 107mm, 122mm MRL; 81mm, 107mm, 120mm mortars; 57mm, 75mm, 106mm RCL; SS-11/12, Dragon, TOW ATGW; 23mm, 23mm SP, 57mm, 57mm SP AA guns; HAWK, SA-7, RBS-70 SAMs. Air Force has Rapier and Tigercat SAMs

IRAQ

Strength: 475,000 including conscripts serving 2 years; 250-300,000 reserves are active in the war

Para-military: 5,000 Security troops, 500,000 People's Army

Army organization: 5 Armd Div, 3 Mot Inf Div, 10 Inf Div (incl Mtn troops), 2 Sp Force Div (6 Bde), 1 Presidential Gd Force comprising 3 Amd Bde, 1 Inf Bde and 1 Cdo Bde, 9 Reserve Bde and 15 People's Army/Volunteer Militia Bde on active service

Equipment includes 4,000+ MBT (T-54/55, T-62, T-72, Tp. 59/69, Chieftain, M47, M60); 100 light tanks (PT-76); 4,000 AFV (BRDM-2, FUG-70, ERC-90, MOWAG Roland, EE-3, EE-9, BMP-1, BTR-50, BTR-60, BTR-152, OT-62/64, VC-TH HOT, M113, Panhard M-3, EE-11); 5,500 guns/howitzers (85mm, 100mm SP, 105mm, 122mm, 122mm SP, 130mm, 152mm, 152mm SP, 155mm, 155mm SP); 40+ SSM (FROG, Scud and possibly SS-21); 108mm, 122mm, 127mm, 132mm MRL; 85mm, 100mm, 105mm SP AT guns; 73mm, 82mm, 107mm RCL; SS-11, HOT, Milan, Swingfire, Sagger, Swatter ATGW; 2,000+ AA guns (23mm, 23mm SP, 37mm, 57mm, 57mm SP, 85mm, 100mm); SA-2, SA-3, SA-6, SA-7, SA-9, Roland SAMs

IRELAND

Strength: 12,000 with 15-20,000 reserves

Army organization: 4 Inf Bde, totalling 11-12 Inf Bn, 1 Tk Sqn, 1 Armd Recce Sqn, 3 Recce Sqn, 3 Fd Arty Regt, 1 AA Regt, 3 Fd Eng Coys, 1 Ranger Coy

Equipment includes 12-14 light tanks (Scorpion); 130+ AFV (AML-60/90, VTT-M3, Timoney); 60 guns/howitzers (105mm, 25-Pdr); 60mm, 81mm, 120mm mortars; 84mm, 90mm RCL; Milan ATGW; 40mm AA guns; RBS-70 SAM

A battery of radar directed, Soviet made 130-mm field guns of the Iraqi army fires on Iranian positions in the long running Gulf War.

ISRAEL

Strength: 140,000 including 95,000 conscripts serving 24-48 months; 500,000 reserves
Para-military: 4,500 Border Guards
Army organization: 11 Armd Div (many cadre only) comprising 33 Armd Bde on mobilization. 9 Mech Inf Bde, 3 Inf Bde, 5 Para Bde, 12 Border Inf Bde, 15 Arty Bde. Air Force controls 15 SAM Bn
Equipment includes 3,600+ MBT (Centurion, M48, M60, T-54/55, T-62, Merkava); 6,500 AFV (RAMTA RBY, M2/3 ½-tr, BRDM-2, M113, BTR-50); 1,200 guns/howitzers (105mm, 122mm, 130mm, 155mm, 155mm SP, 175mm SP, 203mm SP); Lance & Israeli developed SSMs; 122mm, 160mm, 240mm, 290mm MRL; 81mm, 120mm, 160mm mortars; 82mm, 106mm RCL; TOW, Cobra, Dragon, Milan, Picket, 'Togger' (TOW/Sagger derivative), Sagger, SS-10, SS-11 ATGW; 20mm, 20mm SP, 23mm SP, 30mm, 37mm, 40mm AA guns; Redeye, Chaparral, HAWK SAMs

ITALY

Strength: 270,000 including 220,000 conscripts serving 12 months; 520,000 reserves
Para-military: 90,000 Carabinieri, 70,000 public security guards, 50,000 Customs/Finance Guards
Army organization: 3 Corps controlling 1 Armd Div, 3 Mech Div, 2 Mech Bde, 4 Mot Bde, 5 Alpine Bde, 1 AB Bde, 1 Sp Forces Bn, 2 Amph Bn, 1 SSM Bn, 3 SAM Bn, 3 Heavy Arty Bn. Air Force has 12 SAM Gp. Carabinieri have 13 Bn, 1 AB Bn, 2 Cav Sqn
Equipment includes 1,700+ MBT (M47, M60, Leopard 1); 4,100+ AFV (M106, M113, M548, M577, AMX-VCI, VCC-1/2); 1,200 guns/howitzers (105mm, 155mm, 155mm SP, 175mm, 203mm, 203mm SP); 6 SSM (Lance); 81mm, 107mm, 120mm mortars; 57mm, 106mm, Folgore RCL; Cobra, SS-11, TOW, Milan ATGW; 20mm, 40mm, AA guns; Stinger, HAWK SAMs. Air Force controls Nike Hercules, Spada SAMs. Carabinieri have M47 MBT, c.850 AFV (Fiat 6616, M6, M8 Armd Cars, Fiat 242, M113 APC)

Italian para-military units include highly trained police anti-terrorist squads such as the Nucleo Operativo Centrale di Sicurezze, or NOCS.

Israel's unparallelled experience of modern armoured warfare led to the development of the Merkava tank, which was successfully used in Lebanon.

IVORY COAST

Strength: 6-7,000 including conscripts serving 6 months; 12,000 reserves
Para-military: 1,100 Presidential Guard, 4,400 Gendarmerie, 1,500 Militia
Army organization: 3 Inf Bn, 1 Armd Bn, 1 Arty Gp, 1 Para Coy, 1 AA Btty, 1 Eng Coy, 1 Support Coy
Equipment includes 5 light tanks (AMX-13); c.25 AFV (ERC-90, AML-90, Panhard M-3, VAB); 81 mm, 120 mm mortars; 89 mm RCL; 20 mm, 20 mm SP, 40 mm AA guns

JAMAICA

Strength: 2,000 with 1,000 reserves
Para-military: 1,000 Police Mobile Reserve
Army organization: 2 Inf Bn, 1 Reserve Bn, 1 Spt Bn
Equipment includes 15 APC (Commando); 12 mortars (81 mm)

JAPAN

Strength: 156,000, with 45,000 reserves
Army organization: 5 Army HQ. 1 Armd Div, 12 Inf Div, 1 AB Bde, 1 Arty Bde, 2 Arty Gp, 2 Composite Bde, 1 Sig Bde, 5 Eng Bde, 8 SAM Gp
Equipment includes 1,000+ MBT (Tp. 61, Tp. 74); 550+ APC (Tp. 60, Tp. 73); 800 guns/howitzers (105 mm, 155 mm, 155 mm SP, 203 mm, 203 mm SP); 50 SSM (Tp. 30); 130 mm MRL; 75 mm, 84 mm, 106 mm RCL; Tp. 64, Tp. 79 ATGW; 35 mm, 37 mm, 40 mm, 40 mm SP, 75 mm AA guns; Stinger, Tp. 81 Tan, HAWK SAMs. Japan Air Self-Defence Force controls Nike-J SAM (being replaced by Patriot)

JORDAN

Strength: c.70,000 with 30,000 reserves
Para-military: 3,500 Public security/Mobile Police, Civil Militia
Army organization: 2 Armd Div, 2 Mech Inf Div, 1 Royal Gds Bde, 1 Sp Forces Bde, 16 Arty Bn, 4 AA Bn
Equipment includes 800 MBT (M47/48, Centurion, Khalid); 1,250 APC (M113, Saracen); 250 guns/howitzers (105 mm, 155 mm, 155 mm SP, 203 mm, 203 mm SP); 81 mm, 107 mm, 120 mm mortars; 106 mm RCL; Dragon, TOW ATGW; 20 mm, 23 mm SP, 40 mm SP AA guns; Redeye, HAWK, SA-6, SA-8, Rapier, Javelin SAMs

KAMPUCHEA

No reliable data has been released since 1975. The Army is thought to

Japan's advanced arms industry produces weapons solely for the defence of Japan, the Type 74 tank shown not being exported at all.

be between 20 and 30,000 strong. Numerous para-military units include People's Police, Militia and Regional Defence Forces. Vietnam has over 150,000 troops in the country, in more than 20 Divisions.
Equipment known to have been in use includes T-54/55 MBT; M113, BTR APC; 76 mm, 122 mm guns; 82 mm, 120 mm mortars; 107 mm, 132 mm, 140 mm MRL; 82 mm, 107 mm RCL; 14.5 mm, 37 mm, 57 mm AA guns
Opposition includes 30,000 Khmer Rouge, 15,000 Kampuchean People's National Liberation Front and Prince Sihanouk's 5,000 strong ANS

KENYA

Strength: 13,000
Para-military: 1,800 General Service Police
Army organization: 1 Armd Bde of 2 Bn, 5 Inf Bn, 1 Armd Recce Bn, 1 Air Cav Bn, 5 Inf Bn (Cadre only), 1 Para Bn, 1 AA Bn, 1 Eng Bde, 2 Eng Bn
Equipment includes c.90 MBT (Vickers Mk. 3); 150+ AFV (Saladin, Ferret, AML-60/90, Shorland, Saracen, UR-416, Panhard M-3); 40 guns/howitzers (105 mm); 81 mm, 120 mm mortars; 84 mm, 120 mm RCL; Milan, Swingfire ATGW; 20 mm AA guns; Rapier SAM

KOREA, DEMOCRATIC PEOPLE'S REPUBLIC (North)

Strength: 750,000 including conscripts serving 5 years. Reserves estimated between 250-500,000 immediately available and arranged as 23 Inf Div
Para-military: 38,000 Security and Border Guards, c.2,000,000 Civilian Militia
Army organization: 9-11 Corps HQ. 2 Armd Div, 5 Mot Inf Div, 24-40 Inf Div, 6-7 Indep Armd Bde, 8-9 Indep Inf & Lt Inf Bde, 3 Cdo Bde, 4 Recce Bde, 5 AB 'Bn' (totalling up to 100,000 men), 5 Riv Crossing Regt, 3 Amph Bn, up to 70,000 Special Forces (Bureau of Reconnaissance); 2 Heavy Arty Regt, 2 Mortar Regt, 6 SSM Bn, 4 Arty Bde, 2 AA Div, 7 AA Regt
Equipment includes 3,250+ MBT (T-34, T-54/55, T-62, Tp. 59); 150 light tanks (PT-76); 1,500+ AFV (BA-64, BMP-1, BTR-40, BTR-50, BTR-60, BTR-152, Tp. 531); 4,000+ guns/howitzers (76 mm, 85 mm, 100 mm, 122 mm, 130 mm, 152 mm); 2,100 MRL (107 mm, 122 mm, 130 mm, 140 mm, 200 mm, 240 mm); 70 SSM (FROG, Scud); 11,000 82 mm mortars; 120 mm, 160 mm, 240 mm mortars; 45 mm, 57 mm, 75 mm, 76 mm SP, 85 mm, 100 mm SP AT guns; 82 mm, 107 mm RCL; Snapper ATGW; 8,000 AA guns (23 mm, 23 mm SP, 37 mm, 57 mm, 57 mm SP, 85 mm, 100 mm); SA-7 SAM. Air Force controls c.800 SA-2/3

An M48A5 tank comes down a hill in Korea. The US Eighth Army and the Republic of Korea Army operate as one for the defence of the South.

KOREA, REPUBLIC OF (South)

Strength: c.530,000 including conscripts serving 36 months, plus 20,000 Marines; 1,400,000 reserves

Para-military: 3,300,000 Homeland Reserve Defence Force; 3,500,000 Civilian Defence Corps; 600,000 (School) Student Homeland Defence Force

Army organization: 3 Army, 5-6 Corps HQ. 1-2 Mech Div, 19-20 Inf Div, 3 AB Div, 2 Indep Inf Bde, 2 Armd Bde, 2 Sp Forces Bde, 2 AA Bde, 7 Tk Bn, 30+ Arty Bn, 2 SSM Bn, 5 SAM Bn. There are 2 Marine Div

Equipment includes 1,300 MBT (M47/48, ROKIT); 800+ APC (M113, Fiat/OTO 6614); c.2,500 guns/howitzers (105 mm, 155 mm, 155 mm SP, 175 mm SP, 203 mm, 203 mm SP); 5,300 mortars (81 mm, 107 mm); 76 mm, 90 mm SP AT guns; LAW, 57 mm, 75 mm, 106 mm RCL; TOW ATGW; 20 mm, 35 mm, 40 mm AA guns; HAWK, Nike-Hercules, Stinger SAMs. Marines have 40 MBT (M47); 100 APC (LVTP-7); 105 mm, 155 mm howitzers

KUWAIT

Strength: 10,000

Para-military: 18,000 Police, National Guard, Border Guard, Palace Guard

Army organization: 2 Armd Bde, 3 Mech Inf Bn, 1 SSM Bn

Equipment includes 240 MBT (Vickers Mk. 1, Centurion, Chieftain); 500+ AFV (Saladin, Ferret, M113, Saracen, M901); 100+ guns/howitzers (25-Pdr, 155 mm SP); 4 SSM (FROG); 81 mm mortars; SS-11, HOT, TOW, Vigilant ATGW; SA-6, SA-7, SA-8 SAMs

LAOS

Strength: 50,000 including conscripts serving at least 18 months

Para-military: Police, 200,000 Militia

Army organization: 1 Armd Bn, 70 Inf Bn, 11 Provincial Inf Coy, 4-9 AA Bn, 4-5 Arty Bn, Construction Troops

Equipment includes 30 tanks (T-34, T-54/55); light tanks (M24, PT-76); BTR APCs; 135 guns/howitzers (75 mm, 76 mm, 105 mm, 122 mm, 130 mm); 81 mm, 82 mm, 120 mm mortars; 57 mm, 75 mm, 107 mm RCL; 23 mm SP, 37 mm, 57 mm AA guns; SA-7 SAM

LEBANON

Nominal strength: 25-30,000 men in 5 Christian, 1 Druze, 1 Sunni and 3 Shi'ite Brigades. Central authority has to all intents and purposes collapsed, and many soldiers and pieces of equipment have passed to the various militias and private armies currently holding power

Rump of Govt Force (Christian): 15,000, with 90 tanks (M48); 50 light tanks (AMX-13); c.450 AFV (Saladin, Ferret, M113, Saracen, VAB); 122 mm, 130 mm, 155 mm guns/howitzers; 81 mm, 120 mm mortars; 85 mm, 89 mm, 106 mm RCL; Milan, TOW ATGW; 20 mm, 23 mm, 30 mm, 40 mm SP AA guns

Lebanese Forces Militia (Phalange, Christian): 4,500 'regular' with 30,000 reserve. Equipment includes 240 tanks (T-34, M4 Sherman, M48, T-54); 20 light tanks (AMX-30); M113 APC; 100 guns/howitzers (122 mm, 130 mm, 155 mm); 60 mm, 81 mm, 120 mm mortars; 89 mm RCL (RPG-7); 12.7 mm, 14.5 mm, 23 mm AA guns

South Lebanon Army (largely Christian, Israeli backed): c.1,000 armed with 50 tanks (M4, T-54); 122 mm, 130 mm, 155 mm Arty

Progressive Socialist Party (Druze): 5,000 'Regular' plus c.12,000 reserve. Equipment includes c.5 tanks (T-34/54); BTR-60/152 APC; 122 mm Arty; 122 mm MRL; 82 mm mortars

The Sunni Militias (Islamic Unity, Al Mourabitoun and the PLO financed 'Jimudullah' or Soldiers of God) between them muster c.2,000 activists

Amal (Shi'ite): 6,000 'regular', c.10,000 reserve. Equipment includes 50+ MBT (M48, T-54/55); Saladin, VAB, BTR, M113 AFVs; 105 mm, 122 mm, 130 mm, 155 mm Arty; 60 mm, 81 mm, 120 mm mortars; 107 mm, 122 mm MRL; 85 mm, 100 mm AT guns; Sagger ATGW; 14.5 mm, 23 mm AA guns; SA-7 SAM

Islamic Amal; Hizbollah; Islamic Resistance Movement (Extreme Shi'ite, Iranian backed) between them can muster c.2,000. Equipment includes AFV, 130mm Arty; mortars; RCL; AA incl 23mm

LIBERIA
Strength: 6,300. Reserves ?50,000
Para-military: 2,000 National Police
Army organization: 3-5 Inf Bn, 1 Gd Bn, 1 Cdo/special security unit, 1 Arty Bn, 1 Engr Bn, 1 Armd Recce Sqn, 1 Service Bn
Equipment includes c.20 AFV (M3 ½-tr, MOWAG Piranha); c.40 mortars (60mm, 81mm, 4.2-in); 57mm, 3.5-in, 106mm RCL

LIBYA
Strength: 55-60,000 including selected conscripts serving 18 months, plus 13,000 Air Defence Command troops
Para-military: 40,000 People's Militia, 10,000 Islamic Pan-African Legion, numerous other groups such as the Revolutionary Guard Corps, and Muslim Youth
Army organization: 1 Tk, 2 Mech Div HQ. 38 Tk Bn, 54 Mech Inf Bn, 1 National Gd Bde, 41 Arty Bn, 2 AA Arty Bn, 14 Para-Cdo Bn, 6 SSM Bde, 3 SAM Bde. Air Defence command controls 4 AA gun BN, 3 SA-5 Bde, 6 SA-2 Bde, 6+ SA-3 Bde, 9 Bde SA-6/8
Equipment includes up to 3,000 MBT (T-54/55, T-62, T-72); 2,500+ AFV (BRDM-2, EE-9, Fiat 6616, Ferret, Saladin, BMP-1, BMD, BTR-50, BTR-60, OT-62/64, EE-11, Fiat 6614, Saracen); 1,300 guns/howitzers (105mm, 122mm, 122mm SP, 130mm, 152mm SP, 155mm SP); 130 SSM (FROG, Scud); 600 MRL (122mm, 130mm); 450 mortars (81mm, 120mm, 160mm, 240mm); 200 RCL (106mm); 3,000 ATGW (Vigilant, Milan, Sagger); 600 AA guns (23mm SP, 30mm SP, 40mm, 57mm); SA-2, SA-3, SA-5, SA-6/8, SA-7, Crotale SAMs
Note: large amounts of equipment (1,500 tanks, for example) are in storage. SA-5 reportedly Soviet manned. Much equipment (at least 250 armoured vehicles, including 126 T-55 MBTs) reported destroyed in Chad and more than 200 AFVs (including 83 T-55s) captured between January and April 1987

LUXEMBOURG
Strength: 720
Para-military: 470 Gendarmerie
Organization: 1 Lt Inf Bn, 1 Ind Coy
Equipment Commando, BDX APCs; 81mm mortar; LAW; TOW

MADAGASCAR
Strength: 20,000 including conscripts serving 18 months
Para-military: 8,000 Gendarmerie
Army organization: 2 All Arms Bn Gp, 1 Eng Regt, 1 Sig Regt, 1 Service Regt, 7 Construction Regt, support units
Equipment includes 12 light tanks (PT-76); c.100 AFV (M8 Armd Car, Ferret, M-3, BRDM, M3 ½-tr, UR 416); 76mm, 122mm Arty; 81mm, 120mm mortars; 106mm RCL; 14.5mm AA guns

A member of the Shi'ite Amal militia fires a burst from his Kalashnikov in the streets of Beirut. Private armies such as Amal have contributed to the anarchy which has split the Lebanon for a decade and more.

MALAWI
Strength: 5,000 with 500 reserves
Para-military: 1,000 Police
Army organization: 3 Inf Bn, 1 Support Bn (which includes Recce Sqn)
Equipment includes 20 AFV (Fox, BRDM-2); 9 howitzers (105 mm); 81 mm mortars; 57 mm, 3.5-in RCL; 14.5 mm AA; Blowpipe SAM

MALAYSIA
Strength: 90,000; 45,000 reserves
Para-military: 18,000 Police Field Force, 3,100 Home Guard, 1,200 Border Scouts (in Sabah and Sarawak), 350,000 People's Volunteer Corps
Army organization: 1 Corps, 4 Div HQ. 9 Inf Bde comprised of 36 Inf Bn, 4 Cav Regt, 5 Fd Arty Regt, 2 AA Arty Regt, 5 Sigs Regt, 5 Engr Regt, various admin units, 1 Special Service Regt
Equipment includes 1,150 AFV (Scorpion, SIBMAS, AML-60/90, Ferret, AT-105, Commando, Stormer, Condor); 110 howitzers (105 mm); 81 mm mortars; 89 mm, 106 mm, 120 mm RCL; SS-11 ATGW; 12.7 mm, 40 mm AA guns. Police Force has Shorland SB 301 AFV

MALI
Strength: 4,600 including selected conscripts serving 2 years
Para-military: 2,000 Republican Guard, 1,200 Gendarmerie, 3,000 militia, 1,500 Civil Defence Organization
Army organization: 1 Tk Bn, 3 Inf Bn, 2 Armd Car Sqn, 1 Arty Bn, 1 Eng Bn, 1 Para Bn, 1 Sp Forces Bn, 2 AA Coy, 1 SAM Btty
Equipment includes 21 tanks (T-34); 12 light tanks (Tp. 62); 70 AFV (BRDM, BTR-40/152, BTR-60); 85 mm, 100 mm, 122 mm arty; 2 MRL (122 mm); 81 mm, 120 mm mortars; 37 mm, 57 mm AA guns; 6 SAM (SA-3)

MALTA
Strength: 750; 800-900 reserves
Para-military: 1,500 Pioneers & General Duty Volunteers, 1,300 Police
Army organization: 1 Inf Bn (1 Inf Coy, 1 AD Btty, 1 Eng Coy, 1 General Coy)
Equipment includes 81 mm, 82 mm mortars; RPG-7; 14.5 mm, 40 mm AA guns

MAURITANIA
Strength: 8,000
Para-military: 2,500 Gendarmerie, 2,500 other (incl 1,400 National Guard)
Army organization: 1 Inf Bn, 1-2 Arty Btty, 3 Armd Recce Sqn, 2 Armd Car Sqn, 1 Cdo Coy, 1 Para Coy, 1 Camel Corps, 1 AA Btty, 1 Eng Coy
Equipment includes 110 AFV (EBR-75, AML-60/90, Panhard M-3, M3 ½-tr); 81 mm, 120 mm mortars; 57 mm, 75 mm, 106 mm RCL; 14.5 mm, 23 mm, 37 mm AA guns; SA-7 SAM

MEXICO
Strength: 105,000 plus 6,500 Marines
Para-military: 250,000 part-time Rural Defence Militia, conscripted by lot; 60,000 active at any one time
Army organization: 1 Presidential Gd Mech Inf Bde (3 Bn), 2 Inf Bde, 1 Armd Bn, 36 Area Garrisons (which include 21-23 Indep Mot Cav Regt, 65-75 Indep Inf Bn, 3 Arty Regt plus AA, Eng and other support units). Marines form 13 Marine Groups and 20-30 Security Coy
Equipment includes 45 light tanks (M3/M8); 100+ AFV (ERC-90, VBL, DN-3 Caballo, HWK-11, M3 ½-tr); 75 mm, 75 mm SP, 105 mm guns/howitzers; 1,500+ mortars (60 mm, 81 mm, 120 mm); 37 mm AT guns; 106 mm RCL; Milan ATGW; 12.7 mm AA guns

MONGOLIA
Strength: 25-30,000 including c.17,000 conscripts serving 2-3 years. Reserve estimates vary between 40,000 and 200,000+
Para-military: 15-30,000 Police Militia, Internal Security Troops and Border Guards
Army organization: 4 Mot Rifle Div
Equipment includes 650 MBT (T-54/55, T-62); 850 AFV (BRDM-2, BMP, BTR); 650 guns/howitzers (122 mm, 130 mm, 152 mm); 122 mm, 132 mm, 140 mm MRL; 82 mm, 120 mm, 160 mm mortars; 100 mm AT guns; Sagger ATGW; 200 AA guns (14.5 mm, 37 mm, 57 mm); 300 SA-7 SAMs

MOROCCO
Strength: 125-150,000 including some conscripts serving 18 months; 100,000+ reserves
Para-military: 30-35,000 incl Gendarmerie Royale, Sûreté Nationale, others
Army organization: 3 Mech Inf Bde (totalling up to 18 Bn), 1 Lt Security Bde, 2 Royal Gd Bn, 1 Para Bde, 1 AA Bde, 9-14 Mech/Mot Inf Regt, 9 Arty Gp, 7 Armd Bn, 1 Mtn Bn, 3-4 Cdo Bn, 4 Armd Recce Sqn, 4 Camel Corps Bn, 2 Desert Cav Bn, 6-8 Eng Bn
Equipment includes 110 MBT (M48); 70 light tanks (AMX-13); 1,450 AFV (EBR-75, AMX-10RC, AML-60/90, Eland, M8, M113, VAB/VTT, VAB/VCI, VAB/Mortar, UR416, Ratel-20, M3 ½-tr, some OT-62/64); 220 guns/howitzers (85 mm, 100 mm SP, 105 mm, 130 mm, 155 mm, 155 mm SP); 15 MRL (122 mm); c.1,600 mortars (60 mm, 81 mm, 82 mm, 120 mm); 66 mm, 3.5-in, 75 mm, 89 mm, 90 mm, 106 mm RCL; 150 AT guns (90 mm, 105 mm SP); Dragon, Milan, TOW ATGW; 14.5 mm, 20 mm, 20 mm SP, 23 mm, 37 mm, 57 mm, 100 mm AA guns; SA-9, Chaparral SAMs
    Polisario are the main armed opposition. Strength: 4-5,000 active, perhaps 12,000 in all, organized into battalions with T-55 MBT; BMP, EE-9 AFV; 122 mm howitzers; 122 mm MRL; 120 mm, 160 mm mortars; 23 mm SP AA guns; SA-6, SA-7 SAMs. Polisario also have a wide range of captured or salvaged Moroccan Government equipment

MOZAMBIQUE
Strength: 14-15,000 with perhaps 11,000 conscripts
Para-military: 6-9,500 including Border Guard, and local People's Militia
Army organization: 1 Tk Bde (Pres Gd), 7 Inf Bde (each with 1 Tk, 3 Inf, 2 Mot/Mech, 2 Arty, 1 AD Bn), 2 Indep Mech Bn, 7 Indep AA Arty Bn
Equipment includes 250-300 tanks (T-34, T-54/55); c.50 light tanks (PT-76); c.400 AFV (BRDM-1/2, BMP-1, BTR); 250 guns/howitzers (76 mm, 85 mm, 100 mm, 105 mm, 122 mm, 130 mm, 152 mm); 350+ mortars (60 mm, 82 mm, 120 mm); 30 MRL (122 mm); 75 mm, 82 mm, 107 mm RCL; Sagger ATGW; 350-400 AA guns (20 mm, 23 mm, 23 mm SP, 37 mm, 57 mm, 57 mm SP); SA-3, SA-7 SAMs
    Mozambique National Resistance or RENAMO is S. African backed in opposition to Govt. Strength: 10-15,000 fighters

NETHERLANDS
Strength: 65,000 including 41-42,000 conscripts serving 14-16 months plus 2,800 Marines and 145,000 reserves
Para-military: 4,000 Royal Military Constabulary, 22,000 Civil Defence, under Army control and used for disaster relief
Army organization: 1 Corps HQ, 3 Div HQ. 2 Armd Bde, 4 Mech Inf Bde, 1 SSM Bde, 3 AD Bn, 3 Cadre Bde (1 Armd, 2 Mech Inf) filled on mobilization. Air Force have 14 AD Sqn. Marines have 2 Amph Cdo Gp and 1 Mtn/Arctic Warfare Coy
Equipment includes 900+ MBT (Leopard 1, Leopard 2); 2,800 APC (M113, YP-408, YPR-765); c.500 guns/howitzers (105 mm, 155 mm, 155 mm SP, 203 mm SP); 6 SSM (Lance); 700 mortars (81 mm, 107 mm, 120 mm); 84 mm, 106 mm RCL; c.700 ATGW (Dragon, TOW); 35 mm SP (Gepard), 40 mm AA guns; Stinger SAM, Patriot SAM to come. Air Force has 40 mm AA guns, Improved HAWK, Nike Hercules, Stinger, SAMs, Radar units

A Dutch Marine, armed with a heavy
barrelled FN rifle, makes his way
through the Norwegian snow. The
Netherlands Marines operate
alongside the British Royal Marines
on NATO's northern flank.

NEW ZEALAND
Strength: 6,000 plus 1,500-3,000 reserves and 6,500 Territorial Army
Army organization: 2 Inf Bn, 1 Arty Bn, 1 Lt Armd Sqn, 1 SAS Sqn. On mobilization, Territorials and reserves would make up additional 6 Inf Bn, 4 Fd Arty Btty, 1 Med Arty Btty, 1 Recce Sqn, 1 APC sqn, 1 AT Sqn
Equipment includes 26 light tanks (Scorpion); 72 APC (M113); 50+ guns/howitzers (105mm, 5.5-in); 81 mm mortar; 84mm, 106mm RCL

NEPAL
Strength: 30,000
Para-military: 25,000 Police
Army organization: 1 Bde Royal Gd, 5 Inf Bde, 1 AB Bn, 1 Suppt Bde with Arty Regt, 1 Eng Bn, 1 Sig Regt, 1 Cav Sqn, 1 Logistic Bde
Equipment includes light tanks (AMX-13); 25 AFV (Ferret); 15+ howitzers (75mm, 3.7-in, 105mm); 22 mortars (4.2-in, 105mm); 2 AA guns (40mm)

NICARAGUA
Strength: 70,000+ including c.20,000 conscripts serving 2 years; 25,000 reserves are on active service, while all males between 25 and 40 are liable for service and form a reserve of some 250-300,000
Para-military: 5,000 Border Guards, 2,000 State Security Directorate Troops, c.50,000 Sandinista Popular Militia
Army organization: 3 Military Zones. 1-2 Mot Inf Bde, 5 Armd Bn, 10 Inf Bn, 1 AB Bn, 5-6 COIN Bn, 1 Fd Arty Bde of 4 Arty Gp, 1 Eng Bde, 1 AA Gp. Reserve Militia form 150+ 'Bn'. Border Guards form 6 Bn
Equipment includes 110 MBT (T-54/55); 25 light tanks (PT-76); 200+ AFV (BRDM-2, BTR-60, BTR-152); c.70 guns/howitzers (76mm, 122mm, 152mm); 24 MRL (122mm); 60 mm, 82 mm, 120 mm mortars; c.100 AT guns (57mm); c.200 AA guns (14.5mm, 20mm, 23mm, 37mm, 40mm, 57mm); SA-6, SA-7 SAMs

Opposition to the Government comes from a number of the so called 'Contra' rebel groups, most nominally bound to the United Nicaraguan Opposition (UNO). The US backed Fuerza Democratica Nicaraguense (UNO/FDN) has some 20,000 members with up to 12,000 fighters available for operations out of Honduras. On the Southern Front the Union Democratica Nicaraguense/Fuerzas Armadas Revolucionarias Nicaraguenses (UDN/FARN) have up to 3,000 operating out of Costa Rica. The Fronte Revolucionario Sandino and the 2,500 strong, US backed, Democratic Revolutionary Alliance (ARDE) are also in the South. There are also popular movements among the eastern Indian population going by the names 'Misurasata' and 'Misura' (800 strong) and the 3,500 members of the East Coast Indian Unity (UNO/KISAN)

NIGER
Strength: 2,200 including selected conscripts
Para-military: 2,500 Republican Guard, c.800 Gendarmerie
Army organization: 6 Inf Coy, 2 Armd Recce Sqn, 1 Para-Cdo Coy, various Desert Coys, 1 Logistic/Spt unit
Equipment includes 60-70 AFV (M8, AML-60/90, Panhard M-3); 60mm, 81mm, 120mm mortars; 14 RCL (57mm, 75mm); 15+ AA guns (20mm SP, 37mm)

NIGERIA
Strength: 100,000+
Para-military: 200,000 Federal and State Police
Army organization: 1 Armd Div, 2 Mech Div, 1 Composite Div, (the 4 Divisions totalling 4 Armd Bde, 7 Mech Bde, 1 AB Div, 1 Amph Div, 4 Arty Bde, 4 Engr Bde, 4 Recce Bn)
Equipment includes 135+ MBT (Vickers Mk. 3, T-54/55); 50 light tanks (Scorpion); 450+ AFV (Scimitar, AML-60/90, Saladin, EE-9, Ferret, Fox, Saracen, M-3/VPC, AMX-VTT, Piranha 6×6, Steyr 4K7FA); 450+ guns/howitzers (105mm, 122mm, 155mm, 155mm SP); 200 mortars (81mm); 122mm MRL; 106mm RCL; 90 AA guns (20mm, 23mm SP, 40mm); Blowpipe, Roland SAMs

NORWAY

Strength: 20,000 including 13,500 conscripts serving 1 year. Navy has 2,000 coast artillery personnel. There are 150,000 first line reserves, 60,000 second line
Para-military: 70,000 Home Guard, 500 Civil Defence Staff (cadre for a full war strength of c.100,000)
Army organization: 4 Regional Commands. 1 Bde Gp in North with 2 Inf Bn, 1 Tk Coy, 1 Arty Btty, 1 AD Btty. 1 All-Arms Bn Gp in South with 1 Inf Bn, 1 Tank Gp, 1 Arty Btty. 42 Cadre Units will form 3 Div on mobilization, with 13 Indep Bde, 28 Indep Bn, 7 Indep Arty Bn plus up to 60 Home Gd and Spt Units. Air Force has 7-8 AA Bn, 1 SAM Bn. Navy has c.30 Coast defence fortresses
Equipment includes 120 MBT (Leopard 1, M48); 70 light tanks (M24/90); 400+ APC (M113, Bv 206); 400+ howitzers (105mm, 155mm, 155mm SP); 81mm, 107mm mortars; 57mm, 66mm, 84mm, 106mm RCL; TOW ATGW; 20mm, 40mm AA guns; 108 SAM (RBS-70 with more on order). Air Force has 40mm AA guns, 128 Nike-Hercules SAM. Navy coastal fortifications have over 50 Arty, mine, torpedo and SSM batteries, with 75mm, 105mm, 127mm and 150mm guns

OMAN

Strength: 17-20,000 with 1,000 reserves
Para-military: 3-5,000 Tribal Home Guard
Army organization: 1 Royal Gd Regt, 2 Bde HQ, 1 Armd Regt, 3 Arty Regt, 1-2 Recce Regt, 8 Inf 'Regt' (Bn size), 1 Sig Regt, 1 Fd Eng Regt, 1 Para Regt. Air Force controls integrated Air Defence System
Equipment includes 39 MBT (M60, Chieftain); 90 AFV (Scorpion, VBC-90, VAB, Saxon, Saladin, Commando); c.100 guns/howitzers (25-pdr, 105mm, 130mm, 155mm, 155mm SP); 60mm, 81mm, 4.2-in, 120mm mortars; TOW, Milan ATGW; 23mm AA guns; Blowpipe SAM. Air Force controls 28 Rapier Blindfire SAMs

PAKISTAN

Strength: 450,000; 500-520,000 reserves
Para-military: 60-90,000 Civil Armed Forces, 75,000 National Guard, 65,000 Frontier Corps, 15,000 Pakistan Rangers, 7,000 Northern Lt Inf
Army organization: 7 Corps HQ. 2 Armd Div, 16-17 Inf Div, 4 Indep Armd Bde, 5-6 Armd Recce Regt, 5-8 Indep Inf Bde, 1 Special Services Gp (3 Bn), 6-8 Arty Bde; 3 AA Bde, 12 SAM Btty. Air Force has 7 SAM Btty
Equipment includes 1,600 MBT (M47/48, T-55, Tp.59); 120 light tanks (PT-76, M24, Tp.60/63); c.650 AFV (Ferret, M113, K-63, UR 416, AML-60); 100 25-pdr gun/howitzers; 85mm, 100mm, 105mm, 105mm SP, 122mm, 130mm, 5.5-in, 155mm 155mm SP, 203mm SP Arty; 122mm MRL; 81mm, 107mm, 120mm mortars; 75mm, 89mm, 106mm RCL; Cobra, TOW ATGW; 14.5mm, 37mm, 40mm, 57mm AA guns; Stinger, RBS-70 SAMs. Air Force has Crotale, CSA-1 (SA-2) SAMs

Above: Pakistan uses equipment from a number of sources, China being the supplier of these T-59 tanks and the USA providing the M113 APC.

Below: Norwegian reserve troops aim their Recoil-less anti-tank weapon down one of the few roads through the north of the country.

PANAMA
Strength: c.11,000 National Guard
Para-military: Police, Highway Patrol
Army organization: 7 Lt Inf Coy (incl 1 AB, 1 Sp Forces)
Equipment includes 28 AFV (Commando); 60 mm mortars; 3.5-in RCL

PAPUA NEW GUINEA
Strength: 3,400
Para-military: 4,600 Border Patrol (Police)
Army organization: 2 Inf Bn, 1 Eng Bn, 1 Sig Bn, Suppt & Logistic units

PARAGUAY
Strength: 12,500 including 8,000 conscripts serving 18-24 months, plus 500 Marines. Reserves 30,500 plus 100,000 National and Territorial Guard
Para-military: 6,000 Special Police Service and Capital Police Force
Army organization: 1 Army HQ, 1 Presidential Escort Regt, 1 Cav Div (2 Mech, 1 Horse Cav Regt), 8 Inf Div (each 1 Inf Regt & 2 Cadre Regt), 2 Frontier Bn, 1 Army Inf Bn, 1 Army Arty Bn, 5 Eng Bn, 1 Marine Cdo 'Bn', 1 Marine 'Regt' (Bn size), 4 Coast Defence Btty
Equipment includes 2 tanks (Sherman); 2 light tanks (M3); 50 AFV (M8, EE-9, EE-11, M3 ½-tr); 14 Coastal Guns (3-in, 6-in); 35 howitzers (75 mm, 105 mm); 81 mm, 4.2-in mortars; 75 mm RCL; 30 AA guns (20 mm, 40 mm)

PERU
Strength: 80,000 including 40,000+ conscripts serving 2 years plus 3,500 Marines. Reserves total 175-180,000
Para-military: 25-30,000 Guardia Civil, 15,000 Republican Guard, People's Militia recently formed
Army organization: 3-4 Armd 'Div' (Bde size), 1 Cav Div with 3 Mech and 1 Horse Regt, 7-8 Inf 'Div' (Bde size); 1 AB Bde, 1 Jungle Bde, 1 Armd Car unit, 2 Fd Arty Bn, 2 Arty Bn, 1 AA Gp, 1 SAM Gp, 15+ Indep Bn (including 4 Inf, 7 Jungle, Eng). There is 1 Marine Bde with 3 Bn
Equipment includes 280 MBT (T-54/55); 110 light tanks (AMX-13); 450-500 AFV (M8, M113, UR 416, Fiat/OTO 6616); c.280 guns/howitzers (105 mm, 122 mm, 130 mm, 155 mm); 25 MRL (122 mm); 300 mortars (120 mm); 105 mm, 106 mm RCL; 75 AA guns (23 mm SP, 40 mm); SA-3, SA-7 SAMs. Marines have Commando, Chaimite, BMR APCs; 120 mm mortars; 84 mm, 106 mm RCL; 20 mm SP AA guns. Guardia Civil operate MOWAG Roland APC

Main opposition to the Government comes from the 2,000 strong Sendero Luminoso (Shining Path) based in rural areas, and the smaller MRTA based in the cities

PHILIPPINES
Strength: 60-70,000 plus 9,550 Marines. 20,000 reserves are available with a further 75,000 having reserve commitments
Para-military: 100,000+ (including 50,000 Philippine Constabulary)
Army organization: 5-6 Bn Presidential Protection Security Command, 5 Lt Inf Div, 1 Mech Inf Bde, 1 Lt Armd Regt, 4 Arty Regt, 1 MP Special Service Bde, 1 Ranger Regt, 2 Eng Bde. Marines have 3 Bde totalling 10 Bn
Equipment includes c.35 light tanks (M41, Scorpion); 200+ APC (M113, Commando, AIFV, Chaimite, M3 ½-tr); c.250 guns/howitzers (105 mm, 155 mm); 60 mm, 81 mm, 107 mm mortars; 75 mm, 90 mm, 106 mm RCL; 20 mm AA guns; HAWK SAM. Marine equipment includes 80 Amph Assault Vehicles (LVTP-5, LVT-7), 150 howitzers and 107 mm mortars

Main opposition comes from the Maoist New People's Army (11-15,000 strong with perhaps 20,000 supporters) and the 10,000 or more members of the armed wing of the Moro National Liberation Front

POLAND
Strength: c.220,000 including 160,000 conscripts serving 18 months plus 48,000 in Air Defence Command plus Naval Coast Defence Forces. Reserves are 400,000+
Para-military: More than 60,000 Internal Defence Troops, c.30,000 Border Guards, 30,000 Riot Police, 200,000 League for National Defence (citizen's militia)
Army organization: 3 Military Districts controlling 5 Armd Div, 8 Mech Div (5 at low readiness), 1 AB Div, 1 Amph Assault Div, 3-4 Arty Bde, 1 Arty Regt, 3 AT Regt, 4 SSM Bde, 5-8 AA Regt, 1 AA Bde. Air Defence Command controls 10 SAM Regt, and Naval Coast Defences have 6-8 Arty and SSM Bn
Equipment includes 3,500 MBT (T-54/55, T-72); 300 light tanks (PT-76); c.5,000 AFV (FUG/BRDM-2, BMP-1, SKOT-1/2, TOPAS-1/2); c.2,000 guns/howitzers (76 mm, 122 mm, 122 mm SP, 152 mm); 122 mm, 140 mm, 240 mm MRL; 50+ SSM (FROG, Scud); 82 mm, 120 mm mortars; 76 mm, 85 mm, 85 mm SP, 100 mm AT guns (73 mm, 107 mm RCL; Snapper, Sagger, Spigot ATGW; 6-800 AA guns (23 mm, 23 mm SP, 57 mm, 57 mm SP, 85 mm, 100 mm); 250 SAMs (SA-4, SA-6, SA-7, SA-8, SA-9). Air Defence command has 300+ SA-2/3. Coast Defence units have 152 mm Arty, Sagger and SS-C-2b Samlet SSMs

PORTUGAL
Strength: 40,000 including 30,000 conscripts serving 16 months, plus 2,500 Marines (1,200 conscripts). There are up to 500,000 reserves
Para-military: 15,000 National Republican Guard, 13-15,000 Public Security Police, 8,000 Border Guard
Army organization: 6 Commands controlling 1 Mixed Bde (assigned to NATO), 2 Cav Regt, 11-14 Inf Regt (3 Independent), 1 Sp Ops Bde with 1 Cdo Regt, 2-3 Fd Arty Bn, 1 AA Bn, 1 Coast Arty Bn, 2 Eng Regt, 1 Sig Regt, 1 MP unit. There are 3 Marine Bn plus spt units
Equipment includes 50-60 MBT (M47/48); c.340 AFV (Saladin, EBR-75, AML-60/90, Ferret, M113, Chaimite); 200+ guns/howitzers (105 mm, 5.5-inch, 155 mm, 155 mm SP); 50 Coast Defence guns (150 mm, 152 mm, 234 mm); 81 mm, 107 mm mortars; 90 mm, 106 mm RCL; SS-11, TOW, Milan ATGW; 50 AA guns (20 mm, 40 mm); Blowpipe SAM. Marines have Chaimite APC, mortars and raiding boats

QATAR
Strength: 5-6,000
Para-military: c.2,000 Police
Army organization: 1 Gd Bn, 1 Tk Bn, 2 Armd Car Units, 3-5 Inf Bn, 1 Arty Btty, 1 SAM Btty
Equipment includes 24 MBT (AMX-30); 250 AFV (Saladin, Ferret, Saracen, EE-9, AMX-10P, AMX-VTT, VAB); 14 guns/howitzers (25-pdr, 155 mm); 81 mm mortars; HOT, Milan ATGW; 30+ SAMS (Tigercat, Improved HAWK, Rapier, Blowpipe)

ROMANIA
Strength: 150,000 including 95,000 conscripts serving 16 months. Reserves total 450-500,000
Para-military: 17,000 Border Guard, 20,000 Security Troops, 900,000 'Patriotic Guard' (a civil militia), 650,000 Youth Homeland Defence
Army organization: 2 Tk Div (1 at low readiness), 8 Mot Rifle Div (only 1 combat ready, 4 being cadres), 2 AB Regt, 3 Mtn Regt, 2 Arty Bde, 2 SSM Bde, 2 AA Bde with 2 AA Arty Regt, 3 Sam Regt, 1 AT Bde (5 Regt). Air Force has 1 Air Def Div. Navy has 10 Coast Arty Btty, 8 AA Btty
Equipment includes c.1,500 tanks (T-34, T-54/55, T-72); 3,500 AFV (BRDM-1/2, BTR-50, BTR-60/TAB-70/72, OT-180, TAB-77); 1,000+ guns/howitzers (76 mm, 85 mm, 100 mm SP, 122 mm, 152 mm); 50 SSM (FROG, Scud); 82 mm, 120 mm mortars; 325 MRL (122 mm, 130 mm); 57 mm AT guns; Sagger, Snapper ATGW; 550+ AA guns (30 mm, 37 mm, 57 mm, 85 mm, 100 mm); SA-6, SA-7 SAMs. Coast Defence has 100 guns (130 mm, 150 mm, 152 mm); SS-C-2 Samlet anti-ship missiles. Air Force has 108 SA-2 SAMs

A BMP-1 of the Polish Army fords a stream. As with all Warsaw Pact armies, the Poles are largely equipped with Soviet equipment.

RWANDA

Strength: 5,000
Para-military: 1,200 Gendarmerie
Army organization: 8 Inf Coy, 1 Recce Sqn, 1 Cdo Bn, 1 Eng Coy
Equipment includes 28 AFV (AML-60, Panhard M-3); 81 mm mortar; 57 mm AT guns; 83 mm RCL

SAUDI ARABIA

Strength: 40-45,000
Para-military: 25-30,000 National Guard plus c.30,000 irregular (Tribal) reserves; 2,000 Royal Guard, 8,500 Frontier Guard, 15,000 Militia Reserves
Army organization: 1 Regt Royal Guard, 1 Mech Div, 1 Armd Bde, 4 Inf Bde, 1 AB Bde (2 Para Bn plus 2-3 Sp Forces Coy); 3-5 Arty Bn, 5-6 AA Bn, 18 AA Btty, 16-17 SAM Btty. National Guard has 4 Mixed Bn, over 20 Inf Bn, 24 Irregular Inf Bn and 1 ceremonial Cav Sqn
Equipment includes 550 MBT (AMX-30, M60); 1,000+ AFV (AMX-10P, BMR-600P, M113, EE-11, Panhard M-3, VCC-1); 500+ guns/howitzers (105 mm, 155 mm, 155 mm SP); ASTROS MLR; 560 mortars (81 mm, 107 mm); 75 mm, 90 mm, 106 mm RCL; SS-11, TOW, Dragon, HOT, Milan ATGW; 20 mm SP, 30 mm SP, 40 mm SP AA guns; Stinger, Redeye, Shahine, Improved HAWK SAMs
National Guard equipment includes 700+ Commando APC (including TOW and Vulcan variants); 50 howitzers (105 mm); 81 mm mortar; 106 mm RCL

SENEGAMBIA

Strength: c.9,000 mostly conscripts serving 2 years (125 in the Gambia)
Para-military: 6,800 Gendarmerie (400 in the Gambia)
Army organization: 1 Lt Inf Coy in the Gambia. 7 Inf Bn; 1 Eng Bn; 1 Pres Gd (Horsed); 1 Recce Sqn; 2 Para-Cdo Coy; 1 Arty Btty (reserve); 1 AA Gp; 3 Construction Coy
Equipment includes 130+ AFV (M8/M20 Armd Car, AML-60/90, Ferret, M3 ½-tr, Panhard M-3); c.16 guns/howitzers (75 mm, 105 mm, 155 mm); 16 mortars (81 mm, 120 mm); 89 mm RCL; Milan ATGW; 20 mm, 30 mm, 40 mm AA guns

SEYCHELLES

Strength: 1,000 including conscripts serving 2 years
Para-military: 800 People's Militia
Army organization: 1 Inf Bn, 2 Arty units, support coy
Equipment includes c.14 AFV (BRDM-2, Shorland); 3 guns (122 mm); 4 MRL (122 mm); 6 mortars (82 mm); RPG-7 AT; SA-7 SAM

SIERRA LEONE

Strength: c.3,100
Para-military: 800 State Security Division, 2,000 Police, 2,500 Militia
Army organization: 2 Inf Bn, 2 Arty Btty, 1 Mech Coy, 1 Eng Sqn
Equipment includes 24 AFV (MOWAG Piranha, Saladin, Ferret); 10 guns/howitzers (25-pdr); 60 mm, 81 mm mortars; 84 mm RCL; SA-7 SAM

SINGAPORE

Strength: 45,000 including 30,000 conscripts serving 24-30 months. Trained reserves total 170,000
Para-military: 7,500 Police/Marine Police, 700 Gurkha Gd Bn and 30,000 People's Defence Force
Army organization: 1 Div HQ controls 1 Armd Bde, 3 Inf Bde, 6 Arty Bn, 1 Cdo Bn, 6 Eng Bn, 3 Sig Bn. Reserves form 18 Inf, 1 Cdo, 12 Arty, 6 Eng, 3 Sig Bn on mobilization. Singapore Air Force has 4 SAM Sq
Equipment includes 6 MBT (M60); 300+ light tanks (AMX-13); 1,000+ APC (M113, V-150/V-200 Commando, AMX-13); c.150 howitzers (105 mm, 155 mm); 60 mm, 81 mm, 120 mm mortars; 84 mm, 89 mm, 106 mm RCL; 20 mm AA guns
Air Force has Bloodhound, Rapier, Improved HAWK and RBS-70 SAMs

SOMALI REPUBLIC

Strength: 40,000 including c.30,000 conscripts serving 18 months
Para-military: 8,000 Police, 1,500 Border Guard, 20,000 People's Militia
Army organization: 4 Corps, 12 Div HQ. 2 Tnk 'Bde', 20-25 Inf 'Bde', 3 Mech 'Bde', 1 Cdo 'Bde' and numerous Fd Arty and AA units. *Note:* larger formations are severely under strength if manned to more than cadre level. Most 'Bde' are actually Bn size or smaller
Equipment includes 200+ tanks (T-34, T-54/55, M47, Centurion); 560 AFV (BRDM-2, AML-90, BTR-40/152, BTR-50, BTR-60, M113, Commando, Fiat 6614/6616); 76 mm, 85 mm, 100 mm, 105 mm, 122 mm, 155 mm guns/howitzers; 81 mm, 120 mm mortars; 89 mm, 106 mm RCL; Milan, TOW ATGW; 23 mm, 23 mm SP, 37 mm, 57 mm, 100 mm AA guns; SA-2, SA-3, SA-7 SAMs

SOUTH AFRICA

Strength: c.75,000 including 58,000 National Servicemen serving up to 24 months. 140,000 active reserves in Citizen Force plus 150,000 National Reserves
Para-military: 100,000+ Commando Force (local protection units). At least 35,000 Police (who have 20,000 reserves)
Army organization: 11 Territorial Commands, 1 Corps HQ, 1 Corps (Med) Arty Bde, 1 Armd Div (with 1 Armd Bde, 1 Mech Bde, 2 Mot Bde, 3 Fd Arty Bn, 1 Lt AA Regt, 1 Eng Regt), 1 Inf Div (with 3 Mot Bde, 2 Arty Bn, 1 Lt AA Regt plus Sigs & support units), 4 Fd Arty Regt, 1 Med Arty Regt, 4 Lt AA Regt, 7 Eng Sqn, 1 Special Recce Regt, 1 SAM Regt, 3 Sig Regt, 1 Para Bde of 3 Bn (Quick Reaction Force)
Equipment includes 250 MBT (Olifant); 4,500 AFV (Ratel, Eland, Buffel, Hippo, Rhino, Samil, Lynx); c.200 guns/howitzers (25-pdr, 5.5-in, 155 mm, 155 mm SP); 127 mm MRL; 81 mm, 120 mm mortars; 6-pdr, 17-pdr, 90 mm AT guns; 84 mm, 106 mm RCL; Entac ATGW; 20 mm, 35 mm, 40 mm, 3.7-in AA guns; Cactus (Crotale), Tigercat SAMs

SPAIN

Strength: 230,000 including 160,000 conscripts serving 12 months plus 11,500 Marines. Reserves total c.700,000
Para-military: 60,000 Guardia Civil, 45,000 Policia Nacional
Army organization: 6 Military Regions, 2 Overseas commands. Army HQ, 1 Royal Gd Regt. Intervention Force consists of 1 Armd Div, 1 Mech Div, 1 Mot Div, 2 Mtn Div, 1-2 Armd Cav Bde, 1 Indep Inf Bde, 1 Air Portable Bde. General Reserve Force consists of 1 Para Bde, 1 Rocket Arty Bde, 2 Heavy Arty Regt, 7 Coast Defence Regt, 2 Eng Regt, 2 Sig Regt, 2 Railway Eng Regt. The Spanish Legion consists of 3 Regt, 1 Depot Regt, 1 Sp Ops Gp, plus support units. The Marines have 1 Marine Regt, 5 Garrison Regt. The Guardia Civil has 25 Tercios (Regt) plus Railway Security, Traffic and Anti-Terrorist Groups. The Policia Nacional is organized into 26 Inf Bn, 5 Cav Units and 1 Sp Ops Cdo Gp
Equipment includes 900 MBT (M47/48, AMX-30); 120+ light tanks (M41); 1,850 AFV (BMR-600, AML-60/90, VEC, M113); 1,250 guns, howitzers (105 mm, 105 mm SP, 122 mm, 155 mm, 155 mm SP, 203 mm, 203 mm SP); 380 coastal guns (88 mm, 6-in, 8-in, 12-in, 15-in); 105 mm, 140 mm MRL; 81 mm, 107 mm, 120 mm mortars; 89 mm, 90 mm, 106 mm RCL; Milan, Cobra, Dragon, HOT, TOW ATGW; 20 mm, 35 mm, 40 mm, 90 mm AA guns; Nike Hercules, HAWK, Roland, Skyguard/Aspide SAMs. Marine equipment includes 18 MBT (M48); 17 light tanks (Scorpion); 19 Amph Assault Vehicles (LVT-7); 20 howitzers (105 mm, 105 mm SP); 81 mm mortars; 66 mm, 106 mm RCL; TOW, Dragon ATGW. Guardia Civil has BLR APCs

A Ratel 90 fire-support vehicle of the South African army pauses during operations along the border between Angola and Namibia. The South African Defence Forces are considerably more powerful than those of the Black front-line states, and they give the South African Government the power to influence the whole of southern Africa.

SRI LANKA

Strength: 15,000 plus 14-15,000 active reserves

Para-military: 28,000 Police; 56,000 Volunteer Force; 10,000 Auxiliary Defence Troops; Home Guard

Army organization: 5 Inf Bde 'Task Forces', 2 Recce Bn, 2 Fd Arty Regt, 1 AA Arty Regt, 2 Eng Regt, 1 Sig Regt

Equipment includes c.200 AFV (Saladin, Ferret, Saracen, BTR-152, Samil 100); 76mm, 85mm, 25-pdr guns/howitzers; 82mm, 4.2-in mortars; 82mm, 106mm RCL; 40mm, 3.7-in AA guns

Tamil Opposition Forces number between 5,000 and 8,000 members of several groups forming the 'Eelam National Liberation Front' or ENLF. Armed with small-arms, RPG-7 AT launchers and SA-7 SAMs

SUDAN

Strength: 53-56,000 including Air Defence Command. There are c.20,000 Reserves in some 26 Bn mobilized against rebels in the South of Sudan

Para-military: 2,500 Border Guard, 500 Republican Guard, 500 National Guard

Army organization: 1 Armd Div HQ with 2 Armd Bde, 7-10 Inf Bde, 1 AB Bde, 3 AA Arty Regt (Bn size), 1 Eng Regt, 2 AA Bde, 1 SAM Bde

Equipment includes 140 tanks (T-34, T-54/55, M47, M60); c.100 light tanks (M41, Tp.62); c.650 AFV (Saladin, Ferret, AML-90, BRDM-2, Commando, Walid, BTR-40/152, BTR-50, OT-64, AMX-10P, M113, K-63, Panhard M-3); c.150 guns/howitzers (85mm, 25-pdr, 100mm, 105mm, 122mm, 130mm, 155mm SP); 122mm MRL; 120mm mortars; 85mm AT guns; Swingfire ATGW; 20mm, 20mm SP, 23mm, 37mm, 40mm, 85mm, 100mm AA guns; SA-2, SA-7 SAMs

SWEDEN

Strength: 47,000 including 38,000 conscripts serving 8-15 months; 15,000 active reserves plus c.100,000 ex conscripts on refresher

Sweden has powerful armed forces backed by an advanced arms industry producing weapons such as the Bofors RBS-70 anti-aircraft missile.

training. 550,000 troops can be mobilized within 72 hours.

Para-military: 1,000,000+ local defence and Home Guard; c.200,000 Civil Defence Volunteers

Army organization: 6 Independent Military Commands. Peacetime establishment: 50 Regt (Armd, Inf, Cav, Arty, AA, Eng, Sig, Support). Fully mobilized there are 4 Armd Bde, 1 Mech Inf Bde, 19 Inf Bde, 4 Norrland (Arctic trained) Bde, 60 Indep Bn, 100 Indep local defence Bn with a total of 4-500 Indep local def Coy. Swedish Navy has 5 Coast Def Bde with 30 Bn. Air Force has command and control of Air Defence

Equipment includes 650+ tanks (Centurion, S-103); 280 light tanks/tank destroyers (Ikv 91); c.1,000 APC (Pbv 302); 105mm, 150mm, 155mm, 155mm SP guns/howitzers; 81mm, 120mm mortars; 74mm, 84mm, 90mm RCL; Bantam, TOW ATGW; 20mm, 40mm AA guns; Redeye, RBS-70, Improved HAWK SAMs. Naval Coast Defence units have 40mm, 75mm, 120mm (mobile) and 75mm, 120mm (static) guns plus RBS-08, RB-52 and Hellfire SSMs

SWITZERLAND

Strength: 20,000 including 18,500 conscripts serving 4 months. There are between 550,000 and 600,000 reserves recalled for refresher training through the year. 1,100,000 (including Civil Defence) can be mobilized within 48 hours

Para-military: 480,000 Civil Defence

Army organization: (War Establishment) 3 Fd Corps (each with 1 Mech Div, 2 Inf Div), 3 Inf Regt, 3 Cyclist Regt, 3 Eng Regt, 3 Sig Regt, 3 Traffic Regt, 11 Frontier Bde, 3 Fortress Bde, 3 Redoubt Bde, 3 Heavy Arty Gp, 3 Eng Gp, 3 Sig Gp. Air Force has 1 Air Defence Bde, 1 SAM Regt, 7 AA Arty Regt, command and control and logistics units, 1 Fd Bde (3 Regt, 1 Para Coy), 1 Airbase Bde with 3 AA Regt

Equipment includes c.900 MBT (Leopard 2, Centurion, Pz61, Pz68); 1,700+ APC (M113 and variants, MOWAG Piranha); 1,300 guns/howitzers (105mm, 155mm, 155mm SP); 81mm MRL; 3,000+ mortars (81mm, 120mm); 1,340 AT guns (90mm); 83mm, 106mm RCL; TOW, Bantam, Dragon ATGW; 20mm, 35mm SP AA guns; Rapier SAMs. Air Force controls 120+ SAMs (Bloodhound, Rapier) and 20mm, 35mm AA guns

A Syrian tank rolls into the western suburbs of Beirut as part of an attempt to quell factional fighting in the city.

SYRIA

Strength: 320-330,000 including 135-150,000 conscripts serving 30 months and 50,000 active reservists. Total reserves are some 250,000

Para-military: 8,000 Gendarmerie; 1,800 Desert Guard; 25,000 in Defence Coys; plus other groups such as Republican Guard, Internal Security Forces and Ba'ath Militia

Army organization: 2 Corps HQ. 5-6 Armd Div, 2-3 Mech Div, 2 Armd Bde, 2-4 Mech Inf Bde, 1 Sp Forces Div (with 9 Para-Cdo Bde), 3 Arty Bde, 3 SSM Bde, 9 SAM Bn, 1 Coast Def Bde. Air Defence Command has 20 AA Bde with 95 SAM Btty

Equipment includes 4,500 MBT (T-54/55, T-62, T-72/74); 100 light tanks (PT-76); c.3,000 AFV (BRDM-2, BMP-1, BTR-40/152, BTR-50, BTR-60, OT-64); up to 3,500 guns/howitzers (85mm, 122mm, 122mm SP, 130mm, 152mm, 152mm SP, 180mm); 50+ SSM (FROG, Scud, SS-12, SS-21, SS-C-1b Coastal); 122mm, 140mm, 220mm, 240mm MRL; 120mm, 160mm, 240mm mortars; 100mm AT guns; Snapper, Sagger, Swatter, Spigot, Milan, HOT ATGW; 23mm, 23mm SP, 37mm, 57mm, 57mm SP, 85mm, 100mm AA guns; SA-2, SA-3, SA-5 (Soviet manned, possibly withdrawn), SA-6, SA-7, SA-8, SA-9, SA-10, SA-11, SA-13 SAMs

TAIWAN

Strength: 300,000 including conscripts serving 2 years plus 39,000 Marines. Reserves total 1,300,000

Para-military: 100,000 Militia plus various security troops

Army organization: 12 Inf Div, 2 Armd Div, 6 Lt Inf Div, 6 Mech Bde (Cav, Sp Force, Tank), 2 AB Bde, 20 Fd Arty Bn, 4-5 SAM Bn, 1 SSM Bn, 9 Reserve Div cadres. Marines form 2-3 Div plus support units

Equipment includes 300 MBT (M48); 1,000 light tanks (M24, M41); c.1,400 AFV (M8 Armd Car, M18 Tank Dest, M3 ½-tr, M113, Commando); c.2,000 guns/howitzers (75mm, 105mm, 105mm SP, 155mm, 155mm SP, 203mm, 203mm SP); 126mm MRL; Honest John, Hsiung Feng (Gabriel type), Ching Feng (Lance type) SSMs; 81mm mortar; 82mm, 106mm RCL; 300 AA guns (40mm, 40mm SP); 900+ SAMs (HAWK, Improved HAWK, Chaparral, Nike Hercules).

Marines have M47 MBT; LVT-4/5 Amph Assault Vehicles; 105mm, 155mm Arty; 106mm RCL

TANZANIA

Strength: 40,000 including 20,000 conscripts serving 2 years; 10,000 reserves

Para-military: 1,400 Police Field Force, 100,000 Citizen's Militia

Army organization: 3 Div HQ, 8-9 Inf Bde, 1 Tk Bde, 2 Fd Arty Bn, 2 AT Bn, 2 Mortar Bn, 1 SAM Bn, 2 AA Bn, 1 Sig Bn

Equipment includes 30 MBT (Tp.59); 60 light tanks (Tp.62, Scorpion); 70-80 AFV (BRDM-2, BTR-40/152, K-63); 250+ guns/howitzers (76mm, 122mm, 130mm); 50 MRL (122mm); 82mm, 120mm mortars; 75mm RCL; 14.5mm, 23mm, 37mm AA guns; SA-3, SA-6, SA-7 SAMs

THAILAND

Strength: over 170,000 including 90,000 conscripts serving 2 years; 20,000 Marines; 500,000 reserves

Para-military: 50,000 Volunteer Defence Corps, 15-20,000 Border Police, 13-14,000 Rangers, plus Village Scouts and other local defence units

Army organization: 1 Cav Div, 1 Armd Div, 7 Inf Div, 8 Indep Inf Bn, 1-2 Sp Forces Div, 4 Recce Coy, 3-5 Air Mobile Coy, 1 Arty Div, 1 AA Div. Marines form 2 Div

Equipment includes Tp.59, M48 MBT; 500 light tanks (M24, M41, Scorpion); c.1,000 AFV (EE-9, Shorland, M113, M3 ½-tr, Commando, Saracen); 75mm, 105mm, 130mm, 155mm guns/howitzers; LAW, 57mm, 75mm, 106mm RCL; TOW, Dragon ATGW; 20mm SP, 37mm, 40mm, 40mm SP AA guns; Redeye, Blowpipe, Aspide SAMs. Marine equipment includes LVT-7 Assault Amphibians, 24 guns (155mm) and TOW and Dragon ATGW

TOGO

Strength: 4,000
Para-military: 750 Gendarmerie, 900 Police
Army organization: 2 Inf Regt (totalling 1 Mech Bn, 1 Mot Bn, 2 Armd units, 3 Inf Coy plus support), 1 Presidential Gd Regt, 1 Para-Cdo Regt, 1 Arty Btty, 2 AA Btty, 1 Support Bn
Equipment includes 9 tanks (T-34, T-54/55); 80+ AFV (M8/M20, AML-60/90, EE-9, UR-416, M3A1 ½-tr); 4 guns (105 mm); 20 mortars (81 mm/82 mm); 57 mm, 75 mm, 85 mm RCL; 14.5 mm, 37 mm AA guns

TRINIDAD AND TOBAGO

Strength: 1,500 plus 1,000 reserves
Para-military: 4,000 Police
Army organization: 1 Inf Bn, 1 Reserve Bn, 1 Support Bn
Equipment includes 6 mortars (81 mm)

TUNISIA

Strength: 25-30,000 including more than 20,000 conscripts serving 12 months
Para-military: c.3,000 Gendarmerie and c.7,000 National Guard
Army organization: 2 Mech Bde (totalling 2 Armd, 4 Mech Inf Bn), 1 Sahara Bde (of 3 Regt), 1 Para-Cdo Bde, 2-4 Armed Recce Regt, 3-4 Fd Arty Regt, 2 AA Regt, 1 Eng Regt
Equipment includes more than 60 MBT (M48, M60); 100 light tanks/tank dest (AMX-13, M41, SK-105 Kürassier); 300+ AFV (Saladin, EBR-75, AML-90, Fiat 6616, EE-9, EE-11, M113, Steyr 4K7FA, Commando); 80+ guns/howitzers (25-pdr, 105 mm, 105 mm SP, 155 mm, 155 mm SP); 81 mm, 82 mm, 107 mm mortars; 89 mm RCL; Milan, TOW, SS-11 ATGW; 20 mm SP, 37 mm AA guns; RBS-70, Chaparral SAMs. Gendarmerie has 110 APCs (Fiat 6614)

TURKEY

Strength: 520-545,000 including 475-500,000 conscripts serving 18-20 months; 4,000 Marines; 700-800,000 reserves
Para-military: 120-125,000 Gendarmerie
Army organization: 4 Army, 10 Corps HQs. 1 Armd Div, 2 Mech Inf Div, 14 Inf Div, 6 Armd Bde, 2-4 Mech Bde, 11 Inf Bde, 1 AB Bde, 1 Cdo Bde, 8 Armd Recon Bn, 30-32 Arty Bn, up to 20 AA Bn, 4 SSM Bn, 5 Coast Def units, 1 SAM unit. There is 1 Marine Bde of 3 Bn plus 1 Arty Bn. The Gendarmerie has at least 3 Mobile Bde
Equipment includes c.3,700 MBT (M47/48, Leopard 1); 100 light tanks (M24); 3,500+ AFV (M59, M113, plus M8 Armd cars and M2/3 ½-tr in storage); 2,000+ guns/howitzers (75 mm, 105 mm, 105 mm SP, 155 mm, 155 mm SP, 175 mm SP, 203 mm, 203 mm SP); 1,700-1,800 mortars (81 mm, 4.2-in, 120 mm); 57 mm, 75 mm, 106 mm RCL; Cobra, TOW, SS-11, Milan ATGW; 20 mm, 35 mm, 40 mm, 75 mm, 90 mm AA guns); Redeye, Rapier SAMs. Air Force has 72 Nike-Hercules SAMs and more Rapiers. Gendarmerie is equipped with Commando and UR-416 APC

UGANDA

Strength: The Ugandan Army originally totalled some 6-10,000, but men and equipment are being absorbed into the National Resistance Army which won the latest civil war in 1985. The NRA is loosely organized into Bde and Bn formations
Equipment: In the early 1980s included 10 tanks (T-34, T-54/55); 150 AFV (BTR-40/152, Saracen, OT-64); 76 mm, 122 mm guns; Sagger ATGW; 23 mm, 37 mm AA; SA-7 SAMs. Serviceability of this equipment if not destroyed is unlikely to be high

USSR STRATEGIC ROCKET FORCES

Strength: Over 300,000 including c.225,000 conscripts serving 2 years but not counting Naval and Air Force Strategic Forces. 500,000+ reserves
Army organization: 6 Armies controlling 28 Missile Fields, 300 launch control centres. Each Army is broken down into Div, Regt, Bn & Btty. Each Btty controls 1 ICBM launcher
Equipment includes 1,398 ICBM (SS-11, SS-13, SS-17, SS-18, SS-19, SS-24, SS-25, SS-X-26, SS-X-27); 550+ IRBM/MRBM (SS-20, SS-4)

One of the few pictures released of a Soviet ICBM being lowered into a silo. The huge SS-9 missile shown has been replaced in service by the even larger SS-18, but some remain in use as satellite launch vehicles.

USSR GROUND TROOPS

Strength: 1,800,000-2,000,000 including 1,400,000 conscripts serving 2 years; 18,000 Naval Infantry; 3,500,000 reserves with conscript experience within 5 years. Total of 25,000,000 with reserve obligation

Army organization: 5 Theatres of Operations controlling 51 Tk Div, 142 Mot Rifle Div, 7 AB Div, 10 Air Assault Bde, 16 Frontal Arty Div, 16 Sp Forces (Spetznatz) Bde, numerous Arty Bde, Tank Bde, SSM Bde, AT Bde, AD (SAM) Bde, AD (Arty) Bde, Eng Bde, Sig Regt, NBC Regt, Chem Warfare Defence Regt. Naval Infantry have 1 Div, 3 Bde plus 3 Sp Force (Spetznatz) units.

Note: Soviet Divisions are split into three readiness categories, only the first being fully combat ready. Cat 2 Divs require recalled reserves to bring them up to strength, while Cat 3 Divs are cadres only

Equipment includes more than 50,000 MBT (T54/55, T-62, T-64, T-72, T-80); 1,200 light tanks (PT-76); 65,000+ AFV (BRDM-2, BMP-1/2/3, BMD-1/2, BTR-50, BTR-60/70/80, BTR-152, MT-L, MT-LB); 30,000 guns/howitzers (122mm, 122mm SP, 130mm, 152mm, 152mm SP, 180mm, 203mm, 203mm SP); 1,500+ SSM (FROG, SS-1 Scud, SS-12, SS-21, SS-23); SSC-X-4 ground launched cruise missile is entering service; 6-7,000 MRL (122mm, 140mm, 220mm, 240mm); 13,000 mortars (82mm, 120mm, 160mm, 240mm, 240mm SP); 7,000+ AT guns (76mm, 85mm, 85mm SP, 100mm); Swatter, Sagger, Spigot, Spandrel, Spiral ATGW; 21,000 AA guns (23mm, 23mm SP, 30mm, 30mm SP, 37mm, 57mm, 57mm SP, 85mm, 100mm, 130mm);

4,500 SAM systems (SA-4, SA-6, SA-8, SA-9, SA-11, SA-13); c.25,000 man portable SAMs (SA-7, SA-14)

USSR AIR DEFENCE TROOPS (V-PVO)

Strength: 370,000 including over 300,000 conscripts serving 2 years. More than 800,000 reserves

Army organization: 5 Air Defence District commands controlling ABM defences, Air Regiments and Indep Sqn of Fighter Interceptors, Air Defence Regiments and 14 AD Schools

Ground Based equipment includes 9,500 SAM launchers (SA-1, SA-2, SA-3, SA-5, SA-10, SA-12); 100 ABM launchers (ABM-1 Galosh, SH-104 exoatmospheric and SH-08 endoatmospheric interceptor missiles); 7,000 radar locations (OTH-B, early warning, search surveillance, 3D height finders, missile control and 'Civilian' air traffic control)

Most fighters and AWACs type aircraft have recently been transferred to the control of the Air Force

The V-PVO also control Soviet Military Satellites (Launch Detection, Recce, EW, Elint, Ocean Surveillance etc)

A Soviet combined arms attack is rehearsed, with tanks supported by RPG firing infantry and missile firing BMP-1 infantry combat vehicles. The USSR has by far the largest tank force in the world, and the tank lies at the heart of the strategies of the Soviet high command.

USSR PARA-MILITARY TROOPS

Up to 400,000 KGB (Committee for State Security) troops (including the Kremlin Gd Regt, Special Gds, Special Sig Units and more than 250,000 Border troops)

250-300,000 MVD (Ministry of the Interior) Internal Security troops forming 30 Div

5,000,000+ DOSAAF (State leisure and sports organization) which provide pre-military training for 15-18 year olds

KGB, MVD equipment includes tanks and AFV. KGB also has SP Arty, aircraft and ships (including up to a dozen frigates)

UNITED ARAB EMIRATES

Strength: 40-45,000

Army organization: 1 Royal Gd Bde, 2 Inf Bde totalling 9 Inf Bn, 1 Armd Bde, 1 Mech Inf Bde, 1 Arty Bde of 3 Bn, 1 AA Bde

Equipment includes 136 MBT (AMX-30, OF-40); 60 light tanks (Scorpion); 500+ AFV (AML-90, VBC, AMX-10P, AMX-VCI, VCR-TT, Panhard M-3, VAB, EE-11, Saladin, Ferret); c.90 guns/howitzers (25-pdr, 105mm, 155mm SP); 81mm mortars; 84mm, 120mm RCL; TOW, Vigilant ATGW; 20mm SP, 30mm, 35mm AA guns; Crotale, HAWK, Rapier, RBS-70 SAMs

UNITED KINGDOM

Strength: 162,000 plus 7,600 Royal Marines and the RAF Regt. Reserves total 240,000

Army organization: Field Force; 1 Corps HQ, 3 Armd Div, 1 Inf Div. 27 Bde, 14 Armd Regt, 5 Armd Recce Regt, 53 Inf Bn, 3 Para Bn, 1 SAS Regt, 1 SSM Regt, 18 Arty Regt, 3 SAM Regt, 13 Eng Regt. On mobilization, reserves add 2 Armd Regt, 3 Lt Recce Regt, 40 Inf Bn, 2 SAS Bn, 3 Arty Regt, 4 AD Regt, 7 Eng Regt. Royal Marines consist of 1 Cdo Bde (3 Commandos, Bn size) and 1 Sp Boat Sqn. RAF Regt has 5 Lt Armd Sqn and 9 SAM Sqn

Equipment includes 1,200 MBT (Challenger, Chieftain); 270+ light tanks/recce (Scorpion); 5,500+ AFV (Scimitar, Ferret, Fox, Saracen, FV432, Spartan, Saxon, Warrior, Shorland, Humber 'Pig'); 450 guns/howitzers (105mm, 105mm SP, 155mm, 155mm SP, 175mm SP, 203mm SP); MLRS; 12 SSM (Lance); 81mm mortar; LAW, 84mm RCL; SS-11, Milan, TOW, Swingfire ATGW; Blowpipe, Javelin, Rapier SAMs. Royal Marines have 105mm guns, 81mm mortar, 84mm RCL, Milan ATGW; Javelin & Blowpipe SAMs. RAF Regt has 126 AFV (Scorpion, Spartan) and 72 Rapier SAMs. The RAF also operates 64 Bloodhound SAMs and 12 captured Argentine 35mm AA guns

A British army machine-gunner fires his General Purpose Machine Gun across a valley. The GPMG was originally a Belgian FN design.

US Marines storm ashore from their LVTP-7 amphibious vehicles. The US capacity for amphibious warfare is vastly greater than that of any other nation, and at the heart of the US amphibious effort are the Marines.

US ARMY

Strength: 770,000+. Reserves include 450,000 National Guard, 290,000 Active Reserve plus some 440,000 available for call-up if necessary

Army organization: 7 Army HQ, 6 Corps HQ. 4 Armd Div, 6 Mech Div, 1 Inf Div, 1 High Tech Trial Lt Div, 4 Lt Inf Div, 1 Lt Mtn Div, 1 AB Corps (comprising 1 Air Assault Div and 1 AB Div), 13 SSM Bn, 3 SAM Bn, 1 Sp Operations Command (with 8 Sp Forces Gp, 'Delta Force' counter-terrorist unit, 1 Ranger Regt, 4 PsyWar Gp)

Equipment includes 15,000 MBT (M48, M60, M1 Abrams); c.30,000 AFV (M2/3 Bradley, M113 and variants); 5,500 guns/howitzers (105mm, 155mm, 155mm SP, 203mm SP); 337 MRL (227mm); 300 SSM (Pershing II, Lance); 81mm, 107mm mortar; 1,000 RCL (90mm, 106mm); M72, AT-4 AT missiles; Dragon, TOW, Hellfire ATGW; 20mm, 20mm towed AA guns; Redeye, Stinger, Chaparral, Roland, Nike Hercules, Improved HAWK, Patriot, Rapier SAMs

US MARINE CORPS

Strength: c.200,000 including Marine Air; 43,000 reserves

Ground organization: 3 Div each of 9 Inf, 1 Recce, 1 Tk, 1 Eng, 1 Amph, 1 LAV and 3 Arty Bn. 1 Reserve Division. 2 Air Cushion Landing Craft units have been formed

Equipment includes 716 MBT (M60); 3,000 AFV (LVT-7, M113, Light Armored Vehicle); 105mm, 155mm, 203mm SP howitzers; 81mm mortar; TOW. Dragon ATGW; Redeye, Stinger SAMs

URUGUAY

Strength: c.20,000 plus 450 Naval Infantry. Reserves total 120,000

Para-military: Metropolitan Guard, Republican Guard

Army organization: 4 Mil Regions with 4 Inf Div HQ. 3 Armd Bde, 16 Inf Bn, 4-5 Eng Bn, 5 Fd Arty Bn, 1 AA Bn, 7 Cav Units. Army troops include 1 Pres Escort Cav Regt, 1 Inf Bde, 1 Eng Bde, 1 Sig Bde, 1 Bn Naval Infantry

Equipment includes c.65 light tanks (M3A1, M24, M41, Scorpion); c.120 AFV (FN-4-RM-62, EE-3, EE-9, M113, Condor); 46 guns/howitzers (75mm, 105mm, 155mm); 81mm, 107mm mortars; 57mm AT guns; 57mm, 106mm RCL; 20mm, 40 r AA guns

The M1 Abrams has advanced laminated armour, gas-turbine power for notable battlefield mobility and advanced electronic fire-control and night vision systems.

VENEZUELA

Strength: 27,500-34,000 including c.18,000 conscripts serving 18-24 months; 4,500 Marines
Para-military: 20,000 National Guard
Army organization: 5 Div HQ. 1 Armd Bde (3-4 Tk Bn); 6 Inf Bde (totalling 2 Mech Inf Bn, 11 Inf Bn, 13 Lt Jungle Inf Bn); 1 Cav Regt, 1 SP Arty Bn, 1 AD Bn, 2 AA Arty Bn, 2 Ranger (AB) Bn, 5 Eng Bn. Marines have 4 Bn, 1 Arty Bn, 1 Amph Bn, 1 AA Coy. Air Force has 1 Para Bn
Equipment includes 100+ MBT (AMX-30); 70 light tanks (M18, AMX-13); 185 AFV (M8, AML, AMX-VCI, UR 416, EE-11, Commando, Shorland); 100 guns/howitzers (105mm, 155mm SP); 160mm MRL; 81mm, 120mm mortars; 106mm RCL; SS-11, AS-11 ATGW; 20mm SP, 40mm, 40mm SP AA guns. Marine equipment includes c.50 AFV (LVT-7, EE-11, Transportpanzer); 18 howitzers (105mm); 6 AA guns (40mm SP)

VIETNAM

Strength: 1,000,000 including conscripts serving 2-4 years, plus 100,000 Air Defence Force plus 27,000 Naval Infantry. Reserves form the 500,000 strong 'Tactical Rear Force'
Para-military: 2,500,000 Militia Self-Defence, 1,000,000 People's Self-Defence, 500,000 People's Regional Force, 60,000 Border Troops
Army organization: 14 Corps HQ. 57-61 Inf Div, 10 Armd Bde, 2 Marine Div (totalling 10 Marine Bde), 8 Eng Div (incl 1 Transport, 3 Construction), 1 AA Div, 2 Arty Div, 25 SAM Regt, 6 Indep Armd Regt, 5 Indep Arty Regt, 4 Indep AA Bde
Equipment includes 1,600 tanks (T-34, T-54/55, Tp.59, M47/48); 500+ light tanks (PT-76, Tp.60/62, Tp.63, M41); c.3,500 AFV (BRDM, M8, M20, BTR-40/152, BTR-50, BTR-60, Tp.56, K-63, M113, Commando); 2,000+ guns/howitzers (76mm, 76mm SP, 85mm, 100mm, 105mm, 122mm, 122mm SP, 130mm, 155mm, 155mm SP); 107mm, 122mm, 140mm MRL; 60mm, 81mm, 82mm, 120mm, 160mm mortars; 57mm, 75mm, 82mm, 88mm, 90mm, 107mm RCL; 23mm, 23mm SP, 37mm, 37mm SP, 40mm, 57mm, 57mm SP AA guns; SA-7 SAM. Air Defence Command controls at least 60 SAM units with SA-2, SA-3 and SA-9 together with some 1,000 large AA guns (85mm, 100mm, 130mm)

YEMEN ARAB REPUBLIC (North)

Strength: 35-36,000 including 25,000 conscripts serving 3 years. Reserves total some 40,000
Para-military: 5,000 Ministry of National Security, 20,000 Tribal Levies
Army organization: 5 Armd Bde, 7 Inf Bde, 1 Cdo Bde, 1 Sp Forces Bde, 1 Para Bde, 3 Arty Bde, 3 AA Bn. Most 'Bde' units are actually Bn size or smaller
Equipment includes 750+ MBT (T-34, T-54/55, T-62, M-60); 450 AFV (Saladin, Ferret, M113, Walid, BTR-40/152, BTR-60, BMP); 76mm, 100mm SP, 105mm, 122mm, 122mm SP, 155mm guns/howitzers; 70 MRL (122mm); 200 mortars (82mm, 120mm); LAW, 75mm, 82mm, 106mm RCL; Vigilant, Dragon, TOW ATGW; 20mm, 20mm SP, 23mm, 23mm SP, 37mm, 57mm, 85mm AA guns; SA-2, SA-6, SA-7 SAMs

YEMEN (South)

Strength: 24,000 including 18,000 conscripts serving 2 years. There are some 45,000 reserves
Para-military: 30,000 Public Security Force, 15,000 Popular Militia
Army organization: 10 Inf 'Bde' (Regt size), 1 Armd Bde, 1 Arty Bde, 10 Arty Bn, 1-2 SSM Bde, 2 SAM units
Equipment levels are difficult to assess due to heavy losses and damage sustained during the brief civil war in 1986, but the pre-war inventory included 470 tanks (T-34, T-54/55, T-62); c.500 AFV (BRDM-2, BMP-1, BTR-40/152, BTR-60); 250 guns/howitzers (85mm, 100mm, 122mm, 130mm); 120mm, 160mm mortars; 18 SSM (FROG, Scud); 122mm, 140mm MRL; 23mm, 23mm SP, 37mm, 57mm, 85mm AA guns; SA-2, SA-6, SA-7, SA-8 SAMs

YUGOSLAVIA

Strength: 160-190,000 including 120-140,000 conscripts serving 1 year. Reserves 500,000
Para-military: 165,000 People's Militia (Police), 15,000 Frontier Guards, 1,000,000 Territorial Defence Force
Army organization: 7 Military Regions, 3 Corps HQ. 7-8 Inf Div plus 4-5 Reserve Div, 9 Inf Bde, 7-8 Tk Bde, 1-3 Mtn Bde, 6 AT Regt, 6 Fd Arty Regt, 6 Arty Regt, 11-12 AA Regt, 3-4 SAM Regt, 1 Marine Bde, 1 AB Bde. Air Force controls some SAM units. Navy controls 2 Marine Bde and 25 gun/missile coast Arty Btty
Equipment includes 1,000+ MBT (T-54/55, T-72/74, M47); 20 light tanks (PT-76); 1,000 AFV (M3 scout car, M3 ½-tr, M8, BRDM-2, M-80 MICV, BTR-40, BTR-60, M-60 APC); c.1,800 guns/howitzers (76mm, 76mm SP, 85mm, 88mm, 100mm, 100mm SP, 105mm, 105mm SP, 122mm, 122mm SP, 130mm, 152mm, 155mm); 6,000 mortars (82mm, 120mm); 128mm MRL; 4 SSM (FROG); SS-N-2, SS-C-3 anti-ship missiles; 75mm, 90mm, 100mm AT guns; 57mm, 82mm, 105mm RCL; 20mm, 20mm SP, 30mm, 30mm SP, 37mm, 40mm, 57mm, 57mm SP, 85mm, 90mm, 3.7-in AA guns; SA-2, SA-3, SA-6, SA-7, SA-8, SA-9 SAMs

ZAIRE

Strength: 22,000 plus 600 Marines
Para-military: 25,000 Gendarmerie, 25,000 Civil Guard
Army organization: 3 Military Regions. 1 Inf Div, 1 Sp Forces Div (1 Para Bde, 1 Cdo/COIN Bde, 1 Presidential Gd Bde), 1 Indep Armed Bde, 2 Inf Bde. Gendarmerie are organized into 40 Bn
Equipment includes 38 light tanks (Tp.62); 250 AFV (AML-60/90, M113, K-63, Panhard M-3, M3 ½-tr); c.80 guns/howitzers (75mm, 85mm, 122mm, 130mm); 107mm MRL; 81mm, 4.2-in, 120mm mortars; 57mm, 75mm, 106mm, 107mm RCL; 12.7mm, 14.5mm, 20mm, 37mm, 40mm AA guns

ZAMBIA

Strength: 14-15,000; 2,000 reserves
Para-military: 700 Police Mobile Unit, 500 Police Para-Military Unit
Army organization: 1 Armd Regt, 9 Inf Bn (3 Reserve), 3 Arty Btty, 2 AA Btty, 1 Eng Bn, 1 Sig Sqn
Equipment includes 60 MBT (T-54/55, Tp.59); 100+ AFV (BRDM-1/2, BTR-60); c.150 guns/howitzers (76mm, 105mm, 122mm, 130mm); 50 MRL (122mm); 57mm, 75mm, 84mm RCL; Sagger ATGW; 20mm, 37mm, 57mm, 85mm AA guns; SA-7 SAM

ZIMBABWE

Strength: 40-41,000 including conscripts; 25,000 Reserves
Para-military: 15,000 Zimbabwe Police Force, 3,000 Police Support Unit, 20,000 Militia
Army organization: 6 Bde (totalling 1 Armd Regt, 20+ Inf Bn, 1 Cdo Bn, 2 Para Bn), 1 Pres Gd Bde, 1 Arty Regt, 1 AD Regt, 7 Eng Sqn, 7 Sig Sqn
Equipment includes 43 MBT (T-54/Tp.59); 150+ AFV (EE-9, AML-90, Eland, BRDM-2, BTR-152, Tp.63); 25-pdr, 105mm, 122mm Arty; 81mm, 82mm, 120mm mortar; 107mm RCL; 14.5mm, 20mm, 23mm, 37mm AA guns; SA-7 SAM

Index

Page numbers in **bold** indicate an illustration

An asterisk signifies a reference to a detailed entry

315

Index

Index

The publishers would like to thank the following people and organizations for providing the illustrations used in this book:

Aerospatiale; Alvis; ARMSCOR; Arrowpointe Corp; Associated Press; Avibras; Australian Department of Defence; Austrian Ministry of Defence; Belgian Ministry of Defence; Beretta; Bernardini; BMF/SIBMAS; Bofors; Breda; British Aerospace; British Army; British Ministry of Defence; Bundeswehr; Cadillac-Gage; Chartered Industries, Singapore; Creusot-Loire; DAF; ECPA Paris; ENGESA; Euromissile; Fabrique Nationale; Finnish Ministry of Defence; Christopher F. Foss; GAMMA; Terry Gander; General Dynamics; GIAT; GKN; Imperial War Museum; Iraqi Army; Israel Defence Force; Israel Military Industries; Japan Self-Defence Force; Krauss-Maffei; MARS, Lincs.; Martin-Marietta; Mauser; MBB; McDonnell Douglas; MOWAG; Norwegian Ministry of Defence; Oerlikon-Bührle; Pakistan Army; Panhard; Pilot Press; Porsche; Portugal Ministry of Defence; Herman Potgeiter; Press Association; Renault; Rheinmetall; Royal Marines; Royal Ordnance; Short Brothers; SIG; Steyr-Daimler-Puch; Thomson-CSF; Thyssen-Henschel; US Air Force; US Army; US Department of Defense; US Marine Corps; Vickers Defence Systems; Westland.

Thanks are also due to the Weapons Museum at the School of Infantry, Warminster and to the Royal Ordnance Pattern Room for permission to photograph small arms from their collections.